For Cause &
For Country

For Cause & For Country

A Study of the Affair at Spring Hill & the Battle of Franklin

Eric A. Jacobson

co-author
Richard A. Rupp

Manufactured in the United States of America.
Second edition. First Printing.

Editor: Rosemary Hilliard
Cover Design: Paula Rozelle Bagnall

Frontispiece: Battlefield at Franklin and Carter cotton gin, courtesy of the U. S. Army Military History Institute, Carlisle, PA.

Back cover: The Carter House, courtesy of the U. S. Army Military History Institute, Carlisle, PA.

Includes bibliographical references and index.
Hardcover ISBN: 0-9717444-4-0
Softcover ISBN: 0-9717444-6-7

Published and Distributed by:

O'More Publishing
A Division of O'More College of Design
423 South Margin Street
Franklin, TN 37064 U. S. A.
615-794-4254
www.omorecollege.edu

Table of Contents

Illustrations

Photographs

Maps

Acknowledgments

In bringing this project to life and ultimately completing it, I have crossed the paths of many people who are owed a sincere thank you. There is no particular order to this list. Rather it is a simple compilation of those who helped me in ways I cannot ever fully express.

Staff members at the public libraries in Aurora, Illinois and New Washington, Ohio helped find books I desperately needed. Those at the public libraries in Dayton and Cincinnati, Ohio were no less helpful digging up old memoirs and histories. The staff at the Abraham Lincoln Presidential Library in Springfield, Illinois went beyond the call. Those at the Longview Public Library in Longview, Texas were a godsend. Without them I would have had much more difficulty obtaining *MOLLUS* articles. Library assistants at the Hayden Library on the campus of Arizona State University were always available to lend a hand.

John White at the University of North Carolina at Chapel Hill helped time and again with items from the Southern Historical Collection. He was always courteous and patient. The staff at the Tennessee State Library and Archives was nothing short of extraordinary. Even the security personnel were patient with me when I had to get a new entrance card every time I visited because I consistently lost them. The Special Collections Department at George Mason University is owed a thank you. Bob Duncan at the Maury County Historical Society helped answer many questions and we even visited General John Carter's grave together. Without Mr. Duncan I would never have been able to find one of the last unpaved sections of the old Davis Ford Road. I am also indebted to James Redford and other staff at Carnton Plantation for allowing me access to their archive of papers.

Photos assist in telling a story and Randy Hackenburg at the United States Army Military History Institute helped me obtain the wonderful photographs taken of the Franklin battlefield in the early

1880's. Without them the visual story of Franklin would be incomplete. Rick Warwick of the Heritage Foundation of Franklin provided the excellent photographs of Everbright, the Merrill House, and the Neely House.

Maps are also crucial to understanding the complexities of military maneuvers and unit placements. Tim Reese did an excellent job designing the book's various maps. He worked closely and patiently with me to ensure they were exactly as I wanted them. I think they are the best maps of Spring Hill and Franklin anyone has ever done.

I must also extend a very special thank you to Thomas Cartwright and David Fraley, both of whom are the lifeblood of the Carter House in Franklin, Tennessee. They have endured endless phone calls, e-mails, and visits and offered valuable information without hesitation. This work would not be what it is without either of them. If the book comes up short it is through no fault of theirs. Beyond historical information both offered constant encouragement. In the end the latter was worth far more to me.

Conversations with Jimmie French and Virginia Bowman were extremely helpful with questions I had about Everbright Mansion and other general inquiries about the area. Jamie Gillum helped me gain a deeper understanding regarding the fighting at Spring Hill. Tim Burgess offered detailed assistance with the Confederate organization of battle and provided invaluable input regarding casualties. I also want to thank Sam Hood and David Logsdon for their assistance and support.

I also wish to offer a special thank you to Ron Shuff, the current owner of Oaklawn Plantation. He graciously allowed me to tour the historic home south of Spring Hill in the company of current caretaker Jimmy Campbell. I also owe Bill Christmann a debt of gratitude for allowing me to use the unpublished diary of artilleryman Harold Young. The diary is a wonderful and heretofore unknown source of information.

While conducting my research I have traveled thousands of miles across Tennessee, Arkansas, Mississippi, Alabama, and Georgia. I regret I may have forgotten someone who assisted me. If I have done so, it was not intentional.

Oddly enough, I feel compelled to thank Ed Peterson as well. Mr. Peterson was a Federal soldier, so unfortunately I cannot thank him personally. He was a Scandinavian immigrant who volunteered to fight for the Union and he homesteaded the property where I was raised. Ed lived to be an old man and died in the late 1920's. He is buried in my hometown, not far from my grandparents. His service with Company D, 9th Minnesota Infantry led him to Nashville, Tennessee where he fought in the December 1864 battle. It was because of Ed that I originally traveled to Middle Tennessee many years ago. I was familiar with Spring Hill and Franklin so I traveled there after spending some time in Nashville. My life was never the same. Thank you Ed.

Rich Rupp and I met late in this long process, shortly after the original draft of the manuscript was completed. His great-grandfather, Peter Rupp, served in the 183rd Ohio Infantry and saw action throughout the Tennessee Campaign. Rich and I traveled similar paths of discovery, digging through obscure sources, always hoping to find undiscovered details about those fateful November 1864 days. Among other things, Rich read nearly 45 years worth of the *National Tribune* on microfilm, kindly borrowed by his hometown reference librarian from the Library of Congress. Between the two of us we ironed out many critical details regarding units such as the 183rd Ohio, 107th Illinois, 44th Missouri, 175th Ohio, 129th Indiana, and 111th Ohio. I believe strongly, and I am sure Rich does as well, that some of our research is groundbreaking as it pertains to these units. We also believe that the Federal skirmish line at Franklin has been accurately depicted for the first time. Together we reworked sections of the manuscript again and again and the result was a significantly better book.

In Rhode Island, Rich's wife, Jo Ann, became a "microfilm widow" while Rich spent long hours pouring over sources in the library and endless hours on the phone discussing how new information changed various scenarios. For her understanding and support Rich will always be grateful.

I especially want to extend my gratitude to Mark and Rosemary Hilliard. I can never thank them enough for believing in the book and allowing me to tell this story. I can say with all sincerity that a writer could never work with anyone more professional than Mark and Rosemary.

Paula Bagnall designed the book's cover which is, in my opinion, simply incredible. She took my very basic and abstract ideas and molded them into a beautiful piece of work. I only hope the narrative reads as well as the cover looks. Thank you Paula.

In closing, I must thank my wonderful wife Nancy and our beautiful daughters, Madalaine and Braxton. Nancy has listened to me talk about Spring Hill and Franklin for over a decade. She has gotten to know some of the men who fought there far better than she probably ever wanted to. It was at her urging that I finally completed the manuscript.

My hope is that anyone who reads this book will find it to be balanced and understandable as well as enjoyable. I am sure there will be some surprise and disagreement, but I believe deeply that both Spring Hill and Franklin need to have a fresh and grounded perspective. I pray that I have accomplished just that.

Eric A. Jacobson
Spring Hill, Tennessee
February 1, 2006

Preface

In looking over this sad scene, the question irresistibly forces itself upon us, who was to blame for all this? Was it one of the inexplicable decrees of Fate? These questions may never be satisfactorily answered.[1]

So wrote W. J. Worsham, a former Confederate soldier, as he described the battles at Spring Hill and Franklin, Tennessee. He like many others, both Union and Confederate, never fully understood how those fateful conflicts came to pass. Over the course of the last two days of November 1864, some of the most compelling, defining, and bloody action of the entire Civil War unfolded in Middle Tennessee. The story of the men who fought and died there, overshadowed by other events and long neglected by historians, is breathtaking. No doubt Mr. Worsham would agree.

The whirlwind that swept through the Tennessee heartland over one hundred and forty years ago came to be known as Hood's Tennessee Campaign. Soldiers who lived through the campaign discovered that the memories of Spring Hill and Franklin were ones they could not easily shake from their minds. Men on both sides understood that something incredible had occurred there, and a handful took it upon themselves to tell the story as best they could. What those old soldiers left behind was a rich assortment of research material, ranging from well-written essays and a number of books to less polished, but equally rewarding letters, recollections, and reminiscences. For a researcher the reading is engrossing, especially about the

[1] W. J. Worsham, *The Old Nineteenth Tennessee Regiment, C. S. A.*, p. 148.

culpability for Spring Hill, which was an obvious point of contention among former Rebels. Federal veterans who wrote about Spring Hill concluded almost as a whole that they were simply lucky to escape with their army intact. The material covering Franklin becomes even more invigorating. As the soldiers attempt to describe what it was like to be there one is struck by the depth of feeling in the writing. The depictions of the battle are remarkably vivid, from the horror and wild emotions of armed conflict to scenes of unforgettable pageantry. But even hardened veterans were shaken by what they had witnessed at Franklin. Some conceded that for all practical purposes it was impossible to accurately describe the sights and sounds and sensations without having been there. One could not understand the sound of bones being splintered by artillery fire unless you had heard it yourself. Accurate portrayals of men fighting one another like animals with rifle butts, bayonets, axes, and shovels were no less easy to explain. Words never seemed to be enough.

Sources such as *Confederate Veteran* magazine, the *National Tribune* newspaper, and the *Southern Historical Society Papers* were superb places to look for accounts written by former soldiers recounting the campaign's trials in later years. For this project the *National Tribune* was a literal gold mine of information, virtually untapped by previous Civil War scholars. Never before have accounts published in the *National Tribune* been used in a study of either Spring Hill or Franklin. As with any Civil War project the *Official Records of the War of the Rebellion* was a primary source for contemporary information. However, problems using the *Official Records* were immediately obvious. Because of the destruction wrought upon the Confederates not only at Franklin, but also Nashville, very few official reports were filed by Southern officers. The close proximity to the war's conclusion was also a factor that prevented reports from being written. This problem is evidenced by the fact that only one Southern regimental commander ever filed a report about Spring Hill or Franklin. Furthermore, of the seven Confederate division commanders who led their units into battle at Franklin only two filed reports. Although Federal reports are more numerous a number of them are glaringly absent of useful info.

The search for other material, letters, diaries, articles, etc., composed soon after Spring Hill and Franklin took me far and wide. Unfortunately this type of contemporary material is somewhat limited.

The same issues that caused the lack of reports from the officers seems to have passed down to the rank and file. On both sides, once the fighting in Tennessee ended, the survivors focused on getting through the final months of the war and then starting their lives over. Writing about what happened at Spring Hill or the horrors of Franklin was the last thing on the minds of most.

As the veterans grew old and began to pass away the twentieth century saw the emergence of a new group of writers. Thomas R. Hay's magnificent *Hood's Tennessee Campaign* was published in 1929 and offered one of the first objective reviews of what occurred in Middle Tennessee in late 1864. Hay was fortunate to have been working on his project when some of the veterans were still alive. One of those former soldiers was J. P. Young, with whom Hay corresponded regularly. Young, a Rebel cavalryman in 1864, gain notoriety for authoring the first definitive study of Spring Hill. Following Hay's work, however, new books about Spring Hill and Franklin were non-existent. Not until 1983 did another appear in print. *Five Tragic Hours: The Battle of Franklin* was written by James McDonough and Thomas Connelly and although a fine work it is neither footnoted nor lengthy. Almost ten years later, Wiley Sword's *The Confederacy's Last Hurrah: Spring Hill, Franklin, & Nashville* was released and earned its place as a worthy successor to Hay. Sword offered a sweeping look at the Tennessee campaign and provided a magnificent overview of Spring Hill and Franklin.

Books written about the generals who fought there, particularly John Bell Hood, Patrick Cleburne, and John M. Schofield, offered insight into the lost opportunity at Spring Hill and the tragedy of Franklin. Works by Thomas Connelly and Stanley Horn, devoted to the Confederate Army of Tennessee, are also very helpful. General Jacob Cox delivered a much-needed Federal perspective with his books *The Battle of Franklin* and *Sherman's March to the Sea: Hood's Tennessee Campaign and the Carolina Campaigns of 1865.* Cox's *The Battle of Franklin* is absolutely vital to understanding the battle.

I mention all of these because without them my modest work might not have been able to take flight. To them I am indebted for their tireless efforts and groundbreaking achievements.

To stand on the fields of Spring Hill and Franklin, no matter what visible condition they are in, is to tread on truly hallowed ground. What happened there must never be forgotten, for the sacrifices were far too great. As historian and novelist Shelby Foote said, "The Civil War was the crossroads of our being, and it was a hell of a crossroads, the suffering, the enormous tragedy of the whole thing." If you ever have the opportunity, take the time to walk the ground in Franklin that surrounds the intersection of present day Cleburne Avenue and U. S. Highway 31, known formerly as the Columbia Turnpike. Spend just a few moments lingering in the yard of the nearby Carter House. Go to Carnton Plantation and visit the beautiful Confederate cemetery located there. Also, wander the rolling hills south and southeast of Spring Hill. The echoes of late 1864 can still be heard today if you listen carefully.

Although I have chosen not to include the details of the Battle of Nashville here, my intention is not to diminish the importance of that crucial and ultimately decisive battle. Instead, I believe Spring Hill and Franklin deserve to stand alone because to understand Nashville is to fully understand Spring Hill and Franklin. This work has evolved over time into my tribute to the men from both North and South. To most of them sacrifice knew few boundaries. Their bravery, their compassion, their modesty, and their devotion to one another, as well as their idea of what freedom and independence meant, have inspired me to tell their story. May God rest their souls.

Forever.

Author's Note

The various official ranks of both Union and Confederate general officers are used only when a particular officer is first introduced. The repeated use of Brig. Gen., Maj. Gen., etc. tends to slow the pace of the text and thus only Gen. is used following the initial introduction.

Those who are interested may wish to pay special attention to the orders of battle listed for both armies. Consolidated Southern regiments are listed as such and many errors found in previously published orders of battle have herein been corrected. Specifically, a number of regiments, both Union and Confederate, never before listed have been properly included.

Also, the term Ibid. is used in the footnotes only when a source, exclusive of page number, is exactly the same as the prior source. In the case of a footnote with multiple sources, Ibid. is used in the following footnote only if it contains the exact same sources. If the footnote contains even one additional, or less source, Ibid. is not used.

1

The Road to Destiny

Compromise was dead. On December 20, 1860 the very idea of a United States of America began to unravel. In Charleston, South Carolina state delegates gathered and voted unanimously 169-0 to withdraw their state from the Union. The long and painfully debated issue of secession transformed from mere political talk and threats into reality through a simple call of votes. Like a flash of lightning the idea set forth by the Founding Fathers of a "more perfect Union" was suddenly called into question. Within six weeks an additional half dozen states from the Lower South joined South Carolina and an independent government was created at Montgomery, Alabama. By May 1861 four more states made the choice to secede and the final version of the Confederate States of America began its quest for independence.

When the Tennessee state legislature voted on May 7, 1861 to withdraw from the Union, final ratification of the matter was left in the hands of the state citizens. Although it was another month before the people of Tennessee agreed to secession by a vote of 104,913 to 47,238, movements to raise volunteers for defense of the state began almost immediately. By mid-May men and boys were flocking to recruiting stations across the Volunteer State. They came to fight against what they perceived as a threat to their homeland and way of life. It was a personal involvement, a deep rooted connection to mind and soul. At Franklin, Tennessee, in a modest red brick home on the south edge of town, Fountain Branch Carter watched as his three sons left home to join the Confederate army.[1]

---

[1] E. B. Long, *The Civil War Day by Day: An Almanac 1861-65*, p. 71, 83.

Three and a half years later, fate brought one of those brothers back home to take part in perhaps the most incredible infantry assault of the entire Civil War. The story of how the war in the Western Theater, after so much fighting and so much bloodshed, came to Franklin at the end of 1864 is one filled with numerous twists and turns. It is best understood by starting from the beginning, when the war was young and when both soldiers and armies had yet to make names for themselves.

Troops from both North and South began to gather and coalesce into fighting units throughout the summer of 1861. Men loyal to the Union, from states such as Illinois, Indiana, Ohio, Iowa, Michigan, and Missouri, quickly filled out the ranks of the first Federal units assigned to defense of what was then known as the West. Three departments initially made up the basic military structure of the Union forces in this region. They were the Department of Kansas under Maj. Gen. David Hunter; the Department of the Cumberland commanded by Brig. Gen. Robert Anderson; and the Department of Missouri under Maj. Gen. Henry W. Halleck. As for the Confederacy, Gen. Albert Sidney Johnston was appointed to command of Department Number 2, a large collection of both men and land that encompassed portions of Arkansas, Tennessee, Louisiana, Mississippi, and Alabama. Johnston, fifty-eight years old and a close and longtime friend of President Jefferson Davis, had been hand-picked by the Confederacy's chief executive to lead the western Confederate forces.[2]

Sidney Johnston was a 1826 graduate of West Point and had dedicated his entire adult life to serving the United States. He fought against the Black Hawk Indians and in Mexico and took part in the expedition against the Mormons in Utah in 1857. Although a native Kentuckian, Johnston considered Texas his home and when that state seceded he went with her. His first responsibility as a Confederate

---

[2] *The War of the Rebellion: A Compilation of the Official Records of the Union and Confederate Armies*, 128 volumes, (hereafter noted as *OR*), 4, p. 175, 188, 254, 405; *OR* 3, p. 567. All the volumes used herein are from Series I.

department head was the thankless task of maintaining a defensive line which ran from eastern Kentucky to the Mississippi River. Considering the shortage of manpower, it is a true wonder that Johnston maintained the line as long as he did. But inevitable cracks began to develop and fighting soon broke out. Troops commanded by Maj. Gen. Leonidas Polk battled with Federal soldiers under Brig. Gen. Ulysses S. Grant near Belmont, Missouri in November 1861, but the first truly decisive fight erupted in southeastern Kentucky soon thereafter. Holding the eastern section of his line was altogether crucial, and Johnston was fully aware that if the far right caved in, there would be serious problems in Tennessee and Kentucky would surely be lost.[3]

Brig. Gen. George Henry Thomas, a Virginian who remained loyal to the Union, would play a large part in some of the worst days of the Western Confederacy and his first success was manufactured on January 19, 1862 near Mill Springs, Kentucky, just outside of Somerset. Thomas' victory ruptured the enemy's defensive structure and caused Sidney Johnston's Kentucky-Tennessee line to be hastily abandoned. The Southern commander's worst fears quickly began to materialize. Less than a month later, he courted disaster at Forts Henry and Donelson in northern Tennessee, eventually losing both posts and nearly 15,000 prisoners to Grant's troops. Although Johnston was unquestionably burdened with several thoroughly incompetent generals, particularly Brig. Gens. John B. Floyd and Gideon J. Pillow at Fort Donelson, the ultimate responsibility for the loss of the twin forts falls squarely upon his shoulders. Having already ceded Kentucky to Federal control, the failures at Henry and Donelson were serious setbacks that forced Johnston to withdraw deeper into Tennessee. That movement resulted in the forfeiture of invaluable territory and led to the hasty evacuation of Nashville without even so much as a fight. Abandoning Nashville, her factories and stores, and the city's 17,000 citizens was an industrial and psychological loss from which the South never fully recovered. Nashville forever remained the lost jewel of the Confederacy

[3] Patricia L. Faust, ed., *Historical Times Illustrated Encyclopedia of the Civil War*, p. 399; *OR* 4, p. 346, 405, 554. Johnston was also responsible much territory west of the Mississippi River, including Arkansas, Missouri, Kansas, and the Indian Territory.

and the dream of regaining the city would die hard.[4]

In March 1862, the three Federal departments which had largely made up the Western Theater were consolidated into one command - the Union Department of the Mississippi. Command of this new department, created by order of President Abraham Lincoln, was given to Henry Halleck, whose headquarters were based in St. Louis, Missouri. With the simple stroke of a pen, Halleck found himself commanding over 125,000 soldiers spread out over four states.[5]

Even before Halleck took command of this new department, he was picking a fight with Ulysses S. Grant. Halleck treated Grant with pure contempt, ordering him to remain at Fort Henry while Maj. Gen. Charles F. Smith led an expedition south in the direction of Eastport, Mississippi and Paris, Tennessee to feel out the enemy. The shoddy treatment was more than Grant could handle and he asked to be relieved from duty. He did not receive a response and so Grant, diligent as ever, repeated his request. Suddenly Halleck reversed course and sent Grant a telegram on March 13 with orders to assume "immediate command" of the army and "lead it on to new victories." Halleck's duplicity was shocking. In his memoirs, Grant detailed exactly how Halleck tried to discredit him in an effort to have Smith gain permanent command.[6]

By March 17, Grant was back with his army, stationed near Savannah, Tennessee. Meanwhile, while the Halleck-Grant drama had been playing out, Johnston was reorganizing his forces at Corinth in northern Mississippi and planning a masterstroke to recoup his dramatic setbacks. Attacked relentlessly in the press and by many in the Confederate Congress, Johnston knew he had to act quickly before the Union forces did. Along with Gen. P. G. T. Beauregard, the hero of Fort Sumter and First Manassas, who had recently transferred from the

---

[4] *OR* 7, p. 2, 76-83, 159-161, 254, 269-270, 284, 424-427; Benjamin Franklin Cooling, *Forts Henry and Donelson: The Key to the Confederate Heartland*, p. 31. Jefferson Davis was so infuriated by the actions of Floyd and Pillow, both of whom left Fort Donelson before the surrender, that he had them relieved from command.

[5] *OR* 10, pt. 2, p. 28-29; Faust, ed., *Historical Times Encyclopedia*, p. 500.

[6] *OR* 10, pt. 2, p. 3, 15, 21, 32-33; U. S. Grant, *Personal Memoirs of U. S. Grant*, p. 193-195.

East, a plan was developed to strike Grant and his men in camp along the Tennessee River at Pittsburg Landing. The Rebel forces also had for the first time an official moniker. Beauregard chose to label the troops the Army of Mississippi and in a March 5 proclamation called upon them to resist the "subjugation" and "dishonor" of the Southern people. It was a ploy repeated throughout the course of the war to rally the rank and file.[7]

Whether he acted on his own or was emboldened by Beauregard, Sidney Johnston moved aggressively to offset his recent defeats. He decided to hit Grant before Yankee reinforcements could arrive. His comment to a staff officer that he would "fight them if they were a million" said a great deal about Johnston's state of mind in the early spring of 1862.[8]

On April 6 and 7, 1862 the Confederate and Federal armies embraced in a savage struggle in the woods and clearings along the Tennessee River. A tiny log structure, the Shiloh Methodist Church, was at the epicenter of some of the worst fighting. On the first horrific day, which saw some 15,000 blue and gray fall dead and wounded, the Rebels nearly pushed Grant and his shattered Army of the Tennessee into the river. Only a tenacious Yankee defense held out long enough for the Rebel assault to sputter out as the sun went down. That night Northern reinforcements from Maj. Gen. Don Carlos Buell's Army of the Ohio arrived and their appearance, combined with the ravaged and scattered condition of the Confederate troops, forced a dramatic turn of events. Johnston was already dead, killed by a stray bullet during the mid-afternoon hours of April 6. Many have long thought that his death alone caused the entire Confederate effort to falter as dusk approached.[9]

---

[7] *OR* 10, pt. 2, p. 297, 354, 361; Alfred Roman, *The Military Operations of General Beauregard*, Vol. I, p. 210-213.

[8] James Lee McDonough, *Shiloh - In Hell Before Night*, p. 70, 81. Whether Johnston was as confident before Shiloh as his manner indicated has always been a matter of conjecture, but it is clear he told his generals in no uncertain terms the battle was going to be fought there.

[9] *OR* 10, pt. 1, p. 108-109, 387, 390, 405; Roman, *The Military Operations of General Beauregard*, Vol. I, p. 344-351; T. Harry Williams, *P. G. T. Beauregard: Napoleon in Gray*, p. 141-143.

The second day at Shiloh resulted in a crushing Confederate loss. Exhausted and terribly disorganized by their near victory, the Rebels were able to hold off repeated assaults by the revitalized Union troops for several hours. However, momentum was on the North's side and by about 3 p.m. the Southerners were in retreat toward Corinth, fifteen miles to the south. On the blood-soaked fields around Shiloh Church, where over 23,000 American soldiers became casualties, all the horrors of war were readily evident. It was destruction on a scale that shocked even the strong hearted.[10]

For U. S. Grant the victory at Shiloh was a combination of both luck and dogged determination. For the Union the battle had wide-ranging ramifications. Had Grant been defeated at Shiloh it is unlikely he would have ever commanded another army. The career of William Tecumseh Sherman, a division commander at Shiloh, might also have been impacted. Without the leadership of these two men it is questionable whether the North could have achieved four of its greatest victories - Vicksburg, Chattanooga, Atlanta, and the defeat of Robert E. Lee. Shiloh was also grim evidence that the war was not going to be easy or short. Grant, in fact, said that after Shiloh he "gave up all idea of saving the Union except by complete conquest."[11]

Following Shiloh the Confederates again took up ground in and around Corinth. Camp life for the men was largely miserable. Conditions were poor due to a shortage of food and widespread disease, the latter exacerbated by the grueling Mississippi climate. Especially troublesome for Beauregard's army was a lack of good water that only worsened as the weather heated up. Meanwhile, Grant had a troubling situation of his own. His army may have been in better shape, but his personal situation was a different story and once again Henry Halleck was the issue. Only days after Shiloh, Halleck had arrived and taken command of the Union forces. Grant wrote plaintively that he was "little more than an observer" when the army advanced upon Corinth

---

[10] *OR* 10, pt. 1, p. 109, 387-388; Thomas L. Livermore, *Numbers and Losses in the Civil War*, p. 79-80. The Battle of Shiloh resulted in more American casualties than the total losses of the Revolutionary War, the War of 1812, and Mexican War combined.

[11] Grant, *Personal Memoirs*, p. 218; James R. Arnold, *The Armies of U. S. Grant*, p. 72. Arnold states Grant was "fortunate to win" at Shiloh.

at the end of April. Additionally, there were rumors about Grant's drinking making the rounds.[12]

With Halleck at the helm the Federal troops pushed methodically south toward Corinth. It took nearly a month for the Yankees to get there and when they finally arrived, Halleck opted to lay siege to the town. Beauregard knew full well that his men could not withstand a siege, and so on May 29, under cover of night, the Rebel army pulled out of Corinth and marched south to Tupelo. There a new base was established and Halleck, content with his bloodless victory, pursued no further. Beauregard, suffering from the effects of a throat condition, took a leave of absence in June without approval from the War Department and quickly found himself without a job. The relationship between President Davis and Beauregard was anything but friendly, and Davis may have privately relished the chance to rid himself of the Creole general. Yet in Beauregard's place Davis appointed a man who became the focal point of vigorous debate and dissension.[13]

As for the Union forces, Halleck was called back to desk duty in early July and Grant found himself returned to command of the Army of the Tennessee. Buell and his Army of the Ohio were shipped east to Chattanooga and Grant was left to protect western Tennessee and northern Mississippi and prepare for the summer campaign.[14]

Braxton Bragg was not the kind of man people warmed to easily. Cold and impersonal to all but a few close associates, he suffered almost constantly from one physical malady or another, conditions that did little to enhance an already sour disposition. Like Johnston and

---

[12] Grant, *Personal Memoirs*, p. 219-220; Stanley F. Horn, *The Army of Tennessee*, p. 148-149; McDonough, *Shiloh - In Hell Before Night*, p. 222-223; William T. Sherman, *Memoirs of General William T. Sherman,* Vol. I, p. 244.

[13] Horn, *Army of Tennessee*, p. 148, 151-152; Grant, *Personal Memoirs*, p. 226; Jefferson Davis, *The Rise and Fall of the Confederate Government,* Vol. II, p. 60-61; Roman, *The Military Operations of General Beauregard*, Vol. I, p. 403-411; *OR* 17, pt. 2, p. 599, 601, 606, 612, 614.

[14] Grant, *Personal Memoirs*, p. 233-234.

Beauregard, Bragg had attended West Point. A North Carolinian by birth, he graduated fifth in the academy's class of 1837 and served in the Mexican War. Although gifted with a sound military mind Bragg had serious limitations, ones that seemed to prevent him from being able to achieve success on the battlefield. His command would be marred with errors. From the time he took command until the day he stepped down, one golden opportunity after another was allowed to slip away.[15]

Beginning late in the summer of 1862, the first campaign under Bragg got underway. It was actually a dual effort aimed at the Kentucky heartland. With Bragg at the head of one column and Brig. Gen. Edmund Kirby Smith fronting the other, the invasion was an effort to win back the territory lost by Sidney Johnston earlier in the year. Inaugurated just prior to Robert E. Lee's startling trek into Maryland, and carried out in concert with a Southern thrust against Yankee troops occupying Corinth, Bragg's incursion sent a paroxysm of terror through the North. The Confederates seemed to be striking everywhere, and the Federal armies had their hands full trying to hold back the advancing enemy columns.[16]

Initially the Kentucky invasion was a rousing success. Before the end of August, nearly 4,300 Union troops surrendered to Smith at Richmond and at Munfordville on September 17, another 4,000-man garrison capitulated to Bragg.[17] But Federal forces soon coalesced under Don Carlos Buell and on October 7-8, Bragg was forced to fight at Perryville without Smith's help. The battle was a costly one, resulting in combined losses of approximately 7,600. Although the Confederates had enjoyed the upper hand on the battlefield, Bragg knew his force remained isolated and Buell defiantly stood his ground. As a result, Bragg withdrew his troops during the night of October 8 and moved to Harrodsburg where he joined Smith. On October 11, Bragg decided to abandon Kentucky and by the end of the month the Rebel columns were back in Tennessee, exhausted and hungry and their morale sagging.

---

[15] Grady McWhiney, *Braxton Bragg and Confederate Defeat*, Vol. I, p. 21-25, 27-28, 94; Faust, ed., *Historical Times Encyclopedia*, p. 75.

[16] James L. McDonough, *War in Kentucky: From Shiloh to Perryville*, p. 113; *OR* 16, pt. 2, p. 344, 771.

[17] *OR* 16, pt. 1, p. 968; Livermore, *Numbers and Losses*, p. 89; Faust, ed., *Historical Times Encyclopedia*, p. 517.

It was at this time that the seeds of the anti-Bragg movement first took hold. It soon permeated much of the Confederate army and threatened to consume it.[18]

For Gen. Buell the victory at Perryville was not enough to win him favor with President Abraham Lincoln. Buell was a plodding strategist and by the fall of 1862 Lincoln had seen enough generals who fought tentatively and did not follow up victories with vigor. At the end of October, Buell was replaced by Maj. Gen. William S. Rosecrans, an Ohioan whose star had been on the rise since the beginning of the war. Rosecrans, an 1838 graduate of West Point, had achieved one of the Union's first victories at Rich Mountain, Virginia in July 1861. He had also performed tenaciously at bloody Corinth, just days before Perryville. Paralleling Rosecrans' ascension to power was the creation of what became one of the primary Federal forces in the West, the Union Army of the Cumberland. For the next two years, this Federal army would come to grips time and time again with the Confederates in the Western Theater. Theirs would be a struggle to the death.[19]

Following the disastrous Kentucky foray, Bragg's Army of Mississippi and Kirby Smith's Army of Kentucky were consolidated into what became known as the Confederate Army of Tennessee. Shortly after this, in mid-December, President Davis traveled to Tennessee to meet with some of his generals, review the army, and attempt to quell the criticism mounting against Bragg. Like Sidney Johnston, Davis considered Bragg a close friend, a relationship that led Davis to hold a blind trust in Bragg's abilities. Bragg was also a West Point graduate, something in which Davis put much stock. The Christmas visit, however, did nothing to help Bragg's strategic situation. When it concluded, Davis chose to send one of the army's largest divisions, some 7,500 men commanded by Maj. Gen. Carter L. Stevenson, west to bolster the defenses at Vicksburg, Mississippi. An additional brigade totaling about 2,500 from the Department of East Tennessee was also

---

[18] *OR* 16, pt. 1, p. 1087-1088, 1096; Livermore, *Numbers and Losses*, p. 95; McWhiney, *Braxton Bragg and Confederate Defeat*, Vol. I, p. 318, 320-321; McDonough, *War in Kentucky*, p. 308-310; Horn, *Army of Tennessee*, p. 188-189.

[19] *OR* 16, pt. 2, 640, 642; Faust, ed., *Historical Times Encyclopedia*, p. 642-643.

sent to Vicksburg. Davis apparently did not fully appreciate the importance of Middle Tennessee, and while the motives behind his intense preoccupation with Vicksburg are questionable, especially considering Davis was a native Mississippian, he ostensibly weakened a vitally important region in an effort to save the river city. The Southern president also made another critical and far-reaching decision. He threw his complete support behind Bragg, thereby prolonging the internal strife that had begun to infect the army's high command. Both decisions were strategies that would haunt Davis in the months to come.[20]

On December 31, 1862 the Army of Tennessee, acting in response to aggressive movements by Rosecrans' 47,000-man Army of the Cumberland, opened the Battle of Stones River near Murfreesboro, Tennessee with a driving dawn assault. Bragg had about 38,000 men available and he threw practically everything he had at the Federal forces, who were as surprised as Grant's army had been eight months earlier at Shiloh. The fighting was savage and desperate. The Federals, particularly the tough Midwesterners in Brig. Gen. Philip H. Sheridan's Division, regrouped and executed a tenacious defense. All three of Sheridan's brigade commanders were killed, but the Northern troops held on and prevented Rosecrans' entire army from being folded up. By nightfall the fighting ebbed away, leaving in its wake an appalling number of dead and wounded on both sides. It was obvious the Confederates had won the day and Bragg fully expected Rosecrans to withdraw, but January 1 found the Federals right were they had gone to sleep the night before. Only light skirmishing took place on New Year's Day and January 2 saw little action until late afternoon. On that date

---

[20] *OR* 20, pt. 2, p. 385, 462-463; Horn, *Army of Tennessee*, p. 192; McWhiney, *Braxton Bragg and Confederate Defeat*, Vol. I, p. 362-363; Thomas L. Connelly, *Autumn of Glory: The Army of Tennessee, 1862-1865*, p. 38-39; James McDonough, *Stones River: Bloody Winter in Tennessee*, p. 36-37; R. Lockwood Tower, ed., *A Carolinian Goes To War: The Civil War Narrative of Arthur Middleton Manigault*, p. 53. The figure of 10,000 is often accepted as the size of Stevenson's Division. However, McDonough correctly points out that Stevenson's three brigades were joined by the single brigade from East Tennessee to total 10,000. General E. K. Smith stated the total of these four brigades was "an effective force of about 9,000."

Bragg ordered Maj. Gen. John C. Breckinridge, Vice-President of the United States during James Buchanan's administration, to assault a strong position along Stones River. Breckinridge vigorously protested that the assault was nothing short of suicidal. Bragg refused to reconsider, however, and Breckinridge ordered his men forward, only to watch them be cut to pieces. In barely an hour of fighting they suffered some 1,700 casualties. The following day Rosecrans again refused to budge, forcing Bragg to make a decision. After vacillating between standing his ground and retreating, Bragg decided to withdraw and moved the army south to Shelbyville during the night of January 4.[21]

Strewn about the fields and woods surrounding Murfreesboro were approximately 3,000 Union and Confederate dead and altogether the two sides counted some 24,000 casualties. Rosecrans' losses were slightly higher and although he chose not to pursue Bragg, the hard-fought victory was welcomed in the North as the first good news in months. Following the series of defeats in the East at the hands of Robert E. Lee, beginning during the Seven Days Campaign around Richmond and culminating at Fredericksburg, Virginia, the result at Stones River was a marked improvement.[22]

Although no one on either side could have predicted the future, Stones River was where many of the troops who later fought at Spring Hill and Franklin faced one another for the first time. For the next two years, one battle after another pitted these Western soldiers and their respective units against one another.

Through the spring and early summer of 1863, Rosecrans and Bragg faced off in Middle Tennessee. Defense remained their primary mode of thought for months and it was the end of June before the Federal army started moving again. Prodded by Washington for action, Rosecrans had refused to budge until he felt everything was in place. When he finally did order the army forward, the Federal troops pulled off a series of masterful maneuvers. During the Tullahoma Campaign, Rosecrans completely baffled Bragg, outflanked the Army of Tennessee, and forced an eighty-mile Confederate retreat all the way south of the

---

[21] Horn, *Army of Tennessee*, p. 196, 198, 201, 206-210; McDonough, *Bloody Winter in Tennessee*, p. 98-99, 106-108, 176-177, 202; *OR* 20, pt. 1, p. 787; Tower, ed., *A Carolinian Goes To War*, p. 67.

[22] Livermore, *Numbers and Losses*, p. 97.

Tennessee River. The campaign, which cost Bragg over 1,600 prisoners, a half dozen cannon, and "large quantities" of supplies, occurred almost simultaneously with the Confederate defeats at Gettysburg and Vicksburg. It was arguably the most damaging strategic period of time the South had endured during the war and was something from which it never recovered. By the time Rosecrans finally eased up, Bragg's army had been forced to occupy a new position near Chattanooga, Tennessee, just north of the Georgia state line.[23]

After much frantic maneuvering in early September 1863, the two armies again came to grips with one another in the choking forest and underbrush of the northwestern Georgia hills. The battle which erupted along Chickamauga Creek was the bloodiest of the war in the Western Theater. For two days, September 19-20, the brutal fighting raged almost uncontrollably. When the combat finally ended the two armies had suffered nearly 35,000 casualties, more than any battle during the entire Civil War except for Gettysburg. Although Bragg lost almost 19,000 troops, he nearly crushed the Army of the Cumberland on the second day of the battle when a huge hole opened in the blue line as the result of an errant order. Thousands of Confederate troops surged through the gap and exploited the sudden breach. Many of the men who broke through the Union line were largely from Lt. Gen. James Longstreet's Corps, sent west from Robert E. Lee's army in Virginia to assist the Army of Tennessee. Personally leading some of Longstreet's veteran soldiers was Maj. Gen. John Bell Hood, a man whose stamp of influence in the West would be great in the months to come.[24]

What Longstreet's men almost accomplished was the complete destruction of the Army of the Cumberland. Only Maj. Gen. George Henry Thomas, commanding a number of Union brigades atop Snodgrass Hill, was able to organize a patchwork defense and stave off wholesale annihilation, thus allowing what remained of the army to pull back with some sense of order. The Confederates had achieved a resounding victory and thousands of Federals were sent running back to Chattanooga. In the aftermath of the defeat, Rosecrans seemed unable to cope with the results and President Lincoln went so far as to

---

[23] Horn, *Army of Tennessee*, p. 234-238; *OR* 23, pt. 1, p. 10, 425.

[24] Horn, *Army of Tennessee*, p. 263-265, 270; Connelly, *Autumn of Glory*, p. 223-224; Livermore, *Numbers and Losses*, p. 105-106.

describe him as "confused and stunned like a duck hit on the head." Within a month, Rosecrans was relieved of duty and Thomas ascended to command of the Federal army. Meanwhile, Lincoln also brought in U. S. Grant and put him in charge of the Union Military Division of the Mississippi, a post from which Grant could organize and draw up plans for Thomas to employ.[25]

Bragg also failed miserably following Chickamauga. For a time Bragg could not be convinced of the magnitude of the victory, or even that he had won. Not only did many of the enlisted men understand the tremendous opportunity which was slipping away, but a number of the general officers in the Army of Tennessee staged a near mutiny. The anti-Bragg crowd practically accused the commanding general of treason, claiming that he was inept and unfit to command. Chief among his persecutors were James Longstreet, Daniel Harvey Hill, and Leonidas Polk, and the harder they attacked Bragg the more virulent his responses became. It was an ugly and bitter spectacle. Things got so bad that Bragg suspended Polk and preferred charges against the bishop general. He later removed Hill from duty as well. The animosity grew so intense that Davis was forced to travel to Tennessee in early October to try and prevent the army's entire command structure from splintering.[26]

While the Army of the Cumberland was trapped at Chattanooga, the command structure of the Army of Tennessee was rotting away. Bragg may indeed have been unfit for command, but some of the generals who served under him only made matters worse. Inexplicably, Davis could not bring himself to make the necessary changes. He was intent upon maintaining Bragg and instead of sacking him, Davis came

---

[25] *OR* 30, pt. 1, p. 253-254; William M. Lamers, *The Edge of Glory: A Biography of William S. Rosecrans, U.S.A.*, p. 356; Wiley Sword, *Mountains Touched With Fire: Chattanooga Besieged, 1863*, p. 50; Arnold, *The Armies of U. S. Grant*, p. 133-134.

[26] Tower, ed., *A Carolinian Goes To War*, p. 101; Horn, *Army of Tennessee*, p. 275-284; Connelly, *Autumn of Glory*, p. 228-234; Hal Bridges, *Lee's Maverick General: Daniel Harvey Hill*, p. 226-238; Joseph H. Parks, *General Leonidas Polk, C. S. A.: The Fighting Bishop*, p. 340-347. Judith Lee Hallock, *Braxton Bragg and Confederate Defeat*, Vol. II, p. 81-87, 90, 94. Hallock has a much more sympathetic view of Bragg following Chickamauga.

to Tennessee and called a highly unusual meeting. In the conference Bragg was forced to listen as his subordinates were allowed to lambaste him to his face. President Davis was even so foolish as to suggest that Lt. Gen. John Pemberton, the officer who had surrendered Vicksburg, replace Polk as a corps commander. It was an idea that was squelched almost at once. By the time Davis left Bragg's headquarters little had been accomplished, but events quickly shifted back to the battlefield. A new player was in the game.[27]

Maj. Gen. Grant was ushered in to save the besieged Federal army at Chattanooga and by October 26, only days after arriving, he had reopened the Union supply line. Bragg surely was oblivious to the fact that his days as an army commander were ticking away. Grant had a well designed plan and, true to form, he did not delay in launching it. The resulting battles atop Lookout Mountain on November 24 and on Missionary Ridge the following day resulted in decisive victories for the Federals. Bragg helped to seal his own fate by depleting his army. With the Yankees in clear sight Longstreet's troops were sent east to Knoxville to deal with an enemy force there and as late as November 22 Bragg was still shuffling men away to Knoxville. Then the hammer fell.[28]

Maj. Gen. Joseph Hooker, like Longstreet, had come from the Eastern Theater. On November 24 he was pushing 10,000 troops up the slopes toward the crest of Lookout Mountain, partially obscured that morning by a thick blanket of fog rising from the Tennessee River. The Confederates had very few troops actually posted atop Lookout Mountain and by nightfall, although he did not know it until dawn, Hooker had taken possession of the summit and won eternal fame for his part in what became known as the "Battle Above the Clouds."[29]

Grant seized the advantage and by dawn on November 25 he

---

[27] Horn, *Army of Tennessee*, p. 287-288; Hallock, *Braxton Bragg and Confederate Defeat*, Vol, II, p. 97-99; Bridges, *Lee's Maverick General*, p. 236-240. An excellent description of Davis' visit and the bitterness in the high command can be found in Peter Cozzens' *This Terrible Sound: The Battle of Chickamauga*, p. 528-534.

[28] Horn, The *Army of Tennessee*, p. 292-296.

[29] Horn, The *Army of Tennessee*, p. 297-298; Grant, *Personal Memoirs*, p. 379-380.

had Maj. Gen. William T. Sherman's men assaulting Missionary Ridge, where Bragg's main army was waiting. The Federals threw themselves at the Southerners and only a stubborn defense held them back. But disaster was in the air and mid-afternoon brought wholesale disaster to Braxton Bragg and the Army of Tennessee.

George Henry Thomas' troops scaled the seemingly impregnable slopes of Missionary Ridge, pushed the Confederates in the center out of their rifle pits, and sent most of the army into a panicked southward retreat. Watching from a distance, neither Grant nor Thomas could believe their eyes. After clearing away the first Rebel line the heroic Union troops had halted as directed. Then, without orders, they bolted forward and up the slope, knocking aside nearly everything in their path. Bragg was nearly captured and only a valiant rear guard defense by Maj. Gen. Patrick R. Cleburne's Division, similar in valor to that of Thomas at Chickamauga, prevented the army from being torn to pieces by Hooker's pursuing columns.[30]

By November 29, even Bragg realized the futility of continuing as commander of an army that did not favor him and appeared to be falling apart at the seams. He tendered his resignation that day, stepped down officially on December 2, and was replaced in the interim by Lt. Gen. William Hardee. Hardee remained in charge for two weeks and moved aside on December 16 when Gen. Joseph E. Johnston was given permanent command of the beleaguered Southern army.[31]

Johnston wasted little time putting the army back together. He did everything humanly possible, from obtaining new uniforms and shoes and muskets to setting up a system of furloughs that allowed many of the war-weary men to go home for a short while. Yet more than anything Johnston had an air about him that was appealing to the common soldier in the Army of Tennessee. They simply adored him. For some time prior to Bragg's departure there had been calls for Johnston to take command. Although Jefferson Davis, whose

---

[30] Freeman Cleaves, *Rock of Chickamauga, The Life of General George H. Thomas*, p. 196-200; Horn, *Army of Tennessee*, p. 299-301; Grant, *Personal Memoirs*, p. 381-386; Hallock, *Braxton Bragg and Confederate Defeat*, Vol. II, p. 140-141.

[31] *OR* 31, pt. 2, p. 682; *OR* 31, pt. 3, p. 764-765, 775-776; *OR* 52, pt. 2, p. 576.

relationship with Johnston was as strained as it was with Beauregard, found it difficult to put Old Joe at the head of the army, he could not deny the impact his presence had on the men. It was at times electric.[32]

To some, Joseph Eggleston Johnston was the model soldier. A Virginian and a West Point graduate from the class of 1829, Johnston had fought against Indians in Florida and served in the Mexican War during a long and distinguished army career. He eventually rose to become Quartermaster General in 1860, a promotion that made him a brigadier general. When war came over the land Johnston, like Lee, held out until Virginia seceded before resigning his commission and when Johnston quit he was the highest ranking officer to abandon the United States Army. Fifty-six years old when he took command of the Army of Tennessee, it was Johnston's third major assignment of the war. Previously Johnston had led the primary Confederate army in the East, but he was seriously wounded at Seven Pines in May 1862 and Robert E. Lee was elevated to command. Following his recovery, and Lee's many triumphs, Johnston was without an army. Davis chose to assign him a new role heading up the Department of the West, which encompassed Albert Sidney's Johnston's old Department Number 2 and other smaller departments. In neither capacity, however, had Johnston performed with any great success.[33]

Johnston barely had time to settle into his new command, however, before the army's upper command was rocked. In early January 1864, Patrick Cleburne submitted a proposal so shocking that it was kept secret from the public for over thirty years. During a meeting with Johnston and a small group of general officers Cleburne, with support from many of his regimental officers as well as corps commander William Hardee, presented the idea of offering slaves freedom in exchange for loyal service in the Confederate armies. The idea was radical and enraged some of those present to such extremes,

---

[32] Horn, *Army of Tennessee*, p. 311-313; Craig Symonds, *Joseph E. Johnston, A Civil War Biography*, p. 249-250; Larry Daniel, *Soldiering in the Army of Tennessee*, p. 138.

[33] Faust, ed., *Historical Times Encyclopedia*, p. 400.

in particular Maj. Gen. W. H. T. Walker, that Johnston ordered the matter kept quiet. But Walker was indignant and went over Johnston's head and straight to President Davis. Davis agreed with Walker that the plan was outrageous, but he, like Johnston, simply ordered that the proposal be kept silent, deciding the "best policy" was to "avoid all publicity..." As for Cleburne the entire affair may have prevented him from ever again being considered for promotion.[34]

In March of 1864, William Sherman was appointed by U. S. Grant to command three separate Federal armies - Thomas' Army of the Cumberland, Maj. Gen. John B. McPherson's Army of the Tennessee, and Maj. Gen. John M. Schofield's smaller Army of the Ohio. His objective was to move against Johnston's army of nearly 45,000, which was dug in around Dalton, Georgia. During the course of May, Johnston also received about 21,600 reinforcements. Sherman had over 98,000 troops at his disposal and from early May through mid-July he and Johnston performed a dance that repeated itself time and time again. Sherman would push his columns forward and attempt to move them around one of the Confederate flanks, causing Johnston to either pull back and fortify elsewhere or strike if possible. From Dalton to Resaca to Cassville heavy and often bloody fighting broke out as the two armies grappled. Around New Hope Church and Dallas, in mountainous country so thickly forested and difficult to maneuver in that soldiers termed it "the Hell Hole," the combat was exceptionally fierce. But Sherman was undeterred and continued his flanking

---

[34] *OR* 52, pt. 2, p. 586-592, 595-596, 608-609; Connelly, *Autumn of Glory*, p. 319; Craig Symonds, *Stonewall of the West: Patrick Cleburne and the Civil War*, p. 186-191; Howell Purdue and Elizabeth Purdue, *Pat Cleburne: Confederate General*, p. 270-272. It is obvious men like Walker considered slavery and independence to be inexorably linked. Cleburne on the other hand saw independence, even without slavery, as the ultimate goal. This divergence of ideas is a perfect example of the wide schism that existed even among Southerners. As for the proposal, there is no concrete evidence Cleburne was passed over for higher command as a result of it. However, the promotion of other officers to fill vacancies within the army in the latter half of 1864 that might have more logically been filled by Cleburne points to, at the very least, some lingering resentment in the upper reaches of the Confederate government.

movements, forcing Johnston back to near Marietta where the Rebels dug in around Kennesaw Mountain.[35]

Although Johnston's retreat employed mostly sound defensive maneuvering, and he prevented Sherman from dealing any serious blows, the endless backtracking grew increasingly frustrating for Jefferson Davis. Davis' ultimate concern was for the safety of Atlanta, and day after day he wondered when and if Johnston was going to stand and fight. When questioned about his plans, Johnston was unwilling to commit to any sort of definite answer and Davis' apprehension only worsened based on communications received from others. Braxton Bragg, who was serving as the President's chief-of-staff and visited with Johnston in mid-July, offered Davis very little encouragement. Letters penned by Lt. Gen. John Bell Hood only further damned Johnston. Hood pointedly outlined his personal dissatisfaction with Johnston and raised the question of whether the commanding general would ever fight for Atlanta.[36]

Meanwhile, the fighting in the field dragged on. On June 27, Sherman committed perhaps his worst error during the Atlanta Campaign when he decided to attack Joe Johnston head-on. The Federals lurched forward against the fortified Rebel lines stretched along Kennesaw Mountain and the columns of mostly Midwestern boys were decimated. Struggling in the blistering heat and humidity, the blue-clad troops tried with unsurpassed bravery to punch through Johnston's superbly entrenched position. Valor could only accomplish so much, however, and the Yankees were mostly ground to pieces in the face of the murderous enemy fire. When it was all over Sherman had lost nearly 2,500 men in only a few hours, many of them stacked three and four deep in front of the breastworks at a place that came to be known

---

[35] *OR* 38, pt. 1, p. 62-63; *OR* 38, pt. 3, p. 614; Grant, *Personal Memoirs*, p. 405-407; Cleaves, *Rock of Chickamauga*, p. 208; Brooks D. Simpson & Jean V. Berlin, ed., *Sherman's Civil War: Selected Correspondence of William T. Sherman, 1860-1865*, p. 611; Joseph E. Johnston, *Narrative of Military Operations, Directed, During the Late War Between the States*, p. 326-332, 574; Horn, *Army of Tennessee*, p. 322-334.

[36] *OR* 38, pt. 5, p. 882-883; Davis, *Rise and Fall of the Confederate Government,* Vol. II, p. 71; Richard M. McMurry, *John Bell Hood and the War for Southern Independence*, p. 117-120.

as the Dead Angle. Sherman was very blunt in his memoirs when he wrote, "By 11:30 the assault was in fact over, and had failed. We had not broken the rebel line.....This was the hardest fight of the campaign up to that date....." Johnston's stout defense cost his army approximately 500 casualties.[37]

After the Battle of Kennesaw Mountain, Sherman resumed his flanking movements and within days Johnston had given up his position and was swinging the Army of Tennessee ever closer to Atlanta. The Rebels soon crossed over the Chattahoochee River, the last major obstacle between Sherman and Atlanta, and Johnston's army dug in again. It was then that Davis finally reached his breaking point. On the night of July 17 a telegram arrived from Richmond that relieved Johnston of command of the army and turned the reins of leadership over to John Bell Hood. Hood was also promoted to the temporary rank of full general. Hood's claim in his memoirs that the "totally unexpected order so astounded me.....that I remained in deep thought throughout the night" is interesting in light of several writers arguing effectively that Hood had been positioning for the job for some time. That Hood was in deep thought, however, is undoubtedly fact. That same night Hood was sent a telegram by Secretary of War James A. Seddon. In it Seddon warned the young general, "Be wary no less than bold." It was advice Hood would have been well served to follow in the weeks and months ahead.[38]

Some historians later claimed that upon hearing the news of

---

[37] Connelly, *Autumn of Glory*, p. 359-360; Horn, *Army of Tennessee*, p. 335-337; Sherman, *Memoirs,* Vol. II, p. 61; Johnston, *Narrative of Military Operations*, p. 343; Livermore, *Numbers and Losses*, p. 120-121.

[38] Horn, *Army of Tennessee*, p. 339-340; *OR* 38, pt. 5, p. 885; John Bell Hood, *Advance & Retreat*, p. 126; Johnston, *Narrative of Military Operations*, p. 348-349; Connelly, *Autumn of Glory*, p. 417-426. Connelly wrote of Hood's accusations against Hardee and of Johnston's behavior following his removal. Also, Albert Castel in *Decision in the West: The Atlanta Campaign of 1864*, p. 356-357, points out Hood's betrayal of both Johnston and Hardee. Both Connelly and Castel accurately point out that Braxton Bragg did little to quell the misinformation flowing from Hood to Richmond. McMurry said in *John Bell Hood,* p. 118, that Hood's motives by July 1864 were nothing short of ambition.

Johnston's dismissal, scores of men dropped their weapons and went home, vowing never to fight again. One noted writer, however, offers compelling evidence to the contrary. Surely some were disappointed by the change of leadership, but after three years of war many of the men were simply tired of fighting. Desertions were frequent and would continue to be, regardless of who commanded the army.[39]

Hood was just thirty-three years of age when he took command and had suffered two grievous wounds during the prior twelve months. As his troops swarmed toward Little Round Top at Gettysburg on July 2, 1863, shell fragments had sliced into the young general's left arm, tearing it open from the biceps to his hand and virtually mangling the limb. Although saved from amputation, the arm hung useless in a sling from that point on. Only three months later at Chickamauga, while still recovering from his Gettysburg wound, a bullet shattered Hood's upper right leg so close to the hip that doctors were forced to amputate almost the entire limb. It was a procedure so dangerous that patients who went through it died more often than not. But Hood was a bull of a man and although both injuries, especially the latter, sapped his strength and stamina, he dedicated himself to a return to duty. Southern independence remained a singular goal in Hood's mind and it drove him to recover as fast as possible. While his once healthy and muscular figure was never the same, his improvement during the subsequent months was nothing short of remarkable. By early 1864, Hood had been promoted to lieutenant general and was given command of a corps in Johnston's army. But other problems soon came looming, and by mid-year Hood found himself facing yet another Herculean task.[40]

Whether Johnston would have ever attacked the Yankees, or exactly how he planned to defend Atlanta, has been debated since the moment he left the Army of Tennessee. The one thing over which

---

[39] Connelly, *Autumn of Glory*, p. 423-424; Horn, *Army of Tennessee*, p. 345; Daniel, *Soldiering in the Army of Tennessee*, p. 141-147.

[40] McMurry, *John Bell Hood,* p. 75, 79; Jack D. Welsh, *Medical Histories of Confederate Generals*, p. 105-106; John P. Dyer, *The Gallant Hood*, p. 194, 210.

John Bell Hood
(Library of Congress)

there was no debate was that from the moment Hood took command he would attack. He had earned a reputation as an aggressive commander and the losses his troops endured at places such as Gaines' Mill and Antietam, and the injuries Hood suffered, had solidified his place in the minds of friend and foe alike.[41]

Hood's first test as army commander came along the ground south of Peachtree Creek on July 20, when he ordered his troops to attack one of Sherman's three armies, George Henry Thomas' Army of the Cumberland. Although the assault was delayed until late afternoon, once it unfolded the fighting quickly developed into a series of bloody sledgehammer attacks and counterattacks. Yet Thomas' troops were able to hold off the Confederates and thus Hood's first attempt to remove the stranglehold on Atlanta ended in failure. On July 21 heavy fighting continued around Bald Hill and the following day Hood launched another attack in his quest for a decisive victory.[42]

---

[41] Johnston, *Narrative of Military Operations*, p. 350-351, 363-364; Davis, *Rise and Fall of the Confederate Government*, Vol. II, p. 471-472; Hood, *Advance & Retreat*, p. 141-143; Sherman, *Memoirs*, Vol. II, p. 72; Connelly, *Autumn of Glory*, p. 431. Hood's 1st Texas lost 186 of 226 men engaged at Antietam, a casualty rate of 82.3%. This was the highest rate any regiment suffered in any battle during the entire war. See McMurry, *John Bell Hood*, p. 59.

[42] Horn, *Army of Tennessee*, p. 352-355; Sherman, *Memoirs*, Vol. II, p. 72-73; Hood, *Advance & Retreat*, p. 168-171; Cleaves, *Rock of Chickamauga*, p. 229-231.

On paper the plan Hood had developed was well conceived, and with proper execution there would have been a good chance for success. He ordered William Hardee's Corps to move out on an eighteen mile night march and swing northeast around the flank of James B. McPherson's army, Sherman's second largest force. Once there, Hardee was to assail the Union left wing and rear. When he became fully engaged, Maj. Gen. Benjamin Franklin Cheatham, temporarily heading up Hood's old corps, and Maj. Gen. Gustavus W. Smith's Georgia militia were to attack John Schofield. The plan then called for Hardee, Cheatham, and Smith to drive McPherson and Schofield back in disorder upon Peachtree Creek. Meanwhile, the remaining corps, commanded by Lt. Gen. A. P. Stewart, was directed to occupy Thomas and prevent him from lending assistance to McPherson and Schofield.[43]

Problems arose immediately. Hardee was delayed in getting Cleburne's Division removed from the vicinity of Bald Hill without alerting the Union troops to any suspicious activity. So much time was lost that it was after 3 a.m. before the last of the Rebels were on the road. The men, many of whom were already exhausted from fighting all day in the heat, began straggling and the pace of the march slowed to a crawl at times. It was almost noon on July 22 before Hardee was finally able to get into position and by then the broiling sun and choking humidity were causing widespread difficulties. Men were literally falling out of line, prostrated by the heat and complete exhaustion.[44]

As Hardee's four weary divisions readied themselves for the attack, one which even at that late hour was still mostly unsuspected, fate reared its head. McPherson's men were strung out along a line that ran generally from north to south, with the exception of Maj. Gen. Francis P. Blair's Corps. During the night his men, quite fortuitously for them, had been repositioned at a right angle to the main line. Thus Blair was aligned almost east to west and Bald Hill formed the point of

---

[43] Hood, *Advance & Retreat*, p. 174-178; Connelly, *Autumn of Glory*, p. 445-446; Horn, *Army of Tennessee*, p. 354-355; McMurry, *John Bell Hood*, p. 130-131; Samuel Carter III, *The Siege of Atlanta, 1864*, p. 214.

[44] Horn, *Army of Tennessee*, p. 355; Connelly, *Autumn of Glory*, p. 446-447; Nathaniel Cheairs Hughes, Jr., *General William J. Hardee: Old Reliable*, p. 226-227; Carter, *The Siege of Atlanta*, p. 215.

the nearly ninety degree angle McPherson's army held. Meanwhile, during the night Maj. Gen. Grenville M. Dodge's Corps had been ordered to move in rear of the army from right to left and extend Blair's left flank. When Hardee's veterans came marching and howling through the dense woods and underbrush, they unexpectedly came almost face to face with Dodge's surprised troops, who were standing under arms. Dodge had yet to complete his movement to Blair's left and his men suddenly found themselves taking on almost half of Hardee's Corps. In the blink of an eye the battle exploded east of Atlanta.[45]

Hood later blamed Hardee for the failure of the attack, but there is no way Hardee could have foreseen Dodge being where he was. Moreover, Hood did not order Frank Cheatham into the fray until about three hours after Hardee launched his assault. This lack of cohesive action allowed the Federals to focus on one Rebel corps and then another. Pat Cleburne's men achieved the only real success of the day when they struck the angle of McPherson's line southeast of Bald Hill and pierced it, only to be shoved back by a determined Federal counterattack. By the end of the day, Hood had little to show for his masterful plan except for a long list of casualties. Again the new commander had failed to break Sherman's grip on the city.[46]

John Bell Hood's losses, however, were not limited to those in his army. James McPherson, a friend and former West Point classmate, was killed while attempting to stem the Rebel onslaught. As Cleburne's infantry drove toward a gap in the blue line, a handful of gray-clad skirmishers found themselves in the Yankee rear, moving in the direction of a road leading to Bald Hill. It was on this same road that

---

[45] Horn, *Army of Tennessee*, 355-357; Connelly, *Autumn of Glory*, p. 448-449; Hughes, Jr., *General William Hardee*, p. 228-229; McMurry, *John Bell Hood*, p. 131; Carter, *The Siege of Atlanta*, p. 218-219. McMurry states correctly that had "McPherson had access to Hood's plan, he could not have positioned his men better to meet Hardee's onslaught."

[46] Hood, *Advance & Retreat,* p. 179-180; Christopher Losson, *Tennessee's Forgotten Warriors: Frank Cheatham And His Confederate Division*, p. 180-182; Horn, *Army of Tennessee*, p. 357-358; Hughes, Jr., *General William Hardee*, p. 229-231; McMurry, *John Bell Hood*, p. 131-132; Connelly, *Autumn of Glory*, p. 448-450.

McPherson was riding, attended only by a single orderly, when suddenly the Rebel skirmishers and the general caught each other's attention. McPherson reined his horse in so hard the animal almost sat on its haunches. Within seconds, several of the Rebels called on McPherson to surrender and just as quickly as he had stopped, the dashing young general, after tipping his hat politely, spurred his horse to the right and galloped for the woods. He barely got off the road before the Rebel captain at the head of the skirmishers yelled, "Fire!" There was an explosion of musketry and both McPherson and his orderly, Sgt. Andrew Thompson, crashed hard to the ground. McPherson had been shot in the back and Thompson was knocked almost senseless by a tree branch. As the skirmishers approached the fallen men, Thompson came to and saw McPherson about ten feet way, gasping and choking for air. The Rebels hauled Thompson away and within minutes McPherson was dead. Sherman learned of McPherson's death within the hour and was visibly distraught by the news.[47]

Hood was likewise dismayed when he heard what had happened and wrote in his memoirs:

> In connection with this sad event, I will record also the death of my classmate and friend in boyhood, General McPherson, which occurred the same day, and the announcement of which caused me sincere sorrow. Although in the same class, I was several years his junior, and, unlike him, was more wedded to boyish sports than to books. Often, when we were cadets, have I left barracks at night to participate in some merry-making, and early in the following morning have had recourse to him to help me over the difficult portions of my studies for the day. Since we had graduated in June, 1853, and had each been ordered off on duty in different directions, it had not been our fortune to meet. Neither the lapse of years, nor the difference of sentiment which led us to range ourselves on opposite sides in the late war, had lessened my friendship; indeed the attachment, formed in early youth, was strengthened by my admiration and gratitude for his conduct toward our people in the vicinity of Vicksburg. His considerate and kind treatment of them stood in bright contrast to the course pursued by many Federal officers; and his acts were ever characterized by those

---

[47] David Evans, "Gallant Last Ride," *Military History*, 4, August 1987, p. 38-39; Simpson and Berlin, ed., *Sherman's Civil War*, p. 670-672; Sherman, *Memoirs*, Vol. II, p. 77-78.

gentlemanly qualities which distinguished him as a boy. No soldier fell in the enemy's ranks, whose loss caused me equal regret.[48]

When Sherman learned of Hood's appointment to lead the Army of Tennessee, he had asked John Schofield for his opinion regarding the command change. Schofield, who had roomed with Hood at West Point, replied that while the Rebel general was brave, he was also bold to the point of rashness. The assessment could not have been more profound. In two massive assaults since taking command Hood had hit Sherman hard, but unfortunately for the Confederate army little was accomplished. Southern casualties for the two battles totaled some 10,500 whereas Sherman counted barely 5,300. They were the kinds of numbers the Army of Tennessee could ill afford. Sherman rejoiced about the results in a July 29 letter to his wife Ellen, while describing the battle of July 22, that "when night closed.....we found nearly 3000 Dead Rebels." Sherman went on to write that Hood "is a new man and fighter and must be watched.....as he is reckless of the lives of his Men." As for the Confederates soldiers in general, Sherman held a grudging respect. In a July 26 letter to Ellen he wrote, "These fellows fight like Devils & Indians combined, and it calls for all my cunning & Strength."[49]

Hood in the role of the fighter continued to live up to Sherman's billing. On July 28 another attack was launched, one that concluded with results not at all dissimilar to Peachtree Creek and Atlanta. Having learned that Sherman was attempting to transfer McPherson's troops, now commanded by Maj. Gen. Oliver O. Howard, from their position east of Atlanta to the western side, Hood ordered Lt. Gens. Stephen D. Lee's and A. P. Stewart's corps to intercept the Federals. Lee and Stewart were told to work in close conjunction with one another in their effort to attack and destroy the enemy. What developed was not even remotely close to what Hood had planned.[50]

Lee came into contact with the Yankees near Ezra Church and

---

[48] Hood, *Advance & Retreat*, p. 182.

[49] Sherman, *Memoirs*, Vol. II, p. 72; Livermore, *Numbers and Losses*, p. 122-123; Simpson and Berlin, ed., *Sherman's Civil War*, p. 671, 675-676.

[50] Hood, *Advance & Retreat*, p. 194; Horn, *Army of Tennessee*, p. 360; Connelly, *Autumn of Glory*, p. 453.

instead of waiting for Stewart he attacked in piecemeal fashion. Lee's inexperience as a corps commander was evident. His troops were sent crashing into the Northern breastworks, only to recoil before the murderous enemy fire. When Stewart finally came up, he threw his men into the fight as haphazardly as had Lee and with similar result. Night finally concluded the bungled affair, with at least 4,000 killed and wounded Confederates to show for the day's failure. Among the wounded was Stewart, who took a spent ball in the forehead and was forced to spend two weeks convalescing in Savannah, Georgia. Federal losses barely exceeded 600 men. Sherman wrote confidently that the battle was "the easiest thing in the world; that, in fact, it was a common slaughter of the enemy.....All bore willing testimony to the courage and spirit of the foe, who, though repeatedly repulsed, came back with increased determination some six or more times."[51]

The bloody repulses endured by the Army of Tennessee at the end of July were so serious, President Davis telegraphed John Bell Hood in an effort to quell his aggressive behavior. Davis had grave concerns. He could see the advantage Sherman held by remaining behind earthworks and wired Hood, "The loss consequent upon attacking him in his intrenchments requires you to avoid that if practicable." The message was so pointed Hood recalled it in his memoirs, stating that it was a "bold contradiction" to what Davis had wanted following Johnston's removal.[52]

Davis' telegram did, however, have the desired effect and Hood turned to his cavalry in an effort to impede Sherman. As August wore on, while the Federal and Rebel horsemen maneuvered outside Atlanta, Sherman began a relentless day and night shelling of the city. But Sherman was not content solely lobbing shells into Atlanta. His infantry

---

[51] Sam Davis Elliott, *Soldier of Tennessee: General Alexander P. Stewart and the Civil War in the West*, p. 212-214; Hood, *Advance & Retreat*, p. 194-195; Connelly, *Autumn of Glory*, p. 454-455; Horn, *Army of Tennessee*, p. 360-362; Livermore, *Numbers and Losses*, p. 124; Sherman, *Memoirs*, Vol. II, p. 91-92. Horn said Hood's criticisms of the troops at Ezra Church were unwarranted. Connelly said Hood was aware the battle was not progressing well, but he never left Atlanta to offer any personal supervision.

[52] *OR* 38, pt. 5, p. 946; Hood, *Advance & Retreat*, p. 198-199.

slowly sidled around the city toward the southwest, making sure to keep behind their entrenchments in case the Confederates came bounding forward in another wild attack. By the end of the month, it was clear to Hood the Yankees were moving toward Jonesboro to sever the last railroad leading into Atlanta, the tracks running south to Macon. Without the use of that railway the city would be cut off from supply and Hood moved to thwart the effort.[53]

On August 31, Confederate troops from Hardee's and Lee's corps attacked the Union positions near Jonesboro and tried unsuccessfully for several hours to carry the enemy lines. By nightfall, with the offensive having ground to a halt, Hood ordered Lee back to Atlanta based on reports indicating Sherman might assault the city in the morning. Hood must have been unaware that he was leaving Hardee to face nearly Sherman's entire army. As a result, Old Reliable was forced to stand alone on September 1. His vastly outnumbered men, although they fought desperately, were no match for the swarms of Union soldiers thrown at them. Scores of Rebel troops fell in the heavy fighting and hundreds more were captured. Darkness finally allowed Hardee to pull his men out of their precarious position and they moved south to Lovejoy's Station, where entrenchments were hastily erected.[54]

When Hood learned of Hardee's defeat at Jonesboro he realized the futility of holding Atlanta any further. With Sherman holding all of the rail lines around the city, evacuation was the only option remaining. Hood's army, however, was dangerously split. With Hardee on his way to Lovejoy's Station about seven miles south of Jonesboro, A. P. Stewart and G. W. Smith were still inside Atlanta, and S. D. Lee, moving up from Jonesboro, was east of Rough and Ready some six miles south of Atlanta. Lee was halted and ordered to "cover the evacuation of the city." Then around dusk on September 1 Stewart and Smith swung their men into formation and began moving out of Atlanta, tramping southward along the McDonough Road. Soon all three columns were

---

[53] Hood, *Advance & Retreat*, p. 199-203; Horn, *Army of Tennessee*, p. 359, 363-364.

[54] Horn, *Army of Tennessee*, p. 365-366; Connelly, *Autumn of Glory*, p. 462-466; Carter, *The Siege of Atlanta*, p. 308-311; Hughes, Jr., *General William Hardee*, p. 235-240; Simpson and Berlin, ed., *Sherman's Civil War*, p. 695-696; Sherman, *Memoirs*, Vol. II, p. 107-108.

William J. Hardee (Library of Congress)

moving toward Lovejoy's Station to join William Hardee.[55]

The night of September 1 was one of great anxiety for William Sherman. So "restless and impatient" he could not sleep, the Federal commander began hearing huge explosions from the direction of Atlanta at around midnight. Although Sherman could not have known it at the time the sounds were those of a beaten army in hasty retreat. So confused was the Confederate withdrawal from Atlanta that an ordnance train was abandoned and destroyed in the process. It is possible as many as eighty cars filled with ammunition were destroyed. The resulting explosions were so furious that windows were shattered and "houses rocked like cradles..."[56]

On September 2, Hardee was forced to fend off yet another enemy assault. Luckily for him, the Federals applied far less pressure than they had on the previous day and the Southerners were able to repulse the attack. To the north, the sounds of this combat could be heard by the troops winding their way down from Atlanta. It was surely a time of great anxiety for John Bell Hood. Not until the following day did Stewart and Lee arrive at Lovejoy's Station to relieve Hardee's battered corps. Meanwhile, Smith moved his state troops further south to Griffin. The final act of the Atlanta Campaign was as one-sided as the July battles had been. Southern casualties during the fighting around Jonesboro were at least 4,000 and Federal losses amount to about 1,450. For the Confederate psyche, however, the casualties were almost

---

[55] *OR* 38, pt. 3, p. 765; Carter, *The Siege of Atlanta*, p. 314; Hood, *Advance & Retreat*, p. 205.

[56] *OR* 38, pt. 3, p. 633; Sherman, *Memoirs*, Vol. II, p. 108; Carter, *The Siege of Atlanta*, p. 315-316; Horn, *Army of Tennessee*, p. 366.

secondary. Hood later wrote that he was "not so much pained by the fall of Atlanta as by the recurrence of retreat" but his words smack of denial. Hood surely had to understand the enormity of Atlanta's loss overshadowed all else. He knew full well command of the army had been given to him in July to prevent that very thing from happening. The city's fall was a cut which ran deeper than Hood apparently ever understood or chose to admit.[57]

After Atlanta's capture there naturally arose a great deal of finger-pointing, both public and private. Hood chose to blame William Hardee for the losses at Peachtree Creek, outside Atlanta on July 22, and Jonesboro. On the other hand, Hardee was only too willing to reply that Hood's plans were faulty in their inception and thus doomed the army to failure. But Hood went further than simply blaming one of his subordinates. He again accused the troops of performing poorly, if only indirectly, by going so far as to say the attack at Jonesboro on August 31 was "feeble" because the Confederates suffered only about 1,400 casualties. Hood not only made this claim in his official report, but repeated it in his memoirs. Such a charge was both callous and unnecessary. At a time when large numbers of men had deserted and given up the fight for independence, those who continued to toil on deserved better treatment.[58]

Around September 6, the Federal troops remaining south of Atlanta abandoned their positions and retired in the direction of the city. As a result, Hood began shifting his troops west on September 18 and repositioned the army along the West Point Railroad, close to the small town of Palmetto. On September 25, Jefferson Davis arrived at

---

[57] *OR* 38, pt. 3, p. 971; Hughes, Jr., *General William Hardee*, p. 240; Connelly, *Autumn of Glory*, p. 467; Hood, *Advance & Retreat*, p. 206, 209; Livermore, *Numbers and Losses*, p. 125-126. Livermore's calculations do not include the fighting on September 2.

[58] *OR* 39, pt. 2, p. 832; *OR* 38, pt. 3, p. 633, 697-703; Hood, *Advance & Retreat*, p. 206. Hughes said "Generally considered...Peachtree Creek does stand as one of Hardee's poorest performances." He went on to say that Hardee erred in not making a "personal reconnaissance" and that the "attack was delivered piecemeal, and subordinate units were not closely controlled." As a result Hood clearly had reason to be upset with how his plans were executed at Peachtree Creek. See Hughes, Jr., *General William Hardee*, p. 225.

Palmetto to once again try and calm a storm brewing within the Army of Tennessee. Hood's sparring match with Hardee had intensified and the army's morale was as bad or worse than it had been following the disaster at Chattanooga ten months earlier. If it was not clear to Davis that change was necessary as he rode the train from Virginia to Georgia, it should have been apparent soon after he arrived. Years later he wrote succinctly, "The crisis was grave."[59]

After reviewing the troops and conferring with Hood and his corps commanders, Davis made several decisions. Since there was no doubt the rift between Hood and Hardee was irreparable, Davis transferred Hardee to another department on September 28. Hardee was appointed to command the Department of South Carolina, Georgia, and Florida and Hood received what could be interpreted as a message. Davis made a point of telling Hood that the reason for Hardee's transfer had nothing to do with the latter's ability, but rather because Hardee insisted he could no longer serve under Hood. Based on this, it seems Davis did not consider Hood's criticisms of Hardee had much merit. Instead Davis separated the two, convinced Hardee would be happier and more useful elsewhere. Additionally, while Davis chose not to replace Hood as army commander, he appointed P. G. T. Beauregard to head the newly formed Military Division of the West. On paper this meant Hood was to report to Beauregard directly. How well the Texan would respond to this new arrangement with the Creole, however, was an altogether different matter.[60]

Viewing the matter from the perspective of over one hundred and forty years, Davis may have done the best with a bad situation. For him to have brought back Joseph Johnston to command in the fall of 1864 would have been to concede that John Bell Hood's appointment was a mistake. Davis' pride ran far too deep to go to such measures. Even placing Beauregard at the army's helm was really not an option,

---

[59] Steven E. Woodworth, *Jefferson Davis and His Generals: The Failure of Confederate Command in the West*, p. 291-292; Hood, *Advance & Retreat*, p. 209, 252-253; Davis, *Rise and Fall of the Confederate Government,* Vol. II, p. 478.

[60] *OR* 39, pt. 1, p. 805; *OR* 39, pt. 2, p. 879-880; Hughes, Jr., *General William Hardee*, p. 248; Roman, *The Military Operations of General Beauregard*, Vol. II, p. 278-279; Hood, *Advance & Retreat*, p. 255.

since Davis felt little better about the Creole than he did Johnston. The only difference was that by late 1864 he could at least stomach Beauregard. Davis understood that Hood needed some supervision. By elevating Beauregard above Hood some of the critics who were constantly tearing at Davis, from the columns of the Richmond newspapers to the chambers of the Confederate Congress, might be placated. Did Davis have any other choices? Lt. Gen. Richard Taylor was an option, but apparently one not long considered. Even the Army of Tennessee's remaining corps commanders, Lee and Stewart, were far from reasonable selections. Neither Cheatham or Cleburne had any experience managing a corps let alone an army. So Davis was left with Hood, the best of a less than perfect lot.[61]

As for Hardee, Davis had little choice but to send him away. Hood had his share of faults, but Hardee had become a malcontent, behaving in the same poor fashion as Leonidas Polk had when Braxton Bragg headed up the army. But it was with the filling of Hardee's position as corps commander that a unique opportunity may have slipped away. Frank Cheatham was appointed to fill the post, but Pat Cleburne was equally qualified and able. Twice before, when Lee and Stewart were elevated to corps command, Cleburne been bypassed and the fall of 1864 saw it happen a third time. Cleburne's record was impeccable and he had displayed a natural ability to lead men and mold them into fine soldiers. It has long been debated whether there was a reason for Cleburne's snubbing, and although no evidence of a conspiracy against him exists, it does seem that something weighed in the negative. Strikes against him could have been the fact that he was an immigrant and the lack of a West Point education. Perhaps it was

---

[61] Woodworth, *Jefferson Davis and His Generals*, p. 291-293; Connelly, *Autumn of Glory*, p. 470-473; Horn, *Army of Tennessee*, p. 372-375. Although Davis retained Hood he understood great damage had been done to the army and no longer could Hood operate without, in the very least, some indirect guidance. Unfortunately, Davis practically handcuffed Beauregard by preventing him from being able to order Hood to do anything. Hood perceived this and thus paid little heed to anything Beauregard had to say. When one considers the errors made by Davis in the past with the likes of Bragg, his decision to allow Hood to do practically what he wanted is inexcusable.

because Cheatham had some prior experience at the corps level, albeit only temporary. Even Hood's suggestion to President Davis that Cheatham take command of Hardee's Corps was based solely on Cheatham's senior rank over Cleburne. Hood seems not to have factored in any personal feelings about either officer. However, it was the radical proposal to arm slaves which may have tipped the scales against Cleburne forever. Whatever the real reason, Cleburne at the head of the corps that Cheatham went on to command might have changed the Army of Tennessee's history markedly. By 1864 both the Confederate Congress and Davis had displayed an impressive track record of pushing men up the ladder of success who were far from deserving. Pat Cleburne was a man who had earned the right of promotion.[62]

For William Tecumseh Sherman the capture of Atlanta was only part of a significantly larger picture. Federal troops occupied the city on the morning of September 2, before the smoke from Gen. Hood's hasty departure had cleared, and Sherman wasted little time preparing his next move. For some time the idea of a march to the Atlantic seaboard, through the very heart of Georgia, had been on his mind and in a September 4letter to Henry Halleck he struck at the core of his feelings about war. Sherman wrote pointedly, "If the people raise a howl against my barbarity and cruelty, I will answer that war is war, and not popularity seeking. If they want peace, they and their relatives must

---

[62] *OR* 39, pt. 2, p. 720, 842, 880; Losson, *Tennessee's Forgotten Warriors*, p. 196-197; Symonds, *Stonewall of the West*, p. 222-223. Cheatham commanded Hood's old corps until S. D. Lee arrived and he also commanded Stewart's Corps during Old Straight's brief absence following Ezra Church. Losson makes a compelling argument that Cheatham has long been underestimated and was a sound choice for corps command. Symonds says little about the opening in September 1864, but rather focuses on why Cleburne was passed over in July 1864. Symonds relies heavily upon a telegram sent by Hood on July 19 to Secretary of War James Seddon; see *OR* 38, pt. 5, p. 892. The telegram states that Hardee suggested Cheatham for command of Hood's old corps, not Cleburne. Symonds seems to conclude that since Cleburne was bypassed in July there was no reason to promote him in September because Cheatham was available on both occasions.

stop the war."[63]

Sherman understood, with unusual clarity, that many Southern soldiers were highly motivated by events at home. He could see that if war was brought to the homes of the wives and children, mothers and fathers, and brothers and sisters left behind, the average soldier might be more inclined to stop fighting. Sherman knew that while the loss of Atlanta was a deadly blow to the Confederacy it was still just a city. There remained the populace that was largely untouched by the war and Sherman intended to bring it and all of its cruel and harsh realties to the Georgian doorsteps. But first there was the issue of how to handle Hood and the omnipresent Army of Tennessee.

---

[63] Sherman, *Memoirs*, Vol. II, p. 111.

2

The March to the Ohio

By the early fall of 1864 the fledgling Confederate States of America was dying. After three and a half long years of war the South's foundations were rapidly crumbling. The Mississippi River lay firmly in Northern hands, three separate invasions of the North had been turned back, much of the Confederacy's territory was occupied by Federal soldiers, and most importantly the numbers game had turned drastically against the South. Consistently short of men and material, the glaring deficiencies of late 1864 could no longer be offset by elan on the battlefield. Politics also played against the South. Foreign intervention by Great Britain or France on behalf of the seceded states was out of the question and Abraham Lincoln's reelection seemed much more certain following Atlanta. With Lincoln in the White House for a second term pragmatists understood the war would certainly be prosecuted to its bitter end. Times were desperate in the unraveling Confederacy and yet nagging questions lingered among its populace. Chief among them were how long would the fighting be prolonged and could someone in the South perform a miracle to turn the tide?

In the Eastern Theater things were bleak for the Army of Northern Virginia. U. S. Grant had bottled up Robert E. Lee at Petersburg, Virginia following savage and bloody fighting during May and June that made names such as the Wilderness, Spotsylvania, and Cold Harbor famous forever. The struggle around Petersburg soon evolved into trench warfare, filled with endless artillery fire, snipers, monotony, exposure, disease, and death. In many aspects the combat was a precursor to the horrors of the World War I trenches. The Lee-Grant struggle was also war of attrition, one that the Army of Northern Virginia could not possibly win. With his army penned in by the

Yankees, even Lee realized that the fate of both he and his men was likely sealed.

The region of the Trans-Mississippi offered practically little or no hope to Southern independence. Thousands of soldiers who might have been put to use elsewhere languished in Louisiana, Arkansas, Missouri, and Texas, either involved in minor engagements or not actively campaigning at all. Edmund Kirby Smith, commander of the department encompassing these states, was largely unwilling to transfer his soldiers across the Mississippi to assist in areas where military matters were of critical importance. As a result, and almost by default, any hope the Confederacy had by late 1864 fell upon the battered shoulders of the Army of Tennessee and its beleaguered commander John Bell Hood.

Since early in the war there had been talk among some Southerners of driving boldly north through Tennessee toward the banks of the Ohio River. Braxton Bragg had tried such a movement and been unsuccessful, but in the last autumn of the Confederacy the dream materialized again out of the mists of failure. Destiny for Hood's army and the country it fought for was close at hand, and the human drama that unfolded during those October and November days became the stuff of Civil War legend. No one could have possibly foreseen what was about to transpire.[1]

John Bell Hood was born in Owingsville, Kentucky on June 1, 1831, the fourth child of John and Theodosia Hood. The elder Hood was a doctor and his family, although not wealthy, lived a comfortable life and young John Bell grew up with amenities most of the children of his era did not have. Early in life Hood exhibited the occasional streak of wildness and carelessness, traits common among young boys. By the time he was a teenager, Hood had made the decision to pursue a military career. With help from a local congressman, he received an appointment to West Point in early 1849 and in July of that year Hood

---

[1] *OR* 45, pt. 2, p. 636; *OR* 41, pt. 1, p. 121-124; *OR* 41, pt. 4, p. 199, 424; *OR* 52, pt. 2, p. 340.

entered the famed academy on the Hudson River.[2]

For four years Hood studied and trained to become a professional soldier. During his final year of school, he racked up 196 demerits for offenses which ranged from laughing in the ranks, to smoking and not getting his hair cut, and was nearly expelled. Hood was not alone on the edge of expulsion, however, for his classmate John Schofield had the exact same number of demerits. Hood did survive the final months without further incident and graduated forty-fourth out of fifty-two students in the class of 1853. Hood was appointed a brevet second lieutenant in the 4th Infantry Regiment of the United States Army and his first assignment was at a post in northern California. By 1855, Hood was a second lieutenant serving in the 2nd U. S. Cavalry, a unit which boasted among its officers the likes of Robert E. Lee, Albert Sidney Johnston, William Hardee, and George Henry Thomas. By July 1856, Lt. Hood was serving on the frontier. There he became engaged in a fight against Comanche Indians in Texas and was wounded by an arrow in the left hand. Hood spent most of the next few years serving in the Lone Star State.[3]

The outbreak of civil war forced a critical life choice. Hood wasted little time making the decision and resigned his commission on April 17, 1861. By March 1862, the 30-year old Hood was a brigadier general in command of the Texas Brigade and, while his quality as a soldier remained undetermined, he looked every part the dashing soldier. Hood stood six feet two inches tall with broad shoulders and a thin waist. His hair was thick and sandy blond and he had a full beard, making the young commander the very image of dash and elan. Hood was easy to get along with, he enjoyed a good laugh, and was not averse to throwing back a drink or playing cards. Deep inside, however, burned the heart of a relentless fighter. John Bell Hood was born to be a soldier and the Civil War gave him every opportunity to unleash his instincts. The man who finished the war, however, was a far cry from the man who entered into it. The damage done to himself and those who followed him could never be accurately measured.[4]

---

[2] Dyer, *The Gallant Hood*, p. 19-27; Faust, ed., *Historical Times Encyclopedia*, p. 368.

[3] Ibid., p. 27-47; Ibid., p. 368.

[4] Ibid., p. 48; Ibid., p. 368.

When the Confederates pulled out of their Palmetto camps and crossed the Chattahoochee River on September 29-30, they were led by a man desperately trying to redeem himself. John Bell Hood knew that countless eyes were upon him and his army as they struck northward away from William T. Sherman's army, hoping to sever the Federal lines of communication and supply. It was Hood's hope to draw the Yankees out of Atlanta where a great battle might be fought, this time on Southern terms. Initially Hood had some successes. Elements of A. P. Stewart's Corps captured the garrisons at Big Shanty, Acworth, and Moon's Station on October 3 and 4, netting about 600 prisoners.[5]

Samuel G. French (Alabama Department of Archives and History)

On October 5, Maj. Gen. Samuel G. French's Division, also of Stewart's Corps, reached Allatoona, some thirty miles northwest of Atlanta. French had been ordered to fill the railroad cut at Allatoona and, if practicable, destroy the railroad bridge over the Etowah River. Additionally, Hood was aware that a "considerable number of provisions" were stored at Allatoona and only a small enemy force defended the place. He thought that French would be able to overpower the small force posted there. What he did not know, however, was that Sherman had hurriedly shipped troops up the rail line to defend Allatoona and the post was significantly stronger. When French deployed on the morning of October 5, instead of an easy surrender, he was prompted to attack the post. All three of French's brigades took part in the assault and Brig. Gen. John M. Corse's Federal troops put up a tenacious defense. The fighting was exceptionally

---

[5] *OR* 39, pt. 1, p. 801-802, 806, 810, 812-813, 825; *OR* 45, pt. 1, p. 733; Hood, *Advance & Retreat*, p. 255.

ferocious and bloody. Although French had some success and took over 200 prisoners, his division suffered nearly 900 casualties, including Brig. Gen. William H. Young, commander of Ector's Brigade, who was wounded in the leg and taken prisoner. Unable to capture Allatoona, French called off the attack and withdrew.[6]

Even more difficulty was encountered at Resaca on October 12. When Hood demanded the "unconditional surrender of the post and garrison" and said that if forced to attack no prisoners would be taken, Col. Clark R. Weaver, the fort's commanding officer, replied, "In my opinion I can hold this post; if you want it come and take it." Following so closely on the heels of the debacle at Allatoona, Hood chose to bypass Resaca and instead moved north.[7]

On October 13, the Union garrison at Dalton surrendered under an ugly set of circumstances. A large number of the men in Col. Lewis Johnson's command were black soldiers and the mere sight of Negroes in uniform, commanded by white officers, enraged many in Hood's army. Hood met with Johnson and repeated his demand from the previous day that if forced to attack no prisoners would be taken. Johnson protested against what he considered to be "barbarous measures" and said he wanted the black troops treated as prisoners of wars. Hood replied that "all slaves belonging to persons in the Confederacy" would be returned to their masters. Although Johnson was appalled, he saw no other options and handed the garrison over rather than condemn it to death. Johnson said Cleburne's Division, which was at the front of the Rebel army, repeatedly "violated the flag

---

[6] *OR* 39, pt. 1, p. 581, 760, 762-763, 802, 806, 809, 812-815, 818, 820; Sherman, *Memoirs*, Vol. II, p. 146-149; Samuel G. French, *Two Wars: An Autobiography*, p. 225-226; Welsh, *Medical Histories of Confederate Generals*, p. 243. Among those who made the assault on Allatoona was Mary Bowen, wife of Maj. Gen. John S. Bowen, who had died of dysentery shortly after Vicksburg's fall in the summer of 1863. Mary's story was a tragic one, involving the loss of not only her husband, but also a brother in September 1864. After this second death she joined her remaining two brothers in the ranks of Cockrell's Missouri Brigade. See Phillip Thomas Tucker's *The Forgotten "Stonewall of the West": Major General John Stevens Bowen*, p. 322-323.

[7] *OR* 39, pt. 1, p. 752-753; Sherman, *Memoirs*, Vol. II, p. 154-155; French, *Two Wars*, p. 286.

of truce" and seemed "anxious" to attack the black troops. The behavior of Hood's men did not improve when the 751 Federal troops surrendered. The black soldiers were stripped of their shoes and other articles of clothing and Johnson said he had never witnessed such "beastly conduct." The Federal colonel soon found himself in the presence of Maj. Gen. William B. Bate, another of Hood's division commanders, who verbally assaulted Johnson and the fort's other officers. Bate seemed to take "pleasure and delight" in berating the Yankees and Johnson said he had never been spoken to in such a manner.[8]

While Dalton was succumbing to one portion of Hood's army, another was assaulting the nearby blockhouse at Tilton. A. P. Stewart's Corps enveloped that position, but like at Resaca the demand for surrender by the Confederates was initially rebuffed, and with a similarly brazen tone. However, Tilton was a far weaker position and after the two sides exchanged long-range rifle fire for a time, the Rebels rolled several pieces of artillery into position and began shelling the blockhouse. By mid-afternoon the Federal post was crumbling under the weight of the bombardment, forcing Lt. Col. Samson M. Archer's garrison of about 300 to finally capitulate. Hood's troops, however, were not content with simply capturing Federal outposts. The Rebels also ripped up and destroyed every foot of railroad track they could lay their hands on. In his memoirs, Sherman bemoaned how the Southerners "struck our railroad a heavy blow" and that the "repairs called for thirty-five thousand new ties, and six miles of iron."[9]

For William Sherman, the movements of Hood and his army bordered on maddening. The Rebels had inflicted serious damage and

---

[8] *OR* 39, pt. 1, p. 718-721, 807; Sherman, *Memoirs*, Vol. II, p. 155; Hood, *Advance & Retreat*, p. 262. Bate was among those who was deeply opposed to Cleburne's proposal to arm slaves and free them in exchange for service in the Confederate armies. See Steve Davis, "That Extraordinary Document: W. H. T. Walker and Patrick Cleburne's Emancipation Proposal," *Civil War Times Illustrated* (hereafter referred to as *CWTI*), January 1977, p. 15-20. Bate's exchanges with Walker and his behavior at Dalton provide valuable insight into Bate's character and personal feelings.

[9] *OR* 39, pt. 1, p. 752, 758-760; French, *Two Wars*, p. 286; Sherman, *Memoirs*, Vol. II, p. 150-151.

Tennessee-Alabama-Georgia region

were far too dangerous to be left alone marauding deep in the Union rear. Additionally, it was uncertain what Hood was up to and so Sherman was forced to give chase. For another week the cat and mouse game dragged. By October 20, Hood was at Gadsden, Alabama and Sherman was at Gaylesville, Alabama, nearly thirty-five miles away. But events were about to change dramatically. Having grown tired of a pursuit which had earned him little reward, Sherman opted for a new plan. On October 1, he had telegraphed Grant with the idea of leaving Gen. Thomas to defend Tennessee while the rest of the Federal army moved through Georgia, destroying everything it could. Sherman lobbied for the same plan in a wire to Henry Halleck on October 19. The thought of breaking loose from Hood was heavy on Sherman's mind. On October 9, he had wired Grant, stating it was a "physical impossibility to protect the roads, now that Hood, Forrest, and Wheeler, and the whole batch of devils, are turned loose without home or habitation...Until we can repopulate Georgia, it is useless to occupy it, but the utter destruction of its roads, houses, and people will cripple their military resources...I can make this march and make Georgia howl!"[10]

Although at first hesitant to grant Sherman permission for an offensive that involved leaving the Hood's army behind, Grant soon reconsidered and preparations for the March to the Sea began. Sherman was thrilled to abandon his protracted pursuit of Hood, as evidenced by a October 21 letter to his wife Ellen. In it Sherman wrote: "This Army is now ready to march to Mobile, Savannah or Charleston, and I am practising them in the art of foraging and they take to it like Ducks to water. They like pigs, sheep, chickens, calves and Sweet potatoes better than Rations." He also dispensed some final advice to George H. Thomas. In an October 29 telegram Sherman said: "I don't see how Beauregard can support his army; but Jeff. Davis is desperate, and his men will undertake anything possible." He added "we must be expect anything." In his memoirs, Grant remembered this momentous period of time: "On the 2d of November.....I approved definitely his making his proposed campaign through Georgia, leaving Hood behind to the tender mercy of Thomas and the troops in his command."

[10] *OR* 39, pt. 3, p. 3, 162, 357.

P. G. T. Beauregard (Library of Congress)

Tender mercy was quite a choice of words.[11]

While Sherman left Hood to his own devices, Gen. Beauregard could see that the Army of Tennessee's commander had little in the way of a solid plan. In fact, the Creole later wrote that "a great deal had been left to future determination, and even to luck." From Gadsden, following a two day conference with Beauregard, Hood ordered the army to Guntersville, Alabama. From there he intended to cross the Tennessee River and march toward Bridgeport and Stevenson, both of which lay just south of the Alabama-Tennessee state line. Hood had explained to Beauregard that the destruction of miles of the Western & Atlantic Railroad in northern Georgia had already caused Sherman great pains. Furthermore, Hood knew the Federal army relied greatly on the railway coming out of Nashville. From that city the Nashville & Chattanooga Railroad ran south, intersecting with the Memphis & Charleston Railroad near Bridgeport. From there the two lines ran as one to Chattanooga, with the latter continuing eastward into South Carolina. From Chattanooga

---

[11] Simpson and Berlin, ed., *Sherman's Civil War*, p. 738-739; *OR* 39, pt. 3, p. 499; Grant, *Personal Memoirs*, p. 552. Grant at first was as opposed as anyone to Sherman cutting loose from communication and supply and setting out through the Georgia heartland, but he slowly began to see the long term benefits. Grant, however, refused to authorize any movement by Sherman until Thomas had been provided with troops adequate to the challenge of facing an enemy thrust into Tennessee.

the Western & Atlantic wound its way south to Atlanta. Since portions of that line were already destroyed, Hood believed if the Southern army could strike the Federal supply line near Bridgeport, Sherman would be forced to give chase to protect his lifeline. No longer would the Federal commander simply be able to repair the damage. Instead, vital connection points would be cut and Sherman would be forced to fight on Hood's terms. What neither Confederate general knew was that Sherman was finished with railroads and intended to live off the land. Beauregard, although skeptical of Hood's grandiose strategy, nonetheless gave his approval to it, totally unaware of what Sherman was preparing to do in Georgia. It did not take long, however, for Hood's plan of operations to change.[12]

The Confederate army marched out of Gadsden on October 22. But en route to Guntersville, Hood learned the enemy controlled the crossing of the Tennessee River at that place. Without notifying Beauregard, he altered the march and moved his army toward Decatur, Alabama, nearly forty miles to the west. By October 27, the Rebels were at Decatur and Hood began pressing the Federal position with skirmishers the following day. Brig. Gen. Robert S. Granger commanded the Union garrison there and his troops pushed the Confederates back, nabbing at least 125 prisoners in the process. That same evening Sherman sent a telegram to Thomas predicting Hood would never assault the town in force, stating that "Allatoona and Resaca beat him off, and neither was as strong as Decatur." Sherman was absolutely correct. On October 29, Hood chose to abandon Decatur and ordered his men to Bainbridge, Alabama, still another forty miles to the west. But before the march even started, Hood vacillated again. This time he picked a site just four miles beyond Bainbridge, but

---

[12] *OR* 39, pt. 1, p. 802; *OR* 45, pt. 1, p. 647; Connelly, *Autumn of Glory*, p. 484, 488; Roman, *The Military Operations of General Beauregard*, Vol. II, p. 281, 287-291. Beauregard further stated: "It was easy to discover in the details of the plan evidences of the fact that General Hood and Mr. Davis were not accustomed to command armies in the field, especially armies like ours, for the management of which much had to be foreseen, and much prepared or created." Although Beauregard could not always be trusted to give an objective viewpoint, his critique of Hood in this case is quite accurate.

nearer his new supply base at Tuscumbia, Alabama and directly across the river from Florence.[13]

Unlike that of his adversary, Hood's supply system was a woeful operation. When the Confederates moved away from the Atlanta area, their supply base was likewise transferred and Jacksonville, Alabama was chosen as the new site. However, as Hood's plans changed, so did his need for access to the army's necessities. He ordered the base moved to Tuscumbia, but that selection was beset with trouble. To reach Tuscumbia, food, clothing, saddles, blankets, and the like had to be shipped north through Mississippi on the rickety Mobile & Ohio Railroad to Corinth. From there, the supplies took up the track of the Memphis & Charleston Railroad, which ran in an easterly direction to Cherokee Station, Alabama before ending. The distance from Cherokee Station to Tuscumbia was about fifteen miles, but because the railway was destroyed between those points, supplies had to be transferred from the railcars to wagons and pulled by half-starved mules and horses. To make matters worse, the road connecting Cherokee Station and Tuscumbia was an utter disaster and the foul weather only worsened it. Wagons slipped off the road and became hopelessly mired in the axle-deep mud. Animals found themselves stuck in the mire and others collapsed from exhaustion. At times nearly everything ground to a frustrating halt. All things considered, it is a wonder that Hood's commissary team was able to keep the army as well supplied as it was.[14]

Short of rations and wearing threadbare clothing, the Southern troops nonetheless forged onward. By October 30, the vanguard of Stephen D. Lee's Corps occupied Florence, Alabama after driving out a small force of enemy cavalry which had occupied the town. Lee began crossing his troops to the north side of the Tennessee River over a newly erected pontoon bridge that same day. Not until November 2, however, were all of his troops able to cross. The two remaining Rebels

---

[13] *OR* 39, pt. 3, p. 484, 841, 858, 866; *OR* 39, pt. 1, p. 696-697, 812; Roman, *The Military Operations of General Beauregard*, Vol. II, p. 293; Hood, *Advance & Retreat*, p. 270; Connelly, *Autumn of Glory*, p. 485.

[14] *OR* 39, pt. 3, p. 470, 523, 613, 618, 707, 745-746, 816, 845-846, 855-856, 864, 868, 903; *OR* 45, pt. 1, p. 657; Thomas R. Hay, *Hood's Tennessee Campaign*, p. 61-62; French, *Two Wars*, p. 289-290; Connelly, *Autumn of Glory*, p. 484.

corps, Stewart followed by Cheatham, arrived on October 31 and camped on the south bank of the river, just north of Tuscumbia. Also of critical importance to the army's future fortunes was a telegram sent by Beauregard on November 3 to Maj. Gen. Nathan Bedford Forrest, instructing the cavalry commander to have his vaunted command join the Army of Tennessee as soon as possible.[15]

By this time Beauregard was understandably upset with John Bell Hood. Hood seemed unsure of what he wanted to do or where he wanted to go and had repeatedly ignored Beauregard. On November 3, the Creole finally caught up with the Texan and the two had, as one authority wrote, "a tense but momentous meeting."[16]

It was at this conference that the genesis of what became known as Hood's Tennessee Campaign took shape. It was agreed by both men that the Army of Tennessee would march northward in a few days time, converging on either Columbia or Pulaski and making adjustments to enemy movements as necessary. Bedford Forrest, scheduled to join Hood after the onset of the march, would assist in screening the movements of the Confederate columns. His role would be vital in preventing any Yankee cavalry from molesting the forward movement. Yet nothing was to go smoothly for Hood or his army. Unforseen delays lay ahead, ones which allowed the Federals enough time to gather and organize themselves in preparation for the conflict that was to come.[17]

---

[15] *OR* 39, pt. 1, p. 800, 808, 811; *OR* 39, pt. 3, p. 868, 871; Stephen D. Lee, "From Palmetto, GA. to Defeat at Nashville," *Confederate Veteran Magazine* (hereafter referred to as *CV*), 16, p. 257; Hood, *Advance & Retreat*, p. 271. Forrest was ordered by Beauregard through Gen. Richard Taylor to join the Army of Tennessee as early as October 26; see *OR* 39, pt. 3, p. 853. On that date, however, Forrest was immersed in the initial stages of his raid on Johnsonville, Tennessee and unable to comply.

[16] Wiley Sword, *The Confederacy's Last Hurrah: Spring Hill, Franklin, & Nashville*, p. 66.

[17] *OR* 45, pt. 1, p. 648; Roman, *The Military Operations of General Beauregard*, Vol. II, p. 297-298. Beauregard's November 6 letter to Gen. Samuel Cooper, Adjutant and Inspector General of the Confederate Armies, stated that he expected Hood to be on the move by November 9.

The weather in Tennessee in November 1864 was nothing short of horrendous. The rain that had started at the very end of October did not ease up as the first days of November ticked away. The Tennessee River began to rise, camps became flooded, the roads turned to impassable torrents of mud, and the soldiers suffered immeasurably as the cold rain pelted them day and night. Beauregard had hoped to have Hood on his way by November 9 yet that date came and went without any movement. Beauregard grew increasingly concerned and pushed Hood for action. Not only was Hood fighting the elements, but he was desperately concerned about being able to feed his army. In response to a November 17 dispatch from Beauregard about taking the offensive Hood decried the lack of rations, explaining that he had "seven days' rations on hand" but "thirteen days' additional" were needed.[18]

Problems were endless for the Confederates. On the night of November 9, a section of the pontoon bridge spanning the Tennessee was cut by a daring crew of Yankees and subsequently knocked out by the raging river. It took three days for Hood to get replacements shipped up from Corinth, locked together, and put in place by his engineers. Finally, after so much delay, Cheatham's Corps crossed to the Florence side of the river on November 13. On the following day, after a brief spell of decent weather and as the first of Bedford Forrest's horsemen began arriving in camp, the rains came again. The supply train was able to move over the Tennessee on November 14, but following that almost everything ground to a standstill. For almost a week the Confederates were lashed by wind and icy rain and not until November 20 did A. P. Stewart's Corps cross the bridge. After so much delay, Hood finally had his army on the north side of the river. Final minute preparations were quickly conducted and on the morning of November 21 the Army of Tennessee pushed ahead, as "from the different encampments arose at intervals that genuine Confederate shout....."[19]

In his memoirs Hood claimed to have known what lay before him. He wrote, "I hoped by a rapid march to get in rear of Schofield's

---

[18] *OR* 45, pt. 1, p. 648, 1215; French, *Two Wars*, p. 290.

[19] *OR* 39, pt. 1, p. 808; *OR* 39, pt. 3, p. 904; French, *Two Wars*, p. 290; Hood, *Advance & Retreat*, p. 270, 281.

forces, then at Pulaski, before they were able to reach Duck river."[20] Hood said that he knew all or most of the facts regarding the numbers of troops available to George Henry Thomas, but the truth was that the Rebel commander had only basic information. Furthermore, as he readied for the offensive the old and dated dream of the Ohio River and what lay beyond came alive. Hood wrote:

> I decided to make provisions for twenty days' supply of rations in the haversacks and wagons; to order a heavy reserve of artillery to accompany the Army, in order to overcome any serious opposition by the Federal gunboats; to cross the Tennessee at or near Guntersville, and again destroy Sherman's communications, at Stevenson and Bridgeport; to move upon Thomas and Schofield, and attempt to rout and capture their Army before it could reach Nashville. I intended then to march upon that city where I would supply the Army and reinforce it, if possible, by accessions from Tennessee. I was imbued with the belief that I could accomplish this feat, afterward march northeast, pass the Cumberland river at some crossing where the gunboats, if too formidable at other points, were unable to interfere; then move into Kentucky, and take position with our left at or near Richmond...
>
> In this position I could threaten Cincinnati, and recruit the Army from Kentucky and Tennessee; the former State was reported at this juncture, to be more aroused and embittered against the Federals than at any period of the war.[21]

Hood went on to write of moving onward through "gaps in the Cumberland Mountains" to attack U. S. Grant and assist in freeing Robert E. Lee from the Petersburg siege. From there Hood suggested that he and Lee, after defeating Grant, might possibly turn and "annihilate Sherman." It is difficult to imagine which is more confusing, Hood believing in 1864 that such maneuvering was possible, or that a decade and a half after the war's conclusion anyone would believe such claims. Even Jefferson Davis, who held Hood in high regard, wrote in his memoirs that while it pained him to criticize "the conduct of that very gallant and faithful soldier" he considered the

---

[20] Hood, *Advance & Retreat*, p. 281.

[21] Ibid., p. 266-267.

"movement into Tennessee ill-advised."[22]

The facts indicate that Hood must have known Maj. Gens. David S. Stanley and John Schofield and their Fourth and Twenty-Third Army Corps were in the Pulaski area. Yet beyond their presence, Hood seems to have had little idea what else faced him. Thomas had been sent by Sherman to Nashville at the end of September to oversee the defense of Middle Tennessee. It was not an easy assignment. At Nashville some 8,000 garrison troops were available to Thomas and en route from Missouri was Maj. Gen. Andrew J. Smith's Sixteenth Army Corps. Thomas also had at his disposal soldiers based at posts in Murfreesboro and Chattanooga in Tennessee and Decatur, Stevenson, Bridgeport, and Huntsville in Alabama. Although on paper Thomas had a formidable number of troops with which to combat Hood, his immediate problem was that the Federal forces were scattered. Additionally, as Thomas admitted later, "it was impossible to determine which course Hood would take..." What Thomas needed most of all was time to consolidate his troops and every extra day mattered. When the Rebel forces did finally swing north, only Schofield and Stanley and their approximately 23,000 infantry, plus Maj. Gen. James H. Wilson's horsemen, stood against nearly 30,000 veteran enemy infantry and Forrest's relentless cavalry. Thomas had battled the Confederates long enough to know there was reason for concern. Time was running short.[23]

George Henry Thomas was an imposing figure. Nearly six feet tall, Thomas was a large and muscular man who possessed a nearly square jaw covered by a graying beard. His eyes were a deep blue and his brown hair had become tinged with the color of age. As a younger man Thomas was a physical force to be reckoned with, but by 1864 he was more than a little overweight. The extra pounds seemed to make

---

[22] Hood, *Advance & Retreat,* p. 267-268; Davis, *Rise and Fall of the Confederate Government*, Vol. II, p. 483.

[23] *OR* 39, pt. 1, p. 585, 588-590; *OR* 45, pt. 1, p. 32, 52, 56, 678; Sherman, *Memoirs*, Vol. II, p. 162; Horn, *Army of Tennessee*, p. 381-382; Cleaves, *Rock of Chickamauga*, p. 246.

George H. Thomas
(Library of Congress)

the already impressive forty-eight year old Thomas even more so. A Virginian by birth, Thomas had done the unthinkable in the spring of 1861 when he chose to remain loyal to the United States. Vilified by Southerners and mistrusted by many in the North, Thomas nonetheless plodded forward, indicative of his nickname Old Slow Trot. He was a West Point graduate who ranked twelfth in the class of 1840, and it did not take long for Federal authorities to recognize Thomas' talents. Thomas was cool and calculating under fire and made decisions with a clear mind. On the heels of repeated solid performances in the West, Thomas' star ascended to new heights following his performance at Chickamauga where he earned a new nickname - The Rock of Chickamauga. After William Rosecrans' departure, Thomas took command of the Army of the Cumberland and was conspicuous around Chattanooga and steady during the Atlanta Campaign. Therefore it came as no surprise that when Sherman picked someone to take care of Tennessee while he marched across Georgia, the choice was George Henry Thomas.[24]

When William Sherman began the March to the Sea in mid-November he left Thomas "to hold Tennessee" with the Fourth Corps from the Army of the Cumberland and the Twenty-Third Corps from the Army of the Ohio. The Fourth Corps, created in September 1863, was a veteran outfit. The corps was first led by Maj. Gen. Gordon

---

[24] Faust, ed., *Historical Times Encyclopedia*, p. 754; Cleaves, *Rock of Chickamauga*, p. 9, 14, 140, 185.

Granger, who was succeeded by Maj. Gen. Oliver O. Howard. When Howard was promoted to command the Army of the Tennessee following the death of James McPherson, David Stanley took command of the corps and led it through the rest of the Atlanta Campaign. Just before the end of October, the Fourth Corps was encamped near Gaylesville with the rest of Sherman's forces. On October 26, Stanley was ordered to move his men to Chattanooga and "report for orders to Major-General Thomas." Three days later, Stanley received a telegram from Thomas telling him to move the Fourth Corps to Athens, Alabama, with instructions to continue on to Pulaski, Tennessee "unless you learn that the enemy has not crossed the Tennessee." When Stanley arrived at Athens on October 31, he discovered the Rebels had begun shifting to the north side of the Tennessee River. That same day he began moving the Third Division north to Pulaski. By November 4 his entire corps, with the exception of one brigade escorting the supply train, was at Pulaski.[25]

The Twenty-Third Corps had been created in April 1863 and was led by Maj. Gen. George L. Hartsnuff, Brig. Gen. Mahlon D. Manson, Brig. Gen. Jacob D. Cox, and Maj. Gen. George Stoneman during its first year of existence. By the spring of 1864 the corps was the only one remaining in John Schofield's Army of the Ohio and so Schofield took direct command of it. Veterans abounded in the Twenty-Third Corps, especially after the summer of fighting around Atlanta. After a brief period of rest following the Gate City's fall, Gen. Thomas on October 31 ordered Schofield, whose troops were positioned near Rome, Georgia, to move by rail "with as much expedition as possible" to Pulaski. Initially Thomas wanted Schofield to travel to Pulaski through Tullahoma, but he changed his mind and instead ordered the move to Pulaski to occur via Nashville. Because of railroad delays, Schofield was unable to get the first of men moving until November 3 and while these men began arriving in Nashville two days later, it was not until November 7 that the final elements of the Twenty-Third Corps were on their way. When Schofield reported to Thomas in person on November 5, he was told that instead of going to Pulaski

---

[25] *OR* 39, pt. 1, p. 605, 907-908; *OR* 39, pt. 3, p. 442, 445, 448-449, 461, 484, 500-502, 517, 541, 588; Faust, ed. *Historical Times Encyclopedia*, p. 174.

his command would be sent to Johnsonville to help deal with an attack being made there by Nathan Bedford Forrest. Some of Schofield's men reached Johnsonville later that same day only to discover that Forrest was already gone. After reporting this to Thomas, Schofield was ordered on November 7 "to leave at Johnsonville...a strong defense" and move the rest of his command to Pulaski. He chose two brigades from the Second Division to stay behind before returning to Nashville. There the rest of Schofield's Corps joined him on November 9. Two days later Thomas ordered Schofield to move to Pulaski, link up with Stanley and the Fourth Corps, and take "command of the forces assembling there."[26]

Schofield arrived at Pulaski "on the night of the 13th, and assumed command on the 14th of November." The town was occupied by Stanley's Corps, organized into three divisions commanded by Brig. Gens. Walter C. Whitaker, George D. Wagner, and Thomas J. Wood. Whitaker's tenure was brief, however, and he reverted to brigade command on November 25 when Brig. Gen. Nathan Kimball arrived to head up the First Division. The Fourth Corps was alone at Pulaski because none of Schofield's troops from the Twenty-Third Corps joined their commander there. Jacob Cox's Third Division was ordered into position about two miles north of town near Pigeon Creek and Col. Silas A. Strickland's Brigade from Brig. Gen. Thomas H. Ruger's Division was posted at Columbia. Ruger was a newcomer and had just

---

[26] *OR* 39, pt. 1, p. 793-794; *OR* 39, pt. 3, p. 538, 685, 691-692, 768; *OR* 45, pt. 1, p. 340-341; Jacob Cox, *Sherman's March to the Sea: Hood's Tennessee Campaign and the Carolina Campaigns of 1865*, p. 18; John M. Schofield, *Forty-Six Years In The Army*, p. 165; James L. McDonough, *Schofield: Union General in the Civil War and Reconstruction*, p. 100-101; Faust, ed., *Historical Times Encyclopedia*, p. 181. Forrest's Johnsonville Raid was another example of the grief the Confederate general could bring to Union forces. Forrest's cavalry left Corinth, Mississippi on October 19, 1864 and by November 1 had arrived at Johnsonville on the Tennessee River , about midway between Jackson and Nashville. For a week Forrest and his men sparred with the enemy, ultimately destroying 4 gunboats, 14 steamers, 17 barges, and 33 guns. The Confederates also took 150 prisoners and some 75,000 tons of much needed supplies and caused damages in excess of $6 million. See Faust, ed., *Historical Times Encyclopedia*, p. 399.

taken command of his division on November 11, replacing Brig. Gen. Joseph A. Cooper who resumed command of his brigade, one of the two left at Johnsonville. Yet Ruger was not even at Columbia with Strickland, but remained instead at Johnsonville. Not until November 20 was Ruger ordered to move to Columbia, where he arrived three days later.[27]

The Confederates marching north on November 21 were ready for a fight. Many hailed from Tennessee and were returning to their home state for the first time in over a year. Although much more had been lost since the disastrous fall of 1863, there was a common feeling of satisfaction in late 1864 that at least the endless retreating had ceased. Their enthusiasm and hope was evident in a diary entry by Capt. Samuel T. Foster, an officer in Brig. Gen. Hiram B. Granbury's Texas Brigade:

> We left camp this morning at sun up and started for Tenn.
>
> All the regimental commanders call their men out and say that Genl Hood says that we are going into Tenn into the enemy's country, and we will leave our base of supplies here.
>
> That we will have some hard marching and some fighting, but that he is not going to risk a chance for a defeat in Tenn. That he will not fight in Tenn unless he has an equal number of men and choice of the ground and that perhaps we would be short of rations at times, but that he would do his best to keep us supplied.
>
> All this was very nice talk, for we all felt confident that we could always whip an equal number of men with the choice of the ground, and every man felt anxious to go on under these promises from Genl Hood - Commenced

---

[27] *OR* 39, pt. 3, p. 748; *OR* 45, pt. 1, p. 59, 340-341, 357, 378, 380, 886, 958-959, 999; Schofield, *Forty-Six Years In The Army*, p. 166-167. Although Stanley ranked Schofield the latter took overall command because he headed up not only the Army of the Ohio, but also the Department of the Ohio. See David Stanley, *Personal Memoirs of Major-General David S. Stanley*, p. 193. See also *OR* 39, Pt 2, p. 413-414 and pt. 3, p. 64-65, 684 for related information on this topic. It is interesting to note that Grant thought this issue of rank could be a significant problem.

snowing soon after leaving camp. Very cold, with the wind from the north, wind and snow in our faces all day. Came 12 miles passed through Rawhide and camped. Our Regiment is sent forward for a picket about a mile, and I with my Co are ½ mile further as a vidett and stand all night with orders to let no one pass in or out.[28]

The freezing wind and whipping snow that pelted the Southerners on the first day of the march would be remembered as nothing short of miserable. Samuel French wrote that the troops marched through "mud from four to twenty inches deep" and described the day as "bitterly cold, and the snow falling." Maj. Gen. Edward C. Walthall reported the roads were so bad "it was almost impossible" to move the artillery. Harold Young, an artilleryman in Capt. Henry Guibor's battery, A. P. Stewart's Corps, said the road the men traveled upon was the worst he had ever seen.[29]

Many of the men in Brig. Gen. Francis M. Cockrell's tough-as-nails Missouri Brigade, however, seemed to enjoy the inclement conditions. Capt. Joseph Boyce later wrote that the men shouted, "This is the kind of weather we want, regular old Missouri weather. This is none of your Southern rains; this is something decent. Hurrah for old Missouri."[30]

In addition to the weather, many never forgot the forced nature of the march, the lack of food, and the threadbare clothes and shoes. A South Carolinian officer wrote that "seventy of my men had next to no blankets, and as many needed shoes." He said the "roads were in...a terrible condition" and "rations very short, three biscuits only on the 24th and 25th to each man." The suffering was not confined to the men, however, as the same officer mentioned that "no forage" could be found for the horses.[31]

---

[28] Norman D. Brown, ed., *One of Cleburne's Command: The Civil War Reminiscences and Diary of Capt. Samuel T. Foster, Granbury's Texas Brigade, C. S. A.*, p. 145.

[29] French, *Two Wars*, p. 290; *OR* 45, pt. 1, p. 719; Harold Young, November 21, 1864, diary in possession of Bill and Marilyn Christmann of Pembroke, MA.

[30] Joseph Boyce, "Missourians in Battle of Franklin," *CV* 24, p. 102.

[31] *OR* 45, pt. 1, p. 735-736.

Pvt. Sam Watkins was twenty-five years old and a member of Company H, 1st Tennessee Infantry. He had enlisted in the spring of 1861 when the war seemed an adventure, a promise of sights, sounds, and personalities that home could never offer. He and 120 other young men and boys from Columbia, Tennessee and surrounding Maury County had volunteered their services, but by November 1864 only twelve of them were left, and the entire company consisted of just twenty.[32]

Yet Sam Watkins was marching toward home and in his memoirs, he cut to the core of what drove many of the Confederates who had already been through hell and back:

> How every pulse did beat and leap, and how every heart did throb with emotions of joy, which seemed nearly akin to heaven, when we received the glad intelligence of our onward march toward the land of promise, and of our loved ones. The cold November winds coming off the mountains of the northwest were blowing right in our faces, and nearly cutting us in two.
>
> We were inured to privations and hardships; had been upon every march, in every battle, in every skirmish, in every advance, in every retreat, in every victory, in every defeat. We had laid under the burning heat of a tropical sun; had made the cold, frozen earth our bed, with no covering save the blue canopy of heaven; had braved dangers, had breasted floods, had seen our comrades slain upon our right and our left hand; had heard guns that carried death in their missiles; had heard the shouts of the charge; had seen the enemy in full retreat and flying in every direction; had heard the shrieks and groans of the wounded and dying; had seen the blood of our countrymen dyeing the earth and enriching the soil; had been hungry when there was nothing to eat; had been in rags and tatters. We had marked the frozen earth with bloody and unshod feet; had been elated with victory and crushed by defeat; had seen and felt the pleasure of the life of a soldier, and had drank the cup of its dregs. Yes, we had seen it all, and had shared in its hopes and its fears; its love and its hate; its good and its bad; its virtue and its vice; it glories and its shame. We had followed the successes and reverses of the flag of the Lost Cause through all these years of blood and strife.
>
> I was simply one of hundreds of thousands in the same fix.[33]

---

[32] Sam R. Watkins, *Co. Aytch: A Side Show of the Big Show*, p. 216-217.

[33] Ibid., p. 214.

Three columns of Rebel infantry were on the move, each consisting of one corps. On the westernmost road leading north to Waynesboro, Tennessee was Frank Cheatham's Corps, composed of three divisions led by Maj. Gens. Patrick Cleburne, John C. Brown, and William B. Bate. Cleburne's Division, made up of Mississippians, Arkansans, Tennesseans, and Georgians, was arguably the best in the entire army. To the east, on a road leading to Lawrenceburg, was A. P. Stewart's Corps. Stewart, known by his men as Old Straight, had his corps organized into three divisions commanded by Maj. Gens. William W. Loring, Samuel French, and Edward Walthall. While Stewart had the shortest road to travel and Cheatham the longest, the corps commanded by S. D. Lee, moving by way of a backwoods country road between the other two corps, had the most difficult trek. That road led to Henryville, but it was narrow and badly rutted and not at all suited for travel by thousands of soldiers, horses, and hundreds of wagons and artillery caissons. Lee's divisions, led by Maj. Gens. Edward "Allegheny" Johnson, Henry D. Clayton, and Carter L. Stevenson, did as well as could be expected under the circumstances, and by nightfall all three of Hood's corps were near the Alabama-Tennessee state line, having traveled from ten to twelve miles during the day.[34]

Screening the infantry were three columns of Bedford Forrest's cavalry. On the left, or west, the Rebel horsemen galloping northward belonged to Brig. Gen. James R. Chalmers' Division and they aimed for Henryville. At the head of this column rode Forrest himself. On the right, moving up the Lawrenceburg Road, were the divisions of Brig. Gens. Abraham Buford and William H. Jackson. On the north side of the Tennessee River since November 17, the Southern horsemen had been scrapping with their Union counterparts for several days. But the light skirmishing was over. With the army finally in motion, Forrest's men set about pushing their opponents back with vigor.[35]

---

[34] *OR* 45, pt. 1, p. 657, 669, 687, 719, 730, 736; Hood, *Advance & Retreat*, p. 281-282; Elliott, *Soldier of Tennessee*, p. 226.

[35] *OR* 45, pt. 1, p. 752, 763; John Allan Wyeth, *That Devil Forrest: The Life of General Nathan Bedford Forrest*, p. 472; Thomas Jordan and J. P. Pryor, *The Campaigns of General Nathan Bedford Forrest and of Forrest's Cavalry*, p. 612-613. Jordan and Pryor indicate Col. Jacob Biffle also led some 500 men in the direction of Waynesboro.

Brig. Gen. John T. Croxton and his brigade of cavalry, which numbered about 1,000, had been guarding a twenty-five mile stretch of the northern bank of the Tennessee River since October. From the area where the Elk River ran into the Tennessee and then west to Florence, Croxton's men had watched for signs of enemy activity. It was Croxton who first reported with certainty that the Rebels had moved to the north side of the Tennessee and his troops made first contact with the enemy. The information his command provided was incalculable, but Croxton was hopelessly outnumbered and needed help badly. On October 29, Gen. Thomas telegraphed Brig. Gen. Edward Hatch, who was stationed in Clifton, Tennessee with his division of cavalry, to move to Croxton's aid. Hatch moved at once and after passing through Pulaski, he arrived near Lexington, Alabama on November 5 to coordinate a defensive stand with Croxton and take overall field command until Gen. Wilson arrived.[36]

Hatch and Croxton were not the only Federal cavalry ordered to northern Alabama. On October 30, Col. Horace Capron was ordered to move his brigade to northern Alabama and report for duty. Capron was in Pulaski by November 5, but was then diverted to Mount Pleasant on November 15 from which point he sent scouts south to Lawrenceburg and Waynesboro. Three days later, Capron was based at Waynesboro and had begun skirmishing with some elements of Forrest's cavalry, suffering some minor casualties and nabbing a couple of Rebel prisoners.[37]

Hatch's Division also began to scrap with Forrest's advance and it soon became evident that something big was in the works. The sixty-year old Capron again tangled with some of Forrest's men on November 20, a sure sign of things to come. Yet Capron was oblivious to the crisis and actually sent a message to Schofield on November 21 stating there were no Rebels within twenty miles of Waynesboro. This dispatch followed on the heels of a message from a day earlier that said Hood was "certainly not moving in this direction." Others in the Union high command, however, believed otherwise and they worked feverishly

---

[36] *OR* 39, pt. 3, p. 497, 507-508, 514, 527, 535, 541, 547, 550, 582, 588, 590, 607, 634-635; Jerry Keenan, *Wilson's Cavalry Corps*, p. 30.

[37] *OR* 39, pt. 3, p. 525, 652, 885, 909, 936-937; Keenan, *Wilson's Cavalry Corps*, p. 34.

to brace for the enemy strike. Schofield, who perceived Capron's isolation, told him to get out of the Waynesboro area and move toward Mount Pleasant to prevent being cut off. Meanwhile, Hatch had a far better grasp on things. By November 20, he was nearly certain what the Rebels were up to and reported that some of them had already ventured fourteen miles from Florence. Although unsure of the enemy's destination, Hatch provided reliable information confirming that Hood was on the offensive and Forrest was clearing the way. But the question of where Hood was headed remained unanswered. The best guess Hatch and Schofield could initially muster was that he was possibly aiming for Columbia on the Duck River, but both men knew Hood could strike toward any of a number of locations.[38]

Hatch continued to provide remarkably accurate information, as evidenced by a telegram he sent to Thomas on November 21:

> This morning I have information from different scouting parties...which I believe to be true: The head of Lee's corps is twenty miles from Florence, on the Butler Creek road, which strikes the military road south of Lawrenceburg thirteen miles. Cheatham's corps was on the Waynesborough and Florence road; the head of this corps fifteen miles from Florence. Headquarters of Stewart's corps at Wilson's Cross-Roads, six miles from Florence; the corps was moving. The enemy's cavalry on the different roads was near the infantry. This was the state of affairs last night, and has the appearance of an advance on Columbia rather than Pulaski. My advance is now about twelve miles from Lawrenceburg. I am moving that way with small parties on the military road, where we had some skirmishing yesterday. The best information of the strength of the enemy is, infantry, from 30,000 to 35,000, 60 pieces of artillery, and 10,000 cavalry. There is no doubt of their advance. The enemy have one division at Florence, and had not taken up their pontoons last night.[39]

After reading the wire, Thomas included his own comments and forwarded everything to Gen. Henry Halleck in Washington, D.C.:

> I have directed General Schofield to move back gradually from Pulaski and concentrate in the vicinity of Columbia, so as to reach that place before

---

[38] *OR* 45, pt. 1, p. 942, 961-965, 970, 976.

[39] Ibid., p. 970.

Hood could, if he should really move against that place. Hood's force is so much larger than my present available force, both in infantry and cavalry, that I shall have to act on the defensive, Stanley's corps being only 12,000 effective and Schofield's 10,000 effective. As yet General Wilson can only raise about 3,000 effective cavalry.[40]

Early on the morning of November 22, Schofield prepared to pull his men out of Pulaski before they could be cut off by John Bell Hood's advancing columns. He ordered both Jacob Cox and George Wagner to march their divisions to the small village of Lynnville, located roughly ten miles to the north and about halfway to Columbia. David Stanley was also instructed to move his remaining two divisions to the same place the following morning. Thanks to Bedford Forrest's relentless screening, Schofield had no idea where the Rebel army was headed. Forrest even had the Federal commander thinking at one point that the enemy infantry had halted. Indicative of the confusion was a telegram that Schofield fired off to Thomas which read: "I have reports from Waynesborough...and from Lawrenceburg...No indication of any further advance of the enemy...I reckon Hood was unable to move yesterday."[41]

The Rebel infantry and cavalry had not stopped. Instead they kept up the pressure. Cheatham covered another eighteen miles on the second day of the advance and Lee and Stewart also pushed ahead with as much speed as possible. Although the sleet and snow tapered off, November 22 was bitterly cold, forcing the men, especially those without shoes and with tattered jackets and pants, to suffer terribly. Pvt. Willie Smith of the 48th Tennessee remembered the frozen ground and icicles hanging from the trees. He also noted there was not a house in sight for miles. But the Southern troops forged ahead through the desolate and "barren mountainous country..." Ahead of Smith and his comrades Bedford Forrest was having his way with the enemy. By evening the Rebel horsemen had pushed James Wilson's cavalry further both north and east, driving them toward Mount Pleasant southwest of

---

[40] Ibid., p. 970.

[41] *OR* 45, pt. 1, p. 112, 229, 399, 974; Asbury Kerwood, *Annals of the Fifty-Seventh Regiment Indiana Volunteers: Marches, Battles, and Incidents of Army Life*, p. 290.

Columbia and forcing them away from Lawrenceburg.[42]

James Harrison Wilson was only twenty-seven years old when the Tennessee Campaign began and never before had such a task been presented to him. Wilson, an Illinois native, had graduated sixth in the West Point class of 1860, but was not active in the field until 1863. He had developed a friendship with U. S. Grant in 1862 and during the Vicksburg Campaign, where Wilson finally got to display his talent, the relationship strengthened. Wilson was later involved in the battles around Chattanooga and during the first half of 1864 he and Gen. Philip Sheridan worked in unison around Richmond. After the situation in the East became somewhat contained, the young cavalry commander was transferred west in October 1864. Wilson arrived at Gaylesville, Alabama on October 23 and by November 6 he was in Nashville to receive orders from Gen. Thomas. Wilson was put in charge of all cavalry in the Military Division of the Mississippi and he found commands scattered across the West badly in need of reorganization. Having "made all possible arrangements...for expediting the reorganization of the cavalry" Wilson left Nashville after about two weeks and met up with Gen. Schofield "between Lynnville and Pulaski" to field command of the cavalry units opposing the Confederate advance. Wilson would quickly learn, however, that there was no adversary quite like Nathan Bedford Forrest.[43]

At dawn on November 23 the action between the Yankee and Rebel horsemen flared up again, and Forrest wasted little time hammering home his advantage. The skies had cleared and the temperature hovered below freezing, but the conditions meant little to

---

[42] *OR* 45, pt. 1, p. 669, 730; Gerald Allen Kinkaid, Jr., *The Confederate Army, A Regiment: An Analysis of the Forty-Eighth Tennessee Volunteer Infantry Regiment, 1861-1865*, p. 98, Tennessee State Library and Archives (hereafter referred to as TSLA); Nathaniel C. Hughes, Jr., ed., *The Civil War Memoir of Philip Daingerfield Stephenson*, p. 276.

[43] *OR* 45, pt. 1, p. 554-557; Faust, ed., *Historical Times Encyclopedia*, p. 832; McDonough, *Union General in the Civil War and Reconstruction*, p. 101.

James H. Wilson (Library of Congress)

Forrest. He could smell blood and aimed to keep up the pressure.

After two days of rough handling the outmatched bluecoats of Horace Capron's 800-man brigade were on the verge of cracking. The day's fighting began near Henryville and by dusk Forrest, riding at the head of Chalmers' Division, had the Federals pushed all the way to the southern outskirts of Mount Pleasant, some twenty miles north of Lawrenceburg. At Fouche Springs the crackle of rifle fire began to ripple across the landscape when Forrest found his foe "in line of battle in considerable force." Forrest quickly ordered Chalmers to advance Col. Edmund W. Rucker's Brigade toward the enemy front and hold the Federals' attention there. Meanwhile, Lt. Col. D. C. Kelley was told to swing his battalion around the Yankee left while Forrest moved with his eighty man escort around the right. Kelley and Forrest were to meet in the enemy's rear and attack there. Plans went awry, however, and Kelley was not on the scene when Forrest arrived in the Federal rear. He scanned the area. Forrest could see most of the Federal cavalrymen were dismounted and building fires and preparing to encamp for the night. Instead of waiting for Kelley, Forrest ordered an immediate charge into the enemy encampment and soon everything was pure chaos. The sun had set, and in the confusion and growing darkness, Forrest came within inches of taking a bullet when he mistakenly rode up to a small group of Federals. One of the Northerners realized the situation and raised his pistol to fire at Forrest's chest. In a split second Maj. John P. Strange, a member of Forrest's staff, threw out his hand and deflected the enemy soldier's arm as he pulled the trigger, causing the bullet to fly harmlessly into the air. Within moments the rest of Forrest's escort was on the scene and the few Yankees present threw up their hands. Altogether the Confederates bagged fifty prisoners, twenty horses, and even an ambulance. More importantly, they threw the Federal rear into havoc.[44]

In front, James Chalmers and Edmund Rucker pushed their advantage. Hearing the growl of fire from the rear, they charged the Federal position and forced a retreat after some brief fighting. What remained of Capron's Brigade was sent galloping up the road leading to Mount Pleasant and Columbia.[45]

Miles to the east, Jackson and Buford forced Hatch and his Fifth Division out of the Lawrenceburg area and sent the Federals scurrying east toward Pulaski. Before reaching Pulaski, however, Edward Hatch ordered his men north on a road leading to Campbellsville. The Confederates pursued furiously, but the early sunset and frigid conditions brought an end to the action. Encamped on the road four miles south of Campbellsville, Hatch wired Thomas at 10 p.m. that the day had witnessed "a good deal of sharp skirmishing....this evening, before dark, quite spirited."[46]

Although the cavalry had done all of the fighting up to this point, the infantry on both sides was beginning to play an increasingly crucial role. By nightfall on November 23, Hood's three columns, with Cheatham's Corps in the lead, were gathering in and around Waynesboro. A Confederate staff officer reported that the town was entirely deserted. Meanwhile, Schofield had pulled David Stanley's remaining two divisions out of Pulaski around midday. He also ordered Jacob Cox to march out of Lynnville and occupy a new position about ten miles north, near the junction "of Mount Pleasant and Shelbyville road..." Cox's accomplished this and had his men camped by 6 p.m. Stanley's two divisions were in Lynnville by late evening, where they joined their Fourth Corps comrades, the men of Wagner's Division.

---

[44] *OR* 45, pt. 1, p. 752, 763; Wyeth, *That Devil Forrest*, p. 473-474; Jordan & Pryor, *The Campaigns of General Forrest*, p. 614-616.

[45] *OR* 45, pt. 1, p. 752; Jordan & Pryor, *The Campaigns of General Forrest*, p. 616.

[46] *OR* 45, pt. 1, p. 1014.

John M. Schofield (Library of Congress)

For Schofield, however, the night was one of little rest.[47]

It was probably on the evening of November 23 that John McAllister Schofield was forced to admit, if only to himself, that he was in a terrible fix. Thirty-three years of age in the fall of 1864, Schofield was a bit shorter than the average man, had thinning dark hair, and was slightly overweight. His most prominent feature by far was a long beard that extended to his chest. Born in Gerry, New York, a small town southwest of Buffalo near the shores of Lake Erie, to James and Caroline Schofield, he was one of seven children. When Schofield was twelve years old the family moved to Freeport, Illinois and his subsequent years were filled with hard work, church, and a solid public education. The youthful Schofield was calm and well-mannered and displayed obvious signs of intelligence as well as ambition. After finishing school he entered the military academy at West Point in the summer of 1849. In Schofield's first two years there the young cadet performed well in his courses, especially mathematics. Problems, however, loomed on the horizon. On June 18, 1852 he was teaching a math course to candidates hoping to enter the school's summer class when somehow several older cadets made their way into Schofield's classroom and, in some bizarre hazing ritual, had the students "answer indecent questions and draw obscene figures on the blackboard." The episode as a whole nearly ended Schofield's appointment to West Point, and only with the help of Illinois Senator Stephen A. Douglas and after several months was the matter finally

[47] Ibid, p. 112, 357, 669, 730.

resolved in his favor.[48]

Schofield's problems at West Point continued. He, like so many others before and after his term there, enjoyed sneaking away from the barracks late at night for a trip to Benny Havens' tavern. Schofield also loved to smoke and play cards, especially after curfew. He was repeatedly reprimanded for offenses such as being late and inattention and, of course, smoking. During his final year at the academy Schofield racked up 196 demerits, just shy of the 200 that would have led to his dismissal. Amazingly this was the exact same number his classmate John Bell Hood had accumulated. Schofield's grades, however, were markedly better and he graduated seventh in the class of 1853. After leaving West Point with the rank of brevet second lieutenant he served a stint in South Carolina, but returned to the academy in 1855 to teach philosophy in the years before the war. While teaching Schofield worked under the supervision of Professor W. H. C. Barlett. Barlett's daughter Harriet soon caught Schofield's eye and in June 1857 the two were married, a union that resulted in the births of five children.[49]

Schofield transferred in the summer of 1860 to teach physics at Washington University in St. Louis, Missouri, but the outbreak of war threw everything into confusion. Schofield soon filled a spot on the staff of Brig. Gen. Nathaniel Lyon and he was at Wilson's Creek in August 1861 when Lyon was shot and killed. Beyond this exposure to combat, however, Schofield saw no field action until 1864 due to a variety of mostly organizational assignments. Prior to the Atlanta Campaign he took command of the Army of the Ohio, but his force was by far the least used of Sherman's three armies. But as 1864 wound down he found himself in command of two army corps trying to maneuver in the face of an aggressive opponent. Experience could only have been an asset. Schofield, who in later years would greatly downplay what unfolded, was clearly caught off guard by his old school chum. This slowness to action was a problem that William Sherman

---

[48] Faust, ed. *Historical Times Encyclopedia*, p. 661; Schofield, *Forty-Six Years In The Army*, p. 1-2; McDonough, *Union General in the Civil War and Reconstruction*, p. 2-7.

[49] McDonough, *Union General in the Civil War and Reconstruction*, p. 6-10; Schofield, *Forty-Six Years In The Army*, p. 5; Dyer, *The Gallant Hood*, p. 32. Only three of the Schofield children survived to adulthood.

had discerned from careful observation. In a letter to Henry Halleck written days after the fall of Atlanta, Sherman said Schofield was "slow and leaves too much to others..." His analysis is interesting. In Tennessee, Schofield would rely heavily on others, particularly his capable subordinates Jacob Cox and David Stanley.[50]

At 1 a.m. on November 24, Schofield ordered Stanley and Cox to wake their troops and march them to Columbia immediately. Stanley had his bleary-eyed men up by 2 a.m. and on the road within the hour, but Cox, positioned further up the road, did not even receive the dispatch until 4 a.m. Cox roused his men and had them moving north within an hour, on a morning described as "dark and cold." For Schofield the weather might have seemed like an omen. In his message to Cox he said, "...Colonel Capron has been fighting the enemy all day and has been driven back...All information indicates that Hood is nearer Columbia to-night than I am...the question is to concentrate the entire force at Columbia in time." The race was on.[51]

Forrest barely gave his opponent a chance to catch its breath. By 1 a.m. on November 24 he had issued orders to Gen. Chalmers, telling him to pursue the enemy with Col. Rucker's Brigade of 800 troopers. The small village of Mount Pleasant was soon occupied and 35,000 rounds of small arms ammunition were gathered up by the Rebel cavalry. At the first hint of light Chalmers hit Capron's rattled men again, picking up right where he had left off. The Rebels quickly forced their way around Capron's flanks and by 7:30 a.m., less than an hour after sunrise, the Federals were in full flight toward Columbia with the enemy right on their tail. Maj. Henry Connelly of the 16th Illinois Cavalry later wrote that the "only thing that could be done was to get out as promptly as possible, and before Forrest's forces should close in

---

[50] Faust, ed., *Historical Times Encyclopedia*, p. 661; Simpson and Berlin, ed., *Sherman's Civil War*, p. 700; McDonough, *Union General in the Civil War and Reconstruction*, p. 10.

[51] *OR* 45, pt. 1, p. 112, 357, 400, 1020; Kerwood, *Annals of the Fifty-Seventh Indiana*, p. 290.

and capture the command."[52]

Meanwhile, in the vicinity of Campbellsville, the Rebel cavalry was also on the move at dawn. Buford and Jackson forced Hatch north toward Lynnville, rounded up a number of prisoners, killed over a dozen Federals, and captured four stands of colors. Forrest had wanted Buford and Jackson to intercept the Yankee infantry as it moved north toward Columbia, but because they were unable to do so the fight of real consequence became the one waged by Chalmers. On his front things hung in the balance, and although the path to Columbia seemed wide open, a surprise awaited the Southerners.[53]

If nothing else, Nathan Bedford Forrest was intense. Born into the poverty stricken backwoods of the Tennessee in 1821, Forrest had accumulated a fortune by the time the Civil War broke out by becoming one of most successful slave traders in the South. Although he lacked any formal education and struggled somewhat with reading and writing, Forrest refused to let any limitations hold him back. He used both his personality and appearance to his advantage. Forrest stood just over six feet tall, had thick black hair and a goatee, and possessed a physique that invited little trouble. In a day and age when the average man was about five and a half feet tall, Forrest seemed somewhat like a giant. But it was his demeanor, his explosive temper, his flaming eyes when provoked, and his absolute fearlessness that few people ever forgot. Not the kind of man to cross in private, on the field of battle Forrest was able to fully unleash his fury. He may have killed as many as thirty Federal soldiers during the course of the war and had a similar number of horses shot out from beneath him. Forrest had a penchant for immersing himself in hand-to-hand combat, a perfect example of which took place shortly after the Battle of Shiloh. While leading a reckless charge upon the pursuing enemy, Forrest, who was on horseback, was shot at point-blank range by a Federal soldier on the ground. The bullet

---

[52] *OR* 45, pt. 1, p. 752, 763; Wyeth, *That Devil Forrest*, p. 474; Jordan & Pryor, *The Campaigns of General Forrest*, p. 616-617; Henry C. Connelly, Aug. 8, 1887 letter in *Battles & Leaders of the Civil War*, 4, p. 443.

[53] *OR* 45, pt. 1, p. 576, 768.

Nathan Bedford Forrest (Library of Congress)

lodged near his spine, but Forrest, suddenly immersed in a sea of blue, began hacking away with his sword. According to one source, Forrest grabbed a man by the coat, pulled him onto his horse, and galloped away while holding the terrified soldier behind him to prevent the enemy from shooting. When out of range, Forrest let the soldier go and spent the next several weeks recovering from his wound.[54]

Forrest suffered a number of other battlefield injuries. He once dislocated his right shoulder after being thrown from a horse, was wounded just prior to Chickamauga, and was shot at the base of his right big toe at Tupelo, Mississippi in July 1864. Forrest was terribly incapacitated by the latter injury and forced to ride in a buggy for several weeks because he was so weak. A year earlier he had received another wound, but rather than being inflicted by Yankees, it came at the hands of a disgruntled fellow officer named Andrew W. Gould. In June 1863, a disagreement between the two in Columbia, Tennessee spiraled out of control and Gould pulled out a gun and fired. Forrest, who was shot just above the left hip, disregarded the wound and plunged into action. While protecting himself from further shots with one hand, Forrest used his other to unfold a penknife and plunge it into Gould's ribs. Gould turned and ran, but was soon cornered by

---

[54] Faust, ed., *Historical Times Encyclopedia*, p. 269-270; Wyeth, *That Devil Forrest*, p. 65; Jordan & Pryor, *The Campaigns of General Forrest*, p. 146-148; Jack Hurst, *Nathan Bedford Forrest: A Biography*, p. 92-94; Welsh, *Medical Histories of Confederate Generals*, p. 71.

Forrest and hauled away to receive medical attention. Gould's injuries were mortal and he died several days later. Fortunately for the Confederacy, Forrest's injury was not very serious and he recovered in a short time.[55]

By the fall of 1864 Nathan Bedford Forrest was a living legend. He was a savage fighter who possessed a keen instinct for command and strategy, uncommon even among those with military training. Forrest had captured one Federal garrison or post after another and destroyed enough supplies, railroad tracks, and telegraph wire to drive dozens of his adversaries nearly crazy with despair. Now he was called upon to clear the path for John Bell Hood's invasion of the Tennessee heartland.

As Chalmers' cavalry came storming toward Columbia they were greeted by Federal infantry. Jacob Cox and his weary soldiers tramped into the area just before sunup. They "marched by a cross-road some two miles out of town, and reached that on which the fight was going on in time to interpose the infantry skirmishers, moving at double-quick, between Forrest's cavalry and the brigade commanded by Colonel Capron, which was rapidly retreating into the place." A Federal officer remembered how Capron's troops were driven toward Columbia "like a herd in a stampede." Cox quickly placed Brig. Gen. James W. Reilly's Brigade on the right of the Mount Pleasant Pike, Col. Thomas J. Henderson's Brigade on the left of the pike, and allowed Capron's men reform to the rear. Soon Col. Edmund Rucker's Brigade from Chalmers' Division galloped up and began to "vigorously" press the Federal line. Capt. Levi T. Scofield, an engineer officer in the Twenty-Third Corps, recalled how a Rebel captain "on a splendid black charger" was "deliberately shooting our men in the backs of their heads" when he was "dropped from his seat" by rifle fire from the infantry as they moved into position. Chalmers later said that Lt. Col. William A. Dawson of the 15th Tennessee Cavalry, after discharging "all the loads from his revolver," was shot and killed while "endeavoring to wrest one of the enemy's flags from its bearer..." Capt. Scofield also remembered

---

[55] Welsh, *Medical Histories of Confederate Generals*, p. 71-72; Hurst, *Nathan Bedford Forrest*, p. 127-130, 208.

how the "plucky" 100th Ohio, deployed as skirmishers, did much to help stall the enemy's advance. Cox reported that "a lively skirmish ensued," but the Rebels were unable to force a crossing of Bigby Creek and Columbia remained firmly in Federal hands. Additional reinforcements arrived at 10 a.m. when David Stanley's troops began filing into the town. They were complimented by Col. Orlando H. Moore's Brigade of Ruger's Division, which had started arriving in town around 2:30 a.m. on railcars from Johnsonville via Nashville. By late morning thousands of Yankee soldiers were furiously entrenching on the outskirts of Columbia.[56]

The race for Columbia had been a close one. Until early on November 24 the town was barely occupied by Federal troops. Before Moore's and Cox's arrivals, Thomas Ruger had only Col. Silas Strickland's depleted Third Brigade and a single Second Brigade regiment defending the town. Altogether Ruger said there were only "about 800 muskets" available. Strickland was absent the 91st Indiana and 123rd Indiana, both of which were ordered west on November 23 to guard fords over the Duck River at Centreville and Williamsport. This left Strickland with only the 50th Ohio, the recently assigned 72nd Illinois, and the Second Brigade's 111th Ohio.[57]

John Schofield later rather casually dismissed the importance of Cox's arrival at Columbia. He believed Ruger's men were "quite capable" of preventing the enemy cavalry from entering town. While probably true, Schofield ignored the fact that Cox's timely presence made securing Columbia significantly easier than it would have been. Yet even had Forrest gotten into Columbia there is no doubt he would have been unable to hold off the concentrating Union forces. Moreover, the nearest Southern infantry support was still about thirty miles away, well south of Mount Pleasant.[58]

---

[56] *OR* 45, pt. 1, p. 378, 400-401, 763; Stanley, *Personal Memoirs*, p. 199; Levi T. Scofield, *The Retreat from Pulaski to Nashville, Tenn.*, p. 13; Cox, *Sherman's March to the Sea*, p. 65. One of Moore's regiments, th e 111th Ohio, had arrived at Columbia about twenty-four hours earlier at 3 a.m. on the morning of November 23. See *OR* 45, pt. 1, p. 387.

[57] *OR* 45, pt. 1, p. 387, 999-1001.

[58] *OR* 45, pt. 1, p. 670, 730; Schofield, *Forty-Six Years In The Army*, p. 168.

As the action at Columbia wound down, the Rebel infantry was still working its way up the Waynesboro-Mount Pleasant Pike. Moving now as a large single column, the troops forged ahead until nightfall and resumed the march at dawn on November 25. By sundown on that misty and drizzly Friday, Lee's Corps was camped north of Mount Pleasant and the other two corps were strung out south of town. The Confederates kept going the following day under a blanket of gray clouds and ever present rain. Throughout November 26, Hood's gaunt but determined army marched through Mount Pleasant and toward Columbia on the well-constructed pike connecting the two. If the troops were unable to get relief from the weather, at least the new road was in much better condition than some of the horrendous paths they had recently traveled. A Texan from Hiram Granbury's Brigade said the new road was "graveled all over" and was "very hard and solid." An artilleryman who had battled the horrible country paths reported in his diary with exuberance that the road "was splendid..."[59]

Sometime on the afternoon of November 26, as his men passed by, Patrick Cleburne reined in his horse and dismounted north of Mount Pleasant. Cleburne had stopped on the grounds of St. John's Episcopal Church, a magnificent brick structure built by the Polk family on their Ashwood Plantation about two decades before the war. Leonidas Polk, a former corps commander in the Army of Tennessee as well as Episcopalian bishop, had been killed by artillery fire at Pine Mountain outside Atlanta only five months earlier. In fact, it was Polk who had baptized Gen. Hood in early 1864, only months before the bishop's untimely death. Polk's nephew, Brig. Gen. Lucius E. Polk, had returned to Ashwood after losing a leg to artillery fire at Kennesaw Mountain, barely two weeks after his uncle's death.[60]

Cleburne had a close friendship with the younger Polk and it was while speaking with him at the Battle of Richmond, Kentucky that Cleburne was wounded in late 1862. Polk had been injured and Cleburne, seeing him being tended to by medical staff, dismounted to

---

[59] *OR* 45, pt. 1, p. 670, 730; Brown, ed., *One of Cleburne's Command*, p. 146; Young diary, Nov. 26, 1864, in possession of Bill and Marilyn Christmann.

[60] Horn, *Army of Tennessee*, p. 332; Parks, *General Leonidas Polk*, p. 98; Stuart W. Sanders, "The Bishop's Nephew," *CWTI*, Mar. 2001, p. 60.

say a few words. In mid-sentence, however, a minie ball tore through Cleburne's mouth, entered one cheek, took out a couple of teeth, and exited through the other cheek. Luckily for him, the injury was not terribly serious and he was back on duty within weeks. Ironically, Cleburne had a second brush with death on almost the exact same spot where Leonidas Polk was killed. Not only was Pine Mountain well within Federal artillery range, but the Yankees had the distance to it perfectly fixed. Cleburne had scaled the mountain on June 13, 1864 and had to scurry back down when the Federals opened up with a hail of fire. Polk was not so fortunate and he was struck by a solid shot the next day and died instantly.[61]

Perhaps out of respect for his friends, or simply awed by St. John's beauty, Cleburne walked slowly toward the church and the surrounding grove of magnolia trees before winding his way to the rear. Behind the church was located a small cemetery. Pausing for a moment beneath the gray skies and lightly falling rain, Cleburne thought quietly to himself. Several minutes later the general returned and, as he mounted his horse, said to Capt. Charles Hill, "It would not be hard to die if one could be buried in such a beautiful spot."[62]

Cleburne was not the only one who took note of the area's incredible beauty. An artilleryman described the landscape as "Middle Tennessee paradise..." Texas Capt. Sam Foster wrote that it was "the richest country we have seen yet" and recounted how he and his regiment passed "the Polk place in Maury Co. The prettiest place I have ever seen in my life."[63]

Rain continued to fall on November 27 as all three Rebel corps began the job of positioning themselves south of Columbia. Schofield's infantry remained entrenched on the south side of the Duck River and James Wilson's cavalry guarded the fords on the north side to prevent any flanking movements by the Southerners. Schofield, who was headquartered at the Athenaeum, was already in receipt of a telegram from Thomas asking that he try to "hold Hood on the south side of

---

[61] Irving A. Buck, *Cleburne and His Command*, p. 107, 223; Parks, *General Leonidas Polk*, p. 382-383.

[62] Purdue, *Pat Cleburne*, p. 392.

[63] Hughes, Jr., ed., *Stephenson Memoir*, p. 278; Brown, ed., *One of Cleburne's Command*, p. 146.

Duck River..." Schofield knew what his commander expected. But he remained acutely aware that if the Confederates somehow got behind him there would be hell to pay. Believing that Hood would not be foolish enough to attack the strong Union position at Columbia, Schofield remained suspicious of a maneuver around his left flank. In an effort to try and determine the enemy's options, the Federal commander sent scouts out along the river east of town to see whether the fords were usable or not. He also telegraphed Thomas: "The enemy has made no real attack, and I am satisfied he does not intend to attack. My information, though not very satisfactory, leads me to believe that Hood intends to cross Duck River above Columbia, and as near it as he can."[64]

Because of his growing concern, Schofield felt that holding his position south of the Duck River was not feasible. Thus he ordered his troops to pull back across the river and occupy a new position along a ridge approximately a mile and a half from the north bank. The move to this ridge was a necessity because the land adjacent to the river on its north side was "fifteen to twenty feet lower than the banks immediately opposite..." Occupying the ridge was the only way Schofield could prevent the Confederate artillery from moving up, grabbing the heights south of the river, and lobbing shells on top of his troops. With his decision made, Schofield wired Thomas on November 27: "I shall withdraw to the north bank to-night, and endeavor to prevent him from crossing."[65]

That same evening, with his opponent on the move and a bitterly cold wind lashing the area, John Bell Hood had a critically important meeting with his corps commanders and Nathan Bedford Forrest. The conference was held at Hood's headquarters, located east of the Pulaski Pike at Beechlawn, the residence of Mrs. Amos Warfield. Hood explained to those present that he had decided to try and swing a large portion of his army around the Federal left. A lengthy discussion was had "concerning the roads, nature and condition of the country" and what the cavalry's role would be in the morning. Hood also laid out plans for how the infantry would maneuver during the planned flanking

---

[64] *OR* 45, pt. 1, 670, 730-731, 1036, 1044, 1085-1086; Frank H. Smith, *History of Maury County, Tennessee*, p. 26.

[65] Purdue, *Pat Cleburne*, p. 392; *OR* 45, pt. 1, p. 402, 1086.

maneuver.[66]

Hood explained that Forrest would first force a crossing of the Duck River east of town. Once that action was complete, both Frank Cheatham's and A. P. Stewart's corps, plus Edward Johnson's Division from S. D. Lee's Corps, would follow with a quick movement across the river. They would then march around the Federal left flank. Meanwhile, Lee would remain at Columbia with the rest of his corps and almost all of the army's artillery in an effort to keep the Federals occupied. Hood said he hoped to lure Schofield into thinking Lee's artillery and rifle fire was a prelude to a general attack at Columbia. That portion of the plan was critical. If Lee could hold the Yankees in position long enough, the rest of the Confederates would be able to slip behind Schofield's forces and cut him off from Nashville.[67]

By the morning of November 28, Schofield and his men were safely on the north side of the river. A 9:30 a.m. telegram to Thomas reported that "the withdrawal was completed at daylight this morning without serious difficulty." As relieved as he may have been, Schofield's mood was about to change.[68]

Early on November 28, Nathan Bedford Forrest got to work. Following Hood's orders to cross the Duck River and flank the enemy, the "Wizard of the Saddle" broke his cavalry into four sections and started moving. At Holland's Ford, Owen's Ford, and Carr's Mill the Rebels worked their way across the river in the face of little enemy opposition. Only at Hardison's Mill, where Lewisburg Pike crossed the river, did the Yankees offer stiff resistance. At that location Capron's Brigade confronted Buford's Division. When Capron reported to Wilson that the Rebels were engaging him, the young cavalry commander made a serious error.[69]

---

[66] James Lee McDonough and Thomas L. Connelly, *Five Tragic Hours: The Battle of Franklin*, p. 35; Hood, *Advance & Retreat*, p. 282-283; Jordan & Pryor, *The Campaigns of General Forrest*, p. 619; Connelly, *Autumn of Glory*, p. 491.

[67] *OR* 45, pt. 1, p. 687; Hood, *Advance & Retreat*, p. 283.

[68] *OR* 45, pt. 1, p. 1105.

[69] *OR* 45, pt. 1, p. 1122-1123; Keenan, *Wilson's Cavalry Corps*, p. 49; Nathaniel Cheairs Hughes, Jr., *Brigadier General Tyree H. Bell, C.S.A. - Forrest's Fighting Lieutenant*, p. 195-196.

Because Lewisburg Pike was a direct route from the Duck River to Franklin, Wilson believed Forrest might be aiming for that town. To prevent such a move, Wilson ordered his cavalry units to consolidate near Hurt's Cross Roads, about five miles north of Hardison's Mill. This decision allowed the Rebels to continue their crossing of the river largely unimpeded and left Horace Capron's troops virtually isolated. When Edward Hatch pulled his Fifth Division back, Brig. Gen. Richard W. Johnson did the same with the Sixth Division. Johnson, whose new division included the brigades of Capron and Croxton, had just assumed command on November 24, and he rode toward Hurt's Cross Roads with Croxton after sending orders to Capron telling him to fall back. But before Capron was able to withdraw the Confederates came swooping down on him. Johnson said when he reached Lewisburg Pike around nightfall, elements of Capron's Brigade were found "retiring in the direction of Franklin." Told that the Rebels were not far behind, Johnson quickly deployed Croxton "across the pike" and tried to rally some of Capron's troops. The enemy never materialized, but to the south the rest of Capron's Brigade was fighting for its life.[70]

Major J. Morris Young and the 5th Iowa Cavalry had been assigned to Capron's Brigade for less than a week. At about 5 p.m., Young learned from his pickets that not only were the Rebels suddenly behind him, but Col. Capron was nowhere to be found. Because the rest of Wilson's command had pulled back, Brig. Gen. Lawrence S. Ross' Texas Brigade from Jackson's Division, which had crossed the river just a mile west of Hardison's Mill, was able to pounce on several of Capron's unsuspecting regiments. Quickly Ross' men battered the 7th Ohio Cavalry and portions of two Illinois regiments, captured a number of prisoners, took three stands of colors, and sent the Federals scrambling north where Johnson saw them. Capron was also caught up in the retreat. But before the Rebels could finish off the rest of the brigade Maj. Young jumped into action. As he readied his own Iowa regiment, the 8th Michigan Cavalry and what remained of the 14th Illinois Cavalry and 16th Illinois Cavalry came galloping into view. Young placed the 5th Iowa, fully mounted and in column, on the Lewisburg Pike and ordered the 8th Michigan and 16th Illinois to dismount and

---

[70] *OR* 45, pt. 1, p. 589, 1112-1113; Keenan, *Wilson's Cavalry Corps*, p. 49-50.

form perpendicular to the right and left of the Iowans. Then the 14th Illinois "was placed in column of fours, to the left and rear of the Eighth Michigan and parallel to the Fifth Iowa..." Young instructed the dismounted troops to draw the enemy's fire, immediately throw themselves in the saddle, and follow the 5th Iowa, which was going to charge with sabers drawn. In the almost total darkness Young launched his daring plan. It worked perfectly. Within half an hour the Federal horsemen, after scattering Ross' Texans "in all directions" and cutting their way out, were galloping toward safety.[71]

By the time night fell Forrest had largely accomplished his mission. Only Abe Buford's Division remained south of the Duck River and his men were scheduled to cross at dawn, having removed Capron's troops from the scene. But most importantly, the strategic situation had changed dramatically from the prior day. Wilson's cavalry, now positioned far north and east of where it had been, was essentially severed from the main Federal body. This left Schofield both extremely vulnerable and justifiably concerned. In a dispatch sent to Wilson at 5:20 p.m., Schofield said enemy cavalry was approaching the left flank of the infantry. He expressed concern that Wilson had pulled the cavalry pickets away from the river, reminding him that the river "should not be left without cavalry pickets." But Schofield was too late. By the time he prepared the message, Wilson had already abandoned the river. By 9 p.m. he and the cavalry were over a dozen miles northeast of Columbia, encamped near Hurt's Cross Roads.[72]

As November 28 drew to a close Hood's plan was working splendidly. Good luck had also come to bear. Early in the day the army's chief engineer Stephen Presstman examined the south bank of the Duck River east of Columbia, looking for the best place to cross the infantry. During his excursion Presstman was introduced to G. Wash Gordon, a local boy serving as a scout in the 1st Tennessee Infantry. After questioning Gordon rather extensively about his knowledge of the area Presstman became convinced the youth could provide solid

---

[71] *OR* 45, pt. 1, p. 588, 604, 769; Keenan, *Wilson's Cavalry Corps*, p. 50; Hughes, Jr., *Brigadier General Tyree H. Bell*, p. 196.

[72] *OR* 45, pt. 1, p. 1112; Hughes, Jr., *Brigadier General Tyree H. Bell*, p. 197; John E. Fisher, *They Rode With Forrest & Wheeler: A Chronicle of Five Brothers' Service in the Confederate Western Cavalry*, p. 152.

information. Gordon said crossing the river at Huey's Mill would be difficult. He then told Presstman about the Davis Ford, located at a bend in the river about four miles east of town and unguarded by the Yankees. Presstman had Gordon escort him to the ford and when they arrived the engineer could see at once it was suitable for crossing. Quickly Presstman put his miners and sappers to work carving away the river banks and building approaches for the pontoon bridge. Throughout the day the Confederate engineer team worked feverishly, both to prepare the ford and haul the pontoons out of Columbia to the crossing point. All night Presstman and his crew continued their task.[73]

The first troops scheduled to cross the river were moved into position around nightfall. A. J. Batchelor of the 33rd Alabama said his unit was "marched up the river some distance" where it bivouacked for the night "near the river bank." He also recalled a wagon pulling up around dark and distributing ears of corn to the men. Meanwhile, while Batchelor and his comrades got what rest they could, finishing touches were applied to the pontoon bridge. Before dawn it was complete, spanning the width of the Duck River. The general advance was now ready to begin. Forrest's job was complete and the bulk of the infantry was poised to transfer via the Davis Ford to the north bank of the river. Destiny was at hand.[74]

---

[73] Smith, *History of Maury County,* p. 250, 254; Hood, *Advance & Retreat*, p. 283; Keenan, *Wilson's Cavalry Corps*, p. 52.

[74] A. J. Batchelor, "On Hood's Campaign To Franklin," *CV* 18, p. 426.

3

The Roads to Spring Hill

By the time the sun rose at 6:38 a.m. on November 29, 1864, John Bell Hood had been awake for hours. In the saddle by 4 a.m., his mind swirling with determination, Hood knew the day would be a momentous one in his career. The clock of history was ticking fast in a war that had turned sharply against the South and Hood was attempting to radically shift its course. The defining moment of his entire military career lay just ahead of him. As the general prepared to depart he said to Chaplain Charles T. Quintard, "The enemy must give me fight or I will be at Nashville before to-morrow night." Hood then rode off to put his bold plan into action.[1]

Across the river, John Schofield was also wide awake and unsure of what his foe was up to. But things began to take shape before dawn when the Federal commander received a message from James Wilson. Sent by courier from Hurt's Cross Roads shortly after 1 a.m., the dispatch pointed to confirmation that the Rebels were attempting a flanking maneuver:

> I have a prisoner who came with General Forrest to-day from Columbia. The rebel cavalry – Buford's, Chalmers', Jackson's divisions, a part of Roddey's division, and Biffle's regiment (Forrest's escort) – crossed, by swimming, above Huey's Mill. Forrest himself left Columbia at 4:30 p.m. The rebel infantry were then expecting every minute to march. They were building

---

[1] Charles T. Quintard, *Doctor Quintard Chaplain C.S.A. and Second Bishop of Tennessee; Being His Story of the War*, p. 108-109. Sunrise time obtained from the U. S. Naval Observatory and provided specifically for Spring Hill, Tennessee for November 29, 1864.

three pontoon bridges just above Huey's when my prisoner crossed– expected to be ready by 11 to-night (of the 28th). The whole rebel force, except Buford's division, are encamped near Widow Shannon's to-night, on the Columbia and Shelbyville road. Buford is in my front, about Rally Hill. I think it is very clear that they are aiming for Franklin, and that you ought to get to Spring Hill by 10 a.m. I'll keep on this road and hold the enemy all I can. If I had Hammond and Stewart here, I think they could not make anything until their infantry caught up. Communicate with me by Thompson's Station or Spring Hill, and thence eastward. I'll try to get no farther back to-morrow than the Ridge Meeting-House, due east from Thompson's, on this road. I shall probably leave this pike there and move toward Nolensville. Another prisoner confirms the above. Jackson's division is also at or near Rally Hill. There may be no strong advance of the enemy's cavalry till the infantry have crossed, which will be between now and daylight. Get back to Franklin without delay, leaving a small force to detain the enemy. The rebels will move by this road toward that point.[2]

Schofield quickly made preparations for a retreat. He ordered Stanley and two of his Fourth Corps divisions, along with Ruger's Division of the Twenty-Third Corps, to withdraw and move to Spring Hill. He also ordered the wagon train, which had already been moved north to the vicinity of Rutherford Creek, to begin moving toward Spring Hill, escorted by the 120th Indiana. Because the length of the train far exceeded what the 120th Indiana could cover, that regiment was actually assigned to protect the leading elements of the long and creaking procession. Other troops would protect the rest of the wagon train. In the midst of this frantic decision making, Schofield's thoughts also involved Wilson. He believed it likely that the cavalry would be unable to provide any further timely information regarding the enemy's movements. Based on this, Schofield ordered Gen. Thomas Wood, commanding the Third Division of Stanley's Corps, to send out an infantry reconnaissance at 8:15 a.m.[3]

Chosen for the task was Col. L. Sidney Post, who led his 1,600-

---

[2] *OR* 45, pt. 1, p. 1140.

[3] Schofield, *Forty-Six Years In The Army*, p. 210-211; D. W. Smith, "Hood's Last Campaign: Experience with the Wagon-Train from Columbia to Franklin," *National Tribune Newspaper* (hereafter referred to as *NT*), Nov. 20, 1890, p. 4.

man brigade northeast of Columbia to feel out the enemy. But Schofield was not done. He had just received a telegram sent by George Henry Thomas the previous evening that stated, in part: "If you are confident you can hold your present position, I wish you to do so until I can get General Smith here. After his arrival we can withdraw gradually, and invite Hood across Duck River and fall upon him with our whole force, or wait until Wilson can organize his entire cavalry force, and then withdraw from your present position. Should Hood then cross the river we can surely ruin him."[4] In his memoirs Schofield wrote of this momentous morning:

> I was then confronted with the grave question, How long might it be possible to hold Hood back, and thus gain time for Thomas to get up his reinforcements? By holding on to the crossing of Duck River at Columbia until dark that night, and thus preventing Hood from using the turnpike for the movement of his artillery and trains until the next day, we would practically gain twenty-four hours; for he could not move them readily over his mud road from Huey's Mill. To do this, I must not only head Hood off at Spring Hill, but defeat any attempt he might make to dislodge me from the north bank of Duck River.[5]

At the moment of decision, however, John Schofield blinked. At around 10 a.m., based on information received from Post, he rescinded his earlier orders and instead told Ruger only to prepare for the retreat. Meanwhile, Stanley got the exasperating duty of accompanying to Spring Hill both the artillery and trailing end of the cumbersome wagon train. Both decisions would have considerable impact on the day's events.[6]

After weeks of wretched weather the Tennessee skies finally cleared on November 29. Although the morning broke cold, the sun quickly warmed the landscape as it rose above the southeastern horizon, burning the frost from the ground and clearing the fog which hung above the Duck River. At the Davis Ford there was much activity. Frank Cheatham's Corps was the first to cross the pontoon bridge and

---

[4] *OR* 45, pt. 1, p. 122, 1108.

[5] Schofield, *Forty-Six Years In The Army*, p. 213.

[6] *OR* 45, pt. 1, p. 1141-1142.

his men quickly began moving up the Davis Ford Road. It was an efficient and well-timed operation. Soldiers streamed across the bridge with little or no congestion. Patrick Cleburne's Division was on the north side of the river by 7:30 a.m. and it took the advance with Brig. Gen. Mark P. Lowrey's Brigade at the head of the column. It was there, at the very front, where Hood, accompanied by Cleburne and Lowrey, rode confidently northward. Behind him strode the thousands of common men, the heart and soul of the Army of Tennessee. Although some new recruits had joined the ranks the majority of those present were veterans, men who had seen it all. They were men who had continued to fight under circumstances so trying that the average person's spirit would falter and break. Men who had labored on month after month without pay, without food, without decent clothing, and much of the time, without victory. Yet still they battled on.[7]

Pvt. John M. Copley of the 49th Tennessee remembered the persistent optimism of his bedraggled comrades. In a post-war recollection he wrote: "Many of our soldiers were barefooted, and their clothing very ragged; added to this, what little money we possessed was worthless; yet, the soldiers were buoyant and hopeful. When the sun rose...throwing his gentle rays beneath a cloudless sky...our troops were ready for action, and in high spirits at the prospect of having a brush with Schofield's army..."[8]

Did the Confederates understand what their objective was on November 29? Was Hood simply trying to get to Nashville before Schofield or was he trying to eliminate Schofield as a fighting force? Nothing is conclusive, but it does seem Hood was trying to destroy

---

[7] Smith, *History of Maury County*, p. 254; *OR* 45, pt. 1, p. 742; Buck, *Cleburne And His Command*, p. 272; Mark P. Lowrey, "An Autobiography," *Southern Historical Society Papers* (hereafter referred to as *SHSP*) 16, p. 373.

[8] John M. Copley, *A Sketch of the Battle of Franklin, Tenn.; with Reminiscences of Camp Douglas*, p. 30, Southern Historical Collection (hereafter referred to as SHC), University of North Carolina at Chapel Hill.

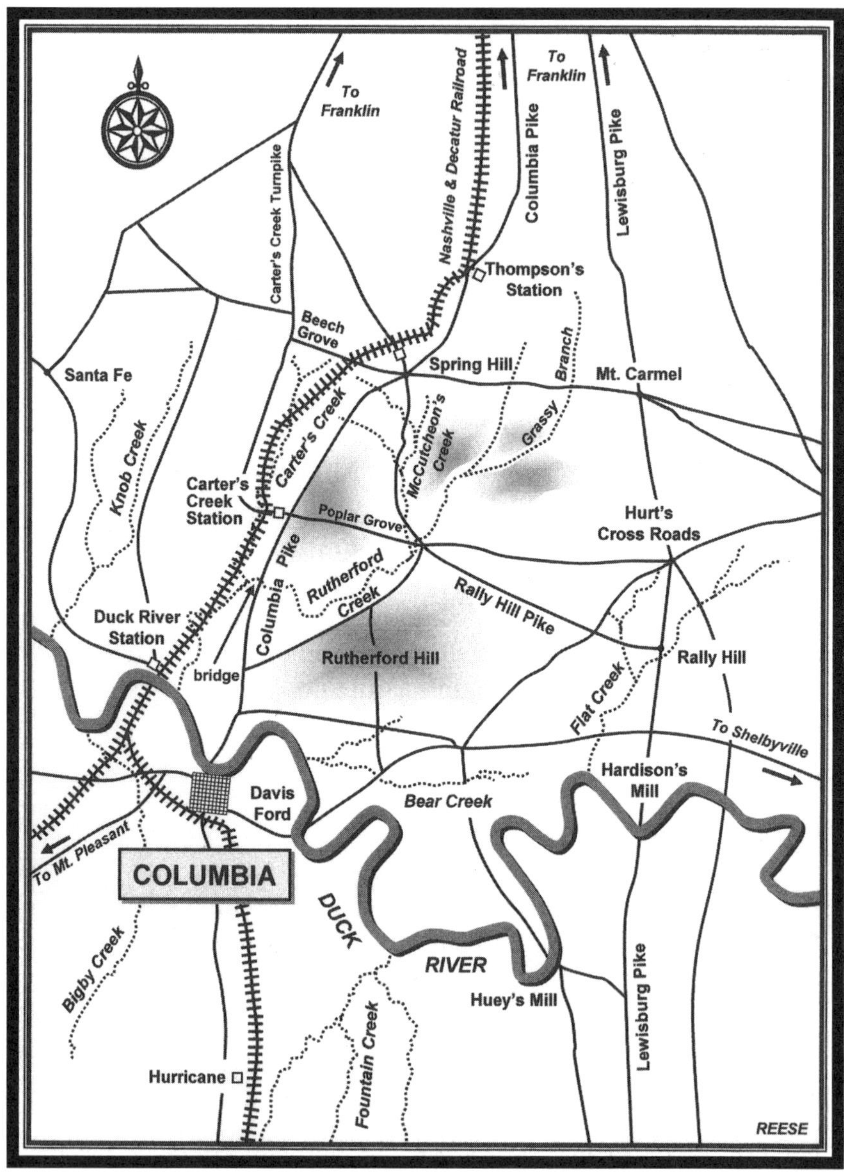

Columbia to Spring Hill vicinity

Schofield, not just beat him to the Tennessee capital. S. D. Lee offered support to Hood's assertion that cutting Schofield's army off and fighting it was the goal when the Southerners left Columbia. Lee had a closer relationship with Hood than did most others, but his recollection is telling. He wrote: "Before starting from Columbia it was understood that the first troops reaching the pike at Spring Hill should cross it or commence fighting and would be supported and reinforced by the other troops as they arrived in succession on the field. A lodgment was to be made on the pike and the march of the enemy stopped." A. P. Stewart wrote that the "forced march" was made "to get in rear of the enemy." Samuel French concurred, stating that Hood had designed "a strategic movement...to gain the Franklin pike in rear of the enemy." Pvt. Edward Y. McMorries said the lead corps was to "pass the enemy and throw itself across the Franklin pike in front" and cut off Schofield's path of retreat. Even more revealing is a letter written by Dr. Urban G. Owen to his wife Laura on November 19, 1864. Owen stated, "Our Gen'ls all say that our route is to get between Thomas' army & Nashville." If a physician was aware of the army's planned movement, it surely was common knowledge among the soldiers.[9]

Although Lee's is the only account that mentions engaging Schofield once the pike was reached, none of the other accounts state anything about continuing on to Nashville. Hood reported that his objective was to "cut off that portion of the enemy at or near Columbia." In his memoirs, Hood said he wished to place his troops across the Columbia Pike and to "attack as the Federals retreated, and put to rout and capture, if possible, their Army..." Hood even went so far as to say that he believed Schofield's force was the only obstruction standing between him and success at Nashville. This argument, made almost fifteen years after the war, is revealing. Obviously by the time he wrote his memoirs, Hood had the benefit of hindsight. However, he remained convinced that had Schofield been defeated Nashville would

---

[9] Lee, *CV* 16, p. 257; *OR* 45, pt. 1, p. 712; French, *Two Wars*, p. 291; Edward Young McMorries, *History of the First Regiment Alabama Volunteer Infantry, C. S. A.*, p. 83; Sadye T. Wilson, Nancy T. Fitzgerald, and Richard Warwick, ed., *Letters to Laura: A Confederate Surgeon's Impressions of Four Years of War*, p. 180.

have fallen. It seems obvious, no matter how flawed Hood's opinion about Nashville may have been, that he wanted to try and erase Schofield from the field. Therefore, it is not at all presumptuous to conclude that Hood's goal on November 29 was, as he stated, to gain control of the pike and force Schofield's hand in battle.[10]

By around 9 a.m., Stewart's Corps had completed its passage across the Duck River along with Johnson's Division of Lee's Corps. The rest of Lee's Corps, Carter Stevenson's and Henry Clayton's divisions, as well as most of the army's artillery, remained behind at Columbia and had been at work since dawn trying to hold Schofield's attention. Col. Robert F. Beckham commanded the Confederate artillery battalions and their fire, combined with the deadly accuracy of sharpshooters posted in and around Greenwood Cemetery, kept the Federals on high alert. One of Beckham's crews doing hard work that morning was Ferguson's South Carolina Battery, commanded by Lt. Rene T. Beauregard, son of none other than P. G. T. Beauregard. Although there were few Northern casualties, Beckham's gunners did a superb job of keeping the enemy pinned down and planting doubt in Schofield's mind when every minute mattered.[11]

Not long into the morning march, the Rebel column, which numbered slightly more than 22,000, pulled to a halt and an impromptu conference was had between Hood and Cleburne. Hood's map differed from the road that lay before him and he wanted some clarification. His guide for the day was a local named John "Sol" Gregory, who was serving in Col. Jacob Biffle's cavalry. Gregory knew every twist and turn between Columbia and Spring Hill and pointed out that while a straight line drawn from the Davis Ford to Spring Hill was only twelve miles, the actual traveling distance was at least seventeen miles. This

---

[10] *OR* 45, pt. 1, p. 652; Hood, *Advance & Retreat*, p. 282. It cannot be determined with certainty what Hood's intentions were by the end of November. Connelly in *Autumn of Glory*, p. 490-493, claimed Hood had no objective beyond getting to Nashville and that he was ignorant of troop strength there.

[11] *OR* 45, pt. 1, p. 669, 1264; Smith, *History of Maury County*, p. 254; Jill K. Garrett and Marise P. Lightfoot, *The Civil War in Maury County, Tennessee*, p. 95; Larry Daniel, *Cannoneers in Gray: The Field Artillery of the Army of Tennessee*, p. 172.

information was confirmed by a guide Cleburne had procured.[12]

Additionally, the road, deeply rutted and washed out in countless spots, was in miserable condition. Harold Young, an artilleryman in Guibor's Missouri Battery, wrote in his diary that it was "the rockiest and roughest road" he had ever traveled on. Only a week before Young had made a similar entry, but in his mind the Davis Ford Road was even worse.[13]

The previous weeks of rain and snow served only to worsen an already bad situation. Although Gregory's news was unexpected Hood knew nothing could be done to alter the situation and so the column was ordered to continue. Shortly after restarting, however, additional trouble cropped up. Schofield's infantry reconnaissance was sighted around 10 a.m. near Bear Creek and Hood suddenly faced the possibility that his left flank was exposed. In response, he ordered a change in the marching formation and split Cheatham's Corps into two columns. Cleburne and William Bate were directed to continue moving up the Davis Ford Road while John Brown was sent into the woods and "open fields" several hundred yards to the east "so as to be ready for attack or defense at a moment's warning." Specifically, Brown was told to protect both Cleburne and Bate and "conform" to their movements. As a further inconvenience, Brown was ordered to detach Brig. Gen. States Rights Gist's Brigade and half of Brig. Gen. Otho F. Strahl's Brigade from his division and send them out as skirmishers.[14]

---

[12] Smith, *History of Maury County*, p. 237-238; Garrett and Lightfoot, *The Civil War in Maury County*, p. 96; Mauriel Phillips Joslyn, ed., *A Meteor Shining Brightly: Essays on Maj. Gen. Patrick R. Cleburne*, p. 243; Mary Miles Jones and Leslie Jones Martin, ed., *The Gentle Rebel: The Civil War Letters of 1st Lt. William Harvey Berryhill, Co. D, 43rd Regiment, Mississippi Volunteers*, p. 119. The name of the other guide was Jim Smith.

[13] Joslyn, ed., *A Meteor Shining Brightly*, p. 243; Young diary, November 29, 1864, in possession of Bill and Marilyn Christmann.

[14] Garrett and Lightfoot, *The Civil War in Maury County*, p. 95-96; John C. Brown, Statement of, in B. F. Cheatham, "The Lost Opportunity at Spring Hill, Tenn. - General Cheatham's Reply to General Hood," *SHSP* 9, p. 537; Frank A. Burr and Talcott Williams, "The Battle of Franklin," *The Philadelphia Press* (hereafter referred to as *PHP*), March 11, 1883, p. 10.

James R. Maxwell was an artillerist in Lumsden's Alabama Battery. He said that while the battery's guns and caissons were left at Columbia the "officers and cannoneers" were ordered to accompany the infantry toward Spring Hill. Maxwell explained the reason for this was that if any enemy batteries were captured during the day they might be properly manned. Specifically Capt. C. L. Lumsden was told to report to Brig. Gen. Daniel H. Reynolds, commanding a brigade in Gen. Walthall's Division, and ensure the battery kept pace "under all circumstances."[15]

Clearing a path north for Hood was Forrest's cavalry. Before sunup he and his men began skirmishing with Wilson, and by the time the Confederate infantry was crossing the Duck River the Federal cavalry was retreating up the Lewisburg Pike. As he gradually pulled back Wilson employed a "fire and withdrawal" system, whereby one of his brigades acted as a rear guard and held the enemy back while the rest of the column withdrew further up the road. Although Forrest had the upper hand, Wilson effectively prevented the Rebel cavalry from overrunning his troops. But it was a hollow achievement. By mid-morning Wilson had his men drawn up near Mount Carmel, five miles north of Hurt's Cross Roads and only five miles east of Spring Hill.[16]

Pressing the Federal rear guard that morning were the men of Red Jackson's Division. When Forrest learned that Brig. Gen. Frank C. Armstrong's Brigade "had struck the enemy" he told Armstrong not to engage the Yankees too heavily because he wanted to try and slip Chalmers' Division around Wilson's flank. Near Mount Carmel all the angles finally came together. As Col. Datus E. Coon's Brigade, positioned behind a rail fence barricade, relieved Brig. Gen. John T. Croxton's exhausted men, Chalmers launched his attack. The Southerners came galloping toward Coon's mostly Illinois troops in column of fours, and suddenly there was a whirlwind of fire, screaming, and cursing. Unexpectedly the Rebels found themselves caught in a murderous crossfire. Coon's men, fighting dismounted, were armed

---

[15] George Little and James R. Maxwell, *A History of Lumsden's Battery, C. S. A.*, p. 54.

[16] Keenan, *Wilson's Cavalry Corps*, p. 54. This method of operation allowed for a rotation of brigades to form the rear guard so that fresh troops could relieve ones who had recently held the post.

with Spencer repeating rifles and they shot Chalmers' men to pieces. The Confederates, enveloped in what was described as a "raking fire," were unable to crack Wilson's defensive line. The blue line crackled with rifle and artillery fire and enemy horses and riders went sprawling to the ground. It did not take long for Chalmers to call off the attack. The Yankee horsemen cheered in celebration, but quickly braced themselves for another charge. To their surprise none was forthcoming, and the abrupt quiet grew unsettling. Wilson, who had seen enough of the enemy's flanking movements, guessed Forrest was probably up to the same thing, and so he withdrew his men from Mount Carmel just after 10 a.m.[17]

Forrest had a plan. Reacting to Wilson's move, he ordered Gen. Lawrence Ross' 600-man brigade to continue after the Yankees, who were moving north toward Franklin. Wilson was so convinced Forrest was attempting another flanking maneuver that at 2 p.m. he notified Thomas "that Forrest is aiming for Nashville, via Triune and Nolensville." Wilson acknowledged that he and Schofield were now completely out of touch and warned Thomas in conclusion, "You had better look out for Forrest at Nashville to-morrow noon; I'll be there before or very soon after he makes his appearance." In his report written in December, Wilson said little about the day's events. He wrote just two sentences, the last of which read, "The enemy attacked us boldly, but were handsomely repulsed; as afterward learned, he turned thence toward Spring Hill, molesting us no more that day." It was truly an understatement of the facts.[18]

Once again Nathan Bedford Forrest had done a remarkably effective job. With Wilson out of the way, the rest of the Southern cavalry, about 4,500 strong, turned their horses west from Mount Carmel and headed down the empty road leading to Spring Hill six miles away. The path to success seemed to be wide open. Ross wrote in his official report: "The Yankee cavalry, completely whipped, had disappeared in the direction of Franklin and did not again show itself that day." The Federal infantry was now on its own and faced with the

---

[17] *OR* 45, pt. 1, p. 559, 576, 588, 753, 1144; Wyeth, *That Devil Forrest*, p. 476-477; Keenan, *Wilson's Cavalry Corps*, p. 54-55; Cox, *Sherman's March to the Sea*, p. 72-73.

[18] *OR* 45, pt. 1, p. 550, 1146.

real possibility of being caught in a stranglehold. Even John Schofield admitted that he did not know where Forrest was and feared he might strike the Union flank, or even worse, come up from behind. There was no exaggerating when he reported that "Wilson is entirely unable to cope with him."[19]

As far as Hood's intentions were concerned, Schofield could not settle on any one idea on the morning of November 29. Col. Post, from a "high ridge where he could see Hood's column marching toward Spring Hill," was able to confirm that the Confederates were unquestionably on the move north, but he could not accurately estimate their numbers. Meanwhile, S. D. Lee's artillery and riflemen kept up their diversion and made life miserable for the Federals. Although Schofield fretted about an attack on his flank, he continued to believe there was just too much activity for the majority of the Rebel army to have slipped across the river. His indecision nearly became his downfall. Luckily his subordinates did not let him down.[20]

It was 8:45 a.m. before the first portion of David Stanley's Fourth Corps left Columbia. The Second Division, commanded by Gen. George Wagner, abandoned its works and headed north with Col. Emerson Opdycke's Brigade leading the way. Opdycke, a thirty-four year old Ohioan, was to find himself immersed in some of the next two days' most hectic action. Gen. Nathan Kimball's First Division also moved north with Wagner's Division. Once Gen. Stanley reached Rutherford Creek, about four miles north of Columbia, his troops joined the army's procession of 800 wagons and roughly forty cannon. Around this time Schofield's concerns about a flank attack caused him to alter plans. He ordered Kimball's Division to halt and occupy a "position to cover the crossing of the creek." Thus Kimball was left behind and Wagner's Division, in company with the seemingly endless stretch of wagons and guns, moved on its own toward Spring Hill.[21]

Kimball's men were not alone at Rutherford Creek. On November 28, Col. John M. Orr, commander of the 124th Indiana, had

---

[19] Ibid., p. 769, 1169.

[20] John K. Shellenberger, "The Fighting at Spring Hill, Tenn.," *CV* 36, p. 101.

[21] *OR* 45, pt. 1, p. 113, 148; Schofield, *Forty-Six Years In The Army*, p. 214; Stanley, *Personal Memoirs*, p. 200-201.

been ordered to guard the same crossing over the creek. Several hours after Kimball's arrival Orr received new orders. He was told to "picket all roads running east for a distance of one mile from the pike, between Rutherford's Creek and Spring Hill, Company B being left on picket on said creek." It was dangerous and thankless work, but Orr complied and began moving north.[22]

The village of Spring Hill was lightly garrisoned by Union troops. Lt. Col. Charles C. Hoefling's 12th Tennessee Cavalry was the only force available for defense until late morning. Hoefling's command, which had only left Nashville on November 26, was under orders to run a courier line between Columbia and Franklin and it numbered only 200 men in Spring Hill on November 29. The remaining fifty or so men from Hoefling's regiment were out running the courier line. But help was on the way. The first support Hoefling received came in the form of cavalry troops from Col. Robert R. Stewart's Brigade. Stewart's 3rd Illinois Cavalry and elements of the 11th Indiana Cavalry, both of which had been guarding crossings over the Duck River, trotted into town after receiving orders to pull back from the area west of Columbia. They arrived at Spring Hill in the nick of time. Ordered by Gen. Wilson to move through Spring Hill and join him on the Lewisburg Pike, Stewart's troops found their path blocked. Suddenly they were immersed in a brewing fight. Understandably Lt. Col. Hoefling was distressed. He had just learned that Forrest was looming nearby, and apparently without opposition, so the appearance of any help was welcome indeed. In a flash the Illinois and Indiana cavalrymen, joined by Hoefling's 12th Tennessee Cavalry, galloped east on the road leading to Mount Carmel to see what could be done.[23]

---

[22] *OR* 45, pt. 1, p. 404, 424, 427-428.

[23] Ibid., p. 558-559, 1061, 1070, 1098, 1111-1112, 1152. Stewart's Brigade had just recently been organized and many of his troops were not at Spring Hill. Even the size of the 11th Indiana Cavalry is unclear. According to Hatch only three companies of the regiment were present at Franklin; see *OR* 45, pt. 1, p. 576. Why the unit was fragmented is unknown. Additionally, there is no record of the 12th Missouri Cavalry being at Spring Hill. The regiment was engaged earlier in the campaign (see *OR* 45, pt. 1, p. 87, 557, 576) and Wilson mentioned it being broken down on November 28 (see *OR* 45, pt. 1, p. 1120), but where it was on November 29 is uncertain. Hatch did

Additional reinforcements soon began arriving at Spring Hill. Around noon four companies of the 73rd Illinois, ordered to precede the wagon train, marched onto the scene and deployed to "stop stragglers and others" from passing through town. The Illinois troops took positions covering the turnpike north of Spring Hill and the railroad west of town. The tiny 103rd Ohio, whose job it was to guard Schofield's headquarters train, also arrived. Extra cavalry support also appeared in the form of Company M, 2nd Michigan Cavalry when it rode into Spring Hill after having left its post on the Duck River.[24]

Two miles east of Spring Hill, not long after 11:00 a.m., the Federal horsemen got their first taste of the onrushing Confederate cavalry. Forrest engaged the Yankee skirmishers and then ordered Armstrong's Mississippi Brigade, "a portion" of Col. Edward Crossland's Kentucky Brigade, and Lt. Col. Raleigh White's 14th Tennessee Cavalry to attack the main body of the enemy. The Rebels charged ahead, but the piecemeal Union force, well positioned on the crest of a hill, checked the advance and threw the Confederates back. Undeterred Forrest called up his entire command, ordered them dismounted, and tried again. By this time the 2nd Michigan company had worked its way into the fray. The Federal line, blazing with Colt revolving rifles, Maynard carbines, and Spencer repeaters, offered stiff resistance and slowed the Rebel movement. Although outnumbered the Yankees gave ground only grudgingly, no small feat in the face of

---

not state the 12th Missouri was present at Franklin on November 30; see *OR* 45, pt. 1, p. 576. Since the regiment had just been assigned to Stewart perhaps it lacked time to rendezvous with its new command. A detachment of the 10th Tennessee Cavalry was also under Stewart's command, but was ordered back to Nashville on November 29. Because it was near Nolensville by November 30 it is unlikely the unit was engaged at Spring Hill; see *OR* 45, pt. 1, p. 1151, 1180, 1184.

[24] *OR* 45, pt. 1, p, 248; Robert J. Hasty, Statement of, *A History of the Seventy-Third Regiment of Illinois Infantry Volunteers*, p. 438; W. H. Bullard, Statement of, *History of the Seventy-Third Illinois*, p. 446; Scofield, *The Retreat From Pulaski*, p. 18; Jacob D. Cox, *The Battle of Franklin, Tennessee, November 30, 1864: A Monograph*, p. 31; Mortimer Hempstead to Dear M., Dec. 1, 1864, contained in Hempstead Journal, p. 171-172, Carter House Archives (hereafter referred to as CHA).

Forrest's veterans.[25]

By around noon, however, the Union troops holding on east of Spring Hill were running out of steam. Forrest had slowly forced them back to the outskirts of town and he refused to yield the initiative. Soon the limited Federal infantry on hand was put to work, constructing crude rail and log breastworks east of town in an effort to buy extra time. In addition to the four companies of the 73rd Illinois, the entire 120th Indiana also marched into Spring Hill. Col. Allen W. Prather's Indiana troops had helped guard the long and winding wagon train as it moved up from Columbia. As the wagons began rolling in they were directed north through town and parked near the railroad depot. Once there drivers began watering and feeding their teams. Prather surveyed the scene. It was clear that Rebel cavalry was pressing in on Spring Hill and every moment counted. Quickly two of the Indiana companies were posted along Columbia Pike near the depot and the remaining eight were rushed east of town. Once in position Col. Prather's troops began throwing up some modest barricades. One of the men remembered working "vigorously" and "using the wood-piles of citizens and anything else available for protection." The 120th Indiana troops, now east of Spring Hill, soon received welcome support when the men of the 73rd Illinois joined them. The officer in command of the Illinois troops had grown concerned that he and his four companies would be cut off and isolated if the Rebel cavalry were successful in "gaining the town..." They "fell back" through town and were soon scrambling behind the crude works erected by the Indiana boys.[26]

Artillery also joined the slowly strengthening Union defense. Lt. Charles W. Scovill's Battery A, 1st Ohio Light Artillery and Capt. Alexander Marshall's Battery G, 1st Ohio Light Artillery was pushed at the double-quick through the infantry column coming up from Columbia. Quickly Marshall's 3-inch rifled guns and Scovill's 12-pounder Napoleons were rolled into position and the artillery teams unlimbered them on the eastern fringes of town. About this same time

---

[25] *OR* 45, pt. 1, p. 753, 987; Fisher, *They Rode With Forrest & Wheeler*, p. 153; Hempstead Journal, p. 172, 174, CHA.

[26] *OR* 45, pt. 1, p. 248; Eli Newsom, "Hovey's Babies," *NT*, May 2, 1912, p. 7; Joseph Edmonds, "From An Indiana Soldier," *NT*, June 11, 1885, p. 3.

David S. Stanley
(Library of Congress)

the cavalry grappling with Forrest's men slowly began withdrawing into the protection of the perimeter drawn up east of Spring Hill. The Federal cavalry had done admirable work holding the Rebels back, but the sheer weight of numbers eventually played against them. They were only too happy to jump behind the barricades thrown up by the infantry and join them in whatever lay ahead. Confidence began to build among some of the Northern troops at Spring Hill. They probably thought they might be able save their skins after all. Yet the threat posed by Bedford Forrest remained omnipresent, and so the ramshackle organization hunkered down behind their hastily erected rails and logs and continued to spar with the Confederates.[27]

Ever vigilant, Gen. Forrest had ridden to a "high hill" on the left of his command after his first repulse. Forrest wanted a better idea of what was going on and he scanned the landscape with his field glasses. From the knoll, located southwest of a tollgate on the Rally Hill Pike, Forrest could see the wagon train moving into Spring Hill and immediately seized upon an idea for another attack. He called on Gen. Buford for a regiment and in short order Buford sent Col. Andrew L. Wilson and the 21st Tennessee Cavalry. Meanwhile, Forrest rode over to James Chalmers, who was in the company of Edmund Rucker, and ordered him to take Wilson's regiment and drive away the Federals in effort to get at the train. Chalmers demurred, explaining that he believed the enemy line contained a sizable infantry force. Forrest responded by saying, "I think you are mistaken. That is only a small

---

[27] *OR* 45, pt. 1, p. 230, 268, 330-331; C. L. Riddle, "The Fight at Spring Hill," *NT*, Apr. 30, 1891, p. 3.

cavalry force." Forrest said to use Wilson's regiment in the effort and added that Chalmers should throw in his own escort company. Reluctantly, Chalmers agreed to try.[28]

Wilson led his mounted Tennesseans in a "gallant charge" across an open field toward the Yankees east of Spring Hill and both he and his men rode into near disaster. The Southerners faced not only the Illinois and Indiana infantry, but the Yankee cavalry, both of which were now backed by the recently arrived artillery. The Rebels never really had a chance. Bullets, canister, and case shot bit into the approaching line and Wilson's men were badly bloodied, barely able to protect themselves from the Federal onslaught. Capt. James Dinkins later wrote that "horses galloped away riderless, and limbs and bark covered the ground. It was a dreadful few minutes, and it all happened very quickly." Wilson took three wounds in the charge and his troops, like their comrades before them, were forced to retire. Behind the Federal works Pvt. Joseph Edmonds of the 120th Indiana remembered that about the time the Rebels withdrew he saw Union reinforcements arriving from south side of Spring Hill. As for Chalmers, the attack turned out just as he thought it would. When he rejoined Forrest the two officers spoke briefly. Forrest looked at Chalmers and asked, "They was in there sure enough, wasn't they, Chalmers?"[29]

At 11:30 a.m. David Stanley, riding with Wagner and Opdycke at the head of the Second Division was still about two miles from Spring Hill. Around this time a visibly shaken courier reported to Stanley that enemy cavalry was attacking the town from the east.

---

[28] *OR* 45, pt. 1, p. 753; Wyeth, *That Devil Forrest*, p. 477; J. P. Young, "Hood's Failure at Spring Hill," *CV* 16, p. 31; James Dinkins, *Personal Recollections and Experiences in the Confederate Army*, p. 230.

[29] *OR* 45, pt. 1, p. 319-320; 753; Wyeth, *That Devil Forrest*, p. 477; Riddle, *NT*, Apr. 30, 1891; Edmonds, *NT*, June 11, 1885; Stanley Horn, "The Spring Hill Legend – A Reappraisal," *CWTI*, April 1969, p. 23-24; Young, *CV* 16, p. 31. Capt. Lyman Bridges stated that this attack was made against Wagner's Division. This author, however, believes the available evidence points to Wilson's attack being turned away prior to Opdycke's arrival. It is possible Opdycke was involved in the final stages of the attack. It seems Forrest's most aggressive actions were largely complete by the time Wagner's Division arrived on the field.

Stanley's deep auburn eyes flared with excitement and he had Wagner order Opdycke to move his brigade at the "double-quick" toward Spring Hill. This was also when the two 1st Ohio Light Artillery batteries were ordered forward and because the guns were horse drawn they reached Spring Hill before the infantry. Opdycke's men immediately picked up the pace and his lead columns reached the town at 12:30 p.m., the ranks filled with scores of panting and wheezing troops nearly on the verge of collapse. But Opdycke kept pushing them to the north and northeast side of Spring Hill, where the Southerners could be seen "advancing in fair view, with quite a force of cavalry."[30]

Quickly Opdycke's Illinois, Ohio, and Wisconsin boys pitched into the Rebel skirmishers and drove them back. With the ground in his front "cleared" Opdycke ordered the 125th Ohio to the north edge of town. There the regiment formed immediately west of Columbia Pike to help guard the army's supply wagons. The 44th Illinois, 24th Wisconsin, and 36th Illinois formed to the left of the Ohioans, extending the Federal line further west of the pike and offering greater protection for the wagons. Meanwhile, the 73rd Illinois took a position northeast of Spring Hill, its left flank extending toward Columbia Pike and its right angling south toward the Mount Carmel Road. The consolidated 74th/88th Illinois, instrumental in driving the Rebels back, was on the skirmish line. With the line in order and skirmishers out, Opdycke and his men took a deep breath and eyed the nearby Rebels warily.[31]

Following on Opdycke's heels were Wagner's remaining

---

[30] *OR* 45, pt. 1, p. 113, 148, 229, 239, 268; W. H. Bullard, Statement of, *History of the Seventy-Third Illinois*, p. 448; Charles T. Clark, *Opdycke Tigers, 125th O.V.I., a History of the Regiment and the Campaigns and Battles of the Army of the Cumberland*, p. 323.

[31] *OR* 45, pt. 1, p. 239, 248-250, 252; Clark, *Opdycke Tigers*, p. 324; George W. Patten, Statement of, *History of the Seventy-Third Illinois*, p. 457; John W. Sherrick, Statement of, *History of the Seventy-Third Illinois*, p. 433. Sgt. Alexander C. Nicholson of Company C, 73rd Illinois said at 4 p.m. the regiment was moved out to support the 88th Illinois and at 5:30 p.m. it was moved to the picket line. He concluded by stating the regiment "was cut up and put in different parts of the line." See *History of the Seventy-Third Illinois*, p. 426-427. Commanding the 24th Wisconsin was Maj. Arthur MacArthur, Jr., whose son Douglas, born after the war, became a World War II hero.

brigades. Col. John Q. Lane had taken command of the Second Brigade just that morning, replacing Brig. Gen William Grose who transferred to head up the Third Brigade, First Division. Lane led his men to the front at the double-quick, threw out Lt Col. J. Rowan Boone's 28th Kentucky as skirmishers, and pushed forward. Fighting quickly broke out as Lane's troops engaged some Rebel cavalry "in heavy force on an eminence half a mile east" of Spring Hill. These horsemen were apparently Col. Edward Dillon's 2nd Mississippi Cavalry of Armstrong's Brigade. Brief but heavy fighting reverberated over the landscape and after about thirty minutes Dillon's troopers disengaged, forfeiting control of the hill to the 28th Kentucky, a portion of which was equipped with Spencer repeating rifles. Lane then ordered Lt. Col. Charles M. Hammond's 100th Illinois to support Boone's Kentuckians. Turned away by Lane's men the Rebel cavalry began sliding to the right of the Federal position, probing for any weaknesses. With little exaggeration Capt. John K. Shellenberger of the 64th Ohio wrote that if Wagner "had arrived a few minutes later, he would have found Forrest in full possession at Spring Hill."[32] Decades later historians and writers could offer little argument with Shellenberger's statement.[33]

Next to arrive was Brig. Gen. Luther P. Bradley's Brigade, which around 2 p.m. formed up on the crest of a hill southeast of town, about a half mile from Lane's right flank. Bradley aligned his men so they could oppose any enemy approach from the direction of Rally Hill Pike.

---

[32] *OR* 45, pt. 1, p. 255, 264-265, 1038; Young, *CV* 16, p. 30; Shellenberger, *CV* 36, p. 101; W. W. Gist, "The Different Point of View in Battle," *CV* 24, p. 550. Grose had replaced Col. John Blake in October 1864. It is uncertain whether Grose was intended as an interim commander only, but that appears to be the case. Grose had no connection to the Second Brigade, Second Division while Lane was the colonel of the 97th Ohio. Blake was in command as late as October 11, but was relieved soon thereafter although no reason is specified. See *OR* 39, pt. 3, p. 214 and *OR* 45, pt. 2, p. 623.

[33] James McDonough wrote in *Union General in the Civil War and Reconstruction,* p. 111, that "the greatest danger for the Union army at Spring Hill was at noon when.....Forrest's defenders might have taken the town from the garrison defenders." Thomas Connelly stated in *Autumn of Glory,* p. 494, that "Forrest probably did not know how close he had come to capturing Spring Hill."

He put four regiments, the 65th Ohio, 15th Missouri, 51st Illinois, and 79th Illinois from right to left, on his main line, held the 42nd Illinois in reserve, and ordered the 64th Ohio forward as skirmishers.[34]

Shortly after Bradley's troops got into position Capt. Henry S. Pickands, a man described as being "as full of mettle as any one that ever commanded men," moved the 103rd Ohio southeast of Spring Hill to occupy a point near John Lane's right flank. There Pickands' regiment, which counted only 200 men in its ranks, "formed in line on the right and left" of Battery A, 1st Ohio Light Artillery and "along the crest of the high ground..." Not much later a section of guns from Capt. Alexander Marshall's Battery G, 1st Ohio Light Artillery also arrived. These 3-inch rifled pieces were commanded by Lt. George W. Bills and he quickly ordered them unlimbered and placed "into a defense thrown up by the One hundred and third Ohio" and next to Battery A's Napoleons.[35]

Out in front of Bradley's line, Lt. Col. Robert C. Brown's 64th Ohio pressed rapidly forward. Brown placed six of his companies in his front line and lined up four in reserve. After advancing about 300 yards over "open country" Brown's troops engaged enemy skirmishers and forced the Rebels back with relative ease. The Ohioans soon passed over the Rally Hill Pike and Brown left one of his reserve companies to guard the pike and protect the regiment's rear. The rest of the men then crossed McCutcheon's Creek. Pvt. William A. Keesy remembered that the creek was cold and "three and a half feet deep" and it did nothing for those who suffered from "already stiffened joints..." Once on the east side of the creek the Federals marched into a cornfield before moving into a cotton field. To this point they had moved effectively unchecked. The 64th Ohio ended up advancing about three-fourths of a mile, and nearly reached the Peters House, before Bradley ordered Lt. Col. Brown to halt the regiment because it was "getting too far

---

[34] *OR* 45, pt. 1, p. 268, 279. The 79th Illinois contained in its ranks a "veteran detachment" of the 27th Illinois.

[35] *OR* 45, pt. 1, p. 331; Michael Dunke, "Spring Hill," *NT*, Mar. 6, 1890, p. 3; Scofield, *The Retreat From Pulaski*, p. 18. Scofield said that Pickands was a colonel, but Pickands was not promoted to major until May 18, 1865.

advanced." But things were about to change.[36]

Nathan Bedford Forrest could see the enemy troops encroaching upon his position east of the Rally Hill Pike. Unwilling to allow this foray to continue, Forrest ordered Col. Tyree H. Bell's Brigade from Abe Buford's Division to move forward and drive off the Yankees. Bell sent his dismounted Tennesseans forward and rather suddenly the luck of the 64th Ohio ended. Pvt. Keesy remembered being met with "a galling fire" and said the enemy "came with a rush and a yell, and swept like a cyclone across that field." Pvt. Francis E. Hoover later wrote that when the Rebels appeared he and his comrades "wheeled about" and began to pull back. Hoover said the Confederates "fired a volley which made our hair stand on end, and away we went helter-skelter and never formed again until on the other side of the creek." Lt. Col. Brown said in no time there was enemy cavalry on both his right and left flanks. Brown quickly called up his reserve companies and placed two on each wing. Yet Bell's men pressed rapidly forward and continued shoving the Northerners back. Soon the 64th Ohio was forced back across both McCutcheon's Creek and Rally Hill Pike. Brown finally concluded that the effort to stem the Confederate advance was "fruitless" and ordered his men to retire to the "hastily constructed defense held by the brigade..."[37]

According to Gen. Bradley, the dismounted Confederate cavalry eventually came within 300 yards of his main line. Having accomplished his mission, Tyree Bell ordered his men to disengage and the Rebels pulled back to the Rally Hill Pike area. Meanwhile, Bradley spoke with Lt. Col. Brown following the 64th Ohio's return and learned that the Rebels were massing additional troops on the right front of the brigade. Bradley was concerned that with both his flanks exposed the enemy would make every effort to turn his position. Bradley felt his right was in far more danger so he directed the 42nd Illinois to support that end of his battle line. Separated from the rest of the brigade by "about 150

---

[36] *OR* 45, pt. 1, p. 268, 283; R. C. Brown, "Battle of Spring Hill," *NT*, June 21, 1883, p. 1; W. A. Keesy, *War As Viewed From The Ranks*, p. 99; Shellenberger, *CV* 36, p. 101.

[37] *OR* 45, pt. 1, p. 283-284, 753; Keesy, *War As Viewed From The Ranks*, p. 99, 101; F. E. Hoover, "Spring Hill and Franklin," *NT*, June 11, 1885, p. 3; Shellenberger, *CV* 36, p. 101.

yards" the Illinois regiment was aligned about forty-five degrees to the main line to protect the vulnerable right flank.[38]

Bradley also ordered the 64th Ohio, which had nearly run out of ammunition during its scrape on the skirmish line, to the far right of his line and the Ohioans took a new position in support of the 42nd Illinois. Meanwhile, the 26th Ohio of Lane's Brigade formed up parallel to the Columbia Pike about a mile and a half south of Spring Hill. Left there by Col. Lane when the rest of his brigade moved into position east of town, the 26th Ohio was under orders to assist in guarding the rest of the wagons as they moved up the pike. Additionally, the 36th Illinois of Opdycke's Brigade was pulled from the east side of town and moved to a position several hundred feet east of Columbia Pike and about a half mile south of Spring Hill. There the regiment was ordered to support a section of Capt. Jacob Ziegler's Battery B, Pennsylvania Artillery, which had been posted by Stanley to further bolster Gen. Bradley's right wing.[39]

In a journal kept for the Fourth Corps, Lt. Col. Joseph S. Fullerton described the Union position at Spring Hill: "A line of battle is formed as follows: Opdycke's brigade faces northeast, its left resting on the Franklin pike north of town; Lane's brigade connects with Opdycke's and faces east; Bradley's brigade connects with Lane's, facing in an easterly direction and sweeping around toward the pike south of the town – the line of battle generally about one mile from town."[40] Such was the design of the Federal defense and with each charge and repulse of the enemy, the blue clad troops holding the line gained confidence, awaiting with set jaws the next Southern rush.

By this juncture even Forrest's characteristic aggressiveness was somewhat curbed. Although he would have been happy to keep up the pressure, Forrest knew his men were running very low on ammunition and the infantry he was facing was not going to be dislodged easily. Gen. Hood had asked via courier around noon that Forrest hold his position "at all hazards" and while that directive had been accomplished Spring Hill remained solidly in Union hands. Indeed Forrest was no fool. He had assaulted the enemy with little success and knew that the

---

38 *OR* 45, pt. 1, p. 268, 275.

39 *OR* 45, pt. 1, p. 230, 245, 255, 268, 336; Young, *CV* 16, p. 30.

40 *OR* 45, pt. 1, p. 148.

Southern infantry's arrival was the best and most realistic chance for victory.[41]

As the action near Spring Hill heated up the Southern infantry continued to draw ever closer. After stopping briefly for rest and lunch at about noon, during which Gens. Hood and Granbury engaged in a rather heated argument about the overall speed of the march, the advance was renewed and "vigorously pursued."[42]

The potential threat raised by Col. Post's troops passed when it became evident they were only observing the Confederate movement. Soon the Rebels passed over Bear Creek and pushed north, marching over brown autumn hills, through wooded valleys, and past "open plantations." Aside from the scenery, however the march was a difficult one. Gen. Brown said the "fields and woods" and "rough ground" did much to fatigue the troops. An Alabama private recalled that "whether on bottom or hills, we sank at every step in mud over our shoes." Yet by mid-afternoon the head of the column was nearing the intersection of the David Ford Road and the Rally Hill Pike southeast of Spring Hill. With his objective within reach Hood's spirits must have soared. From the south the rumble of Lee's artillery at Columbia, much like distant summer thunder, could still be heard and Hood felt confident that Schofield had yet to uncover the flanking movement. If Schofield remained in the dark, Hood knew much of the Federal army was probably still at Columbia and the chance for a decisive victory existed. The only problem was the increasing volume of small arms and artillery fire coming from the direction of Spring Hill. As he rode toward Rutherford Creek, Hood could hear it more distinctly and spurred his horse forward, his heart racing to discover what was happening. Finally, at around 2:30 p.m., he reined up southeast of Spring Hill and prepared to set in motion what he felt was to be the most successful day of his military life.[43]

---

[41] Ibid., p. 753.

[42] Smith, *History of Maury County*, p. 238; D. H. Patterson, "Battle of Franklin," *CV* 9, p. 116.

[43] *OR* 45, pt. 1, p. 736; Hood, *Advance & Retreat*, p. 284; Brown, Statement of, *SHSP* 9, p. 537; McMorries, *History of the First Alabama Infantry*, p. 83; French, *Two Wars*, p. 291.

Riding with Hood that day was Benjamin Franklin Cheatham. Cheatham, born into rolling countryside outside of Nashville, was forty-four years old in the fall of 1864. As a young man, Cheatham served in the Mexican War and at the Battle of Monterey barely escaped death at the hands of artillery fire. Cheatham was not a professional soldier, however, and after returning from Mexico, he dabbled in a variety of projects for the next fifteen years, ranging from farming and local politics to mining for gold during the California Rush of 1849. He stood about five feet eight inches tall and was described variously as muscular, portly, and stocky. Photographs of Cheatham do not deceive. He had thick black or dark brown hair that carried a tinge of gray by the 1860's, and wore a slightly drooping and heavy moustache. His eyes were a light blue color and they sparkled when Cheatham was amused or flushed with excitement. His hobbies included horse racing and thoroughbred breeding, both of which were passions. Until after the war, Cheatham was a bachelor and it was common knowledge that the general liked the company of pretty women and young ladies. Known for his bursts of profanity, which could shake even a strong man, Cheatham also liked his alcohol, whiskey in particular. Like U. S. Grant, rumors floated about that Cheatham was an alcoholic, but like his Union counterpart, there is little evidence for such claims. At worst Cheatham, like Grant, drank too much from time to time and to the detriment of his own image.[44]

As a field commander Cheatham's overall performance was solid. By the spring of 1862, the Tennessean was a major general and commanded a division at Shiloh, where he received a slight shoulder wound. He and his men fought stubbornly at Perryville, Stones River, Chickamauga, and Missionary Ridge. At the Battle of Kennesaw Mountain, during the Atlanta Campaign, Cheatham's Division formed the far left of the Confederate line and had perhaps its finest day. There at the Dead Angle, waves of Federal troops swept toward the Tennesseans and were bloodily repulsed in one of the most decisive fights of the campaign. Yet in spite of Cheatham's successes he never became one of the darlings of the Confederacy. Because in large part he served in the West where the spotlight was considerably less bright,

---

[44] Losson, *Tennessee's Forgotten Warriors*, p. 3, 12, 30; Faust, ed., *Historical Times Encyclopedia*, p. 135.

Benjamin F. Cheatham
(Library of Congress)

Cheatham never gained widespread attention because he was neither flamboyant nor controversial. Cheatham understood what his job was and did it the best way he knew how. The men who served under him largely adored Cheatham. He saw to their needs as best he could and was not reckless with their lives, something a soldier from any era could appreciate. Over time Cheatham and his men developed a close bond. If any Southern general could be termed the common man's general it was Frank Cheatham, because deep in his heart he was one of them. He understood where the rank and file came from, who they were, and what drove them to continue fighting in spite of long odds.[45]

The afternoon of November 29, 1864 saw Cheatham approaching the intersection of the Davis Ford Road and Rally Hill Pike southeast of Spring Hill at the height of his military career. In the soft sunlight and lengthening shadows he readied for orders. But before the day was over things would go terribly wrong for Cheatham. There would forever be more questions than answers about what happened and the maddening gaps of information led to a plethora of stories and accusations. For decades after the fighting stopped, Spring Hill was a focal point of debate and Cheatham, along with his hapless commander John Bell Hood, were the men at the center of the controversy, immersed in a drama that had unfolded one confusing hour after another.

By 3 p.m. Hood was ready. Later he claimed to have pointed to the Columbia Turnpike and asked Cheatham, "General, do you see the enemy there, retreating rapidly to escape us?" To this inquiry, according

[45] Ibid., p. 51, 155-160; Ibid., p. 135.

to Hood, Cheatham answered in the affirmative, whereupon Hood instructed him to "take possession of and hold that pike at or near Spring Hill." Hood then turned to Cleburne and instructed him to go "with General Cheatham, assist him in every way you can, and do as he directs."[46]

The day's many contradictions begin here, because Cheatham refuted the very nature of the alleged conversation. He practically called Hood an outright liar when he said unequivocally that at three o'clock there were no wagons or men moving in the "vicinity of Spring Hill" and the pike was never in view from the crossing point at Rutherford Creek. Cheatham concluded by saying, "Only a mirage would have made possible the vision which this remarkable statement professes to record."[47] Hood's claim is further discredited by the fact that at 3 p.m. there were no Union troops or wagons moving along the pike south of Spring Hill. Also, it is doubtful if not improbable, that Hood could have even seen the pike from his location.[48]

Regardless of the nature of the exchange, the Confederate offensive kicked into gear only minutes later. Cleburne's Division, minus Brig. Gen. James A. Smith's Brigade which had remained at Florence, Alabama to escort supplies, splashed across Rutherford Creek. This occurred near the intersection of the Davis Ford Road and Rally Hill Pike and Cleburne's men began marching up the latter. A member of the 33rd Alabama recalled crossing "a creek near Spring Hill by wading it after removing our shoes and socks and rolling up our pants and drawers..." According to Hood's instructions, once Cleburne's men reached their designated point of deployment, the brigades formed in echelon with Mark Lowrey on the right and Hiram Granbury on the left. Brig. Gen. Daniel C. Govan occupied the reserve position and was centrally located behind the two front line brigades. This alignment,

---

[46] Hood, *Advance & Retreat*, p. 284.
[47] Cheatham, *SHSP* 9, p. 529.
[48] David E. Roth, "The Mysteries of Spring Hill, Tennessee," *Blue & Gray Magazine*, Vol. II, Oct-Nov 1984, p. 26. In this article Roth wrote: "It is a geographical fact, determined by an actual visit to the place, and by reference to a current TVA topographical map indicating a considerably higher elevation (40 feet) of intervening terrain, that Hood could not have seen the road from there."

which meant Granbury would advance on Lowrey's left while keeping his brigade drawn back about one hundred yards, is interesting. It clearly represents Hood's intent to strike at the pike and then wheel Cleburne south to face the Federals as they came up from Columbia. Assisting Cleburne on Lowrey's right was Tyree Bell's cavalry brigade. Bell's men, who had reformed near the Rally Hill Pike after battling with the 64th Ohio, were instructed to move forward dismounted. Bell's men, however, had a serious problem. Most had only about four rounds of ammunition remaining following their earlier action, and because the ordnance wagons were still back at Columbia there was no easy solution to the problem. Bell's men would be forced to improvise.[49]

Cheatham remembered that Hood's verbal orders called for a movement against Spring Hill, not the turnpike, and soon Cleburne's Division was "disappearing over a hill" approximately "one and a half miles from Spring Hill. One of Chalmers' men recalled vividly how "the old rugged veterans of Cheatham's corps came marching up on our left with their battle-flags waving in the mellow sunlight, and we felt that a long-sought opportunity had at last arrived." The seasoned infantry must have been a welcome sight to the cavalry that had fought so tenaciously during the early afternoon hours. The same cavalryman, like so many others, believed it would be only a short time before the pike was captured by the Southerners.[50]

---

[49] *OR* 45, pt. 1, p. 739, 753; Young, *CV* 16, p. 31; Jamie Gillum, *The Battle of Spring Hill: Twenty-Five Hours to Tragedy*, p. 81; Lowrey, *SHSP* 16, p. 373-374. Lowrey recalled that Granbury formed the left flank and Govan was in reserve. This is undoubtedly how Cleburne's Division was aligned instead of the version set forth by Young, which said Lowrey was on the right, Govan in the center, and Granbury on the left with no reserve. This is also the formation Bate's Division used. See *OR* 45, pt. 1, p. 742.

[50] Cheatham, *SHSP* 9, p. 524-525; W. O. Dodd, "Reminiscences of Hood's Tennessee Campaign," *SHSP* 9, p. 520. Cheatham remained unsure why Cleburne moved in the direction that he did. Alethea D. Sayers in *A Meteor Shining Brightly,* p. 247-248, suggested that Hood spoke initially to Cheatham and Cleburne about moving directly on Spring Hill, but later changed his mind and when speaking only to Cleburne the revised plan of striking the pike was put forth. This would explain Cheatham's confusion regarding Cleburne's movement.

With Cleburne on his way, Cheatham was free to set in motion the next part of Hood's order, which was to personally direct Bate and his division across the creek and put those troops into position on Cleburne's left. Although Cheatham, who never filed an official report, but instead wrote and spoke years later from memory, said he did help Bate form up and subsequently sent him in as directed, Bate does great damage to Cheatham's claim. Bate stated that when he was forming his "line of battle" Cheatham was not present. Bate said it was Hood who ordered him to move his division "to the turnpike and sweep toward Columbia." Although Hood is silent on this point, it is unlikely Bate would have reported the facts as such unless they were true, especially in light of events as they unfolded. In addition, such an order from Hood makes sense, especially considering the staggered formation of Cleburne's Division and the obvious result the commanding general was hoping to achieve with it.[51]

Almost before Bate's men were out of sight, as they marched up and over the rolling hills leading toward the Columbia Pike, there came echoing from the direction of Spring Hill the unmistakable sound of small arms fire. Cheatham reported hearing it just as Gen. Brown's Division came into view near the creek and Hood surely heard it also. However, as with Bate's deployment, Hood said nothing about it in either his memoirs or official report. The fight for possession of Spring Hill and the turnpike had began in earnest.[52]

Back in Columbia events had taken a rather sudden turn. Schofield had received confirmation from Col. Post that the enemy was moving in force toward Spring Hill. By 3 p.m. the Federal commander finally "became satisfied" that S. D. Lee's efforts were not the real threat. But the problem facing Schofield at this late hour was clear - whether or not he could save his strung out army from disaster. The sound of artillery fire could be heard rolling in from the direction of Spring Hill and so Schofield ordered Gen. Ruger's two brigades, minus the 111th Ohio, to begin marching northward up the turnpike around 3:30 p.m. Lt. Col. Isaac R. Sherwood's much reduced Ohio regiment, previously directed to guard an old railroad bridge spanning the Duck River, was told to remain at its post "till night" before joining the

---

[51] *OR* 45, pt. 1, p. 742.

[52] Cheatham, *SHSP* 9, p. 525.

retreat. Schofield then mounted his horse to ride at the head of Ruger's column and before vacating Columbia "gave the necessary orders for the withdrawal" of the rest of his command. The remaining troops were instructed to oppose Lee's troops until nightfall before beginning their movement to Spring Hill.[53]

Not long after Ruger left Columbia, his march impacted Col. John Orr and the 124th Indiana. When the day dawned Orr's regiment had been posted where Rutherford Creek crossed Columbia Pike. Following Nathan Kimball's arrival there, Orr headed north with orders to picket roads running east between the creek and Spring Hill. After moving about "two or three miles" Orr received additional orders instructing him to send one of his companies to Ruger to support "his own pickets." Orr must have been puzzled by the order, but diligently he dispatched Company C and again proceeded north. At Poplar Grove, almost exactly halfway between Columbia and Spring Hill, he placed five companies "on a road leading east" and then moved with his remaining three companies in the direction of Spring Hill.[54]

South of the Duck River, it was obvious to S. D. Lee that the Federals were withdrawing at least some of their troops around midday. He soon began an effort to force a crossing to the north bank, where his troops could press Schofield from the rear. By about 4 p.m. a number of daring engineers, exposed to scathing enemy fire, managed to get enough pontoon boats into the water to allow the 23rd Alabama, 31st Alabama, and 46th Alabama of Brig. Gen. Edmund W. Pettus' Brigade to ferry across to the northern bank. The Alabama troops assaulted the 12th Kentucky and 16th Kentucky of James Reilly's Brigade and pushed both regiments back several hundred yards. Additional infantry followed the Alabamians, allowing the Rebel engineers to complete a full pontoon bridge by nightfall.[55]

Casualties at Columbia were minimal, but S. D. Lee's greatest loss was unquestionably the mortal wounding of young Robert Beckham, his artillery chief. While directing fire during the day, Col.

---

[53] Cox, *Battle of Franklin*, p. 27, 32; *OR* 45, pt. 1, 342, 387; Isaac Sherwood, *Memories of the War*, p. 127; Gus Smith, "Battle of Franklin," *MOLLUS*, Michigan, 2, p. 252.

[54] *OR* 45, pt. 1, p. 404, 424, 428.

[55] Young, *CV* 16, p. 26; *OR* 45, pt. 1, p. 403, 687, 693-694.

Beckham was struck down with a freakish injury. A Federal shell struck a rock near him and a fragment of the rock smashed into Beckham's head, splitting his skull and inflicting irreparable damage. Although moved to a nearby home and gently cared for, Beckham "never regained consciousness" and died a week later. Later the young officer's body was escorted to St. John's Church cemetery near Mount Pleasant and laid to rest.[56]

---

[56] *OR* 45, pt. 1, p. 687; Evelyn Sieburg and James E. Hansen II, ed., *Memoirs of a Confederate Staff Officer: From Bethel to Bentonville*, p. 61; Daniel, *Cannoneers in Gray*, p. 172. Beckham remains at rest at St. John's today, his grave marked by a white marble headstone.

4

Passing Right Through Hood's Army

Since the spring of 1862, troops commanded by Patrick Cleburne had struck terror and awe into the hearts of their opponents. From Shiloh to Stones River and Chickamauga through the Atlanta Campaign, the men guided by Cleburne's steady hand had inflicted great losses on opposing troops. At Ringgold Gap, Cleburne and his troops saved the Army of Tennessee from disaster, a performance so exemplary that it earned them a commendation of thanks from the Confederate Congress. With their iron discipline, determined countenance, and blue and white battle flags, Pat Cleburne's troops could be counted on to do the hard, often horrible, work of war and do it well. The end of November 1864 was no different. Once again it was Cleburne and his battle-tested warriors at the front, ready to move on the enemy.[1]

Cleburne's 3,000-man division moved up the Rally Hill Pike nearly a mile and a half, passing Absaolm Thompson's luxurious plantation-style home on their left, before shifting and turning westward at 3:45 p.m. Once they stepped off, Tyree Bell's dismounted cavalry joined the advance on the right. It was a sight to behold as the men of both commands marched in the direction of Columbia Pike with "a promptness and energy and gallantry" that had come to be expected of both Cleburne's and Forrest's well-drilled troops. Frank Cheatham recalled seeing "the left of Cleburne's command...disappearing over a

[1] Purdue, *Pat Cleburne*, p. 254-263.

hill to the left of the road.[2]

Cleburne, astride his favorite horse, Red Pepper, rode directly behind Govan's Brigade in the company of Gen. Forrest, both of whom had swords drawn as they directed the movement of the butternut line over the rolling terrain. The Rebels swept forward mostly unmolested and easily brushed back the Yankee skirmishers who darted back to the main line. But things quickly changed when around 4:15 p.m. Cleburne's right brigade, commanded by Mark Lowrey, suddenly began taking flank fire from some of Luther Bradley's troops. The men of the 42nd Illinois, concealed behind a line of timber and a fence, "poured a deadly volley" into the Rebels and forced Lowrey to begin reforming. Because his troops were nearly perpendicular to the Illinois regiment Lowrey was at a serious disadvantage. Meanwhile, the 65th Ohio joined the fray and poured its fire into Lowrey's line. Henry G. Crum, a sergeant in the 65th Ohio, recalled how the Confederates "passed to the right of us about 100 yards and directly in front of the Illinois men." Crum said the men of his regiment "could not miss" hitting the enemy column when the firing erupted. Cleburne suddenly had a serious problem on his hands. Because his command was formed in echelon, he was unable to easily swing Granbury around to the north to assist Lowrey, who was trying to get his men wheeled to the right. Help would need to come from Govan in the rear. Meanwhile, Bell's men had formed up behind a fence closer to Bradley's left and the two sides exchanged some fire, but the heaviest action remained on the Federal right.[3]

Mark Perrin Lowrey was a Baptist minister who had donned the uniform in defense of his home. Thirty-five years old at Spring Hill, Lowrey had done little with his life until he volunteered for service in the Mexican War. A Tennessee native who had moved to Mississippi when he was fifteen, Lowrey returned from the war and began working

---

[2] *OR* 45, pt. 1, 753; Cheatham, *SHSP* 9, p. 525.

[3] *OR* 45, pt. 1, p. 269, 275, 286; Henry G. Crum, "Spring Hill: Cleburne's Division Was So Roughly Handled It Was In No Mind to Get Across the Road," *NT*, Aug. 17, 1905, p. 3; Young, *CV* 16, p. 31.

with a tutor to conquer his near illiteracy. He also married and by the age of twenty-four had dedicated himself to the Baptist church. Through the years Lowrey became a well known and respected minister who headed up several congregations. When war came again, Lowrey accepted an appointment as a colonel and commanded a regiment of state volunteers before helping to organize the 32nd Mississippi Infantry in early 1862. He first commanded a brigade that same year, was wounded at Perryville, and rose to the rank of brigadier general in 1863. A tall and somewhat thin man with piercing eyes, Lowrey was an able and steady commander.[4]

As Lowrey's Brigade of Alabamians and Mississippians wheeled under fire, Bradley's troops continued blasting away. Groups of Lowrey's men crumpled to the ground and the Yankees furiously reloaded and fired. Some began to holler and cheer and apparently they made a good deal of racket. Lowrey noticed this "cheering and waving of swords and hats" and believed the Federals were preparing to launch an attack. Spotting Cleburne some distance away, Lowrey spurred his horse and galloped over to voice his concern. Lowrey pointed out that the enemy seemed to be readying an assault on his right flank. Cleburne, his eyes flashing with excitement, scanned the field quickly, raised his right hand and "as though he held a heavy whip to be brought down upon his horse" exclaimed, "I'll charge them!" Cleburne then pulled Red Pepper's reins hard to the left and galloped away to bring up Govan's Brigade.[5]

Lowrey returned to his brigade and worked to orient it properly. After getting his men repositioned, reformed, and moving again, Govan came storming up in support on the right. Suddenly it was the Confederates who found themselves in position to deal a heavy blow. Lowrey's line now far outstretched Bradley's right and as Cleburne's two veteran brigades surged forward in a "most determined attack" it was not long before the tables turned. Many of Lowrey's troops began pouring beyond the Federal flank, and as Bradley's refused right wing was "furiously attacked" the 42nd Illinois, its ranks filled with recruits,

---

[4] Lowrey, *SHSP* 16, p. 365-368; Welsh, *Medical Histories of Confederate Generals*, p. 145; Faust, ed., *Historical Times Encyclopedia*, p. 452.

[5] Lowrey, *SHSP* 16, p. 374.

and the 64th Ohio quickly crumbled under the pressure.[6]

In a matter of minutes the rest of Bradley's line started to unravel. When the 42nd Illinois pulled back the 65th Ohio was quickly flanked and also began to take heavy fire, eventually suffering a loss of forty-seven men. Included in this number was the regimental commander, Maj. Orlow Smith. Smith turned command over to Capt. Andrew Howenstine, who in turn was struck down and "left in the hands of the rebels." The reins of leadership were next passed to Maj. Samuel L. Coulter, who was pulled from the 64th Ohio. But there was little Coulter could do, especially with the right flank of the brigade in shambles. Lowrey and Govan quickly rolled up the Federal line and soon the 65th Ohio was "compelled to fall back..."[7]

As the Rebels forced their way into the Federal rear, panic and confusion "beyond human comprehension" erupted among the blue-clad troops. In the 42nd Illinois 110 men were killed, wounded, or reported missing and Maj. Frederick A. Atwater stated that the "colors of the regiment became separated and the sergeant and all the color guard...were killed and the flag was captured by the enemy." It was a bruising and bloody fight. Sgt. John Stark of Company C, 42nd Illinois wrote in January 1865 that the Rebels advanced "on all sides" and poured a "withering and destructive fire" into the ranks. Stark told the heroic story of Cpl. George Wier, who carried the flag of the 42nd Illinois at Spring Hill. Wier, seriously wounded during the fighting, was apparently overcome by the swarming Confederates because Stark said, "It was impossible to save either him or the colors." The Rebels attempted to pull the tattered flag from Wier's blood-stained hands, but the heroic Midwesterner refused to give it up. Pulling himself and the flag up from the ground, Wier stood tall and "defying the whole pack" told the enemy "he would not part with the flag while he lived." Stark went on to write how at that moment a Confederate general rode up, "ordering his men off telling George he was too brave a man to be killed and permitted him to retain the old tattered banner which he had carried so honorably and faithfully..." Stark concluded by saying that Wier died the following evening with his beloved flag lying next to him

---

[6] *OR* 45, pt. 1, p. 269, 275, 284. Gen. Bradley said there was about ten minutes of firing before his right flank began to collapse.

[7] *OR* 45, pt. 1, p. 286; Crum, *NT*, Aug. 17, 1905.

on his deathbed. Considering the furious action and confusion, it is easy to understand how Maj. Atwater believed the colors were lost. As for who the Confederate general was, the most likely possibility is Mark Lowrey, but it may have been Pat Cleburne.[8]

Patrick R. Cleburne
(Library of Congress)

Pvt. William Keesy was caught in the center of the heart-pounding action and remembered the Rebels "simply overwhelming us with superior numbers."[9] Capt. John Shellenberger also provided a description of the clash and how the Rebels rushed Bradley's position and then began to hurl epithets when the pursuit began:

> They pulled down the rims of their hats over their eyes, bent their heads to the storm of missiles pouring upon them, changed direction to their right on double quick in a manner that excited our admiration, and a little later a line came sweeping through the gap between the 42nd and the pike, and swinging in toward our rear. Our line stood firm, holding back the enemy in its front, until the flank movement had progressed so far as to make it a question of legs to escape capture. The regimental commanders then gave the reluctant order to fall back. The contact was then so close that as the men on our right were running past the line closing in on them, they were called on with loud oaths, charging them with a Yankee canine descent, to halt and surrender. When the call was not heeded, some of the men were shot down with the muzzle of the musket almost touching their bodies.[10]

---

[8] *OR* 45, pt. 1, 275; John Stark to I. L. Kipp, Jan. 29, 1865, letter in possession of Lavonne Parrish, Amarillo, TX.
[9] Keesy, *War As Viewed From The Ranks*, p. 101.
[10] Shellenberger, *CV* 36, p. 103.

Cleburne continued to push his developing advantage. Gen. Bradley, as he tried frantically to stem the enemy tide, took a severe wound in the upper left arm and was carried from the field bleeding profusely. But there was little more Bradley could have done. His brigade was coming apart at the seams and once the 65th Ohio pulled back the remaining regiments followed suit. Cleburne's grizzled veterans were on the verge of taking control of the pike when suddenly they began taking fire from the two-gun section of Capt. Jacob Ziegler's Pennsylvania Light Artillery. Battery B's team frantically worked their pieces and the 12-pounder Napoleons found their mark. But within minutes the Pennsylvania gunners found themselves in a fix when the 36th Illinois came rushing straight at them with Hiram Granbury's yipping and howling troops not far behind. Maj. Levi P. Holden later reported how the Illinois regiment was unable to hold its position in support of Ziegler's guns when "the enemy advanced upon us from right, left, and front..."[11]

Hiram Bronson Granbury was thirty-three years old, tall and lanky, and had thick and wavy dark hair. Born and educated in Mississippi, Granbury had moved to Seguin, Texas in 1851 before settling in Waco in 1853, where he became a practicing attorney. He

---

[11] *OR* 45, pt. 1, p. 245, 269, 277-280, 336. Of some debate is whether Cleburne disobeyed orders. Some believe the attack on Bradley was clear disobedience; see Connelly's *Autumn of Glory*, p. 495, and Craig Symond's *Stonewall of the West*, p. 254. See also a letter written by Daniel C. Govan in 1906, printed in *Cleburne and His Command* by Irving Buck, p. 270-276. Govan's statement is interesting because he knew Cleburne personally and would likely have defended him against charges he felt to be false. The author of this work believes Cleburne was obligated to turn and fight Bradley once his flank began to take enemy fire. To attack was the only means by which to eliminate the threat. Even Govan admitted that had Cleburne been allowed an additional twenty minutes the pike would have been in the possession of the Confederates. This indicates Govan felt the real problem was Cleburne's Division being halted, not that Cleburne had attacked Bradley.

married Fannie Sims in 1858, but war soon engulfed the land and Granbury helped organize the Waco Guards, a company of soldiers that eventually became part of the 7th Texas Infantry. Captured at Fort Donelson and imprisoned for a short time, Granbury was later promoted from major to colonel and fought during the Vicksburg Campaign. A subsequent transfer brought him to share the fate of the Army of Tennessee. From Chickamauga, where he was wounded, to Chattanooga he performed well and was elevated to brigade command. After receiving a brigadier general's star in early 1864, Granbury led his men with distinction through the Atlanta Campaign, particularly at Pickett's Mill where he received another wound. But personal issues tugged at the adopted Texan's heart. Fannie had developed ovarian cancer and died in early 1863 and the couple's short marriage bore no children. So as 1864 drew to a close Hiram Granbury was alone, a widower with no children whose country was falling apart.[12]

Granbury's Brigade, unlike Lowrey's and Govan's, had continued moving directly toward the Columbia Pike, and it wound up within a couple hundred yards of the road. When Granbury's men pressed the 36th Illinois it was quickly overwhelmed. Heavily outnumbered, the Illinois troops had little choice but to withdraw, and only limited fighting occurred between them and Granbury's men. Essentially, Granbury's Texans flushed the 36th Illinois from its position. The regiment's precipitate retreat, however, also forced Ziegler's section to limber up and the artillerists and their guns quickly joined the stream of men scrambling north toward Spring Hill.[13]

Pvt. Keesy, who became a well-respected minister in Ohio after the war, wrote a vivid description of the confusion and terror wrought by the Confederate assault:

> In falling back from here we had a lane to cross which had a very high and ginny-hobbled fence on either side of it. This was a serious obstruction for

---

[12] Rebecca Blackwell Drake and Thomas D. Holder, *Lone Star General: Hiram B. Granbury*, p. 7-10, 39, 59, 80; Faust, ed., *Historical Times Encyclopedia*, p. 317; Welsh, *Medical Histories of Confederate Generals*, p. 86.

[13] *OR* 45, pt. 1, p. 245, 336. In *History of the Thirty-Sixth Regiment Illinois Volunteers, During the War of the Rebellion* by L.G. Bennett and William H. Haigh, p. 636-637, the authors gloss over the regiment's retreat.

us in a race for life. In one place a gap was open where a stream of bewildered men were pouring through, but on approaching this place I was startled with the dying wail of more than one poor, unfortunate fellow who had stumbled or tangled in the rails and was being trampled to death. No power there could save one who fell. This rush of men to a central point would likely also draw the enemy's fire, making it doubly dangerous to cross there. I concluded to try my chance and take the risk by running up along the fence a little way and then cross over. As I threw my gun up to mount the fence, it so chanced that a fair-sized Irishman was just getting down between the corner and the rail across it. In throwing up my gun, I accidently thrust the muzzle under his shoulder-belt and in his haste to get away, he dropped down just as I was in the act of withdrawing my gun. Had we both tried for a half day with the material at hand, we could not have made a more satisfactory job of hanging, and I do not think the annals of war can produce a greater job of swearing than that poor fellow did while I detained him in my hurried efforts to detach my gun. The more I pulled downward the tighter it got and the worse he would swear, while the deadly bullets zipped and cut around, and the Johnnies coming after us. I mounted the fence, determined to keep my gun for future use, should I be spared to use it. I lifted that Irishman bodily and detached my gun under a volley of broken profanity and Rebel bullets.

As I ran from the fence across the open field with the hundreds of fleeing men, I heard an "Oh, my God!" and on looking up I saw a man just ahead of me drop his gun and stagger forward, the blood spurting from a hole in his shoulder which looked large enough to put my fist in. [14]

By this stage daylight was fading fast. Sunset occurred at 4:35 p.m. and within half an hour twilight was quickly turning to darkness. Yet Cleburne was not ready to give up the fight and he pushed his brigades onward. Lowrey's and Govan's troops descended the north slopes of the two small hills Bradley's men had initially occupied and moved across a small stream which ran west to east across their bases. As they pushed through a cornfield and open ground beyond the stream, Yankee artillery fire began screaming in from the north. Quickly the Rebels advanced and passed over a slight ridge on the south edge of town before swarming down toward another stream. The enemy they encountered next, however, was not another line of

---

[14] Keesy, *War As Viewed From The Ranks*, p. 102.

"recruits and drafted men who had never been under fire," but a well-crafted and solid line of Yankee batteries.[15]

At Gen. Stanley's behest a number of guns had been strung out south and southeast of Spring Hill on a ridge near the Martin Cheairs home, known today as Ferguson Hall. As Bradley's infantry rallied along this high ground, which commanded the stream below it, the artillery unleashed a furious barrage. The Federal gunners poured a scathing fire into the enemy ranks and staggered the approaching line. Men fell dead and wounded all along Cleburne's front, staining the brown autumn grass and leaves with their blood. Disorganized by their pursuit and manhandled by the artillery, the Confederates were forced to withdraw behind the ridge they had just passed. Many of those lucky enough to escape unharmed pulled back across the cornfield and "concealed themselves in the bed" of the first stream which they had crossed.[16]

Lt. Charles Scovill's Battery A, 1st Ohio Light Artillery did the lion's share of the work. His four 12-pounder Napoleons loosed "spherical case, shell, and canister" upon the enemy and Scovill said 166 rounds were expended by his guns during the day's action. The section of Capt. Alexander Marshall's Battery G, 1st Ohio Light Artillery, repositioned after the earlier fighting with Forrest's cavalry, also contributed to the firestorm. Marshall reported that his battery fired "sixty-seven rounds" during the day and a large number of these were unleashed on Cleburne's Division. Even Jacob Ziegler's retreating section of Pennsylvania artillery rejoined the battery's other two guns near town and "commenced firing again" and "checked the enemy." In addition to stalling the Rebel advance, the stout artillery defense also came close to scoring a significant punch when one of the shells came

---

[15] *OR* 45, pt. 1, p. 114, 269. Sunset time obtained from the U. S. Naval Observatory and calculated for Spring Hill. Civil twilight, the time during which the naked eye can clearly distinguish terrestrial objects, ended at 5:03 p.m. Nautical twilight, during which visibility diminishes to the point of being able to see only the general outline of objects, ended at 5:34 p.m. During astronomical twilight, which ended at 6:05 p.m., sky illumination is so faint that it is practically imperceptible. To the average person it was "dark" by 5:45 p.m.

[16] *OR* 45, pt. 1, p. 114, 320, 330.

within inches of taking Gen. Cleburne out of action.[17]

Through the deepening twilight, Cleburne could faintly discern enemy troops repositioning to the north. Cleburne sensed, even as daylight slipped uncontrollably away, that while his own men were "somewhat scattered" the opportunity still existed for a decisive victory and he desperately wanted to follow up his earlier success. Unsure of exactly what the Federal troops to the north were up to, he guessed they were probably reinforcements and that time was of the essence. According to Lt. Leonard H. Mangum, aide-de-camp to Cleburne and a former law partner, the general ordered him to go to the left, find Gen. Granbury, and give him instructions to "form his brigade on a fence running parallel to the pike, and about two hundred yards from it, so as to be prepared to move on the pike." Cleburne added that in the meantime he would "see Govan." Seconds later a shell exploded above Cleburne and Mangum, and at least three jagged fragments tore into Red Pepper's hip, "causing the animal to rear furiously." Mangum paused before departing to ask if the general was hurt. Cleburne, his battle blood raging, yelled, "No! Go on Mangum, and tell Granbury what I told you!"[18]

The men Cleburne had spotted belonged to Col. John Lane's Brigade. Five of Lane's regiments of Illinois, Indiana, Kentucky, and Ohio troops (not including the 26th Ohio which was south of town along Columbia Pike) had been pulled back by Wagner from the position they had earlier occupied to one nearer Spring Hill. Following Bradley's mauling Lane also changed his "front forward on the First Battalion..." While some of Lane's line remained fronting east, a portion of his command turned to face southeast. Moreover, while he did not say anything about a change of front, Wagner did state that Lane was ordered to send two regiments "to the right to act as a support..." One of those regiments was Lt. Col. Milton Barnes' 97th Ohio. Barnes

---

[17] Ibid., p. 330, 331, 336.

[18] Leonard H. Mangum, "General P. R. Cleburne: A Sketch of His Early Life and His Last Battle," *Kennesaw Gazette*, June 15, 1887; George Williams to Irving Buck, Dec. 4, 1864, Irving Buck Papers, Eleanor S. Brockenbrough Library, Museum of the Confederacy (hereafter referred to as MOC). Special thanks to Scott McKay of Roswell, GA for the transcription.

reported that he and his men were sent "to the right in the rear of the Second Brigade, in time to check further disaster there." The identity of the second regiment Wagner mentioned is not known positively, however, because other than Barnes, none of Lane's regimental commanders filed reports about Spring Hill. But regardless, Col. Lane's partial change of front offered protection for the artillery blasting away at Cleburne's Division and lent support to Luther Bradley's badly routed brigade.[19]

Furthermore, Lane took the initiative to order the 100th Illinois and one company of the 40th Indiana, perhaps 300 men altogether, to his left "to hit the enemy in flank..." These troops took positions very roughly parallel to the Mount Carmel Road, jutting east from the point where Lane's and Opdycke's commands joined together. The presence of this small number of men would have much impact on the unfolding events.[20]

Following Bradley's wounding, Col. Joseph Conrad of the 15th Missouri was elevated to command of the Third Brigade. While Lane redesigned the formation of his own brigade, Conrad worked feverishly to rally the men of the Third Brigade and piece them together along the southern edge of Spring Hill. Conrad placed the shattered 42nd Illinois west of Columbia Pike facing south. The rest of the brigade's regiments were posted east of the pike, fronting south and southeast, in the following order: 51st Illinois, 79th Illinois, 64th Ohio, and 15th Missouri. Into reserve was placed the 64th Ohio. These units reformed along a ridge of land which dominated the ground and stream south of it. This was the same stream Cleburne's men had been stopped short of. Col. Allen Buckner of the 79th Illinois said his men "formed to the left of a large building, in which was corps headquarters..." This building was the Martin Cheairs home. On the left of the line the 15th Missouri, now commanded by Capt. George Ernest, tied in with the right flank of Lane's Brigade. Col. Conrad also threw out skirmishers "about 500 yards in advance" of the main line. Meanwhile, along the main line the troops designed "a temporary line of works" and anxiously awaited any new movements by the Rebels.[21]

---

[19] *OR* 45, pt. 1, p. 230, 255, 265; Young, *CV* 16, p. 32.

[20] *OR* 45, pt. 1, p. 255.

[21] Ibid., p. 269, 279-280.

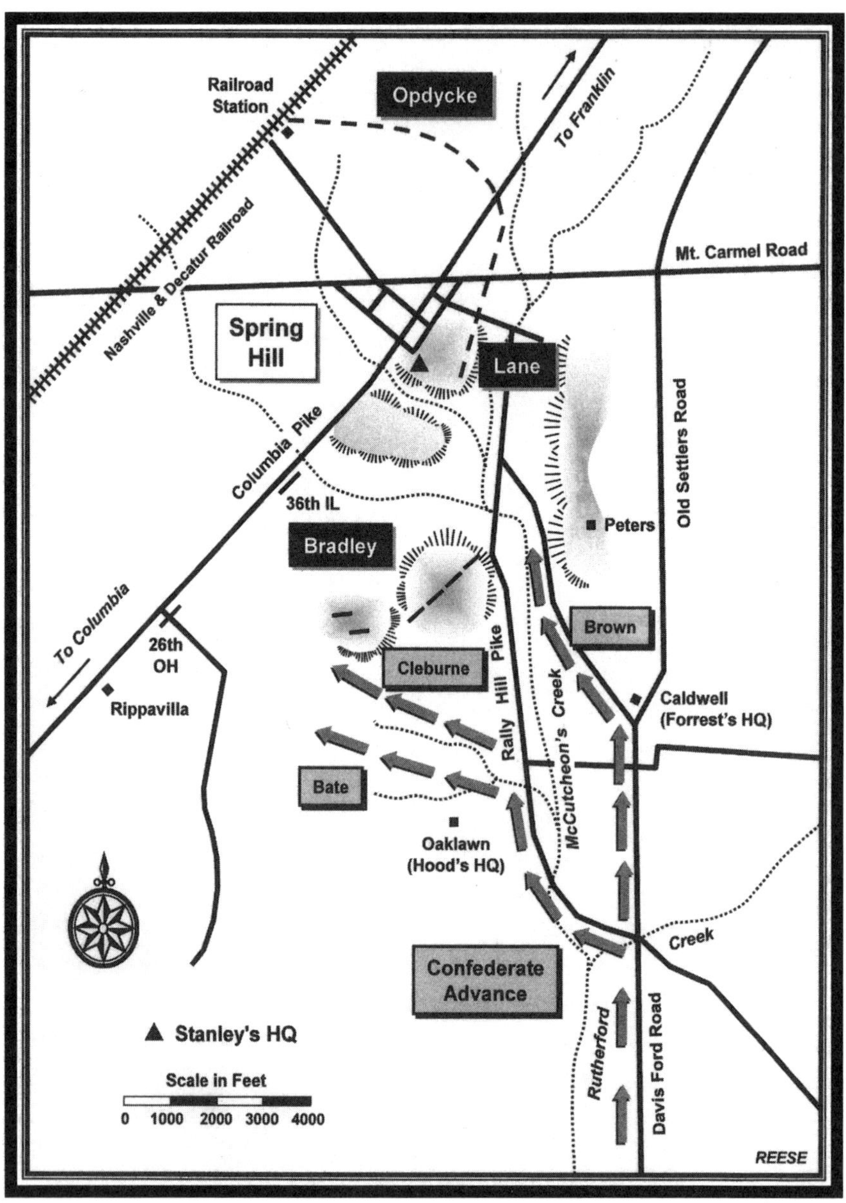

Cheatham's deployment at Spring Hill

Elsewhere things were developing rapidly. Brown's Division splashed across Rutherford Creek soon after Bate's men had crossed and Brown moved his troops north along the Davis Ford Road, in the direction of the Caldwell House, at the double-quick. Not much later orders arrived from Cheatham directing Brown to veer to the left, or west, and shift his division across to the Rally Hill Pike so that he could move into position and "attack to the right of Cleburne." Brown moved by way of a small road that passed near the Peters House and accomplished the movement in reasonable time. His division, still absent S. R. Gist's Brigade and the detachment of Otho Strahl's, hurriedly formed up near a tollgate on the Rally Hill Pike about a mile and a half from Spring Hill. Brown said he "could distinctly see the enemy in force both of infantry and artillery, at Spring Hill..." As Brown readied the attack, however, Cheatham learned that Cleburne's "right brigade has been struck in the flank" and "he had been compelled to fall back and reform his division with a change of front."[22]

This presented an immediate problem for Cheatham. It was nearly 5 o'clock, darkness was falling, and Cheatham, who was preoccupied with delivering an assault on Spring Hill, needed concerted action among his divisions. Hood had other plans, however, namely occupying and holding Columbia Pike with at least one of those divisions. Yet the confusion had only just begun.

As Granbury, Govan, and Lowrey aligned themselves for an all-out push on the Union position, an order from Cheatham was delivered to Cleburne by Maj. Joseph Bostick. It instructed the Irishman to hold his division in place until further notice. Cleburne was understandably dismayed at this turn of events. According to Mangum, "The arrest of his movement on the turnpike was a bitter disappointment to General Cleburne, and he expressed himself very forcibly in regard to the failure that forced it." James Dinkins remembered seeing Cleburne speaking to James Chalmers, explaining that the enemy was "badly paralyzed" and on the heels of his men he had ridden to "within fifty yards of their works without danger."[23]

---

[22] Cheatham, *SHSP* 9, 525; Brown, Statement of, *SHSP* 9, p. 537-538; Purdue, *Pat Cleburne*, p. 399.

[23] Mangum, *Kennesaw Gazette*, June 15, 1887; Dinkins, *Personal Recollections*, p. 232.

Nonetheless, Cleburne's veterans were instructed to await further orders, but remain in line of battle should they need to move at a moment's notice. How close Cleburne was to taking possession of the pike is told by a single sentence from a letter written by Daniel Govan: "Had we not been halted and instead made a determined advance, we could in 20 minutes have captured or destroyed Stanley, together with 800 wagons and his artillery, and have planted our army firmly on the pike." Seeing things in order Cleburne rode to the right.[24]

Cheatham was speaking to Brown and arranging the details of the planned attack when Cleburne trotted up. Cleburne told Cheatham he had "reformed his division" and that the men were awaiting orders. Cheatham, who had just finished speaking with Gen. Hood, gave "orders to Brown and Cleburne that...they should attack the enemy, who were then in sight..." Brown recalled that he "was ordered to form line of battle and take Spring Hill."[25]

According to Maj. Joseph Vaulx, a member of Cheatham's staff, Brown was told by Cheatham that the responsibility for launching the attack was his and that Cleburne would lead his men forward only upon hearing Brown's guns. Bate's Division would then join the assault upon hearing Cleburne's guns. But things soon went awry as words were subsequently passed between Cheatham, Brown, and Hood. As for Brown, he soon became perhaps the most crucial player in the Spring Hill drama.[26]

After giving directions to Brown, Cheatham rode to the left to locate Bate and coordinate the action of his division in the upcoming attack. Very soon, however, Cheatham grew uneasy. He heard no action coming from Brown's direction and asked his accompanying staff, "Why don't we hear Brown's guns?" Cheatham rode only a bit further before deciding to go back and again speak to Brown. After dispatching a staff member to continue on in search of Bate, Cheatham turned back to the east and said to those around him, "Let us go and see what is the matter." Not long into his return trip, however, Cheatham

---

[24] Daniel C. Govan letter to George A. Williams, in *Cleburne and His Command* by Irving Buck, p. 273.

[25] Cheatham, *SHSP* 9, p. 526; Brown, Statement of, *SHSP* 9, p. 538.

[26] Young, *CV* 16, p. 33; Henry M. Field, *Bright Skies and Dark Shadows*, p. 215.

learned why Brown had not launched the attack. One of Brown's own staff officers met Cheatham and informed the corps commander that Brown had been alerted to the presence of Federal troops extending beyond the Confederate right. Cheatham could only shake his head in disbelief.[27]

Brown's men, following their trek up the Rally Hill Pike in column, fronted to the left, or west, upon reaching the area north of the tollgate. Helping to prevent enemy artillery fire from cascading down upon Brown's maneuvering soldiers were a number of sharpshooters equipped with Whitworth rifles. They took positions behind several large trees and peppered the nearby Yankee gunners with bullets.[28]

Brown was ready to send his men forward after talking with Cheatham and connecting his left flank with Pat Cleburne's right, which was located a short distance west of the Rally Hill Pike. Brown threw out "a skirmish line" and advanced his line of battle only about "four hundred or five hundred yards" before trouble was reported. Word came to him from Otho Strahl, whose brigade formed the right of the line, that enemy troops "on a wooded hill" could be seen strung out beyond the Confederate flank. Strahl expressed concern that the Yankees were in a position to easily flank his brigade if the advance continued. Brown quickly joined Strahl, who "pointed out...the position of the Federal line..." Brown agreed with his brigade commander that the risk was too great to resume the forward movement. Concerned about meeting what he termed "inevitable disaster," Brown decided to "suspend the advance and confer with the corps commander." Surely adding to both Brown's and Strahl's unease was the fact that Bedford Forrest's cavalrymen had been withdrawn from their earlier positions "to feed their horses and bivouac out of immediate contact with the enemy's pickets, the infantry being left to hold the ground acquired." What neither Brown nor Strahl discerned in the growing darkness, however, was that the Union force stretched out just north of Mount Carmel Road was not terribly significant. They had stumbled upon the

---

[27] Young, *CV* 16, p. 33-34; Field, *Bright Skies and Dark Shadows*, p. 215-216; William T. Crawford, "The Mystery of Spring Hill," *Civil War History*, June 1955.

[28] Isaac N. Shannon, "Sharpshooters With Hood's Army," *CV* 15, p. 124-125.

extension of John Lane's left flank, which without firing a shot, had halted an entire Rebel division.[29]

John Lane offered no specific information about where he positioned the 100th Illinois and the single 40th Indiana company. He said only that the troops were moved "to my left..." However, Capt. John Shellenberger, a Federal officer, provided some important details after the war. Shellenberger said the 97th Ohio was posted with its left "resting on the Mt. Carmel Road" and the 100th Illinois was "posted several hundred yards in advance of the 97th Ohio, on the opposite side of the road..." Connecting the flanks of the two regiments, according to Shellenberger, was "a part of the 40th Indiana" that was "deployed along the road as skirmishers." Shellenberger must have been mistaken about the 97th Ohio because according to the regiment's commander, Milton Barnes, his men moved to the right of Lane's Brigade as Bradley's fight with Cleburne wound down. Perhaps the 97th Ohio was in the location mentioned by Shellenberger earlier in the day, but another regiment filled that spot around dark. Taken as a whole, however, the information is revealing. If Shellenberger was correct about the unit locations, specifically the 100th Illinois, Lane's extended left flank was less than a mile from John Brown's right when the Rebel advance halted.[30]

Even at this distance Lane's troops, silhouetted by the twilight, would have been visible to the Confederates almost due south along the Rally Hill Pike. The difficulty was that in the dimming light their exact numbers were unknown. But the separation between the two sides was soon further reduced. When Gist's Brigade, the largest in Brown's Division, arrived on the field as dusk was falling it was "immediately

---

[29] Young, *CV* 16, p. 33-34; Brown, Statement of, *SHSP* 9, p. 538; *OR* 45, pt. 1, p. 763; Field, *Bright Skies and Dark Shadows*, p. 215; Jordan & Pryor, *The Campaigns of General Forrest*, p. 622.

[30] *OR* 45, pt. 1, p. 255, 265; John K. Shellenberger, "More About Spring Hill," *NT*, Feb. 1, 1894, p. 1; Shellenberger, *CV* 36, p. 141. The 28th Kentucky likely covered the ground where Shellenberger thought the 97th Ohio was located. Robert Hasty said the "left of the line of the 28th Kentucky" was located to the right of his regiment, the 73rd Illinois. See *A History of the Seventy-Third Regiment of Illinois Infantry Volunteers*, p. 438.

placed in position" on the right. Presumably the other half of Strahl's Brigade was also placed into line. Col. Ellison Capers, commanding the 24th South Carolina, reported being "formed in line of battle, facing the town and apparently about a mile distant." Since Capers' regiment formed the left of Gist's Brigade, his estimate of one mile is not far from being accurate. Also, Capers seems to have been referring to his unit's distance from the town, not the Federal troops.[31]

The arrival of Gist, whose men likely formed in echelon on Brown's right, and Strahl's detachment easily added nearly a quarter mile to the length of the Rebel battle line. When Brown finally got all of his troops into line, John Lane's extended left flank was perhaps a half mile from the Confederate right. Moreover, Lane's line of battle directly in front of Brown's troops was similarly distant. When skirmishers were sent forward, the separation was probably no more than a third of a mile. But it was almost completely dark, leaving the opposing forces to try and estimate the other's distance by what they could hear. It was a night heavy with anxiety and frustration.[32]

When Frank Cheatham arrived "upon the field" and spoke with Brown, which apparently was shortly before Gist and Strahl arrived, he was informed of the "certain disaster" that was sure to result if the line advanced any further. Cheatham said he told Brown to "throw back his right brigade and make the attack." This seems to be a logical response except that Cheatham is the only source for this alleged order. Maj. Vaulx and Gen. Brown, however, told a much different story.[33]

William Brimage Bate was a stocky Tennessean with a thick

---

[31] *OR* 45, pt. 1, p. 736; Brown, Statement of, *SHSP* 9, p. 537-538. There is no account stating when the other half of Strahl's Brigade arrived on the field, but since it had been detached with Gist's Brigade earlier in the day the two likely arrived at Spring Hill together.

[32] Brown's Division numbered about 3,700 effective for duty; see *OR* 45, pt. 1, p. 768. Gist's was the largest brigade and Strahl's was the second largest; see Brown, Statement of, *SHSP* 9, p. 537. Normally a soldier occupied 18-24 inches of space, and if Gist's Brigade numbered about 1,200, in double line of battle it would have spanned some 1,200 feet. This author believes that because Strahl was on the front line, and standard procedure called for a reserve, Gist was formed in echelon on the right flank.

[33] Cheatham, *SHSP* 9, p. 525; Brown, Statement of, *SHSP* 9, p. 538.

shock of black hair and an equally thick beard. Born near Bledsoe's Lick northeast of Nashville in 1826, Bate served in the Mexican War and later became an attorney and state legislator. Although he had no formal military training and volunteered his services as a private, Bate was elected colonel of the 2nd Tennessee Infantry. So badly wounded at Shiloh that his left leg was nearly amputated, Bate was unable to return to duty for months and when he did crutches were required. Elevated to brigadier general at the end of 1862, Bate fought with the Army of Tennessee throughout 1863 and was wounded again in June of that year. He received his promotion to major general in early 1864 and was wounded a third time at Atlanta. This last injury kept him out of service for nearly two months and Bate rejoined the army on October 10, 1864, just in time to take part in the Tennessee invasion.[34]

While developments on the Confederate right flank played out action on the left also became interesting. Gen. Bate, with a force of about 2,100 men, formed his division by placing Brig. Gen. Henry R. Jackson's Brigade on the right, Brig. Gen. Thomas Benton Smith, commanding what was formerly Tyler's Brigade, in echelon on Jackson's left, and Col. Robert Bullock with the Florida Brigade in support of Smith. Bate had moved forward almost a mile when the crackle of small arms fire audible to his right swelled to a roar. It was clear to Bate that "Cleburne had been engaged" and after obtaining a guide to help locate the turnpike, he shifted his command to the right in an effort to link up with Cleburne's left. Without warning, however, the sound of battle to the north faded away. Unsure of what to think Bate pushed onward, but not before again sliding his men to the right in search of Cleburne's elusive left wing. Then, almost suddenly, it seemed as if Hood's plan had success within reach. Night was fast blanketing the landscape when a handful of Bate's advance troops, squinting and struggling to ascertain what lay before them, saw the turnpike come into view barely 100 yards away. These men, Maj. Theodore D. Caswell's sharpshooters, had been deployed as skirmishers and they could see not only the roadway, but also a small number of enemy troops. The time was approximately 5:30 p.m.[35]

---

[34] *OR* 39, pt. 3, p. 826; Faust, ed., *Historical Times Encyclopedia*, p. 44; Welsh, *Medical Histories of Confederate Generals*, p. 15-16.

[35] *OR* 45, pt. 1, p. 742.

The 26th Ohio, which counted only 120 in its ranks, had been ordered by Gen. Wagner to guard a small road south of Spring Hill and provide additional protection for the wagons moving into town. The tiny regiment was standing loosely under arms when out of nowhere bullets began zipping through the air. Three men were hit and went down and within "a short time" the Ohioans had "scattered" in confusion. Not far to the south, moving north along the pike, other Federal troops were approaching. They were the leading elements of Gen. Ruger's column from Columbia, accompanied by Col. John Orr's three companies of the 124th Indiana. Schofield rode at the head of the column, escorted by a company of the 7th Ohio Cavalry. Soon Bate's men and these Federal troops were exchanging fire, the blasts from their muskets punctuating the darkness with light. By this time Bate's main line, positioned just north of Rippavilla, home to the Nathaniel Cheairs family, was within at least 300 yards of the pike. His troops were poised to move astride it when a staff officer approached on horseback. The rider, Lt. Abraham B. Schell, carried a message from Cheatham, which had been delivered by courier. Schell tracked down Bate and, with bullets cracking and whistling in the distance, the lieutenant handed his commander the dispatch. Bate read the note with some bewilderment. It called not only for an immediate halt, but also ordered him to locate and connect with Cleburne's left flank. Bate knew he was operating under direct instructions from Gen. Hood to place his division across Columbia Pike and now Cheatham was countermanding those orders. Reluctant to abandon what he felt was a "good position" Bate instructed Maj. John B. Pirtle to find Cheatham at once. Bate wanted not just confirmation of the order, but felt Cheatham should be aware that the Confederates were in such a spot as to be able to "whip three times their number."[36]

As Bate's men stalled the Federal troops on the pike, with Schofield riding at the head of the column, slid just past the Confederates. Sporadic musket fire continued rattling between the two

---

[36] *OR* 45, pt. 1, p. 230, 255, 428, 742; W. W. Gist, "The Other Side at Franklin," *CV* 24, p. 13; John H. Inglis, "Commander Florida Division, U. C. V.," *CV* 22, p. 159; Cox, *Battle of Franklin*, p. 34; Shellenberger, *CV* 36, p. 141; John Hickman, Statement of, *CV* 22, p. 15; Purdue, *Pat Cleburne*, p. 401.

sides, but mostly the Northerners had an easy passage, even with their hearts in their throats. Along the road troops forming the right flank of Col. Silas Strickland's Brigade chanced upon an interesting prize. Col. Oliver L. Spaulding's 23rd Michigan, which actually belonged to Col. Orlando Moore's Brigade, but had been called up to assist Strickland, had swept out on the right. As Spaulding's flankers advanced a Rebel officer suddenly appeared in their midst. It was Capt. R. T. English of Granbury's staff who had wandered toward the darkened pike trying to identify the troops he could hear marching north. English thought they were possibly Bate's men, but he failed to recognize his error in time and the captain was quickly made a prisoner. Ushered into Spring Hill by 7 p.m., his capture failed to subdue English's attitude. David Stanley said that English was brought to him and "was very saucy" and fully expected the Rebels to "triumph the next day."[37]

The 72nd Illinois almost seemed out of place. Raised in Chicago during the summer of 1862, the regiment had fought at Champion Hill and Vicksburg, a claim that no other unit in either the Fourth Corps or Twenty-Third Corps could match. After a short stint in the field following Vicksburg, the regiment returned to the river city and went on provost guard duty where it remained until October 1864. At the end of October the 72nd Illinois was ordered to join Sherman's March to the Sea, but transportation delays prevented it from reaching Nashville until November 13. By that time it was too late to join Sherman and so instead Gen. Thomas shipped the regiment south to Columbia. There it arrived late on November 16 and was among the first Federal units to enter and fortify the town.[38]

Capt. James A. Sexton and his comrades in the 72nd Illinois,

---

[37] *OR* 45, pt. 1, p. 379, 386; Stanley, *Personal Memoirs*, p. 204; R. M. Collins, *Chapters from the Unwritten History of the War Between the States*, p. 244.

[38] *OR* 39, pt. 3, p. 734; *OR* 41, pt. 3, p. 857; *OR* 45, pt. 1, p. 999; Joseph Stockton, *War Diary (1862-5) of Brevet Brigadier General, First Lieutenant, Captain, Major and Lieutenant-Colonel, 72d Regiment, Illinois Infantry Volunteers*, p. 27, 32-33.

temporarily assigned to Strickland's Brigade, found themselves taking skirmish fire as they approached Spring Hill. In the confusion some of the new recruits from either the 44th Missouri or 183rd Ohio, regiments that had been with the army for barely twenty-four hours, began to fire on the Illinoisans from the rear. Sexton said the men from his regiment threw "themselves upon the ground" to escape injury. In the darkness all was bedlam for a time. After a few moments, however, the green troops were calmed down and the Rebels were scattered, allowing the men of the 72nd Illinois to continue their march. Sexton later wrote:

> Here, we were in such close proximity to the Confederates that we could see their long line of camp fires as they burned brightly; could hear the rattle of their canteens; see the officers and men standing around the fires, or loitering about; while the rumbling of our wagon train on the pike, and the beating of our own hearts were the only sounds we could hear on our side.
>
> After a seemingly endless delay, we were cautiously withdrawn and resumed our march alongside of the wagon train. As darkness came upon us the dangers seemed to increase rather than diminish. The men would not speak above a whisper, lest they might awaken the sleeping foe to an undesirable and unhealthy activity.
>
> Had Hood placed a single Confederate division in a fortified position across the road at this point, it would have been the means of effectually checking the Federal retreat, and dawn would have found our forces cut off from all hope of escape. The enemy would have outnumbered us two to one: it would have been fool-hardy to attack them, and there would have been no possible opportunity of avoiding them.[39]

The 44th Missouri and 183rd Ohio were both new to the field of battle. The Missourians had been recruited during August and September and after being outfitted and drilled for a short time, the regiment was moved to Paducah, Kentucky, arriving there on November 16. Eight days later the 44th Missouri, commanded by Col. Robert C. Bradshaw, was shipped to Nashville via steamer. After disembarking in the Tennessee capital late on November 27,

---

[39] James A. Sexton, "The Observations and Experiences of a Captain of Infantry at the Battle of Franklin, November 30, 1864," *MOLLUS*, Illinois, 4, p. 469-470.

preparations were made to ship the regiment to the Columbia area. The men boarded railroad cars and moved south, where they joined Schofield's forces late on November 28. According to Lt. Col. Andrew J. Barr the regiment was positioned near where the Nashville & Decatur Railroad crossed the Duck River. He also stated the 44th Missouri was put "into position on the right" and attached to Ruger's command, which at Columbia was protecting "crossings and fords on Schofield's right flank." The Missourians, kept under arms the entire night of November 28, barely had time to catch their breath before being ordered north the following day.[40]

The men of the 183rd Ohio were no less harried. Organized during September and October the Ohio recruits, commanded by Col. George W. Hoge, left Camp Dennison on November 19 and proceeded by steamer to Louisville, Kentucky where they were "armed and equipped..." On November 22 they left Louisville by train and pulled into Nashville two days later. Late on the afternoon of November 27 the Ohioans struck their tents and boarded railcars for the move south to Columbia. From available evidence the 183rd Ohio got off the train at Carter's Creek Station, a point on the Nashville & Decatur Railroad north of Columbia. The regiment arrived about sundown on November 28 and it is likely the 183rd Ohio made the trip south from Nashville in the company of the 44th Missouri. The latter regiment, however, was either carried further south or got off the train with the 183rd Ohio and then marched south. But like the Missourians, the 183rd Ohio had barely arrived before being ordered to turn back toward Nashville.[41]

Trailing behind Ruger's primary column was Walter Whitaker's Brigade of Kimball's Division. Whitaker's troops, ordered up by

---

[40] *OR* 41, pt. 4, p. 539, 588; *OR* 45, pt. 1, p. 395; *OR* 52, pt. 1, p. 664; *Supplement to the Official Records of the Union and Confederate Armies* (hereafter referred to as *SUP*), 38, pt. 2, p. 29, 33, 35; *Report of the Adjutant General of Missouri 1865*, p. 275-276; Cox, *Sherman's March to the Sea*, p. 66.

[41] *OR* 45, pt. 1, p. 397; *OR* 52, pt. 1, p. 664; *SUP* 56, pt. 2, p. 396, 400-401; A. G. Hatry, "A Lost Opportunity," *NT*, Jan. 4, 1894, p. 3.

Schofield as he passed them earlier in the day because "the noise of the combat at Spring Hill told of a vigorous attack," were put into position "parallel to the pike" and "on the right of Wagner's line, to cover the march of the rest of the column as it should approach."[42]

That the opposing forces were separated by such a shockingly narrow margin is reinforced by Lt. Col. Isaac Sherwood. Sherwood commanded the 111th Ohio, a small regiment ordered to remain at Columbia and guard a railway bridge until after nightfall. When Sherwood heard the sound of fire coming from the direction of Spring Hill he took it upon himself to move his regiment toward the action. En route Sherwood and his men encountered the diminutive 24th Missouri, which was guarding another point on the Duck River. The 24th Missouri was composed of only two companies totaling seventy-five men and had just been shipped south from Nashville. The rest of the regiment, comprised of soldiers who had enlisted for three years, had only recently been mustered out and the few remaining men were serving out their final days. Sherwood spoke to Capt. Newton Long briefly and the 24th Missouri soon found itself attached to the 111th Ohio. The newly combined commands tramped up Columbia Pike and as Sherwood approached Spring Hill he caught sight of a figure on horseback not far from the road. Sherwood called out to the man and asked what command he belonged to. When the unidentified soldier answered, "General Cleburne's," Sherwood calmly said, "All right," pulled on his horse's reins and quickly galloped away. So concerned for the safety of his own troops and the Missourians was Sherwood that he detoured the men off the pike to the west some three miles and then turned back to the north. Only near dawn would the Ohioans and Missourians find themselves back on the pike again.[43]

About a half mile north of Rutherford Creek, and a few hundred yards west of McCutcheon's Creek, is the magnificent Oaklawn

---

[42] Cox, *Battle of Franklin* p. 32; *OR* 45, pt. 1, p. 342; Cox, *Sherman's March to the Sea*, p. 77.

[43] Sherwood, *Memories of the War*, p. 129; *OR* 45, pt. 1, p. 387; J. R. Shoup, *The 24th Missouri Volunteer Infantry - Lyon Legion*, p. 182-183.

plantation. Even today the land around the home, built in 1835, remains remarkably similar to its nineteenth century appearance. The rolling hills, interspersed with tracts of woodland, are typical of Middle Tennessee and cattle and horses still dot the rural landscape. Absalom Thompson owned Oaklawn and the surrounding acreage in 1864 and as November 29 wound down, visitors approached the stately mansion. John Bell Hood, in the company of his staff and former Tennessee Governor Isham Harris, wanted to know if they could use Mr. Thompson's home as army headquarters for the night. Thompson happily offered his spacious residence to Hood, and with many thanks the general guided his horse toward a small fishing pond just north of the house. After dismounting, Hood sat down on a log near the pond and waited for word as to how Cheatham's Corps was faring. After a short time Hood "dispatched a messenger to General Cheatham" reminding him "to lose no time in gaining possession of the pike at Spring Hill." Hood reportedly received word that the pike would be secured shortly. Hood continued to wait for some indication that the road had been reached, but as twilight began to deepen with no further word from Cheatham, the commanding general began to worry. Additional couriers sent out to locate Cheatham met with no success. Finally Hood turned to Governor Harris.[44]

Three years after the war, in May 1868, a conversation was struck up between Harris and Campbell Brown, son-in-law to Lt. Gen. Richard S. Ewell of the Army of Northern Virginia. Brown kept careful notes of the interesting discussion. According to Harris the sound of Cheatham's initial action with the Federals could be heard from the Thompson House. Soon, however, the firing stopped and "all remained quiet for a considerable time." Harris recalled saying to Hood "that something was the matter" and suggested finding out what was transpiring. Hood agreed and asked Harris to ride forth and "find out the situation." This Harris did and he found much. First he located Gen. Brown who showed Harris the enemy force extending beyond the Confederate right flank. Harris immediately dispatched a rider back to Hood with this information and suggested using Stewart's Corps to correct this problem. Soon thereafter Harris found Cheatham "just

---

[44] Hood, *Advance & Retreat*, p. 285.

beyond Cleburne's line" and the two, in the company of a third party, rode back to Hood's headquarters.[45]

John C. Brown
(Chicago Historical Society)

Maj. Vaulx said that when Cheatham learned about Brown's Division being flanked he asked the officer who delivered the message to ride with him to Hood's headquarters and report "just what you have said to me." Apparently the trio of Cheatham, Harris, and Brown's unnamed staff officer made this trip together. Upon arriving at Oaklawn, Cheatham explained the situation as he understood it to Hood, who replied, "If that is the case, do not attack, but order your troops to hold the position they are in for the night."[46]

Adding some credibility to Vaulx's story is Harris. During his post-war conversation with Campbell Brown, the former governor said that in his presence Hood told Cheatham to "await and conform to the movements of his troops on his right, telling him he had ordered Stewart to move beyond Brown's right until he got across the turnpike..."[47]

John Brown's recollection has striking similarities to both Vaulx and Harris in regards to Hood:

> I formed my line as speedily as worn troops could move, and, after throwing forward a skirmish line, advanced four hundred or five hundred yards,

---

[45] Campbell Brown and Isham Harris conversation, Brown-Ewell Papers, TSLA.

[46] Field, *Bright Skies and Dark Shadows*, p. 216.

[47] Brown-Harris conversation, Brown-Ewell Papers, TSLA.

when I discovered a line of the enemy thrown out of Spring Hill, across and threatening my right flank, and I then discovered for the first time that General Forrest's cavalry, which I had been assured would protect my right, had been ordered to another part of the field, leaving me without any protection on my right flank or support in the rear. I had neither artillery nor cavalry, and was left in a position where I must meet with inevitable disaster if I advanced on Spring Hill. A hasty consultation with my brigade commanders resulted in a determination to suspend the advance and confer with the corps commander. I need not remind you that in a very few minutes you were upon the field and fully approved of what had been done, as also did General Hood a little later, when he directed that the attack should be delayed until the arrival of Generals Stewart and Gist, and in the meantime that the whole command should be held under orders to advance at a moment's notice.[48]

The most critical aspect of Brown's statement is that he mentioned nothing about receiving orders to "throw back his right." How could this be? Cheatham was quite straightforward when explaining that Brown, after being told to attack once, was told to attack a second time. Did Cheatham think that he had passed the second attack order on to Brown just before going to see Hood and actually not send it? Or did Brown get the second order and again delay? Quite intriguing is the fact that Vaulx mentioned nothing about Cheatham's supposed second order. Perhaps Hood did suspend the attack and for some reason Cheatham never got back to Brown as Vaulx seems to indicate. One thing is for certain. As other authors have noted, Cheatham's intended order of attack, Brown followed by Cleburne and then Bate, was quite real because why else would Cleburne not have pushed ahead unless he had been told to wait for the sound of Brown's guns? The question remains why did the delay continue indefinitely after the detection of Union troops on the right.[49]

Earlier, as the last of Brown's troops forded Rutherford Creek, A. P. Stewart's Corps, and Johnson's Division of S. D. Lee's Corps, swung into position and readied for a crossing. John Bell Hood, however, had other plans. In his report covering Spring Hill, composed on April 3, 1865, Stewart wrote:

---

[48] Brown, Statement of, *SHSP* 9, p. 538.

[49] Young, *CV* 16, p. 34; Hay, *Hood's Tennessee Campaign*, p. 93.

In the course of the afternoon, about 3 or 4 o'clock, I reached Rutherford's Creek as Cheatham's rear division was crossing. I received orders to halt and form on the south side of the creek, my right to rest on or near the creek, so as to move down the creek if necessary. Subsequently I received an order to send a division across the creek, and finally, between sunset and dark, an order was received to cross the creek, leaving a division on the south side. Johnson's division, being in rear, was designated to remain.[50]

Hood offered no explanation why he ordered Stewart to align his troops in line of battle south of the creek, and in his memoirs said only that he "sent a staff officer to Stewart and Johnson to push forward."[51] Additionally, why Hood would claim he told Cheatham and Cleburne that not only was Stewart nearby, but Old Straight would be double-quicked to their support when Stewart's men were ordered to do almost precisely the opposite is puzzling. The only real insight into Hood's thoughts regarding this chain of events comes from Stewart himself. On at least two occasions, in an 1881 letter to Capt. W. O. Dodd and a second time in a 1908 conversation with T. G. Dabney, only five days before the general's death, Stewart expounded on the topic. The Dodd letter, in part, is particularly telling:

I was not allowed to cross Rutherford's creek until dark. When I reached the creek, riding in advance of my troops, Cheatham's corps was crossing. A staff officer of his informed me that an attack was to be made. I expected to be hurried forward to support the attack. Instead, I was ordered to form in line of battle before crossing the creek, and about at right angles to it. This, in my poor judgement, was the fatal error. My impression is that Cheatham and his officers thought themselves in great danger of being outflanked and crushed. Had they known my command was coming up to their support, it is likely they would not have hesitated to make the attack. When, about dusk, I received orders to move on across the creek, and rode forward to find the Commanding General, he complained bitterly that his orders to attack had not been obeyed. But he was there himself. I asked him why he had halted me at Rutherford's creek. He replied that he confidently expected Cheatham

---

[50] *OR* 45, pt. 1, p. 712.

[51] Hood, *Advance & Retreat*, p. 285.

would attack and rout the enemy; that there was a road leading to Murfreesboro on the other side of the creek. He wished me there to prevent the escape of the routed foe in that direction. Here, I think, was the error. Johnson's division of Lee's corps was with me. That division, reinforced if necessary by one of mine, would have been sufficient to guard that road. The rest of my command should have been pressed forward to reinforce Cheatham and Forrest.[52]

Likewise, Dabney wrote that Stewart, once he had crossed to the creek's north side, "encountered General Hood by a small fire on the roadside, with a single orderly as attendant." Stewart related that "Hood began to inveigh against Cheatham for not making the attack on Spring Hill, as he was ordered to do." Although almost a half century had elapsed since that fateful November night, Stewart's recollection remained sharp. So clear was his memory that Stewart recalled almost chiding Hood. He said to Dabney, "It was on my tongue to ask Hood, 'Why did you not see yourself that your order was obeyed and the attack made?' but I thought that would appear disrespectful."[53]

Probably within minutes of Hood's initial conversation with Stewart, the courier sent by Isham Harris galloped up with information about Cheatham's stalled attack. Although the news was not good Hood finally had some answers. He proceeded to order Stewart, after giving him a "young man of the neighborhood as a guide," to "move on and place my right across the pike beyond Spring Hill, 'your left,' he added, 'extending down this way.'" Also of note is that Hood's guide John Gregory, who was interviewed in 1903, stated that Hood "seemed very collected, and not excited." Although Hood's demeanor as described by Gregory in comparison to Stewart may seem like a minor point, it well illustrates the surging emotions of the day.[54]

It was shortly after Stewart received his orders that Frank Cheatham and Governor Harris arrived to speak with Hood. Whether Stewart was actually present when Hood and Cheatham conversed is of

---

[52] Alex. P. Stewart, Statement of, in B. F. Cheatham, "The Lost Opportunity at Spring Hill, Tenn. - General Cheatham's Reply to General Hood," *SHSP* 9, p. 534-535.

[53] T. G. Dabney, "Gen. A. P. Stewart on Strong Topics," *CV* 17, p. 32.

[54] *OR* 45, pt. 1, p. 712; Smith, *History of Maury County*, p. 239.

no significance, except that even this simple point cannot be accurately determined. While Stewart maintained the three of them were "at no time together" both Hood and Cheatham claim Stewart was present.[55] Stewart's memory is probably accurate. Considering the mud slinging between Hood and Cheatham after the war neither has much credibility concerning the late afternoon and evening of November 29. Additionally, Stewart outlived both of his old comrades and could have easily added substantive weight to either of their claims. Instead, Stewart remained steadfast in his assertion that the three generals were never together at Spring Hill.

While it would be easy to ignore what Hood and Cheatham said about this particular, and quite significant, meeting at the Thompson House, because of the difficulty in discerning the truthfulness of their writings, each man's version is absolutely crucial to a full understanding of Spring Hill. First came Hood's story, published in 1880 one year after his death:

> I thought it probable that Cheatham had taken possession of Spring Hill without encountering material opposition, or had formed line across the pike, north of town, and entrenched without coming in serious contact with the enemy, which would account for the little musketry heard in his direction. However, to ascertain the truth, I sent an officer to ask Cheatham if he held the pike, and to inform him of the arrival of Stewart, whose Corps I intended to throw on his left, in order to assail the Federals in flank that evening or the next morning, as they approached and formed to attack Cheatham. At this juncture, the last messenger returned with the report that the road had not been taken possession of. General Stewart was then ordered to proceed to the right of Cheatham and place his Corps across the pike, north of Spring Hill.
>
> By this hour, however, twilight was upon us, when General Cheatham rode up in person. I at once directed Stewart to halt, and, turning to Cheatham, I exclaimed with deep emotion, as I felt the golden opportunity fast slipping from me, "General, why in the name of God have you not attacked the enemy, and taken possession of that pike?" He replied that the line looked a little too long for him, and that Stewart should first form on his right. I could hardly believe it possible that this brave soldier, who had given proof of such courage

---

[55] Cheatham, *SHSP* 9, p. 526; Stewart, Statement of, *SHSP* 9, p. 535; Hood, *Advance & Retreat*, p. 286.

and ability upon so many hard-fought fields, would even make such a report. After leading him within full view of the enemy, and pointing out to him the Federals, retreating in great haste and confusion, along the pike, and then giving explicit orders to attack, I would as soon have expected midday to turn into darkness as for him to have disobeyed my orders. I then asked General Cheatham whether or not Stewart's Corps, if formed on the right, would extend across the pike. He answered in the affirmative.[56]

When Cheatham read Hood's book he was appalled. Clearly Hood was attempting to pin the blame for Spring Hill squarely on Cheatham's shoulders and Cheatham was motivated to answer. He immediately began composing a response to Hood's accusations and in late 1881 had the opportunity to read his paper to the Louisville Southern Historical Society. Cheatham's essay was subsequently published in the *Southern Historical Society Papers.* His recollection of the late afternoon conference at the Thompson residence was as follows:

When I had returned from my left, where I had been to get Bate in position, and was on the way to the right of my line, it was dark; but I intended to move forward with Cleburne and Brown and make the attack, knowing that Bate would be in position to support them. Stewart's column had already passed by on the way toward the turnpike, and I presumed he would be in position on my right.

On reaching the road where General Hood's field headquarters had been established, I found a courier with a message from General Hood, requesting me to come to him at Captain Thompson's house, about one and a fourth miles back on the road to Rutherford's creek. I found General Stewart with General Hood. The Commanding General there informed me that he had

---

[56] Hood, *Advance & Retreat*, p. 285-286. P. G. T. Beauregard helped finance the publication of Hood's book for two reasons. Not only did Hood die in the New Orleans yellow fever epidemic of 1879, but so did his wife and their eldest child. Ten children, however, remained behind and Beauregard used the book's proceeds to manage the Hood Orphan Memorial Fund. Hood's book was also a full-fledged assault on Joseph Johnston's handling of the early stages of the Atlanta Campaign and although Beauregard was not especially close to Hood, he was a bitter enemy of Johnston and saw *Advance & Retreat* as an opportunity to taint Old Joe.

concluded to wait till morning, and directed me to hold my command in readiness to attack at daylight.

I was never more astonished than when General Hood informed me that he had concluded to postpone the attack till daylight. The road was still open - orders to remain quiet until morning - and nothing to prevent the enemy from marching to Franklin.

Furthermore, Cheatham stated:

The dramatic scene with which he embellishes his narrative of the day's operations only occurred in the imagination of General Hood.[57]

It is reasonable to believe that by nightfall on November 29 Hood was upset, not only as he remembered, but Stewart also. Whether he berated Cheatham or not will never be known, but it is hard to imagine that by this stage Hood simply gave up the initiative without reason and told Cheatham to wait until morning. Two of Hood's staff officers, Maj. B. H. Blanton and Captain James Hamilton, said they personally delivered orders to Cheatham directing him to attack and neither mentioned anything about the assault being called off by the commanding general.[58] But another member of Hood's staff, Maj. Joseph B. Cumming, provided a tantalizing clue about what might have actually happened. He wrote:

General Hood sent me forward with an order to General Cheatham to attack at once. I delivered the order, and as I had ridden hard to deliver it I returned to Gen. Hood's headquarters at a slow pace expecting every minute to hear the sound of the attack on the pike. It was now getting dark. It was the 29th of November, chilly and drizzling. When I reached Gen. Hood's headquarters, to my astonishment I found Gen. Cheatham there, he having out-ridden me by a different route. He was remonstrating with Gen. Hood against a night attack.[59]

---

[57] Cheatham, *SHSP* 9, p. 526, 530.

[58] Sieburg and Hansen, ed., *Memoirs of a Confederate Staff Officer*, p. 61. Only the last names are mentioned in Ratchford's memoirs and he had Hamilton's rank incorrect. The full names and ranks were obtained from Hood's *Advance & Retreat*, p. 60.

[59] Joseph Cumming, Recollections, p. 72, SHC.

Cumming's statement does great damage to Cheatham if accurate. He effectively refuted Cheatham's claim that it was Hood who was the driving force behind abandoning the offensive. Unfortunately, Cumming said nothing about Hood's response to Cheatham's plea and perhaps he witnessed only part of the exchange. Regardless, the available facts indicate Hood was not ready to abandon all efforts to secure possession of the pike. Even barring a nighttime attack, Hood still wanted troops across the road and so he sent a staff officer galloping after Stewart. As for Cumming it might be said that as an officer on Hood's staff he would be inclined to back his chief's story, but in describing Hood as "physically handicapped, if not wholly disqualified from active service in the field" Cumming comes across as far from partisan.[60]

In the midst of the terse Hood and Cheatham meeting, John Pirtle, the staff member Bate had sent to confirm Cheatham's earlier order halting the movement toward Columbia Pike, finally arrived at Oaklawn. It was around 7 p.m. and Pirtle was not warmly received. Cheatham was in a foul mood. In the yard outside the Thompson House he told Pirtle, with Hood present, that Bate could either pull back as ordered and connect with Cleburne, or he could "report under arrest" directly to Hood. Why Gen. Hood, who had personally ordered Bate's movement toward the pike, did not interject is unknown. His silence indicates the decision to stop the offensive may have already been made. With a quick salute, Pirtle remounted his horse. Message in tow the major raced back through the darkness and delivered the "peremptory order." Bate, still doubting the logic of the situation, started to pull his men away from the pike and began the difficult process of locating Cleburne's left flank in the black of night. Much work remained as almost a full mile separated their positions. For William Bate the night was far from over.[61]

---

[60] Ibid., p. 71, SHC.

[61] Purdue, *Pat Cleburne*, p. 401; Thomas Speed, "The Battle of Franklin, Tennessee," *MOLLUS*, Ohio, 3, p. 52. Speed, a Union officer who served in the 12th Kentucky, spoke to Pirtle after the war about the conversation with Cheatham.

Upon arriving in Spring Hill, John Schofield established his headquarters at the home of William McKissack and began an assessment of the situation. Things did not look good. It was obvious that a good portion of Hood's army was in close proximity to Columbia Pike, as evidenced by the campfires burning in toward the east almost as far as the eye could see. Schofield knew all too well that many of his troops were still strung out along the pike to the south. Additionally, the night had turned cold and blustery. But Schofield remained active. After learning about enemy cavalry lurking near Thompson's Station several miles north of Spring Hill, he moved to clear a path to Franklin if necessary.[62]

As the fates of war unfolded at Spring Hill, the action at Columbia was fast approaching a conclusion. Although the Confederates had managed to lay a pontoon bridge across the Duck River, the main body delayed in making a determined effort to cross.[63]

Jacob Cox took full advantage of his opponent's delay and began pulling the remaining Union troops out of their entrenchments, as Schofield had ordered. Under cover of night Cox fortified the skirmish line and instructed the 12th Kentucky and 16th Kentucky regiments to serve as support for the skirmishers. Cox then moved his division north toward Spring Hill. A captain remembered how the "rearguards were ordered positively to use the bayonet on fence-corner stragglers, and the orders were in several instances obeyed."[64]

With Cox on his way by a little after 7:00 p.m. the final division remaining in Columbia, Gen. Thomas Wood's Third Division of the Fourth Corps, readied for departure. Wood did not specify a departure time in his official report, but the facts indicate his command began its movement north no more than an hour after Cox. The Federal march was not, however, without difficulty. Rutherford Creek crossed the pike about four miles north of Columbia, and because "no sufficient bridge

---

62 McDonough, *Union General in the Civil War and Reconstruction*, p. 113.

63 Richard McMurry in *John Bell Hood* is especially critical of S. D. Lee, calling him "negligent" for his lack of action at Columbia. McMurry notes that Lee was witness to Federal troops leaving Columbia by noon and did nothing to notify Hood; see p. 174.

64 *OR* 45, pt. 1, p. 404; Cox, *Battle of Franklin*, p. 33; Scofield, *The Retreat From Pulaski*, p. 21.

had been constructed" at the intersection, a "protracted and much drawn out" delay ensued. Getting Cox's and Wood's men over the creek turned into a miserable and time consuming effort. Horses and guns became mired in the mud and the men were nearly soaked. Perhaps more than an hour was lost in the effort, but finally the two Federal divisions resumed their march. Because of the delay, however, Nathan Kimball's Division, which had been holding a position along Rutherford Creek since earlier in the day, was not able to fall in line behind Wood until midnight.[65]

Following his brief stop in Spring Hill and conversations with a handful of officers, Schofield pushed toward Thompson's Station with elements of Ruger's Division around 9 p.m. The tiny village had been a busy place during the day and reports of enemy cavalry there weighed heavily on Schofield's mind. What he was not aware of were the details of some rather significant events that had unfolded around the station.[66]

Earlier that morning Alanson P. Cutting was detailed as a military conductor on a railroad train making a run from Franklin to Thompson's Station to drop off a carload of ammunition. Once Cutting completed that task, the train continued south to near Duck River, where it was ordered to return north, take on the baggage of the 44th Missouri and 183rd Ohio, and then proceed back to Nashville. On arriving back at Spring Hill, however, Cutting's train was stopped and he was told to await further orders before moving again.[67]

On November 18, the 175th Ohio had been ordered to guard the railroad from Nashville to Pulaski. Eventually the regiment was scattered along the rail line at the blockhouses over creeks and rivers and had its headquarters at Columbia. Early on November 28, part of Lt. Col. Daniel McCoy's regiment was ordered to leave Columbia and escort some Confederate prisoners and a small number of wagons to Nashville. Around dark that day the Ohioans bivouacked west of

---

[65] *OR* 45, pt. 1, p. 123, 177, 404; Cox, *Sherman's March to the Sea*, p. 79; Scofield, *The Retreat From Pulaski*, p. 21.

[66] *OR* 45, pt. 1, p. 148, 342; Schofield, *Forty-Six Years In The Army*, p. 173.

[67] A. P. Cutting, "This Is How It Was: The Conductor on the Military Railroad Out of Nashville Contradicts Comrade Shellenberger," *NT*, Mar. 22, 1894, p. 3.

Columbia Pike at Thompson's Station, where some of them exchanged pleasantries with members of the 44th Missouri as that unit headed south on railcars. But daylight on November 29 saw the 175th Ohio's plans change radically. Rebel cavalry was detected east of the pike and to the north it appeared as if enemy horsemen were either moving to sever the road or had already done so. Quickly McCoy and his subordinates consulted. Facing the Federals was Lawrence Ross' Texas Brigade. Ross, who could see "a few wagons moving on the pike," quickly ordered up the 9th Texas Cavalry and 1st Texas Legion to "intercept and capture" the enemy goods. He also directed the 3rd Texas Cavalry and 6th Texas Cavalry to attack the railroad depot just west of the pike. At about the same time the 175th Ohio went into action. Barely had the Texans moved out before the Federal wagons suddenly spurred up the pike "as though shot from the muzzle of a cannon." As a result Ross' men were only able to get their hands on one wagon, which was destroyed after the horse team was commandeered. The rest, however, "went thundering through" the Rebel horsemen and headed toward Franklin.[68]

Meanwhile, the 175th Ohio continued its efforts to prevent pursuit of the wagons. The Federal troops flew every flag they could find and did everything else possible to deceive the Rebels into thinking they were facing a much larger force. Then suddenly a section of a southbound train approaching from Franklin became involved in the chaotic scene. The train's engineer, who panicked when he caught sight of the Southern cavalry, abruptly cut his engine loose and beat a hasty path to the Spring Hill station. As he sped away the abandoned cars rolled backward toward a blockhouse on the railroad, just preventing them from being captured by Ross's swarming troopers. By this time the 175th Ohio was slowly drawing back toward Thompson's Station, having done all it could to hold Ross back. As the Confederates pressed in, the Ohioans set fire to the "carload of ammunition" left at the depot earlier in the day and anything else of value. McCoy's men then

---

[68] *OR* 45, pt. 1, p. 769-770, 1117; Keenan, *Wilson's Cavalry Corps*, p. 58; Philip T. South, "Comrade of the 175th Ohio Tells of His Experiences During and After The War," *NT*, Sept. 20, 1923, p. 7; F. M. Posegate, "Battle of Franklin: The Gallant Part Taken by the 175th Ohio," *NT*, Feb. 28, 1889, p. 3.

withdrew toward Spring Hill, arriving there "about dusk." As they tramped south the Rebel horsemen moved in, destroyed the railroad bridge, and after accomplishing "all that could be effected at the station" pulled back.[69]

Although the engagement between the 175th Ohio and Ross' Texans accomplished little aside from saving a few Union wagons, the end result could have easily been a second clash at Thompson's Station between Ruger's Division and Ross' Brigade. Solely by chance did those two forces avoid a nighttime confrontation. Ross said he did not withdraw until "late in the evening" and Schofield admitted he was surprised that no cavalry was discovered upon arriving at the station.[70] Barely a month after Spring Hill, Schofield described this hectic portion of the evening:

> ...I pushed on with General Ruger's division to clear the road at Thompson's Station, which had been occupied by a large body of the enemy's cavalry at dark that evening. On our arrival at Thompson's the enemy had disappeared, his camp-fires still burning, and General Ruger took possession of the cross-roads without opposition.[71]

Ruger's Division was a sadly depleted force at Thompson's Station. Already minus Gen. Joseph Cooper's Brigade, which had been sent from Johnsonville on November 23 to guard the fords on the Duck River at Centreville and Beard's Ferry, Ruger's remaining two brigades were fragmented. Col. Orlando Moore was absent not only the 111th Ohio, but also the 129th Indiana, which about two miles south of Spring Hill had been ordered "back one mile and a half to guard a point until Third Division, Twenty-third Army Corps, and one division of Fourth Army Corps should pass..." Col. Silas Strickland had only two regiments, the 50th Ohio and 72nd Illinois, on hand to help secure the Thompson's Station crossroads. Strickland's other regiments, the 91st Indiana and 123rd Indiana, had been detached from the brigade on November 23 to guard fords over the Duck River at Centreville and Williamsport. In their place Strickland had been given command of the

---

[69] *OR* 45, pt. 1, 769-770; Posegate, *NT*, Feb. 28, 1889.
[70] *OR* 45, pt. 1, p. 770; Schofield, *Forty-Six Years In The Army*, p. 173.
[71] *OR* 45, pt. 1, p. 342.

44th Missouri and 183rd Ohio, both of which remained behind at Spring Hill to help protect the rear of the wagon train.[72]

With Ruger's men in position, Schofield turned to the next order of business. He instructed several members of his staff, headed up by chief engineer Capt. William J. Twining, to ride at a full gallop up the turnpike and not stop until they reached Franklin. Schofield told Twining that once there, he was to immediately telegraph Thomas with the latest information. Twining and his small band of comrades quickly rode off into the darkness and Schofield listened for several minutes until the "clatter of hoofs" could no longer be heard, replaced instead by the dull whistle of the cold wind. Comfortable that at least the immediate road to Franklin was open, Schofield turned his horse south and with his escort in tow, headed back toward Spring Hill. There remained much to do.[73]

Meanwhile, A. P. Stewart was leading his 8,000-man corps north along the Davis Ford Road with assistance from the guide Hood had appointed. In a letter written to J. P. Young in April 1895, Stewart provided significant detail about the events that transpired in the darkness east of Spring Hill. Again Stewart stuck resolutely to his story. The letter to Young was practically the same version as the one Stewart submitted in his official report some thirty years earlier. The letter, in part, read:

> I rode somewhat in advance of the troops, having the guide with me. At a place where the road on which we were moving appeared to curve to the left - now some time after dark - there was a high gate on the right-hand side of the road. The guide said there used to be a road turning off from the one on which we were moving, through that gate, which was the road we wished to find. I inquired if it would take us to the pike beyond Spring Hill. He said it

---

[72] *OR* 45, pt. 1, p. 370, 379, 385, 389, 999; Cox, *Battle of Franklin*, p. 54. Although the 183rd Ohio would remain permanently with the Third Brigade, Second Division, Twenty-Third Corps, the 44th Missouri was a temporary assignment only. Three days after Franklin the 44th Missouri was attached to the Sixteenth Corps.

[73] *OR* 45, pt. 1, p. 342; Schofield, *Forty-Six Years In The Army*, p. 174; Henry Stone, "Repelling Hood's Invasion of Tennessee," *Battles & Leaders of the Civil War*, 4, p. 448.

would, about a mile beyond, near the tollgate. 'Then,' said I, 'that is the road we want.' We rode through the gateway, the head of the column following, and soon passed a house on our left, where someone informed me General Forrest was. I dismounted and went into the house to get such information as Forrest could give me. He said the enemy had left the direct road from Spring Hill to Franklin and taken the Carter's Creek Pike. I think it was just as I was mounting my horse to go on with the guide that the staff officer (whom I did not know) came up and said we were going wrong - on the wrong road - and that General Hood had sent him to show me my position. I inquired when he saw General Hood, and said that, according to the instructions I had received, we were going exactly right. He said he had just come from General Hood. After some further parleying, I concluded (in view of the fact, as General Forrest informed me, that the enemy had abandoned the direct road and taken the Carter's Creek Pike) that General Hood had changed his mind after I left him as to what he wished me to do. So we turned back with this officer to the road we had left and followed it toward Spring Hill (as I supposed) until we came to the line of troops crossing the road, and here I saw General Brown. I was then informed that I was to march on and form on the right and in extension of Cheatham's troops. This was so directly the reverse of what Hood himself had told me he wished - 'Put your right across the road beyond Spring Hill, your left extending down this way' (where I saw him soon after crossing the creek); 'I do not wish you to march your whole corps up to the right; it is too far for the men' - that I felt sure a mistake had been made. So I said to my staff officers: 'Bivouac the men here and I will go to see General Hood and find out what he wishes us to do.'[74]

---

[74] Young, *CV* 16, p. 39; *OR* 45, pt. 1, p. 712-713. It seems that Stewart, after reaching the point where the Davis Ford Road ended and split into two lesser traveled roads, moved a short distance up Old Settlers' Road before turning back south. When again at the split, Stewart moved up an unnamed country road that meandered between Rally Hill Pike and Old Settlers'. This road led past the Peters House and allowed Stewart to pass behind Brown and then beyond Brown's right flank. Stewart believed, based on his talk with Brown, that by connecting with Brown's right he would be unable to extend across the pike. Stewart said Brown's position "was oblique to the pike..." How this error was made in unclear, but it only added to the confusion, especially for later writers.

Gen. Edward Walthall, one of Stewart's division commanders, recalled that it was "10 or 11 o'clock" before the men were ordered into bivouac. Walthall's Division was second in line during the march from Columbia and at Spring Hill it halted "to the right of and near the Franklin pike about a mile above Spring Hill." Gen. W. W. Loring's Division had been the vanguard of Stewart's Corps during the day and according to John S. Collins, an officer on Brig. Gen. John Adams' staff, Loring's troops went into bivouac along "a little dry cobblestone brook..." Collins was obviously referring to a tributary of McCutcheon's Creek which meandered north of the Mount Carmel Road. Even Brown said "Stewart's corps...went into bivouac on the stream in rear of my right..." Specifically, Brown may have been referring to the trailing division of Stewart's Corps, that of Samuel French. French aligned his troops on Walthall's left, but because of where the head of the corps halted some of his men were apparently strung out behind John Brown's right flank.[75]

Most of A. P. Stewart's men had been in formation for nearly six hours, in addition to the long and forced march from Columbia. They were tired, cold, and hungry. Scores threw themselves on the ground and fell fast asleep, others remained awake to eat, smoke, brew coffee, and talk. But as the Confederates settled in and camp chatter began to fill the air, other unmistakable sounds drifted in from the west. The repetitive tread of marching feet, rumble of wagon wheels, and clattering of accouterments could be heard through the darkness. The Yankees were on the move.

It seems that while Stewart spoke with Brown, his corps continued to march northward. Beyond Brown's right there was no road on which to travel, so after moving beyond that point Stewart's men stumbled over unfamiliar terrain in the darkness. The path of a small tributary stream just east of McCutcheon's Creek was the best guide they had. The Confederates crossed the Mount Carmel Road,

---

[75] *OR* 45, pt. 1, p. 720; J. S. Collins, "W. W. Gist's Article Commended," *CV* 24, p. 89; Brown, Statement of, *SHSP* 9, p. 538; French, *Two Wars*, p. 291. Walthall said he followed Loring to Spring Hill and because French formed the advance of the march on November 30, standard military procedure would have had him at the rear on November 29.

passed no more than a few hundred yards in front of John Lane's extended left flank, and followed the stream north. Finally Stewart ordered his troops into bivouac and turned south to find Gen. Hood.

Much of the Spring Hill legend originated on the Confederate right flank, where confusion and inaction reigned in spades. At the center of the action, or lack thereof, was John Calvin Brown. Brown, a native Tennessean, was thirty-seven years old in the fall of 1864 and had been a successful pre-war attorney. He enlisted as a private, but was quickly promoted to colonel of the 3rd Tennessee Infantry. Brown was captured at Fort Donelson and after being exchanged six months later was elevated to brigadier general. For the next two years Brown served dutifully, participated in all of the army's major battles, was wounded four times, and emerged as a major general.[76]

After his division was stalled at Spring Hill by Col. Lane's troops, Brown allegedly received orders to advance regardless of the enemy threat. Yet Brown did not push forward because he claimed, "I received no further orders that evening or during the night to advance or change my position."[77]

Brown also spoke to several officers about his lack of orders on the night of November 29 and if anything, his story remained consistent. In a letter written to J. P. Young by James Chalmers after the war, the cavalry commander told of how he encountered Brown late in the day and asked why he was not assaulting the Yankee position. Chalmers said that Brown "very curtly" replied, "I have no orders." Chalmers was miffed by Brown's tone and replied in turn, "General, when I was circumstanced as you are at Shiloh, I attacked without orders." Brown then said, "I would prefer to wait for orders." Capt. James Dinkins, who rode up with Chalmers, was within earshot of this conversation and confirmed the same basic facts. Chalmers, seeing that Brown could not be moved, rode off into the night.[78]

Brown was also visited by a pair of officers from Brig. Gen. John C. Carter's staff. Carter commanded one of Brown's brigades and

---

[76] Faust, ed., *Historical Times Encyclopedia*, p. 83; Welsh, *Medical Histories of Confederate Generals*, p. 29. Brown was wounded at Fort Donelson, Perryville, Chickamauga, and Ezra Church prior to Franklin.

[77] *OR* 45, pt. 1, p. 736; Brown, Statement of, *SHSP* 9, p. 538.

[78] Young, *CV* 16, p. 34; Dinkins, *Personal Recollections*, p. 232.

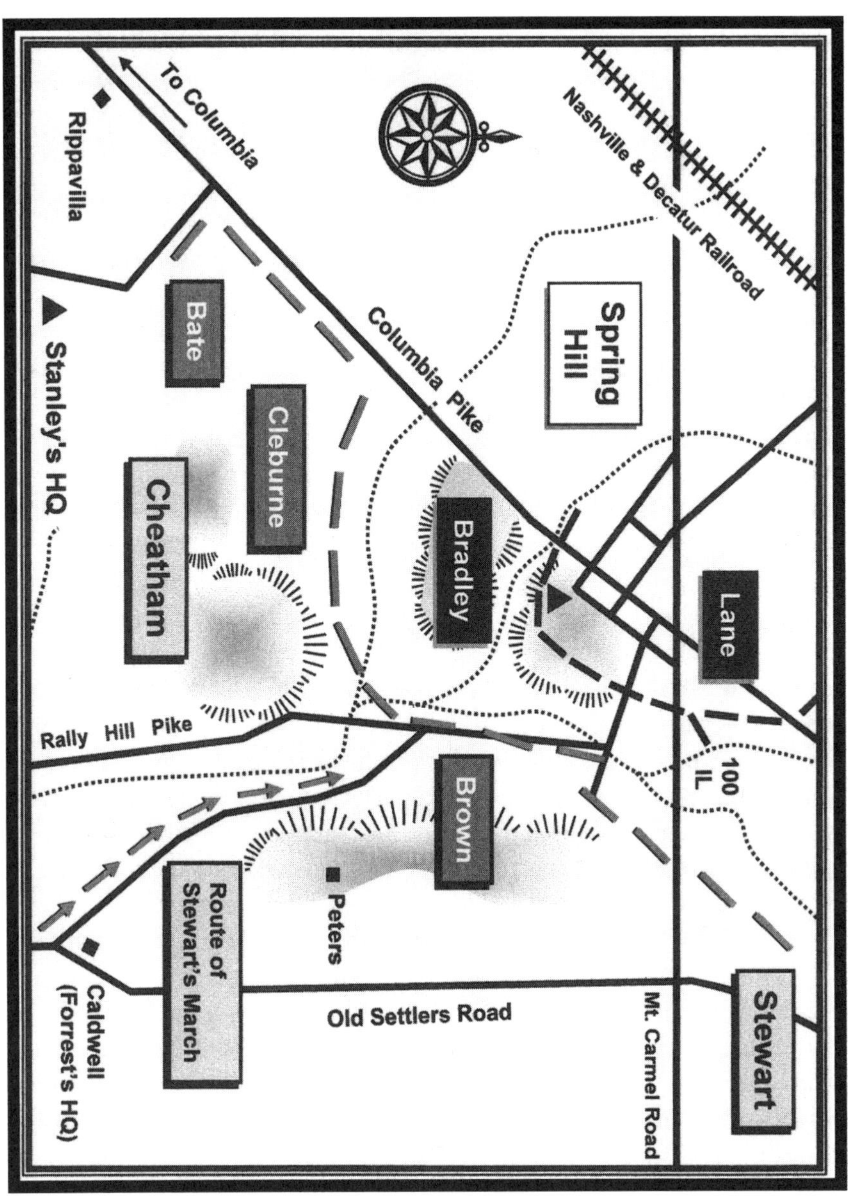

Positions of troops at Spring Hill after dark

the aides, Capt. H. M. Neely and Maj. John Ingram, had first asked Carter why no attack was being made. Carter, who was found sitting beneath a tree, had no information to offer. Riding "a little farther to the rear" Neely and Ingram met Brown and repeated the question. Brown said pointedly, "I don't know, I have no orders." Neely replied to Brown that "if he would take the responsibility of beginning the attack without orders he could safely count on a 'new feather in his cap,' as it would be a quick and easy matter to capture or destroy Schofield's Corps in its present condition." Brown responded similarly, saying, "No, I must wait for orders." This apparently set off Maj. Ingram, who had been drinking. In his disgust, Ingram said sarcastically to Brown, "General, if you will give me your escort company, I will drive that regiment away." Brown, in no mood for such disrespect, snapped at Ingram and told him he was under arrest.[79]

The frustration over the stalled attack was not limited to just a few. Col. Ellison Capers of the 24th South Carolina wrote that the troops "were in momentary expectation of moving" and "could not understand why we did not attack, and every man felt and I heard hundreds remark that for some cause we were losing a grand opportunity." Capers said that he and Gist, joined perhaps by Strahl, rode out on the right where they could hear the Federals "pulling down fences and tearing off plank from houses" as they tried to fortify their lines. The officers could also distinctly hear the enemy horses and wagons. Capers grew so frustrated with the inaction that he drew his revolver and emptied it "at the sound of voices in our front." Just over a month later Capers wrote, "This state of affairs was, and still is, inexplicable to me, and gave us a great disappointment."[80]

Col. Lane believed the Confederates allowed a superb opportunity to elude them. In a 1884 letter to Ellison Capers, Lane said "fewer than five hundred men were between your forces and our train..." Lane reiterated his point, stating that "in your front, covering at least a mile, there were fewer than five hundred men to resist your veterans." What is most interesting about Lane's letter is that he indicated the main Federal line, or at least the section his troops occupied at nightfall, was extremely vulnerable. He made no mention

---

[79] Young, *CV* 16, p. 35.

[80] Young, *CV* 16, p. 35; *OR* 45, pt. 1, p. 736.

of the troops he sent out to flank Brown, only alluding that the force on the main line would have been unable to withstand an attack.[81]

Is it possible that Lane had only 500 men directly opposed to Brown's Division? If so, he must have been referring to only a specific portion of his line, perhaps the segment fronting due east. How Lane had his men aligned at dark on November 29 has never before been accurately depicted. Even now reconstructing the formation of his brigade is difficult, but it is possible to do with reasonable accuracy. Of Lane's six regiments, it is known the 26th Ohio was not on the line east of Spring Hill. The 100th Illinois was not fronting due east, but rather had been positioned by Lane as a rough extension of his left to oppose Brown's advance. The 100th Illinois was probably facing toward the southeast. Also, according to Wagner, two of Lane's regiments were sent to the right to "act as a support" for Bradley's Brigade during its confrontation with Cleburne. It is a fact that Lane changed the "front forward" of at least a portion of his brigade. Lane reported this movement was made based on Wagner's orders. It can be assumed both men are referring to the same action and thus two of Lane's regiments changed front from facing east to facing predominantly southeast. One of these regiments had to have been the 97th Ohio, based upon Milton Barnes' report. The identity of the second is not known, but the only possibilities are the 28th Kentucky or 40th Indiana based on newly discovered evidence.[82]

Lane's line took on an almost snakelike appearance. With his right somewhat refused and his left jutting out in an easterly direction, Lane probably had only two regiments fronting due east. Thanks to a recently discovered letter the identity of one of these regiments is now known positively. Included with a February 1865 letter written by Pvt. James H. Watson of the 57th Indiana was a hand drawn map. Watson clearly indicated that the 57th Indiana was positioned south of the Mount Carmel Road with its right flank resting very near a "grave yard" (the present day Spring Hill Cemetery) and on what he called "east road." This road is today's McLemore Avenue, which is about 1,000 feet south of Duplex Road, formerly known as the Mount Carmel Road. Watson's sketched his unit holding a north to south position, facing

---

[81] Walter B. Capers, *The Soldier-Bishop Ellison Capers*, p. 112-113.

[82] *OR* 45, pt. 1, p. 230, 255, 265.

almost due east. His map does not indicate if the 57th Indiana stretched to the Mount Carmel Road, but it may have come close. Watson estimated the regiment's size to be 450. Pvt. Asbury Kerwood of the 57th Indiana said 280 recruits joined the regiment at Columbia and they numbered "more than one half" of the regiment. If the 57th Indiana had approximately 450-500 men in its ranks, it would have covered slightly more than half the ground between Mount Carmel Road and Pvt. Watson's "east road."[83]

According to Robert Hasty of the 73rd Illinois, the 28th Kentucky formed on the right of Hasty's regiment. Based on this the 28th Kentucky was located to the left of the 57th Indiana, where it would have filled up any remaining ground south of Mount Carmel Road. Hasty's account points to the 28th Kentucky being the second of Lane's regiments that remained fronting east. By eliminating all other possibilities, it appears the 40th Indiana was the other regiment sent with the 97th Ohio "to the right" to "enable Colonel Conrad...to reform his lines."[84]

Based on the approximate size of the 57th Indiana, it seems Lane's reference to only 500 men is invalid. However, there is no evidence to suggest the 28th Kentucky was any larger than the Indiana regiment, and unless it had recently received recruits it was likely smaller. Probably it was about the size of the 57th Indiana before that unit took in recruits, around 150-200 men. So while Lane's recollection of numbers may have been impacted by twenty years worth of time, his basic argument remained sound. Little stood between his force and Brown's men and only his fortuitous placement of the 100th Illinois halted the final Rebel advance.[85]

Although the Confederate offensive at Spring Hill had ground to a halt, there was some continuing troop movement. In the darkness William Bate finally completed the trying task of connecting his

---

[83] J. H. Watson to George Vail, Feb. 25, 1865, letter and map in possession of Gwynne Evans of Spring Hill, TN; Kerwood, *Annals of the Fifty-Seventh Indiana*, p. 289, 295.

[84] *OR* 45, pt. 1, p. 230; Hasty, Statement of, *A History of the Seventy-Third Regiment of Illinois Infantry Volunteers*, p. 438.

[85] J. H. Watson said the 57th Indiana numbered 150 men prior to adding the recruits.

division's right flank with Patrick Cleburne's left. Bate and his men stumbled "with delay and difficulty" over unfamiliar ground for almost three hours before finding their new position at almost 10 p.m. Additionally, Bate reported to Cheatham that his left flank was still vulnerable to an enemy attack and requested "force to protect it." As a precautionary measure, Bate refused his left "to confront any movement from that direction" and shortly thereafter Cheatham directed Johnson's Division of Lee's Corps, which had remained alone near Rutherford Creek following A. P. Stewart's departure, to move up and form on Bate's exposed flank. Bate, however, was still convinced that pulling his men away from the pike was folly and after posting skirmishers, "accompanied by a staff officer and one or more couriers," he rode to Hood's headquarters.[86]

As Bate began his trek, Capt. William Twining of Schofield's staff was finishing his. Galloping into Franklin, his horse nearly broken down, Twining made his way to the telegraph station. Once there he compiled a brief dispatch for Gen. Thomas in Nashville:

> Major-General Schofield directs me to inform you that the enemy's cavalry crossed Duck River in force at daylight this morning...and pushed at once for Spring Hill. Their cavalry reached that point at 4 p.m., and their infantry came in before dark and attacked General Stanley, who held the place with one division, very heavily. General Schofield's troops are pushing for Franklin as rapidly as possible. The general says he will not be able to get farther than Thompson's Station to-night, and possibly not farther than Spring Hill. He regards his situation as extremely perilous, and fears that he may be forced into a general battle to-morrow or lose his wagon train. General Wilson's cavalry have been pushed off toward the east, and do not connect with our infantry nor cover the pike. Thinking that the troops under General A. J. Smith had reached Nashville, General Schofield directed me to have them pushed down the Franklin pike to Spring Hill by daylight to-morrow. I left General Schofield two hours ago at Thompson's Station.[87]

At Oaklawn, following Hood's final meeting with Frank

---

[86] *OR* 45, pt. 1, p. 742; Cheatham, *SHSP* 9, p. 526; William Bate, Statement of, in Cheatham, *SHSP* 9, p. 541.

[87] *OR* 45, pt. 1, p. 1138.

Cheatham, dinner was served by the gracious Thompson family and soon thereafter everyone began to relax for the evening. By around 9 p.m. Hood, along with Governor Harris and Lt. Col. A. P. Mason, retired to the same comfortable downstairs room and set in motion perhaps the greatest prevailing myth about Spring Hill. Numerous authors, in their quest to explain Hood's lethargy, have advanced the claim that Hood likely consumed laudanum on November 29 to numb the pain in the stump of his leg. Because this claim has been repeatedly made, and is promoted verbally on a regular basis, it has become accepted as near fact. Yet to the contrary, there is no evidence that Hood took any sort of drugs, or even alcohol, at Spring Hill. In fact there is scant evidence that Hood's leg, or what remained of it, was causing him any serious difficulties. He was surely tired, probably sore, and may have been in a surly mood, but not a single person who was with Hood that night mentioned anything that lends credence to claims of chemical abuse. Stories also prevail about heavy drinking at Oaklawn by general officers other than Hood, but these, including the only one traceable to a source, seem to be more myth than anything else. The truth is probably far less intriguing than claims of excess and abuse. What seems most likely is that Hood and his staff, weary of mind, exhausted in body, and confident the Federal army was still trapped, simply went to sleep.[88]

---

[88] Roth, *Blue & Gray*, Oct-Nov 1984, p. 22, 28; Smith, *History of Maury County*, p. 238. Roth refers to a story often mentioned in Middle Tennessee about Hood falling from his horse en route to Spring Hill. Even if true, and this author did not uncover any evidence to support it, it does not in any way prove that Hood took laudanum as Roth seems to believe. Also, the source for the alleged drinking at Oaklawn is John Gregory. Gregory was almost 80 years old when Frank Smith interviewed him 1907 and his memory may have been faulty or he was embellishing. In particular, his claim that Granbury and Cleburne were at Oaklawn and drinking "freely" is highly suspect if not an outright falsehood. From all available evidence neither general ever left the front that night and Cleburne was known not to drink. For additional laudanum and drug references, see Sword, *The Confederacy's Last Hurrah*, p. 136, McDonough and Connelly, *Five Tragic Hours*, p. 50, James McDonough, *Nashville: The Western Confederacy's Final Gamble*, p. 69-70 and Anne Bailey, *The Chessboard of War: Sherman and Hood in*

At about 11 o'clock, however, their slumber was broken by several hard knocks on the door to the room. A. P. Stewart had arrived. Stewart, in the company of Bedford Forrest, had made his way through the frosty night air to Oaklawn hoping for some clarification from Hood. What he was told was shocking.[89]

After waking his commander and giving him a few moments to prepare himself, Stewart asked Hood if he had sent the "officer of General Cheatham's staff to place me in position." Hood replied that he had sent the staff aide, whereupon Stewart asked if Hood had changed his mind regarding the objective of cutting the pike north of Spring Hill. Hood said his goal was still the same, but that Cheatham had asked for support on Brown's right flank. Stewart recalled, "I explained to him that in the uncertainty I was in I had directed the troops, who had been marching rapidly since daylight, and it was now 11 p.m., to be placed in bivouac, and had come to report. He remarked, in substance, that it was not material; to let the men rest; and directed me to move before daylight in the morning, taking the advance toward Franklin."[90]

There may have been quite a bit more to this, however, than Stewart related. Governor Harris remembered some obvious tension between Hood and Stewart. Even with the offensive stalled, the commanding general still desired possession of the pike and Stewart brought news that it remained open. Hood asked Stewart if he could not at the very least throw a brigade across the pike. When Old Straight mentioned that his men were tired and had been on the move all day Hood, according to Harris, cut Stewart off and turned to Forrest to ask for his assistance. Hood wanted to know if Forrest and his cavalry would be able to block the pike. Forrest was not optimistic. He told Hood that Buford and Chalmers were out of ammunition and only

---

the Autumn Campaigns of 1864, p. 87.

[89] Jordan & Pryor, *The Campaigns of General Forrest*, p. 622.

[90] *OR* 45, pt. 1, p. 713. According to a January 5, 2006 conversation with Jimmy Campbell, the current caretaker of Oaklawn, it is believed Hood and his staff occupied a downstairs room adjacent to a small porch on the east side of the house. This location would have prevented Hood from having to climb any stairs and would have given him easy outside access.

A. P. Stewart
(National Archives)

Jackson's Division, which had managed to capture some cartridges earlier in the day, might be able to offer some assistance. Harris said that Hood told Stewart to provide Forrest with ammunition. Forrest then left after saying he "would do the best he could in the emergency."[91]

Stewart's statement that an attack was not forthcoming is strengthened by an account made by one of his aides. When Stewart and Forrest rode to Oaklawn two members of Old Straight's staff made the trip as well. One of them was Lt. Bromfield L. Ridley, who after the war published a fine collection of accounts relating to the Army of Tennessee. The other was Lt. James R. Binford, who had been appointed to Stewart's staff just prior to the army crossing the Tennessee River. Binford said that he and Ridley waited outside the Thompson House while Stewart talked to Hood. When the meeting was complete and the men were riding back, Binford asked Stewart is there was going to be a battle. Stewart's reply was simple. He said, "Not that I know of, there are no orders for a fight."[92]

---

[91] Young, *CV* 16, p. 40; Robert Selph Henry, *Nathan Bedford Forrest: First With The Most*, p. 393; Jordan & Pryor, *The Campaigns of General Forrest*, p. 623; Brown-Harris conversation, Brown-Ewell Papers, TSLA.

[92] James R. Binford, *Recollections of the Fifteenth Regiment of Mississippi Infantry, CSA*, p. 100, unpublished manuscript in possession of the Chickamauga National Battlefield Park. Many thanks are due to Lee White for providing the author with a copy.

Hood's next visitor was Gen. Bate, who followed immediately on Forrest's heels. Bate said:

> On my arrival at his quarters I found General Hood in conference with General Forrest, consequently I waited some time for an interview. I informed the General of having, about dark, come near to, in line of battle, and commanded, with my skirmish line, the turnpike south of Spring Hill, and caused a cessation in the movements of wagons, horsemen, etc., which were passing; but I did not 'pass on to the turnpike and sweep toward Columbia' as you (General Hood) had directed me to do, because just at that time I received an order from my corps commander, General Cheatham, to halt and align the right of my division with the left of Cleburne's, which I declined to do until I received a second order to the same effect, and then I did so. General Hood replied in substance: 'It makes no difference now, or it is all right anyhow, for General Forrest, as you see, has just left and informed me that he holds the turnpike with a portion of his forces north of Spring Hill, and will stop the enemy if he tries to press toward Franklin, and so in the morning we will have a surrender without a fight.' He further said, in a congratulatory manner: 'We can sleep quiet tonight.' I said to the General I was glad to hear what he told me, and immediately left.[93]

These conversations are astounding when given even slight evaluation. Hood seems to have understood that Stewart had not secured possession of the Columbia Turnpike. Yet Hood did nothing to force the issue. Forrest then told him there was little he could do to achieve the same goal, but when talking to Bate only minutes later, Hood spoke as if Forrest had virtually given him a guarantee. One is left to wonder what Hood could possibly have been thinking, especially as he spoke with Bate. Additionally, why Hood never wrote of these late night meetings in either his official report or memoirs is disturbing. As a Hood biographer wrote, the general "obviously felt that all was not lost, and in so thinking he made a tragic mistake."[94]

---

[93] Bate, Statement of, *SHSP* 9, p. 541. Bate said Lt. Charles Rogan accompanied him to Hood's headquarters, and that Rogan was either witness to this conversation or Bate told Rogan about it immediately after leaving Hood's room.

[94] Dyer, *The Gallant Hood*, p. 287.

Shortly after 11 p.m. the leading units of Jacob Cox's Division began filling the Columbia Pike south of Spring Hill. What they saw as they moved north was both breathtaking and terrifying. As far to the right as could be seen there was an endless array of campfires flickering in the darkness. The imposing sight meant only one thing. The Rebels were present in great force and might attack at any moment. Levi Scofield, an engineer officer on Cox's staff, recalled how a colonel put his index finger to his lips and told everyone "not to speak above a whisper, and pointed to the camp-fires on the rolling slopes within sight of the road." Scofield also remembered he could "plainly see...the soldiers standing and moving about" and that "in the quiet of the night could hear their voices." William W. Gist, a fifteen year old private in the 26th Ohio, saw "the Confederates walking around their camp fires, and they seemed hardly more than half a mile away." John Shellenberger said that he "could see the glow on the sky made by the...bivouac fires of the enemy" and remembered that the "excessive physical fatigue combined with the intense mental strain" made the night "the most trying in more than three years of soldiering." Gen. Stanley said the march was like "treading upon the thin crust of a smoldering volcano" and that the Confederates could have poured "destruction into the flank of our retreating column." Capt. Bradford F. Thompson of the 112th Illinois related how two sergeants from the regiment found a member of the 4th Florida, Bate's Division, on the pike and "had him by the throat." The Rebel was told if he made "any noise or outcry it would cost him his life..."[95]

From the Rebel viewpoint, Capt. P. H. Coleman of the 1st Florida, also from Bate's Division, said "the conversation of the troops moving on the highway" could be heard as he monitored a section of the picket line. Coleman was not alone. Lt. Cuyler King of the 1st Battalion Georgia Sharpshooters, said he was "within a few hundred yards of the pike" and could hear the Yankees moving up the road. King thought it a "criminal mistake on the part of someone in authority for not getting possession of the pike." Patrick Cleburne could also

---

[95] Scofield, *The Retreat From Pulaski*, p. 21; Gist, *CV* 24, p. 13; Shellenberger, *CV* 36, p. 188; Stanley, *Personal Memoirs*, p. 204; B. F. Thompson, *History of the 112th Regiment of Illinois Volunteer Infantry in the Great War of the Rebellion 1862-1865*, p. 261.

hear the Federals and he sent a courier to Hood with a pointed message: "The enemy is passing in my front." There would be no response.[96]

By about midnight, Cox's Division had moved into Spring Hill, approximately the same time John Schofield returned from his foray to Thompson's Station. Cox's men were "massed by the roadside" and Schofield insisted they keep moving. In his memoirs Schofield wrote that since the road was open "there was no apparent reason for not continuing the march that night." He and Cox spoke for a short time at Gen. Stanley's headquarters before Cox was ordered to take the advance of the army and march immediately for Franklin. Not long after midnight, as Schofield turned to his next responsibility, Cox marched his ragged column out of Spring Hill.[97]

Barely had Cox's men started shuffling out of town before the head of Thomas Wood's Division began filing in at "about midnight..." Meanwhile, John Schofield and David Stanley were engaged in a serious and animated debate. In addition to the thousands of troops strung out along Columbia Pike, the issue of the immense wagon train required full attention. Concerned there was not enough time to move all 800 wagons out of town, Schofield suggested that they be burned. Stanley disagreed with such an idea and was determined "to make an effort to save the train." Based on this impassioned argument, Schofield agreed the wagons should be protected and after seeing Stanley off, he mounted his horse, and accompanied by a small staff, began the twelve mile ride to Franklin. Meanwhile, Stanley readied for the important work that lay ahead.[98]

Born on a farm in Ohio, David Sloane Stanley was thirty-six years old at the end of 1864. Anxious to make a life for himself in the military, Stanley was accepted at West Point and graduated from the academy in 1852, finishing ninth in the class of forty-three. He spent the pre-war years serving in the 2nd U. S. Dragoons at a variety of posts

---

[96] Wyeth, *That Devil Forrest*, p. 479; Russell K. Brown, *History of the First Battalion Georgia Sharpshooters, 1862-1865*, p. 135; Purdue, *Pat Cleburne*, p. 404.

[97] *OR* 45, pt. 1, p. 342, 404; Cox, *Battle of Franklin*, p. 34-35; Schofield, *Forty-Six Years In The Army*, p. 174. Stanley's headquarters was at the Martin Cheairs home, known today as Ferguson Hall.

[98] *OR* 45, pt. 1, p. 114-115, 123.

located across the expanding frontier. When war came Stanley turned down a commission in the Confederate army and remained steadfastly loyal to the United States. Stanley saw his first action at Wilson's Creek in 1861 and the following year, after being elevated to the rank of brigadier general, he fought at Island No. 10. He was also involved in some of the heaviest fighting at Corinth in October 1862. Shortly after Corinth, Stanley was made chief of cavalry in the Army of the Cumberland, a post he would hold for nearly a year. In this capacity he took numerous steps to improve the mounted wing of the army, an achievement for which he has rarely received due credit. Following his stint in the cavalry and a promotion to major general, Stanley returned to infantry command and led a division through the early stages of the Atlanta Campaign before moving up to command of the Fourth Corps in July 1864.[99]

At 1 a.m. the sounds of creaking wagon wheels and teams of straining horses could be heard throughout Spring Hill. The Federal supply train was on the move and it slowly began rolling out of town, preceded by Wood's Third Division. On the north side of Spring Hill, all Federal wagon traffic was forced to cross single file over a bridge spanning a small creek. Capt. John A. Beeman, supervisor of the ordnance train, was given special recognition for his "firmness and coolness" in keeping the road and bridge clear and preventing any panic. One mile north of town Wood's Division "formed parallel to the road and east of it" to protect "the movement of the trains out of Spring Hill..." Meanwhile, the remaining two brigades of Kimball's First Division, after passing "within 300 yards" of the enemy, tramped into Spring Hill around 1 a.m. Corp. Lewis W. Day, an Ohio soldier, was in one of those units and remembered how "to our continual surprise we

---

[99] Faust, ed., *Historical Times Encyclopedia*, p. 712. Stanley was exceedingly critical of the Twenty-Third Corps in his memoirs. Stanley wrote that the Fourth Corps was the only force that could be relied upon in battle and even criticized Jacob Cox and Thomas Ruger. The feud with Cox was one that dragged on for decades after the war. See Stanley, *Personal Memoirs*, p. 189-190.

were permitted to move on, and on, and on" without being molested by the Rebels. Once Gen. William Grose's and Col. Isaac M. Kirby's brigades successfully moved through town, Whitaker's Brigade was withdrawn from its position along the pike and it rejoined the division. Gen. Kimball was soon entirely clear of Spring Hill and his men proceeded "moved on as a convoy to the trains." This allowed the First Division to move at the front of the Fourth Corps en route to Franklin.[100]

At Thompson's Station, the lumbering column of men and material was joined by Thomas Ruger's ramshackle division of the Twenty-Third Corps and soon there were "men marching by the side of the wagons" and "in rear of the trains." By this time, Ruger had been rejoined by the 129th Indiana, which earlier had been left south of Spring Hill to provide flank protection for other units coming up from Columbia.[101]

Some Union troops still at Spring Hill had very pressing issues to deal with. The 36th Illinois had been involved in the afternoon fighting and among the wounded was Pvt. Michael Divine of Company E, who had been terribly injured by musket fire. In the midst of the clash, some of his comrades had carried him to the foot of a nearby tree and laid him down. Unfortunately, during the regiment's hasty withdrawal the young man had been left behind. After sundown his friends in camp heard something cutting through the darkness, a "wailing cry of distress" that all who knew him recognized as Pvt. Divine. Men in time of war often perform brave acts, but few are more heroic than going after a wounded friend or comrade, especially when

---

[100] *OR* 45, pt. 1, p. 114, 123, 177, 195, 342; Cox, *Battle of Franklin*, p. 35; Stanley, *Personal Memoirs*, p. 204; L. W. Day, *Story of the One Hundred and First Ohio Infantry: A Memorial Volume*, p. 286. Sgt. David W. Smith of the 120th Indiana said his regiment was again chosen to escort the wagon train and moved out with it "at dusk in the evening..." See *NT*, Nov. 20, 1890. However, ample evidence points to the wagons leaving Spring Hill later hour so Smith seems to be in error. Based on the 120th Indiana's position at Franklin it is obvious they were the advance regiment in Cox's column marching northward. However, even Cox stated the trains did not leave Spring Hill until after his division had moved on to Franklin.

[101] *OR* 45, pt. 1, p. 342, 385.

risking one's own life. Yet that is precisely what three members of the 36th Illinois did. Cpl. Silas F. Dyer, Sgt. Henry Hanness, and Sgt. Patrick Conner volunteered to retrieve the wounded private. Guided by his "agonizing moans" the three soldiers located Divine, picked him up, and carefully began the return trip. On their way to find him the trio had encountered no Rebel troops, but they were not so lucky going back. Out of the darkness a lone enemy picket suddenly appeared and for several seconds there was silence as all parties exchanged stares. It was a tense situation, broken only when Dyer finally worked up the nerve to move. He walked toward the Southerner and got so close he actually touched the enemy soldier. The Rebel made not a sound nor movement. It was clear to the Illinois soldiers that the picket had decided to allow their mission of mercy to pass unmolested. Quickly the three scampered back to their camp, carrying Divine as gently as possible, and only when long out of range did the Confederate finally fire his gun. That led in turn to a handful of "scattering shots" from other enemy troops. But the good deed was done and Michael Divine was returned to camp and placed in an ambulance. After a short time he succumbed to his wounds, but thanks to three friends and a stranger he did not do so alone.[102]

Other Federals were nearly left behind. Pvt. Tillman H. Stevens was a member of Company I, 124th Indiana, and his unit, along with four other companies, had been posted as pickets several miles south of Spring Hill earlier in the day. Stevens remembered hearing the sound of cannon fire echoing down from Spring Hill, but after dark it "gradually slackened, and finally ceased altogether." For several hours the Indianans waited to be withdrawn from their precarious location. The company only numbered thirty-five men and some of them began to wonder if they had been forgotten. Stevens said it was not until 10 p.m. before someone approached through the darkness and told them to move back to the pike and hurry on to Franklin. When the men got to the road "it was as silent as the grave."[103] Quickly they moved up the

---

[102] Bennett and Haigh, *History of the Thirty-Sixth Illinois*, p. 638-639. The proper spellings of the Illinois soldiers' names and their ranks courtesy of Historical Data Systems, Inc., American Civil War Research Database at www.civilwardata.com.

[103] T. H. Stevens, "The March to Franklin," *NT*, Mar. 19, 1885, p. 3.

pike, afraid of being surrounded at any moment. Stevens later gave a vivid description of the march:

> We passed through Spring Hill just before midnight. Just before coming into this town we came within plain view of Hood's army as they were in bivouac to our right, not more than half a mile. They had thousands of fires burning brightly, and we could see the soldiers standing or moving around the fires. It was a rare and grand spectacle to behold. We were....passing right through Hood's army. The view was grand, the feeling intense; but we kept to the middle of the road, and hustled along toward Franklin.[104]

Around the time Stevens and his comrades were moving through Spring Hill, John Bell Hood received his final visitor of the night. An enlisted man, who apparently fell behind the main body during the day, had discovered Yankee troops clogging the pike. Assuming this would be valuable information for those in command, he somehow made his way to the Thompson House and was escorted to Hood's room. There he informed Hood that upon approaching Spring Hill it was apparent the Yankees "were in great confusion" and the turnpike was choked with wagons, gun carriages, and troops. Hood responded by telling Lt. Col. Mason to prepare an order for Gen. Cheatham, telling him to attack the enemy moving along the pike with at least one regiment. He also instructed Mason to have the private taken to Cheatham so the soldier could tell his story to the general directly. Hood then laid back down and fell asleep for the third time.[105]

Matters only grew more puzzling and bizarre. Cheatham said he received Hood's order via Mason "to fire upon straggling troops passing along the pike in front of my left" and immediately dispatched Maj. Bostick to find Edward Johnson and tell him to "take a brigade, or, if necessary, his whole division, and go on to the pike and cut off anything that might be passing." Cheatham said that Bostick told him Johnson complained bitterly about being "loaned out" and wanted to know why Cheatham had not ordered one of his own divisions to perform the

---

[104] Tillman H. Stevens, "'Other Side' in Battle of Franklin," *CV* 11, p. 165.

[105] Bromfield L. Ridley, *Battles and Sketches of the Army of Tennessee*, p. 436; Brown-Harris conversation, Brown-Ewell Papers, TSLA.

task. Johnson, who had fought with Stonewall Jackson in the Shenandoah Valley and with Robert E. Lee during many of the Army of Northern Virginia's biggest battles, could be contentious even on his best days. Johnson "vehemently objected" to the order and said to Bostick he was unfamiliar with the ground and had no idea about directions. He added that moving soldiers "about in the dark" was dangerous and might result in friendly fire. Politely Bostick reminded Johnson he was only relaying Cheatham's order and the two finally agreed to ride toward the pike and see for themselves what was going happening. In the meantime, Johnson instructed several subordinates to ready the division.[106]

Col. W. H. Sims, commander of sharpshooters in Johnson's Division, recounted the late night activities:

> My command did not reach the encampment near Spring Hill till ten o'clock at night. On my arrival I saw the twinkling camp fires of our army reaching northward far up the pike, stretching, as I was then told, about four miles. Our place of bivouac being assigned to us, my command broke ranks and, being very tired, hastily sought their blankets for sleep. I had wrapped myself in my horse blanket, and was sinking into a much-needed slumber when I was aroused by the adjutant of our brigade with an order from General Sharp to get my troops immediately under arms, that our division (Johnson's) had orders to move perpendicularly upon the pike, and that General Cheatham had orders to sweep down the pike at right angles to us. Our division was soon under arms in line of battle and the guns loaded. We waited hour after hour for the order to come to charge the enemy, who we understood were retreating along the pike four hundred yards in front of us toward Franklin.[107]

As Johnson and Bostick trotted up to the Columbia Pike, they were met by an uneasy silence. The Federals seemed to have vanished. What neither man could have realized was at that moment they had just missed the trailing elements of Nathan Kimball's Division. The only Union troops remaining south of Spring Hill at this hour were the skirmishers Cox had left at Columbia, and they had barely taken up the

---

[106] Cheatham, *SHSP* 9, p. 526-527, 530; Field, *Bright Skies and Dark Shadows*, p. 218-219.
[107] Young, *CV* 16, p. 38.

northward march. Johnson and Bostick remained near the pike for a short time and listened for any enemy activity but heard nothing. Then they turned back and around 2 a.m. reported to Cheatham at his headquarters that "they found everything quiet and no one passing." Word was subsequently sent to Johnson's men that there was to be no advance and the troops "sunk to sleep on the ground where they stood."[108]

What makes this episode so puzzling is that on the morning of November 30, as the Rebel army marched toward Franklin, A. P. Mason admitted to Governor Harris he was so exhausted the previous night that the order called for by Hood was never sent to Cheatham.[109]

Where then did Cheatham get the idea to move on the pike if he did not receive the order? Mason obviously did not send it in writing because he said as much. The answer, however, may be simpler than many historians have previously thought. The barefoot private who went to Hood's room was surely escorted there by some member of the commanding general's staff. In addition, Harris said that Hood told Mason not only to issue an attack order, but to have the private sent to Cheatham "to tell his story." One has to assume that the private was not expected to find his way alone, but rather someone was to accompany him. Although Cheatham said the order he received from headquarters was hand-delivered by courier, it is not implausible that the same person who took the private to Hood's room understood the nature of Hood's order to Mason and delivered the message to Cheatham. Whether the private made the trip from Oaklawn to Cheatham's headquarters is incidental, although he may have gone along as Hood requested if only to add veracity to the situation. Such a theory may seem reaching, but it cannot be discounted because someone obviously gave Cheatham the order to move on the pike.[110]

In his official report, Hood wrote with great feeling about this brief chain of events:

> About 12 p.m., ascertaining that the enemy was moving in great

---

[108] Cheatham, *SHSP* 9, p. 527; Young, *CV* 16, p. 38.

[109] Ridley, *Battles and Sketches of the Army of Tennessee*, p. 437.

[110] Brown-Harris conversation, Brown-Ewell Papers, TSLA; Cheatham, *SHSP* 9, p. 527.

confusion, artillery, wagons, and troops intermixed, I sent instructions to General Cheatham to advance a heavy line of skirmishers against him and still further impede and confuse his march. This was not accomplished. The enemy continued to move along the road in hurry and confusion, within hearing nearly all night. Thus was lost a great opportunity of striking the enemy for which we had labored so long - the greatest this campaign had offered, and one of the greatest of the war.[111]

A Hood biographer, almost one hundred years later, wrote in conclusion:

> Certainly the situation that night called for a personal investigation by Hood to see that orders were being carried out, but it was not made. It is entirely possible that the state of his health made him loathe to leave the warmth of his bed. He had been ill with rheumatism at Florence, and nearly two weeks in the saddle in cold, wet weather had done nothing to help it. Too, it was generally known that long hours in the saddle irritated the stump of his leg and caused him great discomfort. But his health probably was not the only reason. Hood always left too much to his subordinates without giving them adequate supervision.[112]

As promised, Nathan Bedford Forrest did what he could to block the road north of Spring Hill. When Forrest returned to his headquarters at the Caldwell House, he met with Gen. Jackson and the two had a brief conversation. It was agreed that both brigades of Jackson's approximately 2,000-man division, Lawrence Ross' Texans and Frank Armstrong's Mississippians, were available for the job. Ross' command, numbering just under 700 and lingering around Thompson's Station since early afternoon, had already been involved in one engagement there. Around 2 a.m. they reined up east of the pike north of Thompson's Station near the Fitzgerald farm, some four miles from Spring Hill. Ross was aware that the pike was choked with men and wagons, as much by sound as by sight, and he ordered three regiments to dismount while instructing the 9th Texas to guard the brigade's horses. The troopers moved out on foot and slipped forward to within

---

[111] *OR* 45, pt. 1, p. 653.

[112] Dyer, *The Gallant Hood*, p. 288.

100 yards of the pike before bursting forth with a Rebel yell and pitching into the enemy. Causing what Ross termed "a perfect stampede" the Rebels captured thirty-nine wagons and chased off the terrified teamsters and guards who were not killed or captured. Rebel Lt. George "Gris" Griscom said, "The noise and confusion exceeded all I ever heard." Mention was even made of the "continuous uproar of musketry" being heard back at Spring Hill. The Texans were unable to commandeer all of the wagons so Ross ordered a handful of them to be set afire, bathing the immediate area in an eerie glow.[113]

If Armstrong and his men took part in this engagement their involvement was probably limited. Because the brigade had to move from Spring Hill to Thompson's Station, it likely was still a short distance away when the fighting broke out. Neither Armstrong nor Jackson ever filed an official report and Forrest said only that Jackson's command did the fighting. As for Ross, his tiny force held possession of the pike for about thirty minutes, but the Texans were in no position to hold off the large numbers of Federal infantry converging upon them. From the south, Ross began to feel pressure from elements of David Stanley's Corps and there was trouble to the north as well. Some troops who had previously passed were alerted to the chaos near Thompson's Station and doubled back, because Ross said he saw the enemy swooping in from that direction, too. A cavalrymen remembered simply that "the Yanks made it too hot for us." Quickly Ross ordered his men to retire, and for the remainder of the night the Texans "remained on the hills overlooking the pike until daylight, and saw the Yankee army in full retreat."[114]

When Stanley filed his official report he mentioned this episode:

---

[113] *OR* 45, pt. 1, p. 753, 770; P. B. Simmons, Letter of, *CV* 1, p. 163; Martha L. Crabb, *All Afire To Fight: The Untold Tale of the Civil War's Ninth Texas Cavalry*, p. 267; Jordan & Pryor, *The Campaigns of General Forrest*, p. 624; Wyeth, *That Devil Forrest*, p. 477-478.

[114] *OR* 45, pt. 1, p. 177, 753, 770; Simmons, *CV* 1, p. 163; Fisher, *They Rode With Forrest & Wheeler*, p. 155-156. Ross' quite detailed report gives no indication that he had support during the late night attack. Forrest claimed the assault took place at 11 o'clock, but he is mistaken. Ross said he did not even receive the order to attack until around midnight, and by the time he got into position it was surely close to 2 a.m.

My staff officers were busily employed hurrying up the teamsters, and everything promised well, when we were again thrown into despair by the report that the train was attacked north of Thompson's Station, and the whole train had stopped.

It was now 3 o'clock in the morning. General Kimball was directed to push on with the First Division and clear the road. General Wood's division, which had deployed in the night north of Spring Hill and facing the east, had covered the road, was directed to move on, keeping off the road and on the right flank of the train, and General Wagner's division, although wearied by the fighting of the day before, was detailed to bring up the rear. Before Kimball's division could reach the point at which the train was attacked, Major Steele, of my staff, had gotten up a squad of our stragglers and driven off the rebels making the attack; they had succeeded in burning about ten wagons. The trains moved on again, and at about 5 o'clock I had the satisfaction of seeing the last wagon pass the small bridge. The entire corps was on the road before daylight.[115]

Years after the war's conclusion Col. Henry Stone, a member of Thomas' staff, described the belief common among not only former Confederates, but Federal soldiers as well:

When night came, the danger increased rather than diminished. A single Confederate brigade, like Adams' or Cockrell's or Maney's, veterans since Shiloh, planted squarely across the pike, either north or south of Spring Hill, would have effectually prevented Schofield's retreat, and daylight would have found his whole force cut off from every avenue of escape by more than twice its numbers, to assault whom would have been madness, and to avoid whom would have been impossible.[116]

On the Southern side there was the following from Gen. Samuel

---

[115] *OR* 45, pt. 1, p. 115. Maj. John W. Steele won the Medal of Honor for his actions at Spring Hill. Information regarding Steele's medal courtesy the U. S. Army Center of Military History. Kimball said Col. Isaac Kirby's Brigade was involved in driving Ross away. See *OR* 45, pt. 1, p. 177. It is interesting to note that while Stanley and Kimball disagree about how Ross was removed from the pike, they both stated ten wagons were burned by the Rebels.

[116] Stone, *Battles & Leaders*, 4, p. 446.

French, published in his 1901 memoirs:

> The idea of a commanding general reaching his objective point, that required prompt and immediate action and skillful tactics, to turn away and go to bed surpasses the understanding. The truth is, Hood had been outgeneraled, and Stanley with the Federal troops got to Spring Hill before Hood did. What information Hood received of the enemy, when he reached the pike, if any, no one will ever know. Why did he not in person form his line of battle and attack the enemy at Spring Hill? Although we yielded the right of way, the enemy must have been a little nervous, because the slight firing done by Ross's men caused the enemy to abandon about thirty wagons, and I could not but observe what a number of desks containing official vouchers had been thrown from the wagons by the roadside. Had there been a cavalry force with artillery north of Spring Hill and near the pike to have shelled the road, there would no doubt have been a stampede and a wreck of wagons.[117]

Gen. Thomas Wood, barely a month after Spring Hill, spoke for countless others when he said, "The effect of a night attack on a column en route would have been, beyond doubt, most disastrous." Gen. Luther Bradley, in a letter composed three weeks after Spring Hill, said, "It was the most critical time I have ever seen. If only the enemy had shown his usual boldness, I think he would have beaten us disastrously." The passing of years did not alter similar opinions. Levi Scofield wrote, "The proximity of the two armies was such that it seems incredible there were not frequent clashes during the night, or even a general attack to break our line on the night march." Even David Stanley was convinced that the Federal army would have been in ruins if Hood "had taken possession of Schofield's line of retreat.." He wrote that "men will not fight well when their retreat is cut off..."[118]

The one man whose opinion differed with practically everyone else was, of course, Schofield. In his memoirs, *Forty-Six Years In The Army*, Schofield reflected rather casually on how if the Columbia Pike had been captured by Hood's men, the Federal troops would have

---

[117] French, *Two Wars*, p. 292.

[118] *OR* 45, pt. 1, p. 123; Sword, *The Confederacy's Last Hurrah*, p. 152; Scofield, *The Retreat From Pulaski*, p. 21; Stanley, *Personal Memoirs*, p. 203-204.

simply marched via a different route:

> If the enemy had got possession of a point on the pike, the column from Duck River would have taken the country road a short distance to the west of Spring Hill and Thompson's Station, and marched on to Franklin. The situation at Spring Hill in the night was not by any means a desperate one. Veteran troops are not so easily cut off in an open country.[119]

Whether Schofield was actually so calm and determined on November 29 is an open question, but Stanley said Schofield was ready to forfeit the entire wagon train in an effort to escape. There was apparently even some talk of surrendering the entire Federal army on Schofield's part. Furthermore, no one else on either side ever mentioned the road west of Spring Hill, presumably Carter's Creek Pike, as a legitimate avenue of escape. Schofield's comment about veteran troops is also misleading because many of the soldiers under his command were recruits. They were the very troops who could have been easily frightened and routed. Stanley claimed that until late on November 29 the commanding general was unsure of just about everything and said Schofield's aforementioned claims were "the merest bosh." All things being equal Schofield's version of events appears weak at best.[120]

The last Federal troops to reach Spring Hill were the 12th Kentucky and 16th Kentucky, both of which had been left behind by

---

[119] *OR* 45, pt. 1, p. 123; Schofield, *Forty-Six Years In The Army*, p. 216. Connelly in *Autumn of Glory*, p. 501-502, argued that the Federals were not as endangered as both sides indicated. Connelly claimed Schofield had three routes by which to escape had the Columbia Pike been blocked. He listed the roadbed of the Alabama Railroad west of Spring Hill, Carter's Creek Pike further west, and country roads still more to the west. Connelly seems to have based his opinion almost solely on Schofield's version. Stanley Horn, *Army of Tennessee*, p. 388-393, originally believed the Federals were in great danger at Spring Hill, but changed his mind before the release of Connelly's book. See Horn's "The Spring Hill Legend - A Reappraisal" in *CWTI*, April 1969, p. 20-32.

[120] *OR* 45, pt. 1, p. 114-115; Roth, *Blue & Gray*, Oct-Nov 1984, p. 36; Stanley, *Personal Memoirs*, p. 214.

Cox to support the skirmish line at Columbia. The Kentuckians, most of whom expected to be gobbled up by the Rebels, arrived at around 4 a.m. as what remained of Schofield's army was gearing up for the march to Franklin.[121]

West of town, A. P. Cutting's railroad train and the second locomotive that had so ingloriously left its cars to the mercy of the enemy remained on the tracks at the station. Because Lawrence Ross' cavalry had burned the rail bridge north of Spring Hill, they were unable to leave. To prevent the carloads of military goods and ammunition, along with the baggage of the 44th Missouri and 183rd Ohio, from falling into the hands of the enemy, Schofield and Stanley decided earlier to disable the engines and burn the cars. Around 5 a.m. Cutting was told to do exactly that.[122]

At the same time, while Stanley saw to it that the last supply wagon crossed the bridge north of town, Col. Emerson Opdycke's Brigade of Wagner's Division, the only United States troops remaining in Spring Hill, received new orders. Opdycke's men were designated as the army's new rear guard and the men quickly formed into column. Among the first troops to arrive, they were the last to leave. Opdycke knew that serving as the rear guard was replete with peril, so he got his troops on the road and out of Spring Hill promptly, knowing that every minute of separation between his command and the Rebels would count. By the time the first streaks of twilight began to show shortly after 6 a.m. the Yankees were gone. Northwest of town smoke billowed up from the smoldering boxcars and the abandoned locomotives stood nearby. In Spring Hill, although the streets were littered with army debris, not a Union soldier was to be found. Sunrise was at 6:39 a.m. and the Confederate troops who awoke first must have been struck by the ominous silence. It was not to last long. A storm was already brewing.[123]

---

[121] Thomas E. Milchrist, "Reflections of a Subaltern on the Hood-Thomas Campaign in Tennessee," *MOLLUS*, Illinois, 4, p. 459.

[122] Cutting, *NT*, Mar. 22, 1894; A. J. Furnas, "Racing With Hood: A Lively Time in Getting Back to Nashville," *NT*, May 28, 1908, p. 7.

[123] *OR* 45, pt. 1, p. 115, 239. Sunrise time obtained from the U. S. Naval Observatory and provided specifically for Spring Hill for November 30, 1864.

So the Union army had escaped from Spring Hill and, it seemed, the very jaws of defeat. Exhausted, hungry, and cold the blue-clad troops stumbled toward Franklin, shaking their heads at how they had managed to slip past the enemy. What no one in the miles long column could have imagined was what lay ahead. Spring Hill had been just the beginning.

5

The Legend and Legacy of Spring Hill

Among the most pressing and unanswered questions about Spring Hill is why did John Brown not attack? Even if Frank Cheatham did not give Brown orders to refuse his right flank and attack why would Brown, a seasoned veteran of so many battles and campaigns, halt in the face of the enemy? What held Brown back following Gist's arrival? The simple answer is that Cheatham never got back to Brown to issue the second order of attack as Cheatham claimed he did. This is a definite possibility because it does appear that Cheatham was intercepted while returning from the left-center of his line. Perhaps Cheatham then rode directly to John Bell Hood's headquarters without speaking to Brown. Such a scenario boils down to Brown taking matters into his own hands and not advancing without further orders from his corps commander. But this reflects badly on Brown because if it was not unduly obvious to him, it was to practically everyone around him, that an attack had a high chance for success. Brown should have been able to grasp, especially as an experienced divisional commander, that a grand opportunity had been presented to the Confederate forces. What led him to believe that he had absolutely no discretion on the field that night is unknown.

Brown claimed to have completed an official report covering both Spring Hill and Franklin, but said it was lost during the confusing final months of the war. Furthermore, he wrote sparingly about Spring Hill after the war. In fact, other than the letter written to Cheatham as Cheatham was preparing his response to Hood's version of events,

Brown issued nothing on the subject. Allegedly Brown did compose a paper focusing on Spring Hill at some point later in his life. For unknown reasons, however, Brown never published the statement and his family, following his death in 1889, refused to allow the work to become public. Presumably the paper was destroyed and what Brown wrote is pure speculation.[1]

Brown's performance at Spring Hill was the subject of debate for decades after the war. Whispered rumors of Brown's drinking may have made the rounds for years, but his status in the public eye only grew stronger, as evidenced by his election to the Tennessee governorship in 1870 and his reelection in 1872. But rumors die hard and years after his death they resurfaced. S. D. Lee wrote a letter to Col. Ellison Capers in 1902 in which he expounded on the long-lived story. According to Lee, the version he heard "virtually lays the fault at Spring Hill on one not suspected. He was drunk and it was not Cheatham either. John C. Brown, who commanded Cheatham's old Div. either lacked nerve on that day or was drunk (no doubt the latter). Young proves this conclusively in his M.S. - Cheatham to save his friend (B) bore all the odium and even laid fault on Hood. But he was not the one to blame." Lee became so convinced of the story's accuracy that he spoke about it the following year at a United Confederate Veteran's reunion, where he stated Brown was "too much intoxicated to attend to his duties."[2]

This story was even picked up by Maj. James Ratchford. In his memoirs the former staff officer said Brown "was drunk" and that the general had been presented with a number of liquor bottles during the march up from Columbia. Ratchford said Brown had "partaken too freely that day." In fairness to Brown, however, there is no more

---

[1] Brown, Statement of, *SHSP* 9, p. 536; Young, *CV* 16, p. 36. A brief report authored by Brown appeared in *Confederate Military History*, 8, p. 156-158, but it appears to be a post-war composition. Likely it is a continuation of the same report, or statement, that Brown made to Cheatham in 1881 for publication in Cheatham's article. See Cheatham, *SHSP* 9, p. 537-539.

[2] S. D. Lee to Ellison Capers, Nov. 12, 1902, Capers Papers, SHC; Faust, ed., *Historical Times Encyclopedia*, p. 83; Losson, *Tennessee's Forgotten Warriors*, p. 210.

evidence to substantiate this charge than there is of Hood's alleged drug use. However, the story of Brown's drinking remains one of the more dogged Spring Hill rumors.[3]

Apparently even Hood heard the rumors of excessive drinking at Spring Hill. In an April 1879 letter to S. D. Lee, composed just four months prior to his death, Hood wrote cryptically:

> ...I shall at an early day publish my book. And since the officers of the Lines are already much worried about the blunder of one of their numbers, who at the time of the occurrence had too much wine in his stomach.[4]

To whom Hood is referring cannot be known for sure, but likely it was Brown. The only other possibility for such a charge would be Cheatham. Why Hood did not mention a name is puzzling, but perhaps he did not wish to offer any specific information to Lee.[5]

Frank Cheatham's role also leaves unanswered questions. After about 7 p.m. Cheatham was seemingly absent from the scene until approximately midnight. Was he at his headquarters during that period of time? Likely he was because according to Cheatham the attack was suspended by Hood, so it would have been natural to retire for the evening. It is unlikely that Cheatham spent a portion of the evening at the nearby home of Mrs. Jessie Peters. Mrs. Peters was already famous for having carried on a relationship with Confederate Maj. Gen. Earl Van Dorn in the spring of 1863. Their association ultimately led to Mr. Peters shooting and killing Van Dorn. The Cheatham-Peters story, however, has no evidentiary support whatsoever.[6]

Could Cheatham have learned at some point that Brown was intoxicated, either directly or via a staff officer? This idea is interesting if only because it might explain why Joseph Cumming said it was Cheatham, not Hood, making an impassioned case for halting the offensive. Cheatham and Brown had grown close during the war and

---

[3] Sieburg and Hansen, ed., *Memoirs of a Confederate Staff Officer*, p. 61-62.

[4] John Bell Hood to S. D. Lee, Apr. 14, 1879, Lee Papers, SHC.

[5] It is impossible to decipher what Hood knew or had heard about this subject, especially as a result of his untimely death. It cannot be discounted, however, that Hood knew more than he ever divulged.

[6] Losson, *Tennessee's Forgotten Warriors*, p. 212.

Cheatham's natural inclination would have been to try and protect his friend and comrade in arms. Cheatham, reportedly drunk at Stones River, would not have wanted Brown exposed to the same criticism if it could be avoided. Even more importantly, if Brown had been drinking, Cheatham was not about to let him commit his division to battle in an impaired state.[7]

The allegations of drunkenness even extended to Cheatham. To this charge came two strong rebuttals, one from Joseph Vaulx and the other from James D. Porter, a former Cheatham staff member who later served as governor of Tennessee. Vaulx stated unequivocally that the charge "is false." Porter wrote that he was with Cheatham "the entire day from Columbia to Spring Hill" and not only was the general "not intoxicated" but "he did not taste nor see a drop of liquor of any kind."[8]

Among the most intriguing declarations about Spring Hill came from none other than former governor Isham Harris. At the conclusion of a long 1894 letter to Charles Quintard, Harris penned a remarkable three paragraphs:

> As to the Spring Hill matter I decline to discuss it, and I trust that you will pardon me for suggesting that the "War Records" have been published. It is true that they do not settle the question as to who was to blame, nor can you settle it, but my opinion is that in the character of book that I suppose you intend to write, it is much better to omit than to discuss the Spring Hill trouble.
>
> Gen Hood in his official report censures both Gen Cheatham and Gen Stewart and wrote letters to each exonerating them from all blame.
>
> I was there and know much, if not all that occurred, and yet, I cannot fix the responsibility upon any one officer. Let's not open an old sore, and cause it to bleed again.[9]

Harris probably knew as much as anyone about what happened at Spring Hill and he had no axe to grind with anyone. Painfully obvious is the fact that so many years later, Harris understood that Spring Hill remained a deeply embarrassing subject for many. What he

---

[7] Ibid., p. 89-91.

[8] Field, *Bright Skies and Dark Shadows*, p. 218.

[9] Isham G. Harris to Charles Quintard, Dec. 29, 1894, Charles T. Quintard Papers, Duke University Libraries, Duke University.

knew if anything will never be known.

John Bell Hood believed until his death that it was Cheatham who failed to do his duty at Spring Hill. Critical in his memoirs, the words from his official report also ring with disappointment: "Major-General Cheatham was ordered to attack the enemy at once vigorously and get possession of the pike, and, although these orders were frequently and earnestly repeated, he made but a feeble and partial attack, failing to reach the point indicated." Just a week after Spring Hill, Hood was so angered by what had happened that he telegraphed Secretary of War James A. Seddon withdrawing his earlier recommendation that Cheatham be promoted to lieutenant general. The following day Hood went so far as to ask Seddon for someone to replace Cheatham as corps commander. But by December 8 the situation had cooled, as evidenced by another wire Hood transmitted to Seddon. He reported that Cheatham had "made a failure...which will be a lesson to him." Hood concluded by saying it would be best if Cheatham remained in his position and asked Seddon to disregard the previous telegrams.[10]

On the morning of November 30, as the army moved toward Franklin, Harris told A. P. Mason it was imperative that Hood be told Cheatham had not received the late night orders at Spring Hill. It is unclear whether Mason ever did tell Hood, but Harris admitted that he later told Hood what had happened. Harris kept quiet until after Franklin, when Hood made a comment about Cheatham's performance at Spring Hill. From its nature, Harris suspected that Hood had not been told anything so the governor explained what had transpired at Oaklawn. According to Harris' recollection, Hood said Cheatham was owed an apology and one of some sort was made soon thereafter.[11]

---

[10] *OR* 45, pt. 1, p. 652; *OR* 45, pt. 2, p. 659, 665; Hood, *Advance & Retreat*, p. 286-288.

[11] Brown-Harris conversation, Brown-Ewell Papers, TSLA. There is a letter from Harris to Porter included in Cheatham's *SHSP* article that says Mason did speak to Hood about not passing the order on to Cheatham. However, as Harris' conversation with Campbell Brown occurred ten years earlier this author has chosen to use Harris recollection. It is not terribly relevant, however, because no date for the Mason-Hood conversation is mentioned in the 1877 letter.

Cheatham also had vivid memories of what happened. He claimed to have no idea that Hood was upset about Spring Hill until the morning of December 3 when a note was received from the commanding general. In it Hood said he did not hold Cheatham responsible for the inaction at Spring Hill. The following day Cheatham went to Hood's headquarters to talk about the reasons for any blame. Hood was very friendly and agreed that Cheatham was not responsible for the misfortune at Spring Hill. Cheatham said after that meeting the "subject was never alluded" by Hood or anyone else again.[12]

It is clear Frank Cheatham's recollected dates do not fit well with Hood's telegrams to Richmond, and unfortunately Harris did not specify or even suggest when he spoke with Hood. Cheatham's claim also conflicts with Gen. Daniel Reynolds, who met with Hood on December 4 in the company of other officers from Stewart's Corps, and said the commanding general "spoke of the failure to cut off the enemy at Spring Hill...& showed by his remarks that he had ordered some one to strike the enemy there..." Therefore it seems Cheatham did not correctly remember the date on which he talked with Hood. The only other possibility is that Hood sent the December 7 and 8 messages to James Seddon after having spoken to Cheatham. That seems improbable. Most likely Cheatham's memory failed him. But the two men did speak about Spring Hill at some point in early December and both, according to the available facts, left the meeting encouraged. In the conference, however, Hood may have been somewhat two-faced. Although Hood no longer wanted Cheatham removed from command, he never dropped the stigma of blame. Even a December 11 letter from Hood to Seddon stated that Cheatham had "frankly confessed the great error of which he was guilty, and attaches all blame to himself." His official report only further clarified his intent to hold Frank Cheatham responsible for Spring Hill. Even Isham Harris, who was friendly with Hood, thought this behavior was "strongly flavored with duplicity."[13]

---

[12] Cheatham, *SHSP* 9, p. 532-533.

[13] *OR* 45, pt. 1, p. 657; Brown-Harris conversation, Brown-Ewell Papers, TSLA; Daniel Reynolds Diary, p. 112, Daniel Harris Reynolds Papers, Special Collections, University of Arkansas Libraries (hereafter referred to as UAL).

As for A. P. Stewart, it is evident from Hood's own writing that the former Army of Tennessee commander held no ill will. In fact, when Old Straight amended his report on the Tennessee Campaign he included an April 9, 1865 letter written to him by Hood. It read:

> Before leaving for Texas I desire to say that I am sorry to know that some of your friends thought that I intended some slight reflection on your conduct at Spring Hill. You did all that I could say or claim that I would have done under similar circumstances myself. The great opportunity passed with daylight. Since I have been informed that your friends felt that my report led to uncertainty as to yourself and troops, I regret that I did not make myself more clear in my report by going into detail about the staff officer of General Cheatham. I only regret, General, that I did not have you with your corps in front on that day. I feel, and have felt, that Tennessee to-day would have been in our possession.[14]

Apparently, Hood also told Stewart verbally that he was not to blame for Spring Hill.[15] The same cannot be said for how Stewart felt about Hood. E. P. Alexander, the former chief of artillery in Gen. Lee's Army of Northern Virginia, published his wartime memoirs in 1907 and, in a brief section relating to Hood's Tennessee Campaign, wrote of a rumor that both Cheatham and Stewart were absent from their commands at some point on November 29. The book infuriated Stewart who in response wrote to the *Confederate Veteran* spelling out his explicit criticism regarding Gen. Hood:

> The truth is, the failure at Spring Hill was General Hood's own failure. He was at the front with the advanced troops, or could have been, and should have been; and if he gave "explicit orders for an immediate attack and occupation of the pike" and they were disobeyed, the remedy was entirely in his own hands. If it had been true that Cheatham and I disobeyed orders to make an immediate attack and absented ourselves from our commands that evening and Hood had overlooked such offenses, that would have demonstrated his incapacity for the chief command.[16]

---

[14] *OR* 45, pt. 1, p. 713.

[15] Ibid., p. 713.

[16] A. P. Stewart, "A Critical Narrative," *CV* 16, p. 463.

What Stewart neglected to mention in his article was that Alexander reached practically the same conclusion. Alexander wrote: "Undoubtedly, here Hood should have ridden to the front and led the troops into action himself." What came through loud and clear, however, was that Stewart refused to accept any responsibility for the fiasco at Spring Hill.[17]

The "mystery" at Spring Hill led to a great deal of finger-pointing. Although the one absolute answer will probably never be found, one thing is for certain. John Bell Hood was the commander of the army and upon his shoulders must fall the burden of ultimate responsibility. Hood crafted a solid plan, but after about 7 p.m. on November 29, after having been at the front almost all day, he retired to his headquarters and allowed events themselves to take control. Thomas Hay wrote, in words few authors have been able to duplicate, that Hood through "his own neglect or inability to attend to details, was responsible..." Exhaustion on Hood's part undoubtedly played a role that cannot be accurately measured. It is hard to believe that Hood would not have remained at the front, or at least returned to it, if his physical collapse had not been imminent.[18]

Hood said he would have ridden to the front had he believed for "one moment" that Cheatham was going to fail in his effort to bring on the decisive battle. Yet Hood did not do that very thing when made aware of the failure to occupy the turnpike late at night. In his memoirs, however, Hood admitted culpability when he wrote that he "failed utterly to bring on battle at Spring Hill..."[19] This simple statement is often forgotten or ignored by those in the anti-Hood cabal.

Frank Cheatham was also largely responsible for the failure at Spring Hill. Hay was unwilling to lay blame at Cheatham's feet, but Howell and Elizabeth Purdue felt strongly the opposite. It is hard to argue that Cheatham's use of his corps was grossly inadequate. Cleburne, Brown, and Bate seemed to be operating almost independent of one another and while Cheatham did make a genuine effort to get

---

[17] E. P. Alexander, *Military Memoirs of a Confederate*, p. 579.

[18] Hay, *Hood's Tennessee Campaign*, p. 101-102. Hay concluded that Hood's physical limitations could explain the failure to see that his orders were carried out.

[19] Hood, *Advance & Retreat*, p. 287.

them moving in concert, he did little to correct matters when the effort failed. In fact, once the attack stalled Cheatham did practically nothing to get it moving again.[20]

In a letter written by S. D. Lee to Regina Lilly Harrison, his future wife, on December 6, 1864, the general vented his disgust about what transpired at Spring Hill. His condemnation was aimed directly at Cheatham:

> And now...to relate to you one of the most disgraceful and lamentable occurrences of the war, one which in my opinion is unpardonable, and which will prevent our capturing Nashville....I will mention no names. The first Corps reached the turnpike and formed in line of battle near Spring Hill 800 yards from the road one hour before sunset. The Enemy commenced to withdraw from before Columbia about 3 pm and was passing Spring Hill just as our line was formed and the two Corps of the Enemy not exceeding 15,000 men...made their escape to Franklin during the night without being struck a blow. Such another chance will not be presented again during the war...Gen H. gave his Corps Commander 4 or 5 distinct orders to attack and it was not done - his excuse being he was outflanked on the right and did not wish to bring on a night attack - he was ordered also to cut & hold the pike - the opportunity was lost never to be got again - one good Brigade would have stampeded the Yankee Army as they were much alarmed.[21]

Cheatham's worst errors were in halting Cleburne without learning how close the Irishman was to capturing the turnpike, and calling Bate away from the road without ever determining why Bate put up opposition to such a move. At the very least, Cheatham should have been curious why Bate was arguing such an order. Instead he barked at Bate's aide to simply do what he had been told. As far as Brown is concerned, Cheatham committed a serious blunder, regardless of what condition or frame of mind Brown was in. If Brown was drunk, Cheatham should have relieved him. If Brown simply would not move, Cheatham should have done something about it. If Brown did not get the second order to attack, Cheatham should have ridden back to

---

[20] Hay, *Hood's Tennessee Campaign*, p. 101; Purdue, *Pat Cleburne*, p. 406-407.

[21] S. D. Lee to Lilly Harrison, Dec. 6, 1864, Harrison Papers, SHC.

Brown or dispatched a staff officer to investigate the delay. If necessary, Cheatham could have given Brown a third order of attack. In the end, Cheatham did none of these things and the attack never materialized. Cheatham's only defense was that Hood called off the attack, something Hood vehemently denied.

It is very possible that both truth and deception exist in what Cheatham and Hood wrote about Spring Hill. It must be remembered that staff officer Joseph Cumming said he saw Cheatham "remonstrating with Gen. Hood against a night attack..." This is no corroborating evidence to support Cumming, but when other established facts are considered, the real truth about Spring Hill may have been overlooked by all previous historians. Because it was dark when Cumming witnessed this alleged conversation, it is clear the fighting that involved Cleburne had already sputtered out. Presumably Cheatham was concerned not only about the darkness, but the enemy force on Brown's right flank, the overall confusion, and unfamiliarity with the ground. Even some soldiers in the ranks thought a night attack would have been "full of peril." Moreover, Spring Hill was Cheatham's first field action as a permanent corps commander. It was not a role he was far from experienced with, especially in the dark. Cheatham would have had a sound argument for not wanting to press the attack given the circumstances.[22]

Cheatham may have convinced Hood that continuing with the offensive could lead to disaster. Hood would have been obligated to listen to his corps commander, one of the most experienced soldiers on the field that night. Surely neither Hood nor Cheatham ever thought the Federals would march straight up the pike, literally under the noses of the Confederate soldiers and in the dark. Unhappy that his goal could not be achieved, but convinced Schofield could still be trapped in the morning, Hood may have reluctantly agreed with Cheatham.

If the two agreed in principle to halt the offensive until daylight, it does much to explain Hood's demeanor as he received one visitor

---

[22] Cumming, Recollections, p. 72, SHC; Hughes, Jr., ed., *Stephenson Memoir*, p. 280. At Chickamauga, Cheatham's Division was involved in a terrible night attack. One of his brigade commanders, Brig. Gen. Preston Smith, was killed during the attack and Cheatham likely had not forgotten the dangers of nighttime fighting.

after another throughout the evening. A. P. Stewart left Hood's headquarters without any knowledge of an attack and Hood spoke to William Bate only about the enemy surrendering at dawn. Both meetings speak of overconfidence and poor attention to detail on Hood's part, a problem that plagued Cheatham as well. At the very least, Stewart and Forrest should have been notified by Hood of the decision to stop the attack and Cheatham should have informed Bate. As it turned, nothing like that ever happened and the confusion only continued.[23]

If the decision to halt was made and agreed to by both Hood and Cheatham, it would have increased the likelihood that neither man could ever fully tell the truth about Spring Hill. Instead, they dealt in half truths and pointed the finger of responsibility at each other for the rest of their lives.

Beyond Hood and Cheatham, Spring Hill cast a lingering and damaging side effect upon the army. It was described by one man as "a shadow" that "chilled the new found feelings of confidence." The brimming optimism of the troops, felt from the moment they crossed into Tennessee, was dramatically subdued by the morning of November 30. Everyone down to the lowliest private felt the bitter disappointment that was Spring Hill. In years to come, as a way of trying to cope with what had happened, some came to believe that Providence had played its hand at Spring Hill. For them it seemed only God could have saved the Yankees.[24]

J. P. Young, at the conclusion of his exhaustive work on Spring Hill, wrote:

> It must be patent to the most casual observer from what has been narrated above that but for the failure of Hood's subordinates to act promptly at Spring Hill Stanley would have been crushed before nightfall, the wagon train and reserve artillery of the army captured, Schofield entrapped as he approached in the darkness with Ruger's Division, and the remaining divisions of Cox, Wood, and Kimball left at the mercy of Hood at daylight next morning.
>
> It was Providence, not strategy, which saved the Union army that

---

[23] Binford, *Recollections of the Fifteenth Mississippi*, p. 100; Bate, Statement of, *SHSP* 9, p. 541.

[24] Hughes, Jr., ed., *Stephenson Memoir*, p. 280; Dodd, *SHSP* 9, p. 521.

night, and a paralysis scarcely less effective than that which overtook the hosts of Sennacherib fell upon the Confederate army as darkness came on, under the shelter of which Schofield's army moved "rapidly and silently" by on their hurried retreat to Franklin.

Success here and the destruction of his antagonist would have placed Hood in a most exalted position among his people and his name high among the great masters of strategy in the war. The move was faultless; the success of it up to 4 pm startling. Triumph was within his grasp. But failing came, whatever the cause, where least to be expected among those splendid officers and men. General Schofield has been honored by the nation with the highest military office in the gift of the people. Hood, failing through no fault of his own, unless it was his failure to personally see that his orders were obeyed, is reckoned by the average reader of history as mediocre and inefficient. But beyond question General Stewart was right in this: Hood, being present on the field, should have given his orders in person, if necessary, and personally seen that they were obeyed. The fault was not with Cheatham. There is no evidence that he failed in any respect. But General Hood might have seen that no mistakes were made by any one.[25]

John Bell Hood was greatly affected by Spring Hill and accurately viewed the failure there as a tremendous loss. Yet his obsession with it became so great that he bordered on the accusatory and ultimately did little but damage his own reputation. An example of this is how Hood somehow concluded the soldiers of the Army of Tennessee were partially to blame for the failure at Spring Hill. Such an allegation was pure nonsense. In *Advance & Retreat* he wrote:

The best move in my career as a soldier, I was thus destined to behold come to naught. The discovery that the Army, after a forward march of one hundred and eight miles, was still, seemingly, unwilling to accept battle unless under the protection of breastworks, caused me to experience grave concern. In my inmost heart I questioned whether or not I would ever succeed in eradicating this evil. It seemed to me I had exhausted every means in the power of one man to remove this stumbling block to the Army of Tennessee. And I will here inquire, in vindication of its fair name, if any intelligent man of that Army supposes one moment that these same troops, one year previous, would,

---

[25] Young, *CV* 16, p. 41.

even without orders to attack, have allowed the enemy to pass them at Rocky-faced Ridge, as he did at Spring Hill.[26]

Only the first sentence of Hood's account holds any real truth. The men had done whatever had been asked of them and under Hood's command they had indeed charged breastworks. The dead and wounded Southern soldiers piled up in front of the Yankee works at Ezra Church outside of Atlanta were proof enough. Even at Peachtree Creek and during the battle for Atlanta on July 22, the Confederate troops assaulted temporary breastworks. Hood's words dripped with frustration over what might have been at Spring Hill, but the soldiers had nothing to do with the failure. It was the upper command structure of the Army of Tennessee that faltered at Spring Hill, resulting in a mind-boggling tactical paralysis. To think how close the Confederates were to the Columbia Pike and yet remained unable to form any sort of lodgement across the road is hard to fathom even today. There were men present who might well have made a difference, particularly Patrick Cleburne and Nathan Bedford Forrest, but they found themselves handcuffed.

It is interesting to compare Hood's memoirs with a letter he wrote to S. D. Lee on, of all days, November 29, 1865, exactly one year after Spring Hill. The letter does not read quite the same as *Advance & Retreat*, but the similar tone cannot be missed:

The war is over and the time has come for facts to take the place of falsehood. In my shattered condition I may before I die write my own memoirs of this great Struggle just ended. And I desire if you have no objections your military opinion as to the cause of failure at Jonesboro & at Spring Hill. I remember your criticism very well but wish it in written form from you. I have G. W. Smith's and yours will be of much importance to me & to posterity in getting at the facts. Your opinion will of course be worth more than one hundred...who were not in position to judge. If I could have had you in command at Jonesboro & Spring Hill I would have succeeded. I mean this for no idle talk. Tis all over now my dear General. And I expect to die more proud of my defense of Atlanta & my Tenn Campaign than all my career as a soldier - considering the small & dispirited capital I had to work with. Injustice has been

---

[26] Hood, *Advance & Retreat*, p. 290-291.

done me, but that is easy work for a mob when led by bad men. I have never feared but I would get justice, but expect it to be tardy.[27]

When studying Spring Hill one cannot overlook the impact made by the Federals. First there were the men who gallantly defended the town against Bedford Forrest and his troopers early in the day. Then there was George Wagner's Division. Wagner's men often fail to get the credit they deserve. Had it not been for his three tough and solidly veteran brigades, Forrest and Cleburne might well have taken Spring Hill or the pike south of town rather handily. As it was, Wagner's troops put up a defense so stiff that the Rebel offensive came unhinged, and when it did no one was able to get it back on track. Union officer Thomas Speed wrote proudly that even Pat Cleburne, Hood's "best division commander," was unable to fully dislodge Stanley's men.[28]

Among Wagner's brigade commanders, Chicago native Luther Bradley stands out among the Union heroes at Spring Hill. Although wounded and forced from the field, Bradley in no small terms helped to blunt the enemy's momentum. His successor, Joseph Conrad, rallied the men of Bradley's Brigade at a critical juncture. John Lane, elevated to brigade command just that morning, probably did as much as anyone. If Lane did not take the initiative to reposition some of his men before dark, John Brown would not have detected an enemy force threatening his right flank. As corps commander David Stanley was superb. The race to Spring Hill had been close, but the Federal troops had as much to do with the outcome as anything else. They delayed Hood when time was something he had little of.

Lastly, it is easy to forget that the chaos at Spring Hill resulted in significant casualties. Losses are not terribly precise, but both sides combined lost as many as 700 men. Perhaps 250 of that number were suffered by Cleburne's Division alone. In a letter written two weeks after Spring Hill, Capt. George Williams, a staff officer from Govan's

---

[27] Hood to Lee, Nov. 29, 1865, Lee Papers, SHC. By this time Hood was fully aware of how his leadership was being roundly criticized. Hood was genuinely proud of his accomplishments as commander and his anger toward those who saw otherwise is patently obvious.

[28] Speed, *MOLLUS*, Ohio, 3, p. 57.

Brigade, claimed the division lost "about 225" and said that Lowrey's Brigade had suffered the most. In addition to Cleburne's losses, Forrest's cavalry also counted a number of casualties and a handful were inflicted upon Bate's Division. The Federal losses, totaling perhaps as high as 400, were mostly from Wagner's gritty division, particularly Luther Bradley's Brigade.[29]

Spring Hill has earned a reputation as a place of lost opportunities, lucky escapes, and incredible stories. More accurately it is a place where good soldiers and brave men were killed and wounded. It was a place where, in the dying days of a long and bloody war, the struggle for right as both sides saw it continued with unabated ferocity. But Spring Hill only opened the door to something worse and far more tragic.

---

[29] Williams to Buck, Dec. 4, 1864, Buck Papers, MOC. Thomas Wood, who filed the official report for the Fourth Army Corps on January 10, 1865 because of an injury to David Stanley, reported that the Second Division commanded by Wagner suffered some 350 killed and wounded at Spring Hill. See *OR* 45, pt. 1, p. 123. Stanley filed his own report on February 25, 1865 and while no mention was made of the Second Division's total casualties, he wrote that Bradley's Brigade lost only 150 men killed, wounded, and missing. This is a serious error on Stanley's part because Bradley had filed his own report nearly three months earlier and reported his loss to be 198 killed, wounded, and missing. See *OR* 45, pt. 1, p. 114, 269. Wood's figure may be slightly high, but it a far more reasonable number. It should be noted that the Federal cavalry also suffered losses that are included in the total of 400 mentioned in this work. Unfortunately James Wilson did not report casualties by battle, but rather for the period of October 1864 through January 1865. See *OR* 45, pt. 1, p. 568. Confederate casualties are even more problematic. Stanley reported that a Rebel surgeon said the loss had been as much as 500 although as has been shown Stanley's figures are questionable. See *OR* 45, pt. 1, p. 114. No real casualty counts were ever made for the Confederate infantry and Forrest reported his losses for the entire month to be 269. See *OR* 45, pt. 1, p. 760. It is not unreasonable to think Forrest lost as many as 100 men at Spring Hill alone and the infantry suffered upwards of 250.

6

The Gathering Storm

During the cold, clear night of November 29 and into the early morning of November 30 the residents of Franklin, Tennessee slept quietly and peacefully, totally unaware of the cataclysm soon to explode in their midst. Franklin was a small town nestled in a bend of the Harpeth River and had a population of about 900 in 1864. While fully aware of the brutal war being waged along a thousand mile front, Franklin's citizens had largely been spared its horrors. This was due in part to a twist of fate. Because the Federals mostly controlled the Franklin area after Nashville's fall in early 1862, it had been spared from any large-scale action. The only engagement of significance, a sharp fight between Rebel cavalry and occupying Northern troops, occurred on April 10, 1863. Even so, Franklin was far from immune to the long reach of the war. Many of her sons, brothers, fathers, uncles, cousins, and nephews had volunteered to fight for the Confederacy in 1861 when war fever was sweeping the South. Among those units that pledged itself to service was Franklin's local militia which became known as Company D, 1st Tennessee Infantry.[1]

The passing months and years saw more young men leave Franklin as desperate efforts were made by the Confederate government to fill the gaping ranks of the armies and navies. But the war dragged on, relentless and with little good news for the South. Those who lived in Franklin during the war's fourth autumn, in a town sadly absent of young and middle-aged men, tried to remain hopeful during the most

---

[1] Jordan & Pryor, *The Campaigns of General Forrest*, p. 245-248; Stanley, *Personal Memoirs*, p. 131; Sword, *The Confederacy's Last Hurrah*, p. 165.

difficult of times. One of the few positives was that there had been mostly peace in Franklin. But the last day of November 1864, a Wednesday on the calendar, changed all of that forever. War came in blinding, vicious fashion and left behind widespread destruction and scenes of unimaginable, almost unspeakable, horror. The battle to be fought there ensured that Franklin, Tennessee would never again be the same.

Marching with his troops toward what he hoped was safety at Franklin, John Schofield joined the long column of men some distance from Spring Hill. After speaking to a handful of commanders, particularly Jacob Cox, he soon passed the head of the winding blue procession. Before sunup, around 4 or 5 a.m., Schofield rode into Franklin, which was quiet at the early hour. Overhead the stars twinkled in a moonless sky. Having already given Cox basic instructions to mass the lead division "on both sides of the turnpike" Schofield sought out Capt. Twining.[2]

When Cox arrived on the scene, he began filing his bedraggled troops to points east of Columbia Pike, very near a modest red brick home on the southern outskirts of town. Capt. Levi Scofield assisted in directing the soldiers to their positions and recalled that just before their arrival "everything was as still as a grave" and he had an opportunity "to ponder on what the following day would bring forth." Once in place the troops of Cox's Third Division began smoking, boiling coffee, and frying rations. Meanwhile Cox, per Schofield's instructions, watched carefully to ensure that the road remained clear so as to allow the wagons to pass to the rear.[3]

Schofield did not start the day with a plethora of good news. Capt. Twining, who had ridden ahead to telegraph Gen. Thomas late on November 29, handed the visibly exhausted Schofield a reply telegram just in from Nashville:

---

[2] Schofield, *Forty-Six Years In The Army*, p. 221; Cox, *Battle of Franklin*, p. 38.

[3] Scofield, *The Retreat From Pulaski*, p. 21; Cox, *Battle of Franklin*, p. 38.

> Your dispatch of 1 a.m. to-day is received. Please inform General Schofield that Major-General Smith's troops have just arrived at the levee and are still on boats, and that it is impossible for them to reach Franklin to-day. He must make strong efforts to cover his wagon train, protecting it against the enemy, and as well to reach Franklin with his command and get into position there. I will dispatch him further in a few hours.[4]

Schofield almost immediately replied to Thomas:

> Have just seen your dispatch to Captain Twining of 4 a.m. If Smith is not needed for the immediate defense of Nashville, I think he had better march for Franklin at once. He could at least cover my wagon train, if I have to fall back from here.[5]

Barely half an hour later, at 5:30 a.m., after talking with Twining for a short time, Schofield sent another wire to Thomas:

> I hope to get my troops and material safely across the Harpeth this morning. We have suffered no material loss so far. I shall try and get Wilson on my flank this morning. Forrest was all around us yesterday, but we brushed him away during the evening, and came through. Hood attacked us in front and flank, but did not hurt us.[6]

As soon as this last telegram was on its way, Schofield dispatched a message to James Wilson. He had just heard from his cavalry commander, who was now stationed two and a half miles east of Franklin near Triune. Schofield told Wilson he wanted his "immediate flank and rear" covered with at least a portion of the cavalry and concluded by saying that Wilson could find him north of the Harpeth if necessary.[7]

Confident as he may have sounded in his communique to Thomas, Schofield was confronted with serious problems. Not only was he unable to count on reinforcements from Nashville, but the

---

[4] *OR* 45, pt. 1, p. 1168.

[5] Ibid., p. 1168.

[6] Ibid., p. 1169.

[7] Ibid., p. 1177.

pontoons he had requested from Thomas were not yet at Franklin. At the time of the Civil War the town was located almost entirely south of the Harpeth and the road leading to Nashville crossed the river on the north edge of Franklin's town square. Schofield learned shortly after sending the 5:30 a.m. telegram that the wagon bridge spanning the rain-swollen river and at that location was destroyed. Without the pontoon boats to construct a makeshift bridge over which the army and wagons could cross, Schofield was forced to come up with an alternate plan. This he did quickly. He chose to essentially rebuild the wagon bridge and ordered the engineers to lay new "cross beams and stringers" and put down wooden planks. The Nashville & Decatur Railroad bridge was also available to the east and Schofield ordered it planked, thus providing two avenues over the Harpeth. The Federal commander knew, however, that such work was going to take time, not to mention the hours needed to get the wagons and men across once the engineers were finished. Faced with this reality Schofield decided to enhance and fortify the old breastworks south of town. Constructed by Union troops in early 1863, Schofield viewed the works as vital to his defensive scheme.[8]

The Confederate troops stretched out southeast of Spring Hill began to stir before the onset of twilight. The rank and file, after opening their bleary eyes, started by shaking the chill from their bodies. It had been a very cold night, with temperatures at or below freezing, and campfires that had burned out overnight were restarted and soon could be seen painting the clear and ever brightening sky with soft, rolling smoke. What food the Rebels had remaining in their haversacks was hastily cooked or in some cases eaten cold. Hardtack, a staple for both armies, was dug out and chewed heartily. Bacon, salted pork, and beans were not nearly as plentiful as they once had been and by this stage of the war acorns, ripened corn, and sorghum were regular menu items for the often hungry Southern soldier. Men with growling or aching stomachs are usually not choosy, and the average Confederate

---

[8] *OR* 45, pt. 1, p. 342; Schofield, *Forty-Six Years In The Army*, p. 177; Clark, *Opdycke Tigers*, p. 327-328.

soldier by late 1864 was happy to have food of any variety. Coffee, the kind that some said could float a lead weight, was quickly brewed and passed around and slowly the army awoke from its slumber. In little time the troops were moving about, talking and smoking, and readying themselves for what most expected to be another hectic and eventful day of grappling with the Yankees.[9]

Then came the rumor. It spread quickly and was soon confirmed by facts. The Yankees were gone, vanished it seemed. John Bell Hood awoke early and knew very quickly that things had not gone as planned. Hood and his staff readied themselves and left Oaklawn and rode about two miles to Rippavilla, a plantation home owned by Nathaniel Cheairs. Rippavilla, completed in the mid-1850's, stood just east of the turnpike and during the night a number of Confederates camped in the fields north of the house. It was there that William Bate had approached the road and nearly severed it before Cheatham called him back. By the time Hood got to Rippavilla the sun was already up and he was smoldering inside. Painfully obvious not only to him, but to everyone else, was that the entire Federal army had slipped away during the night. Hood issued a handful of brief orders directing the army to be prepared to move immediately. He then put together a list of senior officers to be called together for a breakfast conference at the Cheairs home. Staff officers knew the situation was dire and they left at once to track down the officers Hood wanted to see.

In the ranks there was growing anger and frustration. A soldier from the 27th Alabama remembered that he and his comrades were roused "before daylight" and were mortified to discover the enemy had escaped. He declared the Yankees had "walked right out of the trap..." Sam Watkins, a veteran in the 1st Tennessee wrote: "When we got to the turnpike near Spring Hill, lo! and behold; wonder of wonders! the whole Yankee army had passed during the night. The bird had flown." Mississippian Rhett Thomas said, "I have never seen more intense rage and profound disgust than was expressed by the weary, foot-sore, battle-torn Confederate soldiers when they discovered that their officers had allowed their prey to escape." Gen. Daniel Reynolds, a brigade commander in Edward Walthall's Division, concluded the November

---

[9] Frank Stovall Roberts, "Spring Hill-Franklin-Nashville, 1864," *CV* 27, p. 58.

29 entry of his diary with four simple words: "A great chance lost."[10]

Nathan Bedford Forrest was chomping at the bit. Although obliged to procure ammunition for Abraham Buford and James Chalmers from Walthall, Forrest had most of the Rebel cavalry in the saddle by daybreak. Forrest discovered very early that the Yankees had "passed unmolested on the main pike during the night" and it was clear every minute mattered. Probably he spoke to Hood about the need for an immediate pursuit. Quickly Chalmers' Division was sent galloping across Columbia Pike and then took off up Carter's Creek Pike to cover the army's left flank. Chalmers recalled that when he got to the Carter's Creek Pike it was obvious "no enemy had passed along it." Forrest also ordered Crossland's Kentucky Brigade from Buford's Division to move up the Lewisburg Pike and protect the right wing. Meanwhile, Forrest, with Buford's other brigade, advanced directly up the Columbia Pike toward Franklin. Soon Forrest linked up with Jackson's command, which was still posted near the smoldering wagons at Thompson's Station, and the combined forces pushed forward. Contact with the Yankees first occurred about two miles north of where Jackson had caused a ruckus during the night.[11]

Things quickly escalated and by 8 a.m. the Southern cavalrymen were engaged in a full-blown running skirmish with the rear elements of Col. Emerson Opdycke's beleaguered brigade. Opdycke had been given the use of two guns from Lt. Samuel Canby's Battery M, 4th U. S. Artillery and he put them to quick use. Up and over the gently rolling hills, dotted with small farms and the dying colors of autumn, the two forces sparred with one another. Lt. Adna Phelps of the 73rd Illinois remembered how the Rebels "kept popping away at us at every opportunity..." It was twelve miles from Spring Hill to Franklin and although there were few casualties, Forrest's and Opdycke's men put on a splendid display of maneuvering as they grappled with one another.

---

[10] Noel Crowson and John V. Brogden, ed., *Bloody Banners and Barefoot Boys: A History of the 27th Regiment, Alabama Infantry, C.S.A.*, p. 99; Watkins, *Co. Aytch*, p. 217; Rhett Thomas, Statement of, *History of the Seventy-Third Illinois*, p. 475; Reynolds Diary, p. 111, Special Collections, UAL.

[11] *OR* 45, Pt, 1, p. 753, 764; Dodd, *SHSP* 9, p. 522; Jordan & Pryor, *The Campaigns of General Forrest*, p. 624-625.

The Confederates would rush the Federals and attempt to spill over their flanks, only to have the Yankees put forth a stiff covering fire and pull back, holding the Rebels off long enough to form a new defensive line some distance further up the pike. The Confederates would advance again and start the process over again, bringing the clatter of small arms and artillery to a roar.[12]

Rebel cavalry had also been striking at the Federal column further up the road only a few miles south of Franklin. Around dawn the 111th Ohio and the detachment of the 24th Missouri, fortuitously supported by the 6th Ohio Light Artillery Battery, helped fend off an enemy charge aimed at a section of the wagon train. Only by chance had these particular units found themselves in close proximity to one another on the Columbia Pike. The Ohio battery had left Spring Hill at a very late hour and moved directly up the pike. On the other hand, the infantry had abandoned the road near Spring Hill and moved through the open fields west of it for several miles. It was only about an hour before the Rebels attacked that Lt. Col. Isaac Sherwood had moved his regiment and the attached Missourians back to the pike for the final leg to Franklin. Suddenly all three units found themselves fighting together. Lt. Aaron P. Baldwin, commanding the 6th Ohio Battery, remembered the cavalry "whooping and yelling and firing in every direction." After taking several rounds from Baldwin's Napoleons and a volley or two from the infantry the Southerners beat a hasty retreat. Yet the brief exchange caused such a commotion that Gen. Thomas Wood galloped up and asked Baldwin what had happened. When told about the Rebel attack, Wood offered his thanks and complimented Baldwin "on the spot..."[13]

At Rippavilla emotions were boiling over. Although it remains

---

[12] *OR* 45, pt. 1, p. 239, 338; Henry A. Castle, "Opdycke's Brigade at the Battle of Franklin," *MOLLUS*, Minnesota, 6, p. 391-392; Jordan & Pryor, *The Campaigns of General Forrest*, p. 624-625; Bennett and Haigh, *History of the Thirty-Sixth Illinois*, p. 644-645; Adna Phelps, Statement of, *History of the Seventy-Third Illinois*, p. 451; George Patten, Statement of, *History of the Seventy-Third Illinois*, p. 478.

[13] *OR* 45, pt. 1, p. 123-124, 334, 379, 387; Wilbur Hinman, *The Story of the Sherman Brigade*, p. 669-670; Sherwood, *Memories of the War*, p. 129-130.

unclear exactly who was present at the Cheairs home, it seems John Bell Hood was joined by Frank Cheatham and Nathan Bedford Forrest at the very least. A small number of staff officers may have also attended. Because S. D. Lee had yet to arrive from Columbia he was not present at the meeting. Conspicuous by their absences, however, were Pat Cleburne and A. P. Stewart, both of whom were in the vicinity but apparently not at Rippavilla. Regardless of who shared the breakfast table that morning, Hood wasted little time making his disappointment and anger evident at the "unseemly affair." He was fuming about what had happened, or not happened, during the night and Cheatham took the brunt of Hood's anger. Cheatham's reaction is unknown, but it is not hard to imagine that accusations and finger-pointing flew in both directions for a time. Hood's behavior was described as "a bursting forth of his frustration." At some point in the exchange Cleburne's name came up as blame was being passed around. Hood repeated his displeasure. After a short time the heated conference ended and the army began final preparations for the march to Franklin.[14]

As Cheatham and Stewart formed up, Henry Clayton's Division, the leading element of S. D. Lee's Corps, began to arrive at 9 a.m. Lee had left Columbia at 2:30 a.m. after determining Cox was fully withdrawn. Lee then marched his troops all night to reach Spring Hill as quickly as possible. Upon arriving, however, Lee learned there had been no decisive fight and the Yankees had escaped. When he found Hood the army commander put Johnson's Division back under Lee's direct control. He also told Lee to rest his troops for a short time

---

[14] *OR* 45, pt. 1, p. 687; David Nevin, *Sherman's March: Atlanta to the Sea*, Time-Life Books, p. 95; Horn, *Army of Tennessee*, p. 394; Connelly, *Autumn of Glory*, p. 502; Losson, *Tennessee's Forgotten Warriors*, p. 218. Information about the Rippavilla breakfast is sketchy at best. From a conversation had by the author with Bob Duncan, director of the Maury County Archives, on May 19, 2003 it is apparent that most of what is known has been passed down through the years verbally. Written details beyond those of Gen. Brown are essentially non-existent. Mrs. Cheairs was the source of information regarding the breakfast. She claimed the language used was not appropriate for a woman's ears. Clearly the breakfast was a unsettling event, one that focused around Hood's ire and caused other details to matter very little.

before continuing on to Franklin with the army's trains and most of the artillery. In the meantime Hood said the rest of the army, Stewart in the lead followed by Cheatham, would begin a rapid movement up the road to Franklin to see if Schofield could somehow be stopped.[15]

Not long after the march began John Brown spoke to Maj. Vaulx of Cheatham's staff. Brown said Hood was angry and "he is going to charge the blame of it on somebody." He told Vaulx that the commanding general was "wrathy as a rattlesnake this morning, striking at everything." Brown also said that Hood had spoken to him following the contentious breakfast meeting and given him a lecture on how to handle his troops. Hood said:

> General Brown, in the movement to-day I wish you to bear in mind this military principle: that when a pursuing army comes up with the retreating enemy he must be immediately attacked. If you have a brigade in front as advance guard, order its commander to attack as soon as he comes up with him. If you have a regiment in advance and it comes up with the enemy, give the colonel orders to attack him; if there is but a company in advance, and if it overtakes the entire Yankee army, order the captain to attack it forthwith; and if anything blocks the road in front of you to-day, don't stop a minute, but turn out into the fields or woods and move on to the front.[16]

Some time later Brown received a message from Cleburne asking if the two could meet. Brown said he allowed his troops to pass by on their way north and waited for Cleburne to arrive. When the Irishman rode up Brown could see that he was upset. Brown, in an 1881 letter to Cheatham, recalled the details of this trenchant meeting:

> When he came up we rode apart from the column through the fields,

---

[15] Stephen D. Lee, "Johnson's Division In The Battle Of Franklin," *Publications of the Mississippi Historical Society* (hereafter referred to as *MHS*), 7, p. 77; Lee to Harrison, Dec. 6, 1864, Harrison Papers, SHC; *OR* 45, pt. 1, p. 658, 687; Hood, *Advance & Retreat*, p. 292. Hood stated in his official report that Lee moved to Franklin with only two divisions, but he is in error on this point. Lee made it clear in his report, as well as his article in the *MHS*, that Johnson's Division was put back under his control on the morning of November 30.

[16] Young, *CV* 16, p. 36.

and he told me with much feeling that he had heard that the Commanding General was endeavoring to place upon him the responsibility of allowing the enemy to pass our position on the night previous. I replied to him that I had heard nothing on that subject, and that I hoped he was mistaken. He said: "No, I think not; my information comes through a very reliable channel," and said that he could not afford to rest under such an imputation, and that he should certainly have the matter investigated to the fullest extent, so soon as we were away from the immediate presence of the enemy. General Cleburne was quite angry, and evidently was deeply hurt, under the conviction that the Commander-in-Chief had censured him. I asked General Cleburne who was responsible for the escape of the enemy during the afternoon and night previous. In reply to the inquiry he indulged in some criticisms of a command occupying a position of the left, and concluded by saying that "of course the responsibility rests with the Commander-in-Chief, as he was upon the field during the afternoon and was fully advised during the night of the movement of the enemy." The conversation at this point was abruptly terminated by the arrival of orders for both of us from yourself or the Commanding General.[17]

Patrick Cleburne was an intensely proud man. Although he did not have a short temper, Cleburne had a well-defined opinion of right and wrong. What Cleburne heard on the morning of November 30 obviously angered him. It can be inferred that Cleburne received his information from Frank Cheatham regarding Hood's displeasure with the previous night's events. Cheatham likely told Cleburne that Hood was pointing accusatory fingers at many of the generals, but for a man like Cleburne personal criticism, regardless of who else had been implicated, burned deep. Cleburne knew he had done nothing wrong, yet Hood somehow thought him at least partially responsible for the missed opportunity. Patrick Cleburne was angry and felt as if his honor had been questioned. Duty would come first, but Cleburne was not about to let the charge go unheard.

War has a remarkable way of bringing out greatness in men. War makes heroes and the Civil War generated its fair share during its

---

[17] Brown, Statement of, *SHSP* 9, p. 538-539.

four tumultuous years. Men such as Ulysses S. Grant, Robert E. Lee, Thomas J. "Stonewall" Jackson, William T. Sherman, Nathan Bedford Forrest, and Philip Sheridan became icons as they battled like warriors across the panoramic stage of war. Others were less well-known but equally important. James Longstreet, Winfield Scott Hancock, Jeb Stuart, and George Henry Thomas, to name only a few, occupied supremely vital roles in the opposing armies. The men whom these officers led were an amazing mix of culture, education, religion, devotion, integrity, wealth, and even color. The United States on the eve of the Civil War, much as today, was a country with a high immigrant population. The 1840's and 1850's saw waves of new faces entering the United States and spreading to all corners of the country. In particular, countless thousands of German, Scandinavian, and Irish immigrants left their homes for a new start in America. Among these newcomers was the Irishman Patrick Ronayne Cleburne, a common though intelligent man who joined the Confederate cause and rose to take his place among the greatest field generals of the American Civil War.

Cleburne was born at Bride Park Cottage in County Cork, Ireland on March 16, 1828 to Joseph and Mary Anne Cleburne. Patrick was the third child and second son of a family possessing at least modest if not well-to-do privileges. Not only was Patrick's father a physician, but he was a Protestant, the minority group which ruled the country and largely controlled the mostly poor and often abused Catholics.[18]

Patrick's mother died in October 1829, but within a short time Dr. Cleburne was remarried to Isabella Stuart. From this union came four additional children, the last being born in 1841, Patrick's thirteenth year. Drastic changes, however, were soon to come for the Cleburne family and especially for young Patrick.[19]

Dr. Cleburne died at the age of fifty-one on November 27, 1843 and by 1844 Patrick was serving as an apprentice in nearby Mallow to Dr. Thomas H. Justice. Apparently Patrick had no great desire to pursue a future in medicine, but it was his father's wish, so the younger

---

[18] Purdue, *Pat Cleburne*, p. 5; Joslyn, ed., *A Meteor Shining Brightly*, p. 1; Symonds, *Stonewall of the West*, p. 10.

[19] Ibid., p. 5-8; Ibid., p. 2-4; Ibid., p. 13.

Cleburne set himself to work. In the fall of 1844 Patrick applied for admission to Apothecaries Hall in Dublin, but was rejected based on his academic record, specifically because of troubles with foreign languages and mathematics.[20]

Throughout 1845 Cleburne continued his studies under Dr. Justice. Then in early 1846 he attempted to again pass the entrance examination for apothecary school. This time, however, the result was too much for him to bear. He failed again and in a sudden, almost desperate move, Cleburne did not return to Mallow. He told his family none of this and for several days simply walked the streets of Dublin.[21]

After much thought, Cleburne made a decision on February 27, 1846 that forever changed his life. He left his family behind without so much as a note and enlisted in the British army, where he became a member of the 41st Foot Infantry. Little did he know, however, the trials that lay ahead. There was to be no glory, no fighting in far flung corners of the British Empire. His time was to be spent moving from post to post in Ireland. Additionally, army life in the British ranks during the 1840's was difficult at best and at times could be downright miserable. To make things worse, Ireland was being rocked by the great potato famine that had first appeared in late 1845. By late 1846, the second season of failed potato crops, the situation across the island nation was rapidly deteriorating. Scores of people were starving to death and the relationships between the Irish tenant farmers and the landlords and landowners were collapsing. Into this chaos was thrust the young soldier Patrick Cleburne who surely watched with much concern as his country practically splintered before his very eyes.[22]

By July 1847, the Cleburne family had yet to hear from Patrick. At Mullingar, completely by chance, he was spotted by Capt. Robert Pratt during a drill review. Amazingly, it was Pratt's father who had baptized Cleburne as a boy and Pratt later spoke to Cleburne about his long absence from home. Shortly thereafter Pratt informed Isabella and Patrick's siblings of his whereabouts.[23]

As time passed conditions in Ireland only worsened.

---

[20] Ibid., p. 8-9; Ibid., p. 7; Ibid., p. 16-18.

[21] Ibid., p. 9; Ibid., p. 10; Ibid., p. 21.

[22] Ibid., p. 9-10; Ibid., p. 9-12; Ibid., p. 19-21.

[23] Ibid., p. 10-11; Ibid., p. 17; Ibid., p. 21-22.

Throughout 1848 people literally died everywhere across the vast landscape, and by mid-1849 an estimated one million Irish had perished. It was during 1849 that talk of emigrating to America was first spoken of in the Cleburne family. Because of British tax and rent policy enacted during the Great Famine, families like the Cleburnes were suffering hardships never before experienced. Escape to the United States was for many the only idea that offered any real hope.[24]

With this in mind, Patrick Cleburne paid twenty pounds to gain his discharge from the army effective September 22, 1849. Very quickly arrangements were made for the four oldest Cleburne children to leave Ireland. In addition to Patrick, the others were William, Anne, and Joseph, all three his full-blooded siblings from his father's first marriage. Saying goodbye to his step-mother Isabella was most difficult for Patrick. Both loved each other dearly. It was a relationship that remained strong, and in the following years Isabella also traveled to America to find a new home. Little could she have known, as she hugged and kissed him, what lay ahead for her stepson.[25]

At Cobh Harbor on November 5, 1849 Patrick Cleburne bid farewell to his native Ireland, never to return. He and his two brothers and one sister, four of only six total cabin passengers, boarded the *Bridgetown* along with 258 steerage passengers and crew and set sail for a new life across the ocean. The United States had ended its first war with Great Britain only sixty-eight years earlier and the second one less than thirty-five years previous. The land to which Patrick was sailing, and the people who inhabited it, were nothing like he had ever seen. They held the keys to promise and problems beyond imagination. They would shape his destiny along with millions of his fellow countrymen, some of whom went north and others who went south.[26]

On the southern edge of Franklin the Federal troops were in varying states of relaxation and many were fast asleep. Few had rested since dawn on November 28 and Pvt. Frederick Meinhart of the 65th

---

[24] Ibid., p. 11-13; Ibid., p. 18-22; Ibid., p. 23.

[25] Ibid., p. 14, 23; Ibid., p. 22-23; Ibid., p. 24.

[26] Ibid., p. 23; Ibid., p. 23; Ibid., p. 24.

Looking north along Columbia Pike toward the Carter House on left (U. S. Army Military History Institute)

Illinois recalled being "deathly exhausted..." Many availed themselves of the opportunity to sneak a few minutes of slumber. Included among those nearing collapse was Jacob Cox. He was as spent as his men and after instructing them to get some rest, he and his staff rode toward the red brick home of Fountain Branch Carter. The Carter dwelling, as Cox remembered it, "was on our left hand as we approached the town, and was partly hidden by a grove of trees a little way south of it." Upon arriving at the residence, Cox had the Carter family roused from their beds. After explaining to Mr. Carter and his eldest son Moscow, who was a paroled Confederate officer, that the house was to be used as a "temporary headquarters" Cox was offered the use of the family's front sitting room. As a vivid indication of the Federal officers' state of mind, their first order of business, after "loosening sword belts and pistol holsters," was to immediately lay down upon the carpeted hardwood floor and catch a few precious moments of much needed sleep. It was there, probably less than twenty or thirty minutes later, that a distressed John Schofield found Gen. Cox.[27]

---

[27] Cox, *Battle of Franklin*, p. 39; Robert W. Meinhard, *One Man's War: Frederick Meinhard 1862-1865*, p. 181.

Cox recalled that he had never before seen Schofield so "manifestly disturbed" and that the New York native was "pale and jaded..." In fact, when Schofield began to speak Cox said it was with "a deep earnestness of feeling he rarely showed." Clearly Schofield was under intense pressure.[28] Between the problems with the bridges, the fact that his tiny army was still strung out, and not knowing what Hood might try next, Schofield was understandably worried. Cox recalled with remarkable detail what Schofield told him early that fateful morning:

> General, the pontoons are not here, the county bridge is gone, and the ford is hardly passable. You must take command of the Twenty-third Corps, and put it in position here to hold Hood back at all hazards till we can get our trains over, and fight with the river in front of us. With Twining's help, I shall see what can be done to improve the means of crossing, for everything depends upon it. Let your artillery and trains go over at once. I will give you the batteries from the Fourth Corps, in place of yours, as they come in.[29]

As soon as Schofield finished giving instructions to Cox, which included ensuring that Thomas Wood's Division would be allowed to pass through the main line to take a position north of the river, the two officers parted company again. Schofield rode back to check on the bridges and Cox went to work readying the Federal defensive position.[30]

Jacob Dolson Cox was thirty-six years old at Franklin. Although born in Montreal, Canada while his father was working on a construction project, Cox grew up in Ohio. After graduating from Oberlin College in 1851, he held a job as superintendent of schools in Warren, Ohio before becoming a lawyer. Cox also became involved in politics and in 1858 was elected to serve in the Ohio Senate. There Cox's political leanings became apparent as he helped to develop a radical anti-slavery organization. Soon after war broke out, Cox was

---

[28] Cox, *Battle of Franklin*, p. 39.

[29] Ibid., p. 39.

[30] Schofield, *Forty-Six Years In The Army*, p. 175-176.

appointed to the rank of brigadier general, a promotion based far more on his public image than merit. Yet Jacob Cox, unlike other men similarly elevated to command, would not disappoint. He served under Maj. Gen. George B. McClellan during the war's opening months and in 1862 saw action with the Army of Potomac at South Mountain and Antietam. During much of 1863, Cox oversaw the Union District of Ohio, but 1864 saw him return to field command, where he led his division solidly during the Atlanta Campaign and into Tennessee. But at Franklin a whole new level of responsibility presented itself. Jacob Cox suddenly found himself in control of the primary field operations of a small army and upon his shoulders rested its fate. It was up to Cox to position the troops, strengthen the breastworks and, if necessary, fight to hold back the Rebels. Others may not have been up to the task, but Jacob Cox was ready and able. The day would be the pinnacle of his already solid military resume.[31]

Jacob D. Cox
(Library of Congress)

Already some slight work had been done to the existing fortifications, which were largely worn down. When Cox arrived back along the line where the three brigades of his division were stretched out, he ordered the men to begin strengthening them. Gen. James Reilly was placed in temporary command of the division and the troops quickly went to work. Cox's men were positioned east of Columbia Pike, occupying the ground from the road to the Harpeth River. Col. Israel N. Stiles, in temporary command of Col. Thomas Henderson's

---

[31] *OR* 45, pt. 1, p. 349; Faust, ed., *Historical Times Encyclopedia*, p. 188.

Brigade because of the latter's illness, formed up between the river and Lewisburg Pike, one of the three main roads entering Franklin from the south. His regiments were aligned with Col. Allen Prather's 120th Indiana posted closest to the river and the 63rd Indiana in the center of the brigade. The 63rd Indiana was commanded temporarily by Lt. Col. Daniel Morris because of Stiles' elevation to brigade command. On the right was Lt. Col. Jasper Packard's 128th Indiana. Packard said the right company of his regiment actually rested across Lewisburg Pike. Stiles chose Lt. Col. Emery S. Bond's 112th Illinois to occupy the reserve position. Positioned to Stiles' right was Col. John S. Casement's Brigade, which occupied the ground from Lewisburg Pike to a point just east of a large cotton gin. This gin belonged to the Carter family and would become one of the most recognizable features on the battlefield. Casement placed the 124th Indiana closest to Lewisburg Pike and Stiles' right flank. Absent from Col. John Orr's 124th Indiana was its Company C, which the previous day had been ordered to perform picket duty for Ruger's Second Division. Unfortunately, no one ever relieved the hapless company and it was gobbled up by the enemy. Next to Orr's Indianans came Lt. Col. W. Scott Stewart's 65th Illinois and Lt. Col. John W. Hammond's 65th Indiana formed the right of Casement's Brigade. Major David G. Bower's 5th Tennessee was placed in reserve. The brigade's remaining regiment, the 103rd Ohio, was ordered to the rear to serve as guard for the Twenty-Third Corps headquarters train and to assist with the ordnance trains.[32]

To Casement's right was Reilly's Brigade, which held the section of the line that ran in front of the Carter cotton gin and stretched to Columbia Pike. Only some of Reilly's men were on hand, however, when work on the line began. The 12th Kentucky and 16th Kentucky were absent. They had been among the last troops to leave the Duck River line at Columbia and were trailing at the rear of the army, still hours away from arriving.[33]

James William Reilly, a native of Akron, Ohio, was thirty-six years old at Franklin. Prior to the war Reilly had been an attorney and a state legislator, but he had no military experience. After enlisting in

---

[32] *OR* 45, pt. 1, p. 350, 428-429; Catharine Merrill, *The Soldier of Indiana in the War for the Union*, Vol. 2, p. 759; Cox, *Battle of Franklin*, p. 52-53

[33] *OR* 45, pt. 1, p. 411; Cox, *Battle of Franklin*, p. 52.

the United States Army in July 1862, Reilly was made a colonel and assigned to command of the newly organized 104th Ohio Infantry the following month. For almost a year, Reilly and his men served on garrison duty before fighting at Knoxville, Tennessee and then joining William Sherman for the campaign against Atlanta. Promoted to brigadier general in July 1864, Reilly had proven himself to be a solid and dependable soldier.[34]

Reilly posted Lt. Col. Edwin L. Hayes' 100th Ohio adjacent to the east side of Columbia Pike and Col. Oscar W. Sterl's 104th Ohio held the spot to the left, occupying the ground in front of the gin. A member of the 104th Ohio wrote that the brigade actually centered "around the old cotton gin." Into reserve were placed Capt. James W. Berry's 8th Tennessee, composed of loyal Union men from the eastern part of the Volunteer State, and Lt. Col. Daniel McCoy's 175th Ohio, a regiment of new recruits. Interestingly, the section of the main line occupied by Reilly's men made a sudden change of direction near the cotton gin. Because of where the Carter gin stood a marked salient was created in the breastworks just south of the building. There, 240 feet east of the pike, the line bent backwards sharply at about a forty-five degree angle and ran to a depth of 150 feet. Then approximately fifty feet from the turnpike the line straightened out again and met the road 260 feet south of the Carter House. This salient was to become like a magnet in the hours ahead, and those who lived through the day would never forget what they saw there.[35]

Cox finally had the leading infantry units in their designated locations on the eastern side of Columbia Pike, an first important step. Unable to place any artillery because he had to wait for the Fourth Corps, Cox instead planned where the batteries would be placed upon arrival. Meanwhile, the infantry's work had only begun. Orders were sent down the line instructing the men to have their arms "stacked in rear" and within a short time "intrenching tools" were distributed. Each regiment was directed to work on the ground directly in front of it and the men were organized into work details. Naturally there was a

---

[34] Faust, ed., *Historical Times Encyclopedia*, p. 623.

[35] *OR* 45, pt. 1, p. 350, 411; Cox, *Battle of Franklin*, p. 52; N. A. Pinney, *History of the 104th Regiment Ohio Volunteer Infantry From 1862 to 1865*, p. 59-60; McDonough and Connelly, *Five Tragic Hours*, p. 84.

Carter cotton gin and outbuilding
(U. S. Army Military History Institute)

chorus of grumbling and cursing at the idea of what seemed like senseless manual labor. But the complaining died away, replaced instead by a resonating wall of sound made by the swinging and thrusting of countless pickaxes and shovels. The rich, moist Tennessee dirt soon began moving in massive quantities. Saws and hammers added to the clamor as groups of men searched for additional protection to compliment the fast piling earth.[36]

Among the first local structures seized upon was the Carter cotton gin. The gin, some thirty-six feet square, had a solid wooden and weather-boarded frame supported by thick stone pillars. It possessed some eight feet of clearance between the poplar sills and the ground. According to Moscow Carter this allowed "plenty of head room for the horses, who made the power." The gin walls were comprised of heavy wooden planks, about three inches thick and some nine feet in length. The Federal troops wasted little time ripping much of the weatherboarding and many planks from the gin to further augment their breastworks. Additionally, the men got their hands on a number of wooden beams and poles that came largely from the gin screw press and other related equipment. These items and fence rails found encompassing the gin house property were put to use as head logs. The

[36] Cox, *Battle of Franklin*, p. 51.

men positioned them at the crest of the works, leaving just enough room beneath the log or rail through which to shoot. This would allow a man to fire and only be struck by the luckiest of shots. An Illinois soldier remembered that some of the head logs were laid across railroad ties that had been notched so the logs rested upon them securely. He thought about a "three-inch space" remained to shoot through.[37]

Moscow Carter also recalled that Cox's men tore down the lint shed that was attached to the gin house. This building stood about ten or twelve feet wide and was thirty-six feet long. The Midwestern boys made quick work of it and inserted the various pieces into the works wherever they saw fit. Carter even said the soldiers went so far as to grab the "seed cotton in the gin house" and also threw it into the breastworks.[38]

The Federal soldiers, working and straining by the thousands, also employed teams of horses and wagons to assist them in their efforts. It was a beautifully clear morning, the first decent weather in weeks, and many of the men shed their overcoats and rolled up their sleeves as they worked. Within the first hour or two the works southeast of the Carter House took on an impressive, almost foreboding appearance. They were beginning to look like the type of thing an opposing soldier, especially a veteran, knew could only spell trouble.

While their comrades to the west stripped down the cotton gin, Israel Stiles' men took advantage of a thick hedge of Osage orange growing along Lewisburg Pike and the Nashville & Decatur Railroad. For decades farmers had used hedges just like it as natural boundaries for cattle, horses, sheep, and other farm animals. They knew a fence line was not necessary if Osage orange, also known as bois d'arc, could be used instead. Early settlers had in fact learned to use Osage trees and hedges as natural boundaries from Native Americans.[39]

---

[37] *OR* 45, pt. 1, p. 419, 421; Smith, *History of Maury County*, Interview with Moscow Carter, p. 201-202; Ralsa C. Rice, *Yankee Tigers: Through the Civil War with the 125th Ohio*, p. 156; Meinhard, *One Man's War*, p. 183.

[38] Smith, *History of Maury County*, Interview with Moscow Carter, p. 201-202.

[39] George W. Huckins, "Hung Unto the Rations," *NT*, Sept 5, 1912, p. 7. Huckins said the Osage hedge was "some 20 or 30 feet high..."

The Federal troops at Franklin also viewed the Osage as a potential barrier, and Col. Stiles' men began chopping it apart to construct a crude but very effective abatis. They knew the Osage branches, which were thorny and nearly impossible to break or bend, would cause immense grief to anyone attempting to pass through them. Furiously the Indiana soldiers hacked at the dense and tangled hedge to further shore up their position. One Indiana soldier said, "We went out in front and cut and twisted an osage orange fence till it was about impossible to get thru it." There was so much Osage wood present that troops on the left of John Casement's Brigade also put their axes and hatchets to work and began placing it in front of their works. By mid-morning Stiles' Indiana regiments had an impressive abatis stretched along their front while Casement's men constructed a more impromptu obstruction. Additionally, some of the Osage hedge was left lining both the pike and the railroad. An Indiana officer said some of the boughs were even "piled in the road," apparently a reference to Lewisburg Pike. The same officer recalled that cellar blocks from a nearby burned house were also used in strengthening the breastworks. Combined with the wicked abatis maze, the glowering works made the Federal position appear nearly unbreakable. But the Rebels were nowhere in sight and few of the Yankees actually thought their hard work would be put to use.[40]

While the Union brigades closest to the Harpeth River dug in, Thomas Ruger's depleted division began arriving around 6:30 a.m. Ruger, born in Lima, New York in 1833, had graduated from West Point in 1854 and was a veteran of the Army of the Potomac. During the course of the war he had witnessed his fair share of hard fighting. Ruger led troops at Second Bull Run, Antietam, Chancellorsville, and commanded a division at Gettysburg before going to New York City to help suppress the draft riots that exploded there in the summer of 1863. Thereafter Ruger was transferred west where he participated in the

---

[40] Cox, *Battle of Franklin*, p. 126; Eli Newsom, "Fighting Hood's Army," *NT*, Nov. 8, 1923, p. 3; Park Marshall, *Reminiscence of the Battle of Franklin*, CHA; Merrill, *The Soldier of Indiana*, Vol. 2, p. 758-759. According to Cox the abatis in front of Stiles was more dense than in front of Casement. He said what lay in front of Casement "was more a show of obstruction to the enemy than a reality."

Atlanta Campaign.[41]

Thomas H. Ruger
(Library of Congress)

At Franklin, Ruger commanded only two brigades because Joseph Cooper's Brigade had been assigned on November 23 to guard the ford at Centreville, Tennessee on the Duck River. Moreover, of the two brigades remaining with him, Ruger had to deal with one, Col. Silas A. Strickland's, being a piecemeal outfit. Strickland, an attorney before the war who originally served in the 1st Nebraska Infantry, had transferred to the 50th Ohio Infantry in 1862 as a lieutenant colonel. Soon after joining the 50th Ohio, Strickland was promoted to colonel and elevated to brigade command. Prior to Franklin two of Strickland's regiments, the 91st Indiana and 123rd Indiana, had been shipped away to guard river fords, leaving the veteran 50th Ohio as the only original regiment left in the brigade. While at Columbia the 72nd Illinois was assigned to Strickland and several days later he was also given command of the 44th Missouri and 183rd Ohio, both of which were new units only recently organized. But the four regiments that made up Strickland's Brigade were not even traveling together. The first to arrive at Franklin were Lt. Col. Hamilton S. Gillespie's 50th Ohio and Lt. Col. Joseph Stockton's 72nd Illinois. They were placed on the western edge of Columbia Pike, with the Ohioans holding the ground closest to the road. Supporting these troops would be the 44th Missouri and 183rd Ohio, but Strickland was forced to await their arrival. Because both regiments had been ordered to march out of Spring Hill together and cover the rear of the massive

[41] *OR* 45, pt. 1, p. 389, 396; Cox, *Battle of Franklin*, p. 53; Faust, ed., *Historical Times Encyclopedia*, p. 646-647.

wagon train, they would be among the last troops to arrive at Franklin.[42]

To Strickland's right the strength of the Union defensive line became somewhat less than desirable. Cox had to fill the entire area between Columbia Pike and Carter's Creek Pike, so he decided to position Ruger's other brigade, commanded by Col. Orlando Moore, without a reserve line. It is likely Cox spoke to Ruger, and perhaps Moore, about this and if so there was probably a discussion about how the regiments were to be placed as they arrived.

From available information, it appears that rather than place the regiments from the right flank of the 72nd Illinois heading west, the line was instead filled in from Carter's Creek Pike heading east. The 80th Indiana, commanded by Lt. Col. Alfred D. Owen, was present at about 7 a.m. and took position with its right on the immediate eastern edge of Carter's Creek Pike. Barely fifty yards in front of Owen's right flank was a two-story, white frame house occupied by Samuel S. Moseley which fronted the pike. To the left of the Indianans was Maj. Edgar Sowers' 118th Ohio, followed in the same direction by Col. Oliver Spaulding's 23rd Michigan.[43]

Jacob Cox said Lt. Col. Francis Lowry's 107th Illinois was placed on the left flank of the Michigan troops, but exhaustive research weighs against this. Instead the evidence indicates the 129th Indiana was on the left of the 23rd Michigan. The 129th Indiana's commander, Col. Charles A. Zollinger, wrote in his official report that the regiment arrived "at daylight" and had breakfast. As for the 107th Illinois, Capt. Leander S. McGraw stated that his regiment did not arrive until noon. This was the same arrival time specified by both Lt. Col. Isaac Sherwood and Capt. Henry J. McCord of the 111th Ohio for their regiment. Regarding the 111th Ohio, it is clear from multiple sources that Sherwood's

---

[42] *OR* 45, pt. 1, p. 364, 370, 389, 393, 999; Cox, *Battle of Franklin*, p. 54, 160. Information about Strickland's early career courtesy of Historical Data Systems, Inc. www.civilwardata.com. The Union line west of Columbia Pike extended due west for about 150 feet. At that point, according to Cox, the line began angling toward the northwest. Therefore, the 50th Ohio filled the first 150 feet of the line and carried beyond the angle.

[43] *OR* 45, pt. 1, p. 384, 388. The Moseley House survived the battle and intervening years and is today known as White Hall.

regiment unit formed the left of Moore's Brigade and was on the right of the 72nd Illinois. It does not seem plausible that Moore's first four regiments were placed in line and then forced to sidestep westward to allow for the 107th Illinois and 111th Ohio, as well as the seventy-five men of the 24th Missouri, to take their places. Rather it much more logical that both Moore and Ruger were aware that the 111th Ohio and 107th Illinois were going to be late arrivals and chose to leave space for them to file in on the right of the 72nd Illinois. Strong support for this conclusion comes from Col. Moore personally. In his official report Moore said the 129th Indiana was on the left of the 23rd Michigan. Even Lt. Col. Sherwood indicated the 107th Illinois was located to his regiment's right. Thus it seems clear that the 107th Illinois was positioned between the 111th Ohio and 129th Indiana.[44]

Orlando Hurley Moore was a Michigan native who had joined the U. S. Army in 1856 and served in the 6th Infantry. After the war broke out, Moore served for a time in the 13th Michigan Infantry before being promoted to colonel and taking command of the 25th Michigan Infantry in September 1862. On July 4, 1863, Moore and his men found themselves faced off against John Hunt Morgan and his Confederate cavalry at Tebbs Bend, Kentucky. Morgan's advance was threatening Louisville and Moore had placed his command in position

---

[44] *OR* 45, pt. 1, p. 379-380, 382-383, 385, 387; Cox, *Battle of Franklin*, p. 55; Sherwood, *Memories of the War,* p. 140; Richard G. Young, ed., *Glory! Glory! Glory! The Civil War Diaries of Henry Jackson McCord*, p. 67. The 111th Ohio, along with the detachment of the 24th Missouri, arrived at Franklin late because it had veered west of Columbia Pike at Spring Hill to avoid capture and traveled some distance on that side of the road before returning to it around dawn south of Franklin. The lateness of the 107th Illinois was the result of it being designated for special duty near Spring Hill. According to Sgt. Fletcher Hedges of Company G, in a letter published in the *National Tribune* on Oct. 11, 1906, p. 3, the regiment was "about two miles north of Spring Hill" when it was "turned to the right to do outpost duty in a cornfield." Hedges said the regiment stayed in that location until dawn when it moved toward Franklin.

to contest the enemy's crossing of the Cumberland River. Moore's biggest problem, however, was that he was terribly outnumbered. Morgan closed in and when he presented surrender demands Moore replied that since it was the Fourth of July it was not a good day to surrender. Frustrated by Moore's defiance Morgan launched an attack, but suffered so terribly he was forced to withdraw. Later Moore campaigned in eastern Tennessee and led his troops through the Atlanta Campaign.[45]

Col. Moore's troops held their posts at Franklin in a line that angled gradually to the northwest, much in the same way the line east of Columbia Pike formed a northeasterly arc. In Cox's words the natural strength of this line is described:

> Where the line crossed the road, a gap was left of the full width of the road, for the continuous lines of wagons and artillery crowded it all the morning. On the west of it, the line continued at right angles to the road for fifty yards on level ground, and then bent to the rear, descending the slope somewhat as it did so. This was with the purpose of placing a battery on the summit at the right of the brick smoke-house, which could fire over the heads of the infantry in the front line, and sweep the approaches in the direction of the Bostick place.[46]

As soon as his troops finished filing into line Moore could see an immediate problem. There were not enough men to completely fill the space assigned to his brigade and the colonel asked for assistance. Cox soon learned of the situation and moved to solve the problem. The 44th Missouri and 183rd Ohio had arrived around the same time as the 107th Illinois and 111th Ohio, and Strickland's new regiments were directed into position as reserves. The 44th Missouri occupied the ground closest to the Columbia Pike. Because the size of the regiment, around 720 men, effectively covered the 50th Ohio, 72nd Illinois, and 111th Ohio, the 183rd Ohio was forced to occupy ground further west than previous historians have thought. Cox visited with Lt. Col. Mervin

---

[45] James A. Ramage, *Rebel Raider: The Life of General John Hunt Morgan*, p. 163-164. Other information about Orlando Moore courtesy of Historical Data Systems, Inc. www.civilwardata.com.

[46] Cox, *Battle of Franklin*, p. 55-56.

Clark of the 183rd Ohio at "about noon" and remembered that the men of the regiment were "lying down, with no cover except the natural curve of the ground." This statement indicates at least a portion of the 183rd Ohio was wrapped around the western slope of Carter Hill, where some protection would have been afforded from incoming fire. Surely because of their proximity to the Second Brigade, Cox ordered two companies from the 183rd Ohio to move forward and help fill out Col. Moore's line. According to Moore, the Ohio troops were placed between the left of 23rd Michigan and the right of 129th Indiana, further evidence that the 107th Illinois was not where Cox later believed it to be. One thing was for certain. Cox, Ruger, and Moore understood the line was thin in this area of the field, but agreed that it would have to do.[47]

Like the troops to their left, Ruger's men on the front line went to work building breastworks and digging trenches. The section of line closest to Columbia Pike was especially strong, as dirt and rails were thrown up to form a seemingly impenetrable wall. There the works ran along the southern edge of the Carter garden and they, like those to the east, began to take on a grim and foreboding appearance. Not only did the Union soldiers construct a three or four foot trench on the inside of the works, but they dug ditches on the outside at the base of the embankment. For an assaulting column, this type of fortification presented an immense and potentially deadly problem. An attacking soldier, if he survived the initial charge upon the works, would first hit a ditch up to four feet in width and dug to a depth of perhaps two or three feet. Then the soldier would have to climb over an embankment that was two or three, sometimes even four feet, "above ground level." All the while he would be under a blanket of small arms and artillery

---

[47] Cox, *Battle of Franklin*, p. 55-57; *OR* 45, pt. 1, p. 379, 387, 395; *Report of the Adjutant General of Missouri, 1865*, p. 276; *Missouri Democrat*, Dec. 8, 1864, St. Louis Public Library; William Sparks, "At Duck River," *NT*, Jul. 25, 1918, p. 3. Moore said only one company from the 183rd Ohio totaling fifty troops was sent to fill in his line. However, he was likely mistaken because Spaulding, commander of the 23rd Michigan, recalled two companies, see *OR* 45, pt. 1, p. 386. Also, Wayne Morris of the 23rd Michigan wrote letters on December 2 and 6, 1864 (on file with the Bentley Historical Library, University of Michigan) indicating that two 183rd Ohio companies were present. Possibly the companies were sent forward at different times and Moore knew of only one.

fire.[48]

Bayonets would also come into play at this close range. Scrambling to the top and reaching the parapet under these conditions, however, was only going to be half the problem. If a soldier could actually get to the top he faced about a six or seven foot drop into a trench swarming with enemy soldiers. Needless to say, being on the defense held huge advantages.

The troops near the Carter cotton gin were not the only ones who helped themselves to a variety of goods in an effort to bolster their breastworks. Many of Ruger's men were veterans of the fighting around Atlanta and knew the value of fortifications. They grabbed whatever they could lay their hands on. They ripped down the walnut fence palings and planks from around the Carter garden, over 3,500 feet altogether, and disassembled an outhouse, cook house, carriage house, and buggy house. The large barn, two corn cribs, and other small outbuildings which stood about ninety yards north and west of the house were also not immune. Nearly every wooden item that could be hauled away was removed, including over 200 cedar posts. Incredibly, eight plows were also shoved into the works. If it could be maneuvered by human hands, somehow it found its way to the breastworks.[49]

Near the southwest base of Carter Hill, directly in front of the Federal line, stood a thicket of young locust trees. The trees varied in size, but most had trunks ranging from three to six inches in width. Ruger's troops quickly employed their axes and saws on the hapless trees. Many were used to strengthen the works and others, especially the smaller ones, were made into an abatis. The branches and tops of the trees were also used to make the abatis more dense. The locust

---

[48] Smith, *History of Maury County*, Interview with Moscow Carter, p. 201; Purdue, *Pat Cleburne*, p. 416; A. A. Jones, "Many Days of Fighting: Incidents of the Retreat from Columbia to Nashville," *NT*, June 16, 1898, p. 2. Jones was located east of Columbia Pike and said the ditch to his front was eight feet wide and two feet deep.

[49] Smith, *History of Maury County*, Interview with Moscow Carter, p. 202; Dan M. Robison, "The Carter House: Focus of the Battle of Franklin," *Tennessee Historical Quarterly* (hereafter referred to as *THQ*), 22, No. 1, p. 7; Hudson Alexander, "The Trials and Tribulations of Fountain Branch Carter And His Franklin, Tennessee, Home," *Blue & Gray Magazine*, February 1995, p. 34.

grove stood in a slight hollow and enemy troops moving forward to attack would find themselves coming down a slope from the direction of the Bostick House toward this low-lying area. From there they would have to struggle through the abatis and then scale the works.[50]

Beyond this area, extending to where the line ran into Carter's Creek Pike, the Union soldiers were no less creative, although they had far less to work with. There they hacked down a fruit orchard and used the felled trees in their works. Whatever was not thrown into the works was used to construct a very crude abatis.[51]

Not only did the Union army have strong defensive works on each side of Columbia Pike, there was also a line constructed behind the primary one. This retrenched line became a necessity because Cox had ordered the pike be left open so wagons, artillery, and horses could be moved through the main line. Also, other Union troops who would eventually form up in advance of the main line were to use the opening on the pike. In an effort to ensure the gap would not be exploited, Cox ordered the retrenchment built. It lay almost exactly 200 feet behind, or north of, the main line and actually crossed the road. Approximately forty feet east of the pike a turnout was built so that "army trains could go around it on the left and regain the road."[52]

The retrenched line, made up modestly of dirt and rails, ran due east-west, paralleled the northern edge of the Carter garden, and nearly touched the southern walls of the wooden office building and brick smokehouse. The makeshift line was barely sixty feet from the Carter House. Space for a battery of artillery was made adjacent to the smokehouse on its west side and the retrenchment continued west for about 150 yards.[53]

Apparently Cox wanted the retrenchment only to cross the pike and extend little further. Men from the 44th Missouri, however, began to fortify the extension as it ran through the Carter property. The Missouri troops had their backs almost literally against the Carter yard,

---

[50] Cox, *Battle of Franklin*, p. 55.

[51] Cox, *Battle of Franklin*, p. 55; McDonough and Connelly, *Five Tragic Hours*, p. 85; *OR* 45, pt. 1, p. 364-365.

[52] Cox, *Battle of Franklin*, p. 56.

[53] Smith, *History of Maury County*, Interview with Moscow Carter, p. 201.

and for a span of several hundred feet many of them only had to look over their shoulders to see the house and outbuildings. A lieutenant colonel from the 44th Missouri later wrote of the men throwing up "defenses" so it is clear they improved and extended the retrenchment. Cox wrote that "no second infantry line of trench had been ordered by me" and he had wanted to avoid just such a line so that reserve troops could be moved up rapidly. But Cox was a veteran and knew all too well the nuances and habits of men in uniform. He wrote that "when soldiers at rest have intrenching tools they are apt to use them, and a sheltering ditch may be dug without any authority but that of a regimental or brigade commander." No one could blame the green recruits of the 44th Missouri for trying to protect themselves.[54]

Late in the morning, as the troops were finishing up various sections of the line, the Fourth Corps artillery began to arrive. Earlier, Schofield had ordered Fourth Corps chief of artillery Capt. Lyman Bridges to report to Cox with four batteries immediately upon his arrival at Franklin. This, according to Cox, Bridges did before noon.[55]

After a short discussion, Bridges began placing the guns in carefully selected positions. Cox could see the vulnerability the center of the line posed and had a number of the guns positioned there, not only to protect it, but to inflict the most damage. The 1st Kentucky Light Battery was posted where the 100th Ohio stood, on the eastern side of Columbia Pike. The Kentucky guns were manned mostly by infantrymen who had transferred to the battery after the 3rd Kentucky Infantry's term of enlistment had expired about a month prior. According to Lt. Col. Edwin Hayes, commander of the 100th Ohio, the battery's placement forced three of his companies to move and he recalled how the artillerists began "cutting embrasures" in the works. Hayes subsequently moved his three displaced companies into close support of the 1st Kentucky Battery and had them throw up "a light earth-work."[56]

---

[54] Cox, *Battle of Franklin*, p. 56; *OR* 45, pt. 1, p. 395.

[55] Ibid., p. 57; Ibid., p. 320, 334.

[56] *OR* 45, pt. 1, p. 418; J. Cornelius Smits, "The 1st Ky. Battery: How Its Guns Were Lost and Recovered at Franklin," *NT*, Aug. 25, 1887, p. 3. Embrasures were holes cut in the breastworks through which artilleryman could fire their guns.

Cox also had two guns of Lt. Aaron Baldwin's 6th Ohio Light Artillery Battery placed in the works southeast of the Carter cotton gin, directly to the left of the 104th Ohio. This choice of location was a calculating move. By placing the guns there and having embrasures cut for them, Cox had to know that the ground between that point, which was effectively the corner point of the salient created by the line bending back, and the 1st Kentucky Battery would be a virtual death zone. The slightest angling of either set of guns would create a crossfire of ungodly proportions. Furthermore, Baldwin's other two guns were placed just east of Lewisburg Pike in the works of the 128th Indiana. Cox also had Capt. Bridges ready a position for Battery M, 4th U. S. Artillery east of Lewisburg Pike on high ground near the James McNutt home, located in rear of Israel Stiles' troops. Two of Battery M's guns were present, but the other two remained with Opdycke and the rear guard. As additional support for this sector, the six guns of Capt. Alexander Marshall's Battery G, 1st Ohio Light Artillery were placed some fifty yards behind the Union left and about fifty to one hundred yards west of the Nashville & Decatur Railroad.[57]

Back "in rear of the center" Bridges posted his own battery of the Illinois Light Artillery and Battery A, 1st Ohio Light Artillery near the Columbia Pike, almost due east of the Carter House. Next the four guns of the 20th Ohio Light Battery were rolled into place west of the Carter smokehouse along the retrenched line. The 20th Ohio guns, all 12-pounder brass Napoleons under the command of Lt. John S. Burdick, offered superb support for the infantry. Because the guns were placed higher up the Carter Hill slope, they would be able to fire directly over the heads of the infantrymen on the main line and sweep the ground in their front. Finally, Capt. Bridges directed the four guns of Battery B, Pennsylvania Light Artillery to form up on a slight knoll immediately east of Carter's Creek Pike, almost directly in rear of the 80th Indiana.[58]

These were not the only artillery pieces in place. The big guns

---

[57] Cox, *Battle of Franklin*, p. 58; *OR* 45, pt. 1, p. 320, 331, 338; Merrill, *The Soldier of Indiana*, Vol. 2, p. 760; Hinman, *The Story of the Sherman Brigade*, p. 670; Marshall, *Reminiscence of*, CHA.

[58] Cox, *Battle of Franklin*, p. 58; *OR* 45, pt. 1, p. 320; 330, 335; S. F. Moore, "Short One Brigade," *NT*, May 2, 1912, p. 7.

of the Twenty-Third Corps had arrived around 7 a.m. with the infantry, but in accordance with John Schofield's wishes, they were moved north of the river. Once there, Capt. Giles J. Cockerill was ordered to place Battery D, 1st Ohio Light Artillery within the confines of Fort Granger. The earthen fort, built in 1862 at the behest of Federal Maj. Gen. Gordon Granger, sat high atop Figuers Hill and commanded the open ground in front of the Union left and center. Cockerill's three-inch rifled guns would be able to inflict terrible damage from their location by firing directly into an attacking column or subjecting it to a lethal crossfire. It was the kind of position an artilleryman could only dream of. An Ohio soldier near Columbia Pike looked across the river at the fort and thought that the guns pointing outward looked like "angry dogs of war.[59]

By the time noon rolled around on November 30, the work on the Federal line of defense was largely complete. There remained some minor details to be completed on Orlando Moore's front, but for the most part the backbreaking work was done. For the first time many of the men either sat down or leaned back in the works to soak in the beautiful day. The temperature was approaching fifty degrees, the sky was a late autumn blue, and there was little if any wind. It was Indian summer at its best and the sun's warm rays began to relax the thousands of tired and aching bodies. Commissary boxes were broken open and groups of men sat down to eat, devouring "crackers and raw bacon" and gulping coffee. Many surely had their ears turned to the south at the same time. The deep and resonating boom of artillery was unmistakable and now and again came the faint echo of rifle fire. There was a great deal of chatter about it, but few in the trenches had any idea what was rolling in their direction. They could not have imagined had they tried.[60]

---

[59] *OR* 45, pt. 1, p. 432; Cox, *Battle of Franklin*, p. 49; Keesy, *War As Viewed From The Ranks*, p. 105. The author has visited the remains of Fort Granger and it is a superb position for artillery. From the fort one can look over nearly all of the Franklin battlefield and the ground east of Columbia Pike is in clear and direct view. The position is so dominant that on a clear day the turnpike can be seen emerging from between Winstead and Breezy Hills, a distance of well over two miles.

[60] Pinney, *History of the 104th Ohio,* p. 60.

Around this time the 12th Kentucky and 16th Kentucky arrived following their long and numbing march from the Duck River. The 16th Kentucky was ordered into a reserve position behind the 100th Ohio and "as close to the turnpike as the limbers and caissons" of the 1st Kentucky Battery would allow. The 12th Kentucky was affixed to the left flank of the 16th Kentucky and the Kentuckians promptly went to sleep or began starting fires to cook lunch. The 8th Tennessee was chosen to shore up the left of the reserve line and the 175th Ohio occupied ground only a short distance behind the Tennesseans and Kentuckians. Lt. Frank M. Posegate recalled that the Ohio regiment took a position some 150 yards to the rear of the cotton gin, its right flank "resting if not on the pike, at least very close to it."[61]

Nathan Kimball had been involved in some of the war's heaviest fighting. Born in Indiana in 1822, Kimball was a former school teacher who had served in the Mexican War and when secession came in 1861 he helped organize the 14th Indiana Infantry. He fought at Cheat Mountain in western Virginia during the war's early days and was instrumental in defeating Stonewall Jackson at Kernstown in March 1862. Promoted to brigadier general, Kimball commanded a brigade at both Antietam and Fredericksburg and was badly wounded at the latter battle. Later he fought during the Vicksburg Campaign and even saw action in Arkansas before a transfer took him into the Atlanta Campaign.[62]

Kimball's Division, heading up the Fourth Corps, began arriving at Franklin around 10 a.m. While Walter Whitaker's Brigade took a position "on the summit" of Winstead Hill west of the turnpike, Kimball rested his other two brigades. According to William Grose, his unit relaxed for "about an hour..." Behind Kimball came Thomas Wood's Division. Wood's men quickly streamed by and, according to Schofield's wishes, soon crossed the river where they took a position on

---

[61] *OR* 45, pt. 1, p. 415; Posegate, *NT*, Feb. 28, 1889; Cox, *Battle of Franklin*. p. 59.

[62] Faust, ed., *Historical Times Encyclopedia*, p. 417-418.

the north side.[63]

Kimball's arrival allowed Jacob Cox the opportunity to place troops on the army's right flank. Earlier Cox had notified Schofield that Ruger's right "had no secure point to rest upon." As a result, Schofield sent a dispatch to Kimball instructing him to report to Cox "for position on the line to-day." This apparently caused some confusion in Kimball's mind because Gen. Stanley, commander of the Fourth Corps, was not yet present and Kimball was unsure where Stanley would want the division placed. However, Kimball complied with the order and reported to Cox around noon. At this stage the Yankee line ended at Carter's Creek Pike, so Cox directed Kimball west of the road and told him to spread his three brigades out from the pike to the Harpeth River. According to Cox, he told Kimball to place his brigades "in echelon on Ruger's flank and rear" to protect against "a flank attack from the west."[64]

Emerson Opdycke was a man whose hands were full to overflowing. Since sunup he had been holding off the Rebel cavalry, but Nathan Bedford Forrest was not his only problem. Earlier Opdycke had received a thankless order from division commander George Wagner. Wagner instructed Opdycke "to bring forward all stragglers belonging to the army." So Opdycke and his seven regiment brigade got stuck with double duty and the tasks, combined with a lack of sleep, did nothing to improve the Ohio colonel's already sour mood. The going was not easy. The troops in the Federal column were exhausted, almost on the verge of collapse. A forced march was not an easy task for veteran soldiers and Schofield's army was filled with recruits and draftees. As a result, it did not take long for men to begin falling from ranks and Opdycke was responsible to clean up the mess. Stragglers were "filling the road" and Opdycke noted they were "mostly new men with immense knapsacks." Green soldiers often panic and

---

[63] *OR* 45, pt. 1, p. 115, 124, 177, 195, 208; Peter Cozzens, ed., *Battles & Leaders*, 5, p. 605. Stanley said the First Division arrived "soon after 9 o'clock" and Kimball said the time was noon. Apparently Kimball was referring to the approximate time his men filed into position on the main line.

[64] *OR* 45, pt. 1, p. 177, 348, 1172; Cox, *Battle of Franklin*, p. 60-61; Cozzens, ed., *Battles & Leaders*, 5, p. 605.

Emerson Opdycke
(Library of Congress)

there was plenty of that to go around. Opdycke said some "were so worried" that they resigned themselves to capture. With Forrest's cavalry snapping at their heels, some of the Northerners may have given up hope, but Opdycke had no such inclination. He ordered a number of his veterans to cut off the stragglers' knapsacks and force them north up the turnpike "at the point of the bayonet" if necessary.[65]

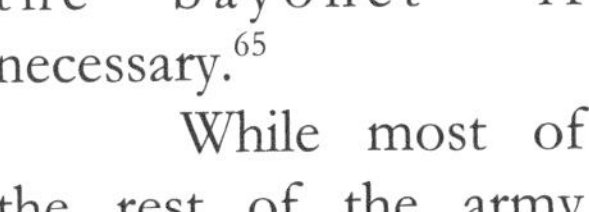

While most of the rest of the army readied itself at Franklin, Wagner's Division, with Opdycke shoring up the rear, continued its trek up the pike. Confederate cavalry continued to harass the column, but shortly before 11 o'clock Wagner's forward troops began cresting the pike as it passed between Winstead and Breezy Hills, about two miles from Franklin. Opdycke said he and his men pulled up "at 11 a.m." Around this time Wagner received orders from David Stanley directing him to halt the division and "allow the troops to get breakfast."[66]

This was positively welcome news for John Lane's and Joseph Conrad's brigades, the latter officer now in command of the Third Brigade following Luther Bradley's wounding at Spring Hill. Quickly the men fell out to begin cooking. For Opdycke and his men, however,

---

[65] *OR* 45, pt. 1, p. 124, 231, 239; Rice, *Yankee Tigers*, p. 155. In Opdycke's estimation only about twenty men ran away successfully and at least 500 were prevented from doing so.

[66] *OR* 45, pt. 1, p. 231, 240.

there was to be no breakfast or rest, but only more action on the line. They were ordered to remain in formation and occupy the "position in the gap" between the two hills as well as "the high point east of the pike," which was the crest of Breezy Hill. Meanwhile, the other two brigades were ordered to Opdycke's left where they began readying breakfast.[67]

Across the pike on Winstead Hill was Whitaker's Brigade from Kimball's Division. Whitaker had positioned two battalions from his command at the crest of the hill, while his remaining troops rested on Winstead's northern slope. Forrest soon moved forward and began pressing the Yankees "in strong force" and with "a heavy skirmish line in front."[68]

This action led Whitaker to recall his troops from the northern slope of Winstead Hill and spread them along the ridge line to his right. The Rebels slowly felt out the enemy position, probing along both Opdycke's and Whitaker's lines, but were unable to exploit any opportunity. The Federals held the high ground and had support from the two-gun section on loan from Lt. Samuel Canby's Battery M, 4th U. S. Artillery. The center section of Capt. Marshall's Battery G, 1st Ohio Light Artillery was also present, having been forwarded by Gen. Stanley to lend assistance. Forrest could see what he was up against and, like at Spring Hill the previous day, understood he would be unable to uproot the opposition without infantry support.[69]

After sparring with the Rebels for about an hour, Whitaker received orders to pull back from the crest of Winstead Hill and join the rest of the division, which was preparing to take positions on the main line. His men quickly descended from the heights and marched toward Franklin.[70]

Once Whitaker withdrew, things developed rapidly atop the hills south of town. Wagner saw Whitaker march toward Franklin and because his troops belonged to the same corps, Wagner assumed he was

---

[67] Ibid., p. 231.

[68] Ibid., p. 195.

[69] *OR* 45, pt. 1, p. 195, 320, 331, 338; Alexander Marshall to Levi Scofield, Oct. 10, 1886, Cox Papers, Oberlin College (hereafter referred to as OBC); Cox, *Battle of Franklin*, p. 65.

[70] *OR* 45, pt. 1, p. 195.

to pull back also. In his official report Wagner stated that he ordered his division "from its advanced position" and followed Whitaker "toward town."[71] The problem was that Whitaker's orders had nothing to do with Wagner, a fact the latter commander soon discovered.

George D. Wagner (Library of Congress)

The three brigades of Wagner's Division began pulling away from Breezy Hill a short time after twelve o'clock. John Lane's command took the lead followed by Joseph Conrad, while Emerson Opdycke was again chosen to form the rear guard. With little delay the Midwesterners of the Second Division began tramping up the pike, their rifle barrels and bayonets gleaming in the warm afternoon sun. Surely Wagner was relieved to finally be approaching the safety of the main defensive perimeter. But as he led his men north a mounted staff officer approached about a half mile from town and handed Wagner written orders from David Stanley.[72]

The dispatch, dated 11:30 a.m., instructed Wagner to "hold the heights you now occupy until dark, unless too severely pressed..." Moreover, it said that Opdycke's Brigade was to be relieved from the rear duty by either Lane or Conrad. Undoubtedly Wagner was unhappy with this news, not to mention what his men thought when the orders to countermarch were sent down the length of the column. Opdycke wrote pointedly that "as my rear was clearing the hill" the brigade "was

---

[71] Ibid., p. 231.

[72] Jacob Cox believed Wagner actually meant a half mile from the Union works. See Cox, *Battle of Franklin*, p. 65.

ordered back there."[73]

No matter what Wagner thought about the orders, it should have occurred to him that he never should have left the heights to begin with. So the division reversed direction, but no sooner were Opdycke's men, some of who were boldly nicknamed the Tigers, back in position on Breezy Hill before trouble appeared. Suddenly visible to the south were "heavy and parallel columns of infantry" that were "approaching rapidly." A member of the brigade said "we had a view of the entire rebel army following us" and recalled how it was obvious the enemy was "not going into camp with all their banners flying." Opdycke and his men had caught their first glimpses of two full Rebel corps. While Opdycke watched the developments a minie ball ripped into his horse's side, missing Opdycke's thigh by only a half inch. Somewhere in the distance a sharpshooter had the Yankee colonel in his sights. Opdycke's horse staggered and Opdycke quickly dismounted, called for a new mount, and looked for safer spot spot on the hill.[74]

On the main line Kimball filed his troops into position. On the left of the division, supporting Ruger, was Grose's Brigade. His left flank regiment was the 84th Indiana, which rested on the western edge of Carter's Creek Pike. To the right Grose placed the 30th Indiana, which consisted of only three companies, the 75th Illinois, and the 9th Indiana. The latter regiment was refused, or drawn back, "about 150 yards" from the main line. Grose placed the 80th Illinois and 84th Illinois into reserve and had the latter regiment cover "a ravine and low piece of ground" between the 75th Illinois and 9th Indiana. Col. Isaac C. B. Suman, commander of the 9th Indiana, said the "small ravine and stream of water" separated his unit from the 75th Illinois by about forty yards. Also present was one company of the 36th Indiana, but it is uncertain where this unit was located. The brigade's remaining regiment, the 77th Pennsylvania, was sent forward as skirmishers.[75]

---

[73] *OR* 45, pt. 1, p. 240, 1174.

[74] Rice, *Yankee Tigers*, p. 155; Glenn V. Longacre and John Haas, ed., *To Battle for God and the Right: The Civil War Letterbooks of Emerson Opdycke*, p. 249.

[75] *OR* 45, pt. 1, p. 177, 208, 220; William Grose, *The Story of the Marches, Battles and Incidents of the 36th Regiment Indiana Volunteer Infantry*, p. 222; Cox, *Battle of Franklin*, p. 61.

Col. Isaac Kirby's Brigade formed the center of Kimball's line. Kirby placed the 21st Illinois, 38th Illinois, and 31st Indiana in his front line and the 81st Indiana, 90th Ohio, and 101st Ohio into reserve. A short time later Kirby moved two companies of the 101st Ohio to the front line, to help "close a gap" between his brigade and Grose's. The remaining eight companies of Lt. Col. Bedan B. McDanald's 101st Ohio would play a very critical role later in the day.[76]

On the right Kimball placed Whitaker's Brigade, just arrived from its rear guard action atop Winstead Hill. Whitaker's men took their positions along a stretch of dominant high ground south of a sharp curve in the river. A portion of the line passed through present day Mt. Hope Cemetery and Whitaker's right flank was described as "resting on the Harpeth River..." On the right was located the 45th Ohio, followed to the left by the 40th Ohio and 21st Kentucky. Into reserve Whitaker placed the 23rd Kentucky, 51st Ohio, and 96th Illinois.[77]

Cox later wrote the "general line of this division was nearly north and south, facing to the west." For protection Kimball's men hurriedly threw up dirt, rails, and whatever else they could find. They did not have near the protection the rest of the troops on the line enjoyed, but Cox did not believe such works were necessary. Primarily he wanted Kimball to protect Ruger's right flank and prevent the Confederates, especially cavalry spotted along Carter's Creek Pike, from slipping around the far Union right.[78]

Three turnpikes approach Franklin from the south. The Lewisburg Pike runs along the western edge of the Harpeth River, the Columbia Pike passes between Winstead and Breezy Hills, and Carter's Creek Pike approaches town from a southwesterly direction. All three roads converge as they approach the town and the distance between them shrinks rapidly. The area south of Franklin is well described as

---

[76] *OR* 45, pt. 1, p. 177, 184.

[77] Ibid., p. 195.

[78] Cox, *Battle of Franklin*, p. 61, 86; *OR* 45, pt. 1, p. 178, 184, 195, 208. The Rebel cavalry seen on this section of the field were from James Chalmers' command.

being similar to an old wagon wheel, with the turnpikes representing the spokes of the wheel and Franklin constituting the hub.

A. P. Stewart's troops turned off Columbia Pike a short distance south of Winstead Hill and Breezy Hill, near present day Henpeck Lane. From there, Stewart was told to march the nearly two miles needed to reach Lewisburg Pike. It was immediately clear as soon as Stewart began filing behind Breezy Hill that he would be able to flank Wagner with ease. Just as concerning to the Northerners was Cheatham, whose troops were nearing the plantation home of William Harrison about a half mile south of the twin hills. They were marching straight up the pike, directly toward the Federal position. In marked contrast to the beautiful Harrison House, which stood just west of the pike, the Rebel soldiers were a ratty looking bunch. But while their clothing may have been a patchwork affair, their polished rifles and steely bayonets stood out, marking them as true soldiers. They were also well-trained and the cadence of their marching feet on the stony roadway could be heard clearly by the Wagner's men atop Breezy Hill. It was a sight to both awe and frighten.[79]

For the Confederate infantry the march to Franklin was unimpeded and mostly without incident. Yet everywhere along the pike were signs of the enemy they were chasing. In their haste to escape, the Federals had left material scattered along both sides of the roadway. Lt. Spencer B. Talley of the 28th Tennessee wrote, "The road was strewn everywhere with the wreck of thrown away stuff that they were unable to carry in their flight." Talley also noted that a large number of wagons had been set afire. Lt. William H. Berryhill of the 43rd Mississippi said the road was "strewn with tents, knapsacks, dirty clothing, books, papers" and "a great many wagons" were on fire.[80]

Staff officer Joseph Cumming rode near the head of the Rebel column and saw piles of Yankee debris. He said there was plain evidence of a "hurried retreat" and not only had wagons been overturned, but others were abandoned with "their teams lying in their harness dead where they had been shot" to keep them out of

---

[79] *OR* 45, pt. 1, p. 240; Elliott, *Soldier of Tennessee,* p. 236-237; Virginia M. Bowman, *Historic Williamson County: Old Homes and Sites*, p. 157.

[80] Spencer B. Talley, Civil War Memoir, TSLA; Jones and Martin, ed., *Civil War Letters of William Harvey Berryhill*, p. 122.

Confederate hands.[81] Col. Ellison Capers of the 24th South Carolina also recalled the burned wagons and "dead mules" that marked the "hasty retreat of the enemy." Sumner Cunningham, a member of the 41st Tennessee who gained post-war fame as the founder of the *Confederate Veteran Magazine*, counted thirty-four abandoned wagons.[82]

With Forrest's cavalry doing the heavy work during the morning hours, Gen. Hood's long, winding column of infantry soaked in the sights with little distraction. In addition to the beauty of the Tennessee landscape and the pleasant weather, the Rebels were especially heartened by the trail of material left behind by the retreating Northerners. Some "enthusiastic young ladies" who lived along the turnpike even turned out and shouted to the passing ranks of gray that the Yankees were on a "dead run."[83]

At around 1 p.m. the Confederates could see the ground begin to rise gradually in front of them along both sides of the pike. To the west, on the left side of the pike, stood the beautiful two-story Harrison House. Directly ahead were Winstead and Breezy Hills and just beyond them lay their destiny.

Stewart's Corps led the advance to Franklin on November 30. Alexander Peter Stewart was a native Tennessean and forty-three years old. An 1842 graduate of West Point, he taught mathematics in the army until 1845 when he resigned and returned home to teach at Cumberland University and Nashville University. About average in height and weight, Stewart was described as having a kind and polite nature. Stewart seemed to have no hidden agendas or confusing personality traits. He was straightforward, both personally and professionally. Stewart, who owned no slaves and had been opposed to secession, joined the Confederacy only when it became clear war was unavoidable. To him the war was based on conflicting constitutional

---

[81] Cumming, Recollections, p. 73, SHC.

[82] *OR* 45, pt. 1, p. 736; Sumner Cunningham, "Disastrous Campaign in Tennessee," *CV* 12, p. 338.

[83] Boyce, *CV* 24, p. 102; Jones and Martin, ed., *Civil War Letters of William Harvey Berryhill*, p. 122.

viewpoints and in the end his own opinions were more closely associated with the South. His nickname, Old Straight, was a perfect moniker and he served exclusively in the Western Theater. Stewart was the epitome of the Army of Tennessee and he was among the South's most reliable and consistent officers.[84]

Samuel French's Division was at the front of Stewart's Corps that day. French recalled how earlier, as the march ensued, Hood had met with him on the road north of Spring Hill. The commanding general said, "Well, General French, we have missed the great opportunity of the war!" French agreed and both men spurred their horses northward. Now, with Stewart arriving and Cheatham following closely behind Old Straight, the next opportunity was close at hand. John Bell Hood surveyed the scene and began his mental preparations.[85]

From atop Breezy Hill it was apparent to Emerson Opdycke there was no possible way Wagner's lone division was going to be able to hold the Rebels back. Yet Opdycke was a fighter and he decided not to stand idly by. He could see no enemy artillery, only infantry and Forrest's cavalry. The two-gun section of Battery G, 1st Ohio Light Artillery that Stanley had earlier sent to Wagner was unlimbered on Columbia Pike between the hills. Lt. Milton Mitchell commanded the section, but Capt. Marshall, the battery commander, had accompanied the two guns to the front and both officers went to work. As Opdycke watched from near the crest of Breezy Hill, the Federal gunners fired "a number of shell and solid shot" at the Confederates.[86]

There was some resulting confusion in the enemy ranks, but for the most part Opdycke was bluffing with the borrowed cannon and the fire had a minimal effect. Marshall said "the firing made no perceptible impression excepting occasionally light would be shone for an instant through the dark lines of men immediately after firing." From where he stood, Opdycke could see cavalry and infantry moving around the south side of Breezy Hill, headed for Lewisburg Pike. He knew once the Rebels reached that road his position on the hill would be untenable.

---

[84] Faust, ed., *Historical Times Encyclopedia*, p. 719; Elliott, *Soldier of Tennessee*, p. 7, 27; Binford, *Recollections of the Fifteenth Mississippi*, p. 103.
[85] French, *Two Wars*, p. 292.
[86] *OR* 45, pt. 1, p. 240, 331; Marshall to Scofield, Oct. 10, 1886, Cox Papers, OBC.

Quickly a courier was sent across Columbia Pike with a dispatch for Gen. Wagner, who at the time was posting some of Col. Lane's Brigade on Winstead Hill to offset the effect of Whitaker's withdrawal. Wagner read the note and wasted little time ordering his men removed from the heights of both hills. Wagner had not been thrilled about returning after having started toward Franklin once already. This time he was indeed being pressed severely and orders were passed to all three of his brigades instructing them to pull back. Wagner also sent a note to Stanley informing him of the movement. In short order the Northerners, staring through sleep-deprived eyes, climbed down from the hills and filed smartly into marching formation. By about 1:30 p.m. Wagner and his men were on their way toward town, trudging up the turnpike and nearing their friends on the main line.[87]

It was obvious John Schofield was feeling better by mid-morning as evidenced by his 9:50 a.m. telegram to George Henry Thomas. Schofield, who had set up headquarters at the home of Dr. Daniel Cliffe, said the trains were "coming in" and that half of the army had arrived from Spring Hill while the "other half" was still some five miles away. He also mentioned there was some ongoing "light skirmishing" and his plan was to have everything, troops and all, over the Harpeth by evening. Furthermore, he said that Wilson was back on the scene, but Forrest's whereabouts were not known. Schofield ended with: "Of course I cannot prevent Hood from crossing the Harpeth wherever he may attempt it. Do you desire me to hold on here until compelled to fall back?"[88]

Thirty-five minutes later, without having received Schofield's 9:50 a.m. wire, Thomas sent a telegram with one all important sentence: "If you prevent Hood from turning your position at Franklin, it should be held; but I do not wish you to risk too much."[89] Schofield's mood plunged when he received Thomas' message, as evidenced by his noon response:

> Your dispatch of 10:25 a.m. is received. I am satisfied that I have

---

[87] Ibid., p. 231, 240; Ibid., Oct. 10, 1886, Cox Papers, OBC.

[88] *OR* 45, pt. 1, p. 1169; Cox, *Battle of Franklin*, p. 280; Bowman, *Historic Williamson County*, p. 106.

[89] *OR*, pt. 1, p. 1169.

> heretofore run too much risk in trying to hold Hood in check, while so far inferior to him in both infantry and cavalry. The slightest mistake on my part, or failure of a subordinate, during the last three days might have proved disastrous. I don't want to get into so tight a place again; yet, I will cheerfully act in accordance with your views of expediency, if you think it important to hold Hood back, as long as possible. When you get all your troops together and the cavalry in effective condition, we can whip Hood easily, and, I believe, make the campaign a decisive one; before that, the most we can do is to husband our strength and increase it as much as possible. I fear the troops which were stationed on the river below Columbia will be lost. I will get my trains out of the way as soon as possible, and watch Hood carefully. Possibly I may be able to hold him here, but do not expect to be able to do so long.[90]

The ability to make sound tactical decisions is probably the most critical factor necessary for an officer to become a successful battlefield commander. It also helps to be able to stare death square in the eye. George Day Wagner was a man who could do both. Wagner was thirty-five years old at Franklin and had been witness to war in all its fury and horror. Born in Ohio, Wagner grew up in rural Indiana. As a young man Wagner was a typical Midwestern farmer, but politics beckoned and he won a seat in the Indiana state house in 1856. This victory was followed by his election to the state senate in 1860. It was war, however, which gave Wagner the opportunity to display talents that might otherwise have gone unnoticed.[91]

Wagner was like countless men who fought to preserve the Union. Through their eyes, the call to duty was one made to prevent the country from disintegrating and all else paled in comparison to that singular goal. Southerners were operating in open rebellion in the eyes of like-minded Unionists, and it was the responsibility of those loyal to the United States to end the insurrection no matter what the cost. It had become necessary to keep the country together by force and Wagner assisted in that cause from the very beginning.

Wagner's first significant action occurred on the second day at Shiloh. There he served under Thomas Wood and the two began a soldiers' relationship that continued all the way to Franklin. Shiloh was

---

[90] Ibid., p. 1170.

[91] Faust, ed., *Historical Times Encyclopedia*, p. 795.

also where Wagner got his first taste of fighting the men who would eventually form the Army of Tennessee. Later that same year, Wagner fought like a bulldog on the Federal left during the savage battle at Stones River. The combat in Wagner's sector, near the Round Forest, was as vicious as armed conflict could be. Although he missed the fighting at Chickamauga, Wagner was right back in the fray at Missionary Ridge. Later, during the Battle of Kennesaw Mountain, troops led by Wagner marched right into the teeth of the Rebel defenses and were repulsed with heavy losses.[92]

After two and a half years of bloody fighting and rising to the rank of brigadier general, the fortunes of war brought George Wagner to Franklin, Tennessee. Bravery and efficient soldiering had been the mark of his military career. But during the late afternoon of November 30 everything came crashing down. His tactical judgement seemed to vanish and his decisions cost the lives of many brave men.

As Wagner and his men moved toward Franklin, they approached a small hill on the western side of the pike. The hill, known locally as Privet Knob, was effectively the halfway point between Winstead Hill and Franklin. Privet Knob, known also as Merrill Hill, was a rock-strewn eminence that rose some seventy-five to one hundred feet above the surrounding terrain. In fact, Lane referred to it as "Stone Hill." It was there that Wagner suddenly decided to make another stand. He ordered Lane's Brigade and the section of guns from Battery G, 1st Ohio Light Artillery to occupy the hill. Meanwhile, Wagner directed his remaining two brigades to continue marching up the pike. Lane's obvious isolation was evident in his report where he wrote of watching "the balance of the army retire to a position in the rear."[93]

---

[92] Faust, ed., *Historical Times Encyclopedia*, p. 795; Larry J. Daniel, *Shiloh: The Battle That Changed the Civil War*, p. 287; Castel, *Decision in the West*, p. 315-316.

[93] *OR* 45, pt. 1, p. 256, 331. Today Privet Knob is still visible as the high ground west of Columbia Avenue, midway between the Carter House and Winstead Hill. In a sketch that accompanied John Lane's official report the hill is said to be "100 Feet High." Also, the hill was flanked on its eastern, southern, and western edges by a low lying stone wall. At the time of the battle there was a corn field on its northern side. See *OR* 45, pt. 1, p. 256 and refer to Atlas.

Barely a half mile further up the road Wagner issued more questionable orders. David Stanley had told Wagner to hold the hills to the south for as long as possible. Nothing in the orders, however, told Wagner that once Winstead and Breezy Hills were abandoned was he to occupy any ground between them and the main line. Wagner exercised reckless discretion when he told Joseph Conrad to form his brigade in the open field, aligning the men so they were positioned nearly parallel to the main line behind them. Capt. John Shellenberger, commanding officer of Company B, 64th Ohio, Conrad's Brigade, said this order was sent to Wagner by Schofield, but there is no evidence to support this claim. There is no doubt Wagner was acting on his own.[94]

Conrad formed his brigade by placing the 15th Missouri, his regiment prior to Bradley's injury, on the west side of the pike. The rest of the brigade was ordered to form up on the road's east side "in a large old cotton field not under cultivation that year." The regiments were aligned as follows: the 51st Illinois anchored on the pike followed to the left by the 79th Illinois, 42nd Illinois, 64th Ohio, and 65th Ohio. Conrad also ordered the 65th Ohio to slightly refuse the left flank. In addition, he "threw out a strong line of skirmishers" nearly "half a mile" in advance of his five regiments. Among the skirmishers was the detachment of the 27th Illinois that had been attached to Col. Allen Buckner's 79th Illinois. Capt. William B. Young commanded the 27th Illinois detachment and his troops added a special punch to the skirmish line. They were armed with Henry repeating rifles.[95]

The position of Wagner's men has been variously quoted as being from several hundred yards south of the main line to as much as a half mile. The latter figure is more accurate. While much of the ground in the Harpeth Valley was effectively flat, there were a number of areas that rose gently and fell away into shallow swales. Conrad posted his men on such a slight rise, a terrain feature not distinguishable

---

[94] *OR* 45, pt. 1, p. 231, 270; Shellenberger, *CV* 36, p. 380. Shellenberger, who wrote extensively about Spring Hill and Franklin after the war, was decidedly anti-Schofield and little friendlier toward Cox. He held them responsible for this action rather than Wagner.

[95] Shellenberger, *CV* 36, p. 380; *OR* 45, pt. 1, p. 270, 278, 280; I. G. Heaps, "In Front at Franklin," *NT*, Mar. 30, 1911, p. 3; Allen Buckner, "Battle of Franklin," *NT*, Feb. 1, 1883, p. 1.

from a distance, especially Winstead Hill. However, the ground had sufficient elevation to prevent the Carter House from being visible from a point just south of it. Meanwhile, at the crest of the rise the Carter House could be seen easily. The distance between the rise and the house was measured by Moscow Carter after the battle and he stated the total equaled 160 rods. A rod is equal to 16.5 feet so the distance was almost precisely a half mile. Moving north from the crest of the rise, the terrain slowly drops away until a low point is reached at the base of Carter Hill. This low-lying area wound west toward the locust grove and was only a short distance in front of the main defensive line.[96]

Emerson Opdycke was a true volunteer soldier. Born in Ohio in 1830, Opdycke had no military experience before the Civil War, but had been involved in the mercantile business. Perhaps his life's greatest excitement prior to the war had been his stint as a prospector in California during the great gold rush. In 1861 he accepted a commission as a lieutenant in the 41st Ohio Infantry and by the fall of 1862 he was a lieutenant colonel in the newly organized 125th Ohio. Promoted to colonel by the time of Chickamauga it was there that Opdycke and his men gained a well-earned name for themselves. They were among the units that had fought so valiantly atop Snodgrass Hill and thereafter the regiment was known affectionately as Opdycke's Tigers. It was a title the men of the 125th Ohio proudly proclaimed for decades after the war. Opdycke next led his men into action at Missionary Ridge and he served with distinction throughout the Atlanta Campaign, during which he was wounded and had his first experience commanding a brigade. Three years of war had molded Opdycke into a fine soldier and solid commander. Bright, opinionated, and very driven Opdycke also had a temper, one that flared when his patience ran low.[97]

---

[96] Cox, *Battle of Franklin*, p. 73-74; Levi Scofield to Jacob Cox, Dec. 23, 1870, Cox Papers, OBC. John Shellenberger said the distance was 470 yards "as measured along the pike." See Shellenberger, *CV* 36, p. 380.

[97] Faust, ed., *Historical Times Encyclopedia*, p. 546-547.

Once George Wagner finished positioning the first of his three brigades he approached Col. Opdycke, who was just then riding up. What Wagner said would have much to do with how lives and careers would change forever. He told Opdycke to begin deploying his troops on the west side of the pike and continue Conrad's line in that direction. Opdycke tried to contain himself. He turned to Wagner and minced no words. Opdycke "strenuously objected" to the order and kept riding north, forcing Wagner to turn his horse around just to continue the conversation. Opdycke said putting troops "out on the open plain" was ridiculous and that doing so would put them "in a good position to aid the enemy and nobody else." He also reminded Wagner that his brigade was exhausted and hungry and pointedly said the men deserved a break. Incredibly, during this entire exchange, Opdycke's Brigade continued marching toward Franklin. The troops passed Conrad and soon left him behind entirely. Meanwhile, Wagner and Opdycke yelled back and forth at one another. This episode continued all the way to the gap in the main line where the two officers passed through, barking at one another in full view of their troops. Adding to the remarkable scene were the regiments of Opdycke's Brigade marching in tow. If the situation had not been so serious and decidedly intense, it might have actually been comical.[98]

Once inside the Union perimeter, Opdycke began looking for a place to rest his men. Because there was no room near the earthworks, Opdycke searched toward the rear. All the while Wagner kept up the pace, bellowing in Opdycke's ear that he was disobeying orders among other things. Finally Wagner had to accept there was nothing more he could do. In sheer frustration he blurted out, "Well, Opdycke, fight when and where you damn please. We all know you'll fight."[99]

It is interesting that Opdycke, when he compiled his official report, said Wagner "was with me in person, and ordered me to fight when and where I thought I should be most needed without further orders." Wagner, on the other hand, wrote in his report that he actually ordered Opdycke "to form in the rear of Carter's house...to act as a reserve..." This is nothing short of a lie on Wagner's part. But the

---

[98] Shellenberger, *CV* 36, p. 380-381.

[99] Ibid., p. 381.

overall truth was far more difficult to explain. Wagner had issued orders so beyond reason that one of his officers became outright insubordinate and risked a potential court martial rather than obey them. Even more incredibly, Wagner stuck to the idea of an advanced line following Opdycke's display. Wagner's focus soon shifted to his other two brigades.[100]

Before he could further tend to Lane and Conrad, the exasperated Wagner stopped at the Carter House to report to Gen. Cox. After Wagner explained the current positioning of his brigades, Cox ordered Opdycke's troops be placed on the west side of the pike in rear of the Carter House. What Cox then said to Wagner was crucial. In accordance with Gen. Stanley's wishes, Cox said "that the orders under which General Wagner was then acting as to the two brigades serving as rear guard should be carried out, and that when the troops were withdrawn within the lines they should be placed in position near Opdycke's Brigade and held in reserve awaiting further orders, and in readiness to support any part of the line." Thus the evidence is clear that Wagner was told explicitly not to allow his advanced troops to become enveloped by the enemy. They were to retire within the main line if matters became too pressing.[101]

Around 2:30 p.m., as Wagner was leaving the Carter House, he received word from Col. Lane that Rebel troops were "advancing in force" and about to swallow up his command. At once Wagner directed Lane to "withdraw his brigade and go into position on the right" of Conrad's position. Pulling Lane back was probably the last responsible order Wagner gave.[102]

After telling Lane to retreat, Wagner rode out to speak with Col. Conrad and give him personal instructions. Conrad, who had been in command of the brigade for less than twenty-four hours, was beginning to fret. The Confederates were plainly visible about a mile away and their numbers were obviously sizable. Conrad said he readied a message for Wagner asking for clarification about whether the brigade "was expected" to hold its exposed position. The dispatch was handed to a staff officer who had just mounted his horse and headed north when

---

[100] *OR* 45, pt. 1, p. 232, 240.

[101] *OR* 45, pt. 1, p. 352; Cox, *Battle of Franklin*, p. 82.

[102] *OR* 45, pt. 1, p. 231, 256.

Looking south from the approximate position of the main Federal line toward Conrad's position. Where the road disappears is the slight ridge upon which Conrad and Lane were positioned. (U. S. Army Military History Institute)

Wagner trotted up shortly after 3 p.m.[103]

Now able to convey his question verbally, Conrad asked if he and his men were supposed to hold their current position. Wagner replied in the affirmative. He told Conrad that both he and Lane were "to hold the line as long as possible..." About this same time Lane, at the head of his column, arrived from Privet Knob and Wagner repeated the order. Lane recalled that he was told to "give battle to the enemy, and, if able, drive him off...." Lane said further that if his troops were "overpowered" they were to check the Rebels "as long as possible" before being allowed "to retire to the main line of works." Wagner, however, was not done. Conrad was told "to have the sergeants to fix bayonets and to keep the men to their places." Many of Conrad's troops were new recruits and the veterans who heard the order believed it was meant to keep the draftees from running. But the order was exceptionally harsh and one officer noted that "never before" had such a directive ever been issued.[104]

---

[103] Ibid., p. 270.

[104] *OR* 45, pt. 1, p. 256, 270; Shellenberger, *CV* 36, p. 381. Lt. Col. Robert Brown of the 64th Ohio said he received the order to "charge bayonets" but did not have his sergeants obey the command.

The time was about 3:30 p.m. when Wagner headed back toward the main line. Behind him the anxious soldiers of Lane and Conrad worked feverishly to erect whatever crude and impromptu earthworks they could manage. At the far eastern end of Conrad's line there was little more than dirt to throw up. The commanding officer of the 64th Ohio said the protective bank covering his regiment's front was "in consequence of no timber....very low." Not only had the area been picked clean of timber, but the Federals had too few spades and shovels. West of the pike things were little better. Trying to find cover on that section of the field was nearly impossible. Like the men across the pike, those in Lane's command were formed up in an old cotton field and there was little with which to build fortifications. The 26th Ohio had "no entrenching tools" and the men dug into the earth with bayonets and tin cups in an effort to throw up some protection. The Ohioans gathered what "rails and loose logs" they could find. The 100th Illinois erected only "some slight works" that were "thrown up hurriedly." The 57th Indiana had only "a succession of short rifle-pits" that offered protection to only "a small number" of the men. A soldier in this regiment remembered how the "slightly undulating" ground in front was completely open. He said only grass was visible for some distance south before it joined a cornfield.[105]

Exactly how Col. Lane positioned his regiments in line remains unclear. Lane provided scant detail in his official report and the regimental commanders are of little help because only one of them ever filed a report about Franklin. What is known positively is that the 40th Indiana formed the extreme left of Lane's line and was posted next to the 15th Missouri of Conrad's Brigade. Also, the 26th Ohio formed the right of Lane's line, but the exact positions of the remaining regiments, the 28th Kentucky, 57th Indiana, 97th Ohio, and 100th Illinois, are not known. Lt. Col. Milton Barnes, commander of the 97th Ohio, noted only that his regiment was placed "in the midst of an extensive open plain" and "near the right center..." However, it is known that the right

---

105 *OR* 45, pt. 1, p. 284; H. Leaming, "The Battle of Franklin," *NT*, Nov. 18, 1888, p. 3; W. W. Gist, "The Battle of Franklin," Tennessee Historical Magazine (hereafter referred to as *THM*), 6, No. 3, p. 223; Kerwood, *Annals of the Fifty-Seventh Indiana*, p. 295; George H. Woodruff, *Fifteen Years Ago: or, The patriotism of Will* County, p. 352.

of Lane's line was refused. Pvt. William Gist, a young soldier in the tiny 26th Ohio, said because of this he and his comrades "were somewhat nearer the works than the rest of the command." Lane also ordered skirmishers to cover the brigade's front. Lt. Col. Barnes said two companies from his regiment were actually left about a half mile south near Privet Knob to serve as skirmishers. Following standard procedure the other regiments surely had at least one company each on the skirmish line.[106]

Jacob Cox said Lane's and Conrad's brigades had their outer flanks "well retired, so that the whole formation was almost wedge-shaped." Additionally, the infantry was still supported by Lt. Milton Mitchell's center section of Battery G, 1st Ohio Light Artillery. By this stage the two gun section of Battery M, 4th U. S. Artillery that had accompanied the rear guard from Spring Hill had been removed to the main line by Lt. J. M. Stephenson. Mitchell and Capt. Marshall had pulled back from Privet Knob with Lane and the Ohio gunners occupied a new position on the pike between the 15th Missouri and 51st Illinois.[107]

Wagner's men were not alone out in the open field. Earlier Col. Silas Strickland had thrown out two companies of skirmishers to cover his brigade front, assigning Company A, 72nd Illinois and Company G, 183rd Ohio to the duty. Col. Orlando Moore also ordered forward a skirmish line numbering six officers and 175 enlisted men to front of his brigade. Pvt. Morris E. Johnson, Company E, 23rd Michigan, was among Moore's skirmishers and said fifteen men from his company were selected for duty. They organized into five man squads and soon began digging impromptu rifle pits. The problem was, as Johnson recalled, there was but one shovel to share among the three groups. Division commander Thomas Ruger said the skirmish line which covered his two brigades was "half to three-quarters of a mile in front"

---

[106] Gist, *THM* 6, No. 3, p. 222; *OR* 45, pt. 1, p. 256, 265, 282; Kerwood, *Annals of the Fifty-Seventh Indiana*, p. 296. Both Col. Lane and Capt. George Ernest confirmed the location of the 40th Indiana in their official reports.

[107] Cox, *Battle of Franklin*, p. 76; *OR* 45, pt. 1, p. 278, 331, 338; Marshall to Scofield, Oct. 10, 1886, Cox Papers, OBC.

of his main line.[108]

Skirmishers were also arrayed ahead of the main battle line east of Columbia Pike. Gen. Reilly said there was "a strong line of skirmishers about a half mile in front" of his brigade. A soldier from the 104th Ohio said his regiment's skirmishers posted "a little in advance on the left" of Conrad's Brigade. Casement's Brigade was covered in part by Company I, 65th Illinois. Pvt. Frederick Meinhart was in Company I and remembered being posted "about one-half to three-fourths" of a mile in front of the main line. On the left, skirmishers were posted in front of Henderson's Brigade, temporarily under the command of Col. Stiles. Pvt. L. H. Brooks was in Company I, 63rd Indiana and recalled being posted ahead of the main line between Lewisburg Pike and the river. Lt. Col Jaspar Packard of the 128th Indiana said two companies from his regiment were chosen for skirmish duty. One of the soldiers from Company K said his unit was sent forward about a half mile and occupied a position "in a beautiful grove dotted with large trees." Very likely this grove was located on Carnton Plantation.[109]

Kimball's Division was also preceded by a skirmish line. On the left of his division the front of Grose's Brigade was covered by an entire regiment, the 77th Pennsylvania. Col. Thomas E. Rose's Pennsylvanians were posted "about a mile from Franklin" along the western edge of Carter's Creek Pike, with six of his companies forming an irregular front line and four companies in reserve. Rose said to his left "were the pickets of General Ruger's command" and on his right were other skirmishers from the First Division.[110]

How the Federal skirmishers were posted at Franklin is not only

---

[108] William Mohrmann, Memoir, CHA; Sexton, *MOLLUS*, Illinois, 4, p. 470-471; Morris E. Johnson, "Battle of Franklin," NT, Jan. 28, 1904, p. 3; *OR* 45, pt. 1, p. 365, 379, 389.

[109] *OR* 45, pt. 1, p. 412; Nelson A. Pinney, "Fierce Work at Franklin," *NT*, Mar. 10, 1887, p. 3; Meinhard, *One Man's War*, p. 184; L. H. Brooks, "As He Saw Franklin," *NT*, Jan. 17, 1895, p. 3; Merrill, *The Soldier of Indiana*, Vol. 2, p. 759; John Enfield, "Comrade Enfield's Exciting Race For Life," *NT*, Mar.15, 1888, p. 3.

[110] *OR* 45, pt. 1, p. 178, 188, 208, 214, 224, 227; Cox, *Battle of Franklin*, p. 136.

unique but has largely been overlooked. The available evidence clearly points to the main line skirmishers being sent forward as much as an hour or two before Conrad and Lane were in position. Based on the distance the skirmishers were from the main line, it is nearly certain that both Conrad and Lane deployed just in rear of the section of the skirmish line that covered the Union center. Only then did they send out their own skirmishers, who moved forward and joined the already established skirmish line.[111]

Everything was now essentially set. Except for the frantic entrenching work, the advanced Federal line was in place. Its shape, as well as the skirmish line, followed the same general course as the main line. As men scraped and clawed for whatever cover they could find, the two guns of the 1st Ohio Light Artillery on the turnpike fired at long range toward the Rebels. As the guns recoiled, their roar echoed slowly across the floor of the Harpeth Valley, mixing strangely with the hazy light of the late Tennessee afternoon. Thus far the day had been mostly quiet, almost peaceful. The low rumble of artillery fire was, however, an ominous sign. It sounded like the thunder of a gathering storm.

---

[111] *OR* 45, pt. 1, p. 365, 379, 389.

7

We Will Make the Fight

Once A. P. Stewart's advance forced the Federals from their position atop Winstead and Breezy Hills, the three divisions of Frank Cheatham's Corps began moving forward. Around 2 p.m. the first of Cheatham's men "reached a line of hills crossing the Franklin pike" and began forming a line of battle "at the foot of the hills."[1]

By this time Gen. Hood had ridden to the crest of Winstead Hill and occupied a spot about halfway down its northern slope. It has been thought that Hood was on Winstead Hill at 1 p.m., but the evidence points to him being there somewhat later. Considering the Federals were abandoning the hill around one o'clock it is not plausible that a commanding general, especially one as incapacitated as Hood, would come into such close contact with the enemy. On his brief sojourn Hood was accompanied only by the staff officers necessary to ensure he did not fall. This was his first chance to get a personal look at the enemy position and Hood scanned it intently. Earlier, when the Confederate army had arrived near the Harrison House, Hood has been visited by Gen. Forrest. Not one to mince words, Forrest said bluntly that the Yankee works looked impressive and attacking them would be costly. Hood replied, "I do not think the Federals will stand strong pressure from the front; the show of force they are making is a feint in order to hold me back from a more vigorous pursuit." Forrest responded, "General Hood, if you will give me one strong division of infantry with my cavalry, I will agree to flank the Federals from their works within two hours' time." Hood told Forrest that he should prepare to support an infantry assault by placing cavalry on both flanks

---

[1] *OR* 45, pt. 1, p. 736.

and be ready to exploit any success the main attack might have. Specifically Hood wanted Forrest to be in a position to cut the road to Nashville if necessary.[2]

As he looked down from Winstead Hill at the enemy line, Hood remained undeterred. He swept the Union works with his field glasses for several moments. Surely he must have been able to see their strength, especially on both sides of Columbia Pike and east toward the river. Likely he saw the guns atop Figuers Hill, protruding from Fort Granger. Moreover, he must have looked at the terrain between himself and the main Union line. For nearly two miles it was mostly flat and almost completely clear of obstruction. Other than a few homes, some areas of timber, and the Nashville & Decatur Railroad running nearly parallel to Columbia Pike, there was little else on the Franklin plain. Any attack would be over open and exposed ground. John Bell Hood digested all of this information. With a firmness he put his glasses back in their case and snapped the cover shut. A soldier standing nearby said Hood spoke to a nearby officer. His words were brief. "We will make the fight."[3]

In deciding to make the attack at Franklin what could Hood have been thinking? Was he a proponent of the frontal assault as many today have come to believe? The facts indicate that Hood, as a student of Lee and Jackson, believed first and foremost in offense. That meant aggressive flanking maneuvers and, if necessary, frontal assaults. During his days with the Army of Northern Virginia, Hood took part in the massive frontal assault at Gaines' Mill. Although very costly the attack was a success. At Gettysburg, before being wounded, Hood pleaded with James Longstreet to be allowed to move his troops around Little Round Top. As an army commander, Hood fought four major battles around Atlanta trying to free it from William Sherman's grip. One of them involved a significant flanking maneuver and another developed into a series of wasted frontal assaults due more in part to errors by Stephen D. Lee than anything Hood did. After entering Tennessee, Hood attempted to flank Schofield and outrace him to Columbia.

---

[2] Wyeth, *That Devil Forrest*, p. 480; Hurst, *Nathan Bedford Forrest*, p. 234. Hurst argued that by using Forrest in this manner, Hood may have prevented the cavalryman from losing his life.

[3] Cunningham, *CV* 12, p. 339.

Having failed in that effort, he tried again to flank Schofield at Spring Hill. When Hood came to Franklin he must have known the fighting there would be desperate and bloody. But Hood was willing to take the chance. Spring Hill had been a chance for a potentially great victory and the opportunity had slipped away. At Franklin, at least in Hood's mind, there seemed to be another chance. He disregarded the option of another flanking movement and instead seized the initiative and chose to attack. In his own words Hood said:

> I hereupon decided, before the enemy would be able to reach his stronghold at Nashville, to make that same afternoon another and final effort to overtake and rout him, and drive him in the Big Harpeth river at Franklin, since I could no longer hope to get between him and Nashville, by reason of the short distance from Franklin to that city, and the advantage which the Federals enjoyed in the possession of the direct road.[4]

This passage is critical to a full and realistic understanding of what Hood was thinking that afternoon. In the same section of his memoirs, Hood also engaged in a baseless attack against the men he commanded as some sort of rationale for ordering the offensive at Franklin. Yet the real reason is right there in black and white. It had nothing to do with Hood's allegation that the men would not attack breastworks, which they had proven they would do. Instead, Hood saw his last true opportunity to stop Schofield slipping through his fingers. From Pulaski to Columbia to Spring Hill the Federals had eluded him. Here was the chance to finish the job.[5]

It has become commonly accepted that Hood ordered the attack at Franklin out of some fit of rage over what had happened at Spring Hill. There is no evidence that Hood was angry by the time he got to Franklin. Surely he had been upset earlier in the day, especially at the Rippavilla breakfast meeting. But claims that Hood was still boiling by the time he viewed the Federal works from Winstead Hill obscures the probable reality. John Bell Hood was a fighting general plain and simple. Did he have to attack because of Spring Hill? No. Did he order the assault simply to punish his men? Unlikely. Hood was

---

[4] Hood, *Advance & Retreat*, p. 291.

[5] Ibid., p. 290-291.

obviously trying to catch his old classmate Schofield before he could team up with Thomas. In his official report covering the campaign, Hood claimed to have captured "dispatches" indicating Schofield was to hold the town until he could strengthen his position. It is true one dispatch from Thomas to Schofield, written at 3:30 a.m. on November 29, was captured by the Confederates. In it Schofield was told to pull back from Columbia, contest any Southern pursuit, and move to Franklin. Once there he was told to secure his army before the next move to a "position behind Franklin" could be made. Hood insisted he had to attack before Schofield could accomplish the goal of securing himself at Franklin. While this reasoning has a sound basis, the ultimate decision to attack was a poor one because the evidence that the Federals were more than secure in their works was right in front of him. Moreover, if Hood did not believe the fortifications at Franklin were already complete or nearly so by the time he saw them, one is left to wonder how closely he reviewed the Federal line.[6]

Hood chose to attack at Franklin with a clear mind. Unfortunately for him this makes his final decision appear all the more reprehensible. Without excuses or innuendo, only the cold and awful reality remains. In war soldiers often die horrible and agonizing deaths. But in war generals use the lives of soldiers as an avenue to accomplish certain objectives, and there are times when the ends must justify the means. For John Bell Hood the decision to attack at Franklin was one that would haunt him to his grave. Many brave men, however, would go to theirs long before the general.

Following his reconnaissance atop Winstead Hill, Hood called for a conference with some of his top generals at the nearby Harrison House. Couriers galloped away to notify the commanders whose presence was requested. Hood was about to learn just how alone he was in believing the attack could be successful.

Hood had not been the only general officer on Winstead Hill scanning the Union defensive line. Frank Cheatham was there as well. While his corps was forming up on the southern side of the hill Cheatham "rode to its summit..." He recalled the day being so "clear and bright" that he could easily see the Yankees on the north side of the

---

[6] *OR* 45, pt. 1, p. 653; Cox, *Battle of Franklin*, p. 25; French, *Two Wars*, p. 299.

Duck River west of Davis Ford

Last unpaved section of the Davis Ford Road

Position of the 42nd Illinois at Spring Hill showing the hill beyond the tree line where the rest of Bradley's Brigade was located.

Oaklawn
Hood's headquarters at Spring Hill

Field beyond the fence where Johnson's Division bivouacked on the night of November 29.

Rippavilla
Scene of breakfast meeting on November 30

View of Franklin from Winstead Hill

The Harrison House
Scene of meeting prior to Battle of Franklin

South side of the Carter House, where a portion of the 44th Missouri was positioned on the retrenched line.

The Carter House yard where vicious hand-to-hand fighting occurred.

Bullet damage to the Carter office building
and smokehouse.

The Truett House
Schofield's headquarters at Franklin

Back porch at Carnton where bodies of six Confederate generals were laid on the morning of December 1.

Carnton front and walkway

The McGavock Confederate Cemetery

St. John's Episcopal Church

Harpeth River. Cheatham said the town of Franklin itself, the "Union line of battle at the Carter House" and Wagner's advanced brigades all seemed to be "within easy gun-shot." But more importantly Frank Cheatham, a seasoned veteran of many fields, saw the looming danger. There was no getting around what the Confederate army was facing. Cheatham remembered the moment vividly:

> I could easily see all the movements of the Federals and readily trace their line. I saw that they were well fortified and in a strong position. I felt that we would take a desperate chance if we attempted to dislodge them.[7]

Patrick Cleburne was also on Winstead Hill for a short time. Cleburne had ridden somewhat in advance of his division and while he waited, the general decided to look over the Yankee position. What he saw did not hearten him. Through a pair of field glasses Cleburne could see the obvious strength of the enemy works. After taking the glasses from his eyes the general said to a nearby aide, "They are very formidable." Cleburne then sat down upon a nearby tree stump and began writing some notes in a small notebook that he pulled from the inner pocket of his jacket. Once he was finished, Cleburne and a staff member began playing a makeshift game of checkers. Using a stick, a board was drawn into the soil and different colored leaves were used for men. Several games were played before a courier from Gen. Hood arrived. Cleburne was told to report to the Harrison House at once.[8]

Attending the meeting at the Harrison residence were, at the very least, Hood, Forrest, Frank Cheatham, and Cleburne. A. P. Stewart apparently was not present, probably because he was directing his corps into position some distance away and was unable to arrive in a timely manner.[9]

The conference in the Harrison parlor was brief and Hood was unable to gather support from any of his generals. Cleburne said the attack would be "a terrible and useless waste of life" and Cheatham added that the Federals had chosen an "excellent position" and were "well fortified." Cheatham looked at Hood and said, "I don't like the

---

[7] Burr and Williams, *PHP*, March 11, 1883, p. 21.

[8] Buck, *Cleburne and His Command*, p. 280-281.

[9] Elliott, *Soldier of Tennessee*, p. 237.

looks of this fight."[10]

Hood listened to his commanders' opinions, but his mind remained unchanged. Forrest also spoke up. Forrest did not have any military training, but he knew a bad field when he saw it. He considered the plan foolish and repeated his assertion that the Yankees could be flanked from their position. Forrest knew where the Harpeth River could be forded southeast of Franklin. Moreover, James Wilson's cavalry had yet to contain Forrest at any point during the campaign. Hood said no and added that the time for flanking movements had passed. He told his generals it was time to drive Schofield "into the river at all hazards."[11]

Outside the Harrison House the Confederate officers said their farewells. Local legend says that Bedford Forrest had some harsh words for Hood before departing. Considering he had physically threatened Braxton Bragg earlier in the war, it is not inconceivable that Forrest shot off a few parting words to Hood. What is more clear is that Hood spoke directly to Pat Cleburne. The Irish general had already mounted his horse on the front lawn when Hood approached him. According to Dr. D. A. Linthicum, Cleburne's chief surgeon, Hood said:

> General, form your division to the right of the pike, letting your left overlap the same. General Brown will form on the left with his right overlapping your left. I wish you to move on the enemy. Give orders to your men not to fire a gun until you run the Yankee skirmish line from behind the first line of works in your front, then press them and shoot them in their backs as they run to their main line; then charge the enemy's works. Franklin is the key to Nashville, and Nashville is the key to independence.[12]

---

[10] Mangum, *Kennesaw Gazette*, June 15, 1887; Burr and Williams, *PHP*, March 11, 1883, p. 21.

[11] Hood, *Advance & Retreat*, p. 293; Jordan & Pryor, *The Campaigns of General Forrest*, p. 626. The footnote on page 626 of the Forrest biography makes it clear that even after the war Forrest remained convinced flanking Schofield had been the best option. Forrest closely supervised the writing of the book and likely the comment would not have been added without the his approval.

[12] Leonard H. Mangum, Statement of Judge L. H. Mangum of Arkansas regarding the death and burial of General Patrick R. Cleburne, p. 1-2, Peacock Papers, SHC.

Patrick Cleburne was a man grounded by common sense and realistic thought. He looked at Hood, a slight smile creased his battle-worn and scarred face, and said, "General, I will take the works or fall in the effort." With a salute Cleburne spurred his mount toward Winstead Hill.[13]

Cleburne arrived atop the cedar-laced hill within just a few minutes. Once there he was soon joined by Hood, William Bate, John Brown, and probably Frank Cheatham. It does seem that A. P. Stewart was present for this meeting. The view of the Federal works "in front of Franklin" was unobstructed and the officers could see "some distance to the right and left." Everything was awash in late afternoon sunlight. After a moment or two, Hood explained to everyone his reasoning behind the planned attack. He said:

> The country around Franklin for many miles is open and exposed to the full view of the Federal army, and I cannot mask the movements of my troops so as to turn either flank of the enemy, and if I attempt it he will withdraw and precede me into Nashville. While his immediate center is very strong, his flanks are weak.[14]

Stewart's Corps, massed west of Lewisburg Pike and about one mile south of Carnton, home to John McGavock and his family, formed the right of the Confederate line. Stewart's divisions were aligned with W. W. Loring on the right, Edward Walthall in the center, and Samuel French on the left. French's Division did not quite reach Columbia Pike, leaving about a half mile between his left and the road for some of Cheatham's men. On Stewart's far right flank, Gen. Abraham Buford's cavalry division was ordered to move in concert with the infantry and cover "the ground from the Lewisburg pike to Harpeth River."[15]

From Cheatham's Corps, Cleburne's Division was ordered to take position on Stewart's left flank and fill the gap between it and Columbia Pike. Brown's Division was placed on Cleburne's left and

---

[13] Ibid., p. 2, SHC.

[14] John Brown, Report of, *Confederate Military History* (hereafter referred to as *CMH*), 8, p. 156.

[15] *OR* 45, pt. 1, p. 754; Elliott, *Soldier of Tennessee*, p. 238.

immediately across the road so that Brown's right flank actually rested on the pike. Getting Bate's men into line was a bit more problematic. They were to form on Brown's left, but an extension of the Winstead Hill range which juts north between Columbia Pike and Carter's Creek Pike was a problem. It effectively prevented Bate from being able to move down the north side of the hill and slide into place next to Brown. Instead Bate had to move around the southern side of Winstead Hill and bypass the protruding ridge. Hood told Cheatham to give Bate "time sufficient to get into position to attack concurrently" with the rest of the corps. Since James Chalmers' cavalry had moved up Carter's Creek Pike from Spring Hill, his troops were to support Bate's left once the division began its movement against the Federals.[16]

As the impromptu meeting broke up, Bate was told "to move at once" and the generals returned to their commands to prepare for the attack. Hood apparently asked no one for input during this final conference. The gathering in the parlor of the Harrison House had made it abundantly clear to Hood what his subordinates thought, and he was not about to go through the same exercise.[17]

The manner in which Hood aligned his forces is interesting. Obviously he was trying to cover as wide a front as possible, but he grossly mismanaged the distribution of Stewart's Corps. While Stewart had ample room to maneuver on the southern end of the field, that span changed dramatically upon approaching Franklin. Because of the meandering course of the Harpeth River toward the northwest, Stewart's men would gradually be forced to shift toward the Columbia Pike they advanced. This type of converging movement would eventually create a logjam between Stewart's troops and those on Cheatham's right, particularly Cleburne's. If Cleburne held his assigned position on the field, Stewart's forces sooner or later would pile onto one another, almost as if they were passing through a massive funnel. It is not known whether Hood was ever aware of the full effect the river was to have on his attack. If not he is culpable for overlooking something that should have been easily detected by looking at a map,

---

[16] Address delivered by General William B. Bate, on occasion dedicating the Battle-Ground Academy on the field at Franklin Oct. 5, 1889, p. 11, TSLA; Brown, *CMH* 8, p. 156.

[17] Brown, *CMH* 8, p. 156.

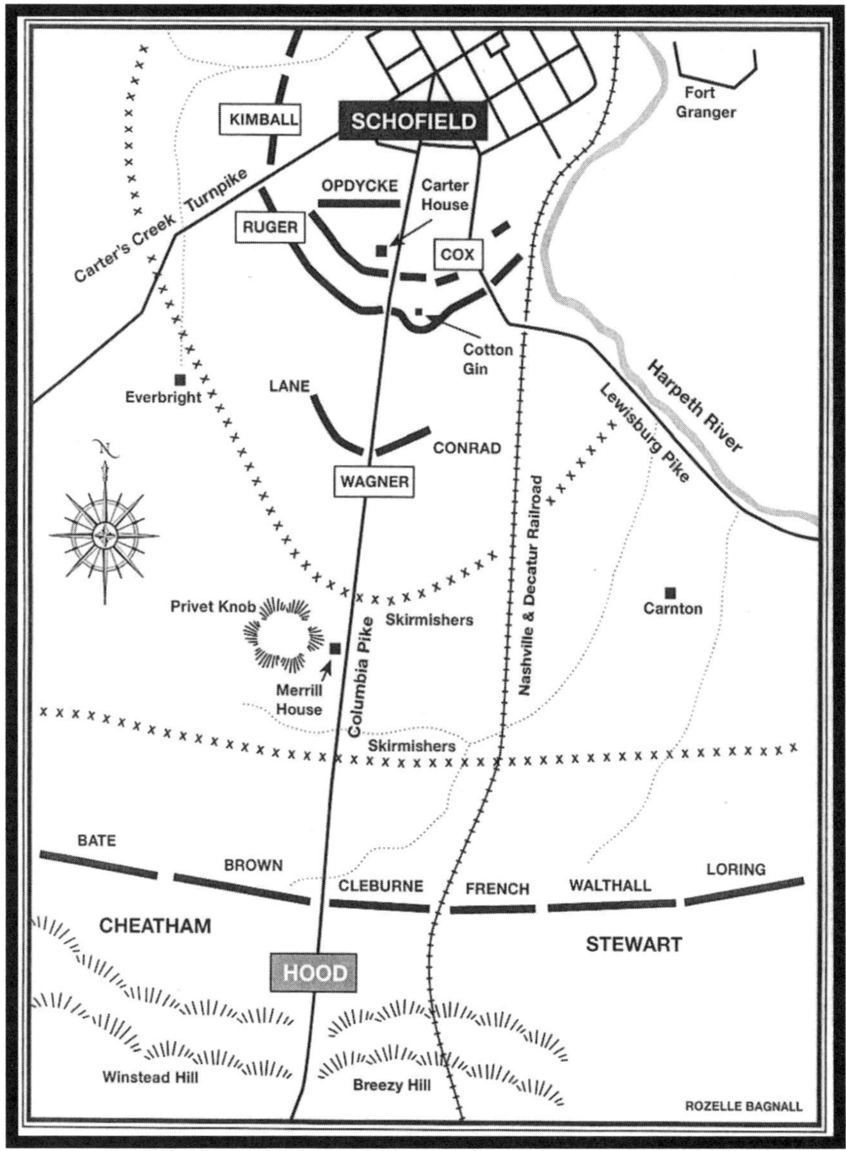

Overview of the Franklin battlefield

talking to a local citizen, or employing even basic reconnaissance. If he ignored it and proceeded anyway, Hood made a serious error in judgment.

Additionally, Hood did not have sufficient troops present to effectively attempt an assault of this magnitude. At three o'clock S. D. Lee's Corps was still en route from Spring Hill and with him was most of the army's artillery. For the second day in a row, Hood had moved without the majority of his big guns and one-third of his infantry. Furthermore, by ordering Bate's Division around Winstead Hill in an effort to extend his line further west, Hood effected a considerable delay. He may have been better served to use Bate as a close support unit on the left of the line, moving behind John Brown or slightly in echelon. Instead, the rest of the troops had to wait for Bate to move into position and unfortunately for them time was not running in their favor. The shadows were lengthening and the 4:34 p.m. sunset was fast approaching.[18]

Hood must have considered the likelihood that a significant portion of the battle would be fought after nightfall. If so, perhaps Gaines' Mill came to mind. The attack there had been launched with the sun about a half hour from setting, and the Confederates were successful in forcing the enemy out of an entrenched position. Whatever Hood was thinking as time ticked away on November 30, 1864 one thing was for certain. After Franklin, John Bell Hood could never again honestly question the bravery of the soldiers who filled the depleted ranks of the Army of Tennessee.[19]

While Bate was moving into position, Brown's and Cleburne's men moved forward and "descended the slopes" of Breezy and Winstead Hills. The sight of the Harpeth Valley opening up before the soldiers, especially for those who called Tennessee home, was exhilarating and a loud cheer rippled back and forth through the ranks. James D. Porter, who served on Gen. Cheatham's staff, recalled the momentous afternoon almost twenty years later. He wrote:

---

[18] Sunset time obtained from the United States Naval Observatory and provided specifically for Franklin, Tennessee for November 30, 1864.
[19] Stephen W. Sears, *To The Gates of Richmond: The Peninsula Campaign*, p. 236.

> It was the grandest sight I ever saw when our army marched over the hill and reached the open field at its base. Each division unfolded itself into a single line of battle with as much steadiness as if forming for dress parade...The men were tired, hungry, footsore, ragged, and many of them barefooted, but their spirit was admirable.[20]

From Winstead Hill, Patrick Cleburne rode across the pike and moved up Breezy Hill. There he met briefly with his brigade commanders and explained to them what Hood had ordered. Cleburne impressed upon them that the Federal works were to be taken at all costs, and his serious tone was brutally obvious. One of Cleburne's brigadiers, Daniel Chevilette Govan, knew his commander well. Both hailed from Arkansas and Govan had commanded a brigade in Cleburne's Division since 1862. Govan was one of Cleburne's most trusted subordinates and had just rejoined the army after being captured at Jonesboro and later exchanged.[21]

Govan never forgot what he saw in Pat Cleburne's steely eyes that afternoon and how his commander's voice reflected an abject sadness. Years later Govan wrote of the fleeting moment:

> General Cleburne seemed to be more despondent than I ever saw him. I was the last one to receive any instructions from him, and as I saluted and bade him good-bye I remarked, "Well, General, there will not be many of us that will get back to Arkansas," and he replied, "Well, Govan, if we are to die, let us die like men."[22]

Cleburne was upset, but it did not stop him from doing his duty. With Stewart's Corps and two-thirds of Cheatham's deploying, jobs that were handled by brigadier generals and other line officers, Cleburne had time to ride forward to Privet Knob. He wanted a closer look at the Union line. The small hill stood practically in no man's land, positioned almost directly between George Wagner's advanced brigades and the Confederates to the south. Privet Knob had recently been occupied by

---

[20] Burr and Williams, *PHP*, March 11, 1883, p. 22.

[21] Buck, *Cleburne and His Command*, p. 290; Faust, ed., *Historical Times Encyclopedia*, p. 316.

[22] Buck, *Cleburne and His Command*, p. 290-291.

a battalion of Rebel sharpshooters who busied themselves picking off Yankees from long distance. When Cleburne trotted up he dismounted and climbed to the crest of the hill. Once there he told Lt. John M. Ozanne that "he had left his field glasses behind" and asked if he could use a scope from one of the Whitworth rifles. Ozanne detached the scope from his own gun and handed it to Cleburne. Kneeling down and laying the long tube across a stump, Cleburne sharpened the focus and deliberately scanned the enemy works. After a moment he said, "They have three lines of works." Then he swept the expanse of the Union lines again and remarked, "And they are all completed." Rising to his feet Cleburne handed the scope back to Lt. Ozanne, thanked him, and descended to the base of the hill. Cleburne quickly remounted, put his spurs to his horse, and "rapidly" rode south along the pike.[23]

Cleburne went to see John Bell Hood almost immediately after returning from his trip to Privet Knob. Seeking to expose his men to as little fire for as long as possible, Cleburne asked Hood if he could be allowed to form his division into columns of brigades. Cleburne assured the commanding general that he would be able to deploy the division into line of battle without difficulty when the time came. Hood approved Cleburne's request and reminded the Irishman it was imperative that the Federals be driven into the river. He also asked Cleburne to report back when the new formation was complete.[24]

It took nearly an hour for the Confederate forces to fully deploy. For many in the ranks it was a time to think deeply and to reckon with one's own mortality. Staring at the distant Federal works over a long and mostly open plain brought home the stark realization to both veteran and recruit alike that "a death-dealing struggle was about to ensue." Chaplain James McNeilly was a firsthand witness to this sort of predilection. Attached to Brig. Gen. William A. Quarles' Brigade,

---

[23] Shannon, *CV* 15, p. 124-125.

[24] Buck, *Cleburne and His Command*, p. 281; Hood, *Advance & Retreat*, p. 293. In his memoirs Hood claimed that when Cleburne returned the Irishman was in high spirits and confident of the chance for success at Franklin as well as Southern independence. Considering the accounts of Cleburne's demeanor during the day by those who knew him best, Hood's statement strains the limits of believability. See *Advance & Retreat*, p. 293-294.

McNeilly was approached before the battle by scores of individual soldiers. They brought to him "watches, jewelry, letters, and photographs" and asked if the chaplain would forward them to family members if they should happen to die. McNeilly related how he had to deny all of the requests because he was also going forward in the advance "and would be exposed to the same danger."[25]

Elsewhere men stood in line silently, awaiting whatever lay ahead. The mood was one of grim determination. George C. Phillips, surgeon for the 22nd Mississippi, said "it was perfectly still" and that he was bothered by the "ominous" silence. Phillips feared the men were "going to be annihilated."[26]

West of the Columbia Pike, in Brown's Division, Gen. Otho Strahl stood ready as his brigade dressed its lines. Strahl, a thirty-three year old Ohio native who had moved to Dyersburg, Tennessee before the war, had only recently returned to active duty following "a dangerous wound" received on July 22 outside Atlanta. Strahl was a veteran of many bloody battles, beginning at Shiloh. Nearly three years of warfare had ingrained in him the difficulties of attacking breastworks and he warned his men that the impending fight would be "short but desperate." Beyond those few words Strahl said little, his face traced with a deep sadness. A private in Strahl's Brigade, J. T. Puckett of the 4th Tennessee, lived near Franklin and had recently received a furlough allowing him to see his family. Rather than abandon his friends just before the battle, however, Puckett pocketed the furlough and said any visiting would have to wait until the fighting was over.[27]

---

[25] George W. Gordon, "Address of Gen. Gordon," *CV* 8, p. 7; James H. McNeilly, "Franklin-Incidents Of The Battle," *CV* 26, p. 118.

[26] G. C. Phillips, "Witness To The Battle Of Franklin," *CV* 14, p. 261.

[27] Brown, *CMH*, 8, p. 159; Sumner Cunningham, "Battle of Franklin," *CV* 1, p. 101; Faust, ed., *Historical Times Encyclopedia*, p. 725; Worsham, *The Old Nineteenth Tennessee*, p. 141; Charles M. Cummings, "Choicest Spirit to Embrace the South: Otho French Strahl," *THQ* 24, No. 4, p. 343; Luke W. Finlay, "Fourth Tennessee Infantry," in *Military Annals of Tennessee*, Vol. 1, John Berrien Lindsley, ed., p. 190. Charles Quintard wrote in *CV* 5, p. 600, that he was given a horse by Strahl at Franklin. He also wrote of speaking to Strahl's aide Lt. John Marsh at the same time. This account contradicts Quintard's own diary. There Quintard related nothing of this story and said he was in

Incredibly there was some wry humor within the ranks. In Francis Marion Cockrell's Missouri Brigade, someone tried to break the mood by quoting the famous English Admiral Horatio Nelson. It was Nelson at the Battle of Trafalgar who called out to his men, "England expects every man to do his duty." Sgt. Denny Callahan loudly replied, "It's damned little duty England would get out of this Irish crowd!" A large number of the Missourians were natives of the Emerald Isle and Capt. Joseph Boyce remembered, "The laugh Denny raised on this was long and hearty. They were noble fellows indeed, laughing in the face of death. Four years of war hardens men..." Boyce was all too correct. These hardy souls had tramped all over the South and fought from Pea Ridge to Corinth and Champion Hill to Vicksburg. Onward they went, battling at Kennesaw Mountain before going to Atlanta and then Allatoona. They had forged a reputation as a force to be reckoned with and were arguably the hardest fighting brigade the war produced on either side.[28]

Of all the soldiers on the field that day, one had thoughts no one else could possibly claim. His name was Theodrick Carter. Known to family and friends as Tod, he was a twenty-four year old captain serving as an aide to twenty-six year old Gen. Thomas Benton Smith, who commanded a brigade in Bate's Division. With the circuit around Winstead Hill complete, Bate moved to attach his brigades to the left of Cheatham's line. Tod Carter finally had a few moments to himself and his heart must have been pounding. Less than two miles away was his home and his family, neither of which he had seen since going off to war in the spring of 1861. If he had field glasses, Tod may have actually been able to catch a glimpse of the house from which he had been absent for so long. No doubt he was aware that Union troops were dug in along his father's property. One can only imagine being in such a situation and the flood of anger and sorrow that came over him. The beautiful Harpeth Valley was Tod's home, and the house he grew up in was about to become the focal point of one of the most ferocious

---

Columbia on November 30.

[28] Boyce, *CV* 24, p. 102; Phil Gottschalk, *In Deadly Earnest: The History of the Missouri Brigade*, p. 463; Phillip Thomas Tucker, "The First Missouri Brigade at the Battle of Franklin," *THQ* 46, No. 1, p. 26.

battles of the entire Civil War.[29]

Around two o'clock, following a meal at Dr. Cliffe's house, John Schofield transferred his headquarters to the home of Alpheus Truett, about a half mile north of the Harpeth River. David Stanley, exhausted and somewhat ill, had joined Schofield earlier following his arrival from Spring Hill and he also moved to the Truett residence. It did not take long for tension to build at the new headquarters.[30]

Schofield reviewed Thomas' last telegram, asking if Hood could be held off at Franklin for three additional days. At 3 p.m. Schofield fired off a response:

> I have just received your despatch asking whether I can hold Hood here three days. I do not believe I can. I can doubtless hold him one day, but will hazard something in doing that. He now has a large force, probably two corps, in my front, and seems prepared to cross the river above and below. I think he can effect a crossing to-morrow in spite of all my efforts, and probably to-night, if he attempts it. A worse position than this for an inferior force could hardly be found. I will refer your question to General Wilson this evening. I think he

---

[29] In *Capt. Tod Carter of the Confederate States Army: A Biographical Word Portrait* by Rosalie Carter, p. 34-36, it states Gen. Smith gave Tod a pass on November 28 allowing him to visit his family. The sketch details how Tod and Sgt. James Cooper, made it from Columbia as far as the home of Green Neely, who owned a home near the northern base of Winstead Hill, by the evening of November 29. Their journey was interrupted, however, by the arrival of Union troops. A secondhand story included in the sketch claims that Tod somehow made his way to the Carter garden before a family member waved him off because the Federals occupied the house. Carter then returned to Winstead Hill. Because the sketch contains an image of the pass Smith signed, the first part of the story is obviously genuine. However, the latter part, which was related by a former slave to a newspaper correspondent years after the war, is highly questionable. It is improbable that Carter would have been able to get near his family's property because the area was swarming with enemy soldiers by dawn. If anything, Carter and Cooper were forced to leave Neely's house to avoid capture by the Yankees and later rejoined their unit.

[30] *OR* 45, pt. 1, p. 115, 349, 353; Bowman, *Historic Williamson County*, p. 112; Cox, *Battle of Franklin*, p. 67, 280; Stanley, *Personal Memoirs*, p. 207.

can do very little. I have no doubt Forrest will be in my rear to-morrow, or doing some greater mischief. It appears to me that I ought to take position at Brentwood at once. If A. J. Smith's division and the Murfreesborough garrison join me there, I ought to be able to hold Hood in check for some time. I have just learned that the enemy's cavalry is already crossing three miles below. I will have lively times with trains again. [31]

Just prior to telegraphing Thomas, word came to Schofield from Gen. Wilson that enemy infantry was pressing toward Hughes' Ford on the Harpeth, some two and a half miles southeast of Franklin. Wilson said he was unsure what the Rebels were up to, but citizens were claiming the river could be crossed anywhere. Fifteen minutes later, Wilson reported that Rebel soldiers had apparently crossed the river at Hughes' Ford. Although he did not know it, these troops were from Forrest's cavalry, specifically William Jackson's Division. Wilson told Schofield that it was his understanding the enemy had already driven in the picket line and was advancing. When Schofield got the dispatch he must have thought his fears about a flanking movement were being realized. He and Stanley spoke briefly. At 3:05 p.m. Schofield notified Wilson that a Fourth Corps brigade would be sent from the north side of the river "to check the crossing of the enemy" at the ford. Brig. Gen. Samuel Beatty's Brigade from Thomas Wood's Division drew this duty and he and his men prepared to move out.[32]

Schofield went through a mental checklist. With Cox in command along the Carter Hill line, Beatty moving to Hughes' Ford, and Wilson shoring up the army's left flank, the troop dispositions were set and Schofield could only anxiously await nightfall. Of some comfort to the Federal commander was the fact that the army's trains would be mostly across the river by sunset. If Hood did not attack, the withdrawal to Nashville was set to begin at 6 p.m. Everything seemed

---

[31] *OR* 45, pt. 1, p. 1170. Of note is that Schofield's telegram sent book is the source of the wording use here. In Thomas' telegrams received book, however, the word "prepared" is instead "preparing" and "below" in the second to last sentence is rather "above." By the time Schofield had his memoirs published in 1897 he had adopted Thomas' wording. See Schofield, *Forty-Six Years In The Army*, p. 223.
[32] *OR* 45, pt. 1, p. 1174, 1178.

to be in place. Schofield and Stanley then stepped outside the Truett home, mounted their horses, and rode toward downtown.[33]

Around the time Schofield and Stanley headed for the town square, the telegraph clicked to life at the downtown station.[34] It carried a message from Thomas. Schofield wanted out of Franklin in the worst way and now Thomas did as well. The wire read:

> Your dispatch of 3 p.m. is received. Send back your trains to this place at once, and hold your troops in readiness to march to Brentwood, and thence to this place, as soon as your trains are fairly on the way, so disposing your force to cover the wagon train. Have all railroad trains sent back immediately. Notify General Wilson of my instructions; he will govern himself accordingly. Relieve all garrisons in block-houses and send back by railroad trains last over the road. Acknowledge receipt.[35]

The problem was that moving up the army's withdrawal at this stage was impossible. The Confederates were massed and ready to advance and there was no time for anything else to be done.

Just nine days previously the Rebels had pushed north from Florence, Alabama. Now a campaign which had been measured by days and hours was reduced to mere minutes and seconds. There was an eerie calm out on the plains south of Franklin, made stranger by the fact that there were almost 40,000 soldiers present. Along the Confederate line there were the hushed sounds of prayers and goodbyes. In the Union trenches there was either stillness or the cold clicking of rifle hammers. An Indiana soldier distinctly remembered the "deep and awful silence..." The sun glided toward the horizon and began sinking into a dark bank of clouds moving in from the west. Golden rays of light blazed through small breaks in the clouds, creating a scene that resembled something out of a dream. But it was all too real. It was madness, the final and dark pages of a time when the idea of a true

---

[33] Cox, *Battle of Franklin*, p. 62, 67, 281; Schofield, *Forty-Six Years In The Army*, p. 177.

[34] Telegraphic messages were received at the station in town and then taken by courier to Schofield and, of course, vice versa.

[35] *OR* 45, pt. 1, p. 1171.

United States was being forged in fire.[36]

While John Schofield clattered toward downtown Franklin and John Bell Hood looked over his army, thousands of other men readied themselves for death.

[36] Kerwood, *Annals of the Fifty-Seventh Indiana*, p. 296.

8

The Devil Had Full Possession of the Earth

Destiny takes its shape in many forms. At Franklin, Tennessee destiny appeared in the form of the long and winding stretch of Federal breastworks. Thousands of Rebel soldiers strained to see those works as final alignment corrections were made to the sprawling line of attack. The Southern line stretched for nearly two miles and was composed of some 20,000 men, including Nathan Bedford Forrest's cavalry. In front of each of the six Rebel divisions was a line of skirmishers, and to the casual observer it might have appeared as if the gray army was on dress parade. But a close look at the faces of the men up and down the line would have told a different story. The troops understood the deadly serious nature of what they were about to attempt and their eyes held the truth.

Previously it had been decided that the attack would commence with the dropping of a flag on Winstead Hill. As the men waited "for the signal to advance" officers moved along the fronts of their units. They chatted with their troops and offered reminders of what was expected of them. But the men knew their duty, they needed few if any prompts. To pass the time some looked at faded photographs and read tattered letters while others read their Bibles. A few pulled out their watches and watched the minutes tick by. One soldier recalled seeing an entire regiment kneel down in prayer. An Alabamian watched as some men almost casually began "picking white beans from the dead vines in a field in our front..." For all too many it was simply a time for reflection. Then, at almost precisely four o'clock, the flag on Winstead Hill came down.[1]

Line officers immediately began calling out various commands. To the sounds of "Attention!" the Confederate rank and file squared their shoulders and almost collectively looked straight ahead, breathing deeply. Then came the orders to "Shoulder arms!" and "Right shoulder shift arms!" The sound of the men wielding their trusted muskets and rifles reverberated in the autumn air. Finally there was heard, "Brigade forward!" and "Quick time march!" Like an enormous human wave eighteen Confederate brigades of infantry stepped forward and some one hundred battle flags sprung into the air. There was barely a breath of air, but the banners were held high aloft nonetheless. The battle flag was the identity of a regiment, brigade, or division and the color bearers displayed them with great pride and honor. Patrick Cleburne's division flag, a blue field encircling a white moon and surrounded by white trim, floated high above the very center of the advancing line. Jacob Cox watched the Rebels as they began marching and said the "martial magnificence" of the sight was something that no one who saw it ever forgot.[2]

In the main Federal line near the gin house, Pvt. Adam Weaver of the 104th Ohio was composing a letter to his girlfriend Charlotte when the Confederates moved forward. He wrote that a nearby captain had asked another officer, "Do you think the Lord will be with us today?" Only moments later Weaver was forced to cut his letter short. He finished by writing, "I must close out this letter, as we are ordered up to our positions. One last look south. The air is hazy, I can hear bands playing, and I see a few Rebels being deployed in a line of battle in the far distance."[3]

Indeed bands were playing. For the first and only time that anyone on either side could remember, army bands accompanied the fighting troops to the front. The brass band belonging to the Missouri Brigade of Samuel French's Division made a good deal of noise as the

---

[1] Burr and Williams, *PHP*, March 11, 1883, p. 23; George R. Sutton, "An Incident at Franklin," *CV* 28, p. 116; Daniel P. Smith, *Company K, First Alabama Regiment, or Three Years In the Confederate Service*, p. 121.

[2] Cox, *Battle of Franklin*, p. 92.

[3] Adam J. Weaver letter to Charlotte, Nov. 30, 1864, CHA.

musicians let loose with "The Bonnie Blue Flag." Nearby another brigade band could be heard playing "Dixie." The music made the scene almost ethereal. Men with fifes and trumpets marched in tandem with the infantry, drums rolled and beat in time, officers barked out orders, and a fine Indian summer day rapidly approached its conclusion. Joseph Boyce, a Missouri officer, said the sun's "slanting rays threw a crimson light over the field and intrenchments in front..." It was a grandeur never before witnessed. But Federal gunners along the Carter Hill line and inside Fort Granger were already sighting in their targets. Soon they would shatter the martial display and transform it into one of horror.[4]

Because of the distance the gray and butternut line was required to travel, at least ten or fifteen minutes elapsed before the Confederate troops closest to Columbia Pike reached the vicinity of Privet Knob. Both to the east and west, the rest of the line kept a near equivalent pace. Officers did good work keeping the formations tight and making sure sections did not lag behind or move too far ahead.

Following behind the expansive line of infantry came the limited Southern artillery. Harold Young was a gunner in Henry Guibor's Missouri Battery and said "it was beautiful to see the entire corps move forward in 2 lines of battle with 150 yards of interveile and the Artillery half way between..." Because so few cannon were available, Guibor's Battery had been split into three two-gun sections. But Guibor, who had served with distinction at places such as Wilson's Creek, Port Gibson, Champion Hill and Vicksburg, was absent. His body, utterly exhausted by years of intense campaigning, had forced him to leave the army at the end of October because of deteriorating health. Yet Guibor's name remained associated with the guns. Two of the battery's sections were located on each side of the Missouri Brigade and the remaining two guns moved up between Walthall's and Loring's divisions. To the west, near the Columbia Pike, Capt. James P. Douglas had his four-gun Texas Battery, "under the immediate command of

---

[4] Boyce, *CV* 24, p. 102-103; Joseph Boyce, "Cockrell's Brigade Band at Franklin," *CV* 19, p. 271; Patterson, *CV* 9, p. 117; Talley, Civil War Memoir, TSLA; Tucker, *THQ* 46, No. 1, p. 26; Binford, *Recollections of the Fifteenth Mississippi*, p.102.

The Merrill House
(Williamson County Archives)

General Cheatham," rolling forward.[5]

In the Merrill House at the base of Privet Knob, the family watched helplessly as the Confederates swarmed past their home and moved toward the Federal position. Lt. Edwin H. Rennolds of the 5th Tennessee later wrote: "The long lines of infantry moved steadily and grandly forward through the open field...The band of the Fifth struck up 'Dixie' and one of Cleburne's the 'Bonnie Blue Flag,' and for once, and only once, we went into battle cheered by the sound of martial music. It was the grandest sight I ever beheld. A battery went galloping up the pike, and, turning aside, unlimbered on a little knoll and opened fire, as the infantry passed, limbering up and advancing again." Capt. Sam Foster of Hiram Granbury's Brigade said "at the command forward the Bands begin to play and we march off to the music..." Barely a half mile away, the

---

[5] Gottschalk, *In Deadly Earnest*, p. 436, 464; Lucia Douglas, *Douglas's Texas Battery*, p. 145, 149, 167; Young diary, Nov. 30, 1864, in possession of Bill and Marilyn Christmann; P. E. Hockersmith, "Douglass's Battery at Franklin," *CV* XIV, p. 352. Bate reported a battery commanded by Stephen Presstman was present near the Bostick House. Presstman was an engineer, however, and had no affiliation with the artillery, so it is unclear how Bate made this error. See *OR* 45, pt. 1, p. 743. In the Douglas book, page 149, a letter from Capt. Douglas dated December 3, 1864 stated an entire battalion was engaged at Franklin. His diary entry concerning the battle on page 212 mentioned the involvement of Courtney's battalion and a single battery from Hotchkiss' battalion. Douglas said Courtney's battalion suffered three killed and seventeen wounded at Franklin, the same number reported by Gen. Edward Johnson on December 3, 1864. See *OR* 45, pt. 1, p. 691.

anxious men of John Lane's and Joseph Conrad's brigades readied for the storm that was bearing down on them.[6]

Sitting on Columbia Pike, at the apex of Wagner's exposed line, was the two-gun section of Capt. Alexander Marshall's Battery G, 1st Ohio Light Artillery. Marshall and Lt. Milton Mitchell, the latter commanding the section, watched as Cheatham's Corps headed straight toward them. They waited until the Rebels cleared the area near Privet Knob and then, from a distance of about 500 yards, Mitchell yelled for his gunners to open fire. The timed shells, once the artillerymen got their range, tore into the Southern ranks, throwing hot and jagged iron everywhere. One of those who fell very early was an officer from the 7th Texas of Granbury's Brigade. Lt. Linson Keener was hit in the upper body by a shell fragment which broke a rib and knocked him unconscious. Keener was lucky. He would survive to tell his tale, but many of his friends would not be so fortunate.[7]

Marshall and Mitchell not only had the advancing infantry to contend with, but the sharpshooters on Privet Knob caused them a great deal of grief. In a matter of minutes, nearly half a dozen men were lying dead or wounded around the guns, the victims of long range minie balls. Isaac N. Shannon, one of the riflemen on the stony knob, singlehandedly dropped four of the Yankee gunners.[8]

Cheatham's men were closing in fast. The Federal cannoneers soon switched from percussion and fused shells to canister. Canister was by far the most lethal weapon Civil War artillerists had at their disposal. Its design was simple. Iron balls were packed with sawdust into a tin cylinder roughly resembling a coffee can. The size of an individual ball depended upon the gun being used. Three-inch rifled guns, like those in Capt. Marshall's battery, used balls three-quarters of an inch in diameter; twelve-pounder smoothbore Napoleons were

---

[6] Gottschalk, *In Deadly Earnest*, p. 465; Edwin H. Rennolds, *A History of the Henry County Commands Which Served in the Confederate States Army, Including Rosters of the Various Companies Enlisted in Henry County, Tenn.*, p. 104; Brown, ed., *One of Cleburne's Command*, p. 147.

[7] *OR* 45, pt. 1, p. 331; John R. Lundberg, *The Finishing Stroke: Texans in the 1864 Tennessee Campaign*, p. 90; Marshall to Scofield, Oct. 10, 1886, Cox Papers, OBC.

[8] Shannon, *CV* 15, p. 125.

loaded with balls one and a quarter inch wide. Each cylindrical container held twenty-seven or twenty-eight balls dispersed into five circular layers. Once rammed into a cannon's muzzle and fired the effect was like a massive shotgun blast. The dispersion ratio for this type of fire was approximately ten percent. That is to say, at a distance of two hundred feet a canister charge would encompass a rough circle some twenty feet in diameter.

The Confederate troops facing Marshall and Mitchell were already deploying into line of battle when the switch in ammunition was ordered. There was no time to waste. Mitchell yelled, "Fire!" Canister peppered Cheatham's exposed troops, inflicting a number of casualties. But the Yankee gunners were not about to stick around and see what the enemy was going to do next. Already some Southern artillery had joined the action and a shell suddenly whistled over Wagner's line. Another "dropped short" and plowed into the ground in front. With that Capt. Marshall decided it was time to go. After belching out a few more rounds the Ohio gunners limbered up their pieces and took off toward the Carter Hill line. The Federal infantry left behind were incredulous. Most figured they should have already been pulled back. Men began cursing and yelling, demanding they be allowed to withdraw. Stewart was obviously going to sweep far beyond their left flank and Cheatham was in the process of rolling up their right. It seemed like utter madness to stay where they were. Straight ahead two full divisions, Pat Cleburne's and John Brown's, were preparing to charge.[9]

Back at the gap in the Federal line, Mitchell's two-gun section arrived and the horses pulled the guns up to the retrenchment. As the pieces turned to go around the end of the retrenched line Alec Clinton, one of the gunners, jumped off the limber, "his face black with powder smoke," and exclaimed, "Old hell is let loose, and coming out there." Clinton was right, but it was a mere prelude of what was to come.[10]

Frank Cheatham followed behind Cleburne and Brown as they led their divisions, seven brigades in all, forward to meet the Yankees. Cleburne and Brown "met several times upon the turnpike road and conferred and acted in harmony" as their approximately 6,500 troops

---

[9] *OR* 45, pt. 1, p. 331; Marshall to Scofield, Oct. 10, 1886, Cox Papers, OBC; Shellenberger, *CV* 36, p. 382.

[10] Scofield, *The Retreat From Pulaski*, p. 34.

The Neely House (Williamson County Archives)

approached Wagner's line. Cheatham watched his men "very closely" and soon set up his headquarters atop Privet Knob. Hood was, Cheatham said, "just back of me on the pike." The commanding general watched the advance from Winstead Hill, but soon descended to the plain below and made his headquarters at the home of Green Neely. From there Gen. Hood watched the battle unfold, lying on a blanket with his head and shoulders supported by a saddle.[11]

On A. P. Stewart's front events escalated quickly. Stewart said his troops "moved forward in fine order," but apparently there were problems with Edward Walthall's Division. Walthall had placed two of his brigades, those commanded by William Quarles and Daniel Reynolds, on the front line and ordered Brig. Gen. Charles M. Shelley, commanding Cantey's Brigade, to form as a reserve. Almost immediately a problem cropped up. Reynolds, forming the front left, faced an "impenetrable brier thicket" so Walthall instructed him to work his way around the obstacle once the advance began. After maneuvering around the thicket, Reynolds was to move at the "double quick and resume his place on the line." According to Walthall, the entire corps had moved only "a short distance" when its formation was disrupted by "broken ground and undergrowth..." Walthall took the opportunity to order Shelley and his brigade to the front of the line because Reynolds, "without fault of himself or his command, had not

---

[11] Brown, *CMH*, 8, p. 157; Burr and Williams, *PHP*, March 11, 1883, p. 24; Cox, *Battle of Franklin*, p. 89-90.

been able to regain his place in the line by reason of the natural obstacles in the way of his march."[12]

Edward Cary Walthall was born in Richmond, Virginia, but Mississippi was the place he considered home. His family had relocated to the Magnolia State when Walthall was ten years old and Holly Springs was where he grew to adulthood. An intelligent young man, Walthall studied law and after passing the state bar in 1852 he became a practicing attorney in Coffeeville. He even won a seat in one of Mississippi's judicial districts in the years before the war. When secession came, however, Walthall's personal life was put on hold and he volunteered for service, even though he had no military experience. Through hard work and attention to detail, Walthall rose through the ranks and by early 1863 had received a promotion to brigadier general. Although wounded at Missionary Ridge, Walthall recovered to fight throughout the Atlanta Campaign. During the summer of 1864, Walthall not only became a major general, but also ascended from brigade to division command. Walthall was thirty-three years old at Franklin and embodied the best of what the South had left to offer, young men who were brave, bright, and educated.[13]

Stewart's Corps, which launched its four o'clock movement from the "beautiful blue-grass pasture lot of Col. John McGavock," resumed its march and moved a considerable distance through "an open field..." The Rebels faced little resistance until they came within range of the rifled guns inside Fort Granger. Capt. Giles Cockerill's Battery D, 1st Ohio Light Artillery, only had to use a few shells to calculate the distance to Stewart's men. The Federal gunners were well-trained and war had made them deadly efficient. They cut the percussion fuses on the shells with such accuracy that the projectiles began exploding directly above the gray ranks and in their midst. Pvt. Joseph N. Thompson of the 35th Alabama, on the right of Brig. Gen. Thomas M.

---

[12] *OR* 45, pt. 1, p. 708, 720. Gen. James Cantey was absent from his brigade's command because of illness for much of 1864. See Welsh, *Medical Histories of Confederate Generals*, p. 34.

[13] Faust, ed., *Historical Times Encyclopedia*, p. 800.

Scott's Brigade, said only the third shot from the Yankees burst right above his regiment, causing the men in line to involuntarily duck their heads. Thompson never forgot how in the following minutes "great gaps" were made "with every shot."[14]

Cockerill's guns inflicted a considerable toll on Stewart's troops. A soldier in the 63rd Indiana, positioned east of Lewisburg Pike, remembered how the Granger artillery "commenced to vigorously shell the belt of timber in front of us..." Undoubtedly the belt of trees were part of McGavock's Grove. The same man said "we saw the rebels pour out of the belt of timber in heavy battle line" and that the explosive fire "mowed them down, making great holes in their ranks..." Col. Marcus D. L. Stephens of the 31st Mississippi said one shot alone killed and wounded seven men from one of his companies. He also described how the incoming shots ripped limbs from the trees.[15]

One shell after another howled into the helpless Southerners, battering their formation and producing a ghastly trail of casualties. Men continued to drop three and four at a time, their bodies collapsing like cordwood into bloody and mangled heaps. But the Rebels showed remarkable, almost iron discipline. After each round did its horrible work the serried ranks closed up as best they could and kept moving.

From the west side of Columbia Pike, the sight of the artillery fire crashing into A. P. Stewart's men was unforgettable. Everywhere the sights were incredible, almost breathtaking. Col. Ellison Capers was in the 24th South Carolina west of the pike and his regiment, part of States Rights Gist's Brigade, was on John Brown's left flank. Some distance in advance and to the left of the South Carolinians stood Everbright mansion, home to the widowed Rebecca Bostick. But it was what Capers saw to his right that he never forgot. As Capers and his fellow Palmetto Staters began to crest the rising terrain around Privet Knob, the ground stretching from Columbia Pike to Lewisburg Pike

---

[14] McNeilly, *CV* 26, p. 117; Joseph N. Thompson, "Battle of Franklin," *Williamson County Historical Society* (hereafter referred to as *WCHS*), 15, p. 58; Joseph N. Thompson, Dec. 15, 1924 letter, Carnton Archives (hereafter referred to as CRN).

[15] McNeilly, *CV* 26, p. 117; Daniel Dawson, "The 63d Ind. At Franklin," *NT*, Aug. 22, 1907, p. 6; M. D. L. Stephens, *Narrative of the Battle of Franklin*, *CRN*; *OR* 45, pt. 1, p. 432, 720.

opened up into view. Capers wrote that "we beheld the magnificent spectacle the battle-field presented - bands were playing, general and staff officers and gallant couriers were riding in front of and between the lines, 100 battle-flags were waving in the smoke of battle, and bursting shells were wreathing the air with great circles of smoke, while 20,000 brave men were marching in perfect order against the foe."[16]

Inside the main Union line, at the Carter House, there was both fear and frantic activity. Soon after Jacob Cox had taken the house as his headquarters Fountain Branch Carter, the owner of the home, had asked the general if there was going to be a battle and if so, should he remove himself and his family from the premises. Cox responded that the family should not leave unless a battle "was imminent" and added it did not appear that Hood was likely to attack. Cox also said as long as the headquarters of the Twenty-Third Corps was in and around the house no damage would come to it. However, he warned Mr. Carter that if he decided to leave and the headquarters happened to be moved, the house could easily be ransacked by Federal troops. Carter took Cox's advice and he and his family chose to stay. For a time it seemed as if the Union general's counsel had been accurate. But then matters abruptly changed. When the Confederates began their advance, Moscow Carter used a heavy cedar ladder to climb to the roof of the house and watch the "martial sight." No sooner had the Yankees made him come down than the battle began erupting south along Columbia Pike. Events unfolded so quickly there was no time for the Carters to evacuate their home. Panic and dread began to spread. Like a violent and unforseen gale the battle that no one thought was coming was doing exactly that and it was heading directly toward the Carter family home.[17]

The Carter House, which still stands, is a red brick building with a front length of fifty-four feet. Today the house looks almost exactly as it did in 1864. The front of the Carter home faces east and at its center are white double doors. When these doors are closed they form an eight-panel colonial pattern. The doors are flanked by beautiful Doric columns and topped with a fanlight transom. Halfway between

---

[16] *OR* 45, pt. 1, p. 737.

[17] Cox, *Battle of Franklin*, p. 198; Smith, *History of Maury County*, Interview with Moscow Carter, p. 202.

the doorway and each end of the house is a twelve-pane window and these are also flanked by Doric columns. Perhaps the most distinguishable feature of the house, especially from a distance, are the stepped parapet walls that adorn each end of the home. Each wall is topped off by prominent chimneys.

Upon entering the house through the double-front door one moves into a twelve by twenty feet hall. On each side of the hall is a room measuring nineteen by twenty feet. There is a fireplace and two windows in each room. One of the windows is a large twelve-pane type, the other is a smaller window near the fireplace. The room on the south end of the house was the family room and the other was the parlor. Six-panel colonial doors open from the family room to a back porch and a door at the end of the hall leads to the porch as well. The porch runs north and south, but has a right, or westerly, wing that fronts a frame ell. This ell contains two small rooms.

The upper section of the house is a half story and has two rooms flanking the stair landing. Each upstairs room measures twelve by twenty feet. Sadly this upper portion of the house was the scene of a tragic accident years before the war. Samuel Carter was only four years old when he fell through the balusters directly above the hall in 1837. He died almost instantly and was one of four Carter sons who died before the war.[18]

Fountain Branch Carter and his wife Mary Armistead Atkinson Carter purchased nineteen acres of land on the west side of the Columbia Turnpike in October 1829. Through the years the Carters watched their family grow to include eight sons and daughters who reached maturity.[19] They also saw their farm swell from its modest beginning to eventually encompass 288 acres. In the 1860 census, Mr. Carter's total value was estimated at $62,000 and he owned twenty-eight slaves. Although not as wealthy as others in the area, Carter had done well for himself. Sadly, however, he had lost his beloved Mary in 1852. Mr. Carter may have been a widower, but he had much to enjoy and loved the company of his family, especially as he moved into his golden years. Little could he have imagined what those years would bring. The fashionable red brick house on the outskirts of Franklin had been the

---

[18] Robison, *THQ* 22, No. 1, p. 3-21.

[19] The Carters had twelve children, but four boys died at young ages.

Carter family home for thirty-five years. Now Mr. Carter and his family would look to their house for protection.[20]

The stone-walled basement of the Carter House is divided into three sections, or rough rooms, and there the family and others sought refuge from the battle. From careful research by a Carter descendant it is now known for certain who went to the basement seeking safety. Fountain Branch Carter and his eldest son Moscow, the paroled Confederate officer, were there. Moscow, like his father, was widowed and he brought his four children with him. They, along with their ages, were: Mary Orleana, 11; Walter Fountain, 10; Annie Josephine, 6; and Hugh Ewing, 4. Moscow's sister, Mary Alice Carter McPhail, was there along with her three children. Mary had come home to Franklin from Texas at her father's behest because her husband, Daniel McPhail, was serving in the Confederate army. Mary's children and their ages were: Alice Adelaide, 8; Marcus, 7; and Orlando, 1. Three other Carter sisters also made their way to the cellar. They were Annie Vick Carter McKinney, Frances Hodge Carter, and Sarah Holcomb. Sallie Dobbins McKinney Carter and her two small children were present, too. Sallie had been married to a Carter son, James Fountain Carter who had died in 1859. Her children were Fountain McKinley Carter, aged 11, and Ruth James, aged 6. There were also at least two of the Carter slaves present and perhaps a third, a small boy. But this was not all. Northeast of Mr. Carter's residence, on the other side of the pike, stood the white-columned, two-story frame house owned by Albert Lotz. Apparently Mr. Lotz believed his home might not make it through the impending battle, so he and his wife and their three children asked if they might take shelter at the Carter home. Mr. Carter agreed and the Lotz family descended the stairs to the basement. His children were Paul, 9; Matilda, 6; and Augustus, 2.[21]

The Carter basement held the fate of some two dozen souls. Outside they could hear the battle approach a furious crescendo and the Carters and their neighbors huddled together and prayed for deliverance. Little more than a mile away Tod Carter sat astride his horse, his hands gripped tightly on the reins. He was just about home.

Around the time the Carters and their friends were finding

---

[20] McDonough and Connelly, *Five Tragic Hours*, p. 100.

[21] Carter, *Tod Carter*, p. 38-39.

refuge below ground, George Wagner was speaking with Levi Scofield east of Columbia Pike. Scofield was standing atop the parapet, speaking with a nearby officer and "urging the men to strengthen the works" while Wagner, with his feet hanging over the edge of the trench, reclined on his elbow. In Wagner's other hand was a crutch he was using because of a fall from his horse earlier in the day. To the south the spattering of fire was growing in intensity. Suddenly an orderly galloped up from one of the advanced brigades with a message. Both the aide, T. C. Gregg, and his horse were completely out of breath and he blurted out to Wagner, "The enemy are forming in heavy columns; we can see them distinctly in the open timber and all along our front." Wagner sat up, looked at the orderly, and said firmly, "Stand there and fight them." Then, turning to Capt. Scofield, and referring to Col. Conrad, Wagner exclaimed, "And that stubbed, curly-headed Dutchman will fight them, too." Confused by the logic of the answer, but not in a position to question it, Gregg turned his horse around and raced back to the advanced line.[22]

As this spectacle was unfolding Capt. Theodore Cox, younger brother of Gen. Cox, was sitting on the Carter House porch talking with Lt. D. C. Bradley. As the two spoke a round of Confederate artillery came crashing in above them. It tore "off a portion of the cornice of the porch" and exploded in the yard. Rattled and now aware that the Rebels were on the move, the two officers jumped on their horses and rode out to find Wagner. When they found him, Scofield had just finished reminding Wagner that the orders were to retreat if it became clear the Rebels meant to engage in a full-scale assault. Scofield's prompting did no good. Another staff aide rode up and told Wagner the Confederates were pushing forward in large numbers. Wagner again repeated his order to stand firm and fight. The aide could not believe what he was hearing. He said plaintively, "But Hood's entire army is coming." Capt. Cox interjected and, like Scofield, told Wagner the general orders were to pull back the advanced brigades if the pressure on them became too great. To drive the point home the young officer said the current situation was not what Gen. Cox desired. In fact, barely

---

[22] Scofield, *The Retreat From Pulaski*, p. 32-33; Cox, *Battle of Franklin*, p. 107; Stanley, *Personal Memoirs*, p. 206; Scofield to Cox, Dec. 23, 1870, Cox Papers, OBC.

an hour earlier Jacob Cox had spoken to Wagner in person. At that time he reiterated both Lane and Conrad were to be withdrawn "whenever the enemy appeared to be advancing in decidedly superior force" to prevent the brigades from becoming "seriously engaged." Wagner nonetheless remained openly defiant to the junior officers and refused to call the brigades in. His temper was flaring and Wagner smashed the ground with his makeshift crutch and yelled, "Go back, and tell them to fight - fight like hell!" Without another word the aide turned around left. Capts. Cox and Bradley followed suit and began a desperate search for Gen. Cox. It was their intent to report "this strange affair" and find out what could be done to prevent Lane and Conrad from being sacrificed.[23]

It remains unclear what caused George Wagner to behave so erratically at Franklin, but whiskey is believed by some to be the cause. Wagner was a dependable and brave soldier and had never before acted as strangely as he did during the afternoon hours at Franklin. Wagner was exhausted, hungry, and in pain from his fall. If Wagner got hold of a whiskey bottle following his altercation with Opdycke and subsequent conversation with Cox, who knows what effect alcohol may have had on him. The evidence for Wagner's drinking or intoxication is limited primarily to a letter which David Stanley wrote in 1883 to Marshall Thatcher. In the letter, Stanley is obviously answering a question Thatcher had asked about Wagner drinking at Franklin. Stanley wrote that Wagner was "full of whiskey" and in "vainglorious condition..." It is interesting that Stanley admitted neither he nor Schofield knew anything about Wagner drinking on the day of the battle, so Stanley was obviously dealing with second hand information about Wagner's alleged intoxication. Whatever the reason for Wagner's erratic behavior, the entire episode involving the non-withdrawal of his two brigades would be among the most hotly debated topics in the post-war years.[24]

Along Wagner's advanced line the pressure on the men was nearly too much to bear. A private from the 26th Ohio said "the

---

[23] Scofield, *The Retreat From Pulaski*, p. 33; Cox, *Battle of Franklin*, p. 336-337; *OR* 45, pt. 1, p. 352; Scofield to Cox, Dec. 23, 1870, Cox Papers, OBC.

[24] Marshall P. Thatcher, *A Hundred Battles in the West - St. Louis to Atlanta - 1861-1865 - The Second Michigan Cavalry*, p. 249.

nervous strain became greater and greater as the time passed and the lines of grey came nearer and nearer." A man from the 57th Indiana recalled that some of the officers realized the regiment would be "swept away like chaff before the devouring flames." Capt. Shellenberger of the 64th Ohio, positioned on the left of Conrad's Brigade, recalled that nothing could be seen of Cheatham's Corps from where he was stationed because of a "small body of timber" located "a short distance in advance" of the regiment. On the left front, however, the ground was mostly "a wide expanse of cleared fields" and "a large part of Stewart's Corps" was easily visible. As Stewart's troops emerged from a line of trees near the river, Conrad's men watched the enemy press forward and deploy from column into line of battle. It was brutally clear to everyone on the blue line what was happening. Making matters even worse was that the troops could not understand why they had been left out in the open and exposed to disaster. Glancing over their shoulders, many wondered aloud why they were not being called back to the main line. One of them yelled out, "Captain, for God's sake, let us get in behind the works. Why, just see them coming! Enough to swallow us up!"[25]

According to John Shellenberger the mood of the troops "grew almost into a mutiny." A sergeant from Company H, 64th Ohio finally stood up and said he was not about to throw his life away based on someone else's stupidity. As he turned to walk away several other men joined him. All were ordered back into the line. Only minutes later the same sergeant and the same group of men again got up and began moving toward the main line. Shellenberger screamed at them, "God damn you, come back here!" Grudgingly the soldiers resumed their spot on the line. But the regiment, as well as the brigade, could not be kept quiet. There was hollering and swearing aplenty and it only increased in volume as the Rebels pushed closer.[26]

The men of Joseph Conrad's Brigade had been able to construct only meager breastworks because of a lack of both digging tools and

---

[25] Gist, *THM* 6, No. 3, p. 227; Shellenberger, *CV* 36, p. 381; Kerwood, *Annals of the Fifty-Seventh Indiana*, p. 296; Keesy, *War As Viewed From The Ranks*, p. 107.

[26] Shellenberger, *CV* 36, p. 381. The sergeant's name was Samuel Libey and he was later killed in the fighting.

View of the area west of Columbia Pike over which a portion of the Confederate army advanced (U. S. Army Military History Institute)

material, other than dirt, with which to build fortifications. But as the Southern forces approached many of the men in the 64th Ohio picked up the few spades and shovels they had and starting digging anew. Soon the regiment's skirmishers became engaged with the enemy and in short order the men of Company E came bounding back. A captain who had been on the skirmish line told John Shellenberger that he "had been face to face with the whole rebel army."[27]

For the advancing Confederates the critical moment had arrived. Although both Rebel corps did not execute a precisely simultaneous movement the next step unfolded very quickly. Most of the two mile long line drew to a halt and officers began bellowing out commands. Then, like some mighty beast unwinding as if to strike, the individual Confederate brigades shifted into attack formation.[28]

Already the Rebels were taking long-range artillery fire from a Union battery located on the Carter Hill line. About an hour earlier the Federal line had been strengthened when a two-gun section from

---

[27] Ibid., p. 381.

[28] Gordon, *CV* 8, p. 7; Mangum, Statement of, p. 2, Peacock Papers, SHC.

Bridges' Illinois Battery was moved into position on the southwestern slope of Carter Hill and two guns from Battery A, 1st Ohio Light Artillery were placed to the right of the 20th Ohio Light Battery.[29]

In Cleburne's Division these developments were unknown. Hiram Granbury's and Daniel Govan's brigades shrugged off the shells fired by the Kentucky Battery and formed as the front line of attack. With his left flank straddling Columbia Pike, Granbury's line of advance was aimed at the heart of the Federal line. Cleburne directed Govan into line on Granbury's right and Mark Lowrey formed as the reserve. Across the pike, John Brown had Brig. Gen. George W. Gordon's Brigade and Gist's Brigade in his forward line, with Gordon closest to the road. Otho Strahl and John C. Carter aligned their brigades as the supporting units and Strahl's men formed nearest the pike. Carter, only 26 years of age, had taken command of Brig. Gen. George E. Maney's Brigade following the Battle of Jonesboro in September.[30]

To Brown's left, William Bate was scrambling to get his troops ready. Gen. Henry Jackson's Brigade formed the right of the line and Gen. Thomas Benton Smith the left. Col. Robert Bullock and the Florida Brigade had been instructed to occupy the reserve. Bullock, like Carter, was new to his command. Bullock had taken over for Brig. Gen. Jesse J. Finley who had been wounded at Jonesboro.[31]

In Stewart's Corps, units also shifted into battle formation. Because Ector's Brigade was on detached duty "guarding the pontoon

---

[29] *OR* 45, pt. 1, p. 320, 326.

[30] *OR* 45, pt. 1, p. 737; Harris D. Riley, "A Gallant Adopted Son of Tennessee - General John C. Carter, C. S. A.," *THQ* 48, No. 4, p. 202; Welsh, *Medical Histories of Confederate Generals*, p. 153; Faust, ed., *Historical Times Encyclopedia*, p. 472. Why Maney relinquished command is unclear. Maney temporarily commanded Cheatham's Division at Jonesboro because of the latter's illness. Because Carter took temporary command of the division at 9 p.m. on August 31 it seems Maney was suddenly relieved of command. Carter later reverted to brigade command following John C. Brown's promotion to division command. Losson, *Tennessee's Forgotten Warriors*, p. 190-192, 198, covers this topic and offers some possible answers. See also Welsh, *Medical Histories of Confederate Generals*, p. 36, 153.

[31] Faust, ed., *Historical Times Encyclopedia*, p. 90; Welsh, *Medical Histories of Confederate Generals*, p. 68.

bridges" Samuel French had just two brigades at Franklin. His division, which passed over the Nashville & Decatur Railroad prior to the final leg of the advance, had Brig. Gen. Claudius W. Sears' Brigade in front and Gen. F. M. Cockrell's hard-hitting Missouri Brigade in reserve. Yet before long the Missourians would find themselves in front, leading the charge. Such a position was familiar territory for Cockrell's men, who had often been used as shock troops. The war had been hard on them and the brigade went into battle at Franklin much reduced in size. Fewer than 700 remained in the ranks as they maneuvered from column into line of battle. Some 350 yards from Conrad's line the Missourians and Sears' Mississippians readied themselves for combat. From the forward right, screaming shells plunged down from Fort Granger. The rifled shots tore huge holes in the ground, showering both brigades with dirt and debris. Some of the enemy fire began to find its mark, striking close and knocking men down. Impatient looks and comments began to ripple up and down the lines. French's men were ready, content with taking their chances near the enemy works rather than waiting for the Federal gunners to get their bead measured again.[32]

Samuel Gibbs French was a transplanted but dedicated Southerner. Born in Gloucester City, New Jersey in 1818, French attended West Point and graduated in 1843. Wounded during the Mexican War, he was given a brevet rank of captain for bravery. Yet by 1856 French had tired of army life and resigned to become a planter in Mississippi, where he married a Southern woman. Tied to the South by both family and business, French sided with the Confederacy and by the end of 1861 was a brigadier general. His early war service took him to several points in the Eastern Theater and led a promotion to major general. Transferred to Joseph Johnston's command in 1863, which brought him to his adopted home state of Mississippi, French ended up with the Army of Tennessee in early 1864.[33]

---

[32] French, *Two Wars*, p. 295, 297; Boyce, *CV* 19, p. 271; Gottschalk, *In Deadly Earnest*, p. 463, 465-466; Tucker, *THQ* 46, No.1, p. 27; Mamie Yeary, *Reminiscences of the Boys in Gray 1861-1865*, p. 117. Gottschalk said when French deployed into attack formation the Missouri Brigade was moved to the front and Sears' Brigade became the reserve. French said this occurred after the charge began.

[33] Faust, ed., *Historical Times Encyclopedia*, p. 292.

On French's right, Edward Walthall stayed with the formation he had earlier reworked. William Quarles and Charles Shelley had their brigades in front and Daniel Reynolds readied his Arkansans as the reserve. On the far right, William Loring had Brig. Gens. Winfield S. Featherston's and Thomas Scott's brigades in the forward line. In support was Gen. John Adams' Brigade of Mississippians.

John Adams was a career soldier. He had traveled far and wide during his many years of service in the United States Army. Born in Nashville in 1825, Adams was a graduate of the West Point class of 1846 and became a second lieutenant in the U. S. Army's 1st Dragoons. He served during the Mexican War and received the rank of brevet first lieutenant for gallant and meritorious service at the Battle of Santa Cruz de Rosales on March 16, 1848. Adams received an 1851 promotion to first lieutenant and by 1856 he was a captain. During an 1853 stint at Fort Snelling in the Minnesota Territory, Adams met and fell in love with Georgiana McDougal, the daughter of a surgeon stationed at the post. The two were married in the spring of 1854 and Georgiana followed her husband across the country as he was assigned to one fort after another. Their happy marriage produced six children, four boys and two girls, all of whom survived long into adulthood. The first was born in 1855 and the last, a girl named Emma, was born in October 1863 in Alabama.[34]

Adams' career in the U. S. Army ended in the spring of 1861 when he resigned his commission and joined the Southern army. His early days in the Confederate armed forces, however, were not particularly noteworthy. Adams served as a cavalry officer for a time and was promoted to brigadier general in December 1862. He became an infantry commander in 1863 and served under Joseph Johnston during the Vicksburg Campaign. By 1864, Adams was serving under Leonidas Polk and he became affiliated with the Army of Tennessee when Polk moved to Resaca in May of that year. Adams served through the summer campaign around Atlanta and he moved with the army as it marched into Tennessee. At Spring Hill he saw no action, but Franklin was an altogether different story. As Adams looked toward the

---

[34] Faust, ed., *Historical Times Encyclopedia*, p. 2. The author is indebted to Ann Gulbransen, a great-great granddaughter of Gen. Adams, for information about the children of John and Georgiana.

Federal line in the fading autumn light, he undoubtedly thought of his wife and children. Surely he considered the possibility that he might never see them again. His heart may have been heavy, but John Adams rode stoically along his line.[35]

In rear of his division Patrick Ronayne Cleburne sat astride a borrowed mount. Red Pepper, his favorite horse, had been so badly injured by shell fragments at Spring Hill that the general could no longer ride him. Now Cleburne guided his new companion, a brown mare belonging to a young aide named Tip Stanton, along the eastern side of Columbia Pike.[36]

It had been a long war, one filled with death, disease, shortages of just about everything, senseless politics, and an opponent with no sense of quit. Through all of it Cleburne had led his men with a sense of duty, honor, and dignity found in few officers on either side of the conflict. The men who served under Cleburne admired him. The very words "Cleburne's Division" and the sight of his unique battle flag had consistently struck terror into the hearts of opposing troops. As his division moved forward at Franklin, Union troops surely caught sight of Cleburne's division flag. The veterans probably understood exactly what they were up against. In the rear of the Rebel division, filled with men and boys from Alabama, Arkansas, Mississippi, and Texas, Cleburne rode back and forth, instructing them to tighten up and ready their bayonets. He told the troops to be prepared for anything and repeated Hood's order to run over the Yankees and shoot them in the back when they ran.

George Wagner came to his senses at the very last moment. According to Col. Conrad, a staff officer from Wagner appeared as the Rebels were coming within musket range. The aide told Conrad that Wagner had just issued orders stating that if the enemy was "too strong" the brigade was to retire to "the main line of works..." Presumably a staff officer was also sent to Col. Lane with a similar message although

---

[35] Faust, ed., *Historical Times Encyclopedia*, p. 2; Bryan Lane, "The Familiar Road: The Life of Confederate Brigadier General John Adams," *CWTI*, Oct. 1996, p. 42.

[36] Mangum, Statement of, p. 3, Peacock Papers, SHC.

he did not mention it in his official report. Conrad quickly decided that the order made little sense at this point. The Rebels were nearly on top of him and Conrad feared that if he ordered a withdrawal the troops would panic, causing all sense of order to dissolve. Instead he ordered the men to hold steady and "commence firing."[37]

Once the Confederates completed their shift into line of battle and dressed their ranks one last time, the power of the assault become plainly evident. From a distance the Rebels appeared impressive, almost mesmerizing. Lt. Col. Jasper Packard, an Indiana officer, said, "I never saw a more magnificent sight." But as they moved into much closer range, with the sun sinking toward the horizon and a dull afternoon haze hanging in the air, they looked almost terrifying. One Federal soldier thought those at the very front seemed "magnified in size" and said they could easily have been mistaken for "phantoms sweeping along in the air." It was like a wave rolling forward, picking up speed with each passing second. Most of the Confederates began moving at the double-quick. At that pace a typical soldier can easily cover one hundred yards in sixty seconds. The men in the advanced Union brigades were horrified. Only about 300 or 400 yards had separated them from three enemy divisions just moments before and now the gap was closing furiously.[38]

Minutes can define a lifetime and create indelible memories of unusual clarity. For some wearing the blue a handful of moments at Franklin, Tennessee did exactly that. Capt. Levi Scofield had turned twenty-four years old and he was serving as an engineer in the Twenty-Third Corps. Years later Scofield's mind remained vividly sharp as he recounted the day's events. Watching the Confederates pour like some Biblical plague toward Wagner's brigades was a sight burned into his mind. A person could live a dozen lives and never have the opportunity to see such a thing. Levi Scofield saw the drama in his prime:

> It was a grand sight! Such as would make a lifelong impression on the mind of any man who would see such a resistless, well-conducted charge. For the moment we were spellbound with admiration, although they were our

---

[37] *OR* 45, pt. 1, p. 270; Cox, *Battle of Franklin*, p. 107-108.

[38] Scofield, *The Retreat From Pulaski*, p. 35; Merrill, *The Soldier of Indiana*, Vol. 2, p. 759.

hated foes; and we knew that in a few brief moments, as soon as they reached firing distance, all of that orderly grandeur would be changed to bleeding, writhing confusion, and that thousands of those valorous men of the South, with their chivalric officers, would pour out their life's blood on the fair fields in front of us. As forerunners well in advance could be seen a line of wild rabbits, bounding along for a few leaps, and then they would stop and look back and listen, but scamper off again, as though convinced that this was the most impenetrable line of beaters-in that had ever given them chase; and quails by the thousands in coveys here and there would rise and settle, and rise again to the warm sunlight that called them back; but no, they were frightened by the unusual turmoil, and back they came and this repeated until finally they rose high in the air and whirred off to the gray sky light of the north.[39]

On and on the Rebels came. Adding to the drama was the sound of thousands of feet treading steadily against the valley floor. It resembled the low but distinct rumble of distant thunder. The screaming and whistling of artillery fire added to the cacophony of sound. But above all else rose the echo of the Rebel yell. Gen. George Gordon, on foot and leading his brigade, remembered that the charge began with "an impetuous rush and a startling shout..." From that moment on the speed and volume only amplified. In front of Gist's Brigade an officer said that Gist and two staff members "rode down our front, and returning, ordered the charge, in concert with General Gordon." He remembered how Gist rode directly in front of the 24th South Carolina and with a wave of his hat "rode away in the smoke of the battle..."[40]

States Rights Gist had a name that embodied for many in the South precisely why the Civil War was fought. Gist was born in South

---

[39] Scofield, *The Retreat From Pulaski,* p. 34. After the war Scofield helped design the Soldiers' and Sailors' Monument in Cleveland, which was constructed in 1894. Standing one hundred and twenty-five feet tall it has a base made of Black Quincy granite and Buff Amherst stone with a sculpture rising above made from bronze. He also designed a number of private homes and put together plans for at least two public schools.

[40] Gordon, *CV* 8, p. 7; G. W. Gordon, "Eleventh Tennessee Infantry," in *Military Annals of Tennessee,* Vol. 1, Lindsley, ed., p. 301; *OR* 45, pt. 1, p. 737.

Carolina in 1831 and it is not hard to imagine, based on his name, how his father Nathaniel felt about the sovereign rights of the states. The outbreak of war saw Gist serve first in his home state and then in Mississippi during the Vicksburg Campaign. Thereafter he was assigned to the Army of Tennessee and served admirably. Wounded in the hand during the Battle of Atlanta on July 22, Gist had a short period of recovery before returning to duty following the Gate City's fall. But his service in John Brown's Division was not without some controversy. Gist's date of rank as a brigadier general preceded that of Brown, who was promoted to major general on August 4, 1864. Yet Gist received no promotion despite his solid record and there was talk that as a South Carolinian he had been bypassed for Brown, who was a Tennessean. Some felt the same thing had occurred in February 1864 when William Bate, another Tennessean, had been promoted ahead of Gist. Additionally, there is evidence Gist may have been headed home to South Carolina thanks to the efforts of P. G. T. Beauregard and William Hardee, both of whom were pulling strings behind the scenes. Unfortunately for the young general he was unable to secure a transfer until the conclusion of the Tennessee Campaign.[41]

Soon the high pitched yip that Federal soldiers had learned to fear could be heard reverberating from all directions. Some of the gray and butternut soldiers began to outpace others as the double-quick pace morphed into almost a full-fledged dash. Like screaming and howling demons they pressed to within 150 yards of Wagner's line. To the east and west other Southern troops began pouring beyond the beleaguered Yankee flanks.

On Joseph Conrad's line the men hunkered down, joined by troops from the skirmish line who had been driven back by the enemy advance. When the Rebels were barely one hundred paces away, a

---

[41] Walter Brian Cisco, *States Rights Gist, A South Carolinian General of the Civil War*, p. 134; Faust, ed., *Historical Times Illustrated Encyclopedia*, p. 312. During Cisco's research he chanced upon a letter in the Ellison Capers file at Duke University indicating Beauregard was going to transfer Gist to South Carolina at the request of Gen. Hardee.

single artillery round screeched over the heads of the Federals. Just as suddenly a second shell exploded not far in front of them. With a flash, Conrad's line let loose a volley. Some of the front line Confederates crumpled to the ground, but the Federal fire served to only momentarily check the advance. Within seconds the rush resumed and fire crackled outward from the Northern units for a few additional minutes. Col. Allen Buckner of the 79th Illinois said his men managed to get off "eight to ten rounds" before the opposing sides were almost face to face. Then, with a crushing blow, Brown's and Cleburne's divisions slammed into the apex of Wagner's line. In almost the blink of an eye the blue clad soldiers straddling the turnpike began to buckle beneath the weight and momentum of the assault. A series of volleys thundered from the Rebel muskets and men began to grapple hand-to-hand. Some used their muskets as clubs. Conrad said he ordered the 15th Missouri, his right flank regiment, to retreat toward the main line, but before he was able to relay the order to his other units the men "had already commenced retiring..." Scores of Federal troops were killed, wounded, or captured in a matter of moments and those who could escape wasted little time dashing for safety. Capt. William Hark of the 15th Missouri was among those who did not get away and was counted among the dead.[42]

It did not take long for the two brigade line to completely implode upon itself. West of the pike Brown's troops, after brushing aside the thin line of Yankee skirmishers, poured toward John Lane's Brigade. But unlike Conrad's command, Lane's men largely avoided any direct confrontation because their line angled away from the pike at a sharper angle than did Conrad's. This led to Cleburne becoming fully engaged slightly before Brown. With pounding hearts Lane's men watched the collapse of Conrad's line. Lane, who could see how untenable his position had become, quickly ordered his troops "to retire to the main line of works." In his official report Lane asserted that the Confederates, moving forward "in heavy columns," struck Conrad's Brigade first. Furthermore, Lane said that of his six regiments, only the 40th Indiana engaged the approaching Rebels and the other five did not fire their guns until they reached the main line. Sgt. Asbury L. Kerwood

---

[42] *OR* 45, pt. 1, p. 270-271, 280, 282; Shellenberger, *CV* 36, p. 382; Losson, *Tennessee's Forgotten Warriors*, p. 221.

of the 57th Indiana said "the brigade on the left of the pike" pulled back first and then the order to "Rally behind the works!" was the only thing that could be heard "above the noise and confusion." Pvt. Sylvester C. Wolford of the 97th Ohio recalled how the men "made a hasty retreat for the main line." Lt. Col. Milton Barnes commanded the 97th Ohio and wrote his wife three days after the battle that he never "came so near being captured before." Pvt. William Gist of the 26th Ohio remembered hearing the firing to his left and saw "the line had given way..." Gist said it was enough to prompt his section of the line to turn and run, but getting back to the main line, was not without difficulty. Lane said the locust abatis "caused some delay which enabled the enemy to get within fifty feet of us..."[43]

East of the pike there was virtual bedlam. An officer on Conrad's left flank said he watched in horror as the entire line leading back toward him disintegrated. It happened with such quickness that it reminded him of "a train of powder burning." He jumped up from his shallow trench, saw the Rebels "coming on a run" and said his first thought was to lay down and "let them charge over." He quickly reconsidered. The terrified captain screamed at his men to fall back and he then ran as fast as possible toward the main line.[44]

A genuine crisis now faced Schofield and shortly before the

---

[43] *OR* 45, pt. 1, p. 256, 265; Gist, *THM* 6, No. 3, p. 227-227; S. C. Wolford, Letter of, *CV* 17, p. 15; Kerwood, *Annals of the Fifty-Seventh Indiana*, p. 297; Milton Barnes to Rhoda Barnes, Dec. 3, 1864, Milton Barnes Civil War Collection, George Mason University (hereafter referred to as GMU). Because there is no evidence to suggest that Cleburne outpaced Brown, it does seem that Lane was aligned at a sharper angle to the Columbia Pike than Conrad. Conrad's right flank regiment, the 15th Missouri, was heavily engaged on the western side of the pike and so was the 40th Indiana, Lane's left flank regiment. Brown's troops engaged those units, indicating he was keeping time with Cleburne across the pike. However, the rest of Lane's line must have angled back significantly toward the main line for his remaining five regiments to have retreated without firing their weapons. An inspection of the ground by the author confirms that Lane's line would have required a sharper angle to follow the direction of the slight rise of ground.

[44] Shellenberger, *CV* 36, p. 382.

Rebel assault commenced he and David Stanley were found just north of the river. Strangely enough, one of Schofield's own staff officers, Maj. William Wherry, had been tracked down by one of Gen. Cox's couriers at Dr. Cliffe's office. Wherry, who was suffering from a terrible toothache, had stopped to have the tooth removed when the courier rode up and recognized the major's horse and orderlies. He told Wherry that Cox believed "the enemy was forming up and about to attack..." Wherry told the courier to come with him and they rode north, where the two encountered Schofield and Stanley just beyond the bridge. As the aides relayed the information "the roll of musketry commenced." Stanley knew the sound of trouble when he heard it and rode immediately toward the front. Schofield meanwhile turned in the direction of Fort Granger.[45]

At the same time, Jacob Cox was watching the shattering of Wagner's brigades with utter disbelief. After speaking with Wagner at the Carter House, Cox had left his headquarters and ridden to the left of the line. From there, atop a knoll behind Col. Israel Stiles' troops, Cox watched the initial Confederate deployment. From the small hill Cox was able to see "behind the rise of ground on which Wagner's two brigades" were positioned. He said the enemy line "could be continuously traced from the Harpeth River...till it was lost near Privet Knob..." Concerned that Wagner was not calling in Conrad's and Lane's brigades, Cox told one of his aides, Lt. James Coughlan, to ride to the center of the main line and make sure the officers there understood not to fire until Wagner's troops were safely inside the Carter Hill perimeter. He also instructed Coughlan to find Col. Opdycke and let him know to have his brigade ready should "any break occur."[46]

Cox watched as the Rebels advanced, dumbfounded that Wagner's troops were not pulling back. Soon "the long lines of Hood's army surged up out of the hollow in which they had formed..." It was patently obvious to him the Southerners were going to engulf the hapless brigades. But it was too late, there was nothing Cox could do. In a matter of minutes the Rebels were all over Wagner's men, shooting

---

[45] Cox, *Battle of Franklin*, p. 280-281; Stanley, *Personal Memoirs*, p. 207; Schofield, *Forty-Six Years In The Army*, p. 177.

[46] Cox, *Battle of Franklin*. p. 82, 91-92, 95.

and bayoneting scores and chasing the rest toward the main line. Now every second mattered. Cox immediately sent another staff officer to find Opdycke and reiterate the need for his brigade to be ready to move. Then Cox dashed toward the center of the line. On his way the battle erupted like a volcano. The guns inside Fort Granger pounded A. P. Stewart's surging lines, especially the right flank, and soon the artillery supporting Israel Stiles and John Casement began raking Stewart. Cox galloped onward and as he passed Lewisburg Pike an enemy shell exploded nearby, frightening away a team of horses which had been strapped to a gun limber. The runaway team and the violent detonation of the shell caused Cox's own horse to rear, nearly throwing him to the ground. The general quickly dismounted and, displaying remarkable coolness under fire, quieted the jittery animal "by rubbing his nose and ears." Cox then threw himself back into the saddle and raced to the center. By his own estimation Cox lost about thirty seconds calming his horse. But on this day thirty seconds seemed like an eternity. What Cox saw when he arrived near the Columbia Pike was chaos and a deepening crisis.[47]

Blunders are not at all uncommon in wartime, especially during battle. But George Wagner erred in the extreme and as a result the fate of Schofield's entire army hung in the balance. There was nothing left of the outlying Union brigades except a wild and uncontrollable crush of men racing along both sides of the Columbia Pike. Over 3,000 Federal soldiers were running for their lives, creating a literal stampede. Four short years after the war Asbury Kerwood shuddered just to recall the scene. John Shellenberger remembered looking back and seeing the Rebels near the line he had abandoned only moments before. They were "loading and firing at will," unleashing a searing multitude of bullets that lashed into the backs of the fleeing Northerners. Men hit went down with cries caused not just by pain, but by the knowledge they were being left to the enemy. Those in the main line were aghast. Their comrades directly out in front were being mauled and run over right before their very eyes. But the vast majority of the Rebels were not even shooting, they were simply charging forward and doing so at breakneck speed. Cries of "Go into the works with them!" could be heard along much of the enemy front. The call was picked up by "a

---

[47] Ibid., p. 96-97.

thousand straining throats" and the charge flooded ahead. Right behind Wagner's men came the Confederates, their shouting growing louder as they came closer.[48]

In one of those bizarre twists of fate and circumstance, the Union troops in the center, both east and west of the pike, were unable to open fire on the Rebels because Wagner's men were largely blocking them. Lt. Thomas Speed remembered how James Reilly's and Silas Strickland's troops stood against the parapet waiting "breathlessly and silent" for their compatriots to get inside the works. Everyone knew that if the order to fire was given, many of their own men would be shot down. Considering the circumstances, Jacob Cox's order not to shoot was incidental. The dilemma was such that if the Federals did nothing, the Rebels coming up the pike were going to burst into the center of the line virtually unchecked. Trepidation coursed along the Yankee line.[49]

Wagner's terrified troops continued to pour en masse toward the Union works. Like a great magnet drawing them in, hundreds began funneling in the direction of the gap in the line through which passed the Columbia Pike. Behind the works the troops had their rifles cocked and ready, their fingers itching to release a shattering volley. The artillerymen were also prepared. The canister was in place and the gunners had their lanyards in hand.

Col. John Casement was ready, too. Casement was a tiny man, only five feet four inches tall, but he was a bundle of furious energy and had been blessed with a full vocabulary.[50] Jumping atop the breastworks in front of his brigade east of the Carter cotton gin he yelled out, "Men, do you see those damn rebel sons-of-bitches coming?" The men cheered wildly. Casement barked back, "Well, I want you to stand here like rocks, and whip hell out of them!" He turned around, faced the

---

[48] Gordon, *CV* 8, p. 7; Kerwood, *Annals of the Fifty-Seventh Indiana*, p. 297; Shellenberger, *CV* 36, p. 382.

[49] Speed, *MOLLUS*, Ohio, 3, p. 77; Kerwood, *Annals of the Fifty-Seventh Indiana*, p. 297.

[50] Charles E. Ames, *Pioneering the Union Pacific Railroad, A Reappraisal of the Builders of the Railroad*, p. 123. Casement was contracted after the war to supervise the construction of the Union Pacific Railroad. Casement was present at the 1869 ceremony when the final spike was driven into the railroad at Promontory, Utah.

onrushing enemy, pulled out both of his revolvers, and emptied them in the direction of the Confederates. Casement then jumped back inside the works and waited with his men for the Rebels to close in.[51]

John Bell Hood's attack was rolling ahead, but confusion was spreading fast. Although Wagner's men had been plowed over a brief delay had ensued in the center of the advancing Rebel line. As a result Stewart's men swung somewhat ahead of the rest of the troops. Meanwhile, on the far left, where the Yankee line angled sharply toward the north, Bate's Division was as far from the enemy as any unit on the field. In the center matters were growing out of control as Cleburne's and Brown's divisions roared forward.

Behind his troops Cleburne was doing what he could. His aide-de-camp Leonard Mangum found Cleburne there, the general's battle ardor clearly up. Earlier, Cleburne had spotted an opportunity for artillery to do some damage and he sent Mangum to place some guns at a particular point. Not much later, Cleburne sent Capt. S. P. Hanley to place the artillery instead and told him to have Magnum return at once. Within moments Mangum galloped up and asked Cleburne what he needed. The general turned to him and spoke just a few words. They were the last ones Magnum ever heard from his venerated commander. Cleburne said, "It is too late. Go on with Granbury." Quickly the Irishman directed his horse to the right and "galloped up to Govan's brigade." Cleburne understood there was no longer time for intricate details. He could see the widening disorder and knew if the attack was to succeed the push had to happen quickly and with furious force. His battlefield instincts remained sharp and aggressive. Mangum watched Cleburne as long as he could. The entire Confederate line was now "rushing madly for the enemy's works." When Cleburne disappeared into the smoke it was the last time Mangum saw him alive.[52]

Lt. Mangum rode furiously toward Granbury's Brigade of Texas veterans. Granbury and Govan were both on foot when Mangum

---

[51] Scofield, *The Retreat From Pulaski*, p. 42.

[52] Mangum, Statement of, p. 2, Peacock Papers, SHC; Mangum, *Kennesaw Gazette*, June 15, 1887.

found them. Granbury was either jogging along the eastern edge of the pike or on the road itself. Govan was close enough to Granbury for Mangum to see both men so likely he was near his brigade's left flank. However, the troops were so co-mingled by this point it was virtually impossible to tell where one brigade ended and another began. Wherever Govan was, he never forgot seeing Pat Cleburne. Govan believed it was Cleburne's intent to smash Wagner's troops into the works and cause a terrific chasm in the main Federal line. Govan was watching his commander when the Irishman's borrowed steed was riddled with fire and killed about eighty yards from the Federal line. A member of Cleburne's escort staff, nineteen-year old Jimmy Brandon, immediately dismounted and gave his horse to the general. Cleburne was swinging into the saddle when the luckless creature was struck by artillery fire and sank to its knees in death. Brandon also fell with a wound to his thigh. The din was now incredible. From where Cleburne stood the cotton gin was almost due north. The rifle fire swelled to a roar as the Yankees on the main line finally decided it was no longer prudent to hold back. The sound of the fire grew ominous, growling and echoing like a nasty storm through the thick, acrid smoke. There seemed to be but one option. Cleburne removed his cap, raised his sword, and plunged forward into the maelstrom. Govan said "he disappeared in the smoke of battle, and that was the last time I ever saw him alive."[53]

Deafening rolls of musketry and peals of artillery fire billowed up from the Union line. The brigades commanded by Israel Stiles and John Casement, straddling Lewisburg Pike, did not have to worry about friendly fire for the most part. Only the right of Casement's line, held by the 65th Indiana, had some minor issues with Wagner's men in their front. The Union left, anchored firmly on the river, was well protected by strong works and Osage orange abatis. It was a defensive dream and the Confederates marched right up and took it in the teeth. With their first volley Casement's troops began to whip the Rebels exactly as he implored them to do. The Federals had a clear and open field of fire and their position commanded the ground in front of them. A "blaze

---

[53] Mangum, Statement of, p. 3, Peacock Papers, SHC; Purdue, *Pat Cleburne*, p. 422-423; Buck, *Cleburne and His Command*, p. 289, 291; Losson, *Tennessee's Forgotten Warriors*, p. 223; Gordon, *CV* 8, p. 7.

of fire" erupted from the blue line that was so intense it appeared to form "a solid plane upon which a man might walk." Adding to the fury were the two and a half batteries supporting this section of the line. From the works straddling Lewisburg Pike to the high ground behind the Indiana regiments of Stiles' command, and sweeping toward the river, the twelve guns poured a torrent of fire toward A. P. Stewart's approaching troops. A two-gun section of Lt. Aaron Baldwin's 6th Battery, Ohio Light Artillery was posted in the works of the 128th Indiana and began working in earnest. To the left rear the four 12-pounder Napoleons of Battery M, 4th U. S. Artillery opened with spherical case and canister. Lt. Samuel Canby's guns sent shock waves through the gray ranks, throwing men about like rag dolls and inflicting horrific casualties. Capt. Alex Marshall's six-gun Battery G, 1st Ohio Light Artillery was composed of 3-inch rifled pieces and his men were posted a short distance from the 4th U. S. Artillery. Like Canby's guns those under Marshall's direction sat on a "well marked knoll" and spewed an iron rain on the Rebels. Marshall opened with canister and his gunners began a methodical and cruel shredding of the enemy troops.[54]

From the early stages of the advance, Stewart's men were forced to contend with the fire crashing down on them from Fort Granger. Bravely they pushed forward, taking losses all the way, but nonetheless making good time. At between 300 and 400 yards from the enemy line the momentum of the advance increased. On Stewart's left the two brigades of French's Division drove forward. Although the evidence indicates the Missouri Brigade began the advance as the reserve unit, Cockrell's men soon assumed the lead position. According to Gen. French, Sears' Brigade became somewhat entangled with elements of Wagner's command and was delayed for several minutes. The Missourians encountered no such impediment and they streamed past Sears' men. Unfortunately for Cockrell and his men, Cleburne's brigades had also been slightly delayed by Wagner's troops. This left the Missouri Brigade horribly exposed on its left flank. Furthermore, the Missourians may have outpaced Walthall on their right, opening up that flank as well. It is very possible the brigade was the first

---

[54] Speed, *MOLLUS*, Ohio, 3, p. 77; *OR* 45, pt. 1, p. 322, 331; Cox, *Battle of Franklin*, p. 47; Merrill, *The Soldier of Indiana*, Vol. 2, p. 760.

Confederate unit to come into contact with the Federals and it paid dearly for the achievement. A Union soldier west of the Columbia Pike said he watched as action east of the road broke out first. He remembered that the "boom of artillery...could be plainly heard above the yelling of the hordes in our front."[55]

Located just east of the cotton gin, the men of Col. John Casement's command decimated Cockrell's Missourians. Casement described it accurately as "terrible slaughter." A soldier from the 65th Illinois recalled how Stewart's Corps "was the first to receive the fire from our main line..." and that Cleburne's involvement with Wagner "threw Stewart's line too far in advance." Even some of Gen. Reilly's men in front of the gin became involved in the fight with Stewart's troops. Col. Oscar Sterl, commanding the 104th Ohio, reported that his "three left companies" joined the barrage. They turned to the left and poured a scalding oblique fire into the Rebels.[56]

The most serious damage, however, was surely done by Casement's Illinois and Indiana troops. Two of his regiments, the 65th Indiana and 65th Illinois, were partially equipped with fifteen-shot Henry repeating rifles and they poured out a volume of fire that was almost

---

[55] Gottschalk, *In Deadly Earnest*, p. 467; Boyce, *CV* 19, p. 271; French, *Two Wars*, p. 297; Tucker, *THQ* 46, No. 1, p. 28; Elliott, *Soldier of Tennessee*, p. 243; James Barr, "Gens. Cleburne and Adams at Franklin," *CV* 10, p. 155; Erastus Winters, *In the 50th Ohio Serving Uncle Sam: Memoirs of One Who Wore The Blue*, p. 121; McDonough and Connelly, *Five Tragic Hours*, p. 120.

[56] *OR* 45, pt. 1, p. 421, 425; Barr, *CV* 10, p. 155; Gottschalk, *In Deadly Earnest*, p. 467; French, *Two Wars*, p. 296. The available evidence points to the Missourians coming under close-range fire from the Federal main line at least briefly before any other unit did. French said the men of Cockrell's Brigade "nearly all disappeared" while at least some of Sears' men were reformed. In addition to eyewitness accounts, one must consider that the Missourians did not have to deal with Wagner's men impeding their progress, that they approached the apex of the Union line, and they suffered a percentage of loss higher than any other Confederate brigade. See Sword, *The Confederacy's Last Hurrah*, p. 225, for the erroneous conclusion that the Missouri Brigade was among the trailing units of Stewart's Corps.

beyond comprehension.[57]

Although men already littered the path the brigade had traveled during the early part of advance, when Casement's troops opened up Cockrell's men began to fall in piles. They struggled to close to within seventy-five yards. The Federals obliterated the Missouri ranks and a Rebel captain said the air "was all red and blue flames, with shells and bullets screeching everywhere..." The barrage of lead and iron was so intense that some of the Missourians actually turned their shoulders into the firestorm and bent down at the knees in the hope of getting through.[58]

Francis M. Cockrell (Library of Congress)

Inside the Union works there were few casualties. The superiority of the position was obvious and the Federal troops took full advantage of the situation. Blue clad officers yelled for their troops to reload and keep firing. A blaze of almost continual fire exploded outward from atop the parapet. The Napoleons at the southeast corner of the cotton gin added to the furor as they split the air with each deadly round.

---

[57] Scofield, *The Retreat From Pulaski*, p. 40; Stevens, *CV* 11, p. 167. The Henry rifle was invented and patented in 1860 by American Benjamin Tyler Henry. The rifle used a .44 caliber rimfire cartridge, the first of its kind, and a trained shooter could fire all upwards of forty-five rounds in a minute. The United States government purchased 1,731 for use during the Civil War.

[58] Tucker, *THQ* 46, No. 1, p. 28; R. S. Bevier, *History of the First and Second Missouri Confederate Brigades 1861 - 1865 and From Wakarusa to Appomattox*, p. 252-253.

Thirty-year old Frances Marion Cockrell was a Missouri native. Raised on a farm, Cockrell was an intelligent man who, after graduating from college, became a practicing attorney in Warrensburg, Missouri in the mid-1850's. A strong supporter of the secession movement, Cockrell served first in the Missouri State Guard under Brig. Gen. Sterling Price. Cockrell fought at Wilson's Creek, Pea Ridge, Corinth, and Vicksburg, where he was captured when the city capitulated. Promoted to brigadier general in July 1863, Cockrell took command of the Missouri Brigade in early 1864. He was struck by artillery fire at Kennesaw Mountain and suffered painful wounds to both hands. The injury invalided the Missourian for almost six weeks. Following this Cockrell rejoined his men and led them through the fall of Atlanta and then into Tennessee.[59]

Outside the blazing enemy works at Franklin, Cockrell fought for his life. Early in the fight, one horse was shot from beneath him. As he urged his men forward Cockrell was blasted from a second horse, struck four times by the relentless fire. He was shot twice in the right arm, took a bullet through the left leg, and was also hit in the right ankle. Cockrell was in agony, but somehow managed to hobble to safety, forced to use his right leg to carry most of his weight because his left was almost useless. Nearby Col. Hugh Garland was shot down while carrying the flag of the 1st Missouri. Garland was seriously wounded in the knee and he lay tangled up in the regimental flag only fifty feet from the Union works. Unable to move because of his wound Garland was helpless, forced to endure from the ground the hurricane that swirled around him.[60]

The Missouri troops refused to quit. Capt. Patrick Canniff desperately tried to get his men up to the Federal breastworks and he spurred his horse forward, hoping to inspire those around him. About ten yards from the ditch at the outside of the works, a minie ball ripped Canniff from his horse. Trembling with shock and pain, as blood

---

[59] Faust, ed., *Historical Times Encyclopedia*, p. 148; Francis M. Cockrell II, *The Senator From Missouri: The Life and Times of Francis Marion Cockrell*, p. 22; Welsh, *Medical Histories of Confederate Generals*, p. 44.

[60] Tucker, *THQ* 46, No. 1, p. 28; Cockrell, *Senator From Missouri*, p. 23-24; Gottschalk, *In Deadly Earnest*, p. 469-470; Welsh, *Medical Histories of Confederate Generals*, p. 44.

poured from the wound to his right shoulder, Canniff tried to rise up on his left elbow. Before he was able to even get his head high enough to see what was in front of him, another bullet crashed into the top of his skull and exploded out near his chin.[61]

Almost everyone was being shot down. Capt. Theodore L. Lanier fell with seven wounds and his blood stained the dirt a dark crimson red. Entire companies almost ceased to exist as the inferno continued. The color bearers of the consolidated 1st/4th Missouri and 2nd/6th Missouri somehow made it through the firestorm and scaled to the top of the breastworks with their flags. Once there they defiantly shoved the wooden staffs into the dirt. Both men were immediately shot down, their riddled bodies tumbling from the parapet while the Yankees gathered up the tattered flags. Another color bearer, Corp. Rankin Black, carried the flag of the dismounted 1st Missouri Cavalry and was wounded and captured. But Black defiantly tore the banner from its staff, hid it inside his jacket, and after nightfall the pugnacious Rebel escaped from the Yankees and made his way to safety. Seventeen-year old Pvt. Thomas Jefferson Neese also scampered to the top of the enemy works. Neese swung his musket around and was ready to use it like a club when a bullet hit him the left shoulder. Stunned by the impact, Neese was grabbed by a couple of Yankees and jerked inside the works. While "in the midst of the enemy" Neese was nearly bayoneted by one soldier only to be saved by another who ushered the young Confederate to the rear.[62]

At the corner of the gin house the two 12-pounder Napoleons commanded by Lt. Aaron Baldwin knocked Missourians down like bowling pins. Canister and spherical case exploded from the mouths of the guns and ravaged the hapless Southern ranks. The Yankees gunners could not miss blowing huge holes clear through the enemy. Frantically the Rebels pushed forward, trying to get out of the line of fire by moving to the right and left of the guns. In one particularly horrible scene a Missouri drummer, no more than 15 years old, jumped in front of one of Baldwin's Napoleons and shoved a fence rail into the smoking

---

[61] Gottschalk, *In Deadly Earnest*, p. 468; Bevier, *History of the First and Second Missouri Confederate Brigades*, p. 255.

[62] Gottschalk, *In Deadly Earnest*, p. 468; W. C. Neese, "Scaling the Works at Franklin," *CV* 11, p. 274; Tucker, *THQ* 46, No. 1, p. 29-30.

tube. What he did not know was that the gun had just been loaded. As the boy strained to jam the rail in as deeply as possible, the gun suddenly went off. In a split second the young boy, who had run forward with his drum still strapped to his back, simply vanished, his body blown away in shreds "so that nothing was ever found of him."[63]

Pvt. Israel O. Gaskill of the 65th Ohio was caught out in front of the breastworks along with the Missourians. Gaskill had been on the advanced line and after the "wild scamper" to the rear he found himself trapped in the ditch near the 6th Ohio Battery guns at the cotton gin. Unable to get over the works after the Union line exploded with fire, Gaskill was forced to endure the horror around him and "wait for an opportunity" to get over the parapet. Eventually the young private found himself "literally covered by corpses" and "stained with blood and grime" and he began screaming for help. In an amazing display of heroism, Lt. Benjamin F. Trescott of the 65th Ohio and Lt. Baldwin, after hearing Gaskill's cries, went over the works, pulled the bodies off their terrified comrade, and all three scrambled back over the parapet to safety.[64]

Col. Elijah Gates assumed command of the Missouri Brigade after learning that Cockrell had gone down. His luck did not last long. An explosion of gunfire enveloped Gates and he emerged with both arms broken and hanging limp at his sides. Lt. Charles B. Cleveland saw Gates and galloped up to lend assistance. Taking hold of the bridle on the colonel's horse, Cleveland helped the badly wounded colonel to the rear.[65]

The Missouri Brigade suffered grievous losses during its assault on the Union line. As the number of men able to fight dwindled, the survivors began drifting to the left, almost as if to escape the repeating rifles in Casement's Brigade and the cannon near the cotton gin. As they passed along the front of the gin, the Missourians joined the bedlam in the center of the Union line and helped wherever they could. When the battle finally ended 419 of the 696 men in the brigade were either killed, wounded, captured, or missing. Gen. French said

---

[63] Scofield, *The Retreat From Pulaski*, p. 46.

[64] Hinman, *The Story of the Sherman Brigade*, p. 661.

[65] Charles B. Cleveland, "With The Third Missouri Regiment," *CV* 31, p. 19-20; Tucker, *THQ* 46, No. 1, p. 28.

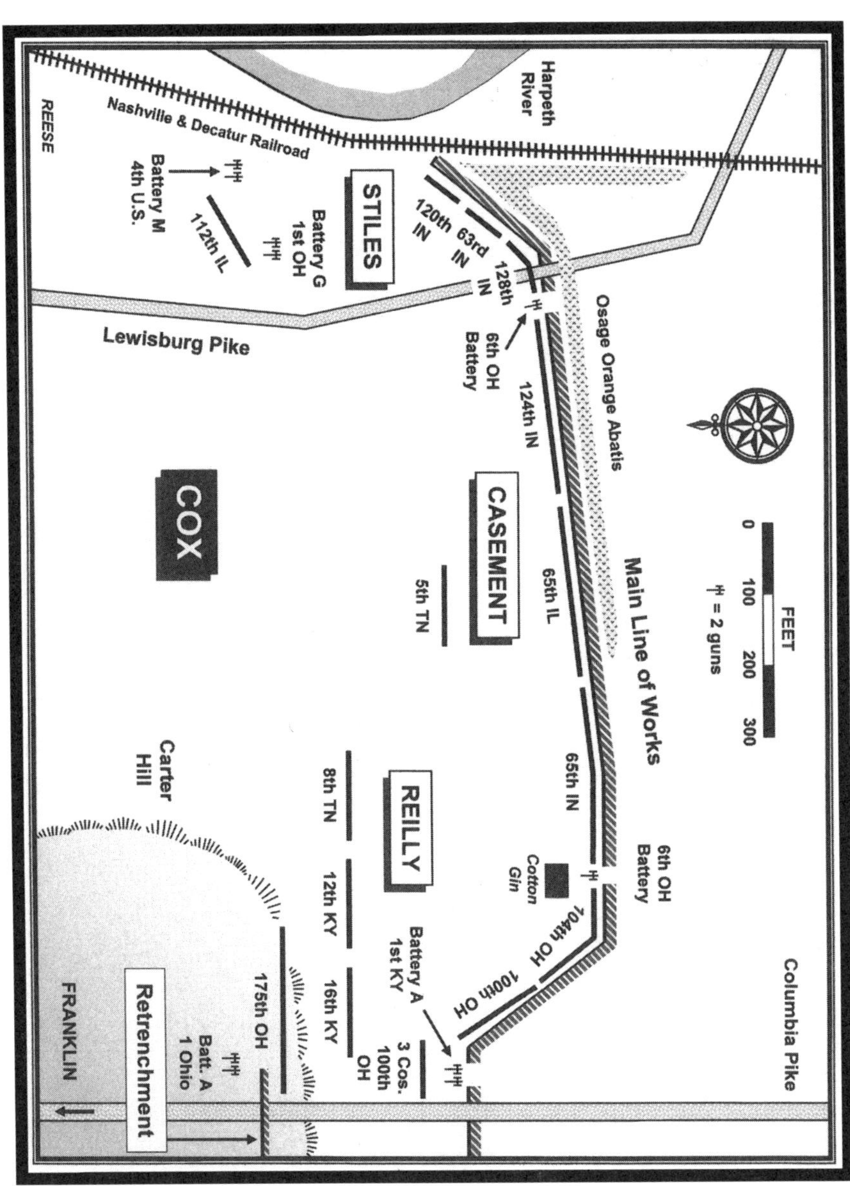

Federal line from Columbia Pike to Harpeth River

"Cockrell's Brigade had nearly all disappeared" and no other Rebel brigade at Franklin suffered a greater loss. Their loss of sixty percent was shocking even by Civil War standards, and served as testimony both to the Missourians' determination and the terrible position they were exposed to.[66]

As the Missourians were battling for their lives, Edward Walthall's Division began moving into contact with the Federals. His troops, once formed up, had an "extensive, open, and almost unbroken plain" over which to travel before reaching the enemy line. The men could see it was not going to be easy. Walthall two front line brigades soon began taking artillery fire and as they closed in rifle fire peppered the ranks. William Quarles' Brigade was ravaged by artillery fire tearing into his right flank. The ground between the cotton gin and Lewisburg Pike seemed alive with fire. Men were falling everywhere and suddenly what had been undetectable from a distance became visible directly ahead. It was the Osage orange abatis. Stretched out along the Yankee line it especially hindered Quarles' men. Officers and soldiers began frantically hacking at the branches with swords and knives. Many clubbed it and swung at the abatis with their muskets hoping somehow to break the snarl of branches and thorns. Walthall said the men "did not falter" until they "reached the abatis fronting the works." He also believed the fire was the most deadly he had "ever seen troops subjected to." Bullets and canister balls crackled through the boughs of Osage and into the bodies of the hapless Rebels. Screams of terror broke out, mixed with a chorus of cursing and yelling. No large body of troops could move through the Osage abatis and the panic of the men increased. Some tried to crawl over the top of the obstructions only to get tangled up and shot to pieces by the Yankees. Others tried to find a way around it, but there were few breaks. Some realized their fate, turned their attention to the enemy, and began firing wildly toward the works.[67]

Walthall's troops faced many of the same Federal troops as had the Missouri Brigade. Casement's regiments methodically tore Walthall's front line to pieces. In the early dim of twilight, the Henry

---

[66] *OR* 45, pt. 1, p. 716; French, *Two Wars*, p. 296.

[67] *OR* 45, pt. 1, p. 720-721; Copley, *Sketch of the Battle of Franklin*, p. 52-53, SHC.

repeaters and Springfield muskets spit out a wall of fire. An audible moan went up from the Rebels. Scores of men fell dead and wounded and bodies toppled into the Osage. There the "mangled and torn remains" created a macabre spectacle as they hung partially suspended in the thorny branches. Countless others, trapped or restricted in their movements, became easy targets for the Federal soldiers. Men were picked off and killed with ease and the wounded were shot repeatedly until they also died.[68]

Capt. William W. McMillan of the 17th Alabama, a regiment in Cantey's Brigade, was among the throng which rushed the Federal line. He said within "10 paces of the works" a bullet slammed into his left thigh, "making a severe wound about 10 inches in length but not breaking the bone, although completely paralyzing the whole limb." McMillan was running when he was hit and the impact flung him flat on his face. After examining the wound and determining he would not bleed to death, McMillan, who was unable to walk, stretched out on the ground. While in this position he was struck in the right hand which severed "the ulna artery" and the captain began bleeding anew. Another ball ripped through his blanket and grazed his ribs and a fourth, nearly spent, "glanced" into his left shoulder. Until nightfall bullets peppered the ground around McMillan when he was convinced by Yankee troops to crawl toward the works and surrender. Two Federal soldiers then picked him up, threw an arm around each shoulder, and carried him to the rear.[69]

As Capt. McMillan's personal drama was playing out, some headway was finally made through the Osage abatis by other men from Walthall's Division. Small seams developed in places and pockets of Rebels began forcing their way through the interwoven wall of branches. Included in this number was Gen. Shelley, commanding Cantey's Brigade, who was on foot because his horse had been killed. At first only a small number of Southerners broke through, but soon larger numbers rushed toward the works. Some Federal soldiers turned their attention to these breaks in the abatis and swept them with scorching fire. But the momentum was unstoppable. Other gaps

---

[68] Copley, *Sketch of the Battle of Franklin*, p. 53, SHC.

[69] Ilene Thompson and Wilbur Thompson, *The Seventeenth Alabama Infantry: A Regimental History And Roster*, p. 106.

Edward C. Walthall (Library of Congress)

developed and groups of Confederates streamed through. Within moments a stampede of men raced for the outside ditch. Waves of them were killed and wounded as they attempted to navigate the open ground between the Osage abatis and the outer ditch. The cost to Walthall's Division was catastrophic. He watched it nearly bleed to death right in front of him. Walthall had two horses killed beneath him, but somehow escaped unharmed. A soldier later wrote with conviction that "Walthall had to fight Death, Hell, and the Devil and each had the advantage of him."[70]

The ditch at the base of the Yankee works quickly became a show of horrors. Those Rebel troops lucky enough to have made it through the Osage orange and across the short expanse between the abatis and the enemy line found just how bad it was. Federal troops started shooting down into the ditch from the top of the parapet. Most of the Southerners could barely defend themselves. Among those trying to stay alive was Col. Virgil S. Murphey, commander of the 17th Alabama. Murphey said men were "disfigured and mutilated and dying" all around him and others were "swept unheralded into eternity." Some of the Rebels tried to scale the works rather than be subjected to the murderous fire. Among those were Murphey and a handful of other

---

[70] *OR* 45, pt. 1, p. 721; Worsham, *The Old Nineteenth Tennessee*, p. 143; Robert Banks, *The Battle of Franklin*, p. 52; William C. Davis, ed., *The Confederate General*, Vol. 5, p. 149.

men who "bounded over like infuriated demons..." They had no luck. Murphey was unceremoniously jerked down and made a prisoner and the rest of his comrades were killed or wounded. The Alabama colonel was fortunate. Behind him dead and wounded piled up along the length of the ditch. Blood and tissue were splattered everywhere and the ground was wet with it. It was enough to shatter raw nerves and some began crying and screaming. Many called out, "Cease firing! Cease firing!" Others shouted, "We surrender! We surrender!" From the vicinity of the cotton gin to the east, the southern face of the Yankee works was covered with men huddling "like sheep in a shambles."[71]

Robert Banks, who had transferred from the 37th Mississippi to the 29th Alabama only five days before the battle, was among those who survived the hail of enemy fire and made it to the ditch. He was there only about five minutes when a nightmare unfolded right before his eyes. Banks saw a young soldier near the works get hit with a bullet. The boy, about seventeen years old with blue eyes and a fair face, immediately cried out that he had been shot and his head tipped backward. In the twilight the scene became all the more frightful. The crowd of soldiers around him was so thick the young soldier could hardly move. Banks saw that nothing could be done for the boy since no one had a bandage or even a rag. Desperately the wounded youth began to gasp and throw about his arms and legs. As the horror played out dead and wounded fell all around the boy. He continued struggling until he was almost lying down, blood still gushing from his wound. In a horrible twist, other soldiers soon began kneeling on the boy's still twitching body as they continued fighting for their own lives. Tragically, the suffering of this single soldier became lost in the larger picture. Banks watched as the boy's life ebbed away, struck by the callousness of man in the face of such misery.[72]

The suffering of Walthall's men dragged on. A soldier in the 49th Tennessee said the "slaughtering of human life" was something that could not adequately be put into words. Most of it occurred in the shadows of twilight and beneath clouds of smoke. Of the 129 men who went into battle under the banner of the 49th Tennessee only thirty-

---

[71] Virgil S. Murphey diary, p. 7, 9-10, SHC; Banks, *Battle of Franklin*, p. 76-77.

[72] Banks, *Battle of Franklin*, p. 66, 77-79.

seven returned. Men fell "on their faces in almost as good order as if they had lain down on purpose..." The Confederates moved ahead almost blindly, unable to see twenty or thirty feet in front of them. The field become blanketed in smoke after the battle began and was heaviest where the fighting was the worst. There was little wind and the only time the smoke cleared was when artillery fire or musket volleys cut through the air. Then large numbers of determined Confederates could be seen clawing their way to the top of the works. But smoke would roll back over like fog, shrouding everything and obscuring the hand-to-hand struggle going on underneath. This slugfest was exemplified by the color bearers of the 1st Alabama, 42nd Tennessee, and 53rd Tennessee. All three got to the parapet only to be either shot or captured and the trio of flags ended up in the hands of the enemy. Pvt. Thomas A. Turner recalled the man who carried the 42nd Tennessee's flag "had his head nearly severed from his body..."[73]

Strange and lurid scenes played out everywhere. One involved a Confederate who made it to the ditch east of the cotton gin. Near him lay the body of a dead Federal soldier who had been on unable able to get back inside the main works. The Southerner noticed the dead Yankee had "two large army pistols" in his belt that were "loaded and capped." Grabbing one gun in each hand the Rebel "emptied them under the head-logs" at the enemy soldiers on the other side. Another episode involved brothers, Joseph Williams and Enoch Williams, both of whom were lieutenants in the 40th Mississippi. Each disappeared into the smoke of battle and they were later found "locked in each other's embrace." Joseph had lost an arm and Enoch had been shot in the stomach. Each had died holding the other's wound, "trying to staunch the flow of blood."[74]

Lt. Aaron Baldwin's 6th Ohio Light Battery only added misery to the scene. His quartet of Napoleons, particularly the two-gun section

---

[73] Copley, *Sketch of the Battle of Franklin*, p. 52, SHC; C. Wallace Cross, *Cry Havoc: A History of the 49th Tennessee Volunteer Infantry Regiment, 1861-1865*, p. 65; *OR* 45, pt. 1, p. 725; J. H. McNeilly, "Bloody Franklin," *CV* 29, p. 5; Thomas A. Turner, "Forty-Second Tennessee Infantry," in *Military Annals of Tennessee*, Vol. 1, Lindsley, ed., p. 518.

[74] Copley, *Sketch of the Battle of Franklin*, p. 54, SHC; Williams brothers account, CHA.

near the cotton gin, inflicted untold agonies on the Confederates who came near them. The ground from Lewisburg Pike to the Carter gin was like hell. The concussions from the guns caused mens' ears to bleed and the dead and wounded actually "piled up like snowdrifts in winter time" before the mouths of the guns. Baldwin said the Rebels "tried hard to force a passage at the right embrasure of the battery." The Southerners were nearly driven mad by the slaughter in front of the works and they tried anything to stop the 12-pounders from firing any longer. Some squeezed their heads into the embrasure and "fired upon the cannoneers." The Yankees in turn used "sponge staves, axes, and picks to drive them back." Pvt. Jacob Steinbaugh actually killed one of the Rebels by throwing an axe through the embrasure. He disabled another by smashing him in the head with a pick. A man from the 104th Ohio, standing beside Steinbaugh, joined in by striking another Rebel in the face with the end of his musket and firing at the same time. Things became so crazed that Baldwin ordered the guns loaded with triple canister. He even told some of his artillerymen to take their socks off and load them with "bullets from the infantry ammunition boxes" and then fire them at the enemy. One Confederate remembered getting his "face blistered and eyebrows burned off" when the guns discharged. Baldwin was never able to forget the dreadful sounds. Because the Rebels were so thick outside the works, every time the guns fired the lieutenant first heard the explosion and then the crunch of bones being broken. Baldwin compared the sound of the firing to the "crashing of an immense forest tree, which had been chopped down" and remembered there were enemy troops literally "swept out of existence with every discharge..."[75]

---

[75] Scofield, *The Retreat From Pulaski*, p. 40-41; *OR* 45, pt. 1, p. 334; Copley, *Sketch of the Battle of Franklin*, p. 55, SHC; Hinman, *The Story of the Sherman Brigade*, p. 671, 673. While Baldwin said "some 550 rounds" were fired at Franklin the report of Fourth Corps artillery chief Lyman Bridges stated the battery fired 480 rounds from Columbia to Franklin. Of the 480 figure, 304 were spherical case and canister. If Bridges' figure is accurate it should be assumed nearly all of the spherical case and canister was fired at Franklin. Even Baldwin said only fifty rounds were fired at Columbia and because the armies were on opposite sides of the Duck River, the fire there would have

As his men struggled against the Federal breastworks, Gen. William Quarles did everything he could to inspire them. Quarles was a 39-year old native Virginian who called Clarksville, Tennessee home at the outbreak of war. He was a solid soldier who had fought at Fort Donelson, Vicksburg, and then led his brigade through the bitter Atlanta Campaign. At Franklin, as he yelled above the roar of battle urging his boys forward, cannon fire ripped into his upper left arm, fracturing the bone and causing considerable muscle damage. Ironically, Quarles was fortunate. All of his staff officers were killed and according to Walthall a captain was in charge of the brigade when the fighting ended.[76]

Capt. Pleasant M. Hope, commander of Company D, 46th Tennessee, was one of the countless brave men in Quarles' Brigade. Killed as he led his men forward, Hope became another casualty in a war that had claimed far too many. Yet this particular soldier left behind a gripping reminder of the human side of the war. Several months before the Battle of Franklin, Hope had written a letter home to his daughter whom he had yet to see. In a period dominated by a lavish Victorian style of writing, his was basic and down to earth. It was also emotional and heart-wrenching:

> It is with pleasure and delight that I write you a few lines, which will be the first letter you ever received, and one too which I hope you will preserve until you can read it.
>
> By the misfortunes of war, I have been separated from your Momma, but by the blessings of God, I hope to soon return to you, never more to leave you, until death shall separate us. My dear and only child, be a good girl, ever love and obey your affectionate Momma, and don't forget your first letter writer, who has not nor never will forget you, who daily prays to God, in his infinite mercy, to spare, bless and protect you amid the troubles of this world,

---

been solid shot or fused shell only. At Spring Hill the battery did not fire a single round. Baldwin said some firing was done on the retreat to Franklin, but did not specify an amount. It is not likely that Baldwin's guns fired, at a minimum, 300 rounds of canister and spherical case during the heaviest fighting at Franklin. See *OR* 45, pt. 1, p. 321-322, 334.

[76] Faust, ed., *Historical Times Encyclopedia*, p. 607; Welsh, *Medical Histories of Confederate Generals*, p. 178; *OR* 45, pt. 1, p. 721.

and should you live to be old, may God bless you and prepare your soul in this life to go to that happy world after death.

Your Father,
P. M. Hope [77]

William Wing Loring was only four days from turning forty-six years of age when he led his division into combat at Franklin. Loring was born in 1818 in Wilmington, North Carolina and as a young man he worked as a lawyer, planter, and was even a politician briefly. Although he did not attend West Point, Loring joined the United States Army and fought gallantly during the Mexican War, where his left arm was amputated after being wounded at Chapultepec. Loring remained in the army until secession came, but then resigned and was appointed a brigadier general in the Confederate army. Perhaps most famous for a showdown he had with Stonewall Jackson in early 1862, Loring was promoted to major general and fought at Champion Hill and Vicksburg in 1863. Nicknamed Old Blizzards by his men, Loring served under Leonidas Polk during the early stages of the Atlanta Campaign and for a short time commanded Polk's Corps after the bishop's death. Subsequently moved back to division command, Loring came to Franklin as a battle-scarred career soldier.[78]

On the Confederate right flank, where Stewart's Corps was hemmed in by the Harpeth River, the losses were awful. Loring's Division approached the enemy line simultaneously with Walthall's, and Loring's advance brigades, Winfield Featherston on the left and Thomas Scott on the right, hardly knew what hit them. The fire from Fort Granger battered the advancing troops long before they came within range of enemy musketry. Moreover, the Rebel approach was fraught with difficulty. Near the river, north and northwest of Carnton, the terrain changed slightly and small undulations rippled up from the ground. As Loring's men swept up and over these rises they took

---

[77] P. M. Hope to daughter, April 25, 1864, CHA. Pleasant's brother, Lt. William L. Hope of the 46th Tennessee was also mortally wounded at Franklin and died several days after the battle.

[78] Faust, ed., *Historical Times Encyclopedia*, p. 447; Welsh, *Medical Histories of Confederate Generals*, p. 144.

Collins' Farm, circa 1915. Lewisburg Pike is on the left and the railroad runs horizontally just beyond the bottom of this photo. Many of Loring's men charged up this slope toward the Union line. (Judge John Henderson Collection)

casualties at every step. They soon approached Collins' Farm, which lay on the western edge of Lewisburg Pike. In that vicinity the two brigades began a mad forward rush. Featherston said his men charged ahead "with a shout." A Union soldier said it was as if "the whole South had come up there and were determined to walk right over us."[79]

The Nashville & Decatur Railroad ran through this section of

---

[79] Stevens, *CV* 11, p. 166; Crowson and Brogdon, ed., *Bloody Banners and Barefoot Boys*, p. 100; Henry George, *History of the 3rd, 7th, 8th and 12th Kentucky C. S. A.*, p. 133; Official Report of W. S. Featherston, April 21, 1865, Featherson Papers, Archives and Special Collections, J. D. Williams Library, University of Mississippi. Special thanks to Bob Jenkins of Dalton, Georgia for bringing Featherston's unpublished report to my attention. There has been ongoing debate about whether Scott or Featherston formed the right of Loring's Division, and hopefully the sources listed here will help answer the question.

the field and some of the troops, particularly Featherston's, became bogged down in the railroad cut. All semblance of order was shattered as the Rebels tried to get across the cut by scrambling down into it and then climbing out the other side. Inside the cut, bodies piled up as the Fort Granger guns took full advantage of the wretched position the Confederates were in. From the fort the Yankee gunners could fire nearly lengthwise into the high-banked cut, and they inflicted a dreadful loss of life. What waited beyond the railroad cut was little better. Through sheer will and determination, Featherston and his line officers kept their men moving forward although they now found themselves lagging slightly behind Scott's troops. Once they cleared the cut, they began moving roughly to the left rear of Scott's charging brigade. In a final and crazed push, the two ragged Southern units bounded toward the Federal line.[80]

The brave men of W. W. Loring's ravaged front line pressed forward, some approaching to within one hundred yards of the enemy breastworks. Along the way the Rebels had been forced to do battle with the Osage orange strung out along the curve of the pike. The Northern troops had done a devilish job with the snarly Osage, creating a "most elaborate" handiwork with "interlocked" branches. Additionally, wooden planks had been sharpened and aligned at chest level with one end "set deep in the ground..." An Indiana officer recalled how the Rebels made "desperate efforts to penetrate" the abatis and that "human nature couldn't stand the destructive fire that was rained upon them..."[81]

Just north of where Lewisburg Pike crossed the railroad tracks, the road veered to the right and approached the Federal line at a nearly perpendicular angle. In addition to the Osage obstructions, very serious space constraints also worked against the Southerners. As a result, many of the Confederates who swarmed into the area of the railroad cut were forced west of the pike, not only to avoid the Osage boughs, but just to maneuver. Scott's men, on the far right, funneled mostly into the area between the pike and the river, but Featherston's command was bisected and his brigade careened both east and west of Lewisburg

---

[80] Elliott, *Soldier of Tennessee*, p. 240.

[81] Merrill, *The Soldier of Indiana*, Vol. 2, p. 759-760; Pat Henry, "Adams's Brigade in Battle of Franklin," *CV* 21, p. 76.

Pike.[82]

Yet the impaired advance was far from over. The next obstacle was the abatis strung out in front of the Federal line, but already devastating enemy volleys were tearing into Loring's ragged line. Men fell everywhere, sprawled in the dirt and grass and screaming from their wounds. Bodies piled atop one another. Like Walthall's troops, the men of Loring's command took as much punishment from the artillery sitting behind the enemy line as they did from the line itself. The Napoleons and 3-inch guns spewed double and triple canister at the Rebels. Earlier, Lt. J. M. Stephenson had received permission to move two guns of the 4th U. S. Artillery further east. Battery commander Samuel Canby said from his new position Stephenson "completely swept the railroad and river-bank." The ground along the Harpeth literally trembled when the Yankee guns fired and deadly fragments of iron screamed over the breastworks and into the swarming ranks outside. Men were lifted "clear off the ground at every discharge." In some areas entire groups of men were nearly blasted apart, their features no longer recognizable in the face of the artillery's graphic power. It was "the most destructive fire" an Alabama soldier said he had ever seen.[83]

Frail human bodies were simply torn asunder. Arms, heads, legs, and pieces of body parts littered the ground in front of the Federal line. Some Southerners came up to the Yankee position "with heads bent low...and caps drawn over their eyes, as if to shut from their sight the fate that awaited them." The Union troops kept up the pressure. Volleys exploded in unison from over the works and scores of Loring's men melted to the earth. A Confederate remembered how the enemy fire "swept our ranks like hail." Shells from Fort Granger plunged to earth like fireballs from the sky, dealing death and misery. The 35th Alabama from Scott's Brigade suffered terribly. When the battle was over the regiment tallied some 150 killed and wounded, nearly one half of its effective force. In Company B alone, out of twenty-one men who

---

[82] Marshall, *Reminiscence of*, CHA. Further evidence regarding Featherston's men veering west of Lewisburg Pike is provided later in the text.

[83] *OR* 45, pt. 1, p. 338; Copley, *Sketch of the Battle of Franklin*, p. 53, SHC; Crowson and Brogden, ed., *Bloody Banners and Barefoot Boys*, p. 99.

went into the battle, four were killed and thirteen were wounded. The 12th Louisiana, the only Bayou State unit at Franklin other than a small company of dismounted cavalry in Granbury's Brigade, also suffered serious casualties, including commanding officer Col. Noel L. Nelson, who was mortally wounded. Gen. Scott, a 35-year old Georgia native, did everything imaginable to keep his men moving forward before his involvement in the fighting abruptly ended. As Scott worked his men toward the Osage orange brush, a shell detonated nearby and he was thrown to the ground by the violent force of the concussion. Scott emerged from the explosion without any obvious physical wound, but was so disoriented that he could barely stand. The general was eventually carried to the rear and his participation in the war ended at Franklin. The concussion caused significant damage to Scott's spine and his kidneys, inflicting bruising so serious only time and extended rest would cure them.[84]

Chaplain James McNeilly moved up with Loring's Division to assist with the wounded. Near the front, McNeilly saw men begin running to the rear and remembered seeing Loring "riding among them trying to rally them." It was one of those fleeting moments burned in time and McNeilly watched intently. After having done everything he could think of, Loring "turned his horse to face the enemy." McNeilly noted that the division commander was dressed in a "full uniform that glittered with golden adornments." For a moment Loring sat on his horse, staring toward the enemy line as bullets creased the air around him. With a look "of grief and of scorn" on his face Loring yelled out, "Great God! Do I command cowards?" He then turned around and galloped after his retreating men in an effort to reform them. Loring surely did not command cowards. Instead, his men faced odds too daunting and deadly, and for the first time many chose their lives above anything else.[85]

---

[84] Field, *Bright Skies and Dark Shadows*, p. 241; Thompson, *WCHS* 15, p. 59; W. Brewer, *Alabama: Her History, Resources, War Record, and Public Men, from 1540 to 1872*, p. 644; Elliott, *Soldier of Tennessee*, p. 240-242; Helen Potts and Helen Hudgins, *McGavock Confederate Cemetery*, p. 37; Crowson and Brogden, ed., *Bloody Banners and Barefoot Boys*, p. 100; *OR* 45, pt. 1, p. 708; Welsh, *Medical Histories of Confederate Generals*, p. 192.

[85] McNeilly, *CV* 26, p. 117.

The combat degenerated into utter brutality. Out of sheer desperation, some of Scott's and Featherston's troops attempted the impossible. The abatis ended near the railroad where the tracks and cut ran along the Harpeth River. There the 120th Indiana held the extreme Federal left flank, but the regiment was unable to butt directly up against the river because of the rail cut. When some of the Rebels got close enough to see this, they pushed into the cut just south of the Union line. Perhaps they thought some of the scathing fire might be avoided by diving into the railroad cut, or that the enemy flank could be turned in. Regardless, the decision was a tragic one.[86]

The 120th Indiana, commanded by Col. Allen W. Prather, held its ground and poured a torrent of fire into the rail cut. Israel Stiles said the Indiana troops deserved "great praise for the heroic manner" with which they executed their duty. Above the din, Confederate officers could be heard screaming at their men to, "Press to the right!" Reacting were the artillerists to the rear. Capt. Alexander Marshall's guns of Battery G, 1st Ohio Light Artillery enfiladed the cut with their fire. Marshall said he found the Rebels moving forward "in strong force" and "on their hands and knees." His 3-inch pieces pumped canister and case shot down on top of the Southerners, blowing many of them to pieces. At the same time, two of the Napoleons from Lt. Samuel Canby's Battery M, 4th U. S. Artillery were moved closer to the railroad. There they "swept the railroad and river-bank" and decimated the enemy ranks. The destruction wrought by these two batteries, ten guns altogether, is difficult to comprehend. At the conclusion of the battle they had fired a total of 1,141 rounds, 796 from the rifled guns and 444 from the Napoleons. The Fort Granger guns also took their toll, even inflicting friendly fire. According to a friend, Maj. Edward B. Brasher of the 120th Indiana was killed by a shell from across the river.[87]

---

[86] *OR* 45, pt. 1, p. 331; Marshall, *Reminiscence of*, CHA. Marshall said the Federal works began within twenty yards of the railroad.

[87] *OR* 45, pt. 1, p. 322, 331, 338, 430; Cox, *Battle of Franklin*, p. 124-125; Marshall, *Reminiscence of*, CHA; S. P. Conner to J. S. Casement, Nov. 10, 1887, CRN. Marshall said several of the rifled guns were placed along the railroad near the present day Highway 96 bridge which spans the Harpeth River. At the time of the battle there was no bridge there.

Incredibly, Featherston's men continued to press the attack. In front of the 128th Indiana, posted mostly east of Lewisburg Pike, portions of three Mississippi regiments slashed their way through the Osage abatis and raced for the smoking breastworks. Men carrying the colors of the 3rd Mississippi, 22nd Mississippi, and 33rd Mississippi, were somehow able to ascend to the top of the enemy parapet. The flag bearers of all three regiments "were wounded and captured with their colors" according to Gen. Featherston. Ensign John J. Cherry, who carried the 3rd Mississippi's flag, later died from his wounds. Lt. Henry Clay Shaw suffered a similar fate. About "fifteen paces from the works" Shaw saw the color bearer of the 33rd Mississippi fall. Instinctively, Shaw picked up the flag and scrambled to the parapet. As he tried to shove the staff into the dirt, Shaw was killed, "his body falling in the trench, the colors falling in the works."[88]

Not mentioned in any official reports were the actions of Sgt. Spence Neal and Col. Marcus Stephens of the 31st Mississippi. Their location on the field was indicative of just how splintered Featherston's command was. After Neal was shot down carrying the regiment's colors, he handed the flag to Stephens who bolted toward the works held by the 65th Illinois. Stephens desperately tried to reach the parapet, but took a bullet in the right thigh and fell into the outside ditch. Others followed the lead of these brave men and scratched their way to the top of the Yankee breastworks, only to find themselves in no man's land. Those not killed outright were dragged down and taken prisoner. Pvt Ira S. Byrd of Company G, 22nd Mississippi, was among the latter. A 16-year old student who had enlisted less than two months earlier, Byrd was captured and later died in prison.[89]

---

[88] *OR* 45, pt. 1, p. 430, 714; D. J. Wilson, Letter of, *CV* 2, p. 186; Merrill, *The Soldier of Indiana*, Vol. 2, p. 760; H. Grady Howell, Jr., *To Live and Die in Dixie: A History of the Third Mississippi Infantry, C. S. A.*, p. 384-385. Col. Stiles indicated the 33rd Mississippi's flag fell outside of the works while Featherston said it fell inside. D. J. Wilson of the 33rd Mississippi said only that the "enemy got the flag." Regardless of where it fell the flag was never recovered.

[89] *OR* 45, pt. 1, p. 430; D. J. Wilson, Letter of, *CV* 2, p. 186; Dunbar Rowland, *Military History of Mississippi, 1803-1898*, p. 293; Alice Hirsh and Edward Hirsh, *Life Story of Isaac E Hirsh, Co. G, 22nd Regiment, Mississippi Infantry, C. S. A.*, attached handwritten roster of Co. G.

As Stewart's Corps became fully engaged in its monumental struggle with the left of the Yankee army, the situation in the center, where Cleburne's and Brown's divisions were driving forward, was a vortex of chaos. Troops from Gen. Wagner's shattered brigades poured through the gap in the Federal line at the Columbia Pike while the more ingenious looked for other avenues. John Shellenberger veered away from the crowd near the pike and with his "body bent over and head down" ran in the direction of the gin house. All at once he crashed violently into a fellow soldier. Both men tumbled to the ground and simultaneously a shell exploded above them. Shellenberger watched as the man he had run into looked about, thinking he had been hit by the shell. For a brief second Shellenberger was so amused he laughed. But suddenly the captain was struck with horror when he got up and realized he could hardly run any longer. With only "fifteen or twenty steps" to go Shellenberger's body had decided it could go no further. Out in the open, just south of the gin, Shellenberger turned and looked toward the Rebels. He nearly looked at death. Spotting a Confederate soldier not far away, Shellenberger watched as the man aimed his musket and fired. A bullet smacked into the man just to the captain's right and with a burst of energy Shellenberger turned and stumbled toward the ditch on the outside of the works. He barely made it there when the troops on the other side raised up and unleashed a crushing volley into the approaching Southerners. Shellenberger then crawled a few feet and when he looked up he saw enemy soldiers flooding the ditch. He remembered them falling "against the outside face of the parapet" and that many lay there "panting for breath" unable to continue. Realizing that staying where he was likely meant being killed with a bayonet, Capt. Shellenberger "sprang up to the top of the breastwork." Without warning, a Rebel soldier stuck his musket up at the Yankee officer and fired. The bullet missed Shellenberger, but he went tumbling down the other side of the works and ended up unconscious at the bottom of the trench.[90]

As John Shellenberger was running for his life and jumping over breastworks, all hell broke loose east and west of Columbia Pike. An Ohio soldier from Col. John Lane's Brigade racing for cover on the west side of the road clearly remembered the emotion of bullets zipping

---

[90] Shellenberger, *CV* 36, p. 382-383.

past him and "expecting in every instant" to be shot in the back. Yet as he and his comrades came up to the main line, they were sickened to see their own men rise up and prepare to fire. Pvt. William Keesy noted the irony of escaping one disaster only to encounter another and be shot by fellow soldiers. Thankfully for Keesy and those near him, the officers were able to keep the men along the main line from firing until most of Wagner's refugees who had not pushed through the gap in the line were able to dive into the ditch lining the works. Keesy tumbled to a stop and looked around. Seconds later an ear-splitting volley erupted right over his head. The Rebels returned fire and minie balls started peppering the outside of the works. Not content with this development, Pvt. Keesy vaulted himself to the top of the embankment and fell inside. There a captain told Keesy to get out of the trench, as he had no time for stragglers and did not want the morale of his men affected. Keesy found his way to the rear and watched as the battle swelled to a monstrous roar.[91]

The Union line had held its fire for as long as it could. The first volleys were paced, but in an instant the entire line came alive and men began firing at will. Keesy said the troops rose up "and a flash of flame shot out in a sinuous line, and the white smoke rose like the foam on the crest of a breaker, while the thunder of that volley shook the firmament." Everyone remaining in front of the works, regardless of what uniform they wore, was in the line of fire. Keesy wrote graphically that the "few straggling blue-coats and the long line of gray went down like over-ripe grain before a blast of wind and hail."[92]

Screaming like furies, Hiram Granbury's hard-hitting Texans and Daniel Govan's Arkansans were less than one hundred yards from the enemy line when the first full volley hit. Instantly the air was alive with bullets. The rifle fire was joined by searing blasts of canister from Capt. Theodore Thomasson's 1st Kentucky Light Battery. Shrouded by billowing clouds of smoke, the front ranks of the Texas Brigade suffered heavy losses as did the Arkansas troops. The crush of men became easy targets for the Federals. Among those who fell early in the fight was Gen. Granbury. Cleburne's aide Leonard Mangum was barely

---

[91] Keesy, *War As Viewed From The Ranks*, p. 109.

[92] Ibid., p. 109.

Hiram B. Granbury (Lawrence T. Jones III Collection, Austin, TX)

ten feet from Granbury when he was hit. The tall, lanky general had just yelled out, "Forward men, forward! Never let it be said that Texans lag in the fight!" Granbury took only a few more steps before a bullet smashed into his lower cheek and exploded out the back of his head. According to Mangum, the general immediately threw both hands to his face as if to find the pain. Granbury then sank to his knees, his hands still on his face. Death came so quickly that his body seized up and his lifeless form remained kneeling as the battle raged all around. Granbury was the first of many general officers lost on the bloody field at Franklin.[93]

Probably within minutes of Granbury's horrifying death the Army of Tennessee, and indeed the entire Confederacy, suffered an irreplaceable loss. East of the pike, perhaps forty yards from the smoldering Union works, Patrick Cleburne was advancing with his men. Bodies covered the field and acrid smoke hung low in the air, almost hugging the ground. There was utter confusion in almost every direction. Cleburne, with his sword in one hand and his kepi in the other, yelled for his men to keep moving. Suddenly the end came, like a flash through the haze. A single minie ball ripped into Cleburne's chest and he staggered to the ground. Blood flowed down his chest and he toppled to the ground, sword still in hand. Struck near the heart, Cleburne probably died almost instantly. He had fulfilled his promise to John Bell Hood. The enemy works would be taken or he would fall

---

[93] Mangum, *Kennesaw Gazette,* June 15, 1887. See also Mangum, Statement of, p. 3, Peacock Papers, SHC.

trying to accomplish the task.[94]

As a division commander, Patrick Cleburne did not need to be on the front line at Franklin. He seemed to approach the battle with some "wild abandon." Even Frank Cheatham said years after the battle that Cleburne "was a little more daring than usual..." As an enduring testament of his devotion to the men he commanded, Cleburne refused to have them assault the Federal works alone. At Franklin they would not go to a place he was unwilling to go.[95]

A fellow Arkansan who fell with Cleburne at Franklin was Lt. Thomas B. Moncrief. In April 1861 a company of soldiers, Moncrief among them, known as the Yell Rifles had been raised to help fill the ranks of an Arkansas regiment. Cleburne was selected as the company's first captain and the unit always remained close to his heart. War had dwindled the ranks of the Yell Rifles and Moncrief was among the last of its original members. His death was the conclusion of another bitter chapter.[96]

Combat along the center of the Federal line was like an inferno. Even Gen. Hood said the "concentrated roar of musketry" reminded him of "some of the deadliest struggles in Virginia" and that it raged with an "intense fury..." Gen. George Gordon, leading his brigade on foot west of the pike, said that when the enemy opened fire it was as if "hell itself had exploded in our faces." The bullets were so thick Gordon thought a handful could have been grabbed from the very air. A Federal soldier east of the cotton gin said he "never saw men in such a terrible position as Cleburne's Division was for a few minutes." He thought it amazing how "any of them escaped death or capture."[97]

Gen. Daniel Govan wrote to his wife after the battle and said

---

[94] Buck, *Cleburne and His Command*, p. 292; Purdue, *Pat Cleburne*, p. 423; Mangum, Statement of, p. 3, Peacock Papers, SHC.

[95] Losson, *Tennessee's Forgotten Warriors*, p. 223; Burr and Williams, *PHP*, March 11, 1883, p. 24.

[96] Purdue, *Pat Cleburne*, p. 429; Faust, ed., *Historical Times Encyclopedia*, p. 145.

[97] Hood, *Advance & Retreat*, p. 294; Gordon, *CV* 8, p. 7; George W. Gordon, "General P. R. Cleburne: Dedication of a Monument to His Memory at Helena, Arkansas, May 10, 1891," *SHSP* 18, p. 267; Barr, *CV* 10, p. 155.

the troops along the pike "bore the brunt of the fight and sustained the heaviest loss." Yet the wave of ragged gray and butternut barely slowed. On both sides of Columbia Pike the Northerners tried desperately to hang on. As the last of Wagner's men attempted to get through the gap in the line, the Confederates came screaming close behind. Lt. Col. Milton Barnes, whose 97th Ohio had been out on the advanced line, said there was "an almost uncontrollable panic among both lines, and for a few moments all was in terrible confusion." Lt. Col. Edwin Hayes of the 100th Ohio said Wagner's troops and the Rebels struck the works "almost simultaneously..." Like a gigantic tidal wave four Southern brigades, with three others in close support, crashed into the Union center. Over thirty regiments, although inferior in size to their blue counterparts, caused a cataclysm that buckled the heart of Jacob Cox's defensive perimeter. At the gap on the pike, a breach almost immediately opened in the Federal line when men from Brown's and Cleburne's divisions began streaming through. An Illinois officer said the Rebels "rushed pell-mell into our works."[98]

Gordon's and Granbury's brigades began to mix almost as soon as they penetrated the enemy position. Groups of Gordon's men actually crossed to the east side of the pike during the whirlwind of action and some of Granbury's were west of the road.[99]

Yet the momentum of the attacking force was not slowed and within moments Union troops were being overwhelmed. Gordon ended up in the ditch east of the pike where the Union line jutted out to the southeast and formed a salient. There was graphic close quarters fighting everywhere. Men kept their heads down and fired under the head logs and over the top of them. The effects of bullets shot from only a handful of feet away were horrific. Muskets were swung like clubs and men threw punches and grappled with one another on the ground. Bayonets were used to perform unspeakable acts.[100]

The clash was uncommon even in a war that had dragged for nearly four years. At Franklin it was as if all sense of morality vanished

---

[98] *OR* 45, pt. 1, p. 265, 393, 419; Daniel C. Govan to his wife, Dec. 4, 1864, Govan Papers, SHC.

[99] Gordon, *CV* 8, p. 7; Losson, *Tennessee's Forgotten Warriors*, p. 224.

[100] Gordon, *CV* 8, p. 8; Gordon, "Eleventh Tennessee Infantry," in *Military Annals of Tennessee,* Vol. 1, Lindsley, ed., p. 301.

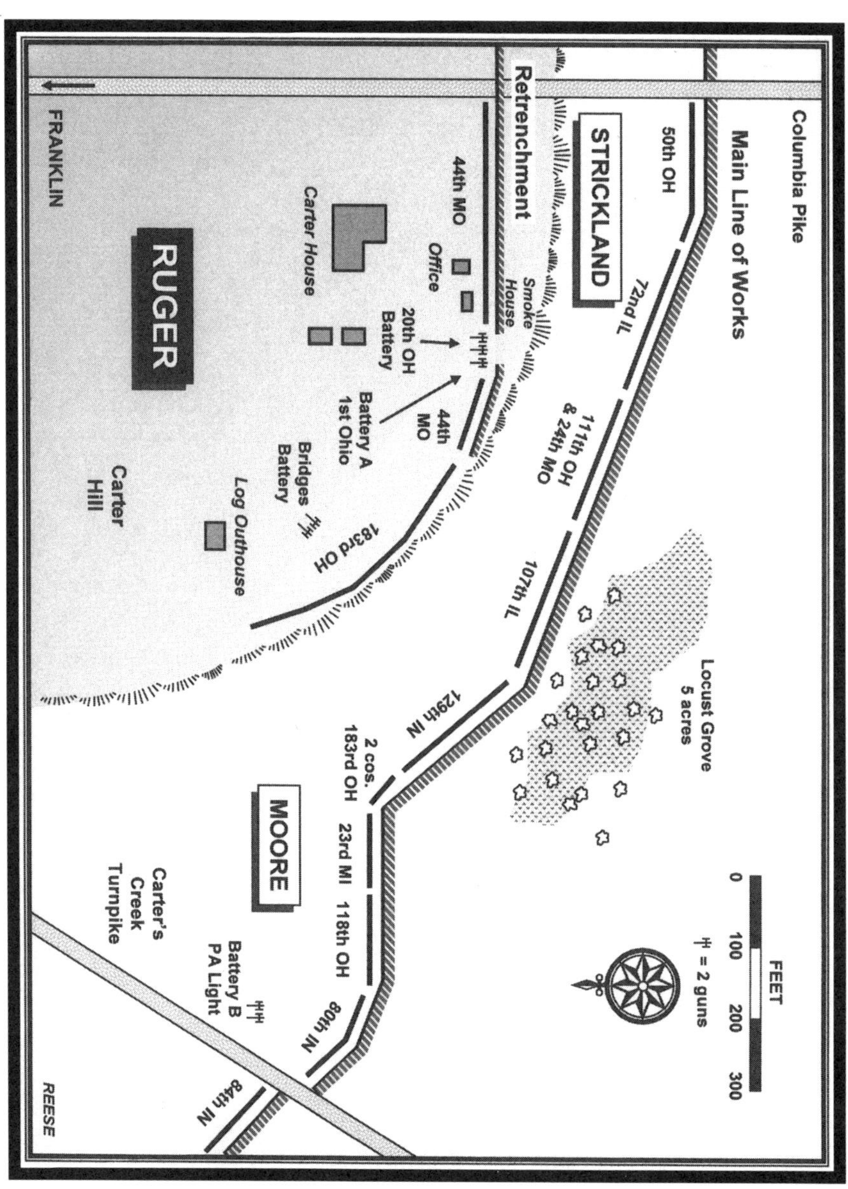

Federal line from Columbia Pike to Carter's Creek Pike

entirely. A war which had started with pomp and grandeur had spiraled into a bloody and gut-wrenching struggle, where victory could only be achieved by absolute extermination of one side or the other.

The battle was not even an hour old when the Union center was pierced. Shortly after 4:30 p.m., with darkness ready to fall, everything hung in the balance. Events unfolded simultaneously and the battle grew muddled. The hours ahead would be no less confusing. The cover of night only exaggerated the situation and brought forth a whole new set of horrors.[101]

In the 50th Ohio, posted on the western edge of the pike, pandemonium broke out. Lt. Thomas C. Thoburn recalled that the Confederates "swept on like a resistless flood, coming in through our front line...and just to the left of where our regiment was stationed." Thoburn was on the right of the regiment, nearest the 72nd Illinois, and he ordered his men to "fix bayonets" and clear out the Rebels who were piling over the breastworks in front. A chill went down the lieutenant's spine when he glanced to the left. The rest of the regiment had completely caved in and the enemy was "sweeping along the rear of our lines in a solid mass." Brown's men had landed a body blow to the Union mid-section. Thoburn sensed disaster and yelled, "Boys, we must get out of here; every man for himself!" Some never got out of the trenches. Erastus Winters was in the 50th Ohio and found himself a prisoner in the blink of an eye. He and his captor crouched down in the trench trying to avoid the fire that was coming in "from all parts of the compass." Men were falling everywhere and two fell almost on top of Winters. He said one fell at his feet and another crumpled against his left shoulder, both men "soaking and staining" his uniform with their blood. The Ohioans who could escape turned and ran toward the retrenched line. Lt. Thoburn immediately noticed an even greater problem when he about-faced. Directly ahead, barely sixty yards away, were the four guns of the 20th Ohio Light Artillery and the two-gun section of Battery A, 1st Ohio Light Artillery. The big Napoleons filled the air with countless iron canister balls and their explosions rocked the ground. The Yankee gunners furiously discharged their pieces in an

---

[101] Sunset was at 4:34 p.m. Information obtained from the U. S. Naval Observatory and provided specifically for Franklin, Tennessee for November 30, 1864.

States Rights Gist (Library of Congress)

effort to stem the gray tide and as they did, Thoburn saw the very real possibility of being "mowed down" by friendly fire.[102]

In the midst of this turmoil was George Wagner, who fought a losing effort almost from the start. As many of his demoralized men rushed for safety, Wagner rode his horse right into the swarming crowd. Although he cursed at them, shook his crutch, and "called them cowards," there was little Wagner could do to staunch the flow. Levi Scofield remembered seeing Wagner's mount being pushed backward in the direction of town by "the surging mass" of soldiers. He said the troops filled the turnpike, but many were also "crowding along in the open ground east of the pike." The last time Scofield saw Wagner the general was still screaming at his troops to halt as the mob pushed in the direction of Franklin.[103]

South of this bedlam, John Brown pushed his advantage. While Gordon's Tennesseans fragmented the Union line west of Columbia Pike and pushed toward the Carter House, Gist's Brigade plowed into the locust grove. Gist's horse was shot through the neck and began rearing onto its hind legs and thrashing violently about. Forced to dismount under fire near a sugar maple tree, the general sprinted forward with the right of his brigade. Already the Georgians and South Carolinians had enveloped the right flank of John Lane's advanced Federal brigade. Now they pushed "the advance force of the enemy

---

[102] Winters, *In the 50th Ohio*, p. 121-122; Thomas C. Thoburn, *My Experiences During the Civil War*, p. 146-147.

[103] Scofield, *The Retreat From Pulaski*, p. 35; Cox, *Battle of Franklin*, p. 105.

pell-mell" into the locust abatis strung along the front of the Yankee breastworks. Many fleeing Northerners "were captured and sent to the rear" and others where shot down by their own men when the main line convulsed to life with volleys of fire. Gist's men approached through this terrific gale along the section of line defended by the 72nd Illinois and 111th Ohio. Many of the Illinois troops, however, had already fled to the rear following the collapse of the 50th Ohio. The Confederates turned up the pressure and flocked toward the works. As they did, Gist was hit in the chest by a bullet and stumbled to the ground, blood rushing from a wound near his heart. Picked up and carried away by litter bearers, Gist mumbled to aide Frank Trenholm that he wanted to be taken home to his wife. His men raced all around on their way to the front. Within moments, they crashed hard into the locust abatis with a South Carolina officer referred to as "a formidable and fearful obstruction..." Although nearly the entire brigade seemed to be slowed by it, the Southerners pressed the attack. Men washed like waves up to the ditch and began a struggle to get over the works. The flag of the 24th South Carolina was planted atop the Yankee parapet and Gist's men battled furiously with what remained of the 72nd Illinois and 111th Ohio. Lt. Col. Joseph Stockton of the 72nd Illinois was urging his men to hold on when suddenly he fell flat on his face. Shot in the back of the neck Stockton felt blood running down his body. He stumbled to the rear, somehow found a doctor in the chaos, and was escorted to safety. Back at the front the battle continued. Capt. William G. Foster of the 65th Georgia managed to get his regiment's flag on top of the enemy works, but the staff was shot in two and the banner fell to the earth. Foster determinedly picked it up and battled on. A participant said it was the "most desperate fighting imaginable..." Lt. Col. Isaac Sherwood of the 111th Ohio faced the storm and remembered how the line to his left was broken and the troops there were "forced back in confusion."[104]

---

[104] *OR* 45, pt. 1, p. 737; Roberts, *CV* 27, p. 58-59; Sherwood, *Memories of the War*, p. 136; Statement of "Uncle Wiley" Howard, Body-Servant of General States Rights Gist, Relative to the Death and Burial of General Gist, p. 2, Peacock Papers, SHC; Stockton, *War Diary*, p. 27-28; Cisco, *States Rights Gist*, p. 142. Appendix One of Cisco's book, p. 152-153, mentions that Janie Gist, the general's wife, learned from someone that her husband had also been shot in the leg.

As his leading units strained against the enemy, Brown ordered his supporting brigades, Strahl's and Carter's, into the fury. Word soon came from Carter that his brigade's left flank was unsupported and in danger of "being threatened..." Brown could see there were no troops beyond Carter's flank, but also knew there was no time for delay. Time spent waiting for William Bate's men to move up and cover the left was time Brown did not have. He chose to keep his units moving. Unfortunately for him a Yankee bullet put him out of commission soon thereafter. As Brown assisted in pushing Carter's men forward near the locust grove a bullet slammed into his leg. The wound was so serious that Brown "fell forward on his horse's neck." The fire in this sector was horrendous and had already taken out nearly all of Brown's aides as well. Only one staff officer and two couriers remained unharmed and they quickly assisted Brown to safety as his division kept grinding ahead.[105]

In what must have seemed like an instant, the Union forces on both sides of Columbia Pike had suddenly given way, unable to withstand the Rebel attack any longer. The first to abandon their posts had been men from the 50th Ohio on the west side of the road. They were soon joined by the 100th Ohio and a portion of the 104th Ohio east of the pike. The commander of the deluged 100th Ohio, Lt. Col. Edwin Hayes, said the Southerners came "in on the right flank and over our works." There were men in blue and gray everywhere, running in all different directions. It was like a riot. Hayes bellowed out to some of Wagner's panic-stricken men flooding the area to get to the rear and reform. He immediately realized he had used the wrong words. Many of the men from his own regiment mistook what Hayes said and thought he had told them to move to the rear. All of a sudden, the entire 100th Ohio broke and retreated toward the retrenchment. Pvt. Haven B. Talbert said he and his fellow Ohioans "had to strike a two-forty gait to get away, as the place was hotter than that mentioned in the Revised Bible."[106]

Col. Oscar Sterl of the 104th Ohio also found his command nearly overrun by swarms of enemy soldiers. Sterl said the ditch outside

---

[105] Brown, *CMH* 8, p. 157; James Van Eldik, *From the Flame of Battle to the Fiery Cross*, p. 259; Field, *Bright Skies and Dark Shadows*, p. 239.

[106] *OR* 45, pt. 1, p. 419; H. B. Talbert, Letter of, *CV* 17, p. 374.

the works was quickly "filled with rebels" and they began vaulting over the parapet. Sterl's regiment was hit hard on its right flank and he watched as the enemy almost buried the 100th Ohio with its numbers. Confederate officers could be heard screaming at their men to "get to the rear and reform" and this only compounded the panic and confusion coursing through the Northern ranks. Sterl watched in disgust as three of his companies nearest to the 100th Ohio also fled to the rear in search of safety.[107]

These developments caused immediate and very serious problems for the men manning the guns of the 1st Battery, Kentucky Light Artillery. Almost before he knew what happened, Capt. Thomasson's infantry support was gone. It only took seconds before "the cannoneers were driven from their posts." Rebel troops, likely from Cleburne's Division, pounced on the battery's four guns and hurriedly began turning them around to fire on the Federals. But the Confederates had a serious problem on their hands. When the Yankee artillerists had bounded away, they took with them the friction primers needed to fire the rifled guns. The crafty Southern infantrymen looked to improvise. A Federal officer nearby saw them pouring gunpowder "from their musket cartridges" into the vent holes. It was obvious to this captain that the Rebels intended to fire their muskets into the vent holes to set off the cannon charges.[108]

Daniel Govan's Arkansans were in the thick of this fighting. Somehow musician James Bradley of the 1st Arkansas ended up near the front and was wounded in his left leg by cannon fire. Pvt. John Ruth of the 6th Arkansas was also wounded, so severely that both of his arms were amputated. He died in a hospital in March 1865. Capt. Samuel L. McAllester of the 8th Arkansas escaped without a wound but was captured in the melee. McAllester, from West Point, Arkansas, was shipped to Fort Delaware and died there of disease in June 1865. He never made it home, and today his remains rest near Salem, NJ.[109]

---

[107] *OR* 45, pt. 1, p. 419, 421.

[108] *OR* 45, pt. 1, p. 326; Shellenberger, *CV* 36, p. 383.

[109] Compiled Service Records of Confederate Soldiers, Arkansas, Microcopy 317, National Archives and Records Administration. Transcription and information courtesy of Bryan Howerton, Little Rock, AR.

Across the road from where Govan's men battled, what was left of the 50th Ohio had largely fallen back to the vicinity of the retrenched line along the south side of Fountain Branch Carter's smokehouse and office building. When the Rebels cracked the center, forcing the 50th Ohio from its position, the regiment lost significant numbers. Over one hundred were killed, wounded, captured, or missing and more than half of those fell into the latter two categories. Among the Ohio soldiers collared and taken prisoner were four privates named Michael Gilmore, Henry Jordan, Lawrence King, and George Shearer. All had enlisted around the same time in the summer of 1862 and had fought togther for two years. At Franklin they all became prisoners and in the days following the battle were shipped to the notorious Andersonville prisoner camp. In a cruel twist of fate all four men survived that horror only to die together aboard the steamer *Sultana* as they were being shipped home in April 1865. It was yet another of the ironic tragedies of war.[110]

As a result of the 50th Ohio's retreat, the next regiment in Col. Silas Strickland's section of the line, the 72nd Illinois, became exposed on its flank by the Rebels flooding inside the main line. Capt. James Sexton said that as "the support on our left gave way" four companies from the Illinois regiment withdrew to the rear toward the support line. For a short time, the remaining six companies held their position on the front line and fought tenaciously. Most hailed from the Chicago area and some knew a good brawl when they saw one. Men were "using the bayonet, and others the clubbed musket..." Sexton said he fired his revolver nine times and the most distant man he shot "was not more than twenty feet away." He also recalled seeing a soldier with "blood streaming down his face from a wound in the head" race toward a group of enemy soldiers and begin swinging a pick axe at them. The insanity had no boundaries. Atop the breastworks the captain saw a

---

[110] *OR* 45, pt. 1, p. 396. Information concerning the 50th Ohio prisoners is courtesy of Historical Data Systems, Inc., www.civilwardata.com. The *Sultana* was a steamer transporting mostly former Union prisoners home shortly following the war's conclusion. The ship had far too many men on board for her size and one of her boilers exploded near Memphis, Tennessee on April 27, 1865. Nearly 1,600 lost their lives in the accident.

Southern officer emerge and demand with "profanely expressive" language the surrender of some of the Illinois troops. Sexton watched in shock as a nearby private shoved his rifle into the Rebel's stomach and shot him, while almost calmly saying, "I guess not." The gaping hole in the enemy officer's mid-section was so big Sexton said he could see light streaming through. The Confederate then doubled over and fell headfirst into the trench, landing almost at the private's feet.[111]

The 72nd Illinois was unable to hold on indefinitely. As they did battle at the front, fire began raking them from the rear. The Federal troops in reserve along the retrenchment, particularly the men of 44th Missouri, were feverishly trying to hold back the Rebels who had passed beyond the main line. Elements of the 44th Missouri had nearly been run over by some of Wagner's men, and before they could recover from that blow the enemy was in their faces. The bedlam caused some of their shots to pass through the enemy ranks and into the backs of the Illinois men at the front. Panicked calls to cease fire went unheeded. Reluctantly, the rest of the 72nd Illinois abandoned the main works and moved "by the right flank" to occupy a new spot along the retrenched line to the right and rear of the 44th Missouri. Once there, however, Capt. Sexton found himself with a whole new set of responsibilities. All of the Illinois regiment's field officers, Lt. Col. Joseph Stockton, Maj. William James, and Capt. Edwin Prior, were down with wounds. Additionally, Lt. Albert S. Packer was dead and Lt. William Stokes lay mortally wounded. This purging thrust Sexton into the role of temporary regimental commander and left him short of lower grade officers. But the young captain took charge and quickly went to work solidifying his regiment's new position.[112]

The Confederates at this point occupied about 200 yards of the main Federal line on both sides of the Columbia Pike. Men like Col. Horace Rice of the 29th Tennessee, Gordon's Brigade, led hundreds of "brave and noble" troops through this massive hole as they pushed into the heart of the enemy defense. Behind them additional Rebel troops

---

[111] *OR* 45, pt. 1, p. 393; Sexton, *MOLLUS*, Illinois, 4, p. 478-479.

[112] Sexton, *MOLLUS*, Illinois, 4, p. 478-479; Cox, *Battle of Franklin*, p. 118, 239-240; *Official Army Register of the Volunteer Force of the United States Army for the Years 1861, '62, '63, '64, '65* (hereafter referred to as *OAR*), 6, p. 330.

surged up through the breach. It was nothing less than the battle's "critical juncture..."[113]

At about the same time that George Wagner was trying to rally his shattered brigades, David Stanley and Jacob Cox arrived near the center. Stanley said the panorama before him was one of "indescribable confusion..." Cox came galloping in from the left of the Yankee line to witness the same wild discord. As he rode behind James Reilly's reserve units in rear of the cotton gin, Cox saw Gen. Stanley on his horse with his "hat in hand" cheering some troops forward. Cox immediately recognized them as men from Col. Emerson Opdycke's Brigade. Barely had Cox looked in that direction when the 12th Kentucky and 16th Kentucky lurched forward to fill the hole on the east side of the pike made by the withdrawal of the Ohio regiments. Moving in tandem with the Kentuckians was the 8th Tennessee and 175th Ohio. Jacob Cox watched the troops react, almost instinctively, to the grave danger at hand. All around him the battle magnified in size and intensity.[114]

North of the Carter House, Opdycke's Brigade was enjoying its first real rest in almost twenty-four hours. The men had stacked their arms and torn boards from a nearby fence to start fires. Soon they were boiling coffee and frying bacon and side pork, readying what one soldier described as an "afternoon breakfast" long overdue. A variety of aromatic smells filled the air, a reminder to many of more pleasant times at home before the war. Yet the respite was short-lived. There was suddenly a loud clamor and then the roar of battle on the other side of Carter Hill. Moments later "a most horrible stampede" of "frightened recruits and panic-stricken men" came pouring over the slight hill. The mob of men streamed past Opdycke's troops, the quickest of foot soon disappearing in the direction of town. Meanwhile, more and more troops continued to spill rearward from the front. Almost to a man the brigade jumped to its feet. Quickly the men gathered their rifles and began forming their respective regiments. Meanwhile, Opdycke rode forward just far enough to see that the soldiers fleeing to the rear were not just Wagner's men as he had first thought. It was clear Federal soldiers were abandoning the center of the main line and Opdycke knew

---

113 Smith, *History of Maury County*, Interview with Moscow Carter, p. 202; Gordon, *SHSP* 18, p. 268.

114 Stanley, *Personal Memoirs*, p. 207; Cox, *Battle of Franklin*, 97-99.

at once he had to get his brigade up to help.[115]

Col. Opdycke was "alive to the situation" and immediately decided to align his brigade and push forward. In the heat of the moment, however, there was a communication breakdown. One unit, Lt. Col. George Smith's consolidated 74th/88th Illinois, shifted to the east side of the road as part of the planned advance, but before anything else could be completed the 73rd Illinois lurched forward. Maj. Thomas W. Motherspaw, commanding the regiment, was astride his horse and could see the chaos near the front. Either Motherspaw believed that Opdycke had already issued orders to charge or he simply acted on his own. Without warning the major called out to his men, "Forward, 73d, to the works!" Motherspaw's men, their hearts pounding, raised a yell and charged. Smith's consolidated command also took off and like dominoes the rest of Opdycke's regiments followed suit. In the 36th Illinois the men rushed ahead after hearing their Lt. Col. Porter C. Olson yell out, "Fall in, 36th! Forward to the trenches!" The 24th Wisconsin's commanding officer, Maj. Arthur MacArthur, flew into his saddle and hollered, "Up Wisconsin!" Sgt. Thomas J. Ford of the 24th Wisconsin said the men were so mad about losing their "nearly cooked dinner" that they felt like whipping "the whole rebel army just at that moment..." Capt. Edwin B. Parsons of the same regiment said there was "no time to form lines" and the Wisconsin troops simply "rushed pell mell to meet the enemy..." Things happened so abruptly that Capt. Edward P. Bates of 125th Ohio was unable "to secure and mount his horse." Opdycke watched, eyes ablaze, for several seconds as his brigade took on a life of its own. His men were veterans of many hard battles and they knew there was no time to waste. Opdycke realized there was nothing else he could do and shouted, "First Brigade, forward to the works!" He then spurred his horse straight into the fury.[116]

---

[115] Castle, *MOLLUS*, Minnesota, 6, p. 393; Rice, *Yankee Tigers*, p. 157; *OR* 45, pt. 1, p. 240, 251.

[116] *OR* 45, pt. 1, p. 240; Rice, *Yankee Tigers*, p. 157; Hasty, Statement of, *History of the Seventy-Third Illinois*, p. 439; Bennett and Haigh, *History of the Thirty-Sixth Illinois*, p. 652; Douglas MacArthur, *Reminiscences: General of the Army*, p. 10; Thomas J. Ford, *With the Rank and File: Incidents and Anecdotes During the War of the Rebellion, as Remembered by one of the Noncommissioned Officers*, p. 16.

Opdycke's men swept forward with their rifles and bayonets forward and ready. Jacob Cox saw them and said they looked "as if breasting a furious gale with strained muscles and set teeth." Quickly apparent was that any troops still moving to the rear were likely to be run over if they did not get out of the way. Stragglers began to peel away to the east and west as Opdycke's Brigade, shaped almost like a wedge, pushed ahead. Many of the rearward bound were heartened by the sight of the Midwestern boys moving up and turned back to join the counter assault.[117]

Only 150 to 200 yards separated the spot where the brigade was resting and the Carter home, so it took only a few moments for Opdycke and his men to get into the thick of things. En route most of the regiments swerved to the west side of the pike because of the high concentration of troops east of the road. As the brigade approached the Carter House and the buildings to its west, the unit's formation began to fall apart. Smith's Illinois regiments "converged towards the pike" and the 125th Ohio found itself on both sides of the house. Much of the Ohio regiment streamed around to the front, or east, side of the home. Capt. Bates shouted at his men, "Come on, boys! We have always whipped them and we will whip them now!" Two companies of the 125th Ohio and most of the 73rd Illinois rushed in the direction of the house's west side where a staked cedar and oak fence formed an obstacle. As a large number of Illinois men struggled with the thick fence palings, which had been securely nailed to crossbars, the 24th Wisconsin moved in to the right. Maj. MacArthur was conspicuous in the storm. Although only nineteen years old, MacArthur had already accomplished much. At Missionary Ridge almost exactly a year earlier, the young MacArthur had stunned those around him when he grabbed the regimental flag from an exhausted color bearer and ran to the crest of the ridge. Once there he planted the flag in the ground for all to see. It was an action that would earn him the Congressional Medal of Honor in 1890. At Franklin he would be no less brave.[118]

---

[117] Cox, *Battle of Franklin*, p. 98; *OR* 45, pt. 1, p. 246, 251, 253.

[118] Clark, *Opdycke Tigers*, p. 338-339; Rice, *Yankee Tigers*, p. 157-158; Adna Phelps, Statement of, *History of the Seventy-Third Illinois*, p. 452. Information regarding MacArthur's Medal of Honor is courtesy of the U. S. Army Center of Military History.

Right behind MacArthur came Lt. Col. Porter Olson and his 36th Illinois. They piled into the already crowded area west of the Carter House and drove toward the retrenched line. Back near the house the struggle continued with the obstinate cedar fence. Men kicked at the fence and bashed it with their rifle butts. An Illinois captain said so many enemy bullets were striking the fence it reminded him "of a boy rattling a stick on a picket-fence as he runs along it." The same officer said "getting over or through that fence" in the face of enemy fire was perhaps the most terrible experience the regiment had undergone during the war. Finally, after "what seemed an age" a hole was made and the Yankees began pouring through like water from a burst dam. As they flooded one side of the yard, Rebel troops from Brown's and Cleburne's divisions suddenly appeared on the other side. The Southerners poured through the area around the smokehouse and office building. In an instant there was a collision right in the middle of the Carter backyard. The force of it was shocking. Capt. George W. Patten said, "Description or imagination is hardly equal to the task of picturing the scene at this time." As the two columns crashed into one another, a maniacal fight to the death exploded right off the steps of the Carter porch. There a core of men who had been at the head of each column battled with fists, muskets, and bayonets. Hundreds of others splintered off in all directions, grappling with the nearest enemy they could find. It was "an indescribable melee" of hand-to-hand combat in its most brutal form. A Federal officer said "hell turned loose would seem almost as a Methodist love-feast compared to the pandemonium that reigned there..."[119]

Maj. MacArthur pushed his horse forward through the throng of men, headed for a Rebel flag he could see not far away. When his mount was shot down, MacArthur struggled ahead on foot and was struck by a bullet that "ripped open his right shoulder..." The enemy flag, however, remained the focus of MacArthur's attention and when he finally got close to it, a nearby Confederate officer took aim and shot MacArthur squarely in the chest. The young Wisconsin major nearly collapsed, but somehow managed to draw his sword and drive it straight through the enemy officer. Incredibly, as the Rebel sank to the ground

---

[119] George Patten, Statement of, *History of the Seventy-Third Illinois*, p. 462; Clark, *Opdycke Tigers*, p. 339.

he shot MacArthur again, this time in the left knee. Finally both men sprawled to the ground covered in blood, their personal battle concluded. With the Southern officer dying and MacArthur faring little better, command of the 24th Wisconsin devolved upon Capt. Alvah Philbrook. Only during one of the battle's first lulls was the desperately wounded MacArthur found and carried to the rear.[120]

The peaceful Carter yard was transformed into a killing zone. After the war a Confederate soldier wrote that at Franklin it seemed "as if the devil had full possession of the earth" and those who lived through the carnage around the Carter House would not have disagreed.[121] Pvt. Stuart F. Hoskinson of the 73rd Illinois said "it was a fight, nearly, to get to the front" as the Federals pushed in one direction and the Rebels the other. For a short time the seething horde of soldiers shot, stabbed, clubbed, and punched at nearly anything in front of them. It was like a gigantic street brawl with thousands of desperate men involved. The struggle became one of wills that grew fiendish in its nature. Once peaceful men, who before the war were farmers, merchants, craftsmen, and teachers, kicked, bit, and choked one another like animals. Some were caught off guard and had bayonets shoved into their backs, stomachs, and chests. Those who actually had time and space to reload their weapons did some of the worst damage. At point-blank range a soldier on the wrong end of a muzzle was doomed. Many were knocked backwards or spun into the ground by a minie ball they never saw coming.[122]

The cannons set inside the epaulement on the west side smokehouse added their thunder to the tempestuousness. Unlucky Confederates who tried to sneak around this corner of the brick structure found themselves staring at the four Napoleons of the 20th Ohio Light Artillery. The explosions from the guns ripped men to pieces and sent body parts flying in all directions. Just before the fighting began, Lt. Charles Scovill had been ordered to take command of the 20th Ohio's guns because the battery's commander, Lt. John Burdick, was a junior officer. Scovill, commander of Battery A, 1st Ohio

---

[120] MacArthur, *Reminiscences*, p. 10; William J. K. Beaudot, *The 24th Wisconsin Infantry in the Civil War: The Biography of a Regiment*, p. 340.

[121] Dinkins, *Personal Recollections*, p. 236.

[122] Hoskinson, Statement of, *History of the Seventy-Third Illinois*, p. 440.

Light Artillery, stepped in and quickly went to work.[123]

When the Rebels first stormed into the yard they came within a hairs-breadth of taking the six Ohio guns. But Opdycke's men ruined any chance of that happening and two sergeants from the 24th Wisconsin, Felix McSorley and Thomas Toohey, pitched in to help the reduced crew man the pieces. With McSorley amd Toohey acting as gunners pro tempore, Scovill hollered out instructions. Although nearly overwhelmed by the enemy and wounded in the chest after dark by a bullet slowed only "by the folds of his overcoat," Scovill held his ground. Preventing the Confederates from capturing these guns and widening their advantage was a key turning point in the battle.[124]

After being wounded, Scovill turned command over to Lt. Henry C. Grant. By the time the battle ended the 20th Ohio Battery had fired 169 rounds and cleared out waves of enemy opposition. To the right of those four guns, two of Scovill's own Napoleons from Battery A, 1st Ohio Light Artillery, with the help of other infantrymen, also turned back a number of Rebel troops.[125]

The bloody struggle on the Carter property drew men like a magnet. Hundreds of Wagner's troops from the advanced line joined the fight as did some from Silas Strickland's command who had earlier fled the main line. One soldier from the 50th Ohio actually got inside the Carter smokehouse and began shooting his rifle out a window on the building's west side. In places the Federal troops were from "four to six men deep..." and the fire they produced was extraordinary.[126]

---

[123] *OR* 45, pt. 1, p. 320, 322.

[124] *OR* 45, pt. 1, p. 253, 330; H. M. Davidson, *History of Battery A, First Regiment of Ohio Vol. Light Artillery*, p. 146. Toohey won the Medal of Honor for his performance at Franklin. Information concerning Toohey's Medal of Honor information is courtesy of the U. S. Army Center of Military History.

[125] *OR* 45, pt. 1, p. 240, 330, 336. Capt. Bates of the 125th Ohio and Capt. Wilson Burroughs of the 73rd Illinois claimed their regiment saved "two guns at the right" and "a battery" respectively. Perhaps both men are referring to the section of the 1st Ohio Light Artillery. See *OR* 45, pt. 1, p. 248, 251. Battery A, 1st Ohio saw only limited action during the battle. Scovill reported the entire battery only fired eight rounds. See *OR* 45, pt. 1, p. 330.

[126] Thoburn, *My Experiences During The Civil War*, p. 148.

Emerson Opdycke was in the middle of the action. Still mounted, he rode into the surging mass of troops and emptied his pistol at the Rebels. He then turned the weapon around and began cracking it over the heads of straggling Union soldiers. One of those who crossed paths with Opdycke was Sgt. Sharon French of the 125th Ohio. French had been sent to the rear to get ammunition from an ordnance wagon when Opdycke saw the sergeant and prepared to belt him across the face. Lt. Ralsa C. Rice saw this and ran up to intervene, explaining to Opdycke what French was doing. A few minutes later Opdycke jumped down from his horse, grabbed a musket, and put it to use keeping his men at the front.[127]

His regimental officers fought just as tenaciously. Lt. Col. Olson, a school teacher before the war, was "everywhere among his men" shouting encouragement and urging them to hold steady. His 36th Illinois suffered higher casualties than any of Opdycke's other units and Olson would be among them. Not long after the regiment began occupying a spot on the retrenchment, Olson was struck in the chest by a bullet that passed through his body. Gasping for air and spitting blood, Olson collapsed to the ground. Two soldiers picked up their commanding officer and carried him through the blistering fire to a point near the Carter House. The regimental historians said Olson was taken to the "shelter of a brick house" so it is likely he was put down on the north side of the Carter residence. Once there a sergeant from Company G ripped down a window shutter and Olson's body was placed on it. Olson was then taken to an ambulance and transported to the rear. Somewhere near the river handsome Porter Olson's struggle finally ended. He said simply, "Oh help me, Lord," and died.[128]

---

[127] Rice, *Yankee Tigers*, p. 161; Clark, *Opdycke Tigers*, p. 341; Longacre and Haas, ed., *Civil War Letterbooks of Emerson Opdycke*, p. 250, 252. Much has been said about Opdycke breaking his pistol over the heads of Rebel troops. This story was concocted by Opdycke after the battle when he was seeking promotion. In a letter written soon after the battle, Opdycke said he broke it over the heads of Federal soldiers. This version is corroborated by Scofield in *The Retreat From Pulaski*, see p. 38. Read footnote No. 10 on page 252 of the Longacre and Haas book to see how Opdycke's story evolved.

[128] Bennett and Haigh, *History of the Thirty-Sixth Illinois*, p. 653-654, 665.

In addition to Olson's mortal wounding, Opdycke lost Maj. Thomas Motherspaw. Shot from his horse, Motherspaw lingered until December 18 before dying of his injuries. But the losses did not stop there. Opdycke also learned that the temporary commander of the 24th Wisconsin had been shot down. Like the 36th Illinois, the Wisconsin troops had finally worked their way up to the retrenchment from where they battled the Rebels. As they grappled with the enemy, Capt. Alvah Philbrook noticed one of the privates dodging the incoming fire. Philbrook walked over, told the soldier to stop moving his head, and added, "Stand up and take it like a man." The captain barely got the last word out of his mouth before a Rebel bullet hit him flush in the forehead and killed him instantly. Without missing a beat the private retorted, "Why the devil in hell don't you stand up and take it like a man." Just then the private felt a bullet crease his scalp, causing a painful wound. Exasperated he said, "Holy Moses, there is nothing like the dodging after all. Every time I heard it before I dodged it and it never hit me." Meanwhile, command of the regiment passed to a third commander, Capt. Edwin Parsons, who collected Philbrook's personal items to ship them back to his family.[129]

In the deepening twilight, made darker by the thick smoke that shrouded much of the field, the character of the battle began to change. Although the action in the yard had been exceptionally violent and involved large numbers of troops, most of the fighting there was over within fifteen minutes. Faced with overwhelming numbers, Brown's and Cleburne's men began to grudgingly pull back from the Carter yard and in the blinding confusion pockets of Southern troops were bagged as prisoners. Sgt. Henry Ross of the 125th Ohio singlehandedly captured forty of the enemy while Cpl. Joseph Wilson, from the same regiment, was actually himself captured before escaping and bringing back with him twenty-five prisoners.[130]

---

[129] *OR* 45, pt. 1, p. 253; Clark, *Opdycke Tigers*, p. 338; Ford, *With the Rank and File*, p. 17-18; *OAR* 6, p. 331.

[130] *OR* 45, pt. 1, p. 251; Cox, *Battle of Franklin*, p. 100. An odd discovery was made near the Carter House by Cpl. John Miller of the 24th Wisconsin. He found the flag of the 51st Illinois, a regiment that had been on the advanced line. Miller returned the flag to the regiment's adjutant the following day. See *OR* 45, pt. 1, p. 253-254.

The Rebels who chose to keep up the fight occupied new positions along the south side of the retrenchment. Opposite the Confederates at least four of Opdycke's regiments jammed together along the low-lying interior line. This secondary line of works, which stretched to a distance of between 300 and 400 yards, also had along its length a number of rallied troops from other commands. The 44th Missouri, which served as the line's anchor, fought furiously. Cocky Union troops could be heard shouting at the Rebels "to come on" if they wanted to fight any more. Pvt. Charlie W. Sears was holding the flag of the 36th Illinois when a Rebel reached out and grabbed hold of the staff. Sears yelled out, "No you don't, unless you take me with it!" Several friends came rushing to his aid and shot the Southerner at point blank range. Sgt. Edward Blake carried the flag of the 24th Wisconsin to the front and planted it atop the retrenched works. When the flagstaff was shattered by enemy bullets Blake tore the colors down, put the flag inside his jacket, picked up a musket, and began firing at the Rebels. Pvt. James S. O'Riley of the 40th Indiana was among those from Wagner's Division who had rallied. O'Riley confronted a Confederate flag bearer near the Carter House and plunged his bayonet through the enemy soldier. O'Riley then "carried off his flag in triumph."[131]

The ground along the retrenchment occupied by the largest concentration of Federal troops extended from the Columbia Pike to a point not far west of the 20th Ohio Battery. In this area Northern troops stood in ranks five and six deep. Yet this was only part of the problem facing the Southerners who had punched through the Union center. Further to the west was the rest of the 44th Missouri as well as the 72nd Illinois, the latter newly positioned after withdrawing from the main line. From this area, approximately where today's Carter House visitor center stands, the right flank of the Missouri regiment and the

---

[131] *OR* 45, pt. 1, p. 238, 260-261; Cox, *Battle of Franklin*, p. 118, 143; Smith, *History of Maury County*, Interview with Moscow Carter, p. 201; Patten, Statement of, *History of the Seventy-Third Illinois*, p. 463; Bennett and Haigh, *History of the Thirty-Sixth Illinois*, p. 657; Beaudot, *The 24th Wisconsin Infantry*, p. 338. Col. Lane reported that O'Riley took the flag of the 15th Alabama, but that is incorrect. See *OR* 45, pt. 1, p. 256. The 16th Alabama's flag was captured elsewhere on the field so it is unclear which flag O'Riley took.

rallied Illinoisans were able to enfilade the enemy almost at will. The Confederates unexpectedly found themselves in a horrific position, one from which they could neither advance or retreat. Tragically no one in the high command of the Southern army was aware of what was happening.[132]

While Opdycke's Brigade and other Federal units battled around the Carter House to stem the Rebel tide there, equally important work was unfolding east of the Columbia Pike near the main line. Between the cotton gin and the road Rebel soldiers, predominantly from Cleburne's Division, forced the 100th Ohio and a good portion of 104th Ohio to flee from their positions behind the main breastworks. The hasty withdrawal by the Ohioans also put the guns of the 1st Kentucky Battery in a terrible fix. A Kentucky artillerist remembered how one moment he was firing his piece and the next he saw a Rebel officer shooting a fellow gunner dead. All of a sudden there were Rebels everywhere, capturing some of the Kentuckians and forcing others to turn and run. In what seemed like the blink of an eye the Union line in this sector, commanded by James Reilly, was in just as much trouble as the stretch west of the road. Fortunately for Reilly he had reserves in exactly the right place.[133]

Two of Reilly's support units, the 12th Kentucky and 16th Kentucky, were located about seventy yards in rear of the main line. Lt. Col. John S. White's 16th Kentucky was next to the pike and lined up behind the eastern extension of retrenchment. Lt. Col. Lawrence H. Rousseau's 12th Kentucky was positioned on White's left flank and the 8th Tennessee and 175th Ohio were in reserve. When the Southerners ruptured the line in the center matters there instantly spiraled out of control. Capt. Morris C. Hutchins of the 16th Kentucky happened to be near the front line when the Confederates broke through. Hutchins barely got his bearings before a Rebel pointed his musket at the captain and ordered him to surrender. Before Hutchins could even respond the Southerner "was shot down by a soldier who stood near..." Hutchins

---

[132] Park Marshall, Letter of, *CV* 24, p. 551.

[133] *OR* 45, pt. 1, p. 326, 419, 421; Smits, *NT*, Aug. 25, 1887.

turned and ran toward his regiment. As he approached, John White could see the look on his face and asked Hutchins what was going on. Hutchins blurted out "that the enemy had carried the first line of works..." White immediately turned to his men, told them to grab their rifles, and ordered a charge to the front. With a hurrah the Kentuckians rushed forward.[134]

In the 12th Kentucky there was also split second decision making. Lt. Rousseau saw "the line of works at and near the old cotton-gin in the angle of the line being abandoned" and he ordered his regiment "forward to the works." A nearby Federal officer said both Kentucky regiments "sprang over the low rifle-pits like tigers" and raised "a shrill shout" that could be heard even above the Rebel yell. Both Lt. Col. Daniel McCoy's 175th Ohio and Captain James Berry's 8th Tennessee also rush forward. With the Kentuckians leading the way, Gen. Reilly's reserves plunged toward the gaping hole between the gin house and the turnpike.[135]

Reilly's troops were not alone in their effort to shove the Confederates back. Emerson Opdycke's charge occurred at essentially the same time as Reilly's, but because of the limited space in which Opdycke's Brigade maneuvered, some of his troops ended up assisting Reilly far more than their own commander. The 44th Illinois from Opdycke's Brigade operated almost exclusively east of the Columbia Pike and moved up behind the 12th Kentucky and 16th Kentucky. Additionally, Smith's consolidated 74th/88th Illinois spent most of its time assisting with the disaster at the main line.[136]

The Kentuckians hit the swarming Rebels first. The two regiments covered the distance from their reserve posts to the front in only a handful of seconds. At nearly point-blank range both units unleashed "a burst of musketry" that "stunned and reeled back the Confederates..." Two companies of Rousseau's 12th Kentucky were armed with Colt revolving rifles and they inflicted heavy losses on the Rebels. A Federal officer said having one hundred Colt rifles was like

---

[134] *OR* 45, pt. 1, p. 417-418; Morris C. Hutchins, "The Battle of Franklin, Tennessee," *MOLLUS*, Ohio, 5, p. 280.
[135] *OR* 45, pt. 1, p. 415-416; Scofield, *The Retreat From Pulaski*, p. 37.
[136] *OR* 45, pt. 1, p. 246-247, 412; Cox, *Battle of Franklin*, p. 113; Clark, *Opdycke Tigers*, p. 338.

Frank M. Posegate, 175th Ohio (Steven E. Williams, Annville, PA)

possessing "five hundred ordinary muskets." It was a fight the outgunned Southerners simply could not win.[137]

The Confederates in this sector had several factors going against them. First, once they got inside the Yankee works all sense of organization broke down. Officers and men alike crowded together with little sense of cohesion. Second, the Rebels were terribly winded from their furious sprint that began on the far side of Wagner's line. Most had covered nearly three-quarters of a mile by the time they got to the Federal works and once inside the job only grew more difficult. There the Confederates came face to face with waves of fresh reserves.

After blasting the disorganized Confederates from close range the 12th Kentucky and 16th Kentucky pitched into their foes. Behind the Kentuckians came the 175th Ohio. Lt. Col. McCoy of the 175th Ohio did not get very far, however, before taking a bullet in the shoulder, forcing Maj. Edward E. Mullenix to take command at the height of the battle. McCoy's regiment, organized barely a month earlier and composed of a mixture of boys and middle-aged men, performed admirably. For a time the Ohioans were immersed in fighting that was hand-to-hand in all directions. Men struck at each other with "picks, shovels, pistols, and butts of guns." The Southerners who tried to fire the guns of the 1st Kentucky Battery were overrun and beaten to the ground. Most got a bullet first, then a bayonet. Lt. James Coughlan, one of Gen. Cox's favorite aides, was killed while cheering the troops on. Lt. Col. White was shot in the face, but wrapped a bandage around

---

[137] Speed, *MOLLUS*, Ohio, 3, p. 78.

his head, which soon became soaked with blood, and kept fighting. Like other spots on the field the confusion in this area was substantial. When the Rebels first penetrated the line the 100th Ohio had fled to the rear along with three companies of the 104th Ohio. Lt. Col. Hayes was horrified to see his entire regiment moving to the rear. He told Sgt. Byron C. Baldwin to run to the rear, grab the colors, bring the flag back, and plant it on the works. As Baldwin took off the 12th and 16th Kentucky were rushing forward. Caught up in their advance were Oscar Sterl's three wayward companies of the 104th Ohio. Quickly Sterl's men changed direction yet again and in a few moments they returned to the front with "fixed bayonets" where the Ohioans quickly "regained their works."[138]

Lawrence Rousseau said when his regiment arrived at the main works there was enough room for him to throw his entire force into line. The 16th Kentucky also flooded the front line, occupying the space near the 1st Kentucky Battery. Soon Capt. Theodore Thomasson's remaining gunners returned to their posts and "the limbers of the caissons" were brought up. Sgt. Baldwin had done his part in bringing the crowd of blue forward. After grabbing the 100th Ohio's flag he raced back to the front, calling for the regiment to follow. With a hurrah they took off for the main line, electrified by what they saw. Before Baldwin could put the flag at the top of the works, however, he was shot down and bled to death with the colors wrapped around his body. But Baldwin's bravery had given the Federals the momentum.[139]

On the right flank of the rallied 100th Ohio came Lt. Col. John Russell's 44th Illinois and George Smith's 74th/88th Illinois, both from Opdycke's Brigade.[140] When Smith's men came crashing down along the pike, the Kentucky regiments were already fully engaged with the

---

[138] *OR* 45, pt. 1, p. 358, 419, 421; J. K. Merrifield, "From 'The Other Side' At Franklin," *CV* 16, p. 554; Speed, *MOLLUS*, Ohio, 3, p. 81; Cox, *Sherman's March to the Sea*, p. 90; Scofield, *The Retreat From Pulaski*, p. 43; Cox, *Battle of Franklin*, p. 114-115; T. W. Williams, "Checking a Pursuing Foe: Schofield's Great Combat at Franklin, Tenn., Nov 30, 1864," *NT*, May 31, 1900, p. 3; South, *NT*, Sept. 20, 1923; Posegate, *NT*, Feb. 28, 1889.

[139] *OR* 45, pt. 1, p. 326, 416, 420.

[140] Ibid., p. 419.

multitude of Confederates. Considering the odds the Rebels faced, they fought with terrific intensity. A private in the consolidated Illinois unit remembered that as he approached the main line, Rebels could be seen everywhere. He saw a Southerner smash a soldier from the 16th Kentucky to the ground with the butt of his gun. Then another Kentuckian "clubbed the Confederate with his musket and knocked him down." By this time the first Kentuckian was back on his feet. He locked his bayonet onto his rifle, "turned it upside down, and plunged the bayonet in the Confederate, who was on the ground." It was one of many such scenes repeated across the battlefield.[141]

The avalanche of Union reinforcements was too much for the Confederates inside the works to overcome. Within fifteen minutes of the Southern breakthrough, the conflict became grossly one-sided. Rebel troops began throwing down their weapons and surrendering. Nearly surrounded and hopelessly outnumbered, many of them could not see the point of throwing their lives away. Federal soldiers rounded them up as quickly as possible and herded them away. Some were even placed "behind the cotton gin for safety." Col. Sterl of the 104th Ohio said 300 of the enemy were "sent to the rear." Opdycke's regiments also scooped up scores of prisoners. Lt. Col. Russell's 44th Illinois captured eighty-three Confederates, but Lt. Col. Smith's 74th/88th Illinois corralled even more. His troops took 210 total prisoners, including ten officers. One of those was a captain from Cockrell's Missouri Brigade named George W. Covell. After his unit's shredding, Covell had followed some of Cleburne's men into the hole in the enemy line. His luck ran out, however, when the attack was stunted. Realizing he had been through about enough, the captain surrendered quietly to Sgt. Israel P. Covey of Company B, 44th Illinois.[142]

Although the main Union line was restored, the Confederates around the gin refused to step down their attacks. They continued throwing themselves at the Federal works with a wild and almost reckless abandon. A Northern soldier recalled how the Rebels tried to

---

[141] J. K. Merrifield, "Opdycke's Brigade at Franklin," *CV* 13, p. 563.

[142] Merrifield, *CV* 13, p. 563; *OR* 45, pt. 1, p. 242, 247, 422.

"shove the headlogs over on our line..." Between the gin and the pike, where so many Federals units converged, the blue clad soldiers stood five and six deep. Soldiers from Joseph Conrad's command who had not fled to the rear also joined in to help. Since there was not enough room for all of them along the works, the men in the rear loaded muskets and handed them up to the front. The men in front "did nothing but fire." Once a rifle was fired it was handed back and the process began anew. For the Confederates on the outside, the relentless fire was more than they could endure. Casualties were appalling. Wounded men gasped for air beneath the piles of dead. Because the Union troops at the front could lean up close against the vertical wall of the breastworks, they only had to expose a hand or an arm when they fired. On the other hand, the Southerners cowered in a ditch on the outside and faced an embankment that sloped down at a convex angle. Thus the Rebels had absolutely no protection from the enemy fire. Moreover, if they tried to scale the works the men had to expose their bodies considerably just to fire into the Yankee trench and that was possible only if they could get to the crest of the parapet. Many who tried this were hit on the way up by bullets from beneath the head logs or gashed by bayonets. Others could fight no more and chose instead to stay in the blood-soaked ditch where they prayed for the horror to pass.[143]

At some point during the desperate fighting, David Stanley's horse was killed and he tumbled to the ground. As he got back on his feet Stanley was hit by a bullet that gashed the back of his neck, causing an extremely painful, but non life-threatening wound. The evidence points to Stanley remaining on the field for a short time and then riding back north of the river to seek medical attention. According to the doctor who examined him, the wound was "probably three inches long and equal in depth to half the diameter of the ball." But the real issue became not so much Stanley's wound, but how long he remained at the front. In his memoirs, Stanley did not even mention being wounded while in his official report, written almost three months after the battle, he stated the injury "did not prevent my keeping the field..." Jacob Cox,

---

[143] John K. Shellenberge, "The Battle of Franklin," *MOLLUS*, Minnesota, 5, p. 511; Jones, *NT*, June 16, 1898; Copley, *Sketch of the Battle of Franklin*, p. 56, SHC.

however, provided ample evidence that Stanley did in fact leave the field shortly after the conclusion of the charge led by Opdycke's Brigade and the Kentucky regiments. Cox said after looking at Stanley's injury and providing him with a new horse, the Fourth Corps commander "rode away toward the town."[144]

Eventually the firing near the cotton gin began to dissipate. The front line Confederate units had been dashed to pieces and some of the survivors began calling over the works begging to surrender. Rebel troops placed their hats and other articles of clothing on the ends of bayonets and began waving them over the parapet. Men began crying, "For God's sake, don't shoot, and we'll give up and come in." A soldier in the 104th Ohio said Col. Oscar Sterl was nearly beside himself with glee. He yelled out, "We've whipped 'em, hurrah, we've whipped 'em." Sterl later said "200 more prisoners" were taken around this time. Additionally, Corp. Newton H. Hall of the 104th Ohio singlehandedly captured two enemy battle flags, an action for which he earned the Medal of Honor.[145]

Five other members of the 104th Ohio were also granted Medals of Honor for capturing Confederate battle flags. The issue of proper credit for these seizures was, however, not without controversy. Col. Conrad made a point of stating in his official report that Lt. P. P. Boyer of the 79th Illinois gathered up three flags "after the firing had ceased" only to have them taken away by members of the 104th Ohio. Maj. Frederick Atwater commanded the 42nd Illinois in Conrad's Brigade and reported that flags taken by his regiment were confiscated by "an officer

---

[144] Cox, *Battle of Franklin*, p. 99-100, 286-287; *OR* 45, pt. 1, p. 116; Welsh, *Medical Histories of Union Generals*, p. 317-318. The only reasonable explanation for Stanley trying to alter the facts is that later he realized he should have remained at the front. His wound was not life threatening, but was serious enough that Cox suggested he seek help. However, in the aftermath of the battle Stanley seemed to have regretted the decision. Stanley was awarded a Medal of Honor in 1893 for his involvement at Franklin, a curious decision considering his limited role. Information about Stanley's Medal of Honor is courtesy of the U. S. Army Center of Military History.

[145] *OR* 45, pt. 1, p. 422; Pinney, *History of the 104th Ohio*, p. 62. Information about Hall's Medal of Honor is courtesy of the U. S. Army Center of Military History.

of the Twenty-third Corps..." Atwater later filed a more detailed report in which he said following his regiment's retreat from the advanced line, it took a position on the main line "behind the same works" as the 104th Ohio. There Cpl. John H. Smith of the 42nd Illinois shot a "rebel color-bearer" and took his flag. According to Atwater the corporal was confronted by "a line officer of the One hundred and fourth Ohio Infantry" who "demanded the flag." Smith protested but gave up his prize. Pvt. John Mollison had the same thing happen to him. After the firing had died down, Pvt. Enoch Downs went over the works "to help one of his wounded comrades..." Nearby Downs "picked up three rebel flags" and took them back inside the works. Upon his return a colonel of the 104th Ohio demanded the flags, stating everything "captured in his front belonged to his regiment." Downs "stoutly protested" but when the Ohio officer threatened to have the young soldier arrested, the private "gave up the colors." In the end Conrad's Brigade ended up maintaining possession of just one flag, the banner captured by Sgt. A. Clark Copeland of the 65th Ohio.[146]

As Rebel prisoners and flag were being gathered up, Pvt. James K. Merrifield, a member of the 88th Illinois, vaulted the works and wove his way through the dead and wounded. He kept going until he got to Col. Hugh Garland of the Missouri Brigade about fifty feet away. Merrifield had apparently seen Garland fall with the flag of the 1st Missouri. By the time Merrifield reached him, the colonel had dead and wounded men sprawled all over him. Merrifield pulled the bodies off Garland and gave the wounded officer a drink of water. After gathering up Garland's sword and belt, which the colonel had asked to be removed, Merrifield also grabbed the flag. Suddenly a bullet zipped past the two men. Merrifield looked up and saw "another line about three hundred feet distant" moving toward the Union position. He turned and fled toward the safety of the works and his flag capture would later

---

[146] *OR* 45, pt. 1, 271-272, 275-276. The names of the other 104th Ohio soldiers who earned Medals of Honor are: Cpl. Joseph Davis, Pvt. John C. Gaunt, Pvt. Abraham Greenawalt, Capt. George V. Kelley, and Pvt. John H. Ricksecker. Whether these men personally captured flags or were simply given flags confiscated from members of Conrad's Brigade is unknown. Information about the medals is courtesy of the U. S. Army Center of Military History.

earn Merrifield a Medal of Honor. Witness to this was Capt. John M. Hickey, who lay only about six feet away. Hickey was "saturated with blood" from two arm wounds and a leg wound. Hickey was so badly hurt that he could not move, and after Merrifield scampered away the captain could see Garland was in the same horrible predicament. Caught between two opposing forces neither man could flee. Bullets again began flying from all directions. Hickey survived the nightmare, but Garland was not so lucky. Hickey watched helplessly as a second shot found Garland only moments later and killed him instantly.[147]

The supporting Confederate brigades crashed into the Yankee line with no less vigor than had the front line units. Mark Lowrey's Brigade came into close contact only minutes after Pat Cleburne's leading units had pounded into the center. Lowrey said as his men approached they experienced "the most destructive fire" he had ever seen. Lowrey's unit had suffered the majority of the Rebel casualties at Spring Hill and at Franklin his losses only multiplied. He said half of his command was struck down before they were even able to reach the Federal works. J. C. Dean, a soldier from Lowrey's 32nd Mississippi Infantry, recalled that the brigade passed through a "deadly hail of lead and iron which made Franklin's field a scene of unparalleled carnage." When the remaining Southerner troops finally got to the breastworks, they crowded mostly into the salient between the cotton gin and the Columbia Pike. Gen. Lowrey recalled how those who were left in his battered brigade "fought the enemy across the parapet." His Mississippians and Alabamians grappled like tigers and some even took part in the struggle around the guns of the 1st Kentucky Battery. In the bedlam the battle flag of the 33rd Alabama was captured by Capt. John H. Brown of the 12th Kentucky and prisoners belonging to one of Lowrey's regiments were netted by Lt. Col. John Russell's 44th Illinois.[148]

---

147 *OR* 45, pt. 1, p. 237; J. K. Merrifield, "Col. Hugh Garland - Captured Flags," *CV* 24, p. 551; Merrifield, *CV* 16, p. 554; J. M. Hickey, Letter of, *CV* 17, p. 14.

148 Lowrey, *SHSP* 16, p. 374; J. C. Dean, "The Battle of Franklin," *CV* 7, p. 27; *OR* 45, pt. 1, 247. Information about the 33rd Alabama's flag courtesy the Alabama Department of Archives and History. Information about Brown's Medal of Honor is courtesy of the U. S. Army Center of Military History.

Lowrey watched as his brave men did everything humanly possible to achieve success. He rode his horse "to within thirty feet of the works" and somehow avoided being hit by enemy fire. His horse was not so lucky, however, and soon took a wound. Convinced "that nothing more could be done" Lowrey turned his injured mount around and rode to the rear. From there he began "gathering up the fragments" of Cleburne's shattered division.[149]

Gen. Claudius Sears' Brigade also washed into the area surrounding the cotton gin. At forty-seven years of age Sears, a former teacher, was nearly the oldest Confederate commander on the field. His Mississippians from French's Division stumbled forward over the bloody bodies of the Missouri Brigade as they charged the Federal position. It was a ghastly but accurate indicator of what awaited Sears' men. Maj. Turpin D. Magee, commanding the 46th Mississippi, was dropped by enemy fire before he got his regiment to the works. One of Magee's soldiers said "it rained fire and brimstone for some time..." Col. Thomas N. Adaire of the 4th Mississippi, as he called upon his men to follow, was shot four times before a shell fragment finally knocked him down near the Yankee line. Behind men such as this came the bulk of the brigade, dodging incoming fire all the way. When Sears' men finally got to the ditch on the outside of the works they began diving and jumping in. The spectacle that greeted them was worse than anything they had seen on the way in. An officer said it was like "a living hell." Bodies of the dead and wounded literally filled entire sections of the ditch. There seemed to be more corpses than living soldiers. Jumbled piles of dead were stacked in places three and four deep. Blood stood in puddles "to the depth of the shoe soles." Pvt. Abner J. Wilkes said the men moved "through dead bodies and through blood." One man believed the Federals did their utmost "to kill every man in that ditch." Even worse was when it became clear to most of the Mississippians no real chance for victory existed. The front line units had been battered to pieces and there was nothing for the reserves to exploit. Their sacrifice seemed to have no purpose. The best Sears' men were able to do was to protect themselves any way they could. For some that meant using the bodies of the dead to stop the Yankee bullets. It was a revolting choice, but with the enemy pouring a

---

[149] Lowrey, *SHSP* 16, p. 374.

terrifying and commanding fire from over the parapet, options were slim. The primal desire to stay alive trumped all else.[150]

Two weeks after the battle, Sears filed a report detailing the names of 177 men from his brigade who reached the "main line of the enemy's works" during the battle. The amazing compilation also remarks whether each of the individual soldiers was killed or wounded. Among the former was Col. William W. Witherspoon, commanding officer of the 36th Mississippi. Sears did not file an official report of the battle, but he obviously felt strongly enough about what had happened at Franklin to put the list on record. His written endorsement echoes through time. It says, "These gallant men merit honorable mention; they were foremost amidst the forlorn hope."[151]

Also pushing toward the front was the Gen. Daniel Reynolds' Brigade of Arkansans from Edward Walthall's Division. Reynolds was surely struck with a certain amount of anxiety as the attack commenced. He was close friends with Gen. Otho Strahl and the two had moved together from Ohio to Tennessee in 1855. They studied law under Judge John W. Harris and were admitted to the Volunteer State bar in 1858. But like so many other talented men of their time, war interrupted and forever changed life as they knew it. Reynolds approached the fiery Yankee line unsure of how his friend was faring. Although able to push his brigade to "within some 15 or 20 steps" of the Federal line in the vicinity of the gin house, Reynolds saw his men subjected to terrible fire. Capt. John W. Lavender of the 4th Arkansas

---

150 R. N. Rea, "A Mississippi Soldier of the Confederacy," *CV* 30, p. 288; Copley, *Sketch of the Battle of Franklin*, p. 55, SHC; Rowland, *Military History of Mississippi*, p. 163, 366; Abner J. Wilkes memoir, p. 13-14, manuscript in the possession of Willard Davis, Prentiss, MS; Faust, ed., *Historical Times Encyclopedia*, p. 663.

151 *OR* 45, pt. 1, p. 716-719. Sears was unable to complete a report about Franklin for two reasons. Shortly after the battle French took leave of absence because of an eye infection and Sears assumed command of the division. At Nashville, Sears lost a leg to artillery fire, was captured, and not released until June 1865. See Welsh, *Medical Histories of Confederate Generals*, p. 73, 193.

recalled rushing "like Demons on to their works." Lt. Levi French of the 2nd Arkansas Mounted Rifles was racing forward when a bullet to the head killed him. His friend Pvt. Newton Park quickly gathered up French's personal items, grabbed the lieutenant's sword, and led the men around him forward. Yet because of the heavy enemy fire and lack of support on either the right or left, the advance stalled. Unable to get all of his men up to the works and unwilling to leave them out in the open, Reynolds pulled the brigade back and out of firing range. In his diary Reynolds wrote succinctly that he had faced "the most terrible fighting" of the war.[152]

Along the ditch near the cotton gin, handfuls of Rebel troops considered their options and chose surrender rather than almost certain death. John Copley and some of his comrades from the 49th Tennessee got the Federals to stop firing just long enough to climb over the works and become prisoners. Pvt. Robert S. Holman was also a member of the 49th Tennessee, but he did not surrender. Instead he got as close to the works as possible, laid down on his back, and aimed his rifle through "a hole where the logs were not joined together well." Every time he saw the hole darken, which Holman assumed meant a Yankee was on the other side, he fired. For almost three hours Holman remained in this position, unsure if he ever killed anyone on the other side of the works or not.[153]

George Gordon remained in the infamous ditch after the first droves of Confederates gave up, telling a nearby soldier that he intended to stay put until night fell. Developments, however, dictated otherwise. Not only was the enemy firing into the salient where Gordon was located, but the Southern reserve units were peppering the area as they advanced. Finally convinced that staying in the ditch was a death warrant, Gordon told the man next to him to put a white handkerchief on his bayonet and wave it above the works. Once this was done the two climbed over the parapet, but their safety immediately came into

---

[152] Cummings, *THQ* 24, No. 4, p. 342; James Willis, *Arkansas Confederates in the Western Theater*, p. 580-581; Elliott, *Soldier of Tennessee*, p. 242; Ted Worley, ed., *The War Memoirs of Captain John W. Lavender, C. S. A.*, p. 108; Reynolds Diary, p. 112; Special Collections, UAL.

[153] Copley, *Sketch of the Battle of Franklin*, p. 60, SHC; Robert S. Holman memoir, in possession of Rayburn W. Qualls, Jr. of Rockville, MD.

George W. Gordon (Library of Congress)

question. The 28-year old Gordon barely got his feet down inside the trench before a Yankee approached and jabbed at the general with the butt of his musket. Gordon dodged and the blow was deflected into his shoulder by a Federal officer who barked out, "He is surrendering." Gordon was then put into the custody of two other men and whisked to the rear.[154]

Not far to the east, Gen. John Adams's Brigade came up in rapid support of Loring's front line. Adams commanded six Mississippi regiments and they could see Featherston's and Scott's brigades taking horrendous losses. Enemy fire passing through the remnants of those advance units soon began hitting Adams' men, causing "considerable damage" and consternation. Lt. William Berryhill of the 43rd Mississippi estimated that about 400 yards from the enemy line, "musketry united with cannon and it...came by the millions." Adams took a bullet in the right arm near the shoulder, but refused to leave the field, saying to an aide, "I am going to see my men through." The next few minutes were a blur, but many soldiers, Federal and Confederate alike, never forgot what they saw. The charge made by Adams and his brigade would be remembered as one of the most extraordinary moments of the battle.[155]

---

[154] Gordon, *CV* 8, p. 8.

[155] Henry, *CV* 21, p. 76; "Gen. John Adams at Franklin: Testimony of Union Officers to His Immutable Valor," *CV* 5, p. 299; Jones and Martin, ed., *The Gentle Rebel: Civil War Letters of William Harvey Berryhill*, p. 122.

As Adams and his Mississippians drew closer to the Union line, they were subjected to the same deadly fire that had so decimated Featherston and Scott. Behind his brigade Adams rode back and forth, urging his men to hold steady and ready themselves for the final leg of the advance. Suddenly and "without orders" a yell rose up from the brigade and the men charged toward the front. It was purely spontaneous, a gut reaction by those who felt the time was now or never, and away they went. Men like these Mississippians were all the South had left by late 1864. They were the bravest of the brave, tattered and gaunt figures clinging to the fading hope of independence. Rebel was a title they wore proudly and many of them would have rather died than live to see the Yankees win the war. Quickly Adams directed a staff officer to each end of the brigade front and told them he could be found in the center if needed.[156]

As the brigade plowed forward, they took heavy fire from the Union works and enfilade fire from Fort Granger. Casualties were already heavy when Adams' troops came up against the Osage orange abatis. Maj. Patrick Henry of Adams' staff said the left of the brigade had a particularly difficult time with the obstruction. He recalled that the left wing was essentially "stopped in the charge by that powerful and impenetrable hedge..." The Rebels, less than 100 feet from the flaming Union works, took sheets of fire "literally in their faces..." One soldier said the front ranks seemingly "melted from the earth." Pvt. John M. Payne of the 14th Mississippi was wounded and "lay in a ravine until after dark" before finally being carried to a field hospital. Capt. William Thompson of the 6th Mississippi was shot in the right leg and carried to the rear "where the bullets were not flying so thick." Thompson remained on the ground in agony until morning, nearly frozen and half-starved. Capt. John L. Collins of the 15th Mississippi was unhurt, but never forgot being enveloped in the hellish spectacle and how his "little mule...opened wide his jaws and began to bray" with distress.[157]

In the midst of the tumult, Pvt. Wesley P. Peacock of the 15th

---

[156] Stevens, *CV* 11, p. 166; Henry, *CV* 21, p. 76.

[157] Henry, *CV* 21, p. 76; John M. Payne, Letter of, *CV* 1, p. 172; William C. Thompson, "A Confederate's Recollection of the Battle of Franklin," *CWTI*, December 1964, p. 24; John L. Collins, "Gallant Mike Farrell," *CV* 34, p. 374.

Mississippi hacked furiously at the "thick hedge row of thorn bushes" with an axe. Peacock, exchanged shortly before the battle, had reached his command without a weapon. When the advance began Peacock picked up the axe and said he would go in with his friends to do what he could. Somehow Peacock remained unscathed and his frantic work actually resulted in a few small pathways through the thorny tangle. Handfuls of men began to push through. Four of the bravest who rushed toward the front were shot down bearing the flag of the 15th Mississippi. Included in the charge were the gunners from Cowan's Mississippi Battery who beforehand were "equipped like infantry" and then ordered forward. It did little good. Largely the Mississippians were in serious trouble, pinned behind the abatis and exposed to merciless fire. Working through the Osage obstructions was compounded by the scores of mutilated bodies scattered throughout it. It was a nightmarish scene, one that defied description. Suddenly John Adams made a bold move on the left of the brigade. Adams was a short distance west of where Lewisburg Pike and the Nashville & Decatur Railroad intersected, and could see his troops had no chance if they remained where they were. Horror and bloodshed was everywhere, and his men were crumbling to the ground "like leaves falling in wintry weather."[158]

As Adams rode out of a small ravine, he could see that to the west the abatis appeared to thin. He looked around at his men and yelled for them to follow him. Adams then spurred his horse, Old Charley, to the left. For a few moments he rode nearly parallel to the Federal line, before turning to the right through an opening in the Osage abatis. Through the smoke and twilight, many of the troops in John Casement's Brigade suddenly caught sight of Adams astride his horse. Most could not believe what they were seeing. Without breaking stride, Adams headed straight for the Federal works. Trailing behind him and squeezing through the abatis were some of his men. A Union soldier who saw Adams remembered how he expected to see the general fall at any moment, but "luck seemed to be with him." Apparently a number of Yankees actually held their fire as they watched the surreal

---

[158] *OR* 45, pt. 1, p. 714; Banks, *Battle of Franklin*, p. 53, 58-59; Yeary, *Reminiscences of the Boys in Gray*, p. 230; Binford, *Recollections of the Fifteenth Mississippi*, p. 105-106.

drama play out right in front of them. According to a soldier in the 65th Illinois, Lt. Col. W. Scott Stewart actually called on his men not to fire.[159]

It did not take long for it to become obvious that Adams was not going to stop. He aimed directly toward the colors of the 65th Illinois and as he came up to the works a volley exploded in his face. In a flash of fire and smoke the incredible ride ended. Old Charley "fell dead upon the top of the embankment" and Adams toppled from the horse near the outside ditch. His body was riddled with bullets, perhaps as many as nine.[160]

John Adams
(Library of Congress)

For a few minutes there was bitter fighting along the works in front of Col. Casement's Brigade as the Federals with "great vigor" turned away the Mississippians who had followed Adams. The final man bearing the flag of the 15th Mississippi was shot as he reached the top of the Yankee parapet and then pulled inside. Both he and the flag were captured. Lt. Thaddeus O. Donoghue of the 14th Mississippi was killed near the guns of the 6th Ohio Battery. Col. Michael Farrell of the 15th Mississippi was horribly wounded in both legs and lost his left to amputation. Farrell, a popular officer, did not have a single living relative nor did he have any money or own any property before enlisting. Those who knew him admired him and said he fought for "principle and constitutional liberty." Col. Farrell's injuries led to his death at John McGavock's home, Carnton, around Christmas. Years later a veteran wrote, when describing the Mississippians, that to

---

159 Stevens, *CV* 11, p. 166; Barr, *CV* 10, p. 155.

160 "Gen. John Adams at Franklin," *CV* 5, p. 300; Ridley, *Battles and Sketches, Army of Tennessee*, p. 47.

"exaggerate their valor would be impossible."[161]

When the Confederates of Adams' command were finally forced back, a slight lull settled over the eastern side of the field. A. P. Stewart's attack was finally exhausted. Seeing that the Rebels were advancing no other units, John Casement ordered a skirmish line out beyond the works. Among "the large number of...killed and wounded" several Union soldiers found Adams and carried him back inside the works. Although mortally wounded, Adams remained coherent enough to ask Casement to please "send him to the Confederate line..." Casement told the dying Adams that as soon as it was safe, he would "be in possession of his friends." Casement then moved off to tend to other duties and by the time he returned Adams had died. Casement had the saddle taken from Old Charley as a souvenir and he also removed Adams's watch and ring so that they might be returned to the general's wife.[162]

Adams' daring ride and resulting death had a profound impact on those who saw it. A great deal of confusion later arose about exactly what happened to Adams after he was shot down. There seems to be no dispute about the fate of Old Charley. His body was stretched over the top of the breastworks and remained there for many days after the battle. But Adams' fate is not so easy to pin down. Little if anything was written about Adams and his fateful ride until years after the guns fell silent. A Union veteran named Edward A. Baker, formerly of the 65th Indiana, began communicating with Adams' widow Georgiana in 1891. In a letter to her, Baker related a story of how Adams charged the Federal line and that both he and his horse fell atop the works. Baker said Adams was trapped beneath Old Charley and when removed and taken inside the works, it was apparent that he was dying. Baker explained how the general asked for some water and then said, "It is the

---

[161] Banks, *Battle of Franklin*, p. 58, 63, 85; Henry, *CV* 21, p. 76; *OR* 45, pt. 1, p. 425, 714; Binford, *Recollections of the Fifteenth Mississippi*, p. 105, 117; James Binford, "Heroism at Franklin: Tributes to Gen. Adams, Cols. Farrell and Rorer," *CV* 10, p. 457.

[162] *OR* 45, pt. 1, p. 425; "Gen. John Adams at Franklin," *CV* 5, p. 300-301. Casement did return the watch and ring shortly after Franklin. He also returned the saddle in 1891. See *CV* article mentioned in this footnote, p. 301.

fate of a soldier to die for his country." This letter was published in an 1897 issue of the *Confederate Veteran* and almost immediately the legend took hold. What was forgotten or ignored by most, however, were other accounts. At the turn of the century, when the Lost Cause mythology was at its peak, Baker's version was easiest to digest, especially for Southerners. Capt. Thomas Gibson, a first cousin to the general and a former staff aide, was among those who stuck resolutely to Edward Baker's account.[163]

John Casement, on the other hand, offered not only a different viewpoint, but his recollection remained largely consistent. In his official report, written only five days after the battle, Casement wrote that when his skirmish line was advanced following the repulse of the final Rebel charge in his sector, Adams' body was found outside the works. Casement said that Adams was already dead when found. Like Baker, Casement also wrote to Mrs. Adams in 1891. In addition to making arrangements for the return of the general's saddle, Casement also told of how Adams had fallen outside the works. Casement explained that after a short time the body was recovered and said although the general was still alive at this point he died shortly thereafter. Although this is a clear contradiction of his official report, as to whether Adams was alive or dead when found, Casement was entirely consistent about the body being found outside the works. There is no mention whatsoever of Adams being found on the works or inside them, or saying anything memorable.[164]

Jacob Cox also found himself involved in the story. In his report written two days after the battle Cox mentioned nothing about Adams. By the time Cox filed a second report on January 10, 1865, Cox had come to learn of Adams' death. His information was obviously gleaned from secondary sources and he wrote, "One general officer (Adams) was shot down upon the parapet itself, his horse falling across the breast-work." Cox elaborated on the story when his first book was published in 1882. There he wrote that Adams' horse was killed on the

---

[163] Edward A. Baker, "Gen. John Adams at Franklin: Testimony of Union Officers to His Immutable Valor," *CV* 5, p. 300-301; Thomas Gibson, "Particulars of Gen. John Adams's Death," *CV* 12, p. 482.

[164] *OR* 45, pt. 1, p. 425; J. S. Casement, "Gen. John Adams at Franklin," *CV* 5, p. 301.

works and the general was "pitched headlong among Casement's men, mortally wounded."[165]

At some later point, however, Cox became familiar with a different version, one told to him by those who had actually witnessed the event. After corresponding with Casement and Capt. Saunders R. Hornbrook of the 65th Indiana, Cox revised his account for publication in his 1897 book. There Cox wrote that Adams and his horse were both shot down and Old Charley struggled to his feet and "dashed wildly forward" to die upon the works. Adams, knocked from the horse and "shot through the thighs," made an effort to "crawl away." He was soon riddled with gunfire and, following the culmination of the Confederate assault, was brought inside the works. Cox said Adams was still alive but "soon died." Cox's varying accounts were attacked by Thomas Gibson, but it appears Cox was simply trying to get the story right by consulting with reliable eyewitnesses.[166]

Other pieces of evidence must also be evaluated. When A. P. Stewart composed his official report he wrote only that Adams was killed and his horse was found "lying across the inner line of the enemy's works." Additionally, none of the regimental commanders from John Casement's Brigade so much as mentioned Adams in their reports.[167]

The post-war years saw the publication of a compelling *Confederate Veteran* article, written by a former member of the 65th Illinois. Oliver W. Case said Adams was shot "not many feet" in front of Company C, 65th Illinois. Case corroborated Casement almost perfectly, stating that "after the battle had ceased" a skirmish line was thrown out. Adams' body was soon found and Lt. George H. Brown and Cpl. Henry Frampton picked up the general and carried him "across the works..." Pvt. Case did not mention whether Adams was still alive or not, but he did say Casement sent forward a stretcher and had the Confederate general moved to a location near the cotton gin.[168]

In the same article, Case mentioned Col. Marcus Stephens of the 31st Mississippi, who had fallen seriously wounded outside the works

---

[165] *OR* 45, pt. 1, p. 348-349, 353; Cox, *Sherman's March to the Sea*, p. 91.

[166] Cox, *Battle of Franklin*, p. 128; Gibson, *CV* 12, p. 482.

[167] *OR* 45, pt. 1, p. 426-428, 808.

[168] O. W. Case, "Gen. John Adams at Franklin," *CV* 1, p. 208.

fronting the 65th Illinois. Stephens had been injured in the assault immediately preceding the one led by Adams. Stephens lay helpless in the outside ditch and was assisted over the works only after Adams' Brigade attacked. It is possible that in the wild confusion of those few moments, with darkness setting in and exhaustion affecting everyone, that some of the Federal troops mistook Stephens for Adams.[169]

Incredibly the story has another twist. Tom M. Gore, a soldier who served in the 15th Mississippi, said that Oliver Case was somewhat mistaken concerning Adams. Gore got within ten feet of the works and spent the night on the battlefield. He insisted that although Adams had been knocked from his horse and was shot repeatedly trying to escape, he was never taken inside the enemy line. The basis for Gore's claim is that Adams' body was found outside the works the following morning. Here John Casement again comes into play. If Casement honored Adams' request to return his body to the Confederate line, then neither Case or Gore is wrong. The two simply reported the facts as they knew them, unaware of any conversation, albeit brief, between Casement and Adams.[170]

There is no absolute conclusion about what happened to John Adams. Unquestioned is that he rode recklessly toward Casement's troops and was shot down at the last moment. Old Charley made his way to the parapet and remained there, but it does appear clear that Adams fell outside. Probably the enemy volley struck him as he prepared to leap the horse over the works. Gen. Adams' frock coat is on display at the Tennessee State Museum and several bullet holes are evident in the upper chest area. It is doubtful he could have survived long after being hit and whether Adams was alive or dead when the Federals carried him inside their line is not terribly relevant.

Thomas Gibson wrote that deferring from Edward Baker's account somehow robbed Adams "of a part of the glory he won on the bloody field of Franklin at the cost of his life." On the contrary, there is no lost glory in relating the true facts of John Adams' ride and death.

---

[169] Ibid., p. 208.

[170] Tom M. Gore, "Death and Identity of Gen. Adams," *CV* 1, p. 264. It is interesting that Gore mentioned Adams had no watch on him when found on December 1. Casement claimed to have removed Adams' watch inside the works.

Instead the story becomes all the more revealing without the gloss. Adams saw his men literally being massacred. Knowing his brigade would be destroyed if it stayed exposed for much longer, Adams did what he could to rally them closer to the front. He rode forward, a conspicuous and lone figure, trying desperately to do the impossible. His final military act was essentially to sacrifice himself so that his men might succeed. His final act as a man was a simple request - to be returned to his troops.[171]

As Adams' charge took place, furious action continued west of the Columbia Pike. In that sector, additional Confederate brigades rushed forward and added their weight to the attack. Gen. John Carter led his Tennesseans toward the Yankee line and tangled locust grove stretched along the enemy front. Carter moved up in support of Gen. Gist and traveled much the same path. As a result, the beating Carter's men took was no less severe. They were pounded without mercy from the front and took awful fire on their exposed left flank. The sound of the battle was like a "continuous roar" and "whole ranks of men" were swept away by the fury. Lt. Spencer Talley said his comrades "were mowed down like grain before the sickle" and the survivors staggered forward "over the dying and the dead." The Rebel troops were also subjected to brutal artillery fire originating from a section of Lyman Bridges' battery of Illinois Light Artillery. Bridges had originally positioned his 3-inch guns on the pike near the Carter home, but shortly before the attack he moved one section west of the house. From there the rifled pieces, which were superbly designed for long-range firing, fired right over the main Federal line and helped splinter both Carter's and Gist's lines.[172]

---

[171] Gibson, *CV* 12, p. 482. It is this author's conclusion that Adams was shot outside the works, carried inside clinging to life, and passed away there. Shortly before the Federal army retreated, Casement had Adams' body taken back over the works and laid among friends where it was found the next morning.

[172] *OR* 45, pt. 1, p. 320, 325; Talley, Civil War Memoir, TSLA; Cox, *Battle of Franklin*, p. 108; Field, *Bright Skies and Dark Shadows*, p. 239.

The youthful Carter was everywhere during his brigade's advance, making every effort to ensure his men did not falter. Carter was a veteran and had been under heavy fire many times before, but Franklin tested all of his skills. The volume of Federal fire was stupefying and his Tennesseans wilted before it. About 150 yards from the Yankee works, as Carter rode recklessly in front of his brigade, a bullet tore into his abdomen and came out his back. It was an awful wound and Carter had to be helped from his horse by staff members. Among them was Capt. H. M. Neely. Carter was in agony and shock and Neely had him removed to a field hospital immediately. Meanwhile, the battle continued and by the time Carter was carried away his brigade had pressed into the heart of the locust thicket.[173]

John C. Carter (Library of Congress)

Col. Charles A. Zollinger commanded the 129th Indiana in Orlando Moore's Brigade and saw firsthand how badly John Carter's men suffered. He said the Rebels endured "heavy slaughter" as they tried to punch a hole in the Federal line. Pvt. George Stanley served in Company G, 129th Indiana and was positioned just west of the locust grove. Stanley later wrote of hearing the screeching Rebel yell and seeing enemy troops rush right up to the edge of the breastworks. He said some were killed right on top of the parapet and others who were

---

[173] J. Harvey Mathes, *The Old Guard in Gray*, p. 170; William B. Turner, *History of Maury County*, Diary of Chaplain Charles Todd Quintard, p. 223; James I. Robertson, "The Human Battle at Franklin," *THQ* 24, No. 1, p. 27.

wounded crawled over and surrendered. Capt. Neely recalled that after Carter's wounding things only got worse. By the time the brigade got to the breastworks it was "in such a shattered condition that it was unable to go over or dislodge the enemy." Some men, however, did make their way over the works and several got far inside the enemy's periphery. One of these was Pvt. Clay Barnes of the 6th Tennessee. Somehow he made it all the way to the retrenched line, battled with a color bearer from the 44th Missouri, ripped away part of the flag, and managed to get back to his regiment.[174]

Though Carter's Brigade was unable to mount a concerted offensive over the enemy works, his men and those of States Rights Gist's command produced enough combined punch to cause upheaval among the Federals. The force of the two Confederate brigades hitting the blue line nearly resulted in more of it rolling up. Already two full regiments, the 50th Ohio and 72nd Illinois, had pulled back from the main works. This left the 111th Ohio with no support on its left flank. Lt. Col. Isaac Sherwood, commanding the Ohio regiment, thought for a moment that "the line was lost." He immediately ordered his troops to fix bayonets. One of the Ohioans remembered seeing a "large muscular rebel" jump over the works and confront a fellow soldier. He said the two poked at each other with their bayonets, but "neither got any advantage..." All of a sudden the Southerner jumped backward and "pitched his gun, bayonet first" at the Yankee. The bayonet sunk into the man's thigh and as the Confederate tried to get back over the works he was shot and "fell on top of the bank dead."[175]

Lt. Fernando Bennett of Company C, 111th Ohio did everything in his power to get help up on the left of his regiment. To the right and rear of the 111th Ohio was the left flank of the 183rd Ohio. Bennett dashed back to the Ohioans and called "upon them in God's name" to move up and help fill the abandoned works. Capt. Daniel Risser, commanding Company B on the 183rd Ohio's left flank, was killed and may have fallen very early in the fighting. The reaction by some of the

---

[174] *OR* 45, pt. 1, p. 385; Mathes, *The Old Guard in Gray*, p. 170; J. H. Lanier, Letter of, *CV* 5, p. 38; George Stanley, "Pushed Back to Nashville," *NT*, Aug. 18, 1910, p. 7.

[175] *OR* 45, pt. 1, p. 387; W. S. Thurstin, *History One Hundred and Eleventh Regiment, O.V.I.*, p. 85, 89 .

183rd Ohio's left indicates this is a definite possibility. The Ohioans closest to Lt. Bennett, green and under fire for the first time and probably without one of their officers, balked and would not move. Some just threw themselves on the ground. Bennett screamed at them to move and pointed toward the empty works with one hand and waved his sword over his head with the other. In an instant a flash of fire exploded and Bennett fell to the ground dead.[176]

Nearby Capt. Patrick H. Dowling, inspector general on Col. Moore's staff and also a member of the 111th Ohio, could see Sherwood's men were in a fix. Feverishly Dowling worked to gather up some of the broken troops and he soon had a small force on Sherwood's left flank. More importantly, he had also requested immediate reinforcements from Jacob Cox. Cox responded by ordering support up from Nathan Kimball. A few moments later eight companies from Col. Isaac Kirby's 101st Ohio came racing up. Using these fresh troops, along with the rallied elements, Dowling helped to construct a short but very effective new line, one that ran "nearly at right angles to the main one..." In doing so, Dowling accomplished two things. The left flank of the 111th Ohio had been solidified and the new line also connected very roughly with some of the troops who occupied the western end of the retrenched line. Moore was effusive in his praise of Dowling, who took a serious arm wound in the course of the action. Moore said the captain "saved the troops from a defeat which otherwise would have been inevitable." Dowling received mention in Sherwood's report and Cox included him in his monograph of the battle. Dowling's actions were truly one of the defining moments at Franklin. Further deterioration of the main line had been prevented and by refusing and extending it to the retrenchment, the Rebels who had punched through the middle suddenly found themselves in a terrible spot. They faced fire from their left, their front, and even from across the pike into their right and right rear. Their initial success had backfired.[177]

Otho Strahl's Brigade also slammed up against the Yankee works. Strahl's Tennessee regiments followed right behind George

---

[176] *SUP* 56, pt. 2, p. 392-393; *OAR* 5, p. 237; Thurstin, *History of the 111th Ohio*, p. 89.

[177] *OR* 45, pt. 1, 184, 380, 387; Cox, *Battle of Franklin*, p. 131; Day, *Story of the One Hundred and First Ohio*, p. 295-297.

Otho F. Strahl
(Library of Congress)

Gordon's men and crowded mostly into the ditch west of the Columbia Pike. Sgt. Maj. Arthur A. Fulkerson, adjutant of the 19th Tennessee, never made it that far. As he struggled with the sharpened locust branches in front of the Yankee works, attempting to open a hole for his comrades to pass through, his body was "riddled with bullets..." For those who hit the ditch it was immediately clear the spot was among the worst on the battlefield. A soldier in the 24th Tennessee remembered the "works were much higher on this part of the line than on the right and around the gin-house." Whether the works were actually higher or the ditch in this area was deeper is not known, but either way it was a significant problem. As a result, it was nearly impossible for the Rebels to scale to the parapet. Individual soldiers were forced to develop a haphazard system involving one man helping another to the top. At the same time Strahl's men were being subjected to a murderous enfilade fire pouring in on their right. Because of the manner in which the Federal line protruded to the southeast near the cotton gin, the Rebels west of the pike were easy targets. The Yankees east of the road were able to sweep the length of Strahl's Brigade almost at will. There was no safe harbor anywhere and volleys ravaged the ranks. The men could not even retreat because the Federals shot at anything that dared move toward the rear. It was like hell on earth. As the minutes ground by it was clear there was little hope for Strahl or his men.[178]

---

[178] B. T. Roberts, "Vivid Reminiscences of Franklin," *CV* 1, p. 339; Cunningham, *CV* 12, p. 339; J. N. Meroney to George L. Cowan, Dec. 3, 1910, CRN.

Sumner Cunningham of the 41st Tennessee recalled fighting until the "ditch was almost full of dead men." There were so many corpses "there was not standing room for the living." Among those killed was Pvt. J. T. Puckett of the 4th Tennessee, the furlough to visit his family still folded in his pocket. Pvt. Charley Nicholson of the 24th Tennessee was shot "seven or eight times" and died on the breastworks. Darkness had nearly covered the field and the troops on opposite sides of the works "fired at the flash of each other's guns."[179]

Nearby, Gen. Strahl helped men to the parapet so they could fire at the Yankees. In quick succession two men who Strahl had assisted were shot down. When a third asked to be hoisted up Strahl said, "No. I have helped my last man up on the works to be shot in my hands." Moments later Pvt. Zack Smith of the 19th Tennessee found his own way to the parapet and began firing at the Federals. Strahl saw Smith and said to him, "Go it, Zack. I will never forget you for this." Soon Strahl called Cunningham over and told him to climb up the embankment and start shooting. As Cunningham fired Strahl loaded guns in the ditch below and handed one up after reach round. Because the enemy had been cleared out of the trenches in their front, Strahl's men were mostly firing over the works at Yankees along the retrenched line. Southern casualties mounted. Cunningham looked to his left and right and could hardly see anyone left in the ditch still capable of fighting. When he asked Strahl what to do, the general said only, "Keep firing." Seconds later a nearby soldier was shot and fell against Cunningham before rolling down into the ditch. At almost the same time, Strahl was hit in the neck with a bullet. Seriously hurt but still alert, Strahl crawled over bodies for about twenty feet. After he found Lt. Col. Fountain E. P. Stafford and turned over command of the brigade, three soldiers named James Beasley, Tom Ledsinger, and Bill Flower picked up Strahl and began carrying him to the rear. They had only gone a few steps before enemy fire ripped through the area, wounding Strahl again. Capt. James W. Johnston and Lt. John Marsh, officers on Strahl's staff, and Lt. Col. Stafford were all killed. When the fire died down Beasley, Ledsinger, and Flower picked Strahl up again

---

[179] Cunningham, *CV* 12, p. 340; Garrett and Lightfoot, *The Civil War in Maury County*, p. 100; Finlay, "Fourth Tennessee Infantry," in *Military Annals of Tennessee*, Vol. 1, Lindsley, ed., p. 190.

and tried to get out of the enemy's range. It was to no avail. Another fusillade of bullets found the group and Strahl was struck in the head. This time the general was killed instantly, ending his involvement in a battle he had foreseen to be so desperate.[180]

Along the section of line where Strahl's troops made their assault, Union soldier Erastus Winters was huddled in the outside ditch with his Southern captor. Initially Winters had been pulled inside the works, but when the firing there became too dangerous he and his captor jumped to the outside of the embankment. Things were no better there. The two were subjected to the same brutal fire Strahl's men were dealing with. When Winters looked around he thought there were not enough Rebels present to form a skirmish line. Those who remained were running out of ammunition and some began to holler over the works asking to surrender. In the noise and confusion no one heeded their calls. Winters could not believe what was happening. His captor had disappeared down the line somewhere and everywhere around him was complete insanity. Winters curled up "against the earthworks as close as possible" and waited out the storm.[181]

The fighting in and around the Carter garden was some of the most vicious of the entire war. The garden occupied about two square acres and it lay just south of the smokehouse and office building. It was positioned roughly between the retrenched and main lines and was heavily occupied by Confederate soldiers, largely from Brown's and Cleburne's divisions. After retreating from the Carter yard following the collision with Opdycke's men, the Rebels hunkered down along the southern edge of the retrenched line and continued their ferocious battle with the enemy. Yet the cards were stacked against them almost from the start.

Through a combination of factors the Southern troops in the

---

[180] Cunningham, *CV* 12, p. 340; E. Shaphard, "At Spring Hill and Franklin Again," *CV* 24, p. 139; Cummings, *THQ* 24, No. 4, p. 354; C. W. Heiskell, "Nineteeth Tennessee Infantry," in *Military Annals of Tennessee*, Vol. 1, Lindsley, ed., p. 377-378; Worsham, *The Old Nineteenth Tennessee*, p. 144, 147; Dyersburg *State Gazette*, May 30, 1907, TSLA; Turner, *History of Maury County*, Quintard Diary, p. 220; Field, *Bright Skies and Dark Shadows*, p. 245.

[181] Winters, *In the 50th Ohio*, p. 122-123.

once genteel garden found themselves nearly surrounded. They had spearheaded the breakthrough of the main Federal line, but once inside enemy territory everything closed around them. Opdycke's charge had sealed off the immediate front and to the left Union troops had been realigned to connect the western edge of the retrenchment with the main line. As a result, the Rebels were exposed not only to fire from their front, but enfilade fire tore into their left as well. This was only part of the problem. Behind them the main works remained empty, but some Southern troops still held the outside ditch and friendly fire crackled into the Carter garden.

Even worse was the fire coming from across Columbia Pike. There the main line had been restored, and Federal troops could not resist shooting across the road and into the backs and sides of the hapless Confederates. The deadly crisscross of fire inflicted grisly losses in the garden. In the darkness the fight only grew uglier as men groped about, firing blindly into the gloom. Casualties mounted as men were shot like animals in a pen. All around the perimeter of the garden thousands of guns flashed over and over, sending flickering shadows dancing along the blood-soaked ground. From inside the garden musket fire sprayed outward, but it grew less and less intense as the minutes dragged by. Rebels soon began surrendering in groups, others battled until silenced by enemy bullets. A corporal from the 101st Ohio recalled how some enemy soldiers who tried to surrender where shot down in the confusion because they held on to their muskets too long. Nearly half of a group of twenty-five were felled by Federal fire before the other half hastily threw their guns to the ground. The scene was, an Illinois soldier said, nothing less than "an awful butchery..."[182]

---

[182] Sexton, *MOLLUS*, Illinois, 4, p. 483; Day, *Story of the One Hundred and First Ohio*, p. 298-300.

9

I Thought I Knew What Fighting Was

By the time William Bate was able to get his division into place for its final advance upon the Federal line the sun had already set. Delays resulting from the path the division had to travel led directly to its late arrival. Because of the prolonged movement around Winstead Hill, Bate's men were obligated to march nearly a full mile more than the rest of the attacking force just to get into position. Apparently they were not fully ready to advance when the other five divisions moved out at 4 p.m. The evidence points to Brown moving forward somewhat earlier than Bate. According to Brown, as his division moved to attack the enemy works word came from John Carter, who was in the second line, that his left flank was not supported. Because Bate was tardy in covering Brown's left, Bate found himself launching his own assault essentially alone.[1]

Bate's first contact with the enemy came near Everbright mansion, home to Rebecca Bostick. Everbright, also known as the Bostick House, was a magnificent two-story modified Greek revival home built in the 1840's by John Dabney Bennett. Rebecca's husband Richard Bostick, who died prior to the war, had purchased the rolling land surrounding Everbright from Fountain Branch Carter and Daniel McPhail. The house, which stood at the crest of a sharp hill overlooking Carter's Creek Pike, faced Columbia Pike. Made of red

[1] Burr and Williams, *PHP*, March 11, 1883, p. 25-26; McDonough and Connelly, *Five Tragic Hours*, p. 141; Brown, *CMH*, 8, p. 157.

Everbright Mansion
(Williamson County Archives)

brick and painted white, Everbright was among the more elegant homes in the area. At home on the day of the battle was Rebecca and at least one of her three sons. In the vicinity of the mansion Bate's skirmish line, composed of the 4th Battalion Georgia Sharpshooters and commanded by Maj. Theodore Caswell, exchanged fire with Yankee skirmishers and drove them off. His front line brigades soon swept past Everbright, which Bate had been told to use as a guidepost for his left flank, and his "line moved steadily on..." At least one battery of artillery seems to have moved in close proximity with the infantry. But Bate soon had a new problem to contend with. James Chalmers' cavalry was nowhere to be seen along Carter's Creek Pike, leaving Bate's line, like Brown's, vulnerable to enfilade fire. As a result, Bate ordered the Florida Brigade, under Col. Robert Bullock's temporary command, from its reserve position and moved it to the left. This decision necessitated additional delay, as the troops marched from their support position to hook up with the front line. Bate even placed two of the Florida regiments west of Carter's Creek Pike in an effort to further shore up his left flank. Finally the Rebel line, "now a single one, without support, charged the works of the enemy."[2]

Although Bate thought Chalmers' Division had not supported him during the attack, the truth was Chalmers did engage the Federal right. The problem was that Chalmers' troops were hidden from Bate's view by "rolling ground, with orchards and woods..." The cavalry, likewise impaired, heard heavy firing rolling in from the distance and Chalmers took this as his signal to advance. What he had heard, however, was the sound of action further east, along the Columbia and Lewisburg Turnpikes, not anything Bate was involved in. The end result was that Chalmers' men engaged their opponents a short time before Bate did, another example of how disjointed the Rebel assault was. Chalmers claimed he started forward at 4:30 p.m., drove back the Federal skirmishers, and "pressed forward...until within sixty yards of the fortifications..." His troops, which fought dismounted, occupied the attention of two Federal brigades, those of Col. Isaac Kirby and Gen. Walter Whitaker. Kirby said after his pickets came racing back the Rebels appeared on an "open ridge directly in our front..." and only "two or three volleys" were needed to force them back. Whitaker reported his troops battled the enemy for "about fifteen minutes" and the encounter was "short but severe." He said the Southerners soon "broke and fled..." Whatever the true scope of the fight, it was all over quickly. Chalmers wrote that his force "was too small to justify an attempt to storm" the Federal position. He withdrew his men behind the protection of some "rolling ground" and held this position out of the range of enemy fire.[3]

John Bell Hood made woeful use of both Nathan Bedford Forrest and his cavalry at Franklin. Not only did he deny Forrest an opportunity to try and flank the Yankee army, Hood broke the cavalry

---

[2] *OR* 45, pt. 1, p. 743; Cox, *Battle of Franklin*, p. 132-133; Bowman, *Historic Williamson County*, p. 142. Additional information about Everbright came from a conversation with Jimmie French, faculty at Battle Ground Academy, on January 7, 2005. Sadly Everbright was torn down in 1937 after falling into great disrepair.

[3] *OR* 45, pt. 1, p. 184, 195, 764; Cox, *Battle of Franklin*, p. 139-140.

into fragments and dispersed them across the field. In addition to James Chalmers' foray on the left, Abe Buford had been ordered to dismount his men and support the Confederate right. This decision left Forrest with only one division, that of William Jackson, with which to maneuver against the Federal cavalry. For the first time since the beginning of the campaign James Wilson held the advantage over his opponent and it was through no mistake of Forrest.

When Wilson arrived in the neighborhood of Franklin, he kept all of his cavalry on the north side of the Harpeth River except for a brigade commanded by the handsome young Brig. Gen. John Croxton. The twenty-seven year old Croxton was a former lawyer, graduate of Yale University, and a dedicated ally of the abolition movement. Early on November 30, Wilson had ordered Croxton to move his First Brigade across the river and occupy a position near Douglass Church on the Lewisburg Pike. From there Croxton would be able to provide protection for the right flank of the Federal infantry as it moved up Columbia Pike from Spring Hill. Wilson's instructions were simply that "if pressed by the enemy" Croxton was to move back across the Harpeth at McGavock's Ford.[4]

By 10 a.m. Rebel cavalry began sparring with Croxton's troops and the two sides exchanged spattering fire until around two o'clock. Then some of Buford's men "made a dash" upon Croxton's position. Shortly thereafter the Federal general learned that other Southern troops were approaching Hughes' Ford to the east Following the tenor of Wilson's directive, Croxton ordered his brigade to retire and most of the Yankee horsemen galloped up Lewisburg Pike. They splashed across the river at McGavock's Ford, well east of Carnton and about a mile and a half southeast of town. Ordered to stay behind was the 2nd Michigan Cavalry with instructions "to contest the advance" of the Confederates for as long as possible.[5]

According to Forrest, Buford's Division went into battle dismounted on the right of Stewart's Corps, "covering the ground from

---

[4] *OR* 45, pt. 1, p. 550, 573; Keenan, *Wilson's Cavalry Corps*, p. 29. Douglass Church was located at the present day intersection of Lewisburg Avenue and Henpeck Lane.

[5] *OR* 45, pt. 1, 573; Keenan, *Wilson's Cavalry Corps*, p. 63; Cox, *Battle of Franklin*, p. 175-176.

the Lewisburg Pike to Harpeth River." Buford's force, supported by Morton's Tennessee Battery, skirmished with the Michigan horsemen for a time before also forcing them to retire across the river. His two brigades, however, gave the infantry little in the way of actual help. Enemy fire soon had the Rebel troopers pinned down and they were obliged to pull back. Later at least one of the brigades, Tyree Bell's, forded the river and engaged the enemy cavalry. Meanwhile, around the time the 2nd Michigan pulled back, Jackson's cavalry "made their appearance" north of Hughes' Ford.[6]

Red Jackson's roughly 2,000-man division, spearheaded by Gen. Lawrence Ross' Brigade of Texans, made quick work of the Yankee pickets posted along the river's edge. Just after 4 p.m., with the infantry assault underway, Ross' men pushed forward to occupy some high ground about a half mile from the Harpeth. As Wilson moved to oppose Jackson word was delivered to Croxton from a subordinate that Rebel infantry was crossing the river "between my position and Franklin..." Croxton understand the gravity of such a development and immediately dispatched the 8th Iowa Cavalry and 4th Kentucky Mounted Infantry to deal with the problem. No sooner had they left, however, before Croxton learned the report was false. In the meantime, Wilson had ordered Gen. Edward Hatch to advance his 2,800-man division and deal with Jackson's troops. Hatch told his men to dismount and they moved forward along with Croxton and his remaining regiments, the 1st Tennessee Cavalry and 2nd Michigan Cavalry, on the right flank.[7]

Although Hatch said the Rebels were "well round" on his left it did not deter him from charging the enemy position. Since the ground in front of the Southerners was steep Hatch gave "the command a moment to breathe" before again ordering the men forward. Soon the two sides were battling head-to-head. Croxton's 2nd Michigan men were armed with seven-shot Spencer carbines and they eviscerated sections of the Rebel line. An eyewitness said Jackson's men withstood the initial barrage from the Spencers, but when a second

---

[6] *OR* 45, pt. 1, p. 573, 754; Cox, *Battle of Franklin*, p. 176; Wyeth, *That Devil Forrest*, p. 481.

[7] *OR* 45, pt. 1, p. 573, 576; Keenan, *Wilson's Cavalry Corps*, p. 64; Wyeth, *That Devil Forrest*, p. 481; Cox, *Battle of Franklin*, p. 177; Hughes, Jr., *Brigadier General Tyree H. Bell*, p. 202.

"storm of leaden hail" ripped through them the line "halted, broke and fled." Lawrence Ross tried doggedly to make some progress against the Federals. The 3rd Texas Cavalry and 9th Texas Cavalry were especially conspicuous in the face of the withering fire and close quarters fighting broke out in places. Pvt. Tom Cellum of the 9th Texas killed a Yankee officer before being shot three times himself. But bravery was not enough for the Confederates. They were hopelessly outnumbered and outgunned. Some of Jackson's troops actually ran out of ammunition and without any realistic chance of victory the Southerners galloped back south of the river around sundown. James Wilson had finally gotten the best of Nathan Bedford Forrest and his jubilation was apparent when, in an evening dispatch to a brigade commander, he stated that Hatch and Croxton had "made a beautiful fight at the same time, driving the enemy's cavalry across the river with great gallantry."[8]

For the Rebels the cavalry encounter was a dismal failure. Hood's dividing of the cavalry made no tactical sense and in the end his decision did practically nothing to bolster the offensive. Had Hood chosen to allow Forrest use of all three cavalry divisions in a concerted movement, there is no telling what might have happened. Forrest had already shown an ability to handle Wilson with relative ease. If Forrest's entire cavalry command had forced a crossing of the Harpeth River at Hughes' Ford even as late as 3 p.m., while the infantry moved out at 4 p.m., John Schofield would have found himself in a dangerous spot. With pressure on his front, and Forrest wreaking havoc in his rear, Schofield would have faced a scenario much different than the one he was handed. But Forrest was handcuffed, essentially relegated to the sideline. On a day where John Bell Hood needed all the help he could get, one of the greatest weapons at his disposal was hardly used.[9]

---

[8] *OR* 45, pt. 1, p. 576, 770, 1179, 1185; Keenan, *Wilson's Cavalry Corps*, p. 65; Crabb, *All Afire To Fight*, p. 268-269; Hay, *Hood's Tennessee Campaign*, p. 126.

[9] Hay, *Hood's Tennessee Campaign*, p. 129-130. Hay raises the very interesting idea that had Forrest, using the entire cavalry, gotten across the river and into Schofield's rear, the Federal commander would have been forced to disengage in the middle of the fight with the Rebel infantry or risk being cut off entirely. Either way the consequences for the Federal army could have been disastrous.

William B. Bate (U. S. Army Military History Institute)

Meanwhile, around the time the cavalry was pulling back, Gen. Bate's men were sprinting toward the Union works, his right brigade under Henry Jackson heading in the direction of the locust grove. The Georgians were raked by artillery fire and had been since they passed Everbright. Jacob Ziegler's Battery B, Pennsylvania Battery and Lyman Bridges' Illinois Battery pummeled the onrushing Confederates. Around 5 p.m. the other two-gun section of Bridges' Battery had been brought forward to the edge of Carter Hill. It did not take long for all four of Bridges' pieces to begin working with the Pennsylvania guns and effect a savage crossfire. Lt. Sidney F. Moore of the 118th Ohio never forgot how the artillerymen fired directly over the top of his regiment. Solid shot, spherical case, and percussion and fused shells screamed outward and blasted holes in Bate's Division. By the time the fighting ended Bridges' men had fired 310 rounds, made up entirely of fused and percussion shells and case shot. When the Southerners got close enough Ziegler's gunners switched to canister. From their position on the east side of Carter's Creek Pike the Pennsylvanians were perfectly placed to fire obliquely into both Jackson's and Smith's brigades. They may have expended as many as 600 rounds during the battle.[10]

The terrain also worked against the Rebels. Beyond Everbright the terrain dropped away, forming "a depression between the enemy

[10] *OR* 45, pt. 1, p. 321-322, 336, 668, 743; Moore, *NT*, May 2, 1912. Ziegler's Battery fired 684 rounds at Spring Hill and Franklin and only fired a small number of rounds at the former place. Unfortunately Ziegler did not specify any exact figures in his report.

and the creek that runs past the Bostick House..." Beyond this hollow, some 150 yards in front of the Federals and located about the center of Orlando Moore's line, the ground rose slightly. As the Southerners raced up this elevation and reached the crest, the Yankees could see them "clearly defined against the sky..." Sheets of fire cascaded from the blue line. Gen. Thomas Ruger, the Federal division commander in this area, watched the enemy line "gradually waste and disappear" under the barrage of incoming fire.[11]

Those who made it through those devastating initial volleys staggered forward. Bodies littered the ground. Among them was Capt. Tod Carter, who with sword drawn had spurred his horse Rosecrantz toward the enemy in a wild dash. Riddled with fire, Carter and his mount had toppled to the ground just south of the shattered locust grove. Thrown over his horse's neck he lay sprawled on the ground gravely wounded, barely 500 feet from his home. Around him flashes of orange and red from thousands of guns pierced the deepening twilight. The final stages of John Bell Hood's desperate and ill-planned assault now approached their conclusion.[12]

Jackson and Benton Smith hammered the center of Col. Moore's line. A horde of their troops funneled toward the weakest point in the Yankee defense. Earlier in the day, Jacob Cox had sent two companies of the 183rd Ohio to help Moore fill out his line. The raw Ohio recruits had been posted between the 23rd Michigan and 129th Indiana, but when the moment of truth arrived they turned and ran before the Rebels even got over the works. As a result, there was an immediate crisis. The sudden gap in the Yankee line was enough of a problem, but Bate's men were also swarming on both sides of the hole and threatening to widen it.[13]

In this chaotic sector the men of the 23rd Michigan, 129th Indiana, and 107th Illinois found themselves bearing the brunt of the pressure. Additional support, however, came when the seven remaining companies of the 183rd Ohio began moving forward from their reserve

---

[11] *OR* 45, pt. 1, p. 365, 743; W. J. McMurray, *History of the Twentieth Tennessee Regiment Volunteer Infantry, C. S. A.*, p. 143.

[12] Field, *Bright Skies and Dark Shadows*, p. 247-248; Carter, *Capt. Tod Carter*, p. 43.

[13] *OR* 45, pt. 1, p. 379-380; Cox, *Battle of Franklin*, p. 133

position. The Ohioans were on slightly higher ground to the rear and a sergeant from the 107th Illinois remembered how the recruits took "telling" fire from advancing Rebels who were shooting high. Maj. August Hatry of the 183rd Ohio, who had been out on the skirmish line and worked his way back to the regiment after the battle erupted, said he found his comrades near the front line battling the enemy. Just before Hatry's arrival, and into the midst of this melee, Lt. Col. Mervin Clark had come dashing forward. Clark was barely twenty-one years old and had served successfully as a captain in the 7th Ohio before being mustered out. His soldierly blood ran strong, however, and after re-enlisting Clark came to serve in Col. George Hoge's 183rd Ohio when that regiment was organized in the fall of 1864. Known as "Clarkie" to his friends he was an inspiration to everyone who knew him. Although accounts of Clark's last moments vary, there is no doubt he was trying to encourage his men and push them toward the front. At least two sources indicate Clark raced toward the breastworks and climbed upon them, from where he implored his men to move forward and bolster the main line. Unfortunately, Clark made a much too inviting target even in the near darkness. Seconds later he was shot and toppled to the ground dead. Yet Clark had prodded many of the green recruits up to the front, rallied some of those in the two companies who had turned and ran, and gained a few valuable moments of time. Orlando Moore already had his contingency plan in motion.[14]

As Mervin Clark heroically performed his duty, Moore called upon two companies from Lt. Col. Alfred Owen's 80th Indiana to move

---

[14] Scofield, *The Retreat From Pulaski*, p. 50-51; Cox, *Battle of Franklin*, p. 237; Willard Musson, "At Franklin: Some Spicy Recollections of an Orderly-Sergeant," *NT*, Feb. 17, 1887, p. 8; R. N. Spohr, "There Was No Shirking: And Col. Mervin Clark Did Not Die as Col. Sherwood Relates," *NT*, Sept. 6, 1894, p. 4. Sherwood claimed that Clark died near the 111th Ohio in both his book *Memories of the War* (see page 140-141) and in a letter published in the *National Tribune* dated Aug. 2, 1894, but his claim is questionable. It does seem that a portion of the left flank of the 183rd Ohio was near the 111th Ohio, but military tactics of the era would have found Clark on the right of his regiment and thus removed from Sherwood and his men by, at the very least, several hundred feet. Also many of Sherwood's post-war writings are riddled with errors and inaccuracies.

to their left and plug the hole in the line. Lt. Sidney Moore of the 118th Ohio remembered the Indianans shuffling "to the left to fill a gap in our brigade line..." Col. Moore also instructed Capt. Ziegler to pull his guns out of their embrasures and "fire upon the ridge upon the left flank" of the brigade. Moore had plans to make sure any Rebels who broke through were going to pay a deadly price. The colonel was also conspicuous to those around him. A young Ohio private never forgot seeing Moore, on horseback with his hat gripped in one hand, bellowing out reassurances to his men and imploring them to give the Rebels hell.[15]

Along the works the action was furious for a time. The Confederates piled into the ditch and fought their way to the parapet time and again. A Michigan officer wrote that the "many hand-to-hand encounters over the works are strongly attested by the number of bayonet wounds received by the men." Capt. Leander S. McGraw of the 107th Illinois said that at one point "four stands of colors were planted upon our breast-works, across which the enemy charged furiously..." McGraw later wrote that he thought he "knew what fighting was," but admitted the action at Franklin "exceeded in severity" anything the he had ever seen. A particularly daring Rebel actually grabbed the Illinois regiment's flag and tried to get away. The man was shot down and Pvt. Bailey Walker of Company G jumped over the works to the enemy side, grabbed the colors, and brought the banner back.[16]

Lt. Joseph R. Wolfe of the 107th Illinois remembered that "a murderous fire" was unleashed on the Southerners, but still they came on "with heads inclined like beasts, striving to stem the pelting of a storm." Wolfe said it was dusk when the enemy made their "most determined" effort and piled to the top of the parapet. Once there the Rebels "were either bayoneted, shot, or knocked down." In one of the battle's many twists, some of the 107th Illinois veterans screamed at the 183rd Ohio troops behind them to lay down, load their muskets, and hand them to the front. It was like the action east of the Columbia Pike

---

[15] *OR* 45, pt. 1, p. 380, 384; Moore, *NT*, May 2, 1912; James Riffle, "Memory of Franklin," *NT*, Oct. 25, 1923, p. 7.

[16] *OR* 45, pt. 1, p. 380, 383; L. S. McGraw to J. J. McGraw, Clinton *Public*, Dec. 8, 1864, ALPL.

as one group of men loaded while another group fired. Lt. Wolfe said the ditch on the outside of the works "was filled with dead and wounded" and he believed the Confederates charged toward the Union line at least eleven times. Lt. Col. Francis Lowry, commanding the 107th Illinois, was mortally wounded during the bitter fighting and leadership of the regiment devolved upon Capt. McGraw. Lowry, shot in the head, was left behind in the hands of Confederate surgeons after the battle and lingered until January 1, 1865 before dying. Lt. Isaac C. Morse of the 107th Illinois was also killed.[17]

To the right of the Illinois troops the men of the 129th Indiana fought to prevent the hole created after the hasty departure of the two 183rd Ohio companies from expanding in their direction. Soon companies C and H of the 80th Indiana arrived to fill the spot vacated by the Ohio troops and they joined the fray. Alfred Owen's veteran soldiers, who had suffered grievous losses at Resaca, Georgia in May 1864, stood firm under the relentless enemy pressure and even netted forty prisoners.[18]

Not far away, Col. George A. Smith of the 1st Georgia Confederate, known also as the 1st Confederate Infantry, was killed desperately urging his men into position on the outside of the Yankee works. Smith was a hardened veteran who had joined the Southern cause in the spring of 1861. In his last moments Smith did everything possible to penetrate the Union line, but death finally caught up with him in the blood-soaked trenches of Franklin. Also struck down and killed was Pvt. Absalom O. Hardy of the 30th Georgia, who carried the regiment's colors.[19]

The 23rd Michigan did its part in sending many Rebels to the grave. The veteran unit welcomed the troops from the 80th Indiana and together they beat the enemy back. Col. Oliver L. Spaulding, the 23rd Michigan's commander, said the Southerners were "repulsed each time, with terrible loss." Pvt. Wayne E. Morris was in the Michigan ranks and wrote that he had never heard such "groaning & praying & pleading"

---

[17] *OR* 45, pt. 1, p. 380, 383; JoeWolfe to Editors, Clinton *Public*, Dec. 15, 1864, ALPL; Musson, *NT*, Feb. 17, 1887; *OAR* 6, p. 371.

[18] *OR* 38, pt. 2, p. 587; *OR* 45, pt. 1, p. 368, 384.

[19] *OR* 45, pt. 1, p. 743; A. P. Adamson, *Brief History of the Thirtieth Georgia Regiment*, p. 45.

before and declared "God knows I do not want to again." Morris said after Franklin he knew all too well "what war is." Col. Moore said Rebels struggling with the 23rd Michigan were twice able to get their flags atop the parapet. Their efforts were in vain, however, as the Michigan troops "cleared the works of the assailants." At one point Col. Spaulding even ordered a company of Michigan troops from the right of the regiment over the works where they fired a volley into some of the Confederates on the outside of the embankment. When their work was done the Spaulding's boys scurried back over the works and resumed firing from there.[20]

While Henry Jackson and Thomas Benton Smith threw their troops against the heart of Moore's Federal line, Robert Bullock tried his luck along Carter's Creek Pike. His Florida troops initially approached on both sides of the road. Along their path the pike veered dramatically to the northeast at almost a forty-five degree angle, some 400 yards from the Northern line. As a result, Bullock's men soon passed over to the west side of the pike entirely. Passing to the right of the Atkins schoolhouse, also known as the Franklin Male Academy, they became heavily involved with a skirmish line commanded by Col. Thomas E. Rose. These troops, composed of Rose's 77th Pennsylvania, put up a remarkably stiff resistance. Only when the sheer number of Confederates began to crack the left of Rose's line did he and his men pull back. Then, at about 250 yards distance, the main Yankee line opened on Bullock's advancing force. Moving toward the front defended by Gen. William Grose's Brigade, on the left of Kimball's Division, the Southerners came up "in good order and with great determination..." Bullock's men marched roughly along the length of a small ravine during their final approach. A small spring fed creek, known today as Sharp's Branch, wound its way through this area and it was a dreadful location for assault troops to find themselves.[21]

Grose said "the destruction...was terrible" as the Rebels pressed to within 100 yards of the blue line. Lt. Col. Edward N. Badger,

---

[20] *OR* 45, pt. 1, p. 380, 386; Cox, *Battle of Franklin*, p. 134; Wayne E. Morris to Libby, Dec. 2, 1864 and Morris to Dear Brother, Dec. 6, 1864, Morris Papers, Bentley Historical Library, University of Michigan.

[21] *OR* 45, pt. 1, p. 208, 224, 227; Cox, *Battle of Franklin*, p. 61.

Nathan Kimball
(Library of Congress)

commanding the consolidated 1st Florida Cavalry (dismounted)/4th Florida Infantry, was shot three times as he led his men forward. Maj. John C. Taylor, commanding the 84th Indiana, said his men "kept up a brisk fire...for about ten minutes..." He also mentioned that fire from a nearby battery, presumably Ziegler's, did much to batter the enemy ranks. Col. John E. Bennett of the 75th Illinois said after his regiment fired its first volley the Rebels halted their advance. Only moments later, and rather suddenly, Col. Bullock's Floridians cracked under the galling fire. Bennett recalled that it took only a few more "well-aimed volleys" to send "the enemy back in confusion." An officer from the 84th Illinois said almost regretfully that his men were not afforded an opportunity to fire on the Rebels. On the right of Grose's line the 9th Indiana fired just a single volley, an oblique salvo that was aimed squarely into the Rebel flank. Capt. Henry W. Lawton of the 30th Indiana remembered this "destructive fire" by the 9th Indiana allowed the skirmishers time to retire to the main line. Lawton said that once his front was clear his own troops "immediately opened" on the Confederates.[22]

Bullock's men were never able to emerge from the ravine during their assault. Lt. Col. Charles H. Morton of the 84th Illinois said the Confederates "were driven back...in every attempt that was made to charge up the ravine." Pinned down by enemy fire and isolated, the Floridians faltered and broke. Maj. Taylor said the Rebels were "compelled...to seek shelter...under cover of a small hill" and Gen. Grose remembered how the enemy's first line "scattered and

[22] *OR* 45, pt. 1, p. 208, 214, 217, 220, 223, 225, 743.

disappeared" and the second line "broke and fell back in confusion."[23]

As with so much that happened at Franklin there is widespread confusion about exactly how Bate's Division assaulted the Union position. Conclusions have been reached ranging from Bullock attacking almost independent of Jackson and Smith, to only one of Bate's brigades even reaching the Federal line.[24]

When reading the official reports written by William Bate and William Grose, it is not easy to decipher the truth. It is clear that Bate did move Bullock up from reserve before his other two brigades reached the Federal breastworks. This is supported by Bate's statement that the line of attack, once extended to protect his left, was a "single one, without support..." On the other hand, Grose mentioned that the Confederates never "got nearer than 100 yards" of his line, which is an obvious reference to Bullock only. Grose could not have been referring to either Jackson or Smith, because other facts indicate those commands did in fact reach the enemy works. The shape of the Federal defensive line on this part of the field was also a significant factor. The Union works turned sharply to the north after crossing Carter's Creek Pike, thus Bullock had further to travel than did Smith and especially Jackson. In fact, he may have had as much as 300 additional yards to cover. This distance, in addition to the ravine through which the

---

[23] *OR* 45, pt. 1, p. 208, 217, 225. Ironically, the commanding officer of the 84th Illinois, Col. Louis H. Waters, was shot in the upper right arm late in the evening by a stray bullet. See *OR* 45, pt. 1, p. 209, 217.

[24] Brown, *History of the First Battalion Georgia Sharpshooters, 1862-1865*, p. 137-138; Losson, *Tennessee's Forgotten Warriors*, p. 233. There is some debate about whether Smith's troops reached the Federal works. In a Dec. 10, 1864 letter written by Henry Jackson to Frank Cheatham, on file at the TSLA, the brigade commander railed against the role of Smith's and Bullock's brigades at Franklin and stated that neither unit ever reached the works. While it seems clear Bullock never reached the Yankee works, this author thinks it improbable that Jackson's Brigade could have alone caused all of the chaos at the breastworks. The size of his entire brigade was little more than that of two of the Union regiments he was facing. It is likely some of Smith's men faltered and turned back, but the available evidence, especially Federal accounts which noted the severity of the fighting, indicate many from his command did reach the works.

Florida Brigade had to move, could have easily delayed its approach to the length of works occupied by Grose's men. Moreover, the arc of the Federal line may have prevented Bullock from ever being able to attack head-on. It is very likely that his men were continually having to right oblique just to try and face the enemy.[25]

During the hectic assault on this part of the Yankee line, Bullock probably became separated from the rest of the division. Evidence for this exists in careful evaluation of the reports filed by Maj. Edgar Sowers of the 118th Ohio and Lt. Col. Alfred Owen of the 80th Indiana. Those regiments formed the right of Orlando Moore's Brigade, with Owen's men being the closest to Carter's Creek Pike. Owen made no mention of an assault on his front and his involvement in the battle was limited largely to sending two companies to help fill the hole made by the withdrawal of the 183rd Ohio. Sowers said the attack was "heaviest on the left" and that his men were able to enfilade the advancing Confederates who moved diagonally across the regiment's front. This account points to Sowers' troops likely firing into the left flank of Thomas Benton Smith's Brigade. Altogether the 80th Indiana and 118th Ohio suffered only fourteen wounded.[26]

Even Oliver Spaulding of the 23rd Michigan said his left was far more "pressed" than his right. Thus while Smith and Jackson attacked the heart of Moore's line it seems that Bullock, after missing Moore's right almost entirely, faced Grose's Brigade west of Carter's Creek Pike. Through a combination of incoming fire, poor terrain, near darkness, the curve of the enemy line, and isolation from the rest of the division, the Florida regiments broke up and withdrew. Gen. Bate reported that his left reformed "between the works of the enemy and Mrs. Bostick's house," but did not have "sufficient numbers to justify another effort" to storm the Federals. With that decision made, and with fragments of Smith's and Jackson's brigades clinging to the outside of the Union

---

[25] *OR* 45, pt. 1, p. 208, 743; Connelly, *Autumn of Glory*, p. 505; McDonough and Connelly, *Five Tragic Hours*, p. 142-143.

[26] *OR* 45, pt. 1, p. 381, 384, 388. Moore reported the losses as one killed and eleven wounded. Moore, however, covered the period November 21-30 and apparently five wounded men from the two regiments had returned to duty by December 8.

breastworks, Bate opted to halt any further offensive movements.[27]

Many years after the war a trio of Ohio veterans attended a United Confederate Veterans reunion in Marianna, Florida. At the reunion the aged Federal soldiers presented the former Rebels with a old and tattered flag that had been captured late in the war. Housed in a Toledo, Ohio museum for almost six decades, the Ohio veterans understood that it had some connection to Florida Confederates. Through the subsequent years it became generally accepted that the flag belonged to the 4th Florida and had been captured by the 111th Ohio at Franklin. Yet the 4th Florida, like the other regiments in Robert Bullock's command, never reached the Federal works. Overlooked was the fact that the 111th Ohio was positioned significantly east of the point the Floridians approached. Furthermore, the Union veterans who showed up at the UCV event were not even former members of the 111th Ohio. Today the flag is held in the collections of the Florida Museum of History in Tallahassee. Recent research has shown that the flag is a type not distributed within the Army of Tennessee by late 1864. In fact, since the flag is not marked in any way there is a question whether it ever belonged to the 4th Florida. However, assuming that it was, the flag was more likely captured at the Battle of Nashville two weeks after Franklin. There William Bate's men, including the 4th Florida, came into close contact with the Federals and suffered serious losses, including several flags.[28]

---

[27] Ibid., p. 386, 743.

[28] Ibid., p. 646. Detailed information about the flag in question was obtained from a February 2, 2005 conversation with Bruce Graetz, curator of the Florida Museum of History. The UCV reunion mentioned was held in 1927. A photo does exist from the reunion showing several individuals holding a very large flag that is often captioned as being the banner of the 4th Florida Infantry captured at Franklin. According to Mr. Graetz, this is most definitely not the flag that is currently held at the Florida Museum of History. Rather it was a silk replica typically used at such veterans gatherings.

With the withdrawal of Bullock's Floridians, the first and most significant portion of the battle drew to a close. Two Confederate corps had attempted to rout the Federal army and drive it into the river. Six divisions had tried everything in their power to bring about victory. The Union defensive perimeter, though badly damaged in spots, had held. It was as if a human wave had roared across the Harpeth Valley, "slamming into the Federal left, rolling northwestward, overflowing onto the Federal center, and dashing itself finally on the Federal right." After 6 p.m. the scope of things changed. What happened over the course of the next few hours would insure the battle's place as one of the darkest moments of the American Civil War.[29]

After witnessing the furious Union counter assaults that had helped to stabilize his line, Jacob Cox briefly reviewed the area surrounding the Carter House. One of the first things he saw through the smoke and deep twilight was that a portion of the main line west of the Columbia Pike remained devoid of Union troops. Riding a short distance to the west, he met with Gen. Ruger and confirmed the front line was solidly held from where the 111th Ohio stood to the right. Cox then rode to the far left to see how his men were faring in that area. Once there he could see that Gen. Reilly's men had everything well in hand. With the abandoned section of the line west of the Columbia Pike fresh in his mind, Cox ordered Lt. Col. Emery Bond's 112th Illinois, the reserve unit of Israel Stiles' Brigade, "to the right centre to assist Strickland in fully regaining the works." Cox also spoke briefly with Reilly and told him to be ready "to sweep with an enfilading fire the enemy who held on in front of the right centre" if Bond's effort failed. Cox then rode back to the center to wait for the 112th Illinois, which had nearly a half mile to travel just to get into position.[30]

During the time that Cox was inspecting his line, the savage combat in and around the Carter garden dragged on. Back at the retrenchment, Capt. James Sexton of the 72nd Illinois was approached by one man after another who insisted the works at the main line should be retaken. As the ranking officer left standing in the regiment, Sexton

---

[29] Michael J. Klinger, "Gallant Charge Repulsed," *America's Civil War*, January 1989, p. 33.

[30] Cox, *Battle of Franklin*, p. 143-147; Thompson, *History of the 112th Regiment of Illinois Infantry*, p. 270.

faced his first critical command decision. He opted to make the effort and passed the word to the other line officers. It was not a wise choice. Sexton ordered the regiment forward and the Illinois troops were able to reoccupy the works with little effort. The problem, however, was not getting there, it was staying. In the near pitch darkness the Confederates were the least of Sexton's difficulties. Union soldiers to the "right and left" mistook the 72nd Illinois for enemy troops and began firing. Bullets peppered Sexton's men and they began screaming that they were friends. A number of them crumpled to the ground. The situation became so serious that the entire regimental color guard was shot down and the flag itself "was shot to shreds..." There seemed to be nothing that could be done to stop the friendly fire, so Sexton ordered his men to withdraw. Without delay they scurried back to the west end of the retrenched line where Sexton decided to "let well enough alone..."[31]

James Sexton's involvement in the battle, however, was far from over. Not long after he got his men back to relative safety an aide called him to the rear. There Sexton was told the 112th Illinois had arrived and that regiment, with assistance from the 72nd Illinois, was to try and regain the main line of works. Sexton, having been exposed to the fire there once already, immediately protested the order. The aide told him, "The other troops will be notified, and you will not be interfered with again." Sexton saluted and grudgingly directed Capt. Spencer B. Carter to escort Lt. Col. Bond and his regiment into place on the right of the 72nd Illinois. Once there and formed up the 112th Illinois advanced toward the main line, although Sexton admitted only a "small portion" of his command moved in concert. He said "the majority of my men were satisfied with their previous experience, and I had no desire to urge them." Bond and his troops soon learned what Capt. Sexton already knew. They approached the works in total darkness and under the "gloom of night and...pall of smoke" the trek was not an easy one. Although Union troops to the east and west were told of the impending advance they were exceedingly jumpy. Their nervousness, coupled with sheer exhaustion, was not in the best interests of the Illinois troops. They were dogged by a mixture of friendly and enemy fire almost from the start and had to move over dead and wounded bodies on their way

---

[31] *OR* 45, pt. 1, p. 393; Sexton, *MOLLUS*, Illinois, 4, p. 480.

to the front. After a few minutes, however, Bond and Sexton got their men up to the works. Then everything broke loose again. Bond said the Rebels were so close on the other side of the parapet that sparking powder from enemy muskets actually burned his face. From right and left friendly fire pelted the Illinois regiments. Bond was even shot in the heel by fire he was convinced had to have originated on his side of the works. It was abundantly clear the position was "untenable" so Bond and Sexton ordered an immediate withdrawal. What was left of the 72nd Illinois pulled back to resume its spot on the retrenched line. Its heroic efforts cost the 72nd Illinois a galling 152 casualties out of 350 men present for duty when the battle began. Meanwhile, the 112th Illinois filed around the western end of the retrenchment and took a position "in support of Strickland's brigade..."[32]

Watching the Illinois troops return from the fiasco at the front fully convinced Jacob Cox of at least one thing. There was no chance he was going to send any more of his men out into the dark to be torn up. If the Rebels wanted to fight any longer they were going to have to come to him.

The sorties by the Illinois regiments were not the only efforts to regain the main works. The 44th Missouri also charged ahead in an attempt to reoccupy the front line, but was bloodily turned back and forced to leave many of their wounded with the dead. Lts. James S. Dunlap, Benjamin E. Kirgan, and Samuel J. Warner were all killed and Col. Robert Bradshaw, the regiment's commander, was among the wounded left behind. Bradshaw had been shot seven times, but somehow survived his injuries. For days following the battle it was thought Bradshaw had been killed, and a letter was even sent to headquarters requesting that a surgeon and chaplain be allowed to retrieve the colonel's body. The charge made by the Missourians may have occurred spontaneously because neither Jacob Cox or Thomas Ruger ever said anything about ordering the attack. The assault, when combined with the regiment's central position on the field, described as

---

[32] Cox, *Battle of Franklin*, p. 161-163; S. N. Munger, "The 72d Illinois at Franklin," *NT*, Feb. 23, 1901, p. 3; *OR* 45, pt. 1, p. 368; *Thompson, History of the 112th Regiment of Illinois Infantry*, p. 271; Sexton, *MOLLUS*, Illinois, 4, p. 480-481. In the *Official Records* the losses for the 72nd Illinois were listed as 149.

being the "hottest" anywhere, resulted in significant casualties for the 44th Missouri. Its losses totaled approximately 163, higher than any other Federal regiment at Franklin.[33]

---

[33] *OR* 45, pt. 1, 343, 367, 395; Cox, *Battle of Franklin*, p. 239-240; *OAR* 7, p. 133; *Report of the Adjutant General of Missouri, 1865*, p. 274, 276; *Missouri Democrat*, Dec. 8, 1864, St. Louis Public Library. Lt. Col. Andrew Barr, author of the 44th Missouri's report to the Adjutant General, claimed the regiment was ordered to make the charge, but he did not specify where the order originated. Barr claimed losses of "about three hundred men" in his A. G. Report. The *Official Army Register* stated the regiment's losses as 142. The 163 figure used here was taken from the *Official Records*.

10

Defeat in a Blaze of Glory

Tragedy and misery enveloped the Confederate Army of Tennessee on November 30, 1864. Barely twenty-four hours earlier, the army had been poised for a great victory and stood ready to deal its opponent a mortal blow. But between the final two sunsets of that long ago November everything went terribly wrong for the Southerners. Opportunity and hope dissolved into trepidation and death. When darkness finally blanketed the thunderstruck field at Franklin, it was as if someone was trying to say the suffering had gone on long enough. What lay hidden beneath the shroud of night, however, was beyond comprehension. And the suffering was not yet over.

Stephen D. Lee was only thirty-one years old at the end of 1864. Yet Lee was a weathered veteran of some of the war's most bitter fighting. A native South Carolinian, Lee was an 1854 graduate of West Point and remained in the United States Army until secession led to his resignation in early 1861. An artilleryman at heart, Lee served on Beauregard's staff at Fort Sumter and inflicted many casualties on Federal troops at Second Bull Run and Antietam while directing the long arm of the army. By 1863 Lee was serving in the Western Theater and he participated extensively in the Vicksburg Campaign. During this period he had his first experience commanding infantry. By 1864, the war took him to Mississippi where he commanded cavalry and fought in tandem with Nathan Bedford Forrest. But with John Bell Hood's ascension to command of the Army of Tennessee there was an opening for a corps commander. The position was filled by Lee and he soon found himself involved in the climactic struggle for Middle Tennessee.[1]

---

[1] Faust, ed., *Historical Times Encyclopedia*, p. 431.

S. D. Lee
(Library of Congress)

Lee had left Spring Hill with his three divisions and most of the army's artillery not long after the last of Frank Cheatham's troops had pulled out. At around 4 p.m., just as the infantry assault was commencing, Lee arrived at Franklin just ahead of his men. Immediately he reported to Gen. Hood, who told him "to go forward in person to communicate with General Cheatham" and be ready to put Edward Johnson's Division into the fight if necessary. Apparently it took Lee some time to find Cheatham. Lee said he did not find his fellow corps commander until "a little after 5 o'clock" and "about dark..." Cheatham was an emotional wreck. Lee said Cheatham "was much wrought up over the terrible battle and the slaughter of his corps." The burly Tennessean told Lee that "assistance was needed at once" and preparations were quickly made to get Johnson's Division ready for an attack.[2]

Just moving Johnson's four brigades into position was difficult work. Lee was completely unfamiliar with the ground and had no idea how his troops were supposed to move against the enemy. When he asked Cheatham for a staff officer to guide Johnson's men forward, or at least someone to explain the "direction and ground over which the division was to charge" the reply he received was chilling. Cheatham looked at Lee and said he had no one left to help. He explained that all of his aides were either dead or already at the front. Cheatham told Lee that Johnson and his troops would simply have to move "to the left of

---

[2] *OR* 45, pt. 1, p. 687; Lee, *MHS* 7, p. 77-78; Burr and Williams, *PHP*, March 11, 1883, p. 25.

the Columbia Pike."[3] Then he pointed toward the front and said:

> Yonder line of fire at the breastworks is where you are needed and wanted at once. There is the place your division is to go, and the sooner you put your men in, the better, as the slaughter has been terrible with my brave men.[4]

Whatever confidence Lee may have had surely began to drain away while talking with Cheatham. It was dark, the terrain was a mystery, and the enemy had been hammering the rest of the army. Although he was a fighter, Lee could not have liked the chances. He knew, however, that Hood was completely serious about continuing the offensive because he had already been told to ready Gen. Henry Clayton's Division "to support the attack." The commanding general's goal of driving the Yankees into the Harpeth River remained unchanged.[5]

Edward Johnson was forty-eight years old in 1864 and his adult life had been dedicated to the armed forces. Born in Virginia, Johnson graduated from West Point in 1838 and fought in the Seminole and Mexican Wars before spending years at various posts in the West. Johnson resigned his commission in the U. S. Army in June 1861 and was a Confederate brigadier general by the end of that year. Seriously wounded in the foot at McDowell, Virginia in early 1862, Johnson was promoted to major general in early 1863. He commanded a division at Gettysburg, where he was again wounded, and in the Wilderness and at Spotsylvania. Captured at Spotsylvania because the McDowell wound had limited his mobility, Johnson was transferred to the Army of Tennessee after being exchanged. He reported for duty on August 22, 1864. Only ten days later he took command of the division formerly led by Maj. Gen. James P. Anderson, who had been terribly wounded at Jonesboro.[6]

---

[3] Lee, *MHS* 7, p. 78.

[4] Ibid., p. 78.

[5] *OR* 45, pt. 1, p. 687.

[6] *OR* 38, pt. 5, p. 983, 1013; Faust, ed., *Historical Times Encyclopedia*, p. 397; Welsh, *Medical Histories of Confederate Generals*, p. 117.

Edward Johnson
(Library of Congress)

Johnson's Division was composed of four brigades led by Brig. Gens. Zachariah C. Deas, Jacob H. Sharp, Arthur M. Manigault, and William F. Brantley. Sharp and Deas formed the front line of the attacking column, with Sharp on the left, while Brantley and Manigault formed a reserve line, with Brantley on the left. Each brigade commander was a veteran and their list of engagements read like an Army of Tennessee history. They had seen action at Shiloh, Corinth, Perryville, Stones River, Chickamauga, Chattanooga, Resaca, and Atlanta. The division was an experienced unit led by hardened officers, but a night attack was a dangerous proposition.[7]

As his troops readied for their advance, S. D. Lee watched the ominous scene in front of him. Johnson's Division had moved forward to the vicinity of Cheatham's headquarters at Privet Knob, about a half mile from the Yankee line, and the men shuffled impatiently in line. With the sun down the temperature was falling and a slight breeze had kicked up. Lee said the enemy works were "lit up by infantry fire on both sides" and wounded men were appearing out of the darkness, struggling toward the rear. Both Cheatham and Bate spoke with Lee and warned him not to fire into those Confederate troops on the outside of the works who were still battling with the Federals. Finally

---

[7] Lee, *MHS* 7, p. 79; Jacob H. Sharp, "Battle of Franklin Remembrances," *CV* 10, p. 502; C. I. Walker, *Rolls and Historical Sketch of the Tenth Regiment, So. Ca. Volunteeres, in the Army of the Confederate States*, p. 122.

at 7 p.m., as prepared as they could be, Johnson's four brigades marched toward the front.[8]

The movement was fraught with difficulty. The darkness made it nearly impossible to keep the brigades in proper alignment, and after only a few hundred yards the advancing ranks began encountering the dead and wounded strewn across the field. Officers tried to keep their troops in good order by yelling out commands into the gloom. It was both maddening and terrifying. Along the Union line the troops there were witness to an incredible display. They could not see the enemy, but they could see fire. The Rebel lines had men carrying torches at each end and the sight of the shimmering flames bobbing up and down, with what seemed like nothing in between, was almost spectral. Many of the Federals could not believe the Confederates were attacking yet again. The very idea seemed to defy any sort of logic or common sense. But on the Rebels came, this time like shadows out of the dark.[9]

It did not take long for the Yankees to open fire. Once they were able to figure out what the Confederates were up to, the night was suddenly torn asunder by light and sound. Sheets of artillery and rifle fire assailed Johnson's men. From the Confederate perspective not only did the main line light up with fire, but so did the retrenched line. Lee said it "looked as if the division was moving into the very door of hell, lighted up with its sulphurous flames." Strangely the encroaching Southerners remained mostly silent. Orders had been given instructing the men not to shout or yell. They were told to get almost on top of the enemy and then make "a spirited dash for the works."[10]

During the advance alterations were made to the alignment of the division. Lt. Col. C. Irvine Walker of the 10th South Carolina, Manigault's Brigade, said one of the reserve brigades was ordered forward to the front line. This had to be Brantley's Brigade. Manigault's troops were then moved to the left, taking a reserve position almost centered on the front line. Walker said these maneuvers, completed "in the open field," were "handsomely and tactically executed." About 100 feet from the Federal works, the three

---

[8] Lee, *MHS* 7, p. 78; *OR* 45, pt. 1, p. 687.

[9] Lee, *MHS* 7, p. 79; Mohrmann, Memoir, CHA.

[10] Lee, *MHS* 7, p. 79; George W. Leavell, "Battle of Franklin Remembrances," *CV* 10, p. 500.

brigades now forming Johnson's front line broke into a haphazard sprint. Manigault's Brigade was not far behind. Gen. Sharp said "within thirty paces...the darkness was lighted up as if by an electrical display." Suddenly the "mighty and defiant" Rebel yell echoed eerily across the field, and Southern troops began pouring into the area dominated by the locust grove. Men jumped into the tangle of brush and pulled on the branches to get through while others crawled on their hands and knees. Rebel soldiers were soon swarming over the breastworks, shooting and howling and battling desperately with the Yankees. Among those who got over the works was the color bearer of the 41st Mississippi from Sharp's aptly nicknamed High Pressure Brigade. Capt. George W. Spooner from the same regiment actually got up on the parapet and walked along it, waving his sword and "encouraging his men." One soldier remembered that Spooner could be seen "through the darkness by the light from the perpetual flash of the guns." Terrific hand-to-hand fighting broke out and a number of Federal troops turned and ran. Sharp's men eventually captured three stands of Union colors. Some of the men from the 41st Mississippi, forming the left of Jacob Sharp's Brigade, hit the enemy line far enough west to allow them to enfilade some of the Federals on the inside of the works. George W. Leavell remembered he could hear groans and cries "above the din of battle." Thirty-one year old Gen. Sharp was among the casualties, struck by a bullet that hit him just below the knee. Sharp tumbled to the earth and said he felt as if his leg "was shivered into splinters."[11]

Manigault's Brigade continued to be shifted as the fighting developed. Eventually they were moved "to the front line on the left of the Division." Lt. Col. Walker said the roar of small arms fire to his right indicated the troops in that direction were "heavily engaged." Indeed they were. Gen. Brantley's five regiments of Mississippians suffered grievously. His brigade took higher losses than any other in Johnson's Division, over forty percent of the total casualties. Even worse, Brantley absorbed nearly sixty percent of the total killed in

---

[11] Lee, *MHS* 7, p. 79-80; Walker, *Historical Sketch of the Tenth Regiment, So. Ca. Volunteers*, p. 122; Lee, *CV* 16, p. 258; *OR* 45, pt. 1, p. 688; Sharp, *CV* 10, p. 502; Leavell, *CV* 10, p. 500-501; E. L. Russell, "Battle of Franklin Remembrances," *CV* 10, p. 502.

Johnson's Division. It seems that for a time, probably before Manigault's men moved to the front line, Brantley's troops were completely unsupported on their left flank. As they came toward the Federal line on Sharp's left, Brantley's men were exposed to a wicked fire. Alerted to the Rebel attack, the Yankees between the locust thicket and Carter's Creek Pike let loose with sheets of musketry. Brantley's Brigade was ravaged and "nearly annihilated" by the fire and only pockets of men were able to press forward to the breastworks. Matters there were little better as a violent "death struggle for the works" ensued. Pvt. Rhea H. Vance of the 29th Mississippi said, "The blood actually ran in the ditch, and in places saturated our clothing where we were lying down."[12]

Zachariah Deas' Brigade of Alabamians hit the Federals right alongside Sharp's men. According to Lee the troops of Deas' command went through the heart of the locust grove. Capt. William O. Baldwin of the 22nd Alabama, who had just turned nineteen years of age, got through the thicket, scaled the enemy works, and shoved the regimental colors into the dirt. Seconds later young Baldwin was shot and killed. Lt. Col. E. Herbert Armistead of the 22nd Alabama was mortally wounded. Also hit was Gen. Deas, who was evacuated and taken to the Harrison House. Among the most bizarre casualties was Dr. Fielding Pope Sloan, regimental surgeon for the 26th/50th Alabama, who was shot in both the right elbow and left lung. Because all the litter bearers were down, Sloan was near the front treating the wounded when he was hit. Sloan, a Tennessee native, had been ordered to duty in the Confederate army in April 1864. Bedridden with complications from his Franklin wounds, Sloan struggled against death for months before succumbing on June 19, 1865.[13]

Many years after the war, Pvt. Milton J. Park recalled the death of his friend Sgt. Milton E. Broome, both of whom belonged to the 39th Alabama of Deas' Brigade. Park said just before moving against the

---

[12] *OR* 45, pt. 1, p. 688, 691; Lee, *MHS* 7, p. 79; Lee, *CV* 16, p. 258; Walker, *Historical Sketch of the Tenth Regiment, So. Ca. Volunteers*, p. 122; Rowland, *Military History of Mississippi*, p. 280.

[13] Lee, *MHS* 7, p. 79; No author, *SHSP* 22, p. 260; Thomas M. Owen, *History of Alabama and Dictionary of Alabama Biography*, Vol. 3, p. 347; Fielding Pope Sloan obituary, "The Last Roll," *CV* 8, p. 84.

Federal works, Broome said "he was going to be killed" in the battle. Broome removed "a gold ring which he wore on the finger of his left hand" and told Park to deliver it to a friend, Lucius House in Dent's Alabama Battery, after the fighting was over. House was told to deliver the ring to Broome's wife Medora after the war. Sadly Broome's premonition turned out to be correct. Park said "a few moments later a shell exploded over our line" and Broome was hit by a fragment, "inflicting a mortal wound." Because of the "rapid advance" Park never saw Broome's body again and assumed he was buried "with no mark to designate his resting place."[14]

Arthur Manigault's Brigade endured a night of horrors. Barely after reaching the front line, the unit "met a ravine too deep to cross" and was forced to move around it to the right. After the men swung back to the left and were finally ordered forward again, word came that Manigault had "fallen dangerously wounded." Command of the brigade fell upon Col. Newton N. Davis of the 24th Alabama, but soon he was also wounded. Col. Thomas P. Shaw of the 19th South Carolina was the next to be shot down. The troops, almost leaderless and stumbling around in the dark, were under fire "from front and flank..." Corp. Luther E. Huffman of the 10th South Carolina survived the chaos, but lost his brother Jacob, who fell "with a bullet through his brain." Lt. Col. Walker tried to find Brantley for assistance, but he could not be located. It was unlikely Brantley would have been able to do anything even had he been found. What remained of his brigade was pinned against the Yankee breastworks, nearly out of ammunition, with a "sheet of fire passing over them..."[15]

Walker took the reins. He consulted with several other officers from the brigade and decided to pull the troops back and place them "under the first cover" that could be found. Walker then sent a message to Gen. Johnson, asking what should be done under the circumstances. Johnson was soon found and approved the withdrawal,

---

[14] Yeary, *Reminiscences of the Boys in Gray*, p. 589-590. Broome is today buried in the McGavock Confederate Cemetery in the Alabama section, Grave 111.

[15] *OR* 45, pt. 1, p. 684, 688; Walker, *Historical Sketch of the Tenth Regiment, So. Ca. Volunteers*, p. 122-123; Lee, *CV* 16, p. 258; Yeary, *Reminiscences of the Boys in Gray*, p. 364-365.

stating he was aware "the entire attack had failed..." Johnson then ordered the entire division to pull back "a short distance..."[16]

Gen. Manigault suffered a terrible wound. The day after the battle he somehow managed to write a letter to his wife describing the ordeal:

> About fifteen minutes after getting under fire, I was struck by a minnie ball...which brought me to the ground. It entered in the back part of the ear & passing thro. & under the skin came out about two inches behind the ear & near the back part of the head. It fortunately was turned in its course by the high projecting bone back of the ear & making a slight groove along the bone passed out as I have described before.
>
> Altho. I was not able to stand without assistance for several hours, still I had use of my legs. After lying on the field for an hour...with the assistance of...a soldier, I walked a mile and a half to the hospital. [17]

Manigault was unable to serve again during the war and the injury remained a nagging problem for the remainder of his life. Complications resulting from the wound were a factor contributing to his early death in 1886.[18] Additionally, in the days following the battle, S. D. Lee was less than impressed with Manigault and his brigade's performance. After Franklin, Lee wrote glowingly of Johnson's other three brigades, stating that they "behaved most nobly" while failing to even mention Manigault's involvement. By the time Lee wrote his official report in January, however, he had obviously reconsidered the valor of the brigade. At that time he wrote that Manigault had been wounded "while gallantly leading his troops to the fight..."[19]

The cost to Johnson's Division was severe. The final count was 587 casualties and probably only the darkness spared it from even greater loss. Lee said the "night charge of this noble division was grand

---

[16] Walker, *Historical Sketch of the Tenth Regiment, So. Ca. Volunteers*, p. 123.

[17] Tower, ed., *A Carolinian Goes To War*, p. XI-XII.

[18] Faust, ed., Historical Times Encyclopedia, p. 473; Welsh, *Medical Histories of Confederate Generals*, p. 153-154.

[19] *OR* 45, pt. 1, p. 688; Lee to Harrison, Dec. 6, 1864, Harrison Papers, SHC.

beyond description." Lee was understandably proud of his men, but unfortunately for them nothing had been accomplished by their sacrifice. The attack only served to further diminish the Army of Tennessee's already sapped strength.[20]

Once it became clear that Johnson's effort had flamed out, the decision was finally made to halt the offensive. The Confederate army had flung itself against the Federal defensive works for nearly four hours before John Bell Hood put an end to the miserable bloodshed. In his memoirs, Hood wrote that the remaining divisions of S. D. Lee's Corps "could not unfortunately become engaged owing to the obscurity of night." Yet darkness had not prevented him from ordering Edward Johnson forward. A more likely reason is that following Johnson's repulse even Hood was forced to concede little else could be accomplished. Dawn would bring new possibilities, however, and Hood was formulating that plan by the time Johnson had withdrawn.[21]

Gen. Marcellus A. Stovall was a brigade commander in Henry Clayton's Division, and although his men were not ordered to the front, they were sent forward to occupy the forward line previously held by George Wagner's men. Not altogether surprising was that several stray shots from the distant Yankee line found targets in Stovall's ranks. He reported one man killed and at least two wounded by the incidental fire. Gen. Clayton understood just how lucky he and his men were when the attack was finally called off. Clayton wrote candidly that his division was "put in position to attack, but night mercifully interposed to save us from the terrible scourge which our brave companions had suffered."[22]

Although there would be no additional large-scale movements against the Federal line, sporadic fighting continued to flare up at different points. It did not take much to get the weary and nervous soldiers on either side to start shooting. Some even thought that under the cover of night they might be able to surprise the enemy. Near the shattered locust thicket, Lt. James A. Tillman of the 24th South Carolina led his company and a handful of survivors from other companies over the Yankee works. In a wild and fearful melee Tillman and his group

---

[20] *OR* 45, pt. 1, p. 691; Lee, *CV* 16, p. 258.

[21] Hood, *Advance & Retreat*, p. 295.

[22] *OR* 45, pt. 1, 697, 701.

battled the Federals, captured the colors of the 97th Ohio, and collared forty prisoners. There was no possibility the daring Confederates could remain where they were, however, and they soon jumped back across the breastworks.[23]

Lt. Col. Milton Barnes, commanding the 97th Ohio, told his wife about how the regiment lost its colors "and color sergeant in the fight..." The loss of the colors was offset, Barnes thought, by "capturing one of theirs in place of it." After Lane's Brigade was routed from the advanced line, many from the 97th Ohio took new positions on the main line and "fought with great desperation..." Among those men was a sergeant named Alfred Ransbottom, who Barnes said saw an enemy flag "in front of the works, leaped over and grabbed it, and returned unharmed."[24]

A Southerner who remained trapped in the ditch east of the pike remembered how the scattered firing punctuated the night. He said from one direction the sound would come rolling down the line "with brief intermissions" and grow louder as it approached. Then the firing would pass by and "die away in the distance, as it receded." The soldier thought it was like a series of aftershocks following an earthquake, "irregular, unmethodical, inconstant."[25]

By around 9 p.m. even this type of irregular musketry began to fade away. Those Southerners who were able to do so pulled back under the cover of night, running to the rear to rejoin what friends and comrades they had left. Officers tried to get the men regrouped as best they could. Many of those who returned from the front, however, nearly collapsed when they finally stopped and would do no more. Exhausted, covered with powder, blood, and dirt, and streaked with sweat, many slipped into an oblivion of sleep. Others sat down around campfires and stared into the flames, their minds filled with a blur of terrifying images. Like an injured animal the Confederates licked their wounds and tried to cope with what had happened. But as the firing

---

[23] Ibid., p. 737-738.

[24] *OR* 45, pt. 1, p. 238, 256, 258, 267, 646; Milton Barnes to Rhoda Barnes, Dec. 3, 1864, GMU. The flag Ransbottom captured, belonging to the 2nd/6th Missouri Infantry, is in the collection of the Missouri State Museum at Jefferson City, MO.

[25] Banks, *Battle of Franklin*, p. 79.

died away a new sound emerged. The screams and cries of the wounded grew louder, piercing the night with their agonizing calls. For those whose nerves were already raw or shattered, the wails were almost enough to drive them mad.[26]

Even before the final Confederate assault had ground to a halt, it was clear at Gen. Schofield's headquarters that the Federal army had won a great victory. But Schofield, who had returned to the Truett House from Fort Granger, could not wait to get out of Franklin. Just before 7 p.m. he issued orders directing the troops south of the river to withdraw from their positions at midnight and move up the Franklin Pike to Brentwood. Pickets would advance to cover the retreat and they were to withdraw once the rest of the army was safely across the Harpeth River. Thomas Wood's Division was ordered to "cover the crossing" and then form the army's rear guard. When Jacob Cox received a copy of this order he was astounded. Convinced that Schofield did not understand the strength of the Federal position or the beating Hood's army had taken, Cox immediately dispatched a staff officer to headquarters. Cox wanted to stay at Franklin and finish the job and believed Schofield should be made aware that there was "no need to retreat." Cox's aide, however, did not meet with success. Schofield said to convey a message to Cox that a "glorious victory" had been won, but since Gen. Thomas had ordered a withdrawal to Nashville "it must be done."[27]

Levi Scofield was convinced the Rebels would have been crushed had the Federal army stayed at Franklin. Almost gleefully he described the "thoroughness of the thrashing" the enemy received on November 30. Scofield opined that the Battle of Nashville was actually fought "eighteen miles south of that city" and it might just as well have taken place on December 1. He said had the Federals remained at Franklin a "great deal more loss and destruction" would have been inflicted upon the "disorganized rebel ranks, while they were so thoroughly disheartened..."[28]

John Schofield very well may have thrown away a chance to

---

[26] Cox, *Battle of Franklin*, p. 166; Reynolds Diary, p. 112, Special Collections, UAL.

[27] *OR* 45, pt. 1, p. 1172; Cox, *Battle of Franklin*, p. 169-170, 338.

[28] Scofield to Cox, Dec. 23, 1870, Cox Papers, OBC.

destroy what remained of the Rebel army. Clearly there were men who wanted to stay and finish what had been started. In fact, the only reason Thomas told Schofield to fall back to Nashville on November 30 was because Schofield was panicking. In all likelihood, had Schofield asked to stay at Franklin and try to eliminate the Rebel army, there is no reason to believe Thomas would not have agreed.

After seeing off Cox's staff aide, Schofield's next task was to telegraph George Henry Thomas and give him some details of the bloody battle. The wire read:

> The enemy made a heavy and persistent attack with about two corps, commencing at 4 p.m. and lasting until after dark. He was repulsed at all points, with very heavy loss, probably 5,000 or 6,000 men. Our loss is probably not more than one-tenth that number. We have captured about 1,000 prisoners, including one brigadier-general. Your dispatch of this p.m. is received. I have already given the orders you direct, and am now executing them.[29]

Thomas' elated reply came soon after:

> Your telegram is just received. It is glorious news, and I congratulate you and the brave men of your command; but you must look out that the enemy does not still persist...Major-General Steedman, with 5,000 men, should be here in the morning. When he arrives I will start General A. J. Smith's command and General Steedman's troops to your assistance at Brentwood.[30]

As Schofield and Thomas exchanged telegrams, the final Confederate assault collapsed against the Union works west of the Columbia Pike. It is frank testimony to the strength of the Federal position that plans to evacuate Franklin were in motion before the fighting had even ended. As Johnson's attack gave way to isolated and spasmodic firing the first steps of the Federal withdrawal began. David Stanley, who was at Schofield's headquarters after getting his neck wound dressed, ordered Capt. Lyman Bridges to withdraw the artillery batteries and move them to the north side of the river. Beginning at 8 p.m. with Lt. Samuel Canby's Battery M, 4th U. S. Artillery and Lt.

---

[29] *OR* 45, pt. 1, p. 1171.

[30] Ibid., p. 1171.

Aaron Baldwin's 6th Ohio Light Battery, the Yankee guns started rolling to the rear. Tragically, only a "few moments" before the 20th Ohio Battery withdrew, its commander Lt. John Burdick was mortally wounded. By 10 p.m. seven of the eight batteries had been removed from the front, leaving only Capt. Theodore Thomasson and his 1st Kentucky Light Battery in place as insurance against any late movements by the enemy.[31]

No Confederate attacks were forthcoming. The Southern army seemed to be swimming in blood, and Union skirmishers who moved out east of the Columbia Pike saw a genuine nightmare. One soldier said what he and his comrades witnessed and heard was "enough to shock a heart of stone." In the ditch outside the works the "dead and dying" were piled up "sometimes eight deep" and the Federals had to be careful as they moved through the carpet of bodies. A wrong step meant treading on an arm or a leg or tripping over them. Pvt. William G. Bentley of the 104th Ohio said the dead "laid in every position imaginable." In every direction the wounded screamed and moaned. Some reached out, grabbing at the feet and ankles of the Northerners as they passed by. Men cried, "O, for God's sake, give me water." Others pleaded not to be killed. Pvt. Andrew J. Moon, also of the 104th Ohio, remembered, "The ground was in a perfect slop and mud and blood and, oh, such cries as would come up from the wounded...." Near the cotton gin the Federals did not find not a single Rebel soldier still able to fight. All of them were either dead or wounded and the rest had withdrawn some distance to the rear in search of safety. There was no apparent enemy resistance, so the blue clad troops withdrew behind their works and watched the final flashing stages of Johnson's assault unfold.[32]

Shortly before Lt. Baldwin pulled his guns from their position

---

[31] *OR* 45, pt. 1, p. 321, 325, 332, 334-336, 338; Cox, *Battle of Franklin*, p. 170, 187. The 20th Ohio Battery was so short of men and horses that Bridges was forced to ask Col. Opdycke "for a company of infantry" to help move the guns.

[32] Pinney, *History of the 104th Ohio*, p. 63; Barbara B. Smith and Nina B. Baker, ed., *Burning Rails as We Pleased: The Civil War Letters of Williams Garrigues Bentley, 104th Ohio Volunteer Infantry*, p. 127; Andrew J. Moon to his sister, Dec. 4, 1864, CHA.

next to the cotton gin, Capt. John Shellenberger went out beyond the breastworks to view the carnage for himself. Prior to this he saw a wounded Federal soldier carried over the works who had been caught on the outside and hit repeatedly by bullets. The man seemed to be insane from his injuries Shellenberger thought, and he crawled around on his hands and knees "moaning in agony." This was only the beginning. Outside the works the Ohio officer was met by horrible sights, visible "even in the dim starlight." He said the "mangled bodies of the dead rebels were piled up as high as the mouth of the embrasure." It was enough to make a person retch. Shellenberger said when he jumped into the outer ditch he came upon a wounded man who was buried in bodies nearly to his shoulders. The Rebel begged "for the love of Christ" to please pull the corpses off him. Everywhere else the captain looked he saw piles of bodies. Heads, arms, and legs stuck out of the grotesque heaps "in almost every conceivable manner." Like the men who had been on the skirmish line, Shellenberger was mortified by the calls for water and help. He said everything around him was "heart rending" in the extreme.[33]

Among the Confederates who never forgot that horrific night was Capt. John M. Hickey. He had been badly wounded early in the fight and remained on the ground for hours hoping and praying as the battle engulfed him. Nightfall brought an end to one horror only to unleash another. Hickey lay south of the cotton gin, unable to move, but all too aware of everything around him. He said when the firing stopped all that could be heard were "the wails of the wounded and the dying..." Hickey, who convalesced after the battle in a Franklin home, said some of the wounded called out for their friends while others prayed to God asking to die. Hickey was never able to shake the anguish from his mind and said the sound of the "throes of death" and "dying groans" were beyond any real understanding.[34]

West of Columbia Pike other strange and anomalous events unfolded. Milton Barnes said the Confederate "dead and wounded lay in perfect heaps." Along the retrenched line an officer from the 72nd Illinois said a group of Rebels on the other side of the makeshift works

---

[33] Shellenberger, *CV* 36, p. 419-420.

[34] Hickey, *CV* 13, p. 14; Mrs. John C. Gaut, in "Anniversary of the Battle of Franklin," *CV* 17, p. 543.

"begged for quarter and were allowed to come in..." He recalled it was the only time that he had ever heard Southern soldiers beg for mercy. Lt. Thomas Thoburn of the 50th Ohio remembered a song breaking out somewhere on the Union line. Through the darkness the words rang clear and crisp. Hundreds of troops joined in and sang, "Rally 'round the flag boys, we'll rally once again, shouting the battle cry of freedom." It was a moment of heavy irony. Only a few hours earlier the Rebels had approached the Federal line with their bands playing songs like "Dixie" and "The Bonnie Blue Flag." Now the bands were silent and the victorious Northern troops let loose with their own anthem, one rooted deeply in the cause for which they fought.[35]

Adding to the human misery south of the Federal works was the weather. It grew colder and windier as the night wore on, only intensifying the suffering. A young Ohio private sat near the Carter House shivering and listened to the gut-wrenching sounds floating through the air. He said most of the enemy troops cried for water, but some in their delirious states of agony called out for their mothers. He and other soldiers later recognized a disturbing fact about the battle. The ratio of killed to wounded was exceptionally high at Franklin. What had happened was that many of those who were wounded early in the fighting were shot again and again as they lay helpless on the ground. One veteran said it was "like the winnowing of grain" as the bullets "sought the victims and crushed out what little life remained." As a result, many who might have otherwise made it through the battle instead joined the long list of the dead.[36]

Lt. Col. Isaac Sherwood stood atop the parapet facing the locust grove and shuddered with disgust. Earlier, a Southern boy had been found near the outside ditch, crawling on his hands and knees gasping and moaning. Terribly wounded, the boy lived only a few minutes longer. Before he died the young soldier cried out, "We are all cut to pieces - Oh, God, what will become of my poor mother?" Sherwood looked out over the ocean of destruction. The darkness and smoke made the visual spectacle difficult to discern, but the sounds were painfully clear. The Confederate wounded cried and prayed in unison,

---

[35] Milton Barnes to Rhoda Barnes, Dec. 3, 1864, GMU; Mohrmann, Memoir, CHA; Thoburn, *My Experiences During the Civil War*, p. 149.

[36] Gist, *THM* 6, No. 3, p. 231; Rice, *Yankee Tigers*, p. 165-166.

filling the Federal officer "with an anguish that no language can describe." Sherwood's life changed forever after what he experienced that harrowing night. Like many others the weight of Franklin's human cost left an indelible mark. One simple sentence he later wrote said it all - "From that hour to this I have hated war."[37]

Abject curiosity continued to draw men up to and over the works. Emerson Opdycke approached the main line after the shooting died down to witness the battle's results in that area for himself. He was no less shocked than anyone else. In a letter to his wife two days later, Opdycke wrote that he had never seen "their dead and wounded lie so thickly piled upon one another; the carnage was awful." Three days following, in his official report, the images remained burned in his mind. He wrote of seeing the Rebels piled "upon each other, dead and ghastly in the powder-dimmed starlight." An officer in the 12th Kentucky remembered how the Union troops stood in their trenches after the hours of fighting. They were mostly silent, making the sounds coming from Confederate seem even louder. He said "the wail that went up from that field...can never be forgotten by those who heard it." Along the Harpeth River the story was much the same. Not long before the infantry began filing out of the trenches, a subordinate was speaking with Col. Israel Stiles about the thrashing the Southerners had taken. He said, "We ought to remain here and wipe hell out of 'em." Stiles replied simply, "There is no hell left in them. Don't you hear them praying?"[38]

Stiles was correct. The Confederates were spent in both body and mind and had nothing left to give. From the Harpeth River to Carter's Creek Pike, the ground in front of the Union works was one vast stretch of nauseating iniquity. Even that, however, did not stop trophy hunters. One of them was a young sergeant from the 74th Illinois named Elijah Kellogg who crawled over the works after dark and began scavenging for Confederate items to confiscate. Kellogg later wrote an account of what he saw and found:

---

[37] Sherwood, *Memories of the War*, p. 138-139.

[38] Longacre & Haas, *Civil War Letterbooks of Emerson Opdycke*, p. 250; *OR* 45, pt. 1, p. 241; Speed, *MOLLUS*, Ohio, 3, p. 97; Milchrist, *MOLLUS*, Illinois, 4, p. 461.

I cannot describe the horror I saw. The smoke of the battle was like a blanket over the ground and the dead and dying were piled on top of each other in front of our line like cord wood. Among the bodies lying at the foot of our breastworks was that of a Confederate officer. He was not much older than I was. His body was almost hidden by those of the men who had followed him. I later learned from a prisoner captured in the vicinity that these men had belonged to Sears' Mississippi Brigade.

The officer had been shot five times, that I could see, piercing his chest, neck, and arm. He had a fine sabre clinched in his hand which I collected. I also found a blood soaked letter in his breast pocket which I had hoped would identify him. About this time the Minnies started whistling around my ears like bees so I quickly scampered back over the works to the safety of our lines with my prize.

Later on while looking at the sabre more closely, I saw where it was made in Memphis, Tennessee; however, the letter proved to be of little help. It was addressed to Dear Brother Lee and signed Your Loving Sister, Agnes.[39]

Sgt. Kellogg received official recognition for his capture of the Confederate sword, as noted in an official report submitted on January 6, 1865. Kellogg kept the sword until after the turn of the century and then donated it to a Grand Army of the Republic post. Kellogg later requested the saber's return, but after his death in 1914 the battlefield trophy disappeared. Not until 1979 was it located after being picked up at an antique store. Shortly thereafter, detailed research showed that the sword had belonged to Capt. Lee O. Paris of the 4th Mississippi, a regiment in Claudius Sears' Brigade. At long last the saber pulled from the dead officer's hand was able to be preserved and protected once again.[40]

Not all scavenging ended with booty, as evidenced by the story of the Federal soldier who climbed over the works and stumbled across Pvt. Robert Holman of the 49th Tennessee. Unlike most of the men in his regiment, Holman had somehow made it through the fighting unscathed, only to find himself approached by an enemy soldier looking to rob the dead. Holman said the Federal had a "light in one hand and

---

[39] James C. Harris, "Souvenir of Franklin," *North South Trader*, July-August 1982, p. 17-18.

[40] Harris, *North South Trader*, p. 16-17; *OR* 45, pt. 1, p. 237.

a pistol in the other" and for a brief moment Holman considered playing dead. But suddenly he changed his mind and when the Northerner got close enough, Holman raised his rifle and called on the man to surrender. The Yankee blurted out that he did not want to be captured and Holman replied, "I don't either, move out!" Quickly Holman and his prisoner moved to the rear and away from the breastworks.[41]

States Rights Gist was one of the multitude of wounded whose injuries were too severe to mend. After being struck down during his brigade's charge, Gist was removed to a nearby field hospital. Following the onset of darkness, the general's body servant Uncle Wiley Howard was told it seemed certain that Gist had been killed. Howard set out on the battlefield to find out what the truth was. After wandering through the dark for a time, Howard found his way to the temporary hospital where he encountered Dr. Wright, a friend to the general. Howard told the doctor he had come to see how Gist was faring. Dr. Wright responded by saying that the general had died at about 8:30 p.m., and although he suffered terribly when first brought in, the pain slowly subsided. Toward the end Gist asked to be taken to his wife and then died.[42]

Gist was not the only general officer being tended to by anxious hands. William Quarles and John Carter were taken to the Harrison House, where the latter man began a tortuous struggle to survive. Near Lewisburg Pike, Thomas Scott was put into a wagon and taken to Carnton for treatment. The setting there was chaotic and deeply disturbing.[43]

---

[41] Holman memoir, personal collection of Rayburn Qualls, Jr.

[42] Howard, Statement Relating to the Death and Burial of General Gist, p. 3, Peacock Papers, SHC.

[43] McDonough and Connelly, *Five Tragic Hours*, p. 61, 161; Mathes, *The Old Guard in Gray*, p. 170; Merrill, *CV* 5, p. 600; Leander Stillwell, *The Story of a Common Soldier*, p. 260. Presumably Carter was moved to the Harrison House on the night of November 30 as stated in McDonough and Connelly's book. Unfortunately, they provided no source information. Chaplain Quintard stated that Carter and Quarles were there on the evening of December 3; see Turner, *History of Maury County*, Quintard Diary, p. 222-223.

Carnton is a beautiful three-story Federal home, modified to a Greek Revival appearance. Made almost entirely of brick, the house sports nine large windows on its south side, five on the upper level and four on the lower, and it has a centrally located two-story veranda. Carnton is adorned by stepped chimneys on its east and west ends and has a massive two-story gallery on the back, or north side, which runs the length of the house. Construction began in 1826 and the home's original occupants were Randal McGavock and his wife Sarah. They had seven children, four of whom survived to adulthood, and the McGavocks passed many happy years at Carnton. Randal died in 1843 and was followed by Sarah in 1854. Upon Randal's death, ownership of the house and surrounding farmland passed to his third son John. In December 1848 John married Carrie Winder and the two soon upgraded the house, attaching the wide porch and gallery to the back of the home. Two dormers were also added in the attic. By the time of the 1860 census, John McGavock owned some 700 acres of land, thirty-nine slaves, and had a net worth of nearly $340,000. Carnton was home to hundreds of farm animals and the expansive plantation grew thousands of bushels of produce each year. Up to the time of the war the McGavocks were among the more wealthy families in Middle Tennessee and their home, inside and out, was indicative of the cream of Southern society.[44]

Carnton is located west of the Lewisburg Pike and W. W. Loring's Division passed over the plantation grounds and around the house as it advanced toward the Federal line. Chaplain Thomas Markham had chosen Carnton as the divisional hospital when he moved past the house. Those slightly wounded who could walk made their way to the rear during the course of the battle and began stumbling toward Carnton around sundown. The conclusion of the fighting, however, changed matters entirely. Stretcher bearers and attendants combed their way through the wreckage south of the Yankee works looking for survivors unable to move. Lanterns and torches cut through the darkness and the wounded were carried from the fields by the hundreds.

---

[44] Information about Carnton and the McGavock family comes exclusively from a booklet entitled *Historic Carnton Plantation*, no author listed. Additional information obtained from verbal discussions with James Redford, staff member at Carnton.

Carnton was soon flooded with scores of bloodied and broken bodies. George C. Estes of the 14th Mississippi was among the wounded and remembered that the house was "full to overflowing with dead and wounded men." Once every room in the McGavock home was filled, expect for one that the family kept for themselves, soldiers were placed on the ground outside. The surrounding yard soon transformed into an endless hospital ward. Joseph Thompson of the 35th Alabama was among those brought to Carnton who had to spend the night outside in the cold. Thompson also recalled that the house was "overflowing" and said there were so many wounded present it was nearly twenty-four hours before a doctor was able to see him.[45]

The McGavocks' daughter, Hattie, who was just nine years old at the time, remembered seeing "swarms of soldiers" spread out beneath "our spacious shade trees and all around the grounds." She also recalled "how the startled cattle came home from the pastures, how restless they became, sniffing and excitedly running about the place, bewildered by the smell of the battlefield." She said the images would be carried with her to the day of her death.[46]

The surgeons at Carnton were completely overwhelmed. Forced to make the lesser but still painfully wounded wait, the medical personnel set aside the more critically injured for amputation. Soon the doctors were sawing off arms and legs by the dozens. Upstairs bedrooms at Carnton still bear stains where blood dripped off the edge of surgical tables and soaked into the floorboards. An officer on Thomas Scott's staff recalled being inside the house in the presence of several men. Scott was there and suffering near paralysis from the artillery concussion which had knocked him out of the battle. Next to him, Col. Noel Nelson of the 12th Louisiana, who was horribly wounded, screamed in agony and tossed back and forth. He cried out, "My poor wife and child!" Nelson's body had been "torn to pieces" by

---

[45] Thompson, Dec. 15, 1924, CRN; George C. Estes, *Some Incidents As Recorded By A Private Soldier In The Southern Army Of The Civil War*, CRN; Thomas R. Markham, "Reminiscences of the Battle of Franklin," *Southern Presbyterian*, Oct. 3, 1893, CRN.

[46] Hattie McGavock Cowan, "Career of Brilliant Cleburne, Arkansas Lawyer Ended by Bullet While Leading His Soldiers in Battle of Franklin," *Memphis Commercial Appeal*, Apr. 19, 1931, CRN.

enemy fire and he screamed for the doctors to give him some sort of drug to ease the pain. Almost mercifully, Nelson died on the morning of December 1. Nearby lay a Mississippi captain who had been hit in both legs by artillery fire. One of his legs was broken and the other was sliced open to the bone. One of his arms was broken and one of his hands had been "torn away." Surgeon George Phillips told the captain there was no point in amputating his most damaged leg because the severity of his other wounds would surely kill him. The stricken officer looked at the doctor and said it would be just fine if his leg were left alone because he did not intend to die anyway. Miraculously the Mississippian did survive and lived for many years following the war.[47]

Conspicuous in the ocean of suffering were the McGavocks themselves. John and Carrie and their children "bent like ministering angels above the dying and dead" doing whatever they could. Carrie ordered the bed sheets and linens torn into bandages, and when they ran out she told the medical attendants to use her tablecloths, towels, and napkins. But even this was not enough. Eventually Mrs. McGavock had "her husband's shirts and her own under garments" put to use mending the myriad of wounds. Those who saw her were awestruck by her selfless actions. Described as "the very impersonation of Divine sympathy" Carrie McGavock never ceased in her work that long and dreadful night. She handed out tea and coffee and went from room to room making sure there was nothing else she could do. William D. Gale, a member of A. P. Stewart's staff, said Carrie was so involved in affairs that her skirt was "stained in blood..." It was no exaggeration when some began referring to her as the Angel of Carnton.[48]

Shortly before midnight the Federal infantry began to withdraw from their positions south of Franklin. According to plan, pickets were advanced to cover the retreat and soon the first Union troops were headed toward town. By this hour Gen. Wagner had managed to get a handle on his wayward brigades, and his reorganized units were the first

---

[47] C. E. Merrill, "Battle of Franklin Recalled," *CV* 5, p. 600. Information regarding the time of Col. Nelson's death courtesy of R. Hugh Simmons of Paoli, PA.

[48] William D. Gale, "Hood's Campaign in Tennessee," *CV* 2, p. 5; C. E. Merrill, "Fearful Franklin - Some Reminiscences of the Bloodiest Battle in History," *Nashville World*, undated, CRN.

ones to cross the river. Some confusion arose, however, when Gen. Kimball's Division arrived at the Harpeth River crossing points. Kimball had originally been ordered to cross first, but someone figured out after the fact that it only made sense to send Wagner over first, since he and many of his men were nearest the river. Through a lapse in communication, Kimball was never notified of the change and was understandably upset when he showed up at the river and became "compelled to wait" for Wagner to finish crossing.[49]

Confederate Gen. George Gordon, captured near the cotton gin, was also near the river along with hundreds of his comrades on their way to Northern prison camps. Gordon remembered the "hundreds of stragglers" who were near the bridge and the Union officers using "swords and pistols" to get them under control. John Copley was among the ranks of prisoners and was being ushered through town when he noticed that his left arm was covered all the way from shoulder to hand "with the blood and brains of some one..." He also noticed with amazement that his haversack and canteen "had been shot away" and his jacket with filled with bullet holes.[50]

Once Wagner got his two brigades over to the Harpeth's north side, Kimball followed quickly behind. Next in line to cross was Gen. Ruger's Division and Col. Opdycke's Brigade. They were to be followed by the final division on the field, Jacob Cox's, which remained under the direction of Gen. Reilly. Before all of the Federal troops were able to get through town and over the river, however, a serious problem arose. A fire broke out in Franklin and quickly spread to a handful of buildings. Of immediate concern was that the light from the blaze "would make it impossible to move the troops without being seen." Cox, still located at the Carter House, recalled how "every man stood out" and they could be "more easily seen than in broad daylight." Orders were quickly distributed to halt the retreating column. Staff officers scurried about and soon found an old fire engine, which they quickly put it to work. Although it took them some time to get the fire under control the blaze was prevented from spreading any further. Eventually the fire was completely extinguished and the withdrawal

---

[49] *OR* 45, pt. 1, p. 178, 232; Cox, *Battle of Franklin*, p. 188-189.

[50] Gordon, *CV* 8, p. 8; Copley, *Sketch of the Battle of Franklin*, p. 63, SHC.

resumed. Cox said that when the Rebels did not make even the slightest effort to impede the retreat, even after the fire started, it proved to him without a doubt that "none but the disabled and the dead remained near our works."[51]

With the initial stages of the retreat complete, the only Federals left at the front were the pickets and skirmishers. Maj. Tristram T. Dow had been put in charge of this line by Gen. Cox and told to remain in position along the line of breastworks for an hour. The Southerners offered no resistance whatsoever and Dow actually "walked some distance" out in front of the works. Dow said the ground was blanketed with bodies and "the cries of the wounded for help were very distressing" and nowhere was there any semblance of a fighting force. The major could not spot even a hint of aggressive action on either side of Columbia Pike. Dow then turned back and resumed his spot on the line. Around 1 a.m. he withdrew the skirmishers and moved toward the river "entirely undisturbed..."[52]

North of the Harpeth, Schofield ordered the main column to halt and wait for Maj. Dow and his command to arrive. When they did, Schofield ordered Jacob Cox to resume command of his Third Division and take the advance. The troops were ordered to move first to Brentwood, where they would eat breakfast and rest briefly, before continuing onward to Nashville. In a few moments the ranks of blue, accompanied by the army wagons, lurched ahead and the movement up the pike began. The last Federal troops to leave Franklin on the morning of December 1 were the men from Wood's Division. At around 3 a.m. some of his troops set fire to the two bridges spanning the river and held their position long enough to ensure nothing could be done to stop the blaze. Within the hour one of the bridges was crumbling into the water, the other was fully engulfed, and the last of Wood's troops were on their way. By 4 a.m. the Yankees were gone.[53]

Although John Schofield's troops and wagons was headed north hours before the sun came up, the last Federal soldiers to leave the Franklin area were actually James Wilson's cavalrymen. They were

---

[51] *OR* 45, pt. 1, p. 117, 355, 366; Cox, *Battle of Franklin*, p. 191-192; Bennett and Haigh, *History of the Thirty-Sixth Illinois*, p. 661.

[52] Cox, *Battle of Franklin*, p. 186, 192.

[53] *OR* 45, pt. 1, p. 117, 126; Cox, *Battle of Franklin*, p. 192.

instructed to hold their positions north of the Harpeth River until nearly dawn and then move out to cover the army's left flank. Shortly before 6 a.m. the Yankee horsemen galloped off, split into two columns, and headed north toward Nashville.[54]

Although John Bell Hood wrote nothing of it in his memoirs, there is no question he fully intended to resume the offensive at dawn. A midnight conference called together at his headquarters was attended by Frank Cheatham, A. P. Stewart, S. D. Lee, and several staff officers. Hood asked for reports from his corps commanders. Stewart and Cheatham gave Hood the unvarnished truth and said their commands were in shambles and could hardly be expected to do anything. In a private conversation with a Federal officer after the war, Lee related how Hood then turned to him and asked, "Are you, too, going back on me?" Lee responded by saying that he had unused troops available and would do whatever was ordered. Hood had grand ideas for the artillery. For the first time since he left Columbia, all of the army's batteries were available so Hood decided to put them to use. He ordered the artillery to be appropriately placed and at 7 a.m. each gun was to fire 100 rounds at the enemy line. Then, once the barrage concluded around 9 a.m., a "general charge" would be made by the entire army.[55]

The idea that Hood actually wanted to continue the offensive is astounding. Even more incredible is that his heavy hearted men, with a sense of duty, did as they were ordered and began preparations for the dawn assault. A brigade from Clayton's Division of Lee's Corps had already been pushed forward to occupy George Wagner's old advanced line and the rest of the division soon followed. Following the midnight war council Carter Stevenson's Division was also ordered up.

---

[54] *OR* 45, pt. 1, p. 560, 589; Keenan, *Wilson's Cavalry Corps*, p. 68.

[55] Gale, *CV* 2, p. 4; Fields, *Bright Skies and Dark Shadows*, p. 250; Scofield, *The Retreat From Pulaski*, p. 53-56; *OR* 45, pt. 1, p. 721. Hood did mention using the artillery in his official report, but said nothing of an infantry assault. See *OR* 45, pt. 1, p. 654. Additionally, Hood claimed artillery was not used during the battle because of women and children being present in the town. There clearly was artillery used by the Confederates, even if on a small scale. Furthermore, Hood's statement is nothing short of a lie when one considers his late night order to fire 100 rounds from each gun at dawn on December 1. See *Advance & Retreat*, p. 293, and *OR* 45, pt. 1, p. 653-654.

Stevenson reported that his men were "put in position preparatory to an assault which it was announced was to be made by the entire army at daylight." E. R. Boaz, a soldier in Stevenson's Division, also recalled the "orders to renew the charge next morning at daylight..." Maj. James W. Ratchford wrote that it was he who delivered the message "to get ready for a renewal of the fight at daylight" to the general officers in Lee's Corps. Clearly Hood intended to use all of the army, not just Lee's fresh troops, and the evidence exists in multiple sources. Like Stevenson, Edward Walthall recalled that the "entire army" was to attack the Federal works at first light. Daniel Reynolds, commanding one of Walthall's brigades, also wrote in his diary of the planned artillery and infantry assault. Maj. Patrick Henry was told that at dawn "a general assault would be made on the works of the enemy." Henry added that it "was a very trying order to men who had been in that bloody battle..."[56]

Maj. Ratchford had an interesting encounter while delivering the message to ready for the dawn offensive. He found Gen. William Brantley, one of Edward Johnson's brigade commanders, "sitting almost stupefied on the ground..." Brantley's unit had suffered higher losses than any of Johnson's four brigades and Ratchford said Brantley did not respond when initially spoken to. Only after Ratchford put his hand on Brantley's shoulder did the general finally speak, mumbling that he had no brigade. When Ratchford asked him where his men were Brantley said, "They're all dead." The young staff officer could not believe what he was hearing and suggested that surely there where survivors. Ratchford added that if Brantley "did not make some effort to get his men together" he would be "compelled to report it to General Lee." Finally roused from his stupor Brantley said he would see how many men were left and moved away into the night.[57]

Capt. William D. Gale was on A. P. Stewart's staff and one of his tasks that night was to begin placing troops for the morning assault.

---

[56] *OR* 45, pt. 1, p. 694, 721; Yeary, *Reminiscences of the Boys in Gray*, p. 63; Sieburg and Hansen, ed., *Memoirs of a Confederate Staff Officer*, p. 62; Patrick Henry, "Hood's Order After the Battle of Franklin," *CV* 26, p. 11; Reynolds Diary, p. 112, Special Collections, UAL.

[57] *OR* 45, pt. 1, p. 691; Sieburg and Hansen, ed., *Memoirs of a Confederate Staff Officer*, p. 62.

When Gale got close to the breastworks, however, he was "struck by the stillness" on the other side. He found another officer nearby and asked him if the enemy had pulled back. When told yes Gale moved ahead to personally inspect the works and confirm it for himself. He found not a single living Yankee anywhere. Exhausted by the recent events and disgusted at the idea the enemy could slip away again, Gale rode to the rear and delivered the startling news to Gen. Stewart. Dawn was fast approaching and Capt. Gale nearly collapsed onto the ground where he got about a half hour's sleep.[58]

Gale was not alone in discovering that the Federals had retreated from their works. Other Confederates who snuck forward learned the same thing and word quickly spread through the surviving ranks. Like Gale, Patrick Henry had been chosen to place troops in position and he worked on the eastern side of the field. When Henry and a friend got close to the works they saw "little torchlights flitting about in our front." When he called out asking what was going on, the major was told the enemy had evacuated. Capt. Sam Foster wrote in his diary that it was about 1 a.m. when he heard the news. A short time later it was reported that a bridge over the Harpeth River was on fire. There was so much confusion and disorganization among the Southerners, no one was sure whether all of the Yankees were over the river or if some remained in Franklin. Orders were sent out to the artillery commanders instructing them to ready their guns. The flames from the burning bridge were visible from the battlefield and using the conflagration as a general target the artillerists opened fire. The problem was that the structure on fire was not the railroad bridge, but rather the footbridge closer to town. At the distance the Rebel gunners were firing, nearly a mile into the pitch black of night, it was difficult if not impossible to be precise. As a result, shells began falling into a residential area on the east side of Franklin. Pandemonium spread like wildfire among the terrified townsfolk as the howling shells crashed into homes and caused extensive damage. A resident said when the guns first opened up he thought the sound "would take my head off." Some 150 rounds were fired before word got to the artilleryman about what was happening. The incident was another tragedy in a day filled with them. Although the barrage inflicted much heartache on innocent

---

[58] Gale, *CV* 2, p. 4-5.

civilians, it had no impact on the retreating Yankees. Gen. Wood said that the "heavy cannonade...did no injury" to his rear guard and his men continued moving without interruption.[59]

Soon after this Confederate troops began slowly filtering into Franklin. Some of the first to enter town were men from cavalry from Gen. James Chalmers' Division. A handful of Yankee stragglers were swooped up, but it was painfully clear that the enemy army had gotten away successfully. The troopers broke ranks and one of the horsemen got a torch and rode south toward the battlefield. He wanted to see what had happened for himself. W. O. Dodd later wrote of seeing the dead "mangled together" and that it was clear entire companies of men had been obliterated by the Yankee fire. As he rode back to town he could not help but think to himself that the lives spent were nothing short of "a useless sacrifice."[60]

For over twelve hours darkness threw its blanket over the Harpeth Valley. They were long and agonizing hours, filled with the mixture of a thousand emotions. All night long and without cessation post-battle horrors engulfed the Franklin area. Yet what darkness had been able to hide the dawn slowly revealed. Those who had combed the field during the night knew full well the situation was beyond bad even before the first streaks of light appeared in the southeast. But even they were totally unprepared for the true magnitude of the Confederate defeat. It was said that even those used to war "had never seen such a sight before."[61]

---

[59] *OR* 45, pt. 1, p. 126; Henry, *CV* 26, p. 11; Field, *Bright Skies and Dark Shadows*, p. 250; Brown, ed., *One of Cleburne's Command*, p. 150; Sword, *The Confederacy's Last Hurrah*, p. 256-257.

[60] Dodd, *SHSP* 9, p. 522-523.

[61] Field, *Bright Skies and Dark Shadows*, p. 251.

11

The Whole Thing is Inexplicable

The morning of December 1, 1864 was cold and frost covered the ground. After two beautiful Indian summer days the weather suddenly changed, bringing in lower temperatures and a deck of mostly unbroken gray clouds. As the dull morning light began spreading over Franklin just after 6 a.m., the gravity of what had happened became horribly clear. Capt. William C. Thompson of the 6th Mississippi was still lying on the ground near the Lewisburg Pike when dawn broke. He was in such pain that he "cared little" about either living or dying. Eventually someone found him and carried him to a field hospital where a doctor dug the bullet out of Thompson's leg without chloroform. Capt. R. N. Rea of the 4th Mississippi was not wounded, but had been through his own hell. After the Federals retreated Rea remained in the ditch near the Carter cotton gin. Around 1 a.m. he got himself out from under "a pile of dead and wounded men" and began wandering the desolate field. It was bitterly cold and Rea was so stiff he "could hardly walk." He saw lanterns moving about and campfires sprinkled across the landscape. By the time the sun came up the captain had recovered somewhat, only to have the light of day expose the great expanse of horror. Rea said it was like nothing he had ever seen, nor wished to see again. Dead and wounded were everywhere and in his estimation one-fourth of the Rebel army had been destroyed.[1]

Capt. William Gale was out early in the morning. After only a short rest he grabbed a cup of coffee and rode toward the now empty breastworks. Gale was out before any burial details had been put

---

[1] McMurry, *John Bell Hood*, p. 176; Thompson, *CWTI*, December 1964, p. 24; Rea, *CV* 30, p. 288.

together and he said the sights were awful. The ditch outside the works "was literally filled with dead bodies" and they were intermingled "in all unseemly deformity of violent death."[2]

Likewise, William L. Truman from Guibor's Missouri Battery traversed the field, curious to see what had caused so many Rebels in the area of Lewisburg Pike to pull back. When he got within "fifty or seventy-five yards" of the works he discovered why. The Osage orange abatis seemed almost diabolical. Truman saw that the attacking units had been greatly impeded, as evidenced by the innumerable casualties strewn all around the abatis. Equally disturbing was a series of "sharpened fence rails" that had been placed in a ditch and pointed outward at a forty-five degree angle. Truman said there were gaps in this line of obstruction where men had forced their way through, but at least two-thirds of them were still "firmly in position." The cost of moving beyond the rails was high. Truman saw that between the abatis and rails and the works "the ground was strewn with dead." Hundreds of men were in the outside ditch and Truman even found Confederate soldiers mixed with Federal dead inside the works. The artilleryman remembered how the head logs "were shot almost to pieces" and it seemed as if the Yankees had all been hit in either the head or face. Truman traveled further west to the locust grove where the destruction was as bad. Trees left standing by the Yankees before the battle were mowed down during it by the fire from both sides.[3]

Harold Young was also from Guibor's Battery. He went into Franklin before sunup to get breakfast and upon returning to the battlefield became "horror stricken..." Death was everywhere. Young said he "saw 250 dead bodies on a space 300 yards square..." He noted that the bodies were "torn and mangled in every possible form..." Young returned to camp, but since no marching orders had been issued, incredibly he returned to the battlefield. By that time details were hard at work and Young recalled seeing collections of bodies numbering "from 25 to 75 in a place" being readied for burial. Young also peered inside the Yankee works and saw a number of dead there as well.[4]

---

[2] Gale, *CV* 2, p. 5

[3] William L. Truman, "First Missouri Brigade at Franklin," *CV* 11, p. 273.

[4] Young diary, Dec. 1, 1864, in possession of Bill Christmann.

A local boy named Hardin P. Figuers combed his way through the battlefield wreckage that morning. He saw the locust thicket and remembered that the trees "were stripped of their bark and every limb by bullets..." Dumbfounded by what he saw, Figuers thought it amazing that trees which stood "four to six inches across the stump" could be toppled by the fighting.[5]

Everywhere on the battlefield the sights had the same tragic undertone. Death lingered in the air and destruction was evident almost everywhere. An officer tried to ride his horse near the works, but the animal refused, its nostrils flaring at the overpowering smell of blood. The man then dismounted and said that from the breastworks outward for almost 200 yards he "could have walked on the dead" by stepping from one body to another. A Missouri captain recalled the "ghastly sight" that was unveiled "to those still living." He added, "Our army was a wreck." One man was struck with the overwhelming feeling that the Confederates had been "led out in a slaughter-pen to be shot down like animals." Near where Gen. Strahl had been killed, Lt. Col. Fountain Stafford was found dead in a pile of bodies with "his feet wedged in at the bottom, with other dead across and under him after he fell, leaving his body half standing." A Tennessean who had seen many battlefields said the tableau at Franklin made him "sick at heart for days afterwards." James Douglas wrote in his diary that along a 400 yard line he had never "seen an equal number of dead..." He said the sight was "sickening, even to an old Soldier..." James Binford of A. P. Stewart's staff said what he saw that morning could never accurately be described with words. He thought there was little sense even to try. Binford remembered Gen. Stewart telling him that the battle was "the most unnecessary loss of human life" he had ever known.[6]

Young Hardin Figuers worked his way past the locust grove and found a severely wounded Rebel soldier near the Columbia Pike. The

---

[5] H. P. Figuers, "A Boy's Impressions of the Battle of Franklin," *CV* 23, p. 6.

[6] Field, *Bright Skies and Dark Shadows*, p. 252; Boyce, *CV* 24, p. 103; Dodd, *SHSP* 9, p. 253; Cunningham, *CV* 12, p. 340; James L. Cooper, "Service With The Twentieth Tennessee Regiment," *CV* 33, p. 181; Douglas, *Douglas's Texas Battery*, p. 212; Binford, *Recollections of the Fifteenth Mississippi*, p. 108.

man's entire lower jaw had been blown away and Figuers saw his "tongue and under lip" hanging almost to his chest. When Figuers asked if there was anything he could do to help, the man pulled out a small pencil and a tattered envelope. He gamely wrote, "No; John B. Hood will be in New York before three weeks."[7]

Capt. John Lavender of the 4th Arkansas never forgot the human destruction he witnessed that morning, but other damage was also long remembered. Lavender said everything seemed to be "full of Bullets." The captains's regiment had assaulted near the cotton gin and he said the building was "honey combed with Bullets." Lavender also recalled a "large Gate Post" about "12 inches Square and about 8 ft high" which stood several yards in front of the works. He said the post was "Shot to splinters on the two sides." Lavender thought it impossible that "such a number of Balls could have hit that Post, and that a man could have Escaped Death in the Range of such a storm..."[8]

The Carter family and their friends remained hidden in the house cellar until after the Yankee army left. When they emerged it was still dark and a handful of Federal troops remained skulking about on the main floor. There were even some hiding upstairs and soon they were escorted down by a Rebel officer. Fountain Branch Carter and his eldest son Moscow looked around the house both inside and out and determined that there appeared to be no irreparable damage. There was blood in the house, some windows were broken out, and bullets and artillery fire had left their imprints, but the family was safe. Considering all that had happened, the Carters must have considered themselves relatively fortunate.[9]

Any relief the family may have felt was swept away shortly before sunup. As Moscow Carter searched the yard and outbuildings a Confederate soldier arrived with terrible news. Moscow was told that his brother Tod had been shot during the battle and was lying wounded somewhere on the field. Moscow immediately grabbed a lantern and left to search for his brother. Not much later Gen. Thomas Benton Smith rode up to the house and asked young Alice Adelaide McPhail, daughter to one of the Carter sisters, if the home was Tod's. When she

---

[7] Figuers, *CV* 23, p. 6.

[8] Worley, ed., *Memoirs of Capt. John Lavender*, p. 108-109.

[9] David R. Logsdon, *Eyewitnesses at the Battle of Franklin*, p. 76.

said it was Smith explained that Tod was badly hurt and he could take someone to where his body was. Within minutes Fountain Branch Carter, three of his daughters, and a daughter-in-law followed Smith into the darkness. It was nearly daylight when they found Tod only "about 150 yards southwest of the smoke house" and delirious from his wounds. He was repeating his friend James Cooper's name over and over. Tod had been shot nine times and the most serious wound was caused by a bullet that had lodged in his skull above the left eye. He was gently carried home by three soldiers and taken to a small room near the end of the house's ell. There the 20th Tennessee's regimental surgeon, Dr. Deering Roberts, extracted the ball from above Tod's eye and "dressed his other wounds." The heartbreak in the room cut deep. His sisters wept and as they bent over his shattered body one of them said, "Brother's come home at last."[10]

There was nothing more that could have been done for Tod Carter. His wounds were so severe that it was only a matter of time. On December 2 the young captain died in the family's front sitting room, another victim of the terrible battle. Tod's body was transported to a small cemetery west of town and quietly buried.[11]

Gen. Frank Cheatham rode into Franklin soon after learning that the Federals had evacuated the town. There he got some food and prepared for what lay ahead. Before sunup Cheatham was aware that great damage had been done to the army, especially his corps, but the Tennessean was sickened when he saw the battlefield at first light. In an interview years later Cheatham said:

> Just at daybreak I rode upon the field, and such a sight I never saw and can never expect to see again. The dead were piled up like stacks of wheat or scattered about like sheaves of grain. You could have walked all over the field upon dead bodies without stepping upon the ground. The first flame of battle had nearly all been confined within a range of fifty yards, except the cavalry fight on the other side of the river. Almost under your eye, nearly all the dead, wounded and dying lay. In front of the Carter House the bodies lay in heaps, and to the right of it a locust-thicket had been mowed off by bullets, as if by a

---

[10] Logsdon, *Eyewitnesses at the Battle of Franklin*, p. 76-77; Carter, *Capt. Tod Carter*, p. 45; Cooper, *CV* 33, p. 181.

[11] Carter, *Capt. Tod Carter*, p. 46.

scythe. It was a wonder that any man escaped alive...I never saw anything like that field, and never want to again.[12]

Burial details began sweeping the field not long after sunup. For the men assigned to this gruesome task, theirs was a thankless and nerve-wracking job. Milton A. Ryan of the 14th Mississippi survived the battle only to be chosen to bury the dead. He remembered how he and his fellow soldiers dug trenches that were "two and one half feet deep and wide enough for two to lay side by side." Once the bodies were put in these trenches Ryan said "an oil cloth or blanket" was placed over the faces of the deceased and dirt was thrown on top. It was revolting work. Along the works the bodies in the outside ditch were simply covered up, usually by pushing down dirt up near the parapet. Texan William Stanton said it looked as if survivors had piled up the dead in certain spots to try and protect themselves from enemy fire. He thought some of the corpses had been shot hundreds of times. Pvt. Stephen C. Trigg of the 3rd Missouri helped bury many of his friends that morning. He said 119 Missourians were laid to rest "in one grave near the pike, between the cotton gin and the pike..." Captain William L. Ritter found himself compelled to walk the field of horrors. He remembered "where Cockrell's Missourians charged" the dead were found "lying thick, piled one upon another, till the earth was hid by the woeful spectacle."[13]

As best as they could, the men in the burial parties identified the bodies of the dead. Crude wooden headboards were erected for most providing basic information such as a name, a rank, and a unit. Yet there were not only Confederate dead to deal with, but the bodies of many Federals as well. Moscow Carter counted fifty-seven dead Yankees in the yard of the family home between the smokehouse and a spot some thirty yards north of the house. Pvt. Robert Holman of the 49th Tennessee said he counted forty-three dead Federals lying near the

---

[12] Burr and Williams, *PHP*, March 11, 1883, p. 27.

[13] Milton A. Ryan, *Experience of a Confederate Soldier in Camp and Prison in the Civil War 1861-1865*, CHA; Lundberg, *The Finishing Stroke*, p. 102; S. C. Trigg, "Why the Band Played at Franklin," *CV* 19, p. 32; Figuers, *CV* 23, p. 7; William L. Ritter, "Sketch of the Third Maryland Artillery," *SHSP* 11, p. 540.

Carter House porch. For the most part, the Southerners buried the Union troops last and little was done to determine the identity of any soldier wearing blue. Additionally, many of the Northerners were nearly stripped naked, their clothing and boots confiscated by Rebel troops who were dressed in tattered uniforms that were nearly falling off. Most of the Yankee dead were gathered up, thrown into the trenches lining the works, and hastily covered up.[14]

Capt. John McQuaide and Chaplain Thomas Markham were also on the field that morning, carefully picking their way through the wreckage. As McQuaide looked at the faces of the dead he suddenly caught sight of one he recognized all too well. Patrick Cleburne's body lay almost peacefully on the ground, surrounded by the countless bodies of his men. McQuaide bent down and looked into the general's "marble features" and thought he must get the body moved at once. Later he wrote:

> The terrible report that Cleburne was missing ran through our ranks that whole dreadful night, and our fears and anxieties were almost disheartening. We almost prayed that he might have been wounded only, or captured; but that was not to be. I and two others were the first to discover his dead body at early dawn the next morning. He was about 40 or 50 yards from the works. He lay flat upon his back as if asleep, his military cap partly over his eyes. He had on a new gray uniform, the coat of the sack or blouse pattern. It was unbuttoned and open; the lower part of his vest was unbuttoned and open. He wore a white linen shirt, which was stained with blood on the front part of the left side, or just left of the abdomen. This was the only sign of a wound I saw on him, and I believe it is the only one he had received. I have always been inclined to think that feeling his end was near, he had thus laid himself down to die, or that his body had been carried there during the night. He was in his sock feet, his boots having been stolen. His watch, sword belt, and other valuables all gone, his body have been robbed during the night.[15]

---

[14] Figuers, *CV* 23, p. 7; Smith, *History of Maury County*, Interview with Moscow Carter, p. 203; Holman memoir, personal collection of Rayburn Qualls, Jr.

[15] John McQuaide, Letter of, *CV* 7, p. 272; Buck, *Cleburne and His Command*, p. 292-293. J. P. Young said Cleburne was found 290 feet east of Columbia Pike. See *Cleburne and His Command*, p. 61 and Young to Hay, May 5, 1921, CRN.

McQuaide made his way east, where he could see an ambulance near the works. He soon found Chaplain Markham, who told McQuaide that John Adams' body had just been found and was being lifted into the rear of the ambulance. McQuaide explained that he had just found Cleburne and asked Markham if he would come "and take charge of it." The team of horses hitched to the ambulance wagon was soon guided to where Cleburne lay. For a few seconds everyone stood silent, unsure of exactly when or how to begin. Finally one of the attendants stepped forward and several men slowly picked up the general's body. It was put on a litter and gently lifted inside the ambulance and placed next to Adams. Soon the sad procession turned around and headed toward Carnton.[16]

Hiram Granbury's body was also found around this time. Two soldiers from the Texas Brigade were detailed to find their commander after dawn, and they soon located Granbury "within twenty steps of the breastworks," still collapsed to his knees with his hands on his face. Nearby the lifeless form of Lt. Col. Robert B. Young was also found and gently the bodies of both men were escorted to Carnton. Other Texans lay strewn everywhere. The 10th Texas suffered terrible losses and seven of its ten company commanders were counted as casualties. The brigade as a whole was in similar shape. Out of roughly 1,100 men who were present at the onset of the battle, some 400 became casualties during the fighting. Granbury's proud unit had been decimated.[17]

The scene at Carnton early on December 1 was little better than it had been throughout the night. What emotion remained was a grim determination to somehow get through the horrible tragedy. Into this spectacle came the wagons bearing the corpses just gathered from the field. Cleburne, Adams, and Granbury were removed and laid on the back porch of the McGavock house. Robert Young joined them only minutes later. The four bodies were placed next to those of Otho Strahl and Lt. John Marsh, both of whom had been brought to Carnton either during the night or around dawn. For many years it was thought that

---

[16] Buck, *Cleburne and His Command*, p. 293; John McQuaide, Letter of, *CV* 10, p. 155; Williams to Buck, Dec. 4, 1864, Buck Papers, MOC. McQuaide said Adams' body was found outside the breastworks.

[17] Lundberg, *The Finishing Stroke*, p. 99-100. Information concerning the 10th Texas losses courtesy Scott McKay of Roswell, GA.

the porch held the bodies of six Confederate generals. But neither John Carter nor States Rights Gist were ever there. Carter was taken to the Harrison House and Gist, after dying in a field hospital, was removed by his body servant and buried at the residence of William White on the morning of December 1. Thus the six bodies were those of Cleburne, Granbury, Strahl, Young, Marsh, and one other officer. The final body was likely that of Adams or Capt. James Johnston, the latter an adjutant from the 4th Tennessee who served on Strahl's staff.[18]

Preparations to transport the bodies of the fallen officers for burial began almost immediately. Carrie McGavock helped with Cleburne's body and took his kepi and sword for safekeeping, which she later hid between her bed and mattress when the Federals came back through Franklin. She also noted that Cleburne wore a small gold locket that was "suspended from his neck by a slender gold chain and worn under his shirt..." Leonard Mangum, one of Cleburne's dedicated aides, showed up at Carnton after learning that the general had been killed. Mangum said Cleburne's face was covered with a "finely embroidered" handkerchief and that his boots, diary, and sword belt were all missing. Later he found the belt in the possession of a soldier "who claimed to have found it." Mangum also hunted down coffins for Cleburne, Granbury, and Young. As Cleburne was being tended to, Gen. Adams' body was taken away. Adams' pre-war home was in Pulaski and the corpse was driven south by his cousin and staff aide Capt. Tom Gibson and another officer. Adams was conducted to his brother's home for a service and the general was subsequently buried at Maplewood Cemetery next to his father and mother. His wife Georgiana, whom Adams had met while serving on post duty at Fort Snelling, Minnesota in 1853, never remarried.[19]

---

[18] Purdue, *Pat Cleburne*, p. 431; Buck, *Cleburne and His Command*, p. 293; Howard, Statement Relating to the Death and Burial of General Gist, p. 3-4, Peacock Papers, SHC. Johnston's body traveled south to Columbia with those of Strahl and Marsh so it may have been at Carnton also. If both he and Adams were on the back gallery the numbers of bodies there would have been seven.

[19] Mangum, Statement of, p. 4, Peacock Papers, SHC; Young to Hay, May 5, 1921, CRN; Purdue, *Pat Cleburne*, p. 432; Lane, *CWTI*, October 1996, p. 46.

The bodies of the remaining three generals and three staff officers were soon transported in two separate wagons. Chaplain Charles T. Quintard left Spring Hill at about 10 a.m. and after riding "several miles" he met one of the wagons moving south from Franklin. In his diary Quintard wrote of it carrying his "beloved friends" Gen. Strahl, Lt. Marsh, and Capt. Johnston. He made no mention of any of the other officers and the facts indicate their bodies were moved at a later hour. As he looked with anguish at his compatriots, Quintard learned many of the battle's terrible details. The next few days were both emotionally and psychologically draining for the chaplain as he tended to one somber affair after another.[20]

Quintard continued on to Franklin and spent a short amount of time there before turning back and returning to Columbia. The bodies of Strahl, Marsh, and Johnston had been taken there "and deposited in the house of Mr. Johnston, brother of the Captain." Those of Cleburne, Granbury, and Young rested at the Columbia residence of Dr. William J. Polk. Cleburne lay in a walnut casket made by a local cabinet maker.[21] While there Naomi Hays, a niece of former President James K. Polk, composed a poem and placed it on Cleburne's casket. It read:

Fare thee well, departed chieftan!
Erin's land sends forth a wail,
And O my country sad laments thee,
Passed so late through Death's dark vale!
Blow, ye breezes, softly o'er him,
Fan his brown with gentlest breath;
Disturb ye not the peaceful slumber,
Cleburne sleeps the sleep of death.
Rest thee, Cleburne, tears of sadness
Flow from hearts thou'st nobly won;
Mem'ry ne'er will cease to cherish
Deeds of glory thou hast won. [22]

---

[20] Turner, *History of Maury County*, Quintard Diary, p. 220.

[21] Purdue, *Pat Cleburne*, p. 432; Turner, *History of Maury County*, Quintard Diary, p. 221.

[22] Mangum, Statement of, p. 4-5, Peacock Papers, SHC.

On December 2, Quintard officiated at two separate funeral services. At noon he led the goodbyes for Strahl, Marsh, and Johnston and at 3 p.m. the ceremony for Cleburne, Granbury, and Young was held. Under military escort the six bodies were taken to Rose Hill Cemetery and buried in likewise separate precepts. Yet within just a few hours a problem arose. It was learned that the officers had been laid to rest in a section of the cemetery that held the remains of Federal troops. Quintard and Mangum were so upset by the situation that they made arrangements for burial elsewhere and had the bodies, with the exception of Capt. Johnston, exhumed on December 3. Mangum was particularly disturbed by the Rose Hill location and spoke to Gen. Lucius Polk about the situation. Polk, who was at home following the serious leg wound he had received in June, offered Mangum the use of a lot at Ashwood Cemetery in the yard of St. John's Episcopal Church. St. John's was where Cleburne had stopped on November 26 and commented on the beauty of the grounds during the army's move north. Mangum did not learn about Cleburne's brief words until after returning to duty several days after the second burial, so it was by pure chance that the general actually ended up being taken at Ashwood. By the evening of December 3, the five officers were again laid to rest. Several days later they were joined by Col. Robert Beckham, who finally succumbed to the head injury he had suffered at Columbia.[23]

John Bell Hood rode into Franklin early on December 1 and saw for himself the immense cost of the battle. Hood could not help but indulge in "sad and painful thought" as he looked upon the brave soldiers who had made the attack. Hardin Figuers never forgot seeing Hood that morning "with his one wooden leg and his long, tawny mustache and whiskers." Hood was emotional as he rode among the men and it did not take long for the horrific sights and sounds to

---

[23] Turner, *History of Maury County*, Quintard Diary, p. 221-222; Purdue, *Pat Cleburne*, p. 432. According to historian Tim Burgess, Capt. Johnston remains buried at Rose Hill. Johnston can be found in the Confederate section, grave number 42. Why he was left there is unknown.

overwhelm him. A nearby soldier said Hood's demeanor transformed from one of sturdiness to melancholy and for "a considerable time he sat on his horse and wept like a child." Hood eventually moved into town and dismounted in the yard of Mrs. William Sykes. A young girl who saw him thought he looked so sad. Hood sat down in a chair, took a few deep breaths, and began planning the army's next move.[24]

Some of Hood's soldiers were beyond simple emotion, ranging instead between nightmarish horror and burning anger. Pvt. Sam Watkins of the 1st Tennessee said Franklin was "the finishing stroke to the independence of the Southern Confederacy. I was there. I saw it. My flesh trembles, and creeps, and crawls when I think of it today. My heart almost ceases to beat at the horrid recollection."[25] Capt. Sam Foster of the 24th Texas Cavalry was enraged. In his diary he wrote:

> Gen. Hood has betrayed us (The Army of Tenn). This is not the kind of fighting he promised us at Tuscumbia and Florence Ala. when we started into Tenn.
>
> This was not a "fight with equal numbers and choice of the ground" by no means.
>
> And the wails and cries of widows and orphans made at Franklin Tenn Nov 30th 1864 will heat up the fires of the bottomless pit to burn the soul of Gen J B Hood for Murdering their husbands and fathers at that place that day. It can't be called anything else but cold blooded Murder.[26]

The losses suffered at the Battle of Franklin were staggering. Confederate casualties are incomplete because no accurate reports detailing the losses suffered by Pat Cleburne's and John Brown's divisions exist. Relatively complete records were, however, compiled by all of the divisions from A. P. Stewart's Corps. Additionally, William Bate and Edward Johnson provided totals for their respective divisions. In Stewart's Corps, the reported loss in killed, wounded, and missing or captured was 2,108. By division the totals were: Loring, 876; French,

---

[24] Hood, *Advance & Retreat*, p. 295-296; Figuers, *CV* 23, p. 7; Yeary, *Reminiscences of the Boys in Gray*, p. 230; Logsdon, *Eyewitnesses at the Battle of Franklin*. p. 83-84.

[25] Watkins, *Co. Aytch*, p. 218.

[26] Brown, ed. , *One of Cleburne's Command*, p. 151.

652; and Walthall, 580. From S. D. Lee's Corps, Johnson's Division reported total losses of 587 and Bate from Frank Cheatham's Corps tabulated 319 casualties. Nathan Bedford Forrest also reported 269 casualties for the month of November, but obviously not all of those men were lost at Franklin. It is safe to assume that not more than half were lost during the battle on November 30.[27]

Cleburne's and Brown's divisions suffered horrendous casualties and while official reports do not exist, the numbers can be surmised with relative accuracy. According to Gen. George Gordon, the percentage of loss by each division was an astonishing fifty-two percent for Cleburne and thirty-one percent for Brown. Even Gen. Daniel Govan said Cleburne's Division "was decimated" and lost "over half of its officers and men." Using the numbers of men who were effective for duty as of the November 6, 1864 field returns it seems Cleburne had at least 2,900 troops at Franklin. The return of November 6 indicates Cleburne had a strength of 3,962, but at Franklin he was minus one brigade, that of Gen. James Smith on detached duty, and he lost a number of men at Spring Hill.[28]

If Cleburne indeed lost fifty-two percent of his remaining force at Franklin, then the division suffered a loss of about 1,500. Brown's losses are somewhat easier to calculate. The November 6 returns show that his division numbered 3,715 effective for duty. A loss of thirty-one percent at Franklin would amount to about 1,150 casualties. Using these figures, and calculating half of Forrest's total loss as having occurred at Franklin, the Confederate army suffered at a bare minimum 5,800 casualties.[29]

The actual numbers, however, were far worse. When the Federals re-occupied Franklin two weeks later, following the Battle of Nashville, a detailed count was made in an effort to determine the true

---

[27] *OR* 45, pt. 1, p. 691, 715-716, 726, 743, 761.

[28] Gordon, *CV* 8, p. 9; Govan to his wife, Dec. 4, 1864, SHC. On a field return dated December 13, 1864 Smith's Brigade is listed as having 892 men effective and present. Considering he saw no action at Franklin and the return was done prior to Nashville, Smith's strength as of the November 6 return was approximately 900. See *OR* 45, pt. 1, p. 680.

[29] Gordon, *CV* 8, p. 9; *OR* 45, pt. 1, p. 678.

Southern loss. There were 1,750 Confederate graves discovered at Franklin and another 3,800 wounded soldiers were counted at hospitals in and around town. In addition, 702 Rebels had been captured and taken to Nashville on December 1. This brought the Army of Tennessee's total loss to 6,252, but that figure is likely still too low. During the two weeks after Franklin a number of wounded men returned to duty and thus were not found in any of the hospitals. Gen. Hood even confirmed the existence of large numbers of "slightly wounded men" several days after the battle. In the estimation of Jacob Cox the total number of Confederate casualties may have been "eight thousand or more."[30]

Federal losses at Franklin are more accurate due mostly to a more solid system of reporting. The official totals reported by Northern authorities were 189 killed, 1,033 wounded, and 1,104 missing and captured. As for the number of killed, however, a review of state roster and regimental muster rolls shows a number slightly in excess of the 189 reported after the battle and even those records are somewhat incomplete. It is not inconceivable that close to 300 Federal soldiers were killed outright at Franklin. Without question a number of the men reported as missing were actually dead, but many of the former were also prisoners taken mostly from the brigades of Cols. John Lane and Joseph Conrad. A number of Col. Silas Strickland's men were also captured. Even Hood referred to 1,000 prisoners being taken in both a telegram after the battle and in his official report.[31]

In total, the Battle of Franklin resulted in at least 8,500 total casualties. Considering the heaviest fighting lasted only about two hours and general combat was over in no more than five, the casualty figures, especially for the Confederates, are shocking. More Rebels were killed than had been in two days of hard fighting at Shiloh and George McClellan lost fewer men during the entire Seven Days Campaign. More Southerners were killed than either Robert E. Lee or John Pope lost at Second Manassas and there were more dead than Ambrose Burnside lost at Fredericksburg. The Army of Tennessee even buried

---

[30] *OR* 45, pt. 1, p. 344, 678-697; *OR* 45, pt. 2, p. 650; Cox, *Battle of Franklin*, p. 212.

[31] *OR* 45, pt. 1, p. 343, 654, 658; *OR* 45, pt. 2, p. 212; Livermore, *Numbers and Losses*, p. 131.

more men than it had at after three days at Stones River. Furthermore, if the Southern dead from First Manassas, Wilson's Creek, Fort Donelson, and Pea Ridge are added together the end result was still less than that at Franklin. It was a bloodbath of unparalleled proportions, one that cost John Bell Hood approximately one-third of the total infantry force sent to attack the Federal entrenchments. It was perhaps the greatest and most useless sacrifice of life the war ever witnessed. A soldier from the 16th Louisiana, spared from the battle, spoke to Gen. Randall L. Gibson about it afterward. Gibson said sincerely and simply, "The whole thing is inexplicable."[32]

Not only had the Army of Tennessee lost sickening numbers of men from its rank and file, but the officer corps was demolished. Fourteen field generals were casualties. Of those, five were killed, eight were wounded, and one was captured. Moreover, fifty-five regimental commanders listed as killed, wounded, captured, or missing. The inner workings of the army from top to bottom was an utter mess. Reviewing a full list of the officers does much to explain how terrible the battle was. The list is produced here, in simple alphabetical order:

Lt. Col. Robert H. Abercrombie, 45th Alabama, wounded.
Col. Thomas N. Adaire, 4th Mississippi, wounded.
Brig. Gen. John Adams, commanding brigade, killed.
Maj. John K. Allen, 30th Mississippi, missing.
Maj. E. Herbert Armistead, 22nd Alabama, wounded.
Col. Frederick A. Ashford, 16th Alabama, killed.
Lt. Col. Thomas M. Atkins, 49th Tennessee, wounded and captured.
Lt. Col. Edward N. Badger, 1st Florida Cavalry / 4th Florida Infantry, wounded.
Col. William H. Bishop, 7th / 9th Mississippi, killed.
Maj. John C. Bratton, 9th Arkansas, wounded.
Capt. J. W. Brown, 7th Texas, missing.
Maj. Gen. John C. Brown, commanding division, wounded.
Col. William N. Brown, 20th Mississippi, wounded.
Capt. Patrick Canniff, 3rd / 5th Missouri, killed.
Col. Ellison Capers, 24th South Carolina, wounded.
Brig. Gen. John C. Carter, commanding brigade, mortally wounded.

---

[32] Livermore, *Numbers and Losses*, p. 77-80, 86, 89, 96-97; R. H. Lindsay, "Seeing the Battle of Franklin," *CV* 9, p. 221.

Lt. Col. William F. Carter, 2nd / 6th Missouri, wounded.
Maj. Gen. Patrick R. Cleburne, commanding division, killed.
Brig. Gen. Francis M. Cockrell, commanding brigade, wounded.
Maj. Sylvester C. Cooper, 46th Tennessee, wounded and captured.
Capt. Aaron A. Cox, 5th Confederate, missing.
Col. Robert F. Crittenden, 33rd Alabama, missing.
Col. Charles J. L. Cunningham, 57th Alabama, wounded.
Col. Newton N. Davis, 24th Alabama, wounded.
Brig. Gen. Zachariah C. Deas, commanding brigade, wounded.
Capt. M. H. Dixon, 3rd Confederate, captured.
Maj. Samuel John Calhoun Dunlop, 46th Georgia, wounded.
Lt. Col. Samuel M. Dyer, 3rd Mississippi, wounded.
Col. Michael Farrell, 15th Mississippi, mortally wounded.
Capt. Rhoads Fisher, 6th Texas Infantry / 15th Texas Cavalry, missing.
Capt. Alfred V. Gardner, 29th Alabama, wounded.
Col. Hugh A. Garland, 1st / 4th Missouri, killed.
Capt. Mordecai P. Garrett, 1st / 15th Arkansas, killed.
Lt. Col. John S. Garvin, 26th Alabama, wounded.
Col. Elijah Gates, 1st / 3rd Missouri Cavalry, wounded.
Brig. Gen. States R. Gist, commanding brigade, killed.
Brig. Gen. George W. Gordon, commanding brigade, captured.
Brig. Gen. Hiram B. Granbury, commanding brigade, killed.
Lt. Col. Algernon S. Hamilton, 66th Georgia, wounded.
Capt. James M. Hicks, 41st Mississippi, wounded.
Col. Isaac N. Hulme, 42nd Tennessee, wounded.
Col. Samuel S. Ives, 27th / 35th / 49th Alabama, wounded.
Lt. Col. James M. Johnson, 30th Mississippi, wounded.
Maj. Samuel L. Knox, 1st Alabama, wounded and captured.
Maj. Joseph E. McDonald, 55th Tennessee, killed.
Maj. Turpin D. Magee, 46th Mississippi, wounded.
Col. Michael Magevney, Jr., 154th Tennessee, wounded.
Brig. Gen. Arthur M. Manigault, commanding brigade, wounded.
Maj. Amzi T. Meek, 2nd / 24th Arkansas, killed.
Col. Virgil S. Murphey, 17th Alabama, captured.
Col. Noel Ligdon Nelson, 12th Louisiana, mortally wounded.
Brig. Gen. William A. Quarles, commanding brigade, wounded.
Maj. George W. Reynolds, 29th Mississippi, killed.
Capt. James J. Rittenbury, 53rd Tennessee, wounded and captured.
Brig. Gen. Thomas M. Scott, commanding brigade, wounded.

Brig. Gen. Jacob H. Sharp, commanding brigade, wounded.
Col. Thomas P. Shaw, 19th South Carolina, wounded.
Lt. Col. William H. Sims, 10th / 44th Mississippi, wounded.
Col. George A. Smith, 1st Confederate Georgia, killed.
Lt. Col. Fountain E. P. Stafford, 31st Tennessee, killed.
Col. Marcus D. L. Stephens, 31st Mississippi, wounded and captured.
Brig. Gen. Otho F. Strahl, commanding brigade, killed.
Maj. William A. Taylor, 24th / 25th Texas Cavalry, missing.
Col. William H. H. Tison, 32nd Mississippi, wounded.
Col. John Weir, 5th Mississippi, wounded.
Col. John A. Wilson, 24th Tennessee, wounded.
Col. William W. Witherspoon, 36th Mississippi, killed.
Lt. Col. Robert Butler Young, 10th Texas, killed.[33]

A grand total of sixty-eight field officers became casualties. In Johnson's Division three of the four brigade commanders were casualties and Brown's Division lost the services of all four. Furthermore, because of Brown's wound Mark Lowrey was promoted to divisional command. W. W. Loring lost two of his three brigade commanders and Samuel French lost one of the two he had at Franklin. In the worst shape, however, was Cleburne's Division. Twelve regimental commanders were lost as well as one brigade commander and, of course, Cleburne himself was killed. Gen. James Smith, who arrived at Nashville on December 6, wrote that Cleburne's Division was "much reduced in numbers, especially officers" when he assumed command. Smith was shocked by what he saw. He said the "tone and morale" of the remaining men was not at all desirable. The division had left not only many of its numbers at Franklin, but its heart as well.[34]

One officer not on the original list who should have been was Gen. John Carter. Badly wounded by a bullet through his body, Carter was transferred from the battlefield to the Harrison House during the night of November 30. Carter was visited on the evening of December 3 by Chaplain Charles Quintard and evidence indicates the young

---

[33] *OR* 45, pt. 1, p. 684-686. Deas and Sharp were not listed in the original reports and Dixon and Murphey, although said to have been missing, were actually captured.
[34] *OR* 45, pt. 1, p. 739; Lowrey, *SHSP* 16, p. 374.

general sent a message to his father in Waynesboro, Georgia stating that he was "living and hopeful." Soon after this, however, Carter took a turn for the worse. By December 7, when Quintard again visited, Carter was "nearing his end." The chaplain said Carter ranged in and out of delirium and was in "frequent and intense" pain. He was administered repeated doses of chloroform to ease his suffering, but Carter could not be convinced that death was drawing near. Quintard finally asked if there was anything he wanted his wife to know. Carter said, "Tell her that I have always loved her devotedly and regret leaving her more than I can express." Quintard sat with Carter until after midnight before leaving. For two more days Carter struggled with complications before he died on Saturday, December 10. Arrangements for his funeral were made by Quintard and Carter was taken to Columbia and buried at Rose Hill Cemetery by Reverend David Pise. His internment there was apparently meant only to be temporary, but Carter's body was never claimed by his family after the war. It is said Mrs. Carter was so devastated by her husband's death that she never again spoke his name. His parents, hampered by the horrendous communication system, did not know about their son's death as late as mid-January 1865. Carter's father, desperate for some information, sent a letter to Frank Cheatham asking if he knew anything about his son's condition. The letter is heartbreaking, especially considering the young general had been dead for over a month when it was written. After his burial, Carter's resting place remained unmarked until the 1930's. It was then that the United Daughters of the Confederacy stepped in and erected a white marble headstone to his memory, some seventy years after his death.[35]

The Confederate army was a physical and psychological wreck on December 1. The survivors were in no condition to keep pushing onward. One Southerner said the men were "disheartened and demoralized" and he believed that the army should have "retired from the State" as soon as the dead were buried. But John Bell Hood had other plans. Considering the condition of his forces, Hood should have

---

[35] Quintard, Being His Story of the War, p. 118 119; Turner, *History of Maury County*, Quintard Diary, p. 222-223; E. J. Carter to Maj. Gen. Cheatham, Jan. 17, 1865, Cheatham Papers, TSLA. Information regarding Carter's wife and his headstone courtesy Bob Duncan, Maury County Archives, Columbia, TN.

chosen to withdraw to the south or at the very least he could have held his position at Franklin. Instead he decided to pursue the Federals to Nashville and circulars were distributed to each of the corps commanders late that morning. Nathan Bedford Forrest had moved out after the Yankees shortly after sunup and Hood chose S. D. Lee to take the advance for the infantry. A. P. Stewart was instructed to follow Lee and move across the Harpeth River by evening and bivouac his men at the "first good place" he could find. Stewart was then told to move his corps to Nashville "at daylight on December 2. As for Frank Cheatham's Corps, even Hood realized what sad condition that portion of his army was in. Cheatham was ordered to move across the river and march his corps toward Nashville on the morning of December 2. Cheatham's command was allowed to spend the rest of December 1 burying the dead, "reforming the broken, decimated ranks" and "caring for the wounded..."[36]

In his memoirs, Hood wrote extensively about why he ordered the army to follow the Yankees to Nashville:

> I could not afford to turn southward, unless for the special purpose of forming a junction with the expected reinforcement from Texas, and with the avowed intention to march back again upon Nashville. In truth, our Army was in that condition which rendered it more judicious the men should face a decisive issue rather than retreat - in other words, rather than renounce the honor of their cause, without having made a last and manful effort to lift up the sinking fortunes of the Confederacy.
>
> I therefore determined to move upon Nashville, to entrench, to accept the chances of reinforcement from Texas, and, even at the risk of an attack in the meantime by overwhelming numbers, to adopt the only feasible means of defeating the enemy with my reduced numbers, viz., to await his attack, and, if favored by success, to follow him into his works. I was apprised of each accession to Thomas's Army, but was still unwilling to abandon the ground as long as I saw a shadow of probability of assistance from the Trans-Mississippi Department, or of victory in battle; and, as I have just remarked, the troops would, I believed, return better satisfied even after defeat if, in grasping at the last straw, they felt that a brave and vigorous effort had been made to save the country from disaster. Such, at the time, was my opinion, which I have since

---

[36] *OR* 45, pt. 1, p. 731, 738; *OR* 45, pt. 2, p. 629-630.

had no reason to alter.[37]

It is clear that until the end of his life Hood did not doubt his decision to move on Nashville. His words speak volumes about the manner in which Hood gambled with the lives of his men after Franklin. He obviously understood the condition of his army following the battle yet still chose to continue onward. His talk of reinforcement from the lethargic Gen. Edmund Kirby Smith was a pipe dream because there was nothing to substantiate the idea that support was forthcoming from the Trans-Mississippi. Moreover, if Hood at the time actually understood how outnumbered the Rebel army was when it got to Nashville, his decision to keep it there is all the more condemnable. It was one thing to fight at Franklin in the manner which he did. It was altogether another to face off against those same Federal troops plus another full army corps and a five-brigade division. Whether he knew the enemy's actual strength or not, Hood acknowledged there was no chance his army could take the offensive. Instead he bet everything on the long hope that George Henry Thomas might somehow slip up. Hood had convinced himself that even if the Confederate army was beaten at Nashville, such a result was better than not having made the attempt. Compounding this train of thought was his unbelievable decision to split the army soon after Franklin.[38]

On December 2, he ordered Gen. William Bate to move his division toward Murfreesboro and tear up the railroad between that town and Nashville and destroy all the bridges and blockhouses. Confederate intelligence was so bad that Bate did not even know Murfreesboro was occupied by an enemy garrison until two days later. He notified Hood of this development and later that same day received belated word from the commanding general that the town was held by "some 5,000 Yankees..." The truth was that the Federals actually numbered almost 8,000. That same day Hood ordered Forrest to move two of his divisions, those commanded by Red Jackson and Abe Buford, to Murfreesboro and join Bate in an effort to overtake the Yankee garrison. Once again Hood played with his cavalry, leaving his right flank at Nashville almost completely unprotected while holding

---

37 Hood, *Advance & Retreat*, p. 299-300.

38 *OR* 45, pt. 2, p. 647.

James Chalmers and his division alone on the army's left. To assist Forrest, two brigades of infantry commanded by Brig. Gens. Claudius Sears and Joseph B. Palmer were also sent to Murfreesboro. On December 7 the attack against the Union garrison got underway. The result was a complete and abysmal failure. Forrest was disgusted with the effort, and wrote in his official report that the infantry, with the exception of the brigade led by Gen. Thomas Benton Smith, made "a shameful retreat..." After the debacle, Bate's Division and Sears' Brigade were ordered back to the main army at Nashville on December 9 and Forrest was told to remain in the Murfreesboro area. Forrest retained Palmer's Brigade and was given another, that of Col. Charles H. Olmstead. Olmstead had taken over James Smith's Brigade when the latter officer assumed command of Cleburne's Division. Ultimately the decision not to bring Forrest back to Nashville would impact Hood greatly in the coming days.[39]

The weather during the second week of December was dreadful. During the day on December 8 there was a sudden shift in temperature as a cold front roared in from the north. By the following day "the ground was covered with sleet and snow." The conditions, especially for the troops exposed to them, were miserable and the inclement weather lasted for nearly a week. Had it not been for this sudden change, Gen. Thomas likely would have lowered the boom on Hood earlier than he did. But the weather eventually broke, and on December 15 the Federal troops came out of their trenches and assaulted what remained of the Army of Tennessee. True to their nature the Southerners fought tenaciously, and although forced to give ground, they held together until nightfall. The next day Thomas ordered his men to attack again. They hit the Confederate right flank hard, but the blue clad troops were unable to make any headway. On the Rebel left, however, the situation was different. Under incredible pressure that wing began to unravel, and when James Wilson's cavalry slipped around the left everything fell apart. As the Yankee horsemen threatened to cut off the Confederate avenue of retreat all sense of order within the Army of Tennessee vanished. When the left folded up the center of Hood's line soon followed, almost like one domino knocking over the other. After the horrors of Franklin and two days of bruising conflict at

[39] *OR* 45, pt. 1, p. 739-740 744-747, 755.

Nashville, the battered Southern army completely collapsed. One historian wrote that it "was simply too much for weary, mortal men to stand." Some of those who had escaped the jaws of war at Franklin were not so lucky at Nashville. Gen. Sears lost a leg to artillery fire and Gens. Edward Johnson, Thomas B. Smith, and Henry Jackson were all captured. Col. Edmund W. Rucker, commanding a brigade in Chalmers' cavalry division, was shot in the left arm and also taken prisoner. By nightfall on December 16, S. D. Lee's Corps was the only large-scale unit able to stand and effectively fight. His men held off the Union hordes, covering Frank Cheatham's and A. P. Stewart's troops as they streamed south toward Franklin.[40]

For the next two weeks, Hood's badly beaten army tried frantically to escape destruction. Like at Franklin, Nathan Bedford Forrest was badly misused. On the night of December 16, Forrest learned of the disaster and immediately got his troops moving. Thanks to the tireless and heroic efforts of his cavalry and a hand-picked infantry division commanded by Edward Walthall, which combined to form the rear guard, Hood was able to escape annihilation. He began crossing what remained of the army over the Tennessee River at Florence, Alabama on Christmas Day. At that point Wilson's cavalry, which had been biting at the heels of the Southerners since Nashville, finally backed off. The disastrous invasion of Tennessee was over.[41]

Once the Army of Tennessee completed its move to the south side of the Tennessee River, the troops were marched to Tupelo, Mississippi to set up winter camp. The first to arrive were those from Lee's Corps who filed in on January 7. They were followed by Stewart's Corps two days later and Cheatham's Corps on January 12. Forrest's command followed but did not go to Corinth. Instead the cavalry found refuge at Verona, just south of Tupelo and next to the battlefield where Forrest and S. D. Lee had fought together just seven months earlier.[42]

As a whole the Rebel army was in ruinous condition, a shell of

---

[40] Horn, *Army of Tennessee*, p. 410, 417; Welsh, *Medical Histories of Confederate Generals*, p. 193; *OR* 45, pt. 2, p. 699, 774; Sword, *The Confederacy's Last Hurrah*, p. 388-389.

[41] *OR* 45, pt. 1, p. 724, 756-758.

[42] Ibid., p. 674, 751.

what it had been only six weeks earlier. According to the November 6 field return, Hood had 28,364 men effective for duty in his infantry and artillery branches, including all staff and escort. For clarity this author has chosen to detail the cavalry separately. The same November 6 return indicated 32,861 infantry and artillery present for duty. The difference between the two sets of numbers is easy to understand. Those listed as "effective" were officers and soldiers who were armed and able to fight. Not included in this number, but listed as "present for duty," were soldiers who were unarmed or served in a non-combatant roles such as medical attendants, cooks, wagon teamsters, and musicians. By the time an inspection report was completed for the army on January 20, the effective total of infantry and artillery was 18,682. Gen. Beauregard had an official field return completed the same day and his effective total for the infantry and artillery was 17,738. The most significant difference between the two reports can be found in the figures for Cheatham's and Stewart's corps. In all likelihood the discrepancy is the result of troops who were given short furloughs and Beauregard's filing did not count those men.[43]

The cavalry totals are somewhat problematic. Because no records exist which accurately detail the number of men Forrest had in his command at the beginning or end of the Tennessee Campaign, any calculations are rough at best. Perhaps the best source for data is Forrest himself. According to him the cavalry numbered 5,000 before Spring Hill and Franklin and totaled only 3,000 when it went into camp at Verona. Using these base figures Hood had about 33,300 effective for duty upon entering Tennessee and, incorporating Beauregard's January 20 report, about 20,700 in mid-January. According to Federal tabulations the Confederates suffered 6,252 casualties at Franklin and 4,462 Rebel troops were captured at Nashville. Southern killed and wounded at Nashville are unknown, but Hood said the number was "very small..." While it is true Hood vastly underestimated the army's casualties at Franklin, where he claimed only 4,500, he seems to have been far more accurate regarding Nashville. According to historian Tim Burgess, who has devoted years of research to Franklin and Nashville casualties, a reasonable estimate of killed and wounded at Nashville is

---

[43] *OR* 45, pt. 1, p. 664, 678; Roman, *The Military Operations of General Beauregard*, Vol. II, p. 633.

1,700. The Federals suffered 2,949 total casualties at Nashville and, considering they were on the offense while the Confederates were fighting behind defensive works, there is no reason to believe, aside from the prisoners taken, that Hood's troops suffered greater losses.[44]

John Bell Hood went to great lengths in his memoirs to try and prove his army did not suffer more than 10,000 casualties during the Tennessee Campaign. There is no doubt the number is greater. Consider the issue of prisoners. In his official report George Henry Thomas said 13,189 prisoners were taken in by Federal authorities from September 7, 1864 to January 20, 1865. That number, however, which includes deserters, is quite misleading. It must be reduced by 1,332 to account for prisoners who were exchanged in September 1864. Furthermore, there were 3,800 Confederate wounded found at Franklin by the Federals following Nashville. Those men were part of the previously mentioned casualty figure of 6,252. However, because they were also incorporated into Thomas' 13,189 figure they, too, must be deducted. By not doing this the 3,800 wounded are counted twice when calculating the campaign's total losses. With a new figure of 8,057 in hand Thomas' report takes on much greater clarity. A total of 1,513 prisoners and 181 deserters were also gathered in September and October so Confederates soldiers were obviously being processed who had nothing to do with the Army of Tennessee. By deducting these figures the prisoner total is lowered to 6,363. The remaining months surely saw a number of other soldiers turn themselves in who were likewise uninvolved with the invasion. S. D. Lee even brought up this issue in a letter written on December 6, 1864. Lee complained bitterly how "upwards of 6 or 7 thousand men went into Nashville ahead of our army to get out of reach of conscription..." Lee's estimate is undoubtedly exaggerated, but it is important to understand that soldiers who were absent without leave may have ended up in the custody of Federal officials in Nashville.[45]

So what were the campaign's total casualties? If one concludes

---

[44] *OR* 45, pt. 1, p. 40, 654, 759; *OR* 45, pt. 2, p. 699. Mr. Burgess has compiled a list of 353 Confederates killed at Nashville. While the list is not complete he believes the true figure is not significantly higher.

[45] Hood, *Advance & Retreat*, p. 308-310; *OR* 45, pt. 1, p. 46-48; Lee to Harrison, Dec. 6, 1864, SHC.

the Franklin losses were 6,252, Nashville's killed and wounded totaled 1,700, prisoners and deserters not rounded up at Franklin amounted to about 6,000, and Forrest lost 2,000 men, then the total Southern casualties amounted to 15,952. If Hood entered Tennessee with some 33,300 effective for duty and in mid-January 20,700 were effective, it is clear a large number of men wounded during the campaign returned to duty before its conclusion. Small additions were also made by new recruits and it is possible some absentees may have even returned to duty.[46]

The losses suffered by the Confederates during the Tennessee Campaign were staggering. Nearly forty percent of Hood's army had been lost and the troops who remained were nearing collapse. The invasion to win back Tennessee ended in abysmal failure.

Word had been circulating for some time that disaster had befallen the Confederate army after Franklin. What Gen. Beauregard found when he arrived at Tupelo only confirmed everyone's worst fears. John Bell Hood was aware that the army was in disastrous condition and two days before Beauregard's arrival he had telegraphed Secretary of War James A. Seddon offering his resignation. Hood also knew that he had been less than honest about the calamity at Nashville. A telegram sent to Beauregard and Seddon on December 17 barely scratched the surface of the truth. Then a suspicious wire was received by Beauregard, sent by Col. George W. Brent who was stationed in Montgomery, Alabama. Brent told the Creole general that S. D. Lee had been in contact from Florence, Alabama and said "he would be glad to have General Beauregard's view in regard to recent events in Tennessee." Brent said he did not understand what Lee's message

---

[46] See Sword, *The Confederacy's Last Hurrah*, p. 426. Sword's primary error was in accepting the 13,189 prisoner figure at face value. As mentioned previously Jacob Cox believed there may have been an additional 2,000 wounded at Franklin who were never counted as official casualties because they returned to duty before the field return of December 10, 1864 was composed. If Cox is correct the campaign's total casualties are indeed higher, but they do not change the facts of the January 20, 1865 field return totals. Such men, although wounded, were effective for duty as of mid-January. See Cox, *Battle of Franklin*, p. 212-213.

meant, but became "apprehensive that some reverse may have occurred." Beauregard became sufficiently alarmed and on December 31 asked permission from Jefferson Davis to relieve Hood and replace him with Gen. Richard Taylor if necessary. Davis responded two days later by approving the request.[47]

Other exchanges of information were buzzing around as well. In a letter to Taylor written on January 2, 1865, Nathan Bedford Forrest pulled no punches when he explained the "Army of Tennessee was badly defeated and is greatly demoralized..." James Cooper of the 20th Tennessee said the men were "thoroughly demoralized, and only a semblance of discipline remained." In an effort to counter the bad news John Bell Hood fired off several telegrams from Corinth on January 3. One went to Secretary Seddon and stated that the army had "recrossed the Tennessee River, without material loss since the battle in front of Nashville..." He made no mention of the true condition of the army. In a second wire to Beauregard, Hood stated only that the troops were being readied for a move to Tupelo so they "may have some rest and obtain a supply of shoes and clothing."[48]

The day following Beauregard's arrival at Tupelo he had a "long and important" conference with Hood. During the meeting Hood confided that he had sent a telegram of resignation to Seddon. Beauregard claimed the commanding general was so "humiliated" and "utterly crushed" by recent events that he did not have the heart to relieve Hood of duty. More likely, Beauregard felt Hood's request would surely be granted so there was no need to get involved.[49]

As Beauregard expected the War Department wasted little time endorsing John Bell Hood's request. On January 17, a telegram from James Seddon arrived at Tupelo instructing Beauregard to relieve Hood at once and appoint Richard Taylor to command of the army. One week later Hood officially took leave of the Army of Tennessee, just over six months after being appointed to lead it. It was surely one of the saddest days of his life. Hood had tried desperately to save Atlanta and reclaim Middle Tennessee for his beloved Confederacy.

---

[47] *OR* 45, pt. 2, p. 699, 731, 749, 753, 781.

[48] *OR* 45, pt. 2, p. 756-758; Cooper, *CV* 33, p. 223.

[49] *OR* 45, pt. 2, p. 781; Roman, *Military Operations of General Beauregard*, Vol. II, p. 331-332; Hood, *Advance & Retreat*, p. 310.

Unfortunately for him, and especially his men, he had success with neither and instead met only crushing defeats. In his farewell address Hood wrote to his men that he alone was responsible for the idea behind the Tennessee Campaign and said he had "strived hard" to do his duty.[50]

Even before John Bell Hood left Tupelo, what remained of the army began moving via the railroad to destination points in the east. There they cobbled together with other Southern forces in an effort to stem William Sherman's advance north through the Carolinas. Through the Confederacy's final and desperate gasps the survivors of the Tennessee campaign were again led by Joseph Johnston. The effort was a futile one, however, as Sherman's legions vastly outnumbered the Rebel troops. The end came soon and following Robert E. Lee's surrender at Appomattox Court House, Johnston did the same with his ramshackle army. Throughout the rest of the spring, the first one to see peace in four years, the men of the former Army of Tennessee slowly filtered home. They had given everything they had and new trials awaited them. But no matter what their future path was to be memories of Spring Hill and Franklin would never far away.[51]

For Hood, without a field command or any specific orders, the last months of the war amounted to little. He stopped in Columbia, South Carolina on his way to Richmond to visit his fiancé Sally Preston, who seemed strangely distant during the visit. Diarist Mary Chesnut also saw Hood and wrote that he talked of his army's terrible defeat and insisted no one was to fault for what had happened in Tennessee except himself. The general was in Richmond, Virginia by February 8 where he finished his official report of the campaign. There he faced a blistering storm of criticism in the newspapers about the handling of the Tennessee invasion. Perhaps only President Davis was treated more harshly by the editors. Hood left Virginia and traveled to South Carolina in early April. There he spent time with Sally again and the painful decision to break off their engagement was made. A major obstacle for the couple seems to have been Sally's sister and her parents, all of whom were steadfastly opposed to any marriage between the two. Hood chose to pursue the matter no further. It seemed pointless to

---

[50] *OR* 45, pt. 2, p. 785, 805.

[51] Ibid., p. 795.

him to try and pursue the woman he loved through the objections of her family. Having been through hell and back, both personally and professionally, Hood finally called off the offensive. He left Sally behind, never to return. The general soon traveled west and finally surrendered to Federal authorities at the end of May 1865. It was said of John Bell Hood at the time that perhaps "now his great sad eyes could laugh occasionally."[52] Only time would tell.

In February 1865, Pvt. James H. Watson of the 57th Indiana wrote a letter home to a friend describing the action at Spring Hill and Franklin. Watson explained that Hood had very nearly whipped the Federal army at Spring Hill. Then, in a single sentence, he summed up what happened to Hood at Franklin. Watson wrote, "On the 30th he hitched into us again but that day was our time to whip, we gave him a whipping he will never forget."[53]

---

[52] McMurry, *John Bell Hood*, p. 183, 188-189; Dyer, *The Gallant Hood*, 305-309.

[53] Watson to Vail, Feb. 25, 1865, letter in possession of Gwynne Evans of Spring Hill, TN.

12

Now There Can Be Peace

In the spring of 1866 John and Carrie McGavock became concerned about the condition of the Confederate graves on the Franklin battlefield. One year after the war's conclusion the Federal dead had already been removed to either private or military cemeteries. A large number of the Northern troops killed at Franklin were transferred to the national cemetery at Murfreesboro. The Southern dead, however, mostly languished where they had been buried in the aftermath of the battle. The South was destitute after the war and only a few families were able to retrieve the bodies of loved ones lost at Franklin. A number of the original wooden headboards used to mark the graves in December 1864 had disappeared and others were becoming increasingly difficult to read. It was clear to Mr. and Mrs. McGavock that something needed to be done.

Moved to action they donated two acres of ground near their home at Carnton as a permanent burial site for the soldiers who had died. The McGavocks and other Franklin citizens soon began fund-raising efforts to garner the money necessary for exhumation and reburial of the Confederate soldiers. Since the troops had originally been buried in plots according to the states for which they fought, the same arrangement was decided upon for the new location. In April 1866 the difficult process of disinterring the dead began and by the end of June it was complete. The total number of bodies buried at what became known as the McGavock Confederate Cemetery was 1,481. There were twelve states represented in a dozen sections with a thirteenth for men whose name or unit affiliation could not be determined. The sections were arranged in two long columns set in the order of platoons in column and an avenue of twelve feet was set between the columns. In death as in life the men would retain their military bearing.[1]

The breakdown of graves is as follows:

Mississippi - 424
Tennessee - 230
Missouri - 130
Alabama - 129
Arkansas - 104
Texas - 89
Georgia - 69
South Carolina - 51
Louisiana - 19
Kentucky - 5
Florida - 4
North Carolina - 2
Unknown - 225

It is interesting to note that not all of these men were killed as a result of the fighting at Franklin on November 30. The North Carolina troops and some of the Louisiana men were killed in the weeks following and were simply moved with the rest of the bodies when the re-burials occurred.[2]

News of the McGavock Cemetery quickly spread and visitors began flocking to it by the summer of 1866. Veterans were especially moved by its quiet beauty. An iron fence was added in 1867 and during the post-war years the cemetery was a powerful reminder of what the country had undergone. The original grave markers were made of cedar and had the name, company, and regiment of each identified man carved into them. With the passage of time, however, weather took its toll on the wooden markers and in 1890 they were replaced with stone markers. Thanks to a complete record of each grave, kept by Carrie

[1] Potts and Hudgins, *McGavock Confederate Cemetery*, p. 3, 23.

[2] Ibid., p. 3. Information concerning the North Carolina troops and handful of Louisiana soldiers courtesy of Thomas Cartwright, Carter House Museum, Franklin, TN.

McGavock in a hand-written journal, it was possible to accurately engrave the new markers. Those states with men in the cemetery were asked to contribute $2.00 per grave to cover the cost of the new stones. Only Mississippi, South Carolina, Louisiana, and Missouri responded with the money requested, however, and the citizens of Franklin raised the balance on their own.[3]

John McGavock died in 1893 and Carrie followed him in 1905. Upon Mrs. McGavock's death, Carnton and the surrounding property was inherited by John and Carrie's son Winder, who was only seven years old at the time of the battle. He died suddenly in 1907 and his widow sold the house and remaining land in 1911. The man who purchased it from her deeded the cemetery into the hands of a local group dedicated to its care and preservation.

The cemetery has been meticulously cared for in the years since the McGavocks died, but Carnton was not quite so lucky. For over sixty years the house was privately owned and in later years fell into disrepair. In 1977 the Carnton Association was formed and the next year the organization obtained the home and ten surrounding acres. Today Carnton has been restored to its nineteenth century splendor although reminders of the battle still exist. The blood-stained upstairs floorboards are alone proof of the horrors witnessed that night. Both Carnton and the McGavock Confederate Cemetery remain humbling reminders of the tremendous sacrifices made at the Battle of Franklin. John and Carrie would be proud.

Memories die hard and the years and decades following the Civil War witnessed efforts to bring home four of the Confederate generals who had perished at Franklin. The first to return to his native soil was States Rights Gist. Gist had been buried at a private residence in Franklin the morning after the battle and in the spring of 1866 his body was exhumed by his family and taken back to South Carolina. On May 10, Gen. Gist was laid to permanent rest at Trinity Episcopal Church in the state capital of Columbia. His wife Janie, who remarried in 1868, lived until 1911.[4]

By the time Patrick Cleburne was brought back to Arkansas, his former fiancé Susan Tarleton had been dead for nearly two years. Sue

---

[3] Ibid., p. 6.

[4] Cisco, *States Rights Gist*, p. 147-148.

was devastated when she learned of Cleburne's death five days after the Battle of Franklin and remained in deep mourning for a year. In 1867 she married another man, but died suddenly less than twelve months later. In 1870 a movement was initiated by the Ladies' Memorial Association of Phillips County to bring Cleburne's remains back to Helena, Arkansas. On April 27, 1870 a small group of men, including former aide Leonard Mangum, arrived at Ashwood Cemetery to complete the first leg of the general's journey home. A ceremony was held in Memphis the following day and on April 29 Cleburne was taken to Helena and buried at Evergreen Cemetery (now known as Magnolia Cemetery) on a bluff overlooking the Mississippi River. In 1891 a beautiful monument was erected over the general's grave and a commemorative speech was delivered by George Gordon, who had fought with Cleburne at Franklin.[5]

Hiram Granbury was also removed from his place at Ashwood and buried elsewhere. Granbury was taken to a Texas town southwest of Fort Worth that had been named in his honor in 1866. Granbury, who had led his Texans up the middle at Franklin and stood with them next to the turnpike at Spring Hill, was placed into eternal rest on November 30, 1893, twenty-nine years to the day after the battle that had ended his life. Sadly, not only was the name on his headstone spelled incorrectly, Granberry instead of Granbury, but the general was forever separated from his wife Fannie. She had died of ovarian cancer in March 1863 and was buried in an unmarked grave in Mobile, Alabama. She and Hiram had been married less than five years and they had no children. Their personal story is another heart-rending episode linked to the great tragedy at Franklin.[6]

Otho Strahl was the last of the Confederate generals to be removed from Ashwood and taken home. Strahl had lived in Dyersburg, Tennessee before the war and on April 4, 1901 friends and veterans had his remains disinterred and transported back to his adopted hometown. Among those involved in Strahl's reburial was Sumner Cunningham, who had been standing in the ditch outside the

---

[5] Joslyn, ed., *A Meteor Shining Brightly*, p. 288-290; Purdue, *Pat Cleburne*, p. 434-437.

[6] Drake and Holder, *Hiram B. Granbury*, p. 39.

Federal works with the general when he was shot and killed.[7]

Lt. John Marsh and Lt. Col. Robert Young remained undisturbed in the quiet cemetery behind St. John's Episcopal Church. They rest there today, along with Col. Robert Beckham. In their midst are the vacant plots where the trio of generals were once buried.

After the war the central figures who were involved at Spring Hill and Franklin traveled many different paths. George Wagner was demoted to brigade command following his disastrous performance at Franklin and chose to resign rather than face further humiliation. Wagner died on February 13, 1869 from the effects of medication he was taking for treatment of a nervous condition. Emerson Opdycke lived in New York City, worked in the dry-goods business, and remained active in veteran affairs. He died on April 22, 1884 after accidentally shooting himself while cleaning a pistol. Jacob Cox lived a long life and served as governor of Ohio and Interior Secretary during U. S. Grant's presidential administration. He resumed his law practice and taught school and wrote extensively about Spring Hill and Franklin. Death called the old soldier home on August 4, 1900. George Henry Thomas was given command of the Division of the Pacific after the war, but he died suddenly at his desk in San Francisco on March 28, 1870. David Stanley commanded the 22nd U. S. Infantry after the Civil War and led the Yellowstone Expedition of 1873. He died on March 13, 1902. James Wilson resigned his commission following the war and worked as an engineer and on the railroad. He returned to serve his country during the Spanish-American War and died on February 23, 1925 at the ripe old age of eighty-eight. John Schofield went on to a long and successful military career. He was briefly Secretary of War under President Andrew Johnson and also served as superintendent of West Point for five years. In 1888 he became commanding general of all U. S. Army forces. Among his most noteworthy accomplishments was the selection of Pearl Harbor in the Hawaiian Islands as a military

---

[7] Sumner Cunningham, "Gen. O. F. Strahl, Buried at Dyersburg," *CV* 9, p. 148-149; Jill K. Garrett, "St. John's Church, Ashwood," *THQ* 29, No. 1, p. 20. This author was unable to find a single source listing the exact date of Strahl's reburial. Cemetery records, historical societies, and libraries were unable to provide the information.

base. Schofield died on March 4, 1906.[8]

Among the Confederates, Nathan Bedford Forrest involved himself with farming and business ventures. More infamously he became involved with the Ku Klux Klan, but called for its disbandment when the organization became excessively violent. He died on October 29, 1877. William Bate went on to serve two terms as Tennessee governor and was a member of the U. S. Senate before dying on March 9, 1905. John Brown became governor of Tennessee twice and also served as president of a railroad company. Brown died on August 17, 1889 and was buried in the same cemetery as Gen. John Adams. Frank Cheatham returned to farming after the war and later held positions as superintendent of the Tennessee State Prison and Nashville postmaster. Cheatham passed away on September 4, 1886. A. P. Stewart had a busy and very noteworthy post-war life. He was a professor at Cumberland University in Tennessee, worked for the Mutual Life Insurance Company, was chancellor of the University of Mississippi, and also served as commissioner of the newly opened Chickamauga and Chattanooga National Battlefield Park. Old Straight died on August 30, 1908 at the age of eighty-six. John Bell Hood worked during the years after the war as a cotton factor and commission merchant and later headed the Life Association of America insurance company. Hood married Anne Marie Hennen in 1868 and the two had a happy life together, enjoying the birth of eleven children including three sets of twins. Hood began working on his memoirs in about 1875 and completed the book early in 1879. But tragedy struck he and his family that summer. Hood lived in New Orleans and yellow fever could strike without warning during the heat and humidity of the summer. It found the Hood home in 1879 and killed the general's wife on August 24. Two days later his eldest daughter Lydia, only ten years old, was stricken and as she worsened Hood became sick with the fever on August 27. Lydia died on August 30 at around noon and her father grew violently ill that afternoon. By evening the end was drawing near. At just after 11 p.m. Hood was wracked with the final violent stages of yellow fever and closed his eyes and died. At forty-eight years of age, John Bell

---

[8] *OR* 45, pt. 1, p. 152; *OR* 45, pt. 2, p. 117; Faust, ed., *Historical Times Encyclopedia*, p. 188, 547, 661, 712, 754, 795, 832-833.

Post-war view of the Carter cotton gin. The Union line ran horizontally across this image. (Carter House Archives)

Hood's abbreviated and often controversial life was over.[9]

Life went on for the Carter family following the Battle of Franklin. In the spring of 1865, Moscow Carter tore down both the advanced and main line of works, not only to prepare some of the ground for planting, but also to return some sense of normalcy to the family's property. A Federal officer who visited Franklin in early May noted that the breastworks, along the length of which had occurred so much death and suffering, were "nearly all leveled down and the fences re-built and the ground under cultivation." Once again the battlefield was a place where crops were grown and animals quietly grazed. Fountain Branch Carter, who had lost so much at the hands of the battle, died on August 22, 1871 and left the house and nineteen acres of land to Moscow. The eldest Carter son lived there until 1896, when the house and property were deeded to new owners after Moscow decided to move east of town to Triune. By the time Moscow Carter left the family home, Franklin was rapidly changing. A beautiful new school,

---

[9] Faust, ed., *Historical Times Encyclopedia*, p. 44, 83, 135, 270, 369, 719; Dyer, *The Gallant Hood*, p. 318-319; McMurry, *John Bell Hood*, 202-203.

the Battle Ground Academy, had been constructed just east of Columbia Pike. The school was dedicated in 1889 and sat on the northeast corner of present day Columbia Avenue and Cleburne Street. A year earlier the cotton gin had been torn down and Moscow donated stones from the foundation pillars to build a cenotaph commemorating Patrick Cleburne. To pay for construction of the monument each child then attending the academy was asked to donate a dime. Unfortunately the school burned in 1902 and it was rebuilt on the west side of Columbia Avenue. While the new academy was being erected, the class of 1903 celebrated their graduation at the Everbright mansion.[10]

By the turn of the century Franklin had undergone significant transformation. There were no plans by the Federal government to design a national battlefield park at Franklin, so development continued unabated on the sacred ground. By the late 1890's most of the property around the Carter House, which was rural at the time of the battle, had been sectioned into lots and streets. When the first Battle Ground Academy burned, George Matthews purchased the property where it had stood and began construction on a new house. Since the home was built almost precisely where some of the Union works had been, many bullets and other artifacts were found. Sadly Matthews also dismantled the Cleburne cenotaph. When a hole was dug for a banana tree near the location of the old salient, two Yankee cartridge boxes were found. The situation was much the same whenever a new home was built along the former Federal line. Construction work to this day regularly yields battlefield items. The author owns a Federal breastplate which was dug up along Columbia Avenue several years ago during routine work by a telephone company. It is not hard to imagine that it may have come from one of George Wagner's troops as the frantic rush toward the works occurred.[11]

---

[10] Robison, *THQ* 22, No. 1, p. 17; Smith, *History of Maury County*, Interview with Moscow Carter, p. 203; Milton Barnes to Rhoda Barnes, May 4, 1865, GMU; William Bate dedication address for Battle-Ground Academy, p. 11-12, TSLA. Information about BGA's comes from a conversation with Jimmie French of Franklin, TN on January 7, 2005.

[11] Robison, *THQ* 22, No. 1, p. 18; Smith, *History of Maury County*, Interview with Moscow Carter, p. 203.

From 1890 until 1949 nearly two dozen bills were introduced in the United States Congress in the hopes of building a memorial park at Franklin. Nothing ever came of any of the bills and the battlefield was effectively lost. The same fate nearly befell the Carter House, but thankfully the State of Tennessee stepped in and purchased the home and several acres of adjoining land in 1951. Included in the purchase were the brick smokehouse, the extended brick kitchen, and the wooden office building, all of which had miraculously survived the handful of owners who occupied the property after Moscow Carter moved out.[12]

Today the Carter House stands in the heart of a bustling city. It still displays its scars from the battle, but the smokehouse and office building are the most vivid reminders of what happened there. The southern faces of both buildings are covered with hundreds of holes and pockmarks caused by the impact of bullets. To gaze upon those exposed walls is to look at history and have it stare right back at you. As you walk between the buildings, treading the same ground as did both Union and Confederate soldiers during a few frantic moments, the emotions can run high. To then stand and look at the Carter House and try to imagine what happened in the yard of a very typical American family is a surreal experience. The battlefield may be mostly gone, but the story survives. What happened at Franklin is timeless. It was real life and death seared into the very fabric of American history. When you begin to understand that the men who fought there were much more than just an old faded photograph or a name in a book their struggle takes on a whole new meaning. They were real men and boys, with real feelings, real families, real dreams, and real opinions about what was right. Theirs is a story that will never die.

---

[12] Robison, *THQ* 22, No. 1, p. 17-18.

Organization of the Confederate Army at Spring Hill & Franklin November 29-30, 1864

Lieutenant General John Bell Hood, Commanding

Cheatham's Corps
Major General Benjamin Franklin Cheatham

Infantry

Cleburne's Division
Major General Patrick Ronayne Cleburne

Govan's Brigade
Brigadier General Daniel Chevilette Govan

3rd Confederate Infantry, 1st / 15th Arkansas Infantry,
2nd / 24th Arkansas Infantry, 5th / 13th Arkansas Infantry,
6th / 7th Arkansas Infantry, 8th / 19th Arkansas Infantry

Lowrey's Brigade
Brigadier General Mark Perrin Lowrey

3rd Mississippi Battalion / 5th Mississippi Infantry,
8th Mississippi Infantry / 32nd Mississippi Infantry,
16th / 33rd / 45th Alabama Infantry

Granbury's Brigade
Brigadier General Hiram Bronson Granbury

5th Confederate Infantry, 7th Texas Infantry, 10th Texas Infantry,
6th Texas Infantry / 15th Texas Cavalry (dismounted),
17th / 18th Texas Cavalry (dismounted),
24th / 25th Texas Cavalry (dismounted),
35th Tennessee,* Nutt's Louisiana Cavalry Company **

* The 35th Tennessee was permanently detached from the brigade and served as the Army of Tennessee's Provost Guard.
** Capt. L. M. Nutt's unit was attached to Company L of the 10th Texas Infantry.

Brown's Division
Major General John Calvin Brown

Gist's Brigade
Brigadier General States Rights Gist

2nd Battalion Georgia Sharpshooters, 16th South Carolina Infantry,
24th South Carolina Infantry, 46th Georgia Infantry,
65th Georgia Infantry / 8th Georgia Battalion

Gordon's Brigade *
Brigadier General George Washington Gordon

11th / 29th Tennessee Infantry, 12th / 47th Tennessee Infantry,
13th / 51st / 52nd Tennessee Infantry, 154th Tennessee Infantry

* Often referred to as Vaughan's Brigade, but Gordon took permanent command of the brigade in July 1864 and so his name is used here.

Strahl's Brigade
Brigadier General Otho French Strahl

4th / 5th / 33rd / 38th Tennessee Infantry,
19th / 41st Tennessee Infantry, 24th Tennessee Infantry,
31st Tennessee Infantry

Carter's Brigade *
Brigadier General John Carpenter Carter

1st / 27th Tennessee Infantry,
4th (provisional) / 6th / 9th / 50th Tennessee Infantry,
8th/ 16th / 28th Tennessee Infantry

* Often referred to as Maney's Brigade, but Carter took permanent command of the brigade in Sept. 1864 and so his name is used here.

Bate's Division
Major General William Brimage Bate

Finley's Brigade
Colonel Robert Bullock

1st Florida Cavalry (dismounted) / 4th Florida Infantry,
1st / 3rd Florida Infantry, 6th Florida Infantry, 7th Florida Infantry

Smith's Brigade *
Brigadier General Thomas Benton Smith

2nd / 10th / 20th / 37th Tennessee Infantry,
15th / 30th Tennessee Infantry, 37th Georgia Infantry,
4th Battalion Georgia Sharpshooters

* Often referred to as Tyler's Brigade, but Smith had been in permanent command of the brigade for over a year and so his name is used here.

Jackson's Brigade
Brigadier General Henry Rootes Jackson

1st Georgia Infantry (provisional), 1st Battalion Georgia Sharpshooters, 25th Georgia Infantry, 29th / 30th Georgia Infantry, 66th Georgia Infantry

Artillery

Colonel Melancthon Smith

Hotchkiss' Battalion
Bledsoe's Missouri Battery, Goldthwaite's Alabama Battery, Key's Arkansas Battery

Hoxton's Battalion
Perry's Florida Battery, Phelan's Alabama Battery, Turner's Mississippi Battery

Cobb's Battalion
Ferguson's South Carolina Battery, Phillip's Tennessee Battery, Slocumb's Louisiana Battery

Stewart's Corps
Lieutenant General Alexander Peter Stewart

Infantry

Loring's Division
Major General William Wing Loring

Adams' Brigade
Brigadier General John Adams

6th Mississippi Infantry, 14th Mississippi Infantry, 15th Mississippi Infantry, 20th Mississippi Infantry, 23rd Mississippi Infantry, 43rd Mississippi Infantry

Featherston's Brigade
Brigadier General Winfield Scott Featherston

1st Battalion Mississippi Sharpshooters, 1st Mississippi Infantry, 3rd Mississippi Infantry, 22nd Mississippi Infantry, 31st Mississippi Infantry, 33rd Mississippi Infantry, 40th Mississippi Infantry

Scott's Brigade
Brigadier General Thomas Moore Scott

12th Louisiana Infantry, 27th / 35th / 49th Alabama Infantry, 55th Alabama Infantry, 57th Alabama Infantry

Walthall's Division
Major General Edward Cary Walthall

Quarles' Brigade
Brigadier General William Andrew Quarles

1st Alabama Infantry, 42nd Tennessee Infantry, 46th Tennessee Infantry, 48th Tennessee Infantry *, 49th Tennessee Infantry, 53rd Tennessee Infantry, 55th Tennessee Infantry

* The 48th Tennessee had been furloughed at Columbia and was not present at either Spring Hill or Franklin.

Cantey's Brigade
Brigadier General Charles Miller Shelley

17th Alabama Infantry, 26th Alabama Infantry, 29th Alabama Infantry, 37th Mississippi Infantry

Reynolds' Brigade
Brigadier General Daniel Harris Reynolds

1st Arkansas Mounted Rifles (dismounted),
2nd Arkansas Mounted Rifles (dismounted),
4th / 31st Arkansas Infantry / 4th Arkansas Battalion,
9th Arkansas Infantry, 25th Arkansas Infantry

French's Division
Major General Samuel Gibbs French

Cockrell's Brigade
Brigadier General Francis Marion Cockrell

1st / 4th Missouri Infantry, 2nd / 6th Missouri Infantry,
3rd / 5th Missouri Infantry,
1st Missouri Cavalry (dismounted) / 3rd Missouri Cavalry (dismounted)

Sears' Brigade
Brigadier General Claudius Wistar Sears

4th Mississippi Infantry, 7th Battalion Mississippi Infantry,
35th Mississippi Infantry, 36th Mississippi Infantry,
39th Mississippi Infantry, 46th Mississippi Infantry

Artillery

Lieutenant Colonel Samuel C. Williams

Myrick's Battalion
Bouanchaud's Louisiana Battery, Cowan's Mississippi Battery,
Darden's Mississippi Battery

Storr's Battalion
Guibor's Missouri Battery, Hoskin's Mississippi Battery,
Kolb's Alabama Battery

Truehart's Battalion
Lumsden's Alabama Battery, Selden's Alabama Battery,
Tarrant's Alabama Battery

Lee's Corps
Lieutenant General Stephen Dill Lee

Infantry

Johnson's Division
Major General Edward Johnson

Deas' Brigade
Brigadier General Zachariah Cantey Deas

19th Alabama Infantry, 22nd Alabama Infantry,
25th Alabama Infantry, 39th Alabama Infantry,
26 / 50th Alabama Infantry

Sharp's Brigade
Brigadier General Jacob Hunter Sharp

7th / 9th Mississippi Infantry, 41st Mississippi Infantry
10th / 44th Mississippi Infantry / 9th Battalion Mississippi Sharpshooters

Brantley's Brigade
Brigadier General William Felix Brantley

24th / 34th Mississippi Infantry, 27th Mississippi Infantry,
29th / 30th Mississippi Infantry

Manigault's Brigade
Brigadier General Arthur Middleton Manigault

10th South Carolina Infantry, 19th South Carolina Infantry,
24th Alabama Infantry, 28th Alabama Infantry, 34th Alabama Infantry

Clayton's Division
Major General Henry DeLamar Clayton

Stovall's Brigade
Brigadier General Marcellus Augustus Stovall

40th Georgia Infantry, 41st Georgia Infantry, 42nd Georgia Infantry, 43rd Georgia Infantry, 52nd Georgia Infantry

Gibson's Brigade
Brigadier General Randall Lee Gibson

1st Louisiana Infantry, 4th Louisiana Infantry, 4th Louisiana Battalion*, 13th Louisiana Infantry, 14th Battalion Louisiana Sharpshooters, 16th Louisiana Infantry, 19th Louisiana Infantry, 20th Louisiana Infantry, 25th Louisiana Infantry, 30th Louisiana Infantry

* Detached and guarding the pontoon train at Florence, AL.

Holtzclaw's Brigade
Brigadier General James Thadeus Holtzclaw

18th Alabama Infantry, 32nd / 58th Alabama Infantry, 36th Alabama Infantry, 38th Alabama Infantry

Stevenson's Division
Major General Carter Littlepage Stevenson

Pettus' Brigade
Brigadier General Edmund Winston Pettus

20th Alabama Infantry, 23rd Alabama Infantry, 30th Alabama Infantry, 31st Alabama Infantry, 46th Alabama Infantry

Cummings' Brigade
Colonel Elihu P. Watkins

34th Georgia Infantry, 36th Georgia Infantry,
39th Georgia Infantry, 56th Georgia Infantry

Palmer's Brigade
Colonel Joseph B. Palmer

3rd /18th Tennessee Infantry, 23rd / 26th / 45th Tennessee Infantry,
32nd Tennessee Infantry, 54th Virginia Infantry,
63rd Virginia Infantry, 58th North Carolina Infantry *,
60th North Carolina Infantry

* Detached from brigade for duty in Columbia.

Artillery

Colonel Robert F. Beckham *
Major John W. Johnston

* Mortally wounded at Columbia on November 29.

Courtney's Battalion
Dent's Alabama Battery, Douglas' Texas Battery,
Garrity's Alabama Battery

Eldridge's Battalion
Eufaula Alabama Battery, Fenner's Louisiana Battery,
Stanford's Mississippi Battery

Johnston's Battalion
Corput's Georgia Battery, Marshall's Tennessee Battery,
Stephen's Light Artillery

Cavalry

Major General Nathan Bedford Forrest

Chalmers' Division
Brigadier General James Ronald Chalmers

Rucker's Brigade
Colonel Edmund W. Rucker

3rd Tennessee Cavalry (aka Forrest's Tennessee Regiment),
5th Mississippi Cavalry; 7th Alabama Cavalry, 7th Tennessee Cavalry,
10th Tennessee Cavalry, 12th Tennessee Cavalry,
14th Tennessee Cavalry, 15th Tennessee Cavalry

Biffle's Brigade
Colonel Jacob B. Biffle

4th Tennessee Cavalry*, 11th Tennessee Cavalry,
19th Tennessee Cavalry

* The 4th Tennessee consisted of only four companies.

Buford's Division
Brigadier General Abraham Buford

Bell's Brigade
Colonel Tyree Harris Bell

2nd Tennessee Cavalry, 18th Tennessee Cavalry,
20th Tennessee Cavalry, 21st Tennessee Cavalry,
22nd Tennessee Cavalry

Crossland's Brigade
Colonel Edward Crossland

3rd Kentucky Mounted Infantry, 7th Kentucky Mounted Infantry, 8th Kentucky Mounted Infantry, 12th Kentucky Mounted Infantry, 12th Kentucky Cavalry, Huey's Kentucky Cavalry Battalion

Jackson's Division
Brigadier General William Hicks Jackson

Armstrong's Brigade
Brigadier General Frank Crawford Armstrong

1st Mississippi Cavalry, 2nd Mississippi Cavalry, 2nd Mississippi Partisan Rangers (aka Ballentine's Mississippi Cavalry), 28th Mississippi Cavalry

Ross' Brigade
Brigadier General Lawrence Sullivan Ross

1st Texas Legion, 3rd Texas Cavalry, 6th Texas Cavalry, 9th Texas Cavalry, 27th Texas Cavalry

Artillery

Captain J. W. Morton

Bryant's Arkansas Battery, Morton's Tennessee Battery, Rice's Tennessee Battery, Croft's Georgia Battery, King's Missouri Battery, Waties' South Carolina Battery

Organization of the Federal Army at Spring Hill & Franklin November 29-30, 1864

Major General John McAllister Schofield, Commanding

Fourth Army Corps
Major General David Sloane Stanley, Commanding

Infantry

First Division
Brigadier General Nathan Kimball

First Brigade
Colonel Isaac Minor Kirby

21st Illinois Infantry, 38th Illinois Infantry, 31st Indiana Infantry, 81st Indiana Infantry, 90th Ohio Infantry, 101st Ohio Infantry

Second Brigade
Brigadier General Walter Chiles Whitaker

21st Kentucky Infantry, 23rd Kentucky Infantry, 35th Indiana Infantry, 40th Ohio Infantry *, 45th Ohio Infantry, 51st Ohio Infantry, 96th Illinois Infantry

* The 40th Ohio Infantry was composed of only six companies.

Third Brigade
Brigadier General William Grose

9th Indiana Infantry, 30th Indiana Infantry *,
36th Indiana Infantry **, 84th Indiana Infantry, 75th Illinois Infantry,
80th Illinois Infantry, 84th Illinois Infantry,
77th Pennsylvania Infantry

* The 30th Indiana Infantry consisted of only three companies.
** The 36th Indiana Infantry consisted of only one company.

Second Division
Brigadier General George Day Wagner

First Brigade
Colonel Emerson Opdycke

24th Wisconsin Infantry, 36th Illinois Infantry, 44th Illinois Infantry,
73rd Illinois Infantry, 74th / 88th Illinois Infantry, 125th Ohio Infantry

Second Brigade
Colonel John Quincy Lane

26th Ohio Infantry, 28th Kentucky Infantry, 40th Indiana Infantry,
57th Indiana Infantry, 97th Ohio Infantry, 100th Illinois Infantry

Third Brigade
Colonel Luther Prentice Bradley, wounded at Spring Hill
Succeeded by Colonel Joseph Conrad

15th Missouri Infantry, 42nd Illinois Infantry, 51st Illinois Infantry,
79th Illinois Infantry, 64th Ohio Infantry, 65th Ohio Infantry,
detachment of 27th Illinois Infantry

Third Division
Brigadier General Thomas John Wood

First Brigade
Colonel Abel D. Streight

8th Kansas Infantry, 15th Ohio Infantry, 49th Ohio Infantry, 51st Indiana Infantry, 89th Illinois Infantry

Second Brigade
Colonel P. Sidney Post

41st Ohio Infantry, 59th Illinois Infantry, 71st Ohio Infantry, 93rd Ohio Infantry, 124th Ohio Infantry

Third Brigade
Brigadier General Samuel Beatty

13th Ohio Infantry, 19th Ohio Infantry, 17th Kentucky Infantry, 40th Missouri Infantry, 79th Indiana Infantry, 86th Indiana Infantry, detachment of 10th Kansas Infantry

Artillery

Captain Lyman A. Bridges

Light Batteries: 1st Kentucky Battery; Battery A, 1st Ohio; Battery G, 1st Ohio; 6th Ohio Battery; 20th Ohio Battery; Battery B, Pennsylvania Light; Battery M, 4th U.S. Regulars; Bridges' Illinois Battery

Twenty-Third Army Corps

Major General John M. Schofield, commanding Nov 29
Brigadier General Jacob D. Cox, commanding Nov 30

Infantry

Second Division
Brigadier General Thomas Howard Ruger

Second Brigade
Colonel Orlando Hurley Moore

23rd Michigan Infantry, 80th Indiana Infantry, 129th Indiana Infantry, 107th Illinois, Infantry, 111th Ohio Infantry, 118th Ohio Infantry, detachment of 24th Missouri Infantry *

* The 24th Missouri Infantry consisted of only two companies and was in the process of being mustered out prior to Franklin. It was temporarily attached to Moore's Brigade at Franklin.

Third Brigade
Colonel Silas Allen Strickland

50th Ohio Infantry, 44th Missouri Infantry, 72nd Illinois Infantry, 183rd Ohio Infantry

The 44th Missouri Infantry and 72nd Illinois Infantry were actually organized into Colonel Jonathan B. Moore's Third Division of Major General Andrew J. Smith's Sixteenth Army Corps, but were temporarily attached to Strickland's Brigade at Spring Hill and Franklin.

Third Division

Brigadier General Jacob Dolson Cox, commanding Nov 29
Brigadier General James William Reilly, commanding Nov 30

First Brigade

Brigadier General James W. Reilly *

* Reilly commanded both the brigade and division at Franklin because Cox was elevated to temporary corps command.

8th Tennessee Infantry, 12th Kentucky Infantry,
16th Kentucky Infantry, 100th Ohio Infantry,
104th Ohio Infantry, 175th Ohio Infantry *

* The 175th Ohio Infantry was an unassigned unit and temporarily attached to Reilly's Brigade at Franklin.

Second Brigade

Colonel John Stephen Casement

5th Tennessee Infantry, 65th Illinois Infantry, 65th Indiana Infantry,
124th Indiana Infantry, 103rd Ohio Infantry

Third Brigade

Colonel Thomas J. Henderson, commanding November 29
Colonel Israel Newton Stiles, commanding November 30

63rd Indiana Infantry, 120th Indiana Infantry,
128th Indiana Infantry, 112th Illinois Infantry

Artillery

Light Batteries: Battery D, 1st Ohio, 15th Indiana,
19th Ohio, 22nd Indiana, 23rd Indiana

Cavalry

Major General James Harrison Wilson

First Division
Brigadier General Edward Moody McCook

First Brigade *
Brigadier General John Thomas Croxton
1st Tennessee Cavalry, 2nd Michigan Cavalry,
4th Kentucky Mounted Infantry, 8th Iowa Cavalry

* Croxton's Brigade was not commanded at Spring Hill and Franklin by McCook; it was temporarily assigned to Sixth Division commander Brigadier General Richard W. Johnson. See *OR* 45, pt. 1, p. 558, 573.

Fifth Division
Brigade General Edward Hatch

First Brigade
Colonel Robert R. Stewart
3rd Illinois Cavalry, 10th Tennessee Cavalry *,
11th Indiana Cavalry, 12th Missouri Cavalry

* The 10th Tennessee Cavalry was serving elsewhere and not present at Spring Hill or Franklin. See *OR* 45, pt. 1, p. 1151, 1180, 1184.

Second Brigade
Colonel Datus Ensing Coon
2nd Iowa Cavalry, 6th Illinois Cavalry, 7th Illinois Cavalry,
9th Illinois Cavalry, 12th Tennessee Cavalry

Artillery

Light Battery: 1st Illinois

Sixth Division
Brigadier General Richard W. Johnson

First Brigade
Colonel Horace Capron replaced in the field by Colonel Thomas J. Harrison on November 30.

5th Indiana Cavalry *, 8th Michigan Cavalry,
14th Illinois Cavalry, 16th Illinois Cavalry

* Although assigned to the brigade, the 5th Indiana Cavalry was not present at Spring Hill or Franklin. See *OR* 45 pt. 1, p. 927, 1005 and *OR* 45, pt. 2, p. 75.

Second Brigade
Colonel James Biddle

3rd Tennessee Cavalry **, 5th Iowa Cavalry *, 6th Indiana Cavalry **,
7th Ohio Cavalry *

* The 5th Iowa Cavalry and 7th Ohio Cavalry were officially constituted as part of the Second Brigade, but operated temporarily with the First Brigade, Sixth Division at Spring Hill and Franklin. See *OR* 45, pt. 1, p. 597, 1113, 1124.

** Neither the 3rd Tennessee Cavalry or 6th Indiana Cavalry were present at Spring Hill or Franklin.

The organization for Johnson's division is based upon orders issued by headquarters on November 17, 1864. By November 30 only the 5th Iowa Cavalry, 7th Ohio Cavalry, 8th Michigan Cavalry, 14th Illinois Cavalry, and 16th Illinois Cavalry were present with the division. See *OR* 45, pt. 1, p. 89, 927, 1205 for November 17 orders, units present on November 30, and reorganization that occurred on December 1.

Bibliography

Abbreviations

ALPL - Abraham Lincoln Presidential Library, Springfield, IL.
B & L - Battles and Leaders of the Civil War.
BHL - Bentley Historical Library, University of Michigan, Ann Arbor, MI.
CHA - Carter House Archives, Franklin, TN.
CMH - Confederate Military History.
CRN - Carnton Archives, Franklin, TN.
CV - Confederate Veteran Magazine.
CWTI - Civil War Times Illustrated Magazine.
MHS - Publications of the Mississippi Historical Society.
MOLLUS - Military Order of the Loyal Legion of the United States.
NT - National Tribune Newspaper.
OBC - Oberlin College, Oberlin, OH.
SHC - Southern Historical Collection, University of North Carolina, Chapel Hill, NC.
SHSP - Southern Historical Society Papers.
THM - Tennessee Historical Magazine.
THQ - Tennessee Historical Quarterly Magazine.
TSLA - Tennessee State Library and Archives, Nashville, TN.
WCHS - Williamson County Historical Society.

Primary Materials

Manuscripts, Letters, etc.

Barnes, Milton. Civil War Collection, Special Collections & Archives. George Mason University, Fairfax, VA.

Bate, William B. Address Delivered by General William B. Bate, on occasion of dedicating the Battle-Ground Academy on the field at Franklin Oct. 5, 1889. TSLA.

Binford, James R. *Recollections of the Fifteenth Regiment of Mississippi Infantry, CSA.* Unpublished. Chickamauga National Battlefield Park.

Brown, Campbell and Harris, Isham conversation. Brown-Ewell Papers. TSLA.

Carter, E. J. to Cheatham, Maj. Gen. Jan. 17, 1865. Benjamin F. Cheatham Papers. TSLA.

Conner, S. P. to Casement, J. S. Nov. 10, 1887. CRN.

Copley, John M. *A Sketch of the Battle of Franklin, Tenn.; with Reminiscences of Camp Douglas.* SHC.

Cowan, Hattie McGavock. "Career of Brilliant Cleburne, Arkansas Lawyer Ended by Bullet While Leading His Soldiers in Battle of Franklin." *Memphis Commercial Appeal*, Apr. 19, 1931. CRN.

Cumming, Joseph. Recollections. Joseph B. Cumming Recollections. SHC.

Dyersburg *State Gazette.* May 30, 1907. TSLA.

Estes, George C. *Some Incidents As Recorded By A Private Soldier In The Southern Army Of The Civil War.* CRN.

Featherston, W. S. Official Report, Apr. 21, 1865. W. S. Featherston Papers, J. D. Williams Library, University of Mississippi, University, MS.

Govan, Daniel to his wife. Dec. 4, 1864. Daniel Chevilette Govan Papers. SHC.

Harris, Isham to Quintard, Charles. Dec. 29, 1874. Charles T. Quintard Papers, Duke University Libraries, Duke University, Durham, NC.

Hempstead, Mortimer to Dear M. Dec. 1, 1864. Letter in Hempstead Journal. CHA.

Holman, Robert Sanford. Unpublished memoir in possession of Rayburn W. Qualls, Jr., Rockville, MD.

Hood, John Bell to Lee, S. D. Nov. 29, 1865. Stephen Dill Lee Papers. SHC.

Hood, John Bell to Lee, S. D. Apr. 14, 1879. Stephen Dill Lee Papers. SHC.

Hope, Pleasant M. to his daughter. Apr. 25, 1864. CHA.

Howard, Uncle Wiley. Statement of "Uncle Wiley" Howard, Body-Servant of General States Rights Gist, Relative to the Death and Burial of General Gist. John Peacock Papers. SHC.

Jackson, H. R. to B. F. Cheatham, Dec. 10, 1864. Benjamin F. Cheatham Papers. TSLA.

Kinkaid, Gerald Allen, Jr., *The Confederate Army, A Regiment: An Analysis of the Forty-Eighth Tennessee Volunteer Infantry Regiment, 1861-1865.* A thesis presented to the Faculty of the U. S. Army Command, 1995. Fort Leavenworth, KS. TSLA.

Lee, S. D. to Capers, Ellison. Nov. 12, 1902. Ellison Capers Papers. SHC.
Lee, S. D. to Harrison, Lilly. Dec. 6, 1864. James Harrison Papers. SHC.
McGraw, L. S. to McGraw, J. J. Dec. 2, 1864. ALPL.
Mangum, Leonard H. Statement of Judge L. H. Mangum of Arkansas regarding the death and burial of General Patrick R. Cleburne. John Peacock Papers. SHC.
Markham, Thomas R. "Reminiscences of the Battle of Franklin." *Southern Presbyterian*, Oct. 3, 1893. CRN.
Marshall, Alexander to Scofield, Levi. Oct. 10, 1886. Jacob Cox Papers. OBC.
Marshall, Park. *Reminiscence of the Battle of Franklin.* CHA.
Meroney, J. N. to Cowan, George L. Dec. 3, 1910. CRN.
Merrill, C. E. "Fearful Franklin - Some Reminiscences of the Bloodiest Battle in History." *Nashville World*, undated. CRN.
Missouri *Democrat.* Dec. 8, 1864. St Louis Public Library, St. Louis, MO.
Mohrmann, William O. Memoir. CHA.
Moon, Andrew J. to his sister. Dec. 4, 1864. CHA.
Morris, Wayne to his brother. Dec. 6, 1864. Wayne E. Morris Papers. BHL.
Morris, Wayne to Libby. Dec. 2, 1864. Wayne E. Morris Papers. BHL.
Murphey, Virgil S. Diary. Virgil S. Murphey Diary. SHC.
National Archives and Records Administration, Compiled Service Records of Confederate Soldiers Who Served in Organizations From the State of Arkansas, Washington, D. C.
Reynolds, Daniel H. Diary. Daniel Harris Reynolds Papers, Special Collections. University of Arkansas Libraries, Fayetteville, AR.
Ryan, Milton A. *Experiences of a Confederate Soldier in Camp and Prisoner in the Civil War 1861-65.* CHA.
Scofield, Levi to Cox, Jacob. Dec. 23, 1870. Jacob Cox Papers. OBC.
Stark, John to Kipp, I. L. Jan. 29, 1865. Unpublished letter in possession of Lavonne Parrish, Amarillo, TX.
Stephens, M. D. L. *Narrative of the Battle of Franklin.* CRN.
Talley, Spencer B. Civil War Memoir. TSLA
Thompson, Joseph N. Letter dated Dec. 15, 1924. CRN.
Watson, J. H. to Vail, George. Feb. 25, 1865. Unpublished letter in possession of Gwynne Evans, Spring Hill, TN.
Weaver, Adam J. to Charlotte. Nov. 30, 1864. CHA.
Wilkes, Abner J. Unpublished memoir in the possession of Willard Davis, Prentiss, MS.
Williams, George A. to Buck, Irving A. Dec. 4, 1864. Irving Buck Papers, Eleanor S. Brockenbrough Library, Museum of the Confederacy, Richmond, VA.

Williams, Joseph and Williams, Enoch. Typescript account of their death. CHA.

Wolfe, Joe to Editors of Clinton *Public*. Dec. 6, 1864. ALPL.

Young, Harold. Diary in possession of Bill and Marilyn Christmann, Pembroke, MA.

Young, J. P. to Hay, Thomas. May 5, 1921. CRN.

Articles & Periodicals

Baker, Edward A. Letter in, "Gen. John Adams at Franklin: Testimony of Union Officers to His Immutable Valor." *CV* V, p. 299-302.

Barr, James. "Gens. Cleburne and Adams at Franklin." *CV* 10, p. 154-155.

Batchelor, A. J. "On Hood's Campaign To Franklin." *CV* 18, p. 426.

Binford, James R. "Heroism at Franklin: Tributes to Gen. Adams, Cols. Farrell and Rorer." *CV* 10, p. 457-458.

Boyce, Joseph. "Cockrell's Brigade Band at Franklin." *CV* 19, p. 271.

_____. "Missourians in the Battle of Franklin." *CV* 24, p. 101-103, 138.

Brooks, L. H. "As He Saw Franklin." *NT*, Jan. 17, 1895, p. 3.

Brown, John C. Report. *CMH* 8, p. 156-158.

Brown, R. C. "Battle of Spring Hill." *NT*, June 21, 1883, p. 1.

Buckner, Allen. "Battle of Franklin." *NT*, Feb. 1, 1883, p. 1.

Burr, Frank A. and Williams, Talcott. "The Battle of Franklin." *Philadelphia Press*, March 11, 1883, p. 7-28.

Case, O. W. "Gen John Adams at Franklin." *CV* 1, p. 208.

Casement, J. S. Letter in, "Gen. John Adams at Franklin: Testimony of Union Officers to His Immutable Valor." *CV* V, p. 299-302.

Castle, Henry M. "Opdycke's Brigade at the Battle of Franklin." *MOLLUS*, Minnesota, 6, p. 385-404.

Cheatham, B. F. "The Lost Opportunity at Spring Hill, Tenn. - General Cheatham's Reply to General Hood." *SHSP* 9, p. 524-541.

Cleveland, Charles B. "With The Third Missouri Regiment." *CV* 31, p. 18-20.

Collins, J. S. "W. W. Gist's Article Commended." *CV* 24, p. 89-90.

_____. "Gallant Mike Farrell." *CV* 34, p. 372-375.

Connelly, Henry C. to *Century Magazine* Editors. Aug. 8, 1887. *B&L*, Vol. 4, p. 443.

Cooper, James L. "Service With the Twentieth Tennessee Regiment." *CV* 33, p. 180-181.

Crum, Henry G. "Spring Hill: Cleburne's Division Was So Roughly Handled That It Was In No Mind to Get Across the Road." *NT*, Aug. 17, 1905, p. 3.

Cunningham, Sumner. "Battle of Franklin." *CV* 1, p. 101-102.

_____. "Disastrous Campaign in Tennessee." *CV* 12, p. 338-341.

_____. "Gen. O. F. Strahl, Buried at Dyersburg." *CV* 9, p. 148-149.

Cutting, A. P. "This Is How It Was: The Conductor on the Military Railroad Out of Nashville Contradicts Comrade Shellenberger." *NT*, Mar. 22, 1894, p. 3.

Dabney, T. G. "Gen A. P. Stewart on Strong Topics." *CV* 17, p. 31-32.

Dawson, Daniel. "The 63d Ind. At Franklin." *NT*, Aug. 22, 1907, p. 6.

Dean, J. C. "The Battle of Franklin." *CV* 7, p. 27.

Dodd, W. O. "Reminiscences of Hood's Tennessee Campaign." *SHSP* 9, p. 518-524.

Dunke, Michael. "Spring Hill." *NT*, Mar. 6, 1890, p. 3.

Edmonds, Joseph. "From An Indiana Soldier." *NT*, Jun. 11, 1885, p. 3.

Enfield, John. "At Franklin: Comrade Enfield's Exciting Race For Life." *NT*, Mar. 15, 1888, p. 3.

Figuers, H. P. "A Boy's Impressions of the Battle of Franklin." *CV* 23, p. 4-7, 44.

Furnas, A. J. "Racing With Hood: A Lively Time in Getting Back to Nashville." *NT*, May 28, 1908, p. 7.

Gale, William D. "Hood's Campaign in Tennessee." *CV* 2, p. 4-5.

Gaut, Mrs. John C. Reminiscence in, "Anniversary of the Battle of Franklin." *CV* 17, p. 542-543.

Gibson, Thomas. "Particulars of Gen. John Adams's Death." *CV* 12, p. 482.

Gist, W. W. "The Battle of Franklin." *THM* 6, No. 3, p. 213-253.

_____. "The Different Point of View in Battle." *CV* 24, p. 550-551.

Gist, W. W. "The Other Side at Franklin." *CV* 24, p. 13-16.

Gordon, George W. Address in, "Confederate Monument at Franklin." *CV* 8, p. 5-11.

_____. "General P. R. Cleburne: Dedication of a Monument to His Memory at Helena, Arkansas, May 10, 1891. *SHSP* 18, p. 260-272.

Gore, Tom M. "Death and Identity of Gen. Adams." *CV* 1, p. 264.

Hatry, A. G. "A Lost Opportunity." *NT*, Jan. 4, 1894, p. 3.

Heaps, I. G. "In Front at Franklin." *NT*, Mar. 30, 1911, p. 3.

Hedges, Fletcher. "Franklin to Nashville." *NT*, Oct. 11, 1906, p. 3.

Henry, Pat. "Adams' Brigade in Battle of Franklin." *CV* 21, p. 76-77.

_____. "Hood's Order After the Battle of Franklin." *CV* 26, p. 11.

Hickey, J. M. to Merrifield, J. K. *CV* 17, p. 14.

Hockersmith, P. E. "Douglass's Battery at Franklin." *CV* 14, p. 352.

Hoover, F. E. "Spring Hill and Franklin." *NT*, June 11, 1885, p. 3.

Huckins, George W. "Hung Unto the Rations." *NT*, Sept. 5, 1912, p. 7.

Hutchins, Morris C. "The Battle of Franklin, Tennessee." *MOLLUS*, Ohio, 5, p. 275-283.

Inglis, John L. "Commander Florida Division, U. C. V." *CV* 22, p. 159.

Johnson, Morris E. "Battle of Franklin." *NT*, Jan. 28, 1904, p. 3.

Jones, A. A. "Many Days of Fighting: Incidents of the Retreat from Columbia to Nashville." *NT*, June 16, 1898, p. 2.

Lanier, J. H. to *CV* Editor. *CV* 5, p. 38.

Leaming, H. "The Battle of Franklin." *NT*, Nov. 18, 1888, p. 3.

Leavell, George W. "Battle of Franklin Remembrances." *CV* 10, p. 500-502.

Lee, Stephen D. "From Palmetto, Ga. To Defeat at Nashville." *CV* 16, p. 257-259.

_____. "Johnson's Division in the Battle of Franklin." *MHS* 7, p. 75-83.

Lindsay, R. H. "Seeing the Battle of Franklin." *CV* 9, p. 221.

Lowrey, Mark P. "An Autobiography." *SHSP* 16, p. 365-376.

McNeilly, J. H. "Bloody Franklin." *CV* 29, p. 5-6.

_____. "Franklin - Incidents of the Battle." *CV* 26, p. 116-118.

McQuaide, John to *CV* Editor. *CV* 7, p. 272.

_____ to *CV* Editor. *CV* 10, p. 155.

Mangum, Leonard H. "General P. R. Cleburne: A Sketch of His Early Life and His Last Battle." *Kennesaw Gazette*, June 15, 1887.

Marshall, Park to *CV* Editor. *CV* 24, p. 551.

Merrifield, J. K. "Col. Hugh Garland - Captured Flags." *CV* 24, p. 551-552.

_____. "From 'The Other Side' at Franklin." *CV* 16, p. 554.

_____. "Opdycke's Brigade at Franklin." *CV* 13, p. 563-564.

Merrill, C. E. "Battle of Franklin Recalled." *CV* 5, p. 600.

Milchrist, Thomas E. "Reflections of a Subaltern on the Hood - Thomas Campaign in Tennessee." *MOLLUS*, Illinois, 4, p. 451-465.

Moore, S. F. "Short One Brigade." *NT*, May 2, 1912, p. 7.

Munger, S. N. "The 72d Illinois at Franklin." *NT*, Feb. 23, 1901, p.3.

Musson, Willard. "At Franklin: Some Spicy Recollections of an Orderly-Sergeant." *NT*, Feb. 17, 1887, p. 8.

Neese, W. C. "Scaling the Works at Franklin." *CV* 11, p. 274.

Newsom, Eli. "Hovey's Babies." *NT*, May 2, 1912, p. 7.

_____. "Fighting Hood's Army." *NT*, Nov. 8, 1923, p. 3.

No author, Fielding P. Sloan obituary. "The Last Roll." *CV* 8, p. 84.

Patterson, D. H. "Battle of Franklin." *CV* 9, p. 116.

Payne, John M. to *CV* Editor. *CV* 1, p. 172.

Phillips, G. C. "Witness to the Battle of Franklin." *CV* 14, p. 261-262.

Pinney, Nelson A. "Fierce Work at Franklin." *NT*, Mar.10, 1887, p. 3.

Posegate, F. M. "Battle of Franklin: The Gallant Part Taken by the 175th Ohio." *NT*, Feb. 28, 1889, p. 3.

Rea, R. N. "A Mississippi Soldier of the Confederacy." *CV* 30, p. 287-289.

Riddle, C. L. "The Fight at Spring Hill." *NT*, Apr. 30, 1891, p. 3.

Riffle, James. "Memory of Franklin." *NT*, Oct. 25, 1923, p. 7.

Ritter, William L. "Sketch of the Third Maryland Artillery." *SHSP* 11, p. 537-544.

Robert, Frank Stovall. "Spring Hill-Franklin-Nashville, 1864." *CV* 27, p. 58-60.

Roberts, B. T. "Vivid Reminiscences of Franklin." *CV* 1, p. 339.

Russell, E. L. "Battle of Franklin Remembrances." *CV* 10, p. 502.

Sexton, James A. "The Observations and Experiences of a Captain of Infantry at the Battle of Franklin, November 30, 1864." *MOLLUS*, Illinois, 4, p. 466-484.

Shannon, Isaac N. "Sharpshooters with Hood's Army." *CV* 15, p. 123-127.

Shaphard, E. "At Spring Hill and Franklin Again." *CV* 24, p. 138-139.

Sharp, Jacob H. "Battle of Franklin Remembrances." *CV* 10, p. 502-503.

Shellenberger, John K. "More About Spring Hill." *NT*, Feb. 1, 1894, p. 1.

_____. "The Battle of Franklin." *MOLLUS*, Minnesota, 5, p. 495-521.

_____. "Federal Blunders at Franklin." *CV* 36, p. 380-384, 419-422.

_____. "The Fighting at Spring Hill, Tenn." *CV* 36, p. 100-103, 140-143, 188.

Sherwood, Isaac. "A Hero of Franklin: Something About the Death of Col. Mervin R. Clark." *NT*, Aug. 2, 1894, p.

Simmons, P. B. to *CV* Editor. *CV* 1, p. 163.

Smith, D. W. "Hood's Last Campaign: Experience with the Wagon-Train from Columbia to Franklin." *NT*, Nov. 20, 1890, p. 4.

Smith, Gus. "Battle of Franklin." *MOLLUS*, Michigan, 2, p. 249-263.

Smits, J. Cornelius. "The 1st Ky. Battery: How Its Guns Were Lost and Recovered at Franklin." *NT,* Aug. 25, 1887, p. 3.

South, Philip T. "Comrade of the 175th Ohio Tells of His Experiences During and After the War." *NT,* Sept. 20, 1923, p. 7.

Sparks, William. "At Duck River." *NT*, July 25, 1918, p. 3.

Speed, Thomas. "The Battle of Franklin, Tennessee." *MOLLUS*, Ohio, 3, p. 44-99.

Spohr, R. H. "There Was No Shirking: And Col. Mervin Clark Did Not Die as Col. Sherwood Relates." *NT*, Sept. 6, 1894, p. 4.

Stanley, George. "Pushed Back to Nashville." *NT*, Aug. 18, 1910, p. 7.

Stevens, T. H. "The March to Franklin." *NT*, Mar. 19, 1885, p. 3.

_____. "Other Side in Battle of Franklin." *CV* 11, p. 165-167.

Stewart, A. P. "A Critical Narrative." *CV* 16, p. 462-463.

Stone, Henry. "Repelling Hood's Invasion of Tennessee." *B & L,* Vol. 4, p. 440-464.

Sutton, George R. "An Incident at Franklin." *CV* 28, p. 116.

Talbert, H. B. to *CV* Editor. *CV* 17, p. 374.

Thompson, Joseph N. "Battle of Franklin." *WCHS* 15, p. 57-59.

Thompson, William C. "A Confederate's Recollection of the Battle of Franklin." *CWTI*, December 1964.

Trigg, S. C. "Why the Band Played at Franklin." *CV* 19, p. 32.

Truman, William L. "First Missouri Brigade at Franklin." *CV* 11, p. 273.

Williams, T. W. "Checking a Pursuing Foe: Schofield's Great Combat at Franklin, Tenn., Nov. 30, 1864." *NT*, May 31, 1900, p. 3.

Wilson, D. J to *CV* Editor. *CV* 2, p. 186.

Wolford, S. C. to *CV* Editor. *CV* 17, p. 15.

Young, J. P. "Hood's Failure at Spring Hill." *CV* 16, 25-41.

Books & Pamphlets

Adamson, A. P. *Brief History of the Thirtieth Georgia Regiment.* Jonesboro, GA, 1987. Reprint.

Alexander, E. P. *Military Memoirs of a Confederate.* New York, 1907.

Banks, Robert. *The Battle of Franklin.* Dayton, OH, 1982. Reprint.

Bennett, L. G. and Haigh, William H. *History of the Thirty-Sixth Regiment Illinois Volunteers, During the War of the Rebellion.* Marengo, IL, 1999. Reprint.

Bevier, R. S. *History of the First and Second Missouri Confederate Brigades 1861 - 1865 and From Wakarusa to Appomattox.* St. Louis, MO, 1878.

Brewer, W. *Alabama: Her History, Resources, War Record, and Public Men, from 1540 to 1872.* Tuscaloosa, AL, 1964. Reprint.

Buck, Irving A. *Cleburne and His Command.* Wilmington, NC, 1995. Reprint.

Capers, Walter B. *The Soldier-Bishop Ellison Capers.* New York, 1912.

Clark, Charles T. *Opdycke Tigers, 125th O. V. I., A History of the Regiment and the Campaigns and Battles of the Army of the Cumberland.* Columbus, OH, 1895.

Collins, R. M. *Chapters from the Unwritten History of the War Between the States.* St. Louis, MO, 1893.

Cox, Jacob. *The Battle of Franklin, Tennessee, November 30, 1864: A Monograph.* Dayton, OH, 1983. Reprint.

_____. *Sherman's March to the Sea: Hood's Tennessee Campaign and the Carolina Campaigns of 1865.* New York, 1994. Reprint.

Davidson, H. M. *History of Battery A, First Regiment of Ohio Vol. Light Artillery.* Milwaukee, WI, 1865.

Davis, Jefferson. *The Rise and Fall of the Confederate Government*; two volumes. New York, 1990. Reprint.

Day, L. W. *Story of the One Hundred and First Ohio Infantry: A Memorial Volume.* Cleveland, OH, 1894.

Dinkins, James. *Personal Recollections and Experiences in the Confederate Army.* Cincinnati, OH, 1897.

Field, Henry M. *Bright Skies and Dark Shadows.* New York, 1890.

French, Samuel G. *Two Wars: An Autobiography.* Huntington, WV, 1999. Reprint.

Géorge, Henry. *History of the 3rd, 7th, 8th and 12th Kentucky C.S.A.* Louisville, KY, 1911.

Grant, Ulysses S. *Personal Memoirs of U. S. Grant.* Cleveland, OH, 1952. Reprint.

Grose, William. *The Story of the Marches, Battles and Incidents of the 36th Regiment Indiana Volunteer Infantry.* New Castle, IN, 1891.

Hirsh, Alice and Hirsh, Edward. *Life Story of Isaac E. Hirsh, Co. G, 22nd Regiment, Mississippi Infantry, C. S. A.*, n.d.

Hood, John Bell. *Advance & Retreat: Personal Experiences in the United States and Confederate States Armies.* Lincoln, NE, 1996. Reprint.

Hinman, Wilbur F. *The Story of the Sherman Brigade: The Camp, the March, the Bivouac, the Battle, and how "the Boys" lived and died, during four years of active service.* Alliance, OH, 1897.

Johnston, Joseph E. *Narrative of Military Operations, Directed, During the Late War Between the States.* New York, 1874.

Jordan, Thomas and Pryor, J. P. *The Campaigns of General Nathan Bedford Forrest and of Forrest's Cavalry.* New York, 1996. Reprint.

Keesy, W. A. *War As Viewed From the Ranks.* New Washington, OH, 1991. Reprint.

Kerwood, Asbury. *Annals of the Fifty-Seventh Regiment Indiana Volunteers: Marches, Battles, and Incidents of Army Life.* Dayton, OH, 1868.

Lindsley, John Berrien. *Military Annals of Tennessee*; two volumes. Wilmington, NC, 1995. Reprint.

Little, George and Maxwell, James R. *A History of Lumsden's Battery, C. S. A.* Tuscaloosa, AL, 1905.

Livermore, Thomas L. *Numbers and Losses in the Civil War in America: 1861-65.* Bloomington, IN, 1957. Reprint.

McMorries, Edward Young. *History of the First Regiment Alabama Volunteer Infantry, C. S. A.* Montgomery, AL, 1904.

McMurray, W. J. *History of the Twentieth Tennessee Regiment Volunteer Infantry, C. S. A.* Nashville, TN, 1904.

Mathes, J. Harvey. *The Old Guard in Gray.* Memphis, TN, 1897.

Merrill, Catharine. *The Soldier of Indiana in the War for the Union*; two volumes. Indianapolis, IN, 1866-1869.

Official Army Register of the Volunteer Force of the United States Army for the Years 1861, '62, '63, '64, '65. Eight volumes. Washington, D. C. 1865.

Pinney, N. A. *History of the 104th Regiment Ohio Volunteer Infantry from 1862 to 1865.* Akron, OH, 1886.

Quintard, Charles T. *Doctor Quintard Chaplain C. S. A. and Second Bishop of Tennessee; Being His Story of the War.* Sewanee, TN, 1905.

Rennolds, Edwin H. *A History of the Henry County Commands Which Served in the Confederate States Army, Including Rosters of the Various Campaigns Enlisted in Henry County, Tenn.* Jacksonville, FL, 1904.

Report of the Adjutant General of Missouri, 1865. Springfield, MO, 1865.

Rice, Ralsa C. *Yankee Tigers: Through the Civil War with the 125th Ohio.* Huntington, WV, 1992. Reprint.

Ridley, Bromfield L. *Battles and Sketches of the Army of Tennessee.* Dayton, OH, 1995. Reprint.

Roman, Alfred. *The Military Operations of General Beauregard in the War Between the States 1861 to 1865*; two volumes. New York, 1994. Reprint.

Schofield, John M. *Forty-Six Years in the Army.* New York, 1897.

Scofield, Levi T. *The Retreat From Pulaski to Nashville, Tenn.* Franklin, TN, 1996. Reprint.

Sherman, William T. *Memoirs of General William T. Sherman*; two volumes. New York, 1984. Reprint.

Sherwood, Isaac. *Memories of the War.* Toledo, OH, 1923.

Smith, Daniel P. *Company K, First Alabama Regiment, or Three Years In the Confederate Service.* Prattville, AL, 1885.

Smith, Frank H. *History of Maury County, Tennessee.* Columbia, TN, 1959.

Stanley, David S. *Personal Memoirs of Major-General David S. Stanley.* Cambridge, MA, 1917.

Stillwell, Leander. *The Story of a Common Soldier of Army Life in the Civil War 1861-1865.* Kansas City, MO, 1920.

Stockton, Joseph. *War Diary (1862-5) of Brevet Brigadier General, First Lieutenant, Captain, Major and Lieutenant-Colonel, 72d Regiment, Illinois Infantry Volunteers.* Chicago, IL, 1910.

Thatcher, Marshall P. *A Hundred Battles in the West - St. Louis to Atlanta - 1861 - 1865 - The Second Michigan Cavalry.* Detroit, MI, 1884.

Thoburn, Thomas C. *My Experiences During the Civil War.* Cleveland, OH, 1963.

Thompson, B. F. *History of the 112th Regiment of Illinois Volunteer Infantry in the Great War of the Rebellion 1862-1865.* Toulon, IL, 1885.

Thurstin, W. S. *History One Hundred and Eleventh Regiment, O. V. I.* Toledo, OH, 1894.

Various Authors. *A History of the Seventy-Third Regiment of Illinois Infantry Volunteers.* Springfield, IL, 1890.

Walker, C. I. *Rolls and Historical Sketch of the Tenth Regiment, So. Ca. Volunteers, in the Army of the Confederate States.* Charleston, S. C., 1881.

War of the Rebellion: A Compilation of the Official Records of the Union and Confederate Armies. 128 volumes. Washington, D.C., 1880-1901.

Watkins, Sam R. *Co. Aytch: Maury Grays First Tennessee Regiment, Or, A Side Show of the Big Show.* Jackson, TN, 1952. Reprint.

Winters, Erastus. *In the 50th Ohio Serving Uncle Sam: Memoirs of One Who Wore The Blue.* Cincinnati, OH, 1905.

Woodruff, George H. *Fifteen Years Ago: or, the patriotism of Will County, designed to preserve the names and memory of Will County Soldiers, both officers and privates - both living and dead: to tell something of what they did, and of what they suffered, in the great struggle to protect our nationality.* Joliet, IL, 1876.

Worsham, W. J. *The Old Nineteenth Tennessee Regiment, C. S. A.* Knoxville, TN, 1902.

Wyeth, John Allan. *That Devil Forrest: The Life of General Nathan Bedford Forrest.* New York, 1959. Reprint.

Secondary Materials

Articles and Periodicals

Alexander, Hudson. "The Trials and Tribulations of Fountain Branch Carter And His Franklin, Tennessee, Home." *Blue & Gray Magazine*, February 1995.

Crawford, William T. "The Mystery of Spring Hill." *Civil War History*, June 1955.

Cummings, Charles M. "The Choicest Spirit to Embrace the South: Otho French Strahl." *THQ* 24, No. 4, 1965.

Davis, Steve. "That Extraordinary Document: W. H. T. Walker and Patrick Cleburne's Emancipation Proposal." *CWTI*, January 1977.

Evans, David. "Gallant Last Ride." *Military History*, 4, August 1987.

Garrett, Jill K. "St. John's Church, Ashwood." *THQ* 29, No. 1, 1970.

Harris, James C. "Souvenir of Franklin." *North South Trader*, July - August 1982.

Horn, Stanley. "The Spring Hill Legend - A Reappraisal." *CWTI*, April 1969.

Klinger, Michael. "Gallant Charge Repulsed." *America's Civil War*, January 1989.

Lane, Bryan. "The Life of Confederate Brigadier General John Adams." *CWTI*, October 1996.

Riley, Harris D. "A Gallant Adopted Son of Tennessee - General John C. Carter, C. S. A." *THQ* 48, No. 4., 1989.

Robison, Dan. "The Carter House: Focus of the Battle of Franklin." *THQ* 22, No. 1, 1963.

Robertson, James I. "The Human Battle at Franklin." *THQ* 24, No. 1, 1965.

Roth, David E. "The Mysteries of Spring Hill, Tennessee." *Blue & Gray Magazine*, Vol. II, October-November 1984.

Sanders, Stuart W. "The Bishop's Nephew." *CWTI*, March 2001.

Tucker, Phillip Thomas. "The First Missouri Brigade at the Battle of Franklin." *THQ* 46 No. 1, 1987.

Books & Pamphlets

Ames, Charles E. *Pioneering the Union Pacific Railroad, A Reappraisal of the Builders of the Railroad.* New York, 1969.

Arnold, James. *The Armies of U. S. Grant.* New York, 1995.

Bailey, Anne J. *The Chessboard of War: Sherman and Hood in the Autumn Campaigns of 1864.* Lincoln, NE, 2000.

Beaudot, William J. K. *The 24th Wisconsin Infantry in the Civil War: The Biography of a Regiment.* Mechanicsburg, PA, 2003.

Bridges, Hal. *Lee's Maverick General: Daniel Harvey Hill.* Lincoln, NE, 1991. Reprint.

Brown, Norman D., ed. *One of Cleburne's Command: The Civil War Reminiscences and Diary of Capt. Samuel T. Foster, Granbury's Texas Brigade, C. S. A.* Austin, TX, 1980.

Bowman, Virginia McDaniel. *Historic Williamson County: Old Homes and Sites.* Franklin, TN, 1971.

Carter, Rosalie. *Capt. Tod Carter of the Confederate States Army: A Biographical Word Portrait.* Franklin, TN, 1978.

Carter, Samuel, III. *The Siege of Atlanta, 1864.* New York, 1973.

Castel, Albert. *Decision in the West: The Atlanta Campaign of 1864.* Lawrence, KS, 1992.

Cisco, Walter Brian. *States Rights Gist: A South Carolinian General of the Civil War.* Shippensburg, PA, 1991.

Cockrell, Francis M., II. *The Senator From Missouri: The Life and Times of Francis Marion Cockrell.* New York, 1962.

Cooling, Benjamin Franklin. *Forts Henry and Donelson: The Key to the Confederate Heartland.* Knoxville, TN, 1987.

Connelly, Thomas L. *Autumn of Glory: The Army of Tennessee, 1862-1865.* Baton Rogue, LA, 1998. Reprint.

Cozzens, Peter. *This Terrible Sound: The Battle of Chickamauga.* Chicago, IL, 1992.

_____, ed. *Battles and Leaders of the Civil War.* Volume 5. Chicago, IL, 2002.

Crabb, Martha L. *All Afire to Fight: The Untold Tale of the Civil War's Ninth Texas Cavalry.* New York, 2000.

Cross, C. Wallace. *Cry Havoc: A History of the 49th Tennessee Volunteer Infantry Regiment, 1861-1865.* Franklin, TN, 2004.

Crowson, Noel and Brogden, John V., ed. *Bloody Banners and Barefoot Boys: A History of the 27th Regiment, Alabama Infantry, C. S. A.* Shippensburg, PA, 1997.

Daniel, Larry. *Cannoneers in Gray: The Field Artillery of the Army of Tennessee.* Tuscaloosa, AL, 1984.

_____. *Shiloh: The Battle That Changed the Civil War.* New York, 1997.

_____. *Soldiering In the Army of Tennessee: A Portrait of Life in a Confederate Army.* Chapel Hill, NC, 1991.

Davis, William C., ed. *The Confederate General.* 1991.

Drake, Rebecca Blackwell and Holder, Thomas D. *Lone Star General: Hiram Bronson Granbury.* Raymond, MS, 2004.

Dyer, John P. *The Gallant Hood.* New York, 1995. Reprint.

Elliott, Sam D. *General Alexander P. Stewart and the Civil War in the West.* Baton Rogue, LA, 1999.

Faust, Patricia L., ed. *Historical Times Illustrated Encyclopedia of the Civil War.* New York, 1986.

Fisher, John E. *They Rode With Forrest & Wheeler: A Chronicle of Five Brothers' Service in the Confederate Western Cavalry.* Jefferson, NC, 1995.

Garrett, Jill K. and Lightfoot, Marise P. *The Civil War in Maury County, Tennessee.* Columbia, TN, 1966.

Gillum, Jamie. *The Battle of Spring Hill: Twenty-Five Hours to Tragedy.* Franklin, TN, 2004.

Gottschalk, Phil. *In Deadly Earnest: The History of the Missouri Brigade.* Columbia, MO, 1991.

Hallock, Judith Lee. *Braxton Bragg and Confederate Defeat,* Volume 2. Tuscaloosa, AL, 1991.

Hay, Thomas Robson *Hood's Tennessee Campaign.* Dayton, OH, 1976. Reprint.

Henry, Robert Selph. *Nathan Bedford Forrest: First With the Most.* New York, 1992. Reprint.

Horn, Stanley. *The Army of Tennessee.* Norman, OK, 1993. Reprint.

Houp, J. Randall. *The 24th Missouri Volunteer Infantry "Lyon Legion."* Alma, AR, 1997.

Howell, Jr., H. Grady. *To Live and Die in Dixe: A History of the Third Mississippi Infantry, C. S. A.* Jackson, MS, 1991.

Hughes, Nathaniel C., Jr. *Brigadier General Tyree H. Bell, C. S. A. - Forrest's Fighting Lieutenant.* Knoxville, TN, 2004.

_____. *General William J. Hardee: Old Reliable.* Baton Rogue, LA, 1992. Reprint.

_____, ed. *The Civil War Memoir of Philip Dangerfield Stephenson, D. D.* Conway, AR, 1995.

Hurst, Jack. *Nathan Bedford Forrest, A Biography.* New York, 1994.

Jones, Mary Miles and Martin, Leslie Jones, ed. *The Gentle Rebel: The Civil War Letters of 1st Lt. William Harvey Berryhill, Co. D, 43rd Regiment, Mississippi Volunteers.* Yazoo City, MS, 1982.

Joslyn, Mauriel P., ed. *A Meteor Shining Brightly: Essays on Maj. Gen. Patrick R. Cleburne.* Milledgeville, GA, 1997.

Keenan, Jerry. *Wilson's Cavalry Corps.* Jefferson, NC, 1998.

Lamers, William M. *The Edge of Glory: A Biography of General Williams S. Rosecrans, U.S.A.* Baton Rogue, LA, 1999. Reprint.

Logsdon, David, ed. *Eyewitness at the Battle of Franklin.* Nashville, TN, 2000.

Long, E. B. *The Civil War Day by Day: An Almanac 1861-1865.* New York, 1985.

Longacre, Glenn V. and Haas, John, ed. *To Battle for God and the Right: The Civil War Letterbooks of Emerson Opdycke.* Urbana, IL, 2003.

Losson, Christopher. *Tennessee's Forgotten Warriors: Frank Cheatham and His Confederate Division.* Knoxville, TN, 1989.

Lundberg, John R. *The Finishing Stroke: Texans in the 1864 Tennessee Campaign.* Abilene, TX, 2002.

McDonough, James L. *Schofield: Union General in the Civil War and Reconstruction.* Tallahassee, FL, 1972.

_____. *Shiloh: In Hell Before Night.* Knoxville, TN, 1977.

_____. *Stones River: Bloody Winter in Tennessee.* Knoxville, TN, 1980.

_____ and Connelly, Thomas L. *Five Tragic Hours: The Battle of Franklin.* Knoxville, TN, 1983.

_____. *Nashville: The Western Confederacy's Final Gamble.* Knoxville, TN, 2004.

McMurry, Richard M. *John Bell Hood and the War for Southern Independence.* Lincoln, NE, 1992.

McWhiney, Grady. *Braxton Bragg and Confederate Defeat,* Volume 1. Tuscaloosa, AL, 1991. Reprint.

MacArthur, Douglas. *Reminiscences: General of the Army.* New York, 1964.

Meinhard, Robert W. *One Man's War: Frederick Meinhard 1862-1865.* Winona, MN, 1980.

Nevin, David. *Sherman's March: Atlanta to the Sea.* Alexandria, VA, 1986.

Owen, Thomas M. *History of Alabama and Dictionary of Alabama Biography.* Volume 3. Spartanburg, SC, 1978.

Parks, Joseph H. *General Leonidas Polk, C. S. A.: The Fighting Bishop.* Baton Rogue, LA, 1990. Reprint.

Potts, Helen and Hudgins, Helen. *McGavock Confederate Cemetery.* Franklin, TN 1989.

Purdue, Howell and Purdue, Elizabeth. *Pat Cleburne: Confederate General.* Gaithersburg, MD, 1987. Reprint.

Ramage, James A. *Rebel Raider: The Life of General John Hunt Morgan.* Lexington, KY, 1986.

Rowland, Dunbar. *Military History of Mississippi, 1803-1898.* Spartanburg, SC, 1988. Reprint.

Sears, Stephen. *To The Gates of Richmond: The Peninsula Campaign.* New York, 1992.

Sieburg, Evelyn and Hansen, James E., II, ed. *Memoirs of a Confederate Staff Officer: From Bethel to Bentonville.* Shippensburg, PA, 1998.

Simpson, Brooks D. and Berlin, Jean V., ed. *Sherman's Civil War: Selected Correspondence of William T. Sherman, 1860-1865.* Chapel Hill, NC, 1999.

Smith, Barbara B. and Baker, Nina B., ed. *Burning Rails as We Pleased: The Civil War Letters of William Garrigues Bentley, 104th Ohio Volunteer Infantry.* Jefferson, NC, 2004.

Smith, Frank M. *History of Maury County.* Columbia, TN, 1969.

Supplement to the Official Records *of the Union and Confederate Armies.* 100 volumes. Wilmington, NC, 1998.

Sword, Wiley. *The Confederacy's Last Hurrah: Spring Hill, Franklin, & Nashville.* New York, 1993.

_____. *Mountains Touched With Fire: Chattanooga Besieged, 1863.* New York, 1995.

Symonds, Craig L. *Joseph E. Johnston: A Civil War Biography.* New York, 1992.

_____. *Stonewall of the West: Patrick Cleburne and the Civil War.* Lawrence, KS, 1997.

Thompson, Ilene and Thompson, Wilbur. *The Seventeenth Alabama Infantry: A Regimental History And Roster.* Bowie, MD, 2001.

Tower, R. Lockwood, ed. *A Carolinian Goes to War: The Civil War Narrative of Arthur Middleton Manigault.* Columbia, SC, 1992.

Tucker, Philip Thomas. *The Forgotten "Stonewall of the West": Major General John Stevens Bowen.* Macon, GA, 1997.

Turner, William B. *History of Maury County.* Nashville, TN, 1955.

Van Eldik, James. *From the Flame of Battle to the Fiery Cross.* Las Cruces, NM, 2001.

Welsh, Jack. *Medical Histories of Confederate Generals.* Kent, OH, 1995.

_____. *Medical Histories of Union Generals.* Kent, OH, 1997.

Williams, T. Harry. *P. G. T. Beauregard: Napoleon in Gray.* Baton Rogue, LA, 1995. Reprint.

Willis, James. *Arkansas Confederates in the Western Theater.* Dayton, OH, 1998.

Wilson, Sadye T., Fitzgerald, Nancy T., and Warwick, Richard, ed. *Letters to Laura: A Confederate Surgeon's Impressions of Four Years of War.* Nashville, TN, 1996.

Woodworth, Steven. *Jefferson Davis and His Generals: The Failure of Confederate Command in the West.* Lawrence, KS, 1990.

Worley, Ted R., ed. *The War Memoirs of Captain John W. Lavender, C. S. A.* Pine Bluff, AR, 1956.

Young, Richard G, ed. *Glory! Glory! Glory! The Civil War Diaries of Henry Jackson McCord.* Fairfax, VA, 2002.

Index